W9-DGF-620

BRUCE CATTON
NEVER CALL RETREAT

"No finer narrative history of the Civil War has ever appeared. . . . Catton's major triumph is in the art of history. He manages to combine the great sweep of history with its sum of individual actors, major and minor, its incidents, anecdotes, asides."   —*Los Angeles Times*

"A solid, thrilling book . . . superb history—the best that has come from the author's prolific pen. . . ."   —*Baltimore Sunday Sun*

"It is rather *amazing* to find a historian who can give a running account of the events of a war which was fought on more than one front, give the political and military history of the war at the same time without impairing the readability of the work or giving it a 'patchy' aspect. This book accomplishes this feat, too. . . . The three volumes of his history will become classics."   —*Nashville Banner*

Books by Bruce Catton

Published by POCKET BOOKS

Bruce Catton

NEVER CALL RETREAT

PUBLISHED BY POCKET BOOKS NEW YORK

POCKET BOOKS, a Simon & Schuster division of
GULF & WESTERN CORPORATION
1230 Avenue of the Americas, New York, N.Y. 10020

Copyright © 1965 by Bruce Catton

Published by arrangement with Doubleday & Company, Inc.

All rights reserved, including the right to reproduce
this book or portions thereof in any form whatsoever.
For information address Doubleday & Company, Inc.,
245 Park Avenue, New York, N.Y. 10017

ISBN: 0-671-80651-3

First Pocket Books printing August, 1967

15   14   13   12   11   10   9   8

Trademarks registered in the United States and other countries.

Printed in the U.S.A.

To the one-time members of E. P. Case Post Number 372, Grand Army of the Republic, who now sleep in the village cemetery at Benzonia, Michigan, this book is affectionately dedicated.

Foreword

THE CENTENNIAL HISTORY OF THE CIVIL WAR by Bruce Catton is a project begun in 1955 by Doubleday & Company, Inc., in conjunction with *The New York Times*. As originally planned, this is a three-volume work constituting a modern history, based on the fullest as well as the most recent research. The three volumes, which are entitled THE COMING FURY, TERRIBLE SWIFT SWORD, and NEVER CALL RETREAT, may be read and understood separately.

In the foreword of Volume One of the original publication of the work, Mr. Catton wrote of Mr. E. B. Long: "As Director of Research for this project he has made a more substantial contribution than it is possible to acknowledge properly." Mr. Catton also noted the "able assistance given by that indefatigable and charming person, Mrs. Barbara Long."

Contents

Chapter Five: THE IMPOSSIBILITIES

Chapter Six: ACT OF FAITH

Chapter Seven: HIS ALMOST CHOSEN PEOPLE

List of Maps

Following page 266

On the above listed maps the black arrows or bars indicate the Confederate forces, the blue bars or arrows indicate the Federal forces. In both cases, when the arrow lines are interrupted or dotted, it means either retreat or regrouping.

The Centennial History of the Civil War

VOLUME THREE

NEVER CALL RETREAT

CHAPTER ONE

In the Rapids

1. Castles in the Air

OFFICIALLY, Jefferson Davis was traveling incognito; and yet, as the Chattanooga newspaperman wrote, a live President was still something of a curiosity in Tennessee, and the trip got a good deal of attention. The reporter considered Mr. Davis "decidedly handsome for a middle-aged gentleman," and said that he wore a perpetual expression of good humor, combining graceful manners with an impressive senatorial dignity; and he commended him for going about without ostentation or parade, his only luggage one leather valise, his only attendant a single body servant. It was inspiring (said the reporter) to contrast this republican simplicity with the pretensions of the "miserable despot of abolitionism" in Washington, who never went abroad without a file of armed dragoons and who lived "in constant apprehension of the assassin's dagger in his own capital."[1]

Mr. Davis was making this trip in the middle of December 1862, drawn from Richmond to the Mississippi Valley by grave problems of command, of strategy and of public morale. A few days earlier he had confessed to a committee of the Confederate Congress that the war had entered its most dangerous period, and on this trip he saw nothing to make him revise that opinion; yet in public he was serene, and in Knoxville, the most dissident of all Confederate cities, he told an attentive audience that "the Toryism of east Tennessee" had been greatly exaggerated. Two days later, at Murfreesboro, he assured an enthusiastic crowd that if the Southern people persevered a little longer final victory would be theirs.

Perhaps it was easy to be hopeful at Murfreesboro. The powerful Army of Tennessee was in camp there, and this army had never looked better. It had recovered from the bewildering Perryville campaign, in which a valiant thousand-mile march brought nothing but an inconclusive battle and a missed opportunity; it had had plenty of rest, for once it was properly shod and clothed, it had more than 45,000 veterans in its ranks, and morale was high. Even its generals were feeling confident. Braxton Bragg, the army commander, a dyspeptic martinet who ordinarily radiated an infectious gloom, seemed sprightly, and he assured the President that the army was ready for anything. It was nobly supported, he said, by the patriotic people of Tennessee, who, "having felt the heel of the tyrant," were furnishing men and supplies in abundance. He believed he could whip the Yankee army that held Nashville if that army could ever be induced to come out and fight.[2]

Mr. Davis was ready to agree. He reviewed the army, was impressed by what he saw, and impressed those who saw him. His old friend Leonidas Polk, the Episcopal Bishop who was now a lieutenant general commanding an army corps, wrote to Mrs. Polk with innocent enthusiasm: "We have had a royal visit, from a royal visitor. The President himself has been with us." The review was "a great affair," and the Bishop said Mr. Davis told him that the soldiers who passed in review were "the best-appearing troops he had seen, well appointed and well clad."

Bishop Polk had the President's trust and affection, he was a West Point graduate (of a long-gone vintage, to be sure) and he was a devout patriot; and on both sides in this war men were commissioned general for less impressive reasons. He could still wear episcopal vestments over his uniform. In this month of December he officiated at a wedding, marrying General John Hunt Morgan, the famous Kentucky cavalryman, to pretty Mattie Ready of Murfreesboro, with Bragg and his staff, and other generals, looking on; and this was a storybook affair with a storybook romance back of it. A few months earlier, Mattie Ready was living in Federally occupied territory. She did not then know Morgan, but she defended him with much spirit when she heard Federal officers deride him, and one of them demanded her name—he would write it down, and see that she was listed as a confirmed rebel. She gave it to him, and added defiantly: "But by the grace of God I hope one day to call myself the wife of John Morgan." After the Federals were gone Morgan heard the story, laughed, then rode around to see her; liked what he saw, courted her, and now made her his wife. . . . So went the story. A day or so after the wedding, Morgan and his squadrons went riding hard to the northward, to go raiding far behind the Federal front and spread alarm along the wild Kentucky border. The ceremony at army headquarters went into the Confederate legend, along with bride and bridegroom and the memory of candlelight glinting off the brass buttons and sword-hilts. The good bishop assured his wife that the wedding had been a historic occasion.[3]

So the legend was flourishing, and the fine review at Murfreesboro would fit into it; but meanwhile the Confederate cause itself was displaying ominous symptoms, and that was why the President had come to Tennessee. He was not really worried about what this army at Murfreesboro might do, and he did not need to see the troops march past in order to know that they would give a good account of themselves when it was time to fight. But he had come to the Mississippi Valley just when the Federal Army of the Potomac was making another "forward to Richmond" campaign, and at such a moment Jefferson Davis did not leave the Confederate capital for any small reason. What had wrenched him away from Richmond was his recognition of the fact that no matter what happened in Virginia the Confederacy was very probably doomed unless it could reverse the tide that was beginning to flow in the west. The problem in the east could be left to Robert E. Lee; that in the west demanded immediate presidential attention.

The danger could be stated in simple terms. Thirty thousand veteran Federal soldiers led by the aggressive Major General Ulysses S. Grant were marching out of western Tennessee down the line of the Mississippi Central Railroad, heading for Vicksburg. Vicksburg, a one-time cotton-shipping port that sprawled up the slopes of a chain of hills overlooking a hairpin bend in the Mississippi, roughly halfway between Memphis and New Orleans, had been given river batteries of moderate strength and it was occupied by an inadequate garrison. It was one of the places which the Confederate nation had to possess if it were to win its independence.

As long as they held Vicksburg the Confederates owned a 150-mile stretch of the great river, the segment running south from Vicksburg to Port Hudson in Louisiana, where there were also fortifications and a garrison; and as long as this much of the river was held the Southern Confederacy was still a valid whole, an unbroken nation stretching from Virginia tidewater to the Rio Grande, the authentic cotton kingdom as planned by the founding fathers. But if this bit of the river were lost—as it would be if Vicksburg fell, for Port Hudson could not stand alone—then the Confederacy would begin to die, its western states broken off forever, all of the Mississippi Valley held by the government at Washington. Then there would be no good way to save what was left of Tennessee, or the Gulf States either, and once these were gone the remnant of the nation could hardly hope to survive.

Obviously, General Grant had to be stopped, and the President had come west to see about it. Yet if it was easy to say what had to be done it was extremely hard to say what it was going to be done with. To oppose General Grant there was in northern Mississippi a field army less than 24,000 strong, somewhat frayed from its experiences in the recent battle of Corinth. Elsewhere in the Department of Mississippi—the state itself, and that part of Louisiana which lay east of the river—there were no more than 10,000 men, most of them tied down in garrison duty at Vicksburg and Port Hudson. Unless help could be brought in from outside the Department the game was going to be lost. But all of the troops that might conceivably be brought in were urgently needed (according to their commanding officers) somewhere else, and could not be summoned without inviting disaster.[4]

To accept this argument was in effect to admit that the Confederacy was being tried beyond its strength, an admission Mr. Davis would never make. In Arkansas and in Tennessee the Confederacy had upward of 80,000 soldiers; surely, with the nation's life at stake, some of these could be brought into Mississippi? Surely, strategic brilliance could find a way to make up for lack of brute strength? Mr. Davis showed a cheerful face in public, but his generals were giving him very little to be cheerful about. It might be that strategic resources in these parts were as limited as resources of manpower.

Or it might be that Mr. Davis was calling for an answer that did not exist.

During the war, and after it, Mr. Davis was accused of failing to see the gravity of the Mississippi Valley problem; of interpreting all of the war in terms of what happened in Virginia, and of ignoring the catastrophe that began to take shape when Grant marched south across the Mississippi line. This charge does injustice to a sorely harried man. Mr. Davis understood perfectly the implications of the Federal drive to open the Mississippi Valley—after all he was a westerner himself, his own plantation lying only a few miles downstream from Vicksburg—and he gave the matter full attention the moment the campaign began. The real trouble was that the crisis called on him to take a gambler's chance and he did not feel that he ought to gamble.

Neither his vision nor his nerve was at fault. It simply seemed to Mr. Davis that it was necessary to win in front of Vicksburg without risking loss anywhere else, and although no general could show him how to do this (because in fact it could not be done) it had to be admitted that the situation in the western Confederacy now was most peculiar.

Before he left Richmond, Mr. Davis told General Lee that he had to go west "to bring out men not heretofore in service and to arouse all classes to united and desperate resistance," and after his departure a War Department official made an entry in his diary: "Private information from many sources represents the tone and temper of the Mississippi Valley as very unsound. *They are submitting.*" Although he had spoken so bravely at Knoxville, the President sent a somber appraisal back to the Secretary of War: "The feeling in East Tennessee and North Alabama is far from what we desire. There is some hostility and much want of confidence in our strength."[5]

East Tennessee, to be sure, had long been recognized as an area badly infected with Yankeeism, but the worst report of all came from Mr. Davis' own state, Mississippi. Senator James Phelan said frankly that "the present alarming crisis," far from arousing the people, had made them despondent, and he went on to assert: "The spirit of enlistment is thrice dead. Enthusiasm has expired to a cold pile of ashes. De-

feats, retreats, sufferings, dangers, magnified by the spiritless
helplessness and an unchangeable conviction that our army
is in the hands of ignorant and feeble commanders, are
rapidly producing a sense of settled despair, from which, if
not speedily dissipated by 'some bright event or happy
change,' the most disastrous consequences may be appre-
hended." It was essential for the President to "plant your
foot upon our soil" and, thus anchored, to "unfurl your banner at the head of the army"; and in fact Mr. Davis went to
Mississippi as soon as he disposed of his business in Tennessee.

Unquestionably the command situation had caused trouble. Mr. Davis had recently taken steps from which he hoped
good would come, but the generals who served the Confederacy in the west were oddly assorted and, in some cases,
oddly selected as well. Collectively they presented a problem to each other, to the President, and to the country.

Until recently the Mississippi army had been in command
of Earl Van Dorn, one of the President's favorite officers—
curly-haired, alert, a man of much energy, not all of it
properly channeled. It was Van Dorn on whom the Yankees
had inflicted costly defeat at Corinth in October, and on
Van Dorn the people of Mississippi now were blaming their
troubles. Senator Phelan said frankly that in the common
belief Van Dorn was "the source of all our woes," and he
added that the man's private life as well as his military competence had been called into question: "The atmosphere is
dense with horrid narratives of his negligence, whoring and
drunkenness, for the truth of which I cannot vouch; but it is
so fastened in the public belief that an acquittal by a court-
martial of angels would not relieve him of the charge."[6] Van
Dorn knew what was being said about him, and grew
despondent, writing to his wife that his command had brought
him nothing but "misfortune, criticism, falsehood, slander
and all the vile things belonging to the human heart." He
recovered his bounce presently; before 1862 was out he
would strike a blow that helped to compel Grant to beat a
hasty retreat, and in the spring, unacquitted by angels, he
would be shot to death by a Tennessee civilian who considered himself an outraged husband.[7] Meanwhile his mere
existence offended the patriotic.

But Van Dorn, after all, had been relieved weeks earlier,

and now in December he commanded only cavalry. The Department of Mississippi was in the hands of Lieutenant General John C. Pemberton, a transplanted Yankee whose morals were above reproach but who could neither reassure civilians nor inspire soldiers; a man dedicated but wholly without good luck.

Pemberton was in his late forties, a Pennsylvanian with two brothers in the Northern army. He seems to have been in love with the South from boyhood. At West Point, where he was in the class of 1837, he was known as a states' rights advocate, most of his cadet corps chums were Southerners, and in 1848 he married a Virginia girl. When secession came he was a captain of engineers, and he apparently had impressed his superiors in the War Department because they offered him a colonelcy. He rejected it, resigned and went South, getting a commission from Jefferson Davis, whom he had also impressed. He rose rapidly in the Confederate service, commanded at Charleston in the summer of 1862, and in the fall struck Mr. Davis as just the man for Mississippi.

Pemberton was diligent and he took hold with a firm hand, reorganizing his staff departments, shaking up supply services, pushing the work on fortifications and organizing a steamboat line to bring foodstuffs from the trans-Mississippi. For the first time the department got competent administration, and a newspaper editor held that Pemberton had brought order out of chaos: "If after the well-nigh fatal blunders of his predecessor it is possible to defend ourselves against the Yankees we believe he will do it."[8]

Yet the man could not win people. In a spot that called for inspirational leadership he was uninspiring. He made no impact on the state's discontent; Senator Phelan morosely told Mr. Davis that hardly anyone in Mississippi so much as realized that Pemberton was in command, and some of those who did realize it recalled darkly that he was after all a Yankee, and doubted that his heart was in the Southern cause. Something flinty about his personality made him hard to work with. Across the river in Arkansas, grumpy Lieutenant General Theophilus Holmes wrote that although the government did well to remove Van Dorn its choice of Pemberton did not help matters much, "as Pemberton has many ways of making people hate him and none to inspire confidence."[9]

Holmes himself was one of the most baffling aspects of the command problem. He was in his late fifties, rigid, half-deaf; along the James River in the previous spring, in the midst of a thunderous Yankee bombardment, with his troops on the verge of panic from the fury of the shelling, he had emerged from his headquarters hut, hand cupped behind an ear, and innocently asked if he had not heard firing somewhere. He led a division without distinction during the Seven Days campaign, and he was one of the men Lee carefully weeded out as soon as that campaign ended. Now he commanded the whole Trans-Mississippi Department, and he was unhappily the sort of general who sees his difficulties clearly but is quite unable to do anything about them.

It must be admitted that enough difficulties were visible in Arkansas to frustrate almost anyone. The people of the state were discontented, Governor Henry M. Rector was loudly complaining that the troops his state sent east under Van Dorn in the spring had never been returned, and Holmes had grave command problems of his own. His chief lieutenant was Major General T. C. Hindman, who had done wonders during spring and summer in the way of raising and equipping troops, but who did not seem able to use them effectively. Early in September Hindman had led two divisions into southwest Missouri, and on September 30 these troops won an opening engagement at Newtonia and caused the more optimistic to hope that the long-anticipated reconquest of Missouri was at hand. But Hindman was called away to confer with Holmes at Little Rock, and while he was away the reinforced Federals advanced again; whereupon the little Confederate army hastily retreated and in its panic virtually fell apart. (It developed that of the two top officers Hindman had left behind, one was drunk when the Yankees advanced and the other had just ceased to be drunk and suffered from a massive hangover.) Hindman managed to put most of the army together again, but early in December he got into a battle with Federals led by Brigadier General James G. Blunt at Prairie Grove, Arkansas, near Fayetteville and not far from the old battlefield of Pea Ridge. Hindman was badly beaten, his army was driven off toward Little Rock, and now the Federals had practically all the state north of the Arkansas River.[10]

Still, no matter how defectively they were led, Holmes did

have 25,000 troops in Arkansas, and he seemed the logical man to send help to Pemberton. Pemberton thought so, at any rate, and so did Van Dorn, and so for that matter did the Secretary of War. But Holmes had only the loosest grip on his department, and the Richmond government had an even looser grip on Holmes, and it turned out finally that although everyone agreed that Holmes' soldiers ought to go to Pemberton's rescue there was no power anywhere that could get them to do so. In October Secretary of War George W. Randolph tried to bring this about and succeeded only in disconnecting himself from his seat in the cabinet.

Randolph sent a telegram, suggesting that Holmes collect all available forces and take them across the Mississippi, assuming command of his own and Pemberton's troops in a campaign against Grant. This immediately got Randolph into trouble with Mr. Davis, who felt that Holmes should send troops east but that Holmes himself ought to stay west of the river, and who coldly rebuked Randolph for trying to move generals and armies on his own initiative. Offended, Randolph resigned; his resignation was quickly accepted, and his place presently was filled by a gaunt, aristocratic Virginia planter, James A. Seddon, who had a better understanding of the limits within which a Confederate Secretary of War must operate. Then, concluding that what the situation needed was an area commander with broad powers, Mr. Davis turned to General Joseph E. Johnston, who was recovering from a grave wound received in May at the Battle of Seven Pines. In effect, Mr. Davis gave Johnston control of everything west of the Appalachians and east of the Mississippi—control, subject of course to presidential approval—and instructed him to go west and restore the situation.[11]

General Johnston was to have his own place in the Confederate legend. He was Little Joe, the Gamecock, graying, winsome, courtly but at times fiercely, absurdly, ruinously touchy; a gifted defensive strategist the value of whose services to the South was limited by two small failings. His canny appraisal of the military realities was so precise that it never quite left him room for the risk-everything sort of offensive thrust which the Confederacy's situation occasionally demanded; also, it unfortunately was in the long run impossible for him and Jefferson Davis to work together with mutual confidence and understanding. This appointment to western command exposed both of these qualities to the open air.

Johnston's assignment was to use Bragg and Pemberton to defeat Grant, and he quickly concluded that this combination was less logical than it looked. Bragg and Pemberton were separated by the Tennessee River, by Grant's army, and by the fact that the only really good route from Murfreesboro to central Mississippi was extremely roundabout, wandering by way of Chattanooga, Atlanta, Montgomery, and Mobile—800 miles and more, involving the use of half a dozen railroads. It would be much better, said General Johnston, to use Holmes and Pemberton against Grant. His own authority ought to embrace these two armies, joining Mississippi and Arkansas instead of Mississippi and Tennessee.

The protest was not heeded. Opening headquarters at Chattanooga on December 4, Johnston got word from the War Department that Pemberton was in full retreat, that Holmes had been "peremptorily ordered" to send reinforcements, and that the President, anticipating delay in Holmes' movement, wanted Johnston to order troops down from Bragg. Johnston protested that Pemberton's retreat took the man constantly farther away from Bragg, which made Bragg's army a most illogical source of support, but this did no good—partly because he could not get Richmond to see his point and partly because Richmond was oddly helpless. Holmes, it finally appeared, was not going to send any men east of the Mississippi—the Federals were too menacing, his army was too weak, and the people of Arkansas were likely to give up the cause if this army moved away. Pemberton pleaded, the War Department ordered, and Mr. Davis sent Holmes a long, patiently persuasive letter, pointing out that Arkansas and Holmes' army would both be doomed if the Confederacy lost Vicksburg; and all of this did no good at all. When Mr. Davis got to Chattanooga he told Johnston that there was no help for it; Johnston must send at least a division of General Bragg's troops down to help Pemberton.[12]

Holmes would not act, Richmond could not make him act—and Mr. Davis, so often accused of behaving with bureaucratic and dictatorial firmness toward his generals, was in this case unwontedly pliable. Perhaps the truth was that the vast country west of the Mississippi was so far away, and the situation there was so delicate, that the central government could not enforce its will without subjecting the Confederate fabric to an unendurable strain. Holmes believed that this was so. He argued that if his army came east of the river and the Federals as a result captured Little Rock, "the whole valley of the Arkansas will be stampeded and the political party which has constantly cried out that the country is deserted by the government will pave the way to dangerous disloyalty and disgust." The warning was cloudy, but Holmes at once made it more explicit: if his troops went east the Confederacy would probably lose Arkansas, and to lose Arkansas was to lose the entire trans-Mississippi country. And so, "under these circumstances, and with the greatest reluctance, I hesitate to obey your last order."[13]

Rarely did a Confederate officer tell Jefferson Davis, "I hesitate to obey," and escape destruction. Holmes was one who did; probably because Mr. Davis saw his point before he made it. Several days before he left for Tennessee the President had told General Lee that he wanted Holmes to send troops to Mississippi "if it can safely be done." The fatal difficulty in the Mississippi Valley was that what imperatively had to be done could not be done safely, and because it could not be done safely it was not done at all. Joe Johnston wrote to his friend Senator Wigfall that the failure to bring Holmes' troops east of the river "has blown away some tall castles in the air."[14] Some of these dissolving air castles were central to the vision of Confederate independence.

2. Battle without Logic

JUST BEFORE President Davis and General Johnston left Tennessee for Mississippi an urgent telegram arrived from Richmond: the powerful Federal Army of the Potomac, 120,000 strong and backed by abundant reserves, had crossed the Rappahannock River in Virginia and was attacking General Lee's army at Fredericksburg. Lee had rather more than half as many men as the Federals had, with no reserves worth mentioning, and Fredericksburg was hardly fifty miles north of Richmond. A Federal victory here (not unlikely, when the odds were figured) could mean the end of everything, and Mr. Davis immediately telegraphed for more news. A twenty-four-hour wait brought no answer, and as he resumed his journey the President wrote to Mrs. Davis to say that he was most anxious.

General Johnston did not share his anxiety. He could see much trouble ahead in Mississippi, but in Virginia everything was different. He remembered that the high ground back of Fredericksburg offered almost perfect defensive positions, he felt that General Lee was being presented with victory by some incomprehensible act of Yankee generosity, and he wrote his own characteristic comment, half jocular, half rueful: "What luck some people have. Nobody will ever come to attack me in such a place."[1]

General Johnston's professional appraisal was sound. Fredericksburg turned out to be a top-heavy Confederate victory, and Lee's only regret arose from the fact that the beaten Federals were able to get back to their own side of the Rappahannock after the fighting ended. He doubtless would have agreed that he was lucky to be attacked here; he was able to repulse the invader without using more than half of his outnumbered army, and it was this battle that drew from him the exultant, desolating cry: *It is well that war is so terrible—we should grow too fond of it.* After its retreat the Federal army that looked so dangerous in its advance was glad to lie in camp, painfully recuperating, meditating on its casualty list (which contained more than 12,000 names) and on the varieties of human folly that had created the list. The President who needed to worry about Fredericksburg was not Jefferson Davis but Abraham Lincoln.

In a sense what happened there happened to Mr. Lincoln personally. In the Emancipation Proclamation he had given the nation a new imperative, and as an inescapable sequel he had given the Army of the Potomac a new leader. When he did this he took a prodigious risk. To remove Major General George B. McClellan was to wrench out of this army its central personality; the President had rested the entire Union cause on the belief that these soldiers could win even though they lost the leader who had molded them in his own image, but now their new leader failed them abysmally. Strategically, Fredericksburg cost the North nothing that could not be restored; spiritually, it was fearfully expensive. The nation could endure agony better than ignominy.

Fredericksburg was a strange and terrible battle, fought on a frozen plain between bleak hills and a ruined town—a battle that began in wintry sunlight and ended with mist floating up from the river to cloak many hundreds of bodies that lay in fields and leafless thickets—and its meaning was veiled. All of the material strength the mighty republic could bring to the battlefield had been displayed here. The soldiers had fought as well as ever. What made the battle so tragic, to Northern eyes, was that heroism and endurance had been so prodigally displayed and so miserably wasted. That strange and inexplicable quality which Mr. Lincoln later called the last full measure of devotion was still there, but Fredericksburg proved that by itself this was not enough. Mr. Lincoln now had to think of how it was to be used.

The soldier who replaced McClellan was Major General Ambrose E. Burnside. He was handsome, likable, imbued with a humility not previously known in the army's headquarters tents,[2] and he did his conscientious best only to become the architect of unrelieved catastrophe. If it is true that he was much too limited a mortal to command the nation's largest army, it is also true that he could have been served ever so much better than he was served, both by his subordinates and by the War Department. It is true, further, that he had not angled for the job and that when the time came he gave it up with a good grace. Finally, the campaign which he devised and tried to carry out was well planned; up to a point it was fairly well executed. It came a little closer to success than is usually realized. Actually, it could have worked.

Burnside took command on November 7, when the army was loosely grouped around Warrenton, Virginia. Lee's army was divided, half of it twenty miles away at Culpeper and the other half up beyond the Blue Ridge in the Shenandoah Valley. McClellan had been shifting to the southwest, hoping to destroy the segment at Culpeper. Burnside distrusted this plan, and with some reason. There were approximately 35,000 Confederates in the valley, potentially in his rear, and they were led by Stonewall Jackson: altogether this was not unlike the layout that made so much trouble for the unfortunate John Pope.[3] Burnside proposed, instead, an immediate move to the southeast. A march of rather more than thirty miles would put him in Falmouth, across the Rappahannock from Fredericksburg and on the railroad that went down from Aquia Creek on the Potomac, ten miles northeast of Falmouth, through Fredericksburg to Richmond. His base at Aquia Creek would be safe, and if Burnside got into Fredericksburg quickly he would actually be nearer to Richmond than Lee was at Culpeper. Advancing along the railroad, he could compel Lee to fight, near the Confederate capital, with the odds all in favor of the Federals. Burnside put his plan on paper and when the major general commanding all the armies, Henry W. Halleck, came to Warrenton for consultation Burnside showed him the paper and asked for its approval.

Halleck had more authority than he liked to use. His guiding star was the conviction that nothing of any importance could be done without prior clearance at the White House. This now and then made it impossible for him to act at all, but during the last six months he had been in a position to see what happened to generals who ignored the President's wishes, and understandably he was most cautious. Now he took Burnside's program back to Washington, and on November 14 he sent word that the President thought the plan would work if Burnside moved rapidly.

This Burnside could do. He got two army corps on the road the next morning, and on November 17 they were in Falmouth, looking across the river to Fredericksburg which was occupied by the merest handful of Confederates. On this day Lee, still at Culpeper, notified President Davis that the Yankees seemed to be getting out of Warrenton but that it was not yet clear where they were going; he had anticipated that they might go to Fredericksburg, but so far there was nothing to show that they were actually doing it. To the War Department Lee wrote that the Yankee move might well be the first step in a program to transfer the Army of the Potomac to the James River.[4] Undeniably, Burnside was off to an excellent start. He had in fact done what few Federal generals were ever able to do: he had stolen a couple of days on Robert E. Lee. If he now used that time properly he might win a dazzling success.

Burnside was not, unfortunately, able to use the time at all, and the campaign that began so briskly slowed down until it became a blind drifting to disaster.

All Burnside needed to do, once his advance guard was at

Falmouth, was to cross the river into Fredericksburg and begin his move toward Richmond. To do this of course he had to have bridges, and the War Department had promised that the pontoons, timbers, and engineer troops to build bridges would be waiting for him at Falmouth. They were not there—were in fact nowhere in sight, nor did anyone from General Halleck on down know where they were or how their arrival might be expedited. Lacking bridges, the army sat down and waited; and as it waited time went by, and many thousands of armed Confederates got into Fredericksburg, prepared to dispute the crossing.

Burnside's military secretary explained the situation in a plaintive and revealing letter from Falmouth:

"It was promised us before we left Warrenton that by the time we arrived here our pontoon trains should be here in readiness for us to cross at once—had this been the case we should have occupied the city the first night and been ready to move on the rebels the next day, but we had to wait here *four days and a half* before a single pontoon train came in & meanwhile all we could do was to see the rebels gather their forces & fortify the heights till now they have a *very large* force & in a very strong position to operate against us with."[5]

The non-arrival of the pontoons was of course no fault of Burnside's, but it did bring into glaring relief the quality that may have been his greatest single defect as a soldier—his utter inability to adjust himself to an unexpected development requiring a quick change in plan. He could not improvise. He had to follow his original plan, even though the delay had ruined it; Lee had ample time to assemble his entire army on the high ground which Joe Johnston recalled so wistfully. The pontoon bridges were laid at last, under fire and at some cost in human life, on December 11, and the army formed columns of assault on the Confederate side of the river and marched off to fight on December 13— almost exactly one month after the President said that Burnside had a good plan if he carried it out fast, and more than three weeks after Burnside had massed his army in and around Falmouth.[6]

What followed was not so much a battle as a military tragedy. Half of Burnside's tactical program was hopeless from the start and the other half was made hopeless in the performance; his poor plans were faithfully executed and his good plans were atrociously bungled. Neither for the first time nor for the last, it was proven that there was amazing, heart-breaking valor in the ranks of the Army of the Potomac—and, in its chain of command. an equally amazing lack of the ability to put that valor to effective use.

In front of Fredericksburg the Rappahannock River flows nearly north to south. West of the town there is a low ridge known as Marye's Heights. At the time of the battle there was a sunken road flanked by a stone wall running along the base of this ridge, and on the crest there was a fine pillared mansion with lawns and open grounds around it. The ridge runs north to the river (which curves westward, upstream from Fredericksburg) and opposite what was in 1862 the southern end of the town the ridge ends in the shallow valley of a stream known as Hazel Run. South of Hazel Run there is an irregular chain of little wooded hills, going south for about three miles and ending in an insignificant knoll that looks down on a looping curve in the railroad that goes on to Richmond. Beyond the knoll a country road ran across the tracks—Hamilton's Crossing, they called it; the name was remembered because it marked the southern end of the battlefield.

None of this elevated ground, from Marye's Heights to Hamilton's Crossing, is really very high. but Lee's army occupied all of it and for purely defensive purposes the position was extremely strong. To be sure, it was not good for anything more than defense. Burnside had artillery planted all along the Yankee side of the river, and Lee had no scope for a counteroffensive. But as a place on which the Army of the Potomac might easily break its back the Confederate position here was ideal.

Burnside's battle plan called for two offensive blows, one of which was supposed to puncture the Confederate left center while the other overpowered the Confederate right. It was hoped that the two columns of assault, carrying out their assignments, would eventually join hands in the Confederate rear; and of course if they did this Burnside would win his battle and the road to Richmond would be wide open. To do it, however, Burnside's men must carry Marye's Heights by direct frontal assault, and this was little less than a military impossibility; what with the guns on top of the ridge and the infantry packed into the sunken road behind that stone wall, this position simply could not be taken by storm. Furthermore, the assault on Lee's right would encounter the seasoned army corps of the fabulous Stonewall Jackson, who had boasted with fair accuracy that no one ever drove his troops out of a place they had been ordered to hold. Still, this was Burnside's plan, and on the morning of December 13 the army undertook to put it into effect.

There was a heavy fog that morning, and the Confederates on their hills looked east over a filmy white sea that hid everything except the church spires of Fredericksburg. They could see no Yankees, but they could hear them; there were bugle calls, going from corps to division to brigade to regiment, and there was the muffled, shuffling tramp of great masses of marching men, and the clank and clatter of gun carriages jolting along frozen roads. Then, around eleven o'clock in the morning, a wind shredded the fog and drew it away, and under the clear sunlight the waiting Southerners could see their enemies.

They could see all of them at once, as if the footlights had suddenly lit up some unimaginable stage, and in no other battle did they see anything quite as breath-taking. Here was the Army of the Potomac, on the move and coming out to fight; it seemed to be made visible all in one instant, the wind rippled in its flags and the sunlight sparkled from musket barrels and bayonets and the brass fieldpieces. Out of Fredericksburg came long columns-of-four, marching west toward Marye's Heights. Other columns moved down the country roads to the south, and by the river still more columns were coming across on the pontoon bridges. Below the town, battle line upon battle line began to swing forward through the brown fields toward Stonewall Jackson's position, and under Marye's Heights the endless columns fanned out to make more battle lines. Far beyond, across the river, quick flashes of light flickered up and down the length of Stafford Heights as the powerful Federal siege guns began to feel for their targets.

Southeast of Hamilton's Crossing, Jeb Stuart's horse artillery was taking position to open fire on the Yankee left, and on Marye's Heights the massed guns began to lay crisscross lines of fire on the plain where the Federal assault was taking shape. A little earlier, posting his guns, tough James

Longstreet, lieutenant general commanding the left of Lee's army, asked his chief of artillery if there were guns enough to cover the approaches, and the artillerist laughed at him. Once he opened fire, he said, not even a chicken could live on the open ground between Fredericksburg and the sunken road.[7] It was only a moderate overstatement.

Burnside had divided his army into three masses which he called Grand Divisions, each commanded by a major general in whom he had confidence and with whom the battle plan had been discussed earlier. The hardest assignment, the assault on Marye's Heights, had been given to the Right Grand Division, led by Edwin Vose Sumner. Sumner was a rigid Old-Army type, a man of boundless courage and fidelity and the simplest mental processes; admirable, and yet a little out of date. He had been an army officer since 1819, which was long before most of the men in his command had been born, and he had a roaring parade-ground voice and a dogged heads-down quality that led his juniors to refer to him as the Bull of the Woods. Burnside had ordered him to stay on the Yankee side of the river, fearing that if Sumner were anywhere near the scene of action he would insist on getting all the way up in the front line. Burnside's order probably saved Sumner's life, because the front line of his Grand Division this day was a deadly place and the old man would unquestionably have been in it if his orders had permitted it.

Sumner was brave and so were his men, but bravery was not enough. He sent his two army corps into action unimaginatively, after the Antietam system, one division at a time, so that the attack on the heights became a long series of battles and the defense never had to bear the weight of one massive blow. Each division had to cross the wide plain where the dead grass was blistered by Longstreet's artillery, and the men who were not killed by the gunfire had to march up toward the stone wall that concealed the sunken road. The wall was a quarter of a mile long, there were six ranks of infantry behind it enjoying almost perfect protection, and the blue brigades coming up elbow to elbow offered a target that could not be missed.

The mustering of Burnside's hosts was impressive to see. Watching from the hilltop where he had his headquarters flag, Lee knew a moment of doubt and cautioned Longstreet that this pressure might break his line. Longstreet refused to worry, asserting that if every man in the Federal army came up to assault Marye's Heights, "I will kill them all."[8] From the start of the battle to the end of it, not one Federal soldier got within 100 feet of the stone wall.

The failure was not for want of trying: nearly half of the Yankee army set out to get there. After Sumner's people wore themselves out Burnside sent in his Center Grand Division. This was under Joseph Hooker, whom the newspapers called "Fighting Joe" and who was everything Sumner was not. He was smart, adaptable, his mental agility unhampered by the slightest trace of loyalty toward any superior: there was no reason to doubt his fidelity to the Union cause, but he did see the war mostly in terms of opportunity for Joe Hooker, and there was no opportunity in front of Marye's Heights. He sent back word that the assault could not succeed, and when his orders were repeated he rode back to headquarters to protest in person, doing it so vigorously that Burnside's military secretary considered him "ungentlemanly and impatient." It did no good; orders were orders, and Hooker's division began to advance over ground littered with dead and wounded from Sumner's command.

Hooker was right. The case was hopeless, and the new divisions got no farther than those that had gone in earlier. Toward the end of the day a curious additional handicap developed. Brigadier General Andrew A. Humphreys, leading a division through the smoky twilight toward the blazing wall, believed that his men might actually have stormed the position if the prostrate survivors of former attacks had not kept trying to stop them. Humphreys' soldiers waded through a sea of clutching hands; wounded and unwounded men wanted to see no more men killed in an attempt to do the impossible, and they reached up to grab feet and pants legs, throwing the advance into such disorder that it gave way under fire as all the others had done. And at last, "finding that I had lost as many men as my orders required me to lose," Hooker suspended the attack.[9]

Different participants said different things, all of them meaning much the same. Old Sumner spoke of the fearful musketry that swept the plain and said that "no troops could stand such a fire as that." Hooker remarked that the soldiers "were put to do a work that no men could do," and one of the infantrymen involved said that he and his comrades "might as well have tried to take Hell." The next day a general officer visited Burnside and found him pacing restlessly back and forth in his tent, repeating "Oh, those men! Those men!" The visitor asked what he meant, and Burnside gestured toward the field where so many had fallen, saying: "I am thinking of them all the time."[10]

Haunted thus by ghosts, Burnside also was plagued by a tragic might-have-been. This half of the battle never could have been a success, but the other half was different. His blow at Stonewall Jackson could have been a victory. It did not actually come very close to it but the possibility was there, and Burnside did not need to shoulder all of the blame for the failure.

In his assault on Lee's right Burnside used his Left Grand Division, under William B. Franklin. A favorite of the departed McClellan, Franklin was careful, competent, and uninspired; the sort of general who is unlikely to make a serious blunder and equally unlikely to capitalize on a blunder made by his opponent. On this day at Fredericksburg, Franklin followed the strict letter of his orders and came to failure. It seems likely that even after the battle was over he did not quite see the success that might have been won if his orders had been more intelligently drafted by General Burnside or more intelligently interpreted by himself.

Burnside wanted Franklin to use his entire force to fight his way into Lee's right rear, but the written orders he sent down did not say it that way. They told Franklin to get ready for a rapid move down the Old Richmond road, which ran past Jackson's front and gave access to roads that led directly to the Confederate rear. They also told him to send, at once, "a division at least" to seize the rising ground north of Hamilton's Crossing. Two of Hooker's infantry divisions and two divisions of cavalry were put at his disposal, so that he commanded nearly half of the Federal army. He was instructed, finally, to be prepared "to move at once, as soon as the fog lifts."[11]

This opaque writing led to trouble. Franklin thought he had simply been told to strike a moderate blow and stand by for further orders. Dutifully enough, he sent out a single division to attack Jackson's line, with another division in support. He also moved a division south to keep Stuart's pestiferous horse artillery at a distance; using two fieldpieces, Stuart's brilliant young gunner, Major John Pelham, managed to delay Franklin's deployment for most of the morning. But by noon Franklin was ready to take additional action as soon as headquarters told him to do so.

He got no further orders, but unexpected opportunity did present itself.

The division that attacked Jackson was a good one; three brigades of Pennsylvanians under crabbed, reliable Major General George Gordon Meade. It crossed the railroad tracks, crashed through stubby thickets and small timber, and—incredibly—broke the Confederate line. If the breakthrough had been exploited, Burnside could have won his battle in spite of the odds.

Jackson's army corps, approximately 35,000 strong, had been posted farther down the Rappahannock, and Lee had been a little tardy in ordering it up to the line it held on December 13. Placing his men in haste, Jackson apparently had been careless. At any rate there was a gap in his line just where Meade's men hit him, and the Pennsylvanians went straight through it, crumpling the brigades on either side, driving off the support troops, and actually reaching the higher ground Burnside wanted occupied. There they were, 4,500 of them, right in the middle of Jackson's 35,000, touching the chance of victory. Afterward Meade cried bitterly: "The slightest straw almost would have kept the tide in our favor."[12]

Meade's men needed help they did not get. The division that had been assigned to support them got started late, floundered up ineffectively, never came in contact with them, and was broken and driven away without giving them the slightest help. Jackson was quick to organize a counterattack, and when it struck it struck with power; the Pennsylvanians were assailed in front and on both flanks, nobody in all the Federal army showed any sign of coming to the rescue, and at last the division broke and ran for it, more than a third of its men out of action. The triumphant Confederates swept out into the open as if they would drive the whole Federal left into the river, but Franklin's artillery halted them and when the day ended nothing whatever had been accomplished. Burnside's failure had been complete. He had lost more than 12,000 men, his opponent had lost fewer than half that many, and the battle had done nothing except demonstrate that the strength of the Army of the Potomac lay in its rank and file rather than in its generals.

It demonstrated too the prankish fate that governs battles. The command failure had been abysmal; and yet if Sumner and Franklin had changed places, each man taking his own limitations to the other man's assignment, and each working under Burnside's hazy directives, the battle might have been very different. Franklin, sticking to the letter of his orders, would have tapped at Marye's Heights with one division, bringing one more up in support, and letting it go at that; and an infinity of useless death and suffering would have been avoided. Sumner, fighting heads down, would have hit the break in Jackson's line with as many of his 60,000 as he could get to the scene, and something important might have come of it; and you can imagine the whole battle turned inside-out if you imagine one change in the assignments of two men. There is not much logic in war.[13]

Burnside wanted to renew the attack next day but was talked out of it, and for two days the armies stayed in skirmish-line contact, neither daring to strike at the other; then Burnside moved his men back across the river to their old camps, took up his bridges, and tacitly confessed that the whole adventure had been a failure. Lee was left in full possession of the town and the battlefield.

The town was wrecked—abandoned by most of its inhabitants, it had been heavily bombarded and then had been looted by the Federal troops—and the battlefield was ghastly, especially the plain below Marye's Heights. On the night after the battle a thick white fog filled the river valley, and Federal stretcher bearers who went out to bring in the wounded felt that they were groping along the shore of some nightmarish lake, the town all hidden, starlight coming down on what looked like a ghostly expanse of misty water. At first this unearthly landscape seemed to be silent, and then the rescue parties realized that the night was not quiet at all; the cries of the wounded men echoed all about them, the noise dying away now and then with only a single agonized scream quavering across the darkness, then rising as thousands of men joined in a disorganized chorus.[14]

After the stretcher bearers worked, needy Confederates

came out to take uniforms and shoes from dead Yankees who would need them no more; and when light came the field was monstrous to see, with hundreds of frozen naked corpses lying in front of the stone wall. One Confederate confessed that "it was an awful sight to see them strewing the ground stark and stiff in the dim starlight," and another remarked: "All the Yank dead had been stripped of every rag of their clothing and looked like hogs that had been cleaned. . . . It was an awful sight. I pitied these poor dead men and could not help it."

Jeb Stuart, as a professional soldier, took a more detached view, and in a letter to Custis Lee he exulted: "The victory won by us here is one of the neatest and cheapest of the war. Englishmen here who surveyed Solferino & all the battlefields of Italy say that the pile of dead on the plains of Fredericksburg exceeds anything of the sort ever seen by them." What had happened to the buildings of the town, however, moved Stuart profoundly, and he added: "Fredericksburg is in ruins. It is the saddest sight I ever saw."[15]

3. The Politics of War

DURING MANY unrewarding months of war, public men in Washington had become convinced that the country's woes came from bad leadership. This belief was pessimistic but comforting, because there was always somebody to blame for misfortune, and so whenever bad news arrived eloquent letters were written. Thus Congressman William H. Wadsworth of Kentucky, a border state conservative, took heart after Fredericksburg in the reflection that "a nation which Lincoln and his controllers could not destroy in two years is immortal," and he wrote that the President was reported to have said that if a worse place than Hell existed he was in it. The ultra-radical Senator Zachariah Chandler asserted that folly reigned supreme, and complained of "fool or traitor generals." Senator Chandler doubted that Mr. Lincoln was strong enough for the situation, sharing this doubt with Republican Editor Joseph Medill, who said that "Lincoln is only half awake and will never do much better than he has done."[1]

General Burnside, to be sure, manfully tried to take all

the blame. He wrote bluntly, "for the failure in the attack I am responsible," he assured General Halleck that the administration had given him proper support, and he told a friendly newspaperman that an army commander who met with disaster had to assume the responsibility.[2] Yet the storm that grew out of this battle centered first of all about the White House—the discontent of the Army of the Potomac officer corps could be aired somewhat later—and it reflected the fact that the very men who most passionately shared Mr. Lincoln's desire for a speedy and unconditional victory were the ones who would most quickly and bitterly criticize him for failing to win it.

Some of these were men of action like Senator Chandler, coarse-gained, tough; others were men of thought, reflective liberal-intellectuals like the historian, George Bancroft, former Secretary of the Navy; and they objected deeply to the fact that although Mr. Lincoln seemed to know where he wanted to go he obviously lacked their own certainty about the best way to get there. Weeks before the battle was fought, Bancroft summed up the complaint in a letter to his fellow liberal, Francis Lieber: "How can we reach our President with advice? He is ignorant, self-willed, and is surrounded by men some of whom are almost as ignorant as himself. So we have the dilemma put to us, What to do, when his power must continue two years longer and when the existence of our country may be endangered before he can be replaced by a man of sense. How hard, in order to save the country, to sustain a man who is incompetent."[3] Perhaps the saddest thing about being a good liberal is that at times one is compelled to meditate in that vein.

It was hard to be sure about President Lincoln. Some men thought him a Cromwell, bent on destruction and subjugation; to others he looked like a trimmer, seeking no more than political advantage. He refused to modify the Emancipation Proclamation, which he was to issue in final form on the first day of 1863, but he urged Congress to amend the Constitution so as to provide Federal compensation for any slave state that would abolish slavery before 1900. This seemed to involve a long delay, and the Ohio Congressman Albert Gallatin Riddle spoke for most abolitionists when he declared hotly that the war and slavery ought to end together on some date ever so much nearer than

1900. Mr. Lincoln continued to support his old plan for colonization of freed slaves in some land far away; yet he also asserted that the common objection to permitting freedmen to remain in the United States "is largely imaginary if not sometimes malicious."[4] He told one acquaintance that it was pointless to try to make formal definitions of political programs because events were moving too fast; political issues were swept away as soon as they were formed, and "no party will have time to mature until after the war." He told this man, as he told all others, that he was determined to crush rebellion, but he added an oddly phrased qualification—he hoped "to carry a truce in the belly of this war," to be delivered if the South offered to return to the fold. Rebellion that voluntarily ceased to be rebellion need not be crushed; neither it, nor the men who had made it.[5]

A clearer statement of purpose came in a letter he wrote a few weeks after Fredericksburg to the aggressive Douglas Democrat from Illinois, John A. McClernand. As a war Democrat whose support was so valuable in the early days of the war, McClernand had been made major general, and now he was trying to subdue rebellion in the Mississippi Valley. To his intense disgust he was subordinate to U. S. Grant, but he still had a direct line of communication to the White House, and when he reported that prominent Confederates, friends of his in the old days, wanted to know the terms on which they could have peace Mr. Lincoln hastened to give him a frank reply.

Reunion, said the President, was the most and the least he had ever asked. He had tried for nearly a year and a half to get it without touching slavery, and when he found this impossible he had drafted the Emancipation Proclamation, giving fair warning in advance. The proclamation would stand, yet secessionist slave states could still escape serious injury: "Let them adopt systems of apprenticeship for the colored people, conforming substantially to the most approved plans of gradual emancipation; and, with the aid they can have from the general government, they may be nearly as well off, in this respect, as if the present trouble had not occurred, and much better off than they can possibly be if the contest continues persistently." Time was running out, and "if the friends you mention really wish to have peace upon the old terms they should act at once. Every day makes the case more difficult."[6]

Inasmuch as "the old terms" promised peace upon reunion, with no harm to the peculiar institution, this was strange talk to come from the author of the Emancipation Proclamation; but what Mr. Lincoln was really saying was that the war even now was not entirely and irrevocably a military operation. Men were shooting at each other instead of arguing and debating, but it was still possible for them to recognize the fact of their continuing common interest. Once they admitted that this interest endured in spite of all they had been doing to each other, they could have recourse to the saving devices of politics. They could eventually make a deal, the winner accepting less than the maximum so that the loser could save more than the minimum. Despite all the fury and the bloodshed, this was still a political contest. That was why McClernand had been made a major general in the first place; it was also why he was now in the Mississippi Valley, engaged in a venture which outraged strategy but which made excellent sense politically.

Late in the summer of 1862, when Mr. Lincoln was preparing to proclaim emancipation even though he knew that this would cost him the support of many thousands of war Democrats (beginning with General McClellan and working down to the irreplaceable rank and file) McClernand took leave from his post as division commander in Grant's army and went to Washington to lay a proposition before the President.

Reduced to its elements, the proposition was simple. McClernand would rekindle the flame of patriotism among middle western Democrats and would personally persuade them to send a host of new recruits into the army, despite their hatred of abolitionists and black Republicans. In return, McClernand wanted an independent command, with authority to capture Vicksburg and reopen the Mississippi Valley, despite the fact that both General Halleck and General Grant understood this to be Grant's assignment. To divide the command of the all-important Mississippi campaign might well be dangerous folly—off beyond the picket lines, Confederate Joe Johnston, vexed by the ruinous independence of General Holmes, could have testified on that point—but General McClernand and President Lincoln, veterans of western politics, were considering not so much the object of the campaign as the base on which it had to rest. The drive to open the Mississippi would never succeed unless the whole weight of a united northwest were massed behind it. Here McClernand had something to offer, and Mr. Lincoln made up his mind to use him.

So McClernand went west in October, armed with confidential orders instructing him to raise and organize troops in Indiana, Illinois, and Iowa. He was to forward these to such place as General Halleck might designate, and "when a sufficient force, not required by the operations of General Grant," had been assembled, McClernand could organize and command an expedition against Vicksburg. Vicksburg taken, he was empowered to go on down to New Orleans; reaching which place, at the head of a victorious army, he would unquestionably be the hero of the war with immense political rewards awaiting him.[7]

It was a bright opportunity, and McClernand went to work vigorously and effectively. By the beginning of December he had sent thousands of soldiers to the chosen staging point of Memphis, and as he tied up the loose ends in his headquarters at Springfield, Illinois, he waited for formal orders to go down to Memphis and assume command. Waiting with rising impatience, he began to see that the arrangement he had made was not quite as solid as it looked.

The administration had given him a fair promise but it contained a big loophole, perfectly visible to a lawyer as competent as McClernand once the first burst of enthusiasm had passed. McClernand remained under the control of General Halleck, who was also a competent lawyer, and his striking force was to consist of troops who—in Halleck's opinion—were not needed by General Grant. Grant had begun his campaign against Vicksburg and obviously needed all the men he could get, and although Grant had never been one of Halleck's favorites the general-in-chief had no use at all for McClernand. whom he considered vainglorious, contentious, and unskilled; nor did he like McClernand's program. Grant was already making Joe Johnston's argument for unity of command in the Mississippi Valley, and Halleck would presently give him control of Federal troops from beyond the river. There was no chance whatever that Halleck would now approve an independent command for

McClernand, and although he could not countermand Mc-
Clernand's orders he could lay down the conditions under
which they must be carried out. Halleck in short had all of
the resources by which an ingenious administrator can modify
a distasteful directive, and he knew exactly how to use them.

Grant moved south from Grand Junction, Tennessee—just
north of the Mississippi-Tennessee line, fifty miles east of
Memphis—early in November, following the line of the
Mississippi Central Railroad, planning to come in on Vicksburg from the east. He had left Sherman in Memphis to
bring down promised reinforcements, and a few days after
his advance began he notified Halleck that reinforcements
were not arriving. Halleck telegraphed that plenty of troops
were on the way, then added mysteriously: MEMPHIS WILL
BE MADE THE DEPOT OF A JOINT MILITARY AND NAVAL EX-
PEDITION ON VICKSBURG. Grant had been hearing rumors
about McClernand, and this seemed to give them substance.
He sent Halleck an urgent inquiry: AM I TO UNDERSTAND
THAT I LIE STILL HERE WHILE AN EXPEDITION IS FITTED
OUT FROM MEMPHIS, OR DO YOU WANT ME TO PUSH AS FAR
SOUTH AS POSSIBLE? AM I TO HAVE SHERMAN SUBJECT TO
MY ORDERS, OR ARE HE AND HIS FORCES RESERVED FOR SOME
SPECIAL SERVICE?

Halleck's reply was bland: YOU HAVE COMMAND OF ALL
TROOPS SENT TO YOUR DEPARTMENT AND HAVE PERMISSION
TO FIGHT THE ENEMY WHERE YOU PLEASE.

Memphis unquestionably was in Grant's department, and
if Grant could not keep this joint military and naval expedition from being launched he might at least assert control
over the military part of it. He immediately revised Sherman's orders. While Grant continued to advance along the
railroad line, Sherman was to collect the troops at Memphis,
take them down the river with transports and gunboats as
soon as the Navy was ready, and head for the mouth of
the Yazoo River, a few miles above Vicksburg. Moving a
short distance up that stream he was to put his men ashore
and attack the Vicksburg defenses from the north while
Grant was coming in from the east. Pemberton could not
possibly get together enough men to meet both threats, and
one or the other was almost certain to succeed. And if it
happened that Sherman and all the troops left Memphis

before ardent McClernand got there . . . well, Halleck's hint was broad enough.[8]

As the first two weeks in December passed McClernand suspected that something like this was being attempted, and he sent angry protests to Washington. Secretary Stanton's reply was as bland as the message Halleck had sent to Grant: McClernand was by no means being superseded, he was about to be announced in War Department orders as commander of a corps in Grant's army, the plan for the amphibious assault on Vicksburg stood, and as soon as McClernand reached Memphis he could take charge of the expedition because he outranked everybody in Grant's department except Grant himself.

This reassurance was in fact somewhat deflationary, because to command a corps under Grant was not quite the same as to be at the head of an independent army. Still, McClernand could make the best of it; he was to remain leader of the expedition against Vicksburg, and all he needed now was a signed order from Grant telling him to go to Memphis and start his campaign.

But this order was strangely late in reaching him. Nobody except McClernand (who had no control over it) seemed to be in a rousing hurry about it; and anyway there was unanticipated interference by armies of the Southern Confederacy. McClernand's advance toward greatness began with a humiliating anticlimax.

Shortly before this, fortified by renewed assurances from Washington that he could control all activities in his department, and still officially ignorant of any special orders affecting McClernand, Grant notified Halleck that Sherman would command the amphibious expedition and he ordered Sherman to get under way as soon as men, transports, and naval support were properly organized. Halleck sent a quiet warning: Sherman would be his own choice, but the President might insist on naming a commander for this expedition. Then, on December 18, Grant at last got a positive directive from the general-in-chief: the troops in his department were being organized into four army corps, their commanders designated at Washington. The troops at Memphis, plus a division that was being made available from beyond the Mississippi, would form two of these corps; McClernand would command one of them and Sherman would have the other. Finally: "It is the wish of the President that General McClernand's corps shall constitute a part of the river expedition and that he shall have the immediate command under your direction."[9]

This of course could not be evaded and Grant did not try to evade it. He did exactly what he was supposed to do; that is, he immediately sent a message to McClernand, at Springfield, explaining the situation and telling him to go at once to Memphis, where Sherman would turn over the command and give him all of the written and oral orders and information that had been issued to date. Grant added that he hoped McClernand would find the expedition ready to move, and he pointed out that quick action was essential; he promised, also, that he himself would co-operate by menacing Pemberton along the line of the railroad. To complete the transaction he ordered a copy of this message transmitted to Sherman at Memphis.[10]

Now Grant and his troops were at Oxford, Mississippi, and any messages he sent to his subordinates had a long way to go. His line of supply and communication ran straight north along the railroad all the way to Columbus, Kentucky, more than 175 miles away. The fact that on its way through western Tennessee the railroad and its telegraph system passed within fifty miles of Memphis did not help, because Confederate cavalry and guerrilla bands had broken all land communication with Memphis. The message to Sherman, therefore, had to be sent to Columbus by telegraph and then had to go down the river to Memphis by steamboat. Similarly, the message to McClernand had to go to Columbus, to be forwarded thence by boat to Cairo, Illinois, where it could be telegraphed on to Springfield. It was possible for energetic enemies to interfere with all of this, because no matter how diligently the Federals tried to guard this line it remained painfully exposed.

One of the first men to realize this was the Confederacy's General Johnston. Shortly after he took command in the west he telegraphed to General Bragg, urging him to strike that vulnerable line with his cavalry. Apparently Bragg never got this telegram but that did no harm because he thought of the same thing independently and told Nathan Bedford Forrest to assemble his cavalry and go to work; after which he optimistically told President Davis that if this stroke succeeded it might compel Grant to retreat.[11]

The odds were much against success. Forrest's cavalry was miserably equipped and totally untrained; indeed, it barely existed at all, for it was still being organized when Bragg gave Forrest his orders. The men were the rawest of raw recruits, hundreds of them had neither weapons nor horses, those who were armed carried nothing better than shotguns or flintlock muskets, hardly anyone had any clothing or blankets except what he had brought from home, and supplies were so skimpy that Bragg warned Forrest the men would have to find their own food and forage once they set out. To get at Grant's railroad this cavalry must first cross the Tennessee River, which had no bridges and few boats and was much too deep to wade. Once across they would be in a region swarming with many thousands of Yankee soldiers who had been carefully posted all along the railroad for the specific purpose of beating off raids like this; and no matter how the raid went, in the end these Confederates would have to get back across the river with many times their number hotly pursuing them. By any logical appraisal of the prospects, this expedition had no chance . . . except that it was being led by Forrest.

Forrest was self-made all the way, a brigadier general with no military background whatever and no social background worth mentioning, a man who would be wholly out of place in the gallery of Confederate officers were it not that he was, inexplicably, a military genius: the best man in either the Confederacy or the Union for the kind of exploit Bragg was demanding. The measure of his capacity lies in what he now accomplished. He completely disrupted all of the Federal plans—Halleck's, Grant's, McClernand's, everybody's—and with excellent assistance from the romantic Van Dorn, who launched a simultaneous strike at Grant's immediate rear, he made Bragg's hopeful prediction good: Grant did have to retreat, getting out of Mississippi entirely and going all the way back to Memphis. Quite incidentally, Forrest armed, equipped, recruited and fed his cavalry while he was doing all of this. When the raid ended he had more men than he had when it began, all of them excellently mounted, armed, clad and fed by the United States government.

Forrest's cavalry started from the town of Columbia, south-

west of Murfreesboro, on December 11. Forrest crossed the
Tennessee River at Clifton, swimming his animals and taking
his men over, a troop at a time, in an old flatboat; then he
struck west, routing a Federal cavalry detachment on the
way, and coming up to the railroad junction town of Jackson, Tennessee, where Grant's Mississippi Central stemmed
off of the principal north-south line, the Mobile & Ohio.
Veering away from Jackson, which the Federals held in
force, Forrest went rampaging north along the Mobile &
Ohio, capturing Union supply and ammunition dumps, brush-
ing off hostile patrols, seizing the horses, weapons, and other
equipment he needed, and utterly ruining the railroad for a
stretch of sixty miles or more. Grant sent powerful contingents of cavalry and infantry to destroy this marauder, but
Forrest was extremely elusive. One Federal column at last got
in his path at Parker's Cross Roads, a converging column
came up from Forrest's rear, and there was a sharp fight in
which Forrest lost 300 men; but at last Forrest broke away,
shook off his pursuers, got to the Tennessee, retrieved the
flatboat he had used earlier, and got his expedition safely
over to Confederate territory on the eastern side of the river.
He had put 2500 Federals out of action, had captured ten
pieces of artillery and 10,000 small arms, and had completely broken Grant's communications with the outside world
for ten days.[12]

The first result was that neither McClernand nor Sherman
got Grant's December 18 orders until many days later. Obeying his earlier orders—which, as far as he knew, were still
in force—Sherman started south from Memphis on December 20. McClernand, receiving his own orders only after this
force had reached the vicinity of Vicksburg, could do no
more than get on a steamboat in frantic pursuit, complaining
bitterly that because of "petty jealousy *somewhere* in high
authority" he had been the victim of exceedingly sharp practice.[13] He was correct in his belief that neither Halleck nor
Grant wanted him to command the Vicksburg expedition; but
both men had dutifully followed the President's directive, and
neither could really be blamed for the fact that Forrest's
troopers cut the Mobile & Ohio telegraph line on the evening of December 18 just in time to prevent transmission of
Grant's dispatches.

Grant was in an even more embarrassing position than

McClernand. With his line of supply coming down from Columbus, Kentucky, he had planted his advance base at Holly Springs, Mississippi, thirty miles north of his army's position near Oxford, and he supposed that the garrison of 1500 men he had posted there was strong enough to protect it. But on December 20, just when Forrest was doing his worst a hundred miles to the north, Earl Van Dorn with all of Pemberton's cavalry, 3000 men or more, slipped by the Federal patrols and came storming in to Holly Springs and demanded that the town be surrendered. The Union commander was a Colonel R. C. Murphy, and he caved in at once, surrendering without more than token resistance. Van Dorn's soldiers went through the supply dumps like a swarm of locusts, destroying everything Grant's army possessed— $1,500,000 worth of food, ammunition, and equipment, by Van Dorn's estimate, including three solid freight trains waiting to be unloaded. A jubilant Southern reporter saw panicky Yankees in flight "clothed very similarly to Joseph when the lady Potiphar attempted to detain him," and wrote breathlessly of "tents burning, torches flaming, Confederates shouting, guns popping, sabres clanking, abolitionists begging for mercy, 'rebels' shouting exultingly, women *en dishabile* clapping their hands frantic with joy, crying 'Kill them! Kill them!'" Grant announced "the disgraceful surrender" with "pain and mortification," and said Holly Springs could easily have been held; and scapegrace Colonel Murphy was dismissed from the service.[14] Van Dorn got away unharmed, and Grant's army, finding itself with no supplies and no means of getting any more, went dejectedly northward in retreat.

Between them, Forrest and Van Dorn destroyed any chance that the amphibious expedition might succeed, whether with or without McClernand. This operation had been keyed to the expectation that Grant's advance would keep Pemberton from reinforcing the Vicksburg garrison, and when Grant's advance became a retreat Pemberton had no problem. Sending reinforcements on ahead, Pemberton reached Vicksburg on December 26 to find Sherman's men disembarking along the Yazoo River. When the Federal assault was made on December 29, on low ground along Chickasaw Bayou just north of Vicksburg, Pemberton's men beat it off without difficulty. Sherman lost more than 1700 men, accomplished nothing at all, and withdrew to a cheerless camp at Milliken's Bend, on the west side of the Mississippi twenty miles above the Confederate stronghold. There, at last, McClernand caught up with him, assuming command of a force which had just had to confess a humiliating failure.[15]

4. In the Mists at Stone's River

WINTER IN TENNESSEE (said a man who campaigned there) "means cold, and snow, and rain, and boundless mud," and neither the Federals at Nashville nor the Confederates at Murfreesboro really wanted to be active before spring. The main bodies of the armies were only thirty miles apart, but this was more of a distance than the map showed because the country between them was firmly held by Braxton Bragg's cavalry. Bragg's new cavalry chief, Major General Joseph Wheeler, was young and somewhat full of himself— he had a gay way of telling his staff, when he had a raid in the making: "The War Child rides tonight!"—but he was diligent and active, and he was providing a solid cavalry screen behind which Bragg's infantry could remain quietly on the defensive.

Bragg wanted to remain on the defensive as long as possible because he felt too weak to do anything else. On General Johnston's orders he had lately sent a solid infantry division, 9000 men under Major General C. L. Stevenson, off to Mississippi to help General Pemberton; General Johnston believed that helping Pemberton thus might eventually cause the loss of both Tennessee and Mississippi, but President Davis insisted and Johnston issued an order which both he and Bragg disliked very much. So Stevenson's division was gone, probably for good; Forrest's men were off to the west, harrying the Mobile & Ohio country, and Morgan's were raiding far to the northward, in Kentucky; as Christmas came Bragg had fewer than 40,000 men of all arms, and it was greatly to his interest to stay inactive.

Besides this, he gained much simply by remaining at Murfreesboro. Middle Tennessee was a productive land of plenty, and as long as Bragg's army controlled it the Confederacy could draw large supplies of food, forage, leather, cloth, and other essential materials.[1] Naturally, Bragg wanted to stay where he was.

His opponent, Major General William S. Rosecrans, wanted to drive him away but refused to be hasty about it. When he took over the command from Don Carlos Buell at the end of October, Rosecrans was appalled to find that a third of his army was either in the hospital or absent without leave, and that much of the rest was badly drilled and miserably equipped. Like Grant, he dangled at the end of an exposed supply line, which was an irresistible temptation to Confederate raiders; with good reason Rosecrans refused to advance until he had built up a reserve of at least two million rations. He also wanted to strengthen his cavalry so that it could keep the jaunty Confederate troopers from riding circles around it, and his entire army clearly needed a refit and a general reorganization. His reasons for delay were numerous and compelling, and he explained them to Washington in much detail.[2]

By this time Washington had grown weary of hearing commanding generals explain their excellent reasons for inaction. Early in December Halleck notified Rosecrans that the President was most impatient, and warned him: "If you remain one more week in Nashville I cannot prevent your removal." Rosecrans replied that he had wasted no time, listed the evil things that would happen if he moved prematurely, and stoutly closed: "To threats of removal or the like I must be permitted to say that I am insensible." Halleck told him that this was very well, but the President had repeatedly said that there were "imperative reasons why the enemy should be driven across the Tennessee River at the earliest possible moment." The President had not said what these reasons were, but it was important for the Federals to win a decisive victory in Tennessee and Rosecrans must go ahead and win it: "There is a pressure for you to advance much greater than you can possibly have imagined."[3]

In point of fact Rosecrans put heavy pressure on himself. He was a driver, and his army was responding to him; the enlisted men were already calling him "Old Rosey," a sure sign of enthusiastic affection. They especially liked the way he inspected regiments. If he saw a soldier with worn-out shoes or a ragged coat he would tell him: "Go to your captain and demand what you need! Go to him every day until you get it! Bore him for it! Bore him in his quarters! Bore him at meal time! Bore him in bed! Don't let him rest!" Warming to his exhortation, he would explain that this demand for relief would bounce upward, through regiment, brigade, division and corps until it reached army headquarters, where "I'll see then if you don't get what you want!"

The men believed that Rosecrans worked so hard that he always stayed up until two in the morning, usually until four, sometimes all night; his aides would fall asleep in their chairs while he worked, and he would tweak their ears, pat their heads paternally, and send them to their cots. He insisted on having young men on his staff—"sandy fellows," he called them, "quick and sharp," who lacked experience and thus had no fixed habits of thought and action to overcome. From his troop commanders he demanded precision. One brigadier sent him a report on Confederate movements, opening with the sentence: "Permit me to give you the following positive information." The brigadier quickly got the report back, with the endorsement: "General Negley will please call at headquarters and explain on what grounds he rests his belief that the information within is positive." Asserting that in a moving army he could not discipline errant officers by court-martial, Rosecrans demanded and got from Secretary Stanton authority to muster out of service officers guilty of pillage, drunkenness, or misbehavior in the presence of the enemy.[4]

Before Christmas Bragg heard that the Federals might be getting ready to retreat, and he told Wheeler to press their outposts and see what was going on. Wheeler did, and found no sign of a withdrawal; on the contrary all of Rosecrans' army was south of the Cumberland and a forward movement seemed likely. Probably the news was about what Bragg expected. Even though Forrest and Van Dorn had spoiled Grant's plans they had done no harm to Rosecrans, and the strategic picture in Tennessee was unchanged: the Federals had the initiative, and Bragg's army could do nothing but wait for the enemy to make the next move. Bragg's men were quite willing to wait; as veterans they did not care how long active campaigning might be postponed, and while they waited they were in good spirits. There was plenty to eat, for once, and plenty to wear, and the camps were healthy. On Christmas Day the weather was mild and the officers paid calls and got up horse races, while the men played games, including that now-forgotten favorite of country school yards, prisoner's base. Some of the headquarters officers planned an elaborate ball for December 26.[5]

The ball was never held, because on the morning of December 26 the cavalry sent word that the Yankees were on the march, heading for Murfreesboro. Rosecrans had things ready at last, twenty days' rations in the warehouses, 45,000 men organized in three commands under Major Generals George H. Thomas, Alexander McD. McCook, and Thomas L. Crittenden. (Technically, these commands were known as wings; actually they were army corps, and they would be regularized as such a bit later.) On Christmas night Rosecrans had these officers, and his own staff, at headquarters for an eve-of-campaign drink and a final word. For a time he was the genial host; then, abruptly, he banged a glass down on a table and made his little speech: "We move tomorrow, gentlemen! We shall begin to skirmish probably as soon as we pass the outposts. Press them hard! Drive them out of their nests! Make them fight or run! Strike hard and fast! Give them no rest! Fight them—fight them, I say!" He pounded his open palm with his fist, while imperturbable Pap Thomas grinned at him; and as the generals left to go to their tents Rosecrans gave each man a grip of the hand and repeated: "Fight! Keep fighting! They will not stand it!"[6]

This vibrant enthusiasm was for the high command. For lesser ranks there was a long hike in the mud. Bragg's army was spread out on a thirty-mile front, at right angles to the line of the Federal advance, so Rosecrans had to send his men forward in separate columns, each adjusting its march to the progress of its neighbors. It made for slow going, and alert Confederate cavalry skirmished along every rise of ground to make the going even slower. The miserable December weather was the worst handicap of all, and the Federal army needed five days to get from Nashville to Murfreesboro. Hard rain driven by cold gusty winds turned the roads into mud and soaked the marching men to the skin; when the rain stopped dense fog covered bivouacs in the dripping second-growth timber, and when more wind came in the morning to blow the fog away it brought rain again so that it was hard for anybody to cook breakfast. The Confederates were doing about as much marching as the Federals were, because Bragg's extended line had to concentrate, and they got as cold and wet and muddy; Bragg wrote feelingly, afterward, about their "seven days exposure to the inclemency of winter weather without cover and with most insufficient diet." One of his brigades dug shallow rifle pits on an exposed hillock and had to huddle there for forty-eight hours, forbidden to make fires either for warmth or for cooking, their blankets as wet as their clothing.[7]

By December 30 the two armies were groping into close contact a few miles west and northwest of Murfreesboro, the Federals astride the turnpike that ran back to Nashville. The ground was rocky, broken by small hillocks and ridges, with scrub timber separating the brown fields; at irregular intervals there were dense thickets of cedar, wet and black under the gray sky. Across this landscape innumerable parties of skirmishers were prowling. They collided, fired at each other —often enough without doing any damage—and by these small, haphazard encounters, repeated over and over again, the two armies clumsily collected the bits of information that told each one where its enemy was. Slowly, brigade by brigade, the Federal army began to form an irregular line of battle, between three and four miles from flank to flank, facing generally toward the east. Just out of range and mostly out of sight in the woods, Bragg's army was similarly drawn into position facing toward the west. One of Bragg's divisions lay north of the Nashville turnpike; all the rest were to the south, with the lazy meandering loops of Stone's River to the rear, between the army and its base, Murfreesboro. There were several bridges over the river, and it had numerous fords, and ordinarily it was no great barrier; with all the rain that had been coming down lately, however, it was due to rise, and if Bragg's army had to retreat in a hurry the river might be a problem.

Bragg had no intention of retreating. The strange irresolution that sometimes came over him in a time of crisis was not in evidence now; even though the Federals were on the offensive, obviously preparing to make an assault, Bragg intended to strike first, gambling that he could catch his foe off balance, throwing his full weight into one smashing blow, North of the turnpike and east of the river he had one division, more than 7000 men under Major General John C. Breckinridge, who had once been a Vice-President of the United States. These men would hold their ground, guarding the immediate approach to Murfreesboro and serving as the army's general reserve. With everybody else—close to 30,000 infantry and artillery, led by the two corps commanders, William J. Hardee and Leonidas Polk—Bragg would attack the Federal right, south of the turnpike and west of the river. He devised this plan on December 30, while the cold rain continued to beat down on the waiting armies, and ordered the assault to take place as soon as daylight came on December 31.

By strange coincidence Rosecrans had made a plan which was almost an exact duplicate of this; he too would defend with his right and attack with his left. McCook's corps had taken position opposite Hardee and Polk, the right end of his line drawn back slightly, and McCook's assignment was simply to hold his ground. Thomas was in the center and Crittenden was on the left, and they would smash at the Confederate right, Crittenden going beyond Stone's River to get at Breckinridge. This attack, like Bragg's, was to be launched at daybreak.

The last day of 1862 came in cold and windy after a wet night. The sky was beginning to clear, although a mist was drifting up from the river valley, and Rosecrans, Crittenden and their staff officers stood chatting behind the Federal left. Out of sight in the surrounding woods, Federal soldiers were working with damp bits of wood to make smoky little fires to boil coffee. As soon as they finished breakfast the battle would begin; some of Crittenden's men were already starting to ford the river. Then, far to the southward, there was a rolling, crackling noise, snapping and sputtering and sounding (as one of the headquarters men remembered it) for all the world like a cane brake on fire. It grew louder, spreading to right and left across sodden fields and woods that the commanding general could not see, and it was punctuated by salvos of artillery fire which overlapped and became a pounding unbroken roar, an ominous bass for the rising treble of the musketry. The uproar came nearer, and there was the far-off sound of the falsetto Confederate battle cry. Down the lanes that led back from McCook's rear came ambulances and supply wagons, rocking and careening as panicky teamsters flogged their horses. Fugitive infantrymen began to appear, singly, then in disorganized squads, finally in a confused broken flood. All chance for a Federal offensive vanished. McCook's entire army corps had been routed, and unless Rosecrans could form a new line and find men who could hold it he might lose his whole army.

Bragg had planned better and moved faster, and his men had not waited for breakfast. Hardee's corps had been posted far beyond McCook's flank, and when his brigades charged, wheeled toward the right and struck the end of McCook's line, that line broke into fragments. Running back to find new defensive positions the Federal brigades lost contact with one another; the Confederates came in a division at a time, each unit striking with crushing force, and whenever a Federal unit formed to make a stand it was flanked, crumpled, and driven back. One of McCook's divisions led by a black-haired, bandy-legged young general named Phil Sheridan swung back like a gate in a gale of wind, rallied, and for a time held on valiantly, a mile away from its original position, facing toward what had been the Federal rear an hour earlier. Then Bishop Polk began driving his men in beside Hardee's, Sheridan's line gave way, and Rosecrans was desperately pulling men over from the extreme left to save the day.

The fresh levies and the remnants of the ones that had been routed began to form up, late in the morning, on or near the Nashville turnpike. That fact measures the extent of the disaster; at daybreak this had been a safe roadway, slanting back on a long diagonal from the army's center to behind its left, and troops that had been posted to attack toward the east were now trying to beat off an onslaught from the southwest and west. Rosecrans' tortured army was bent far back on itself, like a jackknife with its blade nearly closed. If the Confederates could break the Federal grip anywhere on the turnpike the blade would snap shut and the Union army would be gone.

At the angle in the line—the place where the knife blade joined the handle—there was a four-acre patch of trees known as the Round Forest, and by the middle of the morning it was the most important spot on the battlefield. Hardee's men had driven their foes in a huge semicircle and were fighting within musket shot of the pike, but the Federal line had stiffened at last and these Confederates, who had had fearful losses, could do no more. Now Bishop Polk ordered an all-out attack on the Round Forest, which Thomas and Crittenden had packed with infantry backed by a powerful array of artillery—Thomas had been building up a row of guns ever since the battle started, in preparation for this moment of crisis—and the noise of combat became unendurable, so that charging men paused in the fields to pluck cotton from the open bolls and stuff it in their ears. Federals who lay in line of battle northwest of the woods were amazed to see dozens of rabbits, driven wholly out of their wits by the uproar, scampering along the line and trying to crawl under the prostrate soldiers for shelter. Someone remembered that distracted flocks of little birds kept circling over the woods while the fighting was going on.

Spearhead of the attack on the Round Forest was a brigade of Mississippi troops under Brigadier General James R. Chalmers. These were the lads who had huddled for two days in damp rifle pits, unable to build fires, soaked and half frozen; the order to attack struck them as a positive relief, and they swung forward to expend on the hated Yankees the fury generated by forty-eight hours of misery. They charged on the run but the Federal musketry tore them apart; they re-formed, came on again, were broken by artillery fire, General Chalmers was shot down, some regiments lost half a dozen color bearers in rapid succession—and at last the survivors, completely fought out, went back to their rifle pits. A Tennessee brigade charged beside them and captured two batteries, but the Yankee line remained unbroken. By an extremely narrow margin the Federals kept the Round Forest.

They probably would have lost it except for an unexpected echo from the one fragment of Rosecrans' original battle plan that was ever put into effect. Earlier in the day Crittenden had started his corps across Stone's River to lead the attack on the Confederate right. He had to bring it back almost at once because of Hardee's attack, but the simple fact that he had made this unproductive move had a profound effect two hours later. For at the height of the action, when it seemed clear that the Confederates would storm the Round Forest if they could get a little more weight in their attack, Bragg sent for his reserve—Breckinridge's division, far off on the right—and Breckinridge replied that he could send no help because he was about to be attacked by the Yankees. He was of course entirely wrong, but he was going by the best information he had; Crittenden's advance had been reported to him, but somehow the withdrawal had not been noticed, and so Bragg's reserve remained out of action all morning, waiting for an attack that was never made. By the time the misunderstanding was cleared up it was too late; the Federal grip on the Round Forest was too strong to break.

Once his tactical plan had been knocked out of his hands, Rosecrans could do little more than shore up his collapsing lines and show his troops that their commanding officer was still undaunted, and this much he did with unflagging spirits. He seemed to be galloping along the lines all day long, a dead cigar clenched in his teeth, black hat jammed down on his head, his overcoat all streaked with blood—a shell had taken off the head of his chief of staff, riding beside him, and the general had been spattered. If the soldiers needed a general's words to hearten them, Old Rosey was the man. He reined up once by a line of infantry to demand: "Men, do you wish to know how to be safe? Shoot low! Give them a blizzard at their shins!" Gunners in a battery that was hard pressed remembered that he galloped up and told their captain: "Be a little more deliberate and take good aim—don't fire so damned fast!" Usually he rode alone, except for one or two of those sandy fellows on his staff, and one admiring enlisted man said that with his rumpled hat, stained coat, and stubby cigar "he looked more like a third-rate wagon master than a great general, as he is."[8]

If his day was heroic it was frustrating, a continuous process of staving off disaster. When night came and the fighting ended the Federal army was still in one piece and it was not running away, but it had unquestionably taken a beating. It had lost more than a fourth of its numbers, the Confederates had captured twenty-eight pieces of artillery, there had been a cloud of stragglers drifting back toward Nashville throughout the day, and Joe Wheeler had gone rampaging around in the army's rear, destroying wagon trains and threatening to cut the army off from its base entirely. At nightfall Bragg confidently expected the Federals to retreat, and he telegraphed to Richmond that he had won a noble victory and that "God has granted us a happy New Year."[9]

For the enlisted men of the two armies, New Year's Eve was not at all happy. The rain began again, the gloomy thickets dripped in the cold dark, and the fields where so many thousands of wounded men lay were deep with mud. Confederates who wandered across the ground they had won saw hideous things. Here a soldier leaned against a tree, an overturned coffee mill between his spread legs; a Minié ball had struck him while he was getting breakfast and he had bled to death. By a path leading to a spring sprawled another dead Federal, still gripping the bail of an oaken bucket. A Confederate had been cut entirely in two by a shell; another soldier had been killed by the windage of a near miss and lay contorted, his face blackened, not a wound on his body; farther on there were two men who had been killed by the same cannon ball, which had passed through their chests, removing their hearts and leaving "a hole big enough to put your arm through." One Rebel remembered seeing a blue-coated soldier whose skull had been broken open like a melon, his intact brain lying on the ground near his body. A Texas soldier wrote that "the seens on the battle field was aufle" and asserted that "the hogs got a holt of some of the Yankey dead before the night was over." A man from Louisiana saw horrors when the moon broke through the rain clouds: "The earth was burdened with the Yankee dead. They were crossed and piled over each other, nearly all of them lying on their backs, with their faces so ghastly turned up to the moon."[10]

New Year's Day brought disillusionment to General Bragg, because the Federal army clung to its position. There had been a tense meeting of the Federal high command, late the night before, in which everybody agreed with Thomas' terse verdict: "This army *can't* retreat," and Rosecrans ordered his battered divisions to hold their ground.[11] With that decision, the battle of Stone's River began to change from a Confederate victory to a Confederate defeat. Bragg held his army in position on January 1 but he did not resume the attack—could not, because his army had worn itself out. His men had fought magnificently, but there were not enough of them, and it did no good to reflect that they almost certainly would have won decisively if Stevenson's missing division had been there to help. Bragg's army had suffered the astounding loss of approximately one-third of its total effective strength, and although Federal losses had been higher numerically, and almost as high proportionately, a genuine renewal of the Confederate offensive was utterly impossible.[12] In sheer desperation, Bragg ordered Breckinridge to attack the Federal left on the morning of January 2, but the case was hopeless, and the massed Federal artillery quickly broke Breckinridge's brigades to fragments. On January 3 there was another odd pause on the battlefield, while the two mangled armies stared at each other from their wretched bivouacs, and by nightfall it was clear that Bragg had only one option left: retreat. Of infantry and artillery, the only arms that would be effective in a renewed engagement here, he now had no more than 20,000 men. It was reported that Rosecrans was being reinforced, and although this was not true it was obvious that he could get reinforcements long before Bragg could hope to get any. Stone's River was rising behind Hardee's men, if they did not retreat now they might not be able to later—and at last, on the night of January 3, the Confederate army tramped through Murfreesboro and headed south.[13]

It did not have to go far because the Federals were too cut up to pursue. Rosecrans' army stumbled into Murfreesboro like an exhausted man collapsing on his cot, and it spent the better part of six months there, recuperating. This was much too long, yet there was some excuse: this army was only a third as large as the Federal army that had fought at Fredericksburg, yet it had equaled the Fredericksburg losses. These armies at Stone's River had in truth fought each other almost to death and each was out of action for a long time.

To use such a word as "victory" in connection with a shambles like Stone's River is to risk twisting the word out of its meaning. Yet in a negative but vitally important way Rosecrans' army did win something there. It kept the Confederacy from knocking the props out from under the campaign against Vicksburg. Grant's advance could be resumed, because this blow at the roots of Federal power in the west had failed precisely as the earlier blow at Shiloh had failed. (There is a strange similarity between these two mismanaged battles, Shiloh and Stone's River.) Now there was shattering proof of Johnston's gloomy forecast that the essential help for Pemberton's army could not come from Tennessee; and as the cards lay if that help could not come from Tennessee it could not come from anywhere. The retreat of Bragg's army was clear announcement that those cavalry blows at Grant's communications had been mere episodes rather than a turning of the tide.

This was perfectly clear to Abraham Lincoln, who understood the strategic score as well as anybody. Months later, when Rosecrans thought himself in disfavor at the White House, Mr. Lincoln sent measured words of reassurance:

"I can never forget, whilst I remember anything, that about the end of last year, and beginning of this, you gave us a hard-earned victory which, had there been a defeat instead, the nation could scarcely have lived over."[14]

5. Paralysis of Command

RETURNING FROM his visit to the Mississippi Valley after the first of the year, Jefferson Davis faced two major problems. One was the situation created by the Emancipation Proclamation, which Abraham Lincoln issued, as he had promised to do, on New Year's Day; the other was the matter of the war in the west, whose gravity was underlined by the victory General Bragg had first won and then lost at Stone's River. The first problem was largely political, and the other was purely military, but at bottom the two were ominously alike: each one required Mr. Davis to transcend the limitations that the war itself imposed on him and find a solution which a President of the Confederacy could hardly hope to attain.

As always, Mr. Davis presented a cheerful face to the public. On the night of January 5 there was a serenade in front of his house in Richmond, with Captain J. B. Smith's Silver Band on hand to make music. The crowd was small, because the affair had not been announced in advance, but Mr. Davis made a short speech with much spirit. He assured his listeners that their fight for independence was even nobler than the struggle of 1776, because that one was at least waged against a manly foe while the patriots of the 1860s "fight against the offscourings of the earth." He drew laughter by remarking that some of the Yankees whose latest "on to Richmond" drive had been broken up at Fredericksburg did actually get to Richmond—many hundreds of them, as closely guarded prisoners of war—and he treated Stone's River as a victory that might well cause the states of the northwest to break away from the old Union. War, to be sure, was "an evil in every form in which it can be presented," but it was a crucible in which Southern unity was being created: "With such noble women at home, and such heroic soldiers in the field, we are invincible!"[1]

Even an invincible people, however, could feel outrage. For the Confederate Congress a week later Mr. Davis had a prepared speech which was deeply charged with emotion. He spoke of the Emancipation Proclamation as "a measure by which several millions of human beings of an inferior race, peaceful and contented laborers in their sphere, are doomed to extermination," and he continued: "Our own detestation of those who have attempted the most execrable measure recorded in the history of guilty man is tempered by profound contempt for the impotent rage which it discloses." He proposed to turn over to state authorities any Federal officers captured in areas covered by the proclamation, "that they may be dealt with in accordance with the laws of those States providing for the punishment of criminals engaged in exciting servile insurrection," and he went on to explain what the evil effects of the proclamation must be. The proclamation, he said, created a situation which could have only three possible consequences—"the extermination of the slaves, the exile of the whole white population from the Confederacy, or absolute and total separation of these States from the United States"—and the mere fact that it had been issued amounted to a confession by the Federal government that it could no longer hope to subjugate the South by force of arms.[2]

To Edward A. Pollard, the Richmond editor who was becoming Mr. Davis' most bitter and captious critic, this was simply an attempt "to drown public indignation in a volume of furious words," and after the war Mr. Pollard denounced Mr. Davis for "the mean patience with which he submitted to an act of the enemy which despoiled a whole people of their property, and consigned them to a loss and ruin unequaled in all the penalties of modern war."[3] Mr. Pollard, demanding some inconceivable retaliation that could neither have been attempted nor made effective, spoke for nothing more than personal bitterness, and his remark endures only as a historical oddity. But Mr. Davis was speaking for many people, not all of them living in the South, or in the 1860s either, and he was expressing a deep and tragic conviction that the kind of society that was supposed to lie somewhere beyond Mr. Lincoln's proclamation of freedom was simply beyond human attainment.

Yet emancipation had been proclaimed, and after the beginning of 1863 the war would be different because of it. The leaders of the Southern nation were bound to give the matter thought. It was no longer possible to hope that the war's current might yet be reversed; they were in the rapids now, they and all of the American people with them, and although the future might seem unthinkable they were heading toward it at an accelerating pace. Wispy Alexander Stephens, the Vice-President of the Confederacy, reflected on the matter and was moved to deep pessimism.

Stephens did not think the war could last longer than one more year: it would break down, somewhere, "we may not have peace but we shall have a smash-up." The Emancipation Proclamation was irrevocable, President Lincoln could not possibly put back into slavery men whom he had now declared free, and as a result there was no chance at all for "a restored Union with slavery as it was." Ahead there lay only war, and although hardly anybody wanted the war to continue there was no way to stop it. "A large majority on both sides are tired of the war: want peace," wrote Stephens. "I have no doubt about that. But as we do not want peace without independence, so they" (the people of the North) "do not want peace without union. There is the difficulty. I think the war will break down in less than a twelvemonth; but I really do not see in that any prospect for peace, permanent peace. Peace founded upon a treaty recognizing our separate independence is not yet in sight."[4]

It was Stephens' hard fate to see problems so clearly that he became immobilized. He had stated the case with flawless accuracy: wherever this war was taking the people of America, it must take them first through destruction. Stephens could say no more than that. If the facts as he saw them demanded either a broadening of war aims or a change in the way the war was being fought, someone else must chart the course.

This responsibility of course belonged to Mr. Davis, who did not dream of trying to evade it. On the matter of war aims he was completely inflexible, and no proclamation from Washington could make the slightest difference to him. The

Southern struggle defined itself, and the fact that the world in which that struggle must be waged was now being redefined most drastically mattered not at all. To the end Mr. Davis would abide by the defiant sentence he had flung to the world at Montgomery, two years earlier: "All we ask is to be let alone." The only problem he would even recognize was the matter of how that aim was to be achieved. He would apply himself to military matters.

As far as the military front in Virginia was concerned there seemed no immediate ground for worry. The eternal wastage of war was creating problems of supply, transportation, and recruitment, to be sure, but these could be thought about later, or perhaps, with sufficient dedication, could simply be overridden. The encouraging point was that the Federals in the east showed no sign of coming up with a soldier who could cope with General Lee. Until they did, the President could contemplate the Virginia front with serenity.

The trouble was in the west, where the Federal advance would certainly be resumed before long. It would move with greater force than before. To meet the new advance with equal force was out of the question. The only hope lay in superior generalship. What was needed in the Mississippi Valley was the kind of strategic brilliance that, in the east, had produced the miracle of the Seven Days. To ask for that, to be sure, was to ask for a good deal, but nothing less would do. It was the President's task to find the right man and put him to work.

As a first step it was necessary to take a long look at General Braxton Bragg, whom nobody suspected of having that sort of brilliance. Mr. Davis liked General Bragg as a man and admired him as a soldier, and after the war Mr. Davis' critics complained that he clung to Bragg too long and defended him much too warmly; but the fact remains that in the winter of 1863 the President tried to remove Bragg from his command and was kept from doing it by none other than General Joseph E. Johnston.

On January 22 Johnston was inspecting the defenses of Mobile, Alabama, when he got a telegram from the President telling him to go at once to Bragg's headquarters at Tullahoma, Tennessee, stopping en route at Chattanooga to pick up a letter of instructions. Obeying, Johnston found that the letter ordered him to take soundings among Bragg's subordinates and let the President know whether Bragg had lost the confidence of his army. Obviously, the President was meditating a change in command and would base his decision largely on Johnston's report. Going on to Tullahoma, where he spent three weeks investigating, Johnston got a look at an extremely odd state of affairs.[5]

Bragg was under heavy criticism for the retreat from Murfreesboro, and much of it rested on the charge that he had ordered the retreat against the advice of his corps and division commanders. This was not true; the retreat had first been urged by Polk's division commanders, Major Generals B. F. Cheatham and J. M. Withers, Polk himself had endorsed their proposal, and by the time the withdrawal began there was virtually unanimous agreement that nothing else was possible. But Bragg had a genius for the maladroit, and after the battle in an attempt to quiet the criticism he made it much worse. Polling his officers on the matter of the retreat, he phrased his letter so clumsily that they considered themselves asked to say whether or not he had lost their confidence. Without a dissenting vote his corps and division commanders replied that this was unfortunately the case. They admired and respected him as a man and a patriot, they said, but they did think the army needed a new commander.[6]

Bragg was deeply dejected. He wrote to a friend that he feared his usefulness was impaired and confessed that he wondered "whether it would not be better for the President to send someone to relieve me," and he wrote to Mr. Davis urging him, "as a favor to myself and justice to the cause we both represent and ardently support" to disregard personal feelings and dispose of the matter for the general good. Mr. Davis bleakly commented that "it is not given to all men of ability to excite enthusiasm and to win the affection of their troops," and he added that only men who had that gift "could overcome the distrust and alienation of their principal officers."[7] Mr. Davis would act after he got General Johnston's report.

It was logical to refer the case to Johnston but it was also unfortunate. Strategic planning in the west was already partly paralyzed because the general and the administration had such different ideas, and this action simply made the paralysis worse. Mr. Davis and the War Department believed that Johnston controlled the armies of both Bragg and Pemberton, with ample powers, and hence controlled the situation in the Mississippi Valley. Johnston felt that these armies were so far apart and faced such different problems that he really controlled nothing. He told his friend Senator Wigfall: "These armies cannot, in the nature of things, form one command. The mistake of the government has been, and is, trying to make them one." Richmond now was preparing to exercise the authority that Johnston thought it should have been exercising all along, but it was asking him to say what it ought to do. Johnston was proud, oddly sensitive, beset by inner resentments. The administration might not get the advice it was expecting to get.

Johnston methodically completed his investigation and then, to Richmond's surprise, reported bluntly that "the interests of the service require that General Bragg should not be removed." Bragg's generals had lost faith in him but Johnston believed that the enlisted men had not; Johnston held that the army was in very good spirits, and pointed out that its numbers were actually larger in mid-February than they had been before the battle of Stone's River—the last fact, he said, being due to Bragg's excellent system of rounding up absentees and making soldiers out of them. All in all, Johnston felt that Bragg had done well and "has just earned, if not won, the gratitude of the country." There was one additional point, which may have been controlling. If Johnston called for Bragg's removal, he himself would undoubtedly be put in the man's place; he knew that both Polk and Hardee had begged the President to take such a step. So Johnston wrote stiffly that "the part I have borne in this investigation would render it inconsistent with my personal honor to occupy that position."[8]

Richmond did not like Johnston's finding. Secretary Seddon wrote to him, pointing out that Johnston had ample authority to assume the direct command of either of the two armies in his department; if he did not want to displace Bragg, could he not establish himself with Bragg's army and direct all of its field operations, letting Bragg keep his present title and serve as an administrator or executive officer? As delicately as he could, President Davis made it more pointed: since Johnston already was in command in the west, "the removal of General Bragg would only affect you in so far as it deprived you of his services"; instead of taking

Bragg's place, Johnston would simply be asked to get along without him. Mr. Davis was as sensitive to matters of punctilio as anybody, and he assured General Johnston: "I do not think that your personal honor is involved, as you could have nothing to gain by the removal of General Bragg." Mr. Seddon wrote a second letter, expressing his appreciation of "the nobility of spirit" which moved General Johnston and going on to make a frank appeal: "Let me urge you, my dear general, to think well, in view of all the great interests to our beloved South involved in the decision, on this line of action, and if possible make the sacrifice of your honorable delicacy to the importance of the occasion and the greatness of our cause."[9]

This did no good. For once the administration was handling Johnston with gloves on, and it was accomplishing nothing at all. Accordingly, on March 9, Secretary Seddon sent a flat order: "Order General Bragg to report to the War Department here for conference. Assume yourself direct charge of the army in Middle Tennessee." Johnston replied that he would obey; yet when he returned to Tullahoma he found that Mrs. Bragg was extremely ill, and he notified Richmond that he could not send Bragg off at such a time . . . and a bit later, when Mrs. Bragg recovered, Johnston himself fell ill and informed the President that inasmuch as he was unable to serve in the field Bragg's services were indispensable. In the end, Bragg kept his command.[10] Like General Holmes, General Johnston had found it inadvisable to obey a direct order from Richmond.

Johnston was so guarded, and so politely formal, that about all that Richmond could understand was that he simply would not take Bragg's place as commander of the Army of Tennessee and that he did not think his existing command enabled him to do an effective job. To Senator Wigfall Johnston wrote more frankly. He told Wigfall what he had told Mr. Davis, that Bragg had done well and ought to be retained; if he must be relieved, however, Johnston thought that General Longstreet, "the senior Lieut. Gen. & highest in reputation," was undoubtedly the man for the place. He complained that Richmond did not understand the importance of central Tennessee and did not realize that the westerners in Rosecrans' army were twice as dangerous as the easterners in the Army of the Potomac; actually, troops from Virginia

should be sent west to reinforce Bragg. And, for himself: if
he were to have a new assignment, he wanted "to be replaced
where the Yankee missiles found me"—in short, he wanted
to go back to command the Army of Northern Virginia.

He expounded this thought more fully in a second letter
to Wigfall. He had been told, he said, that the President and
Secretary of War "think they have given me the highest military position in the Confederacy," with full control over all
the armies east of the Mississippi and west of the mountains.
If the job was that big, he said, "ought not our highest military officer to occupy it? It seems to me so—that principle
would bring Lee here—I might then with great propriety be
replaced in my old command." But he did not think the
western command was actually the highest in the Confederacy; it set up a system that could not work, "it is giving
each army two generals who are to command in succession,"
and its result could only be strategic confusion. Would not
Senator Wigfall delicately convey these ideas to Mr. Seddon?
It might be, of course, that Richmond would not agree and
would continue to think it necessary to have one-man control of the armies in Tennessee and Mississippi. If so, "it
seems to me that the assignment of Lee to this command & of
me to my old army would be a good and pleasant solution of
the question."[11]

This good and pleasant solution was never adopted, which
is not surprising in view of the fact that the very existence
of the Confederate government had come to depend (at
least in the minds of the men who controlled that government) on the presence in Virginia of Robert E. Lee; and the
paralysis in western command was not remedied, perhaps because as things stood no real remedy was possible. The central authority was too insecure and unsteady, the tradition of
regional independence was too great. The inexorable pressure of the Federal armies, each one stronger than any force
that could be brought against it, was driving the elements of
Confederate strength apart rather than bringing them together.
At the moment when Richmond found itself unable to bend
Joe Johnston to its will, Johnston himself began to find that
Pemberton was unmanageable; a War Department inspector
sent west to study the situation reported, in April, that Johnston "receives no intelligence from General Pemberton, who

ignores his authority, is mortified at his command over him and receives his suggestions with coldness or opposition."[12]

Yet although the Mississippi Valley was far from Richmond, it was nevertheless the place where the Confederacy could receive mortal injury, and President Davis was well aware of it. General Josiah Gorgas, emerging from a long conference with the President late in March, wrote that "he is at present evidently wholly devoted to the defense of the Mississippi and thinks and talks of little else." A few days later the President composed a letter to the several Senators and Congressmen from Arkansas, who had complained that their state was suffering invasion because too many of its troops were serving east of the river. To these men Mr. Davis tried to explain the military principle which he saw so clearly but about which he seemed able to do very little: "Our safety—our very existence—depends on the complete blending of the military strength of all the states into one united body, to be used anywhere and everywhere as the exigencies of the contest may require for the good of the *whole*."[13]

This was admirably put; and yet this military principle cut squarely across a political principle that lay at the heart of the Confederacy's creation—the belief that a central authority strong enough to enforce such unity would be an unendurable menace to human freedom. Vice-President Stephens knew about this, and worried about it; and it seemed to him that "our President is aiming at the obtainment of power inconsistent with public liberty." Whether the public liberty thus menaced would survive total defeat in the present war was a matter to which Mr. Stephens did not address himself publicly, but he wrote to a friend: "Our country is in a sad condition; worse than the people are at all aware of. It is painful to me to look towards the future. I shrink from it as from a frightful gulf towards which we are rapidly tending."[14]

6. A Question of Control

ATTORNEY GENERAL EDWARD BATES was a border state moderate in his attitude toward slavery. He opposed it enough to be a Republican but not enough to seem out of place in Missouri, and Editor Joseph Medill of the Chicago *Tribune* once unkindly referred to him as a fossil taken from the quarry in error. But Mr. Bates was at least a thorough realist, and now he thought it important for people to understand exactly what war and emancipation were going to mean.

Writing to Robert C. Winthrop of Massachusetts shortly after the first of the year, Mr. Bates insisted that if the slaves were set free—by proclamation, by the accident of war, or however—then they were not just partly free. They were altogether free, and so must come under the protection of the Constitution: "In the language of the Constitution they will be 'free persons.'" This was something for Northerners to think about. There were Northern states like Illinois that had laws barring the ingress of free Negroes, and Mr. Bates felt that the people of these states ought to reflect on the change:

"If blacks be, in constitutional law, citizens, and if the state legislature can exclude for color, then why not for race, religion, nativity or any other discretionary cause? The Constitution was made as it is for the very purpose of securing to every citizen common & equal rights all over the nation, and to prevent local prejudice & captious legislation in the states." There was no escape from it: "We must take the Constitution as we do our most beautiful shrubbery—if we will have roses, we must take them along with the thorns."[1]

This was the enormous vista that was beginning to open, and there were loyal Unionists who did not at all like the looks of it. On January 7 Mr. Lincoln told a friend in Kentucky that he hesitated to send to that state certain arms that were wanted by home-defense units because he did not know how they might be used. "The changed conduct towards me of some of her members of Congress, and the ominous out-givings as to what the Governor and Legislature of Kentucky intend doing," he confessed, "admonish me to consider whether any additional arms I may send there are not to be turned against the government."

When the war began he had said that to lose Kentucky would be about equal to losing the war itself. Now the danger was visible. A week earlier the administration had been warned by Major General Horatio G. Wright, commanding Federal troops in Ohio and Kentucky, that the state authorities were apt to take Kentucky clear out of the Union if the Emancipation Proclamation went into effect. Wright thought he should keep several good regiments near the Kentucky capital, Frankfort, and he also thought that if an ordinance of secession were presented he should arrest everyone who voted for it; and altogether he wanted advice from headquarters. On the day the President wrote so gloomily to his Kentucky friend, General Halleck notified Wright that his projected course of action was approved and that he could go even further if he had to.

As it happened, this particular crisis finally dissolved. Kentucky did not try to secede, Stone's River having served notice that the Confederate tide after all was ebbing in those parts, and although a committee of the Kentucky House of Representatives not long after this reported that "the Rebellion cannot be conquered under the present policy of the government," and denounced Emancipation, suspension of habeas corpus and the arming of Negroes as acts of tyranny and crimes against civilization, nothing concrete was actually done.[2]

Yet the fact that the crisis had emerged was symptomatic. The war had taken on this new dimension. Having dared to invoke freedom the nation now must take the consequences; as Mr. Bates was pointing out, the formula that had been adopted to insure victory was also the formula for a social revolution. As the new year began the overriding question was how the people of the North (ultimately, the people of the whole country) would respond to that revolution. It was more than they had bargained for; they were not in the least prepared to meet it, or even to think about it; and it might well be more than they would accept. But it was beginning to happen, the only way to avert it was to give up the war itself, and responsible men in Washington could only wonder if firmer leadership was not needed to meet the profound state of public unrest.

To a certain extent this was a reflection of the military situation: unrest rose when military affairs went badly and sank when they went well. Of late affairs had been going badly, and Presidential Secretary John Nicolay expressed it accurately when he told his wife that "little disasters still tread on each other's heels"—the latest little disaster being a sudden blow by which Confederates in Texas had overwhelmed a Federal force of occupation at Galveston, capturing the revenue cutter *Harriet Lane* and reoccupying the city.

Editor Medill found himself in the mood of Alexander Stephens, and he wrote: "An armistice is bound to come during the year 1863. . . . We have to fight for a boundary." Congressman Elbridge Spaulding of New York told the Congress on January 12 that the cost of the war now was $2,500,000 a day, "Sundays included"; the government's income amounted to no more than $600,000 a day, and in little more than a year the public debt would reach $2,000,000,000. Captain John A. Dahlgren of the Washington Navy Yard entered the President's study a few days before Christmas just in time to hear a caller warn the President that the findings of the Committee on the Conduct of the War in regard to bungling generalship at Fredericksburg had better be made public at once because of public excitement. To this, Dahlgren noted, Mr. Lincoln replied with some heat that he did not like to swear but "why will people be such damned fools?"[3]

But it went further than little disasters, oppressive fiscal arrangements and an itch to have defective generalship dissected in public. The determination to restore the Union at any cost had been, originally and for most Northerners, a determination to restore a cherished past; as sincerely as Mr. Davis himself, the average Northerner wanted to be let alone so that he could enjoy things as they used to be. Now he was beginning to see that things would never again, not this side of Jordan, be as they used to be. Instead of restoring the past the war was destroying it.

Increased public unrest, in short, rested at least partly on an uneasy awareness that the price of victory was likely to be an illimitable commitment to the future, Mr. Lincoln's hope that he might carry a truce in the belly of the war was an expression of his own anxiety; for a war in which no truce was possible was bound to bring such a commitment, and neither he nor anyone else knew how that commitment would finally be met. But the immediate necessities of war were controlling. If the war was to be won at all it was necessary for him to assert firmer direction, first over his own administration and next over the nation's biggest army, the Army of the Potomac.

The two went together. War, as Prussian Clausewitz held and as Mr. Lincoln knew by instinct, is an extension of politics; and by 1863 the converse also was true—politics was an extension of war. The war itself was a brutal and fearfully definitive substitute for a political debate and a national election. To appoint a general—any general—was of necessity to play a political card, even though all that was actually wanted was a man who could beat the Rebels. To deal with elected persons or with the voters who had elected them was always to speak and act from a platform built by the armies. The Emancipation Proclamation itself, which would change American politics forever, had come into existence as a military expedient. War and politics walked together now, not merely hand in hand but in one body.[4]

Mr. Lincoln's effort to assert firmer control was complicated by a singular fact. Basic to the situation was a widespread feeling that it was necessary for someone to control Mr. Lincoln himself—that his presidency was a sort of vacuum that needed to be filled by a man or men more dedicated, earnest, and forceful than he was. Both radical Republicans and conservative Democrats had this idea. The conservatives, to be sure, had suffered a check when General McClellan ceased to command the Army of the Potomac, but the radicals were hard at work. They wanted total war and total emancipation, and they felt that this reluctant administration was not likely to give them either. The reason, as they saw it, was that Mr. Lincoln was too weak and that Secretary of State William H. Seward was too strong; now they proposed to force Seward out of the cabinet and manage the administration themselves, using Secretary of the Treasury Salmon P. Chase as their principal instrument. In the middle of December thirty-two Republican Senators caucused for two days, listened to denunciations of Seward, agreed that there should be a partial reconstruction of the cabinet, and named nine of their number to call on Mr. Lincoln and tell him what he ought to do.[5]

Several factors were at work, not least the profound discontent of Chase, who had been complaining that the President overrode his cabinet and reduced it to an administrative nullity. In a sense Chase was right. The President was not a good administrator. He did not try to make an operating mechanism out of his cabinet, and probably the idea never occurred to him. He listened to everybody and then did what he thought best, and even when he let his ministers see the first draft of the Emancipation Proclamation he said that he had already made up his mind about it but that he would like to hear what they had to say. It was at least clear that the cabinet did not manage the administration, and the situation was not eased by Seward's total willingness to let people believe that he himself did.

The Senators felt that the President should be guided and directed by a "cabinet council." Inasmuch as they agreed that the Senate ought to control a President's cabinet selections, they were actually demanding top control for the legislative branch. They were attacking not merely the President but the presidency; they were offended, not by Mr. Lincoln's supposed weakness, but by the fact that if he became strong he could use his strength. When they sat down with him in the White House on the evening of December 19—nine Senators, seven of them staunch radicals—they were in effect notifying Mr. Lincoln that he must remake his cabinet so that the administration would be in complete harmony . . . with itself, and with them.

Mr. Lincoln had no intention of doing this. He had told a friend that all of the responsibilities of the administration "belong to that unhappy wretch called Abraham Lincoln," and as he tried to meet those responsibilities the last thing he needed or wanted was a contrived or enforced harmony. Precisely because he was leading a divided country he needed diverse counsels. He had his own grave doubts about the era that lay ahead, and so did most of his fellow citizens, and the true strength of his leadership had to arise from his ability to work out his doubts as he went along. Only so could he hope to carry all factions with him. To choose between Seward and Chase would be to commit himself to one faction or another before it was time—to entrust the fate of the nation to the men who had no doubts at all. He needed to keep both ministers, and yet it would be difficult. Learning about the Senate caucus, Mr. Seward had quietly submitted his resignation.

The December 19 meeting brought no result. The Senators voiced their complaint and demanded Seward's removal; Mr. Lincoln listened, said he would think it over, and invited the Senators to come back the next evening. They agreed, and the President arranged a small surprise. On this second meeting, as soon as the Senators had been greeted and seated, Mr. Lincoln asked them if he might not bring in the cabinet.

Somewhat struck, they agreed to this, whereupon Mr. Lincoln brought in everybody except Seward, and permitted Senators and ministers to regard each other briefly.

Then he began to talk. He outlined the history of his administration, taking up one issue after another and telling how each one had been handled. He remarked that nobody could expect all cabinet members to think alike on everything, and he confessed that the pressure of the times had kept him from having frequent or extended cabinet sessions. However, he added, once he had settled upon a policy, all of the ministers always agreed on it. The cabinet had not been overridden; if it had not directed the President, it had always at least gone along with him. Having said all of this, Mr. Lincoln turned to his cabinet and asked each man, one after another, whether he had not given a true statement of the case.

True in substance: possibly stretched a little, here and there. On some points—notably the reinstatement of McClellan after the Second Battle of Bull Run—some cabinet members had been in most determined opposition, and had reluctantly accepted an accomplished fact only because there had been nothing else they could do. But in the main the account was close enough to accuracy, and the question provided infinite discomfort for Secretary Chase, who had provided most of the source material for the Senators' bill of particulars.

Dignified, able, dedicated, and always conscious of his own rectitude, Chase could not, in front of the President and his colleagues, brand himself a disloyal member of the official family by repeating here the complaints he had made elsewhere. He was hopelessly trapped between duplicity and integrity, and now he could only agree lamely that the President's account was correct, adding that he did think there might perhaps have been fuller discussion on some points. One after another the others confirmed the President's story. Stony-faced, the Senators listened.

Having polled his cabinet, the President then asked the Senators if they still thought that he ought to dismiss Secretary Seward.

The Senators had been both outmaneuvered and let down, the support they relied on most having failed them. In addition, it was all too clear by now that if the President dismissed his Secretary of State he would also dismiss his Secretary of the Treasury, which was not at all what anybody wanted. Only four Senators, at last, said that they still thought that Seward ought to go. The meeting ended. As people began to leave, Senator Lyman Trumbull of Illinois—an old acquaintance who could speak bluntly—stopped by the President's side and said angrily: "Lincoln, somebody has lied like hell!" Mr. Lincoln replied: "Not tonight."[6]

It remained for the President to pick up the loose ends, and the next morning he picked up the only one that mattered. Secretary Chase came to see him, remarked that the evening's conference had given him much pain, and hesitantly produced, or began to produce, a letter, saying that he had written his resignation. This of course was a gesture: Chase did not want to leave the cabinet, but if he put a resignation on paper and then waved the paper about it might have good effect. But this was no morning for gestures by Chase. To his dismay, Mr. Lincoln promptly took the letter away from him, saying with undisguised elation that at last his problem was solved; after which he permitted Chase to go back to his office.

The next day the President let it be known that both Seward and Chase had submitted resignations, that neither resignation had been accepted, and that both men would remain in the cabinet. In the language of politics, a to-whom-it-may-concern: the President would continue to work with both conservatives and radicals, he had not yielded to the pressure of Seward nor to that of Chase, and he had not wilted under the heat applied by Senators. Regardless of what had been supposed previously, he and nobody else was running the administration.

It remained to be seen whether he could also control the Army of the Potomac.

As the new year began this army could hardly be said to be under anybody's control. General Burnside could not manage it effectively. This was partly because he lacked competence; far worse was the fact that some of his principal officers were grimly determined to make everyone in the army and out of it understand that he lacked it. The army's discipline, its morale, the very possibility of its future usefulness were beginning to collapse under pressure of resentments, enmities, personal shortcomings and thwarted ambitions even more sharply edged than the combination that had beset the cabinet. Mr. Lincoln began to see how things were going on December 21, when he got a singular letter signed by Major General William B. Franklin, commander of Burnside's Left Grand Division, and Major General William F. Smith, who led the VI Army Corps in that Grand Division.

Serenely going over their commanding officer's head, these two soldiers told the President that Burnside's present plan of campaign—an overland approach to Richmond, via Fredericksburg—was bound to fail: the line of supply would be too long and too exposed, and there were too many good positions south of Fredericksburg where the Confederates could post themselves strongly and repulse assaults. It would be better to take the army down to the James River, as McClellan had done. With an ample garrison retained to protect Washington and the Potomac River crossings, let 250,000 men be massed on both banks of the James, as close to Richmond as possible. Thus the Rebel army should be destroyed, and even if it escaped the capture of Richmond would be assured. The generals wrote that they submitted their views "with diffidence," but they felt it was their duty to present them as "suggestions to some other military mind in discussing plans for the future operations of our armies in the east."[7]

The letter was odd on two counts. To begin with it asked the impossible. Obviously, if the government could find the resources to put 250,000 men on the James, at the same time holding an adequate covering force in front of Washington, any general, even one with the most moderate capacities, could go on and take Richmond. As Mr. Lincoln was painfully aware, no such forces could be assembled. The other oddity lay in the fact that Franklin and Smith were the staunchest of McClellan men, fully representing the McClellan point of view—which held that that professional soldier's campaign had been ruined because an amateur President insisted on reaching over the professional's shoulder to interfere with strategy. (After all, it was Mr. Lincoln who had held back Franklin's division, when McClellan wanted it in front of Yorktown in the spring of 1862.) Now they were urging the same amateur President to reach over the shoulder of another professional and interfere with strategy anew.

As professional soldiers they were taking a most unprofessional way of undercutting their commanding officer.

They were not the only ones. To the White House, two days before the end of the year, came two of their subordinates—Brigadier General John A. Newton, head of the 3rd Division in Smith's Corps, and Brigadier General John Cochrane, who led the 1st Brigade in Newton's division. (A former Republican Congressman, Cochrane was the only nonprofessional in the lot.) Having cleared the matter with Franklin and Smith, these two men told the President that Burnside planned a new movement and that the army was so thoroughly demoralized that the move could lead to nothing but disaster. Deeply disturbed, Mr. Lincoln, after they left, had an inconclusive talk with General Burnside—who unsuccessfully demanded that these talebearers be cashiered for their irregular conduct—and finally he sent a stiff note to General Halleck, giving that officer much the same assignment that Jefferson Davis gave to General Johnston: go down to the army, see what the situation really is, examine Burnside's plan and either tell the man to go ahead with it or forbid him to move at all. He closed the letter with the comment: "Your military skill is useless to me if you will not do this."

Halleck would not do it. Instead he offered to resign, and Mr. Lincoln's letter finally came to rest in the files with a notation in the President's hand: "Withdrawn, because considered harsh by General Halleck." Like Mr. Davis, Mr. Lincoln was finding that one of his principal armies was all but totally out of his reach. Without in the least intending to, his professional soldiers were confirming him in his belief that the President must take his responsibilities as commander-in-chief seriously and keep a firm hand on the military.[8]

Another malcontent was Major General Joseph Hooker— "Fighting Joe," hard, colorful, aggressive, chief of Burnside's Center Grand Division, a better combat soldier than those others but a man irrationally consumed by ambition. Hooker did not call at the White House. He simply talked— so loosely that the President's secretaries wrote him down as "the most indiscreet and outspoken of all." He was saying now that Burnside was incompetent, that President and administration were imbecile, and that "nothing would go right until they had a dictator, and the sooner the better." Hooker differed from the others in this: their basic complaint was that the army commander was not McClellan, and his was that the commander was not Joe Hooker. His words were heard in Washington, in the White House, and elsewhere . . . and meanwhile officers of lower rank were resigning "with insolent expressions against the government for its conduct of the war." Even those who did not resign had complaints. Among them was Brigadier General G. K. Warren, who led a good brigade in the V Corps and who wrote: "We *must* have McClellan back with unlimited and unfettered powers. His name is a tower of strength to everyone here; and the repose of winter is absolutely necessary. . . . The remedy must begin in Washington. No human intelligence can mend matters here till that is done."[9]

What could Burnside do? His army was being systematically and ruinously demoralized—not by its losses at Fredericksburg, but by the leaders who tried to capitalize on those losses. Before January ended Burnside learned that he could do nothing at all. On January 20 he led his army up the Rappahannock, planning to cross the river above Lee's left and strike the Confederate flank with irresistible force, and as military plans go his scheme was not bad. But by this time his army had become unusable.

The night before the move began an artillery officer at Franklin's headquarters found that Franklin's and Smith's staff officers were "talking outrageously," predicting failure, and he wrote: "Franklin has talked so much and so loudly to this effect ever since the present move was decided on that he has completely demoralized his whole command and so rendered failure doubly sure. His conduct is such that he certainly deserves to be broken. Smith and they say Hooker are almost as bad." (The trouble here was that Franklin and Hooker were leading the Grand Divisions which had the primary parts in this march.) The next day, when the march had begun, the same gunner wrote that "the disaffection produced by Franklin's and others' talk was very evident. The whole army seems to know what they have said, and their speeches condemning the move were in the mouths of everyone."

The next day, as a matter of fact, the high heavens intervened; there was a drenching rain, the roads turned to bottomless mud, and the army got irretrievably bogged down, unable to advance even if it had wanted to. Guns, horses, mules, and pontoons disappeared from view in the mire, the foot soldiers tried in vain to plod across open fields, and the same artillerist, visiting Franklin's headquarters, "found him, Smith and their staffs in quite a comfortable camp; doing nothing to help things on, but grumbling and talking in a manner to do all the harm possible." Major General George G. Meade, a sober regular with no ax to grind, wrote to his wife: "I am sorry to say there were many men, and among them generals high in command, who openly rejoiced at the storm and the obstacle it presented," and Franklin himself confessed that he considered the storm "almost a providential interference in our behalf." In any case, Burnside was defeated. He got his army back to camp, at last, and had to confess that the situation was beyond his control.[10]

He offered the President a choice: purge the officer corps of nine or ten troublemakers, starting with Franklin and Hooker, or accept Burnside's resignation and start over again with someone else. The President did not hesitate. The general purge was to be avoided, possibly because the army by now was too frail to survive a major operation, but there would be a new commander and certain other changes. On January 25 the War Department announced that Burnside had been relieved at his own request, that Sumner and Franklin were being sent to other duties . . . and that General Joseph Hooker had been appointed Burnside's successor.[11]

Along with his new appointment, General Hooker got a letter from Abraham Lincoln.

"I think," wrote Mr. Lincoln, "that during General Burnside's command of the army you have taken counsel of your ambition, and thwarted him as much as you could, in which you did a great wrong to the country and to a most meritorious and honorable brother officer. I have heard, in such a way as to believe it, of your recently saying that both the army and the Government needed a dictator. Of course it was not for this, but in spite of it, that I have given you the command. Only those generals who gain successes can set up dictators. What I now ask of you is military success and I will risk the dictatorship. . . . I much fear that the spirit which you have aided to infuse into the army, of criticising their commander and withholding confidence from him, will now turn upon you. I shall assist you as far as I can to put it down. Neither you nor Napoleon, if he were alive again, could get any good of an army while such a spirit prevails in it. And now beware of rashness. Beware of rashness, but with energy and sleepless vigilance go forward and give us victories."[12]

To give an officer a blistering rebuke and a prized promotion all in one breath was, to say the least, unusual. Mr. Lincoln seems to have been gambling that Hooker's driving energy, his qualities of leadership, his fame as a combat soldier and, not least, his insatiable ambition, would enable him to bring the army back to fighting condition. In addition (and it was a point of substantial importance) Hooker was not a McClellan man, and the McClellan faction in the officer corps, a source of so much of the current discontent, could take no comfort at all from his elevation. To put Hooker in command might be dangerous, but the President felt strong enough to run the risk; meanwhile, the appointment told all and sundry where final authority lay.

Four days before he turned the army over to Hooker, Mr. Lincoln did one other thing. To his desk came the findings of a court-martial which had convicted Major General Fitz John Porter of willful disobedience of General John Pope's orders at the Second Battle of Bull Run. Porter was alleged to have contributed to Pope's defeat by refusing to make an attack that—in Pope's belief, if not in everyone's—would have saved the day. Years later, a board of officers appointed by President Rutherford B. Hayes reviewed the case in the light of fuller evidence and exonerated Porter, and in 1886 a special act of Congress relieved him of the burden imposed by the wartime court and restored his old rank in the Regular Army. But in 1863 the court-martial convicted him, ordering that he be stripped of his rank, dismissed from the service, and "forever disqualified from holding any office of trust or profit under the government of the United States." And on January 21 President Lincoln approved these findings. General Porter was cashiered.[13]

What made the Porter case important in the tangled story of army politics was that he had been closer to McClellan than any other officer and that during the period immediately before the Battle of Bull Run he had been deriding General Pope in much the same way Franklin had recently been deriding General Burnside. Now he was publicly broken—ostensibly for disobeying orders but at least partly as a warning to all malcontents. What was done to him may have been unjust, but it was at least a powerful object lesson. Any officer who doubted the firmness of the President's control over the army had only to think about General Porter.

CHAPTER TWO

Parting of the Red Sea Waves

1. The Land of Cotton

LOUISIANA LOOKED LIKE a storybook land, all color and warmth under the December sun. As the steamers came up the river the Federal troops could see endless rows of orange trees in fruit, groves of live oaks at the edges of sugar plantations, manor houses elegant and imposing with white pillars fronting broad lawns. Here and there, near the levee, were slave-quarter cabins, with Negro women waving a welcome. After ten days on the crowded transports the soldiers were willing to be pleased; they lined the rails and cheered, and as the convoy drew nearer to New Orleans they felt that "the scene went on increasing in richness." Major General Nathaniel P. Banks was bringing reinforcements to take over on the lower Mississippi. He was under orders to do many things—among them, to close out the strange pro-consular reign of General Ben Butler—and as he reached the end of his journey it appeared that he was coming to a place that was rich, orderly, and contented.

The appearance was deceptive. Beautiful as the land was, New Orleans itself was almost lifeless. Few people were on the streets, little business was being done, and an officer on Banks' staff felt that the place "looked like a decayed city of the old world." General Butler received General Banks with much pomp, trim sentries guarding his doors, a well-drilled troop of dismounted cavalry to do the honors; yet the whiff of something spoiled and corrupt, which had drawn attention in faraway Washington, was inescapable, and it was clear that even the junior officers of the occupation forces had been doing themselves very well. Mere lieutenants of infantry lived in huge town houses, "where they use the plate, drink the wine cellars dry, and in various ways spoil the Egyptians." Most of them were looting and plundering without restraint, believing that General Butler expected it of them. The visiting staff officer found it a relief to go aboard Rear Admiral David Glasgow Farragut's flagship, *Hartford*, where everything was clean, orderly, and austere, and he wrote: "Oh, for a country where quarter-deck government is in the ascendant."[1]

Of quarter-deck government New Orleans had seen not a trace, and early in January General Banks wrote to General Halleck that the "immense military government" that he had taken over was so busy running the city, collecting taxes, imposing fines and regulating a cunningly devised trade in contraband goods that it had no time to fight the war. The contraband trade he found appalling because it was so crooked, and he wrote that no military operations could be carried on with this mess in the rear. He had been in office only a few days when a citizen came to him with a contract, cleared by the Confederate authorities, for the exchange of Secessionist cotton for Unionist salt, and unblushingly offered Banks $100,000 if he would approve the deal.[2] This, it appeared, was standing operating procedure. The staff officer who had sighed for quarter-deck government noted that Banks "begins to accept the certainty of the fall of the Republic," and to his wife Banks wrote frankly:

"I never despaired of my country until I came here. The strongest government in the world could not bear up under such responsibility and wrong. Everybody connected with the government has been employed in stealing other people's property. Sugar, silver plate, horses, carriages, everything they could lay hands on. There has been open trade with the enemy. No attention has been given to military affairs. . . . We can never succeed, under such direction—our people must give up stealing or give up the country, one or the other."[3]

This of course was one of the things General Banks had been sent to New Orleans to correct. His charter of authority was uncomfortably broad. He was to straighten out the weird tangle Butler had created; he was to extend the area of Federal authority so that cotton grown inside the Union lines could reach New Orleans legitimately and not by graft; he was to take care of the hordes of fugitive slaves who kept presenting themselves; and, most important of all, he was to lead an army up the Mississippi, making contact with General Grant, taking that officer and his army under his own command and seeing to it that the river was opened to Union commerce from its headwaters to the Gulf. His military skills were limited—he had suffered much grief at the hands of Stonewall Jackson in Virginia, eight months earlier—but he was a good patriot, with an honest man's capacity for shock at the sight of blatant corruption, and he would do his best. He published the preliminary draft of the Emancipation Proclamation for the information of Louisiana, sent 10,000 men upstream to take a firm hold on Baton Rouge, and got down to work.[4]

The work he had to do was too much for any one man to handle. Along with everything else, he was supposed to bring about the reconstruction of Louisiana as a loyal state in the Union, and hardly anyone in Louisiana wanted to be reconstructed. Part of the fault was Butler's: he had offered nothing but oppression tempered by venality, and so Banks would be both conciliatory and upright. But the trouble went deeper. As far as anyone in Louisiana could see the Confederacy right now looked like a winner, and anyway the war had got past the point where conciliation was possible. The indigestible fact was that Mr. Lincoln had proclaimed freedom for the slaves, and although the flexibility of his proclamation gave General Banks a certain amount of elbow room it was still true that to consent to reunion meant to accept emancipation. This was unacceptable, because of an irrational factor that was almost as strong in the North as in the South; the race that had enslaved the Negro did not in its heart believe that it was possible to live beside the Negro if he lost his chains.

Jefferson Davis, as humane a man as ever lived, had said that emancipation must mean extermination of slaves, and S. L. M. Barlow's Washington tipster, T. J. Barnett, warning at the end of December that the government meant business about emancipation, added as a matter of course that "scenes of horror whose bare imagining chills the heart and congeals the blood" would be bound to follow.[5] Abraham Lincoln himself felt a touch of this fear, and he still hoped that the freed Negroes might be sent to some colony far from the United States. The least common denominator here was the belief that the races could not get along as equals. White America had to believe that the Negro was inferior and in need of restraint, because otherwise the whole idea of slavery was morally wrong from the beginning and the Northerner who tacitly consented to it was as guilty as the Southerner who lived with it.

This had especial weight in Louisiana. Before Banks' arrival Brigadier General Godfrey Weitzel, leading Union troops in a campaign along the bayous west of New Orleans, protested vigorously when Butler sent him a couple of colored regiments. Since these regiments arrived, said Weitzel, symptoms of a slave insurrection were appearing everywhere. The countryside was in terror, he could not post detachments to keep people safe without breaking up his whole brigade, the moral effect was deplorable, and "I cannot command these Negro regiments." Weitzel was not pro-slavery; he was just a professional who felt that the very idea of turning Negroes into soldiers was outrageous. (He had no way to know that he himself would be the first Union general to lead an army into Richmond and that half of his army then would be composed of Negroes.)

Another soldier who foresaw violence was Brigadier General J. W. Phelps, a regular from Vermont who commanded Camp Parapet, upriver from New Orleans. Early in the summer Phelps told Butler that the fugitive slaves in Louisiana were tough and unruly men who might make real trouble, and he felt that the only remedy was to put them in the army and discipline them. He explained: "Many of the slaves here have been sold away from the border states as a punishment, being too refractory to be dealt with there." These slaves, he went on, wanted justice rather than revenge, but the bad treatment they had had "promises more terror to the retribution when it comes."

Phelps had touched a sore point. By grim tradition, the troublemaking slave farther north was always sold down the river as a last resort; and this gulf coast cotton belt *was* down the river, the end of the line, the ultimate destination for the Negro who refused to be meek and obedient. There was possibly a special reason for men here to be nervous about what might happen if the Negro were made free.

Ben Butler was finally to be the abolitionists' hero, but he was oddly reluctant to use Negro troops. He tried to calm

Weitzel by saying that it was war itself, and not Negro regiments, that spread fear across the plantations, and he rebuked Phelps so sternly that the man finally resigned and went back to Vermont, complaining that Butler wanted to do nothing with the Negroes but make camp laborers out of them. Butler had written to Stanton earlier that the fugitive slaves were usually the worst men on the plantation, not the best, and he said he did not want or need Negro troops, adding that in any case "I believe that this war will be ended before any body of Negroes could be organized, armed and drilled so as to be efficient." Now Butler was gone, and Banks was learning that the problem was unexpectedly intricate.[6]

He began simply enough by introducing decency and restraint into Federal rule. He got the lieutenants and other ranks out of those town houses, and he reported presently that he had "reduced officers and soldiers in this city to the accommodations provided by the Army regulations." He canceled an existing directive which provided for the closing of any church wherein prayers for the President of the United States were not offered, and he ended the free-and-easy system of bribery, writing to his wife: "I thank God every day that I have no thirst for money—when I see how great the wrongs are to the country committed by the men who are seeking it. I feel that I would as soon be covered with loathsome disease as to share with them their desires & their profits."[7] Then he undertook to end the stagnation of local business by reviving agriculture and trade in the occupied area, feeling that people would accept Federal authority more readily if it meant prosperity.

Here the case was difficult. There were cotton and sugar plantations that produced nothing because the slaves had all run away. Banks wanted to get the planters back in business, but if they were to produce they had to have gangs of laborers and the laborers refused to co-operate. Banks had publicly explained that the war was bound to mean the end of slavery, even though the Emancipation Proclamation did exempt occupied Louisiana, but these abandoned plantations would never start raising crops again unless the Federal government lent a hand; and on January 29 Banks issued a regulation to govern the subject.

The gist of this was that slaves who had left their "employment" must nevertheless work for a living and that the occupation authorities would see to it that they did. A Sequestration Committee of army officers was appointed to devise a yearly system of paid labor for the idle plantations. When the program was accepted by the planters, "all the conditions of continuous and faithful service, respectful deportment, correct discipline and perfect subordination shall be enforced on the part of the Negroes by the officers of the government." A member of the Commission wrote that as he understood this a planter would compensate his workers by setting aside one-twentieth of his crop for their benefit; once he agreed to this the army would make sure that he got his laborers. Banks assured the Commissioners that he would not use force and would depend entirely on moral suasion to make the slaves return to their masters; but he rejected a clause stipulating that the whole deal would rest on the consent of the slaves, and it was undeniably true that moral suasion exerted by a government which controlled all of the food and had all of the bayonets could look remarkably like outright compulsion, especially when the government talked stiffly about correct discipline and perfect subordination. The planters displayed enthusiasm for the operation, and the system went into effect; not quite slavery in the old style, but not exactly freedom either. Banks considered it a proper first step in the transition from slave to free labor.[8]

At the very least it was designed to conciliate Secessionist planters, even though it would evoke bitter complaint from the radical Republicans up north; and the general now was ready to approach the purely military part of his assignment. Like all of his other tasks, this one turned out to be larger than he had originally supposed.

In his entire department Banks had approximately 36,000 men, of whom about 31,000 could be listed as present for duty, equipped, which was how the army described men who could be used in combat. Most of these were only partly trained and had never made a campaign or fought in a battle, and many of them had been enlisted for nine-month terms. There were numerous places that had to be garrisoned, starting with New Orleans itself, and General Banks found that when all of these were taken care of he would have a field army of between 12,000 and 14,000 men. This was the force

with which he was supposed to go up the Mississippi and
join hands with General Grant.

That after all was the central part of his assignment. It
was an attractive assignment, because Banks' commission as
major general dated a long way back and he would outrank
any Federal general he met; and he had a War Department
directive specifically telling him to assume command over
Grant, or any other Federal commander in the Valley, as
soon as he made contact. The trouble was that Grant's army
was somewhere on the far side of Vicksburg, more than 150
miles from Baton Rouge in an air line, much farther by the
winding course of the river. Between Grant and Banks was
General John Pemberton, with a Confederate army of unknown strength, and when Banks started up the river he got
no more than twenty-five miles from Baton Rouge before
he ran into the southern anchor of Pemberton's Mississippi
River defensive line—a formidable set of trenches and gun
pits on high ground overlooking the river at a place called
Port Hudson. Port Hudson was held by some 11,000 men,
ably commanded by Major General Franklin Gardner, and
Banks quickly concluded that he was not strong enough to
take the place. One way or another he would have to go
around it.[9]

Not far above Port Hudson the Red River came in from
the northwest to join the Mississippi. It drained a rich
agricultural country, it was the highway for most of the supplies the Confederacy got from the trans-Mississippi, and
if the Federals possessed it they could impose a severe
handicap on Pemberton. By going west of the Mississippi
and using two rambling waterways, the Atchafalaya and the
Teche, Banks could get up to the Red River without going
near Port Hudson. He would have to be careful, because the
Confederates had troops in west Louisiana and also in Mobile, and unless he guarded his rear carefully these might
squeeze in behind him and pinch him off from his base.[10]
Still, to take Port Hudson seemed impossible, and Banks
settled at last for a drive toward the Red River.

It may have been his best choice. But the Red River was
a man-trap, a road that led off to the northwest, off to
nowhere. A Federal army moving up this river would keep
getting farther and farther away from Grant, Pemberton,

and the Mississippi; much worse, it would be moving straight into one of the richest cotton-producing areas on earth.

Cotton was all-corrupting, no matter how honest a soldier might be; Banks had been around New Orleans long enough to see what it could do. But he knew that in theory at least cotton could get to the market without bribery, as a New Englander he understood the importance of cotton, and after the move got under way he wrote Halleck a long letter about the high attractions of this Red River country.

If a Federal army could get on the Red River and stay there, he said, suppressing guerrillas and enabling planters to send produce direct to the New Orleans market, something between 50,000 and 150,000 bales would be brought into circulation. This would make millions of dollars for the government, the Red River people would find that Federal rule meant money in the pocket and so would abandon the Secessionist heresy, and domestic and foreign manufacturers would be partly relieved from "the cotton starvation under which they are suffering." General Banks wanted to know how the administration felt about it.[11]

The administration was both repelled and fascinated; and in the end the lure of Red River cotton would waste an army and a fleet, destroy most of General Banks' military reputation, and make this part of the war look like nothing nobler than a gigantic cotton raid. These fruits, however, were for the future. In this winter and spring of 1863 Banks' troops campaigned laboriously along the Atchafalaya and the Teche, fighting against the landscape almost as much as against Secession. (The ground was swampy, rivers were numerous, water was high and the objectives were diverse.) They fought battles, skirmishes and the false alarms that beset green troops at night in strange country, and by late April they made it possible for Banks to go to the Red River. First, though, there was a joint army-navy nudge at Port Hudson. It did not accomplish very much, but after it was over Admiral Farragut believed that Banks had missed a fine chance. Port Hudson, said the admiral, might have been had.

The admiral, to be sure, was impatient. He had had an unhappy winter; neither he nor his ships were being used as he felt they should be used, and he was eager to wipe out the memory of the loss of *Harriet Lane* at Galveston. To a fellow sailor he wrote angrily that this was "not only the most unfortunate thing that has ever happened to the Navy, but the most shameful and pusillanimous"; and it was followed by other misfortunes. The blockading flotilla at Mobile somehow let C.S.S. *Florida* slip out in mid-January to begin a spectacular career as a commerce raider, and Farragut's plan to recapture Galveston failed when U.S.S. *Hatteras* was sunk by a new, English-built Confederate cruiser named *Alabama* —a ship the Navy would be a long time forgetting. Farragut wrote: "I hope we shall soon have some good luck, for I am sick of disasters," and early in the spring he began peering up the Mississippi to see if good luck might not be found there.[12]

The Navy's luck recently had been no better on the river than on the gulf. Rear Admiral David D. Porter, commanding the flotilla that was attached to Grant's expedition above Vicksburg, sent the ram *Queen of the West* down past the Vicksburg batteries in broad daylight on February 2. This craft reached the mouth of the Red River and seized a number of Confederate supply steamers, doing so well that two weeks later Porter sent the new ironclad *Indianola* down to help. But *Queen of the West* meanwhile ran aground and was captured, and using this vessel and some of their own gunboats the Confederates then captured *Indianola* as well, and now they had a fairly formidable little navy on the river between Vicksburg and Port Hudson. Farragut growled that "Porter has allowed his boats to come down one at a time & they have been captured by the enemy, which compels me to go up & recapture the whole or be sunk in the attempt, the whole country will be in arms if we do not do something."[13] To Banks, Farragut said that they simply must get past Port Hudson.

The situation was presently made easier by a farce-comedy sequence. The Confederates on the river understood that Porter was getting one or more of the new, supposedly irresistible ironclad monitors, and Porter took an old scow, had his carpenters build a false turret-and-pilot-house superstructure (at a total cost of $8.61) and sent the thing drifting downstream in dead of night. The Vicksburg batteries fired at it without effect, the scow continued down the river, and the word went out that a live Yankee monitor was loose. Panicky, the crew of captured *Indianola* ran their vessel ashore and blew her up, *Queen of the West* fled incontinently down to the Louisiana waterways, the fake ironclad came to rest peacefully on a sandbar, and affairs on the Mississippi returned to the status quo. But it seemed clear that a Federal squadron near the mouth of the Red River could do the Confederacy much harm, and Farragut determined to go ahead.[14]

Over a bottle of wine in his cabin on *Hartford*, Farragut spoke his mind to General Banks.

"General," he said, "we have more men and more resources than these traitors and five times as much money. We must beat them in the end, but we must do it by poking them, butting them whenever we see them. By God, shall a United States ship of war hesitate to go in and destroy a dozen of these wretched Mississippi steamers? I am sick of hearing my officers talk of cotton-clad boats and impregnable rams. They should pitch in and destroy them."

At this point, apparently, the elderly admiral paused to pour another drink. He went on: "What matters it, General, whether you and I are killed or not? We came here to die. It is our business and must happen sooner or later. We must fight this thing out until there is no more than one man left, and that man must be a Union man. Here's to his health."[15]

The attempt was made on the night of March 14. Banks was ready to do no more than make a diversionary attack, but that did not stop Farragut. He had four sea-going cruisers, *Hartford*, *Richmond*, *Monongahela*, and *Mississippi*, along with gunboats *Albatross*, *Genesee*, and *Kineo*, and while Banks was starting his columns up toward the Port Hudson lines the squadron got under way.

It ran into trouble at once. The current was strong, the river made a hairpin turn right where the powerful Confederate batteries could do their worst, General Gardner had placed locomotive headlights to play on the water and light up the targets, and the army never did get into action. *Mississippi* ran aground and was destroyed, *Monongahela* also went aground, stayed there under fire for nearly half an hour, and at last staggered back downstream, *Richmond* was disabled by a shell through her steam pipes, and only *Hartford* and *Albatross* got past the batteries and went on to safety upstream. Farragut was isolated, he had acted without orders, and for all he knew he might be in line for a sharp reprimand from the Navy Department. Still, he did have *Hartford* and *Albatross* up above the batteries, and he set to work to patrol the river, lamenting that if he had only one more warship he could make the blockade of Port Hudson air tight.

Not long after this an army officer at Baton Rouge wrote to him commiserating him on the disaster that had befallen his squadron and offering any kind of help the army could supply. Farragut replied that as far as the disaster was concerned, men in battle had to take their chances and "were we to be deterred by the apprehension of such accidents there would be no battles fought." Port Hudson, he added, would surely have fallen if Banks' army had attacked while the fleet was engaging the water batteries. He would be glad to get further assistance from Banks' army, he said, "but I look for General Grant's forces before that day."[16]

2. In Motion in All Directions

FROM THE BEGINNING, General Johnston suspected that the Federals in the Mississippi Valley held a winning hand if they played it right. That Van Dorn and Forrest had made Grant retreat from Oxford was of course good, and Sherman's repulse at Chickasaw Bayou was still better; but even before the rejoicing had died down Johnston told President Davis that "it would be very embarrassing" if Grant brought all the rest of his army down to join Sherman, whose force was resting unhappily at Milliken's Bend. Johnston felt that the Confederacy had too much ground to cover here, and that the Federal commander could always concentrate, at one pressure point or another, an army too big for the defense to dislodge.

"Should the enemy's forces be respectably handled," wrote General Johnston, "the task you have set me will be above my ability."[1]

Grant was about to make the very move that Johnston feared. He could see, as readily as his opponent could do, how this move would embarrass the Confederacy, and besides his hand was forced by the presence at Milliken's Bend of the irrepressible General McClernand.

Full of energy and resentment, McClernand reached Milliken's Bend on January 4 and informed the 30,000 Union soldiers there that they were now the Army of the Mississippi and that he was the army's commander.[2] This fractured Grant's published orders styling McClernand a corps commander in Grant's army, but Grant was many miles away. Having given himself promotion, McClernand might well make it stick if he won victories while Grant was still extricating himself from the desolation of western Tennessee. McClernand's immediate problem was to find where such a victory could be most readily won and quickly seen.

Now he was helped by a man who detested him, General Sherman, who told him about the Post of Arkansas.

Halfway between Vicksburg and Memphis the Arkansas River flows into the Mississippi from the northwest, and about fifty miles up the Arkansas the Confederates had built Fort Hindman, commonly known as the Post of Arkansas or simply as Arkansas Post. It was not part of the Vicksburg defense apparatus but it did lie on the flank of any Federal supply line that came down the Mississippi, and to knock it over would obviously be a good deed. McClernand had been talking about opening the Mississippi and cutting his way to the sea but he had not focused on anything specific; now Sherman gave him an objective and he took it with enthusiasm. He sent Grant a dispatch that spoke rather vaguely about making a diversion in Arkansas, promising to return to the big river after he accomplished his purpose; then, with the Army of the Mississippi and Porter's river fleet, he set off for Fort Hindman.

This gave Grant the impression that the ambitious McClernand had gone thrashing off into the wilds for some improbable end of his own just when it was essential that he stay at Milliken's Bend to await the advance of General Banks, who was going to be ever so much later than General Grant then supposed. Grant sent an indignant complaint to Halleck (getting in return formal authorization to remove McClernand from command if he saw fit) and he wrote a dispatch to McClernand telling that officer to get back to Vicksburg "unless you are acting under authority not derived from me."[3]

Before this message reached McClernand, however, the victory had been won. Arkansas Post was well laid out and adequately garrisoned, but nobody had ever imagined that the Yankees would come after it with a whole fleet and an army of 30,000 men, and it fell on January 11 after a brisk assault and bombardment. McClernand found that he had taken nearly 4800 prisoners at a cost of about 1000 of his own men and he sent word of his victory to Grant, telling his own troops meanwhile that "a success so complete in itself has not hitherto been achieved during the war." He wanted to go on up the Arkansas and take Little Rock, which would have been another glittering victory although it would have taken him a long distance from Vicksburg; he gave it up when Porter told him there was not enough water farther up the Arkansas to float gunboats and transports, and at last McClernand got his command afloat and steamed back to Milliken's Bend.[4]

Grant had to reverse himself: the blow at Arkansas Post had been a good move, even though it did Pemberton no especial harm. (The reversal came more easily when Grant learned that the move had been Sherman's idea in the first place.) But Grant had to be on the Mississippi himself. The big campaign against Vicksburg was going to be made from the river because the President and the Secretary of War said so. In Grant's absence McClernand would command because he ranked everyone but Grant, and the man obviously had Banks' own weakness for going off on a tangent. Grant could do nothing but make the river expedition as strong as possible and then take charge of it in person. By the end of January he had his headquarters at Young's Point, on the west bank a few miles below Milliken's Bend, and he had made it clear to McClernand that the commander of the Army of the Mississippi was Grant and nobody else. He had concentrated some 40,000 troops at Vicksburg and he had perhaps 15,000 more waiting at Memphis to come down when needed. Now his task was to find out just how the army at Milliken's Bend was going to come to grips with Pemberton.

The problem was hard because the Federal army was on the wrong side of the river. It had to be there because it could not put its camp and its base on the eastern side; there was no place to land east of the river that was not covered by Confederate guns. Before they could beat their enemies the Federals must first get at them, and to do this they had to defeat geography itself. Right here geography was very much on the side of the Southerners.

North of Vicksburg on the east side of the Mississippi,

running almost all the way to Memphis, was the vast area of the Yazoo Delta, two hundred miles from north to south and up to fifty miles across; flat, swampy, seamed with rivers and bayous, black-soil farming land that had never been properly drained and was half under water. To march an army with its guns and supply trains across this land and reach the high ground east of the Yazoo and Tallahatchie rivers was wholly impossible. To be sure, the Yazoo entered the Mississippi a little below Milliken's Bend, but when Sherman tried to take this route in December he had floundered helplessly into defeat. A little farther up the Yazoo, a dozen miles north of Vicksburg, there were strong Confederate batteries at Haynes' Bluff, barring the way to Federal transports. Pemberton's northern flank looked perfectly secure.

The western flank was no softer. Vicksburg sprawled along the side of a long bluff, protected by numerous batteries and trenches for infantry. The Federals might have landed a storming party along the waterfront, but no one imagined that such a storming party could fight its way uphill and seize the town and its fortifications. Whatever else it might do, Grant's army could not take Vicksburg from this approach.

Before he even got to Young's Point, Grant notified Halleck that although he did not know what would have to be done he did think that "our troops must get below the city to be used effectively."[5] This was sound as Gospel; unhappily, to get the army below Vicksburg looked no easier than crossing the Yazoo Delta looked. The Louisiana country west of the river was flat, crisscrossed by innumerable little streams, with wandering country roads that were utterly inadequate for the use of an army with its guns and trains; and even if the army did somehow manage to march forty or fifty miles downstream it would still be on the wrong side of the Mississippi. To fight Pemberton, Grant's army had to reach the high ground east of the river, and it could not cross the river without transports—of which the Federal government had none below Vicksburg. It was not enough for Grant to get his army south of Vicksburg; he had to get steamboats down there too, accompanied by gunboats, and the frowning batteries along the Vicksburg waterfront looked like an impassable barrier.

By logic, Grant probably should have taken the whole army back to Memphis and made one more attempt to come down overland, along the railroad line east of the Yazoo Delta. But logic was powerless now. For better or worse the government was committed to a river campaign. To retreat, confessing failure, and to start all over again would probably be too much for the Northern people to take. Grant had to solve this problem where he found it, and he found it at Milliken's Bend.

There were several things he could try, and he put the army and navy to work on all of them.

He might bypass the Vicksburg batteries by digging a canal. Right above the city the river made a 180-degree turn; opposite Vicksburg there was a narrow peninsula, four miles long by less than a mile wide, very low, protected along most of its length by levees. If the levees were cut and a ditch were dug at the base of the peninsula the river might well scour the ditch out and create a deep channel. Then gunboats and transports could float down, avoiding the Vicksburg batteries altogether, to find a proper landing place somewhere south of Pemberton's fortifications. An unproductive beginning had been made in the preceding summer, when Farragut's cruisers and a brigade of Butler's troops tried unsuccessfully to take Vicksburg. Grant remembered this, and he sent an engineer officer down to study the situation even before McClernand got back from Arkansas Post. The engineer said the thing might conceivably be done, and so in February Grant brought in dredges and a boatload of picks and shovels and put Sherman's corps to work as canal diggers.[6]

There were other ventures, each one requiring thousands of soldiers and sailors to work unproductively in the mud. None of these ventures looked promising, but all of them were tried more or less simultaneously.

Fifty miles above Vicksburg a placid bayou known as Lake Providence lay west of the Mississippi. Through swamps, ponds, and stagnant rivers it seemed to offer a waterway which, after wandering halfway across Louisiana, led at last into the Red River; and if this waterway could be widened, deepened and cleared of dead logs so that steamboats could use it the army could float along and get into the Mississippi not far above Port Hudson. Up to Lake

Providence came engineers, followed by working parties with full equipment, and another job of canal digging got under way.

More than a hundred miles above Lake Providence, on the east side of the Mississippi, there was a desolate expanse of mud, water, and trees known as Yazoo Pass. In the old days the Mississippi used to discharge flood waters here, and some years before the war men had built a levee to keep the Yazoo Delta from being drowned. Now details came to blow up the levee, and a torrent of foaming brown water went spilling off through the pass and on into the Coldwater River; and after the turbulence subsided a little, gunboats and transports went through, seeking to go on to the Tallahatchie River and from that into the Yazoo itself. This waterway was exceedingly roundabout, and it was even less simple than it looked, because many large trees had to be hauled out of the channel and for miles the boats cruised along rivers so narrow the growth on the banks knocked down their smokestacks. The route was a sailor's nightmare, and the officer Porter put in charge of this flotilla went half out of his mind, collapsed physically, and presently died in the hospital, apparently of exhaustion coupled with sheer frustration. But the flotilla kept on going; if it got through Grant could put his army on the east side of the trackless Yazoo Delta, north of Vicksburg, and then he could get on with the campaign.

There were still other possibilities. Another canal was begun, on the west bank near Milliken's Bend, at Duckport, and details assembled more picks and shovels to connect forgotten bayous and sloughs so that steamboats could reach the Mississippi twenty miles south of Vicksburg. There were moments when this idea looked good, and eventually one light-draft steamer made the trip; but then the water level of the Mississippi receded, the waterway became impassable, and one more project went for nothing.

Last of all there was a plan that involved no digging but that almost cost Porter a flotilla of gunboats. All of the innumerable bodies of water in the low country seemed to connect with one another, and it developed that by going a few miles up the Yazoo, turning north into Steele's Bayou, and then threading a tortuous course through rivers nobody had ever heard of—Black Bayou, Deer Creek, Rolling Fork, and Sunflower River—steamers could get back into the Yazoo several miles above the Confederate works at Haynes' Bluff. This involved a 200-mile journey to reach a point that was only about twenty miles away, but anything was worth trying and Porter took eleven gunboats and tried it. He came to a halt, at last, miles from nowhere, in a stream so narrow his vessels could not turn around and so thick with saplings that they could not move forward, and he had to back out ignominiously lest his squadron be hung up there forever. Grant's army might reach dry land east of Vicksburg someday, but it obviously was not going to do it by this route.

Nor by any of the others; all of them, vigorously tried, turned out to be impractical. The winter wore away and the army toiled mightily without making progress, and in the North it began to seem that the whole campaign was a dismal failure. There was some grumbling by the higher officers. Major General Frank P. Blair, division commander under Sherman and brother to Postmaster General Montgomery Blair, said that the army was wearing itself out and complained that "this business of working our men to death when there are hundreds of thousands of Negroes who could be had to do the work in the mud and water is disgusting beyond all measure." Brigadier General Cadwallader C. Washburn of the cavalry rendered his own gloomy verdict: "There is no push in this Army, and there is very little Common Sense among Generals. I fear Grant won't do. He trusts too much to others and they are incompetent." To the people who begged him to remove Grant and put someone better in his place, Mr. Lincoln could give no answer better than a grim: "I can't spare this man. He fights."[7]

He would fight if he could ever reach a battlefield, but by spring he was still in the swamps. Yet the morale of his army remained good, and the rank and file complained, not of its own hardships but of the rise of defeatist sentiment back home. Typical was the outburst of a Missouri soldier: "There is a strong feeling growing up in the army against all the enemies of the government, whether at home or abroad, and meetings are being held, strong resolutions are being passed and letters are being written home by officers and men (for publication) sustaining the President and denouncing the

Traitors everywhere." Talk about the army's extensive sick list, said this soldier, was "all gammon . . . True, there is sickness and death, but no more than is usual with new Regiments the first winter in the field." An Illinois soldier wrote that his regiment was healthy and happy, and said that as soon as these canals were finished "we are going round and cut a canal across the upper part of Florida, thereby cutting that invaluable state off from the 'Confed' and give the alligators a deed for it."[8]

The winter's work apparently accomplished nothing, yet a strange thing was happening. Trying half a dozen ventures at once and failing in all of them, Grant nevertheless was preparing General Pemberton for defeat. As spring approached, Pemberton felt that he was under a constantly increasing pressure. He knew that this unceasing coiling and shifting of his powerful enemy would sooner or later find a weak spot in his inadequate line of defense. He could not see Grant's failures: he could only see that the Federals were moving all over the map, making moves that might be feints and might be real. It was impossible to tell where the heavy blow was going to be struck. He became first anxious and then confused and out of many small confusions there came at last a large and fatal confusion.

At the beginning, in January, Pemberton had been optimistic enough. Sherman's assault at Chickasaw Bayou had failed so completely that Pemberton proudly remarked that 100,000 Yankees could not have succeeded there. He kept on strengthening Vicksburg's defenses, and he told a fellow officer that if he had to (although he would not tell higher authority) he could spare 8000 men to help Bragg in Tennessee. He did not complain greatly—not then, anyway—when Johnston ordered him to send Van Dorn and three-quarters of the 6000 cavalry in the department off to work with Bragg's cavalry, and in the middle of the month Pemberton considered the possibility of taking the offensive. He had 15,000 men at Grenada, east of the Yazoo Delta and 120 miles north of Vicksburg, under the Major General W. W. Loring whom Lee had found so touchy in that long-forgotten West Virginia campaign eighteen months earlier, and he ordered Loring to prepare his command for a northward movement up the line of the Mississippi Central Railroad.[9]

But the Federals who had been so badly beaten came back,

powerfully reinforced, and the river above Vicksburg was full of gunboats, mortar schooners, transports, and supply vessels—more than a hundred of them had come down, Pemberton was told, in three days, and Grant in person had come with them—and there was every evidence that a big push was in the making. Pemberton was guarding a line fully two hundred miles long, and his immediate defenses at Vicksburg ran for more than fifteen miles, from Haynes' Bluff on the north to Warrenton south of the town. He sent a sober dispatch to Johnston: "Enemy in full force again opposite the city, with indications of attempting to force his way below. This necessarily separates my command. Must have large force at Warrenton." He ordered the Vicksburg entrenchments strengthened and told the garrison commander to alert the waterfront batteries and prepare for an early attack. Loring heard no more about an advance up the railroad. Instead he was warned that the Yankees might try to break through Yazoo Pass and that it would be well to get ready to block them.[10]

So far there was no real cause for alarm, yet there were many places where the enemy might cause trouble. The canal opposite Vicksburg looked as if it might work, and, in the middle of February, Pemberton told Mr. Davis that this would enable the Federals to run downstream, and said that "either from above or below there is a possibility that troops may be landed and Vicksburg be invested by land or water." He was fairly well supplied with food and ammunition but he did not have enough to stand a siege, and he feared that Federal operations on the Yazoo would cut off the supplies he was getting from the delta country. Loring built a makeshift fort, duly christened Fort Pemberton, where the Tallahatchie and Yalobusha rivers join to form the Yazoo, and armed it as well as he could. Pemberton confessed he could send him no heavy guns but told him this position must be held even if he had to use infantry as boarding parties to capture armored gunboats: he had been informed that the Federals planned to go east from the Yazoo and assault Grenada with 50,000 men. He notified Mr. Davis that the progress of the canal compelled him to fortify Grand Gulf, where high bluffs overlooked the Mississippi twenty-five miles below Vicksburg, and to do this he would have to have more artillery. Then he learned that Porter was going up Steele's Bayou, and he had to detach men from Vicksburg to put up batteries there.[11]

Actually, it was impossible for Pemberton to tell what was happening. On March 11 the Federal gunboats came down the Tallahatchie to Fort Pemberton and opened fire. The river channel was so narrow that they had to come in single file, bows-on, and the country roundabout was so badly flooded that it was impossible to land infantry or artillery; the attack failed dismally, and the invaders went back up the Tallahatchie. But Pemberton had no way to know that this attempt had been written off; two weeks later Loring called for more guns and more infantry; Pemberton tried to find reinforcements for him, and told Johnston that as spring dried the roads it might be possible for the Federals to march east from the Tallahatchie to strike the Mississippi Central Railroad near Grenada. The commanding officer at Vicksburg held that Porter's expedition up Steele's Bayou would probably be the main Federal effort; he continued to think so as late as April 2, although by that time Porter had taken his gunboats back to the Mississippi and the whole project had been given up. Pemberton began to complain bitterly that since Van Dorn and the cavalry had been sent away he could not find out what Grant's people were doing. Something menacing apparently was being prepared in northern Mississippi, and the Federals appeared to be making some sort of move on the west side of the big river. It was reported that 30,000 Federals were going to attack Port Hudson; also, that troops in west Tennessee were about to become aggressive in northern Mississippi. Early in April Pemberton sent an expressive report to Richmond: "Enemy is constantly in motion in all directions."[12]

This was a good summary of what the general knew about the situation. He was being bewildered just as John Pope had been bewildered in Virginia, eight months earlier, and when the crisis came he would have to do what Pope did—make life-or-death decisions based on a total inability to understand what his enemies were trying to do. Grant's endless maneuvers had got the Federals not one foot nearer the high ground east of the Mississippi, but they had inflicted crippling damage on Grant's opponent.

Finally, at the end of March, Grant committed himself. He would march his army down the west side of the river, he would run gunboats and transports past the batteries, and then he would cross the river and attack Vicksburg from the south and east. On March 29 McClernand's corps was put to work, corduroying roads, building bridges, filling in swamps, and in a few weeks these westerners had built a road seventy miles long, winding down from Milliken's Bend to a riverside hamlet named Hard Times. The road was not very good but it would do for one march. Grant notified Porter to be prepared to run the batteries, first with gunboats and then with transports.

Now Porter warned him: this was the point of no return. The gunboats could probably pass the batteries going downstream, but they could never come back because against the current they moved so slowly that the batteries would destroy them. Once they went down the river Grant's whole campaign would stand or fall on this one thrust. Grant agreed. This was going to be it.

Pemberton learned no more than that the Yankees were trying some sort of raid over on the Louisiana side, and again he appealed for cavalry. He sent reinforcements to Loring at Fort Pemberton, believing that the Tallahatchie expedition was still a hovering menace. Then his intelligence service told him that the Yankees at Memphis were seizing river steamers, for some inscrutable purpose of their own; thirty boats, it was reported, all of them empty, had started down the Mississippi.

Not long after this Pemberton was warned—first by Johnston, who was in Tennessee, and then by President Davis— that there was reason to think that Rosecrans' army in central Tennessee was being reinforced, apparently by Grant; could Pemberton send some of his troops to help General Bragg? This struck Pemberton as reasonable; those empty steamers obviously were coming down to carry Grant's men somewhere, and the best information Pemberton could get indicated a return to Memphis. On April 12 Pemberton sent a message to Johnston: "Will forward troops to you as fast as transportation can be furnished—about 8000 men. Am satisfied Rosecrans will be reinforced from Grant's army."[13]

Then he began to suspect that this movement of the Federals might be a ruse. He had second thoughts, and on April 16 he wired Johnston that he did not think Grant was sending very many men away; as a result he could send Bragg only two brigades instead of the three he had promised.[14]

And on the night Pemberton wrote that dispatch Porter

ran past the Vicksburg batteries with gunboats, empty transports and some loaded coal barges and went steaming on
down the river to join the vanguard of Grant's army on the
Louisiana shore south of Vicksburg. Early the next morning
Grant went riding down McClernand's new road to look after
things in person.

3. The Needs of Two Armies

THE RIVAL ARMIES along the Rappahannock that winter were
under very different handicaps.

South of the river there was a shortage of material goods,
not yet acute but still touching the army's nerves and muscles.
In Richmond a mob rioted for bread, sacking jewelry stores
in an excess of fervor, and in camp General Lee found that
inadequate supplies imposed narrow limits on the possibilities
open to the Army of Northern Virginia, whose meat ration
had been cut to four ounces a day.

North of the river there was plenty of bread but a dire
shortage of less tangible rations. The Army of the Potomac
seemed to be hungry for some value not listed on the commissary tables; perhaps, despite the millions of words that had
been spoken to, by and about this army it was still waiting
for The Word, which if it had been uttered had not pene-
trated to all ranks.

Characteristic complaints were heard on each side of the
river.

An officer in Brigadier General Harry T. Hays' Louisiana
brigade, in Stonewall Jackson's corps, wrote to his Congressman to say that of 1500 men present for duty, 400 had no
shoes. Many men had no blankets, many had neither underwear nor socks, hardly anyone had an overcoat, there were
no tents, and everybody was hungry all the time. Troops from
other states, said this officer, were eased over the rough spots
by contributions from home, but this brigade had not had
anything from Louisiana since the fall of New Orleans. General Lee told Mr. Davis that unless supplies could be increased, "I fear the efficiency of the army will be reduced
by many thousands of men."[1]

North of the river an officer in the battle-tried 20th Massachusetts assured his brother that there would be no blessing

on Northern arms until the wrong done by the removal of McClellan had been righted; he urged the brother to "lift your voice like a trumpet and show the people their sins and Abraham his transgressions." A soldier who had the ear of leading Democrat Barlow declared the enlisted men were deserting because they "will not fight to put niggers on a par with white men," and he said he anticipated "a general uprising in the North to put an end to this war and decapitate some of the leading men in the Cabinet." Brigadier General Marsena Patrick, Provost Marshal of the Army, wrote in his diary that "the President has the names of about 80 officers who are to be dismissed the service for having spoken disrespectfully of him in reference to the removal of McClellan and the Porter court martial."[2]

Thus each army lacked nourishment, whether for the body or for the spirit. In neither case was the outlook promising.

In the Confederacy there was a relative abundance of meat, grain, and forage, but the railroads that brought supplies to the Army of Northern Virginia were falling apart, the horses that handled the short hauls had too much to do and too little to eat, and the army was hungry. It was also beginning to be seen that a man taken from civil life and turned into a soldier cannot at the same time stay in a shop and make things for soldiers to use; a dismaying lesson, because the army desperately needed soldiers now but could not use them properly unless it got the goods and services these men used to produce before they became soldiers.

In some ways the Army of the Potomac seemed to be in an even worse fix. Needing food for the spirit, its only immediate resource was Joe Hooker, who never was noted for his spiritual qualities.

Hooker indeed had nothing to offer but the resources of a hard-boiled soldier; yet these, for the moment and up to a point, turned out to be enough. He had the insight to realize that the plight of his army looked worse than it really was. Morale was far down, but to a large extent the soldiers had simply been suffering from an acute case of poor administration. There was plenty of food, but it was so bad the army actually was showing symptoms of scurvy. Camps were miserably policed, hospital services were atrocious, discipline was slipshod and the generals were visibly warring among themselves. The men were veterans denied the veteran's one consolation, the feeling that his closed military society would get on with its job no matter how the winds of politics blew; this military society obviously was in no shape to get on with any job. More than anything else the soldiers needed to feel that they were being used sensibly by a general who knew what he was doing. If Hooker could evoke that feeling he would have a different sort of army.

His immediate task happened to be within his means. He was neither cursed nor blessed with any profound convictions about what the war ought to mean; he was at the moment the favored soldier of the radical Republicans, but this was a marriage of convenience, and Hooker's driving force was a simple desire to be a winner. In the Army of the Potomac he had an instrument that he could win with if he knew how to handle it. He played it on that basis.

He began by shaking up the army's housekeeping services; quartermaster and commissary and medical departments. Rations suddenly improved, filthy camps were made clean and tolerably comfortable, hospitals became places where sick men might recover. Discipline grew tighter, so that it was much harder for unhappy men to slip away and go home—a point of some importance, because desertions had been averaging two hundred a day; at the same time liberal grants of furloughs did something to ease the homesickness that caused the desertions.

Hooker believed that idleness was "the great evil of all armies," especially of this one. He asserted that perhaps a majority of the officers, especially those of rank, were hostile to the government's policy and he said that when the army had nothing to do these disaffected persons "began to show themselves and make their influence felt in and out of camp." He got rid of some of the worst of the troublemakers; more important, he ended the idleness by sternly putting the army to work, and there were incessant drills and reviews, with regular classes of instruction for company and regimental officers. Periodically there were spectacular parades, with the dashing commanding general riding his horse, evoking cheers and making the men feel like soldiers once more. (This worked fairly well because the enlisted men liked Hooker, considering him a two-fisted fighter; also, he shared with McClellan the knack of *looking* like a good general.) Within weeks a Wisconsin officer wrote that "the army is in excellent condition as far as the health and spirit of the men are concerned," and an army historian asserted that in a comparatively short time "the busy scenes in camp once more betokened a healthful state."[3]

Hooker abolished the Grand Divisions, considering them cumbersome. Possibly this was a mistake, because it threw too much detail work on army headquarters, and in the stress of battle it would be hard for the army commander to keep his hand on all of the controls; Hooker may have felt that he had no subordinates capable of handling 40,000 men in the field. He did put through one badly needed reform, consolidating the army's cavalry into one corps of four divisions under command of Brigadier General George Stoneman. Previously the cavalry regiments had been distributed all through the army, and it had never been possible to bring together a contingent that could cope with Jeb Stuart's superb Confederate brigades. Now the Federal cavalry had a chance to do cavalry's proper job, and there was a striking improvement in its fighting capacity. Stoneman, to be sure, was no Stuart, and it remained to be seen whether either he or Hooker would know how to use the troopers effectively. But at least the possibility of effective use was there.[4]

So the army began to get back into fighting trim. It was at work once more, doing things that appeared to make sense, and the conditions under which it lived and worked were about as tolerable as they ever are in an army camp. The malcontents who had done so much to destroy morale were muzzled, Franklin and Smith and their staff officers were gone, and the ugly lesson taught by the cashiering of luckless General Porter was being absorbed. What one officer after the war remembered as "a military aristocracy . . . defying the government at home with only a little less disdain than Davis manifested at Richmond" had been brought into line.[5] The army at least was not going to be made impotent by its own discontent.

Yet a question mark remained. General Hooker was immensely pleased with everything, announcing that he commanded "the finest army on the planet" and assuring President Lincoln that the question was not *whether* he would capture Richmond but simply *when:* and this led the President to wonder whether the general was not a little too self-confident, uttering brave words to cloak an inner doubt.

There was an odd gap in Hooker's relationship with Washington. He treated General Halleck with disdain, dealing directly with the President and almost entirely ignoring the general-in-chief, building up a body of ill-will that might some day have to be paid for. He had been sharply critical of many of his generals, and if trouble came they could be counted on to be critical in return. They served him dutifully and with diligence now, but they did have reservations.[6]

Beyond this, the real test of army and general alike would come on the field of battle, where General Lee would apply his own searching and pitiless analysis; and although this army had been reorganized and shaken out of despondency it still retained a queer feeling of separateness that made it unlike all other Federal armies. In the other armies the men were and incurably would remain civilians in arms, men who had dropped their ordinary pursuits to do an unpleasant job but not changing very much: in this army it was subtly different, with the men standing somehow apart from everything they had been before they became soldiers, relying only on themselves and not expecting a great deal from presidents, generals, or the people back home. One veteran remarked after the war that "the capability of enthusiasm seemed to have died out of the army at this time . . . the rank and file of the Army of the Potomac had begun to consider themselves better soldiers than their commanders."[7]

This put an especial burden on Joe Hooker, who might have thought about it with profit if he had been the reflective type. This army would respond well enough to his professional skill, but what it particularly wanted from its commanding general (although it could never formulate this desire) was some indication of the moral stature that could lead the army to surpass itself. Nobody would know whether it was actually going to get this until it reached the battlefield, and that day could not be postponed for long, because as soon as spring came Hooker was bound to take the offensive. He was driven to this, not merely because the government expected it but also because there were in his army forty-three regiments of short-term soldiers, 20,000 effectives in all, who would go out of the service in May. Hooker had to do whatever he was going to do before these trained men left the army. Their departure would rob him of the equivalent of a good-sized army corps.[8]

General Lee's difficulties were different. If Hooker knew that he must move promptly, General Lee at times had to wonder whether he could move at all. He and his men had already created their share of the undying Confederate legend, which told of an undernourished army made victorious by brilliant leadership and unending valor but desperately lacking the material support an army had to have; and in this legend there was, by the winter of 1863, altogether too much truth for comfort.

In the middle of February, Lee admitted that he could not take the offensive. The rivers were too deep for fording, he lacked pontoon bridges, the roads were impassable—"we have mud up to our eyes"—and the horses and mules that pulled the army's guns and wagons were so badly run down that "the labor and exposure incident to an attack would result in their destruction and leave us destitute of the means of transportation." The Federals were massing troops around Norfolk, possibly to move up the James toward Richmond, and Lee had to send James Longstreet and two good divisions down to the south side of the James to meet this threat. When he ordered the move he warned Longstreet that "the horses are in such a reduced state, and the country so saturated with water, that it will be almost impossible for them to drag the guns."[9] Fortunately it had been possible to make the move by rail, but the warning was ominous. Ordinary cross-country movements were out of the question unless Lee could count on drier roads and stronger animals.

Stronger animals he could not get. In ordinary times the southern states got most of their horses from Missouri, Kentucky, Tennessee, and western Virginia—precisely the areas largely held by the Federals. The army used up animals as prodigally as it used up men, and now it was becoming extremely difficult to find replacements. Within a few months an army inspector concerned with such matters would warn that Confederate sources of supply were almost exhausted and that "nothing is left us but to procure animals from the enemy's country." To make matters worse, it was impossible to get enough food for the animals the army did have. The northern part of Virginia, from Rappahannock tidewater all the way to the Shenandoah, had been stripped of everything; to get hay and grain for his livestock Lee had to send wagons seventy miles from the army, but with bad roads and weakened teams these wagons carried pitifully small loads. The army was beginning to face a problem as dire as a modern army would face if it ran out of gasoline. Lee put it bluntly to Secretary of War Seddon: if underfed horses were overworked now they would be entirely out of action by spring, when active campaigning began, and "without forage for the horses provisions for the infantry cannot be transported."

To make the difficulty more acute, it was discovered that when the Federal threat on the James River faded (as it did, before winter ended) Longstreet and his divisions had to stay down there in order to collect supplies from the unravaged land between the lower James and the Carolina border. In effect, Lee had to use a fourth of his undersized army on a food-collecting expedition in order to keep the rest of the army alive. In March he cut the army's transportation to the lowest possible limit, pointing out that this necessity arose "from the difficulty of procuring animals and forage and from the increased demand for transportation of subsistence when the army shall be removed from the vicinity of the railroads."[10]

It would not have been quite so bad if the railroads had been adequate, but the railroads were in deplorable shape.

There had been a shortage of rolling stock from the beginning, and most Southern railroads were lightly built, all of which meant that there was an extraordinary need for ample repair and maintenance work. But this need could not be met because most of the mechanics were in the army, and every attempt to get them out of the army was blocked by the army's need to keep every soldier it had. A quartermaster officer complained that "there is not a car, engine or machine shop in the country able to do half the work offered it for want of men and material," and by fall it was estimated that fifty locomotives were idle because they could not get new iron tires for their drive wheels. One War Department official said flatly that "the railroads are worn out," noted that the man responsible for railroad service said he could do nothing unless he got more mechanics, and added: "General Lee has fought all winter against this."[11]

What Lee was fighting was the War Department system of "details"—an attempt to solve industry's worst problems by detailing soldiers with mechanics' training for temporary service in shops and factories. Like every other army commander Lee opposed this bitterly, suspecting that most requests for details were politically inspired and knowing all too well that he was critically short of combat men anyway. In February this led to an exchange of letters with Secretary Seddon, who came about as close as any Confederate Secretary of War ever came to giving General Lee a rebuke.

Seddon complained that practically all of the War Department's requests for details were being turned down at Lee's headquarters. These requests, Seddon went on, "are not transmitted incautiously but are sent by me reluctantly and stintingly, and only when on large considerations of public interest the requirements of the general service, in my judgment, demand them." Would not General Lee consider this matter, give more weight to the Department's measured judgment, and permit "only strong controlling considerations of a military character" to lead to a disapproval?

General Lee would not. He remarked that when a man got a government contract "his first endeavor appears to be to get his friends out of the army to help him." Hundreds of soldiers, he said, went home on sick leave and then pulled every imaginable wire to promote a safe detail in some shop; of the thousands who had been detailed for special purposes, hardly one ever got back to the army, some regiments were almost useless as a result, and the whole thing had given Lee "the impression of waning interest on the part of the people in our cause." If the Department flatly ordered the details he would of course obey, but if he were allowed any discretion he would disapprove as long as life remained.[12]

Lee and the Confederacy were beginning to face a most baffling problem.

The problem came out of all-out war—by definition, a war in which complete victory is the only thing that matters. To fight so calls for maximum effort in two conflicting areas— the army needs every man it can get and so does industry, and the rival needs have to be balanced. Eighty years later, in the Second World War, the same struggle was fought in Washington, and army and industry accused each other of vast stupidity. All ended well in the 1940s because the most highly industrialized nation on earth found that it could meet both requirements; but in the 1860s one of the world's least industrialized nations could do nothing of the kind. The Confederacy could have an adequate army, or it could support its army adequately; it could not conceivably do both because it did not have the resources to do both. It could only wrangle about those details. In this winter of 1863 it was being warned about ultimate disaster but the warning did no good because the disaster was inescapable. The Confederacy had got into the sort of war it could not win.

One trouble was that it was so hard to identify the problem. In the field, brave men faced the foe; at home they wrestled with high prices and low salaries, found that butter cost $2 a pound and pantaloons $40 a pair, noted that a Negro cobbler could make more money than a member of Congress, and concluded that villainy was afoot: "all patriotism is in the army; out of it the demon avarice rages supreme."[13] On April 2 Mr. Davis was called in haste to quell a riot on Richmond's Main Street, where some hundreds of people were demanding bread and were indiscriminately looting bakeries, jewelry shops, millinery stores and other places. As always, the President faced up to it. He mounted an empty dray, called on the mob to behave itself, emptied his pocket to toss what money he had with him into the crowd, and then summoned the militia, which fixed bayonets, loaded its muskets with ball cartridges, and ended the disturbance.[14] The business meant nothing in particular except that the shortage of transportation was beginning to bind; this was a war in which a collapse of railroads might be as deadly as a collapse of armies.

Early in April Secretary Seddon drew Lee's attention to the need for reinforcing the western armies. Lee replied that the natural thing would be to send troops from Virginia, but railroad service being as it was this would be cumbersome and slow "and if we rely on that method we may always be too late." Should Hooker remain on the defensive, he went on, the Army of Northern Virginia could relieve the pressure on other fronts by invading Maryland: however, "this cannot be done in the present condition of the roads, nor unless I can obtain a certain amount of provisions and suitable transportation." A week later he confessed that he could reach no satisfactory conclusion in the matter. He doubted that Hooker would remain inactive much longer. When Longstreet returned, it might be possible to hold Hooker in check and clear the Federals out of the Shenandoah Valley, but "if it is decided that it will be more advantageous to reinforce Gen-

eral Johnston, these operations will have to be arrested."
Stonewall Jackson was working hard on a plan to march all
the way into Pennsylvania and cripple Northern industry by
breaking up operations in the anthracite coal fields, and he
had his topographical engineer prepare detailed maps of the
country between the Potomac and the Susquehanna, but Lee
at this time could make no elaborate plans. On April 16 he
could tell Mr. Davis only that it was going to be necessary to
assume the offensive by May, if possible; still, "at present we
are very much scattered, and I am unable to bring the army
together for want of proper subsistence and forage."[15]

Lee was beginning to show the strain physically. To his
daughter Agnes, who had been hoping to visit him, he wrote
that "the only place I am to be found is in camp, and I am
so cross now that I am not worth seeing anywhere." He told
Mrs. Lee that he felt "almost worn out" and feared that "I
may be unable in the approaching campaign to go through
the work before me," and shortly after this he wrote: "As
for my health, I suppose I shall never be better. Old age
and sorrow is wearing me away, and constant anxiety & labor,
day and night, leaves me but little repose." Early in April
his doctors warned him that he was threatened "with some
malady which must be dreadful if it resembles its name but
which I have forgotten." He had a hard cold and suffered
from sharp pains in the chest and back, and the doctors
"have been tapping me all over like an old steam boiler before condemning it."[16]

The wry humor with which he talked of his symptoms
shows clearly that his real concern was not the state of his
own health. He seemed this winter to be approaching a new
concept of Confederate strategy, as if he began to feel that
final victory would be won by a dogged endurance based
on superior spiritual resources; and here, typically, he was
thinking about the flaws in his opponent's armor. Handicapped as they were in all material things, the Confederates
might yet wear the Yankees out by greater dedication to the
cause. On April 19 General Lee explored this thought in a
letter to Mrs. Lee:

"I do not think our enemies are so confident of success as
they used to be. If we can baffle them in their various designs this year & our people are true to their cause & not so
devoted to themselves & their own aggrandisement, I think

our success will be certain. We will have to suffer & must suffer to the end. But it will all come right. This year I hope will establish our supplies on a firmer basis. On every other point we are strong. If successful this year, next fall there will be a great change in public opinion at the north. The Republicans will be destroyed. I think the friends of peace will become so strong that the next administration will go in on that basis. We have only therefore to resist manfully."[17]

4. A Bridge for the Moderates

AMONG THE MOST prominent friends of peace in the North was Congressman Clement Laird Vallandigham of Ohio. He was a Democrat and a lame duck, having been gerrymandered into defeat in the 1862 election, but he would remain a member of Congress to the end of the present session and he planned to run later in the year for governor of Ohio. He was going to run on a peace platform, and on January 14 he arose in the House of Representatives to demand that the war be stopped.

He was not, he hastened to emphasize, a disunionist. On the contrary he devoutly wanted the Union restored, and his big objection to the war (one of his big objections, at least) was that the way it was being fought made reunion impossible. He believed that the sections would return to fraternal embrace once the shooting stopped, and he wanted the war ended so that this could happen.

Vallandigham subjected the past to rigid analysis and took the future on faith. He was smooth, persuasive, an uncommonly able orator, offering a politician's mixture of principle and self-interest whose proportions no one could quite make out; he was speaking today partly as an old-fashioned Democrat trying to bedevil the Republicans, partly as a gubernatorial candidate exploiting a useful issue, and partly too as a spokesman for genuine resentments, fears, and ideals. He pointed out that he had never supported the war and he thanked God that "not so much as one drop of its blood is upon my garments."

On the record, he held, the Northern war effort had been a failure. The rebellion was still going on, the Union was not yet restored, and the Constitution was dishonored. The

South not only was unconquered; it never could be conquered. War for the Union had been abandoned, and it had been replaced by "war for the Negro," which was proving a bloody failure. Vallandigham had a solution:

"Stop fighting. Make an armistice—no formal treaty. Withdraw your army from the seceded states. Reduce both armies to a fair and sufficient peace establishment. Declare absolute free trade between North and South. Buy and sell. . . . Recall your fleets. Break up your blockade. Reduce your navy. Restore travel. Open up railroads. Re-establish the telegraph. Reunite your express companies. No more monitors and ironclads, but set your friendly steamers and steamships once again in motion. Visit the North and West. Visit the South. Exchange newspapers. Migrate. Intermarry. Let slavery alone. Hold elections at the appointed times. Let us choose a new President in sixty-four.

"And when the gospel of peace shall have descended again from heaven into their hearts, and the gospel of abolition and hate been expelled, let your clergy and the churches meet again in Christian intercourse, North and South."

Three things, said Vallandigham, he hated with equal fervor—abolition, forced reunion, and the idea of Southern independence. The crisis of the war, he felt, was at hand; if peace came now all would be well, but if it did not "I see nothing before us but universal political and social revolution, anarchy and bloodshed, compared with which the Reign of Terror in the French Revolution was a merciful visitation."[1]

Read in the light of General Lee's letter (which also looked forward to the election of a different President in 1864) this is less persuasive than the orator intended it to be. The Southern Confederacy had been fought for so hard and believed in so much that its creators would not now abandon it unless they were forced to, and they were hard men to convince. By 1863 it was folly to suppose that the old Union would quietly restore itself as soon as men stopped killing one another. The only possible way now to have a peace acceptable to the South was to draw a boundary and make a treaty between two independent nations; this speech ignored that point and addressed itself to men who took the impossible for granted.

Vallandigham in short was speaking for those numerous

war-weary Northerners who were already becoming known as Copperheads. His speech did not need to be logical; it was an attempt to stir the emotions rather than the reason. It came from, and it reached out to, something massive and enduring in the heart of the North—a poignant longing for the good old days when life was simpler, a longing made all the more terrible by the fact that it was so hard to say where the old simplicities had gone. Vallandigham was speaking for people who were often accused of treasonous intent, as he himself was accused. Whatever his own inner motives may have been, the people who looked to him for leadership desired no victory for the South and no defeat for the North; they simply wanted something that had been shattered put back together again. Not only were they conservatives, resentful of the changes war was bringing; they were also lovers of liberty, dismayed by what the war seemed to be doing to freedom.

They were not, of course, the only lovers of liberty. Their bitterest political opponents loved it as much as they did. The trouble was that freedom had so many facets. Under the twisting pressure of war the administration was going in opposite directions at the same time. It had issued a notable proclamation, promising freedom to people who had never had it; almost in the same breath it had proclaimed suspension of the privilege of the writ of habeas corpus, curtailing freedom for people who had always had it. In some strange way these two acts went together, inseparable as liberty and union in the old oration, as if the freedom that had always been enjoyed was a hardy growth that could survive temporary infringement whereas the other freedom was so new that it had to take precedence. What bothered so many of Vallandigham's followers was the belief that neither proclamation was really needed in the first place, and that the American people had stumbled into a bog.

It was certainly true that the effort to win the war was curtailing personal liberties. Newspapers were being suppressed on the mere say-so of army officers, and thousands of Americans had been put in prison solely because some official thought that they ought to be there. One did not need to be a friend of the Confederacy to feel that arbitrary arrests were wrong and that the policy that countenanced them was dangerous. The suppressed newspapers eventually resumed publication and the people imprisoned eventually got out, but the government undeniably was using a power American governments were not supposed to have.[2]

It was almost impossible for anyone to say where ordinary political opposition to the party in power ended and opposition to the Union cause began. The government was drafting men into the army. The decision to draft was both an act of politics and an act of war. As an act of politics it could be attacked; but how could an editor, a politician, a judge, or a private citizen oppose the draft without at the same time helping the Confederacy? The privilege of the writ was suspended in order to help the draft; was this suspension a proper step toward winning the war or a despotic attempt to silence criticism? It might be either, or indeed it might be both, but it made the way of the political opposition uncommonly difficult.

This was where Vallandigham stepped into a fatal trap. He made a party of moderates look dangerously immoderate, and he turned the war rather than the conduct of the war into an issue. He enabled Republicans to answer all complaints with the simple word "Copperhead!" Because he said what he said, supporters of the administration could—and infallibly would, because they also were immoderate men—charge that opponents of Abraham Lincoln were really friends of Jefferson Davis. They would ring all the changes on the argument that the Democrats were nothing more than an anti-war party.

So the ground on which Northern Democrats stood began to get dangerously narrow. There were Democrats who saw this and protested vigorously. One was another Democratic Congressman from Ohio, Samuel Sullivan Cox of Cincinnati, picturesquely known as Sunset Cox because he liked to describe the beauties of the sunsets along the Ohio River. Cox wrote to Democratic Editor Manton Marble of the New York *World* to say that although "there is a large element in our party West for peace" no one should get a wrong idea about it. Western Democrats, said Cox, did not want peace at any price; they stood with the border state Unionists, and they wanted peace only "whenever honorable and possible—not an armistice, not a hollow truce, not any cessation of hostilities which will jeopardize Kentucky, West Virginia, Tennessee, and Missouri." They wanted peace with victory, and they would not be handed over to Secessionists: "If we are beaten it will be because of this erratic course."[3]

It went beyond a question of immediate political advantage. Abraham Lincoln was a moderate man bringing in immoderate change; that is, he had ordained emancipation, with ultimate results which both Attorney General Bates and the middle western Democrats saw clearly, but he had his own grave doubts about what those results were going to be. If there was one man in the United States to whom the Northern Democrats could have talked frankly about the need to keep it all within bounds it was the President of the United States. He had argued for gradual emancipation and for an impossible scheme of colonization, simply because as a conservative middle westerner he doubted that the two races could get along together once the bars were down. Yet he himself was taking the bars down, striking at slavery with a rail-splitter's ax, wedge, and mallet because he believed that the Union could not otherwise be saved. The conservatives who were so concerned with the ultimate problem of reconstruction—although this fateful word had not yet passed into common currency—were cutting off their access to him, and now the only people who supported his war program seemed to be the Republican radicals. The very men who most deeply shared his brooding skepticism were being driven, by the fear of change, into a position where they could not exercise a moderating influence.

Sunset Cox was not the only man who detected the profound tactical error that was being committed. Back in December, at the time of the cabinet crisis, Tipster Barnett tried to tell S. L. M. Barlow that the conservatives must not "permit the President's ear to be opened exclusively to a majority of the present Congress." The radical tide, said Barnett, was in full flood, and if the conservatives failed to present a program the President would listen to, he would soon find that the radicals were his only supporters. Barnett was a man of no especial importance but he was in a good position to know how Mr. Lincoln's mind was working and how the war was going, and as winter wore away to spring he tried harder and harder (and with no success whatever) to persuade Democratic leaders that their strategy was "quite as mad as that of those whom they stigmatize." The power of the Rebellion was visibly waning, he argued; the Con-

federacy had "deathless spirit" but it was in a desperate
state, and "even awkward and bumbling licks will soon bring
it down." Instead of looking ahead to the opportunities that
would be open then the Democrats were confining themselves to untempered criticism.

Who was to blame (Barnett asked) for the fact that the
radical Republicans seemed to be controlling the President's
actions? What had the conservatives ever done to give him
better counsel? "One or two lazy adventures of this sort was
attempted, and not by men of great vim—and then an opposition was organized to his administration *per se*. And so he
has been left to the mercy of men against whom were all his
pre-dispositions; and events have drifted him into the whirl-
ing vortex of their fanaticism." The conservatives had won
notable victories at the polls in the autumn of 1862, but
their triumph had been mismanaged even worse than the
Army of the Potomac itself; they had altogether ignored the
fact that "Mr. Lincoln, if he believes the men to be true to
the country, is quite as glad to listen to conservatives as to
anybody."[4]

Barnett had part of the picture but not all of it. The
President was by no means following the advice of the radicals in these days, and he had not given up the attempt to
get some of the conservative counsel Barnett was talking
about. Late in March he sent an anxious letter to Governor
Horatio Seymour of New York, one of the Democrats who
had come into high office through the fall elections. Seymour
was no Vallandigham. He was of course a partisan politician,
as every governor had to be, an able and consistent opponent
of the politician who occupied the White House, but he was
a loyal Unionist not tainted with open or secret leanings toward the Confederate cause; and Mr. Lincoln's letter, most
carefully phrased, was an attempt to find some sort of meeting ground.

"You and I are substantially strangers," wrote the President, "and I write this chiefly that we may become better
acquainted. I, for the time being, am at the head of a nation
which is in great peril; and you are at the head of the greatest State of that nation. As to maintaining the nation's life,
and integrity, I assume and believe that there cannot be a
difference of *purpose* between you and me. If we should dif-
fer as to the *means,* it is important that such difference should

be as small as possible—that it should not be enhanced by unjust suspicions on one side or the other. In the performance of my duty, the co-operation of your State, as that of others, is needed—in fact, is indispensable. This alone is a sufficient reason why I should wish to be at a good understanding with you. Please write me at least as long a letter as this—of course, saying in it just what you think fit."

Governor Seymour's reply was phrased with equal care: "I assure you that no political resentments, or no personal objects will turn me aside from the pathway I have marked out for myself—I intend to show to those charged with the administration of public affairs a due deference and respect and to yield them a just and generous support in all measures they may adopt within the scope of their constitutional powers. For the preservation of this Union I am ready to make every sacrifice."[5]

Perhaps the two men were a little too careful. President and governor had been courteous and restrained, but if there was to be a useful bridge between the administration and the conservatives it was not going to be built here. Yet it was important to build it somewhere, and Mr. Lincoln kept on trying. Now he reached out to one of the most turbulent areas of all, border state Missouri, to see how the moderate approach would go there.

Missouri badly needed a moderate approach and seemed most unlikely to get it. The state's Unionists, who had a comfortable majority when united, had fallen into what the President described as "a pestilent factional quarrel," disagreeing bitterly over the degree to which emancipation should be adopted and the restraints that should be enforced upon citizens who still felt sympathy for the South. Governor Hamilton R. Gamble, who had been put in office in the summer of 1861 after the late Nathaniel Lyon wrenched control of the state government away from the secessionists, was trying to put through a law for gradual emancipation, and he believed in mild treatment for dissenters. To the Republican radicals this was no better than appeasement, and they had rallied behind the military commander of the Department of Missouri, the elderly and conscientious Major General Samuel R. Curtis, who had won the notable victory at Pea Ridge a year earlier and who believed in stern measures for patriots of doubtful loyalty. The President had tried without success to settle this quarrel, and at last—remarking that "as I could not remove Gov. Gamble I had to remove Gen. Curtis"— he relieved Curtis of his command.

First choice to succeed Curtis was General Sumner, who was going to be displaced anyway by Hooker's abolition of the Grand Divisions. Sumner was simplicity itself, with a passion for doing exactly what his superiors told him to do; perhaps, in Missouri, such a man could be used. Attorney General Bates, who kept a watchful eye on affairs in his home state, approved of the choice. But Sumner never got there. He was worn out physically and emotionally, and on his way west he fell ill of pneumonia and died—rousing himself, characteristically, on his deathbed to take a glass of wine and ceremoniously drink a toast to the United States of America. Now it was necessary to find another man, and Mr. Bates was gloomy. "Good men do tell me," he wrote to a friend, "that patience and passive valor are great virtues, and I partly believe it and try to cultivate them. But I fear that my supply of these good articles is ebbing pretty low." After long consideration, the President sent Major General John M. Schofield out to take Curtis' place.

Schofield was young, vigorous, a West Pointer who had served with Lyon at Wilson's Creek (he would eventually get a Medal of Honor for his work there) and he had been fighting most recently along the Missouri-Arkansas border. Mr. Lincoln gave him sage but brief counsel along with his letter of appointment: Schofield was to use his own judgment, keep the peace and repel invaders without harassing or persecuting people, and keep out of the factional row if he could. "If both factions, or neither, shall abuse you," said the President, "you will probably be about right."[6]

A few weeks later the President sent more specific advice. The governor of Missouri had called a constitutional convention and a plan for gradual emancipation was being adopted, and now Schofield wanted to know what he should do when this plan went into effect. Should he give military protection to slaveowners in their exercise of human property rights during the time when emancipation was proceeding gradually? In other words, would the United States Army uphold slavery up to the time the cut-off point was reached? This presented the author of the Emancipation Proclamation with a nice question, and in his reply Mr. Lincoln carefully drew a line between the extremes. In substance, he said that slavery had to die but that there could be some flexibility if the slaveowners themselves consented to its death. His letter to the general read thus:

"Desirous as I am that emancipation shall be adopted by Missouri, and believing as I do that *gradual* can be made better than *immediate* for both black and white, except when military necessity changes the case, my impulse is to say that such protection should be given. I cannot know exactly what shape an act of emancipation may take. If the period from the initiation to the final end should be comparatively short, and the act should prevent persons being sold, during that period, into more lasting slavery, the whole would be easier. I do not wish to pledge the general government to the affirmative support of even temporary slavery, beyond what can be fairly claimed under the constitution. I suppose, however, that this is not desired; but that it is desired for the military force of the United States, while in Missouri, to not be used in subverting the temporarily reserved legal rights in slaves during the progress of emancipation. This I would desire also. I have very earnestly urged the slave states to accept emancipation; and it ought to be and is an object with me not to overthrow or thwart what any of them may in good faith do to that end.

"You are therefore authorized to act in the spirit of this letter, in conjunction with what may appear to be the military necessities of your department."[7]

5. *The Way of the Liberated*

THE TROUBLE WAS that events were moving too fast. The Emancipation Proclamation had been nothing more than a statement of intent, written by a man who supposed that there would be time to make all necessary adjustments. What was happening in Missouri was a case in point: the people of this state were trying to work out a slow transition, and the President was willing to allow a margin for trial-and-error expedients in the hope that other slave states would fall in line. But emancipation came with such a rush that there was no time to adjust anything. Men found that they were living with it while they still wondered whether it ought to happen at all.

In his notable speech Congressman Vallandigham warned that nothing of the kind could possibly occur. The institution had too many roots and the roots went down too far in too many hearts. Sudden change was out of the question.

"You cannot abolish slavery by the sword; still less by proclamations, though the President were to 'proclaim' every month," he cried. "Neither, sir, can you abolish slavery by argument. As well attempt to abolish marriage, or the relation of paternity."[1]

This was a perfectly logical argument, robbed of its meaning by the fact that what Vallandigham considered impossible was actually being done. Slavery *was* being abolished by the sword and by proclamation, by fire and by sudden uprising of the spirit; perhaps because there was no other earthly way to do it. The greatest single change in American life arrived without the benefit of any advance planning.

To begin with, the proclamation was taken with deadly seriousness by the people most concerned, the Negroes themselves. To others it might be no more than a piece of paper that would mean much or nothing depending on how the war went; to the Negroes it was the parting of the Red Sea. It meant freedom now and everywhere, as fast as the word could travel, and the Negroes acted on this belief. Even though it had always been buttressed by unlimited force, slavery in America really existed by the consent of the governed. This consent, to be sure, came largely because the governed were utterly helpless, but it was a basic element in the institution, and the worst nightmares of slaveholding society arose from the fear that consent might some day be withdrawn, with violence. Now, almost overnight, the consent was gone. The Negro was using no violence; he just was not consenting any more, and he never would consent again no matter what happened because he had at last been told that he did not have to.

The lack of violence may have been at least partly due to the fact that the proclamation had been issued. The feeling that the Federal government was on their side relieved the Negroes from the desire to start the war for freedom on the plantations; the dreadful nightmares failed to come true because the slaves believed that they were or soon would be under the protection of the United States Army. Some time earlier Mr. Lincoln had told an acquaintance that the proclamation was essentially conservative, sparing the slaveowners possible horrors and making servile insurrection unnecessary.[2] Now events were bearing him out.

Because the Negro response was so strong, Mr. Lincoln began to see that the problems that came with freedom would have to be solved in America. His long-held idea that it might be possible to avoid these by transferring the Negroes en masse to some far-off colony began to fade when he realized that the colored folk not only wanted freedom but wanted to be Americans, enjoying their freedom in America and not elsewhere. He still gave the colonization project some support but he no longer really fought for it; the place he had suddenly taken in the Negroes' hearts made it impossible. On January 1, just after the signing of the final draft of the proclamation, the abolitionist Benjamin Rush Plumly wrote to him to tell how the free Negroes of Philadelphia had held watch-night services in their churches, praying, singing, weeping, and displaying "the solemn joy of an old Jewish Passover." Plumly, who had attended some of the meetings, tried to tell the President how these people felt:

"The Black people trust *you.* They believe that you desire to do them justice. They do not believe that *you* wish to expatriate them, or to enforce upon them any disability, but that you cannot do *all* that you would . . . Someone intimated that you might be forced into some form of colonization. 'God won't let him,' shouted an old woman. 'God's in his *heart,*' said another, and the response of the Congregation was emphatic.

"Another thought there must be some design of God in having your name 'Abraham,' that if you were not the 'Father' you were to be the 'Liberator' of a people. One minister advised them to thank God that He had raised up an honest man for the White House, whereupon they broke, five hundred strong, into that ringing hymn, 'The Year of Jubilee.' "[3]

In the deep South the slaves held no prayer meetings of celebration. They simply walked away from the plantation whenever they heard that there was a Federal army within range and presented themselves to their liberators with a touching faith that a new day had come; beginning thus a tragic pilgrimage that cost many thousands of them their lives and plunged all of them deep into utter misery but that did not quite destroy the appeal of the vision that led them on. Before the winter was out the army in the Mississippi Valley area alone was caring for 30,000 or 40,000 of them— men and women and children whose helplessness was absolute, who had no resources except impossible expectations, and for whom no one on earth was really responsible.[4]

The army was giving them atrocious care because it had been taken completely by surprise; and so had government, President, War Department, and everyone else. To turn nearly 4,000,000 slaves into free people demanded long-range planning if anything ever did, partly because the problems of transition were so intricate and partly because meeting these problems would inevitably set patterns that would affect Negro life for generations to come. If there had been plenty of time the administration doubtless would eventually have created a special department to handle all of this, with expert planners, a suitable appropriation and a man of cabinet rank to take charge; but that word "eventually" fell out of the language the moment the other word, "freedom," went down the lanes and the grapevine telegraph to the slave cabins, and everything that was done had to be improvised by men whose real concern was something quite different.

There was no way out of it. The soldiers in the field had to do the job simply because they themselves stood where the Red Sea waves had parted. The chaplain of an Ohio regiment in Grant's army wrote that the in-gathering of fugitive Negroes was "like the oncoming of cities." Some of the slaves had fled from their masters and some were adrift because the masters themselves had fled, and all of them were waifs in a baffling world where the only certainties they had ever known were gone forever. They came to the army camps because for the moment they were totally helpless, self-reliance and initiative being traits which had gone undeveloped under slavery. They came because they could think of no other place to go and knew only that they had to be on their way somewhere; as the chaplain said, "a blind terror stung them and an equally blind hope allured them, and to us they came."[5] The army had to take some sort of care of them because otherwise the army itself would be swamped.

So the army set up concentration camps, whenever and

wherever they seemed to be needed; near enough to be under army protection, remote enough to be out of the army's way. For shelter there were condemned army tents, or makeshift cabins improvised out of stray bits of lumber. Army rations were issued, supplemented by foodstuffs gathered in the neighborhood and later by produce from little vegetable plots cultivated by the Negroes themselves. Sometimes army blankets and clothing could be had; more often, as the business got organized, such things were sent to the camps by charitably minded folk in the North. There were armed guards, to keep order, and at least in theory medical care was available. This was nearly always inadequate, sanitary arrangements barely existed, and a representative of the Western Sanitary Commission, after inspecting a chain of these camps in the Mississippi Valley, wrote that many of the inmates were a good deal worse off than they had been under slavery.

The death rate, naturally, was appalling. By the middle of the summer a camp near Natchez, Mississippi, was having from fifty to seventy-five deaths every day—rather more than half the number recorded at notorious Andersonville Prison in its worst days, although the Natchez camp held only a fraction of the number confined at Andersonville. Part of this came because the whole operation was done on the spur of the moment, with the left hand, and part of it came because so many of the refugees were physically unfit to begin with. Early in the winter Grant notified Halleck that most of the planters who moved South took their healthy, able-bodied slaves with them, abandoning the old, the very young, and the infirm; Frank Blair's notion that all of the canal-digging around Vicksburg might be done by sturdy contrabands was in error because so many refugees were not sturdy enough, and Grant said he was not letting any more Negroes come within his lines, adding tersely: "Humanity dictates this policy."[6]

But the tide kept rising. As a practical matter there was no way to keep the Negroes out, the container which had held them being in process of collapse. The camps multiplied, and the dictates of humanity were all but inaudible. A white woman sent to the Mississippi Valley by the Western Sanitary Commission to work with the refugees was appalled by what she saw in a camp near Helena, Arkansas. The hospital was "a wretched hovel," the streets were so deep with mud that army wagons stuck there, their mules dying in harness, the refugees themselves lived in quarters "void of comfort or decency," and conditions were so bad that the mere idea that there could ever be an improvement seemed to this woman to be impossible. Many of the refugees, she said, seemed to have come to the camp simply to die, "and they do die, very rapidly." Writing in February 1863, she noted that "the carcasses, filth and decay . . . will make the mortality fearful when warm weather comes."

To make matters worse, "the barbarities from our soldiers are unparallelled," and the refugees were often treated with incredible brutality. This woman cited one example: "One man came to Mr. Sawyer" (the army chaplain detailed to take charge of the camp) "and said that his wife had lived in a tent with soldiers, had been sick; they being ordered away pulled up the tent and left her on the ground, she had died, and now he wished her buried. Storming terribly as it was, the good chaplain started, but found her so far out that she could not be buried that night, for the teams could not get there and back, so they covered her as well as they could with a blanket and left her. In the morning they found her babe a few months old lying with her under the blanket, some person having become tired of it placed it there for the chaplain to see."

Her recital went on, a catalog of horrors. One group of twenty plantation hands came to camp, were robbed by the soldiers of the little they owned, and thirteen of them died of sickness and exposure. Their owner presently came to camp and asked the survivors if they did not want to go back to slavery. "They did not wish to go, faltered, changed their minds daily for a week, we encouraging them all we could, but as destitution, persecution and death stared them in the face the sad sufferers went back." A Federal gunboat brought in eighty-two Negroes, along with a load of cotton; the cotton, having good cash value, was promptly sent North for disposal, but the eighty-two Negroes were dumped at the Helena camp, and "one of the women, a cripple, came to me today, said they had been so abused and starved already that they wished themselves back." One surgeon ordered that contrabands suffering from diarrhea be tied up and flogged, on the theory that this would break them of the abominable habit of soiling their bedding; "it was often done, and to some that were dying."

People in the North sent clothing for the inmates, and here the Sanitary Commission agent found an unexpected problem. When a child died the Negroes who were all but naked would use the very best garments they had to clothe the dead child for burial. It was useless to try to explain that the clothing was desperately needed for the living. The parents could think only of the children who had died, who never in their brief lives had worn good clothing, and their answer invariably was: "We want them to look pretty."[7]

By slow degrees the worst abuses were corrected, and although many people died most of them after all lived; and the authorities tried to work out a system by which these fugitives could become self-supporting. Abandoned plantations were taken over, leased on one-year terms, and the contrabands were put to work for wages: $7 a month for able-bodied men, $5 for women, half-price for children. One investigator reported that "This plan would have answered a tolerable purpose had the lessees of the plantations been honest, upright, humane men; but with few exceptions they were adventurers and camp followers, who were ready to turn their hands to any opportunity of getting gain by the oppression of the poor, the weak or the defenceless." The army appointed commissioners to supervise the business, but mostly the commissioners sided with the lessees rather than with the Negroes. The investigator noted that wages were based on the slave-hire rate that prevailed when cotton sold for 10 cents a pound; it sold for 70 cents now, $2 a head was deducted for medical care which often was not provided, and in many cases wages stopped on rainy days.

This exploitation was not confined to the Mississippi Valley. In the vicinity of Port Royal, South Carolina, the story was about the same. A number of plantations there were sold to Northerners who set up a share-crop system. One man acquired thirteen plantations, employing 400 former slaves, "not one of them able-bodied, all being old men, old or feeble women, or children." He raised sea island cotton, investing $40,000 altogether and clearing an $81,000 profit for his year's effort. On an average, his workers got $16.50 a month. In some instances small plantations were leased and operated by the Negroes themselves, and this seemed to work out fairly well except that the Negroes often feared to bring their crops to market because soldiers and civilian speculators either swindled them or took their produce by force.

A Federal officer said that he "found the prejudice of color and race here in full force, and the general feeling of the army of occupation was unfriendly to the blacks. It was manifested in various forms of personal insult and abuse, in depredations on their plantations, stealing and despoiling them of their crops and domestic animals and robbing them of their money." It was considered that the system set up by General Banks in Louisiana was the worst of all, labor being enforced by the army "often with great rigor" with everything arranged for the benefit of the planters. Here, as elsewhere, there was heavy mortality in the camps.[8]

Dawn was a long way off, and if there was a light in the sky the light was streaky, blood-red against the darkness. Yet the slaves kept on coming in, and on the whole what they came to seemed to matter less to them than what they were getting away from. After a few months of it General Grant told his friend and patron, Congressman Elihu B. Washburne of Illinois: "Slavery is already dead and cannot be resurrected. It would take a standing army to maintain slavery in the South if we were to make peace today guaranteeing to the South all their former Constitutional privileges." Grant went on to say that he himself had never been an abolitionist, "not even what could be called anti-slavery"; he was simply telling what he saw.[9]

Grant was not overstating the case. The great change was taking place, and as the winter passed Negroes were not only coming into the army's lines: in increasing numbers they were coming into the army itself, the administration having at last made up its mind to put Negroes in uniform and make soldiers out of them.

Before the proclamation was issued this looked like too risky a step to take, and in the summer of 1862 President Lincoln had refused to take it. But after the proclamation came out he changed his mind, remarking to General John A. Dix at Fort Monroe that inasmuch as "we have it, and bear all the disadvantage of it (as we do bear some in certain quarters) we must also take some benefit from it, if practicable." He asked Dix if he could not raise Negro regiments, using them to garrison places in the rear areas so that the white troops there could be freed for field service. To Andrew Johnson, military governor of Tennessee, he wrote that the nation needed nothing so much as to have a man like Johnson—"an eminent citizen of a slave-state, and himself a slave-holder"—raise Negro troops. "The colored population," wrote Mr. Lincoln, "is the great *available* and yet *unavailed* of force for restoring the Union. The bare sight of 50,000 armed and drilled black soldiers on the banks of the Mississippi would end the rebellion at once. And who doubts that we can present that sight, if we but take hold in earnest?"[10]

The hope that this spectacle would of itself end the rebellion turned out, of course, to be a wildly optimistic miscalculation, but a decision of immense importance had been made, and the administration pushed the program with energy. Authority to recruit and use Negro regiments had been granted by Congress much earlier, and before the winter was out the War Department sent Adjutant General Lorenzo Thomas to the Mississippi Valley to see that such units were raised, officered, drilled and used. Halleck sent a private letter to Grant, remarking that he understood many of Grant's officers mistreated Negro refugees and tried to make them return to their masters and ordering him to "use your official and personal influence to remove prejudices on this subject and to fully and thoroughly carry out the policy now adopted and ordered by the government." This policy, in brief, was "to withdraw from the use of the enemy all the slaves you can, and to employ those so withdrawn to the best possible advantage against the enemy."

As Grant hardly needed to be told, this marked a significant change in the administration's attitude toward Secession, and Halleck underlined it:

"The character of the war has very much changed within the last year. There is now no possible hope of a reconciliation with the Rebels. The Union party in the South is virtually destroyed. There can be no peace but that which is enforced by the sword"—by the sword, the instrument which Mr. Vallandigham considered wholly impotent in this case.[11]

It was a long, painful process; a revolutionary change embraced reluctantly and from dire necessity. The nation had not been driven to war by its desire to free the slaves; instead it had been driven to free the slaves by its desire to win the war.

Now it had to change its thinking, and this was hard to do. Under the revolution involved in the act of changing slaves into free men, even into soldiers, there lay a profounder revolution involving the way individual men looked at their fellow human beings. Men of unquestioned good will found old habits of thought hard to break. Presidential Secretary John G. Nicolay this spring went to a Washington party where the Haitian Chargé d'Affaires was a guest, attended by his Secretary of Legation: two men of color, accepted on an equal footing in a roomful of whites. "They were quiet and well behaved, and said to be quite intelligent," wrote Nicolay. "But on the whole it was rather difficult to dissociate them in one's mind from the other colored waiters in the room."[12]

It was difficult: even more so for men not conditioned as Nicolay had been conditioned. Colonel Edward S. Bragg of the 6th Wisconsin was a distinguished combat soldier, leader of one of the best regiments in the Army of the Potomac, and he found adjustment impossible. A few weeks before the Battle of Gettysburg he wrote thus to his wife:

"I understand there is a Negro regiment in town, but as I am confined to my room I have not had my nerves shocked by seeing 'a woolly head and black face' decked out in Uncle Sam's uniform. I wish a white man was as good as a Negro and elicited as much sympathy and attention. A man must be either 'a foreigner or a black' to receive early notice at the hands of our exceedingly discriminating public.

"A little nigger just came in my room, with 'our corps' badge on his hat which was given him by a Lieutenant—by the aid of a knife I soon destroyed the 'Cuffie's' plumage. What an ass a man must be to put his uniform on a dirty nigger that didn't belong to him."[13]

Something irrevocable was happening. A good many Cuffies were putting on the country's uniform this spring, and they had no illusions about the way they were regarded. One Federal officer intimately connected with the enlistment of Negro soldiers wrote frankly: "They were fully aware of the contempt, often times amounting to hatred, of their ostensible liberators. They felt the bitter derision, even from officers of high rank, with which the idea of their being transformed into available soldiers was met." But they had their own point of view, which was expressed bluntly by Frederick Douglass, the one-time slave who was the acknowledged spokesman for free Negroes in the North. He put it this way:

"Once let the black man get upon his person the brass letters, *U. S.;* let him get an eagle on his button, and a musket on his shoulder, and bullets in his pocket, and there is no power on earth which can deny that he has earned the right to citizenship in the United States."[14]

For when the Negro put on his country's uniform it followed logically that at last he had a country.

CHAPTER THREE

Remorseless Revolutionary Struggle

1. Ironclads at Charleston

THE GENERAL usually signed himself simply as G. T. Beauregard; which seems a pity, because there was a fine resonance to his surname when the three given names marched ahead of it, and the general was a resonant man. To say "Pierre Gustave Toutant Beauregard" is to get a little of the flavor of him; and yet the fact that he cut the name down when he signed official papers was fully in character, because he was a conscientious worker. Like Jeb Stuart, he was both flamboyant and competent, and his habit of devising strategic plans far too elaborate for the Confederacy's resources did not keep him from making good use of the limited means that were available.

It was necessary to be most practical now, because after two years the war was returning to the city where it began. General Beauregard was back in South Carolina, back in Charleston where two years earlier he had drawn a famous "circle of fire" around Fort Sumter. He had taken Fort Sumter after a spectacular but almost bloodless bombardment, and then for a little while the war had been a matter of high spirits and hope and waving flags, with history pivoting neatly on one heroic but inexpensive act of defiance. Since then General Beauregard had been at Shiloh and the palmetto flags had been carried to such places as Gaines' Mill and Sharpsburg, and all of 1861's innocence was gone forever. Now Fort Sumter was Beauregard's to defend, and the war had a new grimness. The Yankees had built and manned a whole fleet of ironclad warships—dark vessels, clumsy and ugly and inexpressibly menacing—and they were planning to use this fleet to destroy the fort and the city and to kill secession in the place where secession began.

So, at any rate, said the Northern press, which had never learned discretion; and so said the omens along the South Carolina coast, studied intently by General Beauregard. It was clear that the Federal naval commander, Rear Admiral Samuel F. Du Pont, was trying to test his new ironclads under battle conditions. The Navy Department had given him nine of them, led by U.S.S. *New Ironsides,* his flagship, a ponderous steam frigate with a high freeboard and no turrets, mounting a heavy broadside battery behind stout iron plating. There were seven monitors—eight, originally, but the vessel that gave this class its name, the original U.S.S. *Monitor,* had foundered in a mid-winter gale off Cape Hatteras. In addition there was U.S.S. *Keokuk,* listed as an "experimental ironclad," a low-hulled craft mounting two 11-inch guns in fixed citadels, bow and stern, looking like a monitor but differently arranged. As the new monitors came down they were sent to bombard Fort McAllister, on the Ogeechee River near Savannah. It appeared, from all of these trials, that the monitors could stand a heavy fire without being hurt very much, and one of them, U.S.S. *Montauk,* showed her hitting power on February 28, 1863, by reaching out past the fort to sink C.S.S. *Nashville,* a former blockade runner converted into a commerce raider, highly regarded by Confederate navalists. Admiral Du Pont's enthusiasm was temperate, for although the monitors escaped serious damage they had not hurt Fort McAllister very much either. General Beauregard got that point, too, and was comforted thereby. What was more important was the obvious conclusion that the Yankees were tuning up for an attack on Charleston.[1]

The fact that Beauregard commanded at Charleston indicated that he was not liked in Richmond. The army he led at Shiloh had long since been turned over to Braxton Bragg, and when the government in the fall of 1862 looked for a good man to assume the all-important defense of Vicksburg and the Mississippi River it bypassed Beauregard and chose General Pemberton. Pemberton then was on duty at Charleston, and when he went west Beauregard was ordered to Charleston as his replacement, one of the Confederacy's most famous soldiers going in to substitute for one of its most obscure. Charleston at the time was an inactive sector, and

the obvious implication was that the administration did not
care much who commanded there.

The war had brought changes to Charleston. The city was
as determined as ever, but the early springtime rapture was
gone. Gone too was Secession Hall itself, destroyed in the
fall of 1861 by a fire which with notable impartiality also
destroyed the home of James Louis Petigru, the city's one
unreconstructed Union loyalist. Petigru was the man who
greeted passage of the original ordinance of secession by
remarking that the state was too small for a republic and too
large for a lunatic asylum, and not long after the war began
he wrote to Maryland's Reverdy Johnson that every day he
saw "manifestations of an enthusiasm in which I have not
the slightest participation." Nothing ever shut him up, and
diarist Mary Chesnut wrote tartly that his career proved
that in South Carolina "if you have stout hearts—and good
family connections—you can do pretty much as you please."
In an odd way the city was rather proud of him; like the
village atheist, he testified by his mere existence to the stal-
wart orthodoxy of his community. Now the old man himself
was gone, dying on March 3, 1863, as his city was preparing for new trials.[2]

Beauregard took over in Charleston in September 1862,
and concluded that trouble was coming. (He was entirely
right; Du Pont had already been notified that the Federal
government was going to go all-out to capture Charleston,
even though it was not then ready to set a date.) Beauregard
concluded also that Pemberton had left a good deal of work
for him to do. The defensive installations, he said, were badly
located, incomplete and poorly armed, and he applied himself
to their improvement. He noted as he did so that the South
Carolina authorities were most helpful but that the Richmond
government, at least after Mr. Seddon became Secretary of
War, was somewhat apathetic. But whether he was helped
much or little he worked hard. New guns went into forts
and batteries, floating mines (torpedoes, as they were called
then) were planted in ship channels at the harbor entrance,
buoys were anchored so that gunners in Fort Sumter and Fort
Moultrie would know precise ranges, ingenious floating en-
tanglements to jam propellers and paddle-wheels were put
afloat, new works were erected to cover secondary approaches to the city, more troops were brought in. From the

far-away Rappahannock General Lee wrote to the President predicting a Yankee attack on Charleston and offering to contribute reinforcements if necessary. By the middle of the winter the Charleston defenses were strong.[3]

Admiral Du Pont had this forcibly brought to his attention. On January 30 the Federal gunboat *Isaac Smith* went prowling up the Stono River a dozen miles south of the entrance to Charleston harbor and came under heavy fire from concealed batteries; was disabled with a shot through her steam drum, lost nine men killed and sixteen wounded, and hastily surrendered. (The Confederates repaired her and put her on duty as a guard ship off Fort Sumter.) The next day two small lightly armored Confederate rams, *Chicora* and *Palmetto State,* slipped down past the fort on a misty dawn and took the Federal blockaders by surprise, overpowering the wooden gunboats *Mercedita* and *Keystone State* and forcing their captains to strike their flags. With other scattered Federal vessels hit, and momentary confusion prevailing, the ships that had surrendered managed to hoist their flags again and got away, but for a time the two rams controlled the sea approach and their officers insisted that not a Federal warship was in sight. This led Beauregard to issue a formal proclamation that the blockade had been broken and that Charleston was an open port again—technically an important point, since under international usage a broken blockade could not be re-imposed until the blockading government had given due notice to all neutral powers, which would take several weeks. The embarrassed Federal naval officers insisted that the blockade had not really been lifted. They got their cruisers back on station in a matter of hours, and things went on about as before. But they could see that Charleston was being defended with a good deal of energy, and Captain Percival Drayton of U.S.S. *Passaic* wrote gloomily that the city was "almost the strongest place by sea in the world."[4]

It seemed to Admiral Du Pont that the Federal government had entirely too much confidence in the monitors. It believed that they were invulnerable, it remembered how the navy's wooden warships had overpowered forts at Port Royal Sound and on the lower Mississippi, and it apparently felt that if the ironclads boldly steamed in and pounded Fort Sumter Charleston would quickly fall. It was so confident that the Navy Department notified Du Pont that as soon as this

Charleston affair was over he must send all but two of his monitors down to the Gulf to open the Mississippi. The administration did not want to lay siege to Charleston: it wanted the job done right away, navy-style, before Congress adjourned.[5]

Washington was overlooking several points. Du Pont, Farragut, and others had done well against strong forts by steaming boldly past them, taking a hammering but gambling that their own volume of fire would keep the Confederate gunners from inflicting crippling damage before the fleet got out of range. This could not be done at Charleston. The harbor was a blind alley, and the attacking fleet would have to anchor within easy range and slug it out until one side or the other was put out of action. Nothing that had happened yet in this war weakened the age-old naval axiom that ships could not fight forts. They could rush them, but unless the forts were unusually weak—like Fort Henry, in Tennessee—they could not overpower them.

In addition, when the monitors went in to attack Fort Sumter they would encounter a weight of fire no ironclads had yet faced. Beauregard had forts and batteries all around the harbor, and although his guns were not as heavy as the immense 11-inch and 15-inch monsters the monitors carried he had many more of them and they could fire much faster. The monitors would have to take half a dozen shots for every one they got off. They would also have to steam into a carefully prepared mine field. Worst of all, if a monitor was lost inside the harbor the Confederates would unquestionably raise it, repair it, and so come into possession of an instrument that could break any blockade the wooden cruisers could maintain; a prospect that gave Admiral Du Pont the cold shivers.

Du Pont suspected that the only proper approach was a joint army-navy operation, with the army coming up to Charleston on dry land while the navy gave its support; and here, if he had known it, Beauregard agreed with him. Long after the war Beauregard wrote that if the Yankees had sent troops inland on James Island, north of the Stono River, they could have struck the weakest part of the Confederate line: the weak works that lay in their path could have been stormed, they then could have built batteries that would command the inner harbor, and they would have been able to force "an immediate surrender."[6] But although the Federals had plenty of troops in the area, and would eventually try the siege operation, right now they wanted the job done quickly and cheaply and Du Pont had his orders. And so on the morning of April 7 the sluggish ironclads were prodded into line and they came steaming up the deep-water channel, headed for Fort Sumter.

The monitors were formidable but cantankerous. When the wind was right they could steam at a little more than four miles an hour, and on ordinary sea passages they were towed by sturdier vessels. When they cast off the tows they were almost unmanageable, and they had a way of swinging around and drifting sideways the moment their propellers stopped turning. Each skipper peered out of his pilothouse through tiny peep-holes which allowed him to see very little; the big guns could be fired only once in five minutes; in any seaway water came in under the base of the turrets; and the mechanism by which the guns recoiled, came back into battery and then were trained on their targets was easily deranged. When a shot hit a turret the jar was as likely as not to put the guns out of action for a time; it could also knock bolt-heads loose and send them flying around inside like lethal shell fragments. Still, the turrets had nine inches of armor, and if the ships were hard to control they were also hard to sink, and the morning of April 7 was windless with a calm sea; and at last the monitors came in, black smoke trailing from their funnels, Sumter and Moultrie and all the batteries waiting for them. As the first ships came into view Sumter hoisted all of its flags and saluted the Confederate colors with thirteen guns, a band got on the parapet and played *Dixie*, and all along the Charleston waterfront eager crowds watched to see what would happen. The world's first salt-water action by an ironclad fleet was about to begin.[7]

It began in a good deal of confusion. Monitor *Weehawken* led the line, pushing an ungainly raft that was supposed to clear torpedoes out of the way but that actually made it nearly impossible for the ship to move at all; *Weehawken* slowed almost to a halt, sheering to right and left and throwing the whole line into disorder as the other monitors stopped their engines to avoid collision and swung off every which way. Then the flagship, *New Ironsides*, had to anchor because she drew too much water for the channel, and the line was further disarrayed as the monitors went stumbling past her; the disorder was so great that *Keokuk*, which had been last in line, was presently leading the whole fleet, steaming straight for Fort Sumter.

It was well after noon when the firing began. It started deliberately: one range-testing shot from Sumter, two answering shots a few minutes later from one of the monitors, then a shattering broadside from Sumter's entire battery; and at last most of the ships were within fifteen hundred yards of the fort, and all of the gun crews afloat and ashore went into action. The noise was irregular, with brief moments of dead silence broken first by single shots, then by the reverberating crash of battery fire. In the patchy smoke the gunners could see the heavy round shot from the big guns arching toward their targets; once in a while through all the tumult they could hear the smashing thud of a solid shot hitting Fort Sumter's masonry walls, or the sharp, bell-like clang of a shot striking the iron turret of a monitor. A Confederate gunner was probably right when he estimated that the next hour saw the most powerful bombardment yet fired anywhere.

Sumter was garrisoned by seven companies from the First South Carolina Regular Artillery, disciplined men under a good officer, Colonel Alfred Rhett. Rhett had his guns firing by battery, at first, but to get more accuracy he changed presently to individual fire; the smoke made it hard to see, the low hulls of the monitors were almost invisible, and the whole fleet seemed to be drifting slowly through a bewildering forest of water spouts as near-misses sent up enormous splashes. Rhett had trained some first-rate marksmen, and as his fire became slower it grew more effective. The monitors were hitting, too. Sumter was struck again and again, and when one of the terrible 15-inch shot hit the walls the whole fort seemed to quiver, down to its bedrock foundations. Here and there the walls were broken open, a shell exploded in the barracks and started a fire (perilously near the magazine, but quickly extinguished), showers of bricks spattered around the gun emplacements when shot struck the parapets, two embrasures were destroyed, and at times it looked as if the fort must eventually collapse. Yet casualties were astonishingly light, and before long the defenders realized that although the fort was a most uncomfortable place to be in it was not really being hurt badly, and their confidence rose. Moultrie was in action, and so were all of the shore-side batteries whose guns would bear, and although the firing went on for the better part of two hours it was clear enough after thirty minutes or so that this Federal attack was an outright failure.[8]

Back on *New Ironsides,* Du Pont could see only that the battle could not be finished today, and in late afternoon he hoisted the recall signal, planning to make repairs overnight and resume the fight next morning. But when the fleet withdrew, and the monitor captains came aboard and told what had happened to them, he realized that he had been defeated, and came to a conclusion that would make him most unpopular in Washington: he would not renew the attack because to do so might turn failure into disaster. Then and there he made up his mind that Charleston could never be taken by the navy alone, and he refused to modify that conclusion even though it finally cost him his command.[9]

The monitor captains described a strange battle: only one ship had been seriously damaged, the casualty list was almost too small to be worth mentioning, and yet the fleet had failed conclusively and the only thing to do was to accept defeat and to revise all former ideas about monitors. These vessels might indeed be almost unsinkable, but they were complicated pieces of machinery rather than warships and under the hammering of Beauregard's guns they had simply lost their fighting power; pound those invulnerable turrets hard enough, and the guns inside the turrets could not be worked. In the history of navies there never was a fight like this one, either before or afterward.

Du Pont had sent eight ironclads into action, *New Ironsides* having anchored outside effective range. One of the ironclads, experimental *Keokuk,* armored much more lightly than the regular monitors, had been hit ninety times in thirty minutes of action; her hull had been pierced at or near the waterline nineteen times, her twin gunhouses had been riddled, and when she staggered back after the cease-fire she was ready to founder—did founder, in fact, early next morning, when a moderate sea came up, sinking at the edge of the ship channel, the top of her funnel still above water. The seven monitors were as seaworthy as monitors ever were, but four of them were unable to do any more fighting without undergoing repairs and all of them needed more or less attention.

Nahant, for instance, had fired only a few shots before the blows she received (she was struck thirty-six times) jammed her turret; unable to revolve the turret she could not train her guns on any target. On *Passaic,* the 11-inch gun was disabled early in the action, and it was almost impossible to revolve the turret. *Patapsco* also got a jammed turret, lost the use of one of her two guns, and in the entire action was able to fire only ten shots. *Nantucket* could not use her 15-inch gun because the hits she received jammed a port stopper, a ponderous iron shutter that closed the gunport when the gun was run in for reloading; she also found that after she had been hit a number of times it was hard to turn the turret. *Weehawken* was able to maintain her fire, but she was struck fifty-three times, and after the action parts of her side armor were so badly splintered that a lucky waterline hit could have sunk her. *Catskill* and *Montauk* got off with minor damage, but *Montauk's* skipper, Captain John Worden of the original *Monitor,* was convinced that this fleet could never take Charleston and warned Du Pont not to continue the attack.[10]

To be sure, all of the damage to turrets, gun carriages, port stoppers, side armor, and so on could be repaired in a few days, but there was nothing to show that the story would not be repeated in the next engagement. Indeed, the story would probably be worse because if the monitors pushed on to really close range they would reach the torpedoes and obstructions that clogged the ship channel, and would have to try to remove these things under a heavier fire than they had yet taken. Worst of all, they could not maintain anything approaching the volume of fire the Confederate gunners could inflict on them: for the job ahead of them their hitting power obviously was inadequate. Captain John Rodgers of *Weehawken* put it accurately in a letter to Secretary of the Navy Gideon Welles: "The punishment which the monitors are able to stand is wonderful, but it cannot be denied that their gun gear is more liable to accident than was foreseen. Battles are won by two qualities, ability to endure and ability to injure. The first we possess to an unrivalled degree—the latter one more sparingly."[11]

It was the inability to injure that was decisive. The mon-

itors carried the heaviest guns yet put into modern battle
action, but they did not have many of them and they could
not fire them very often. In the entire battle they got off
about 140 shots, hitting thirty or forty times; Beauregard's
gunners had fired more than 2200, scoring an estimated 440
hits. Sumter had been damaged, but working details were
busy all night and by morning the fort was just about as
strong as ever. The Confederates had lost four men killed and
ten wounded, and although the navy's casualty list (incurred
mostly on *Keokuk*) came to no more than one man dead
and twenty-two wounded it was clear that Beauregard could
play this kind of game all year. The monitor captains concluded almost unanimously that the percentage here was
all against the fleet.[12]

It would have been hard to arrange a battle more likely
to cause misunderstanding in Washington. From the beginning, President Lincoln had felt that Du Pont was unen-
thusiastic and slow, and the man's constant request for more
ships sounded unpleasantly like McClellan asking for more
troops; the President told Secretary Welles before the battle
that he thought Du Pont and McClellan were much alike
and said that he "was prepared for a repulse at Charleston."
Now all he could see was that the admiral had thrown in
his hand after a short fight which killed hardly any sailors
and did the ships little harm, and his faith in Admiral Du
Pont declined. The Navy Department sent Chief Engineer
Alban C. Stimers down to examine the ironclads, and Stimers
said he was "agreeably disappointed" to find that neither the
side armor nor the turrets of the monitors had been pen-
etrated. He felt that the harbor obstructions could be removed if the fleet really tried and concluded that "the
monitor vessels still retain sufficient enduring powers to
enable them to pass all the forts and batteries."

Du Pont formally accused Stimers of falsehood and conduct unbecoming an officer, but it did no good; Secretary
Welles chided Du Pont for it, and went on to express his
regret that Du Pont had abandoned, "after a single brief
effort, a purpose that the nation had deeply at heart." President Lincoln sent down a curt order: Du Pont was to hold
his position inside the bar near Charleston, if he had left
that position he was to return to it at once, and he was not
to let Beauregard build any more batteries on Morris Island,

a sand-spit south of the harbor entrance. The President added: "I do not, herein, order you to renew the general attack. That is to depend on your discretion, or a further order."[13]

All of this was rather unfair, for Du Pont was a good man who had done his best; handicapped because he served when the navy was embracing machinery, the embrace being so new that keeping the machinery from harm could seem more important than making the fullest use of it. Perhaps what was chiefly bothering the President was a thought old Admiral Farragut had voiced earlier in the winter. Farragut told David Strother that he believed ironclad ships and rifled guns were going to ruin the fighting forces. In the old days, said Farragut, wooden walls and smoothbore guns at close range were good enough, and men went in and fought to the finish. Nowadays what men fought with seemed to mean more than the men themselves; the old fighting spirit was bound to decline once it was permissible to shirk a fight because one did not have enough armor or modern rifles. . . . Admiral Du Pont patched up his monitors, President Lincoln and Secretary Welles began to think about a replacement, and *Harper's Weekly* deplored the failure to take Charleston and concluded simply: "The most obvious of all inferences is that it insures the indefinite prolongation of the war."[14]

2. Men Trained for Command

APPRAISING THE STATE of the Union from the American Legation in London, Charles Francis Adams felt that it was time to think about getting another President. It seemed to him this spring that the United States government was like a big machine running on its own momentum, and to find the right man for Mr. Lincoln's place was infinitely important. On the whole, Mr. Adams felt that the next President probably ought to be a general, because generals were properly trained for command; at the same time, no general really looked like a presidential candidate because of course the man chosen ought to be a *victorious* general and the North did not seem to have any of these. National prestige was gone, and "it needs some extraordinary genius to bring it back."

Musing thus, Mr. Adams went on to remark that neither North nor South had any real advantage in the matter of leadership. Presidents and generals on both sides were about equal and about average.

"Jefferson Davis is perhaps in some respects superior to our President," wrote the American minister to England. "But after all, he is not a superior man. His generals are respectable in the field, but they seem to be wholly without marking qualities. There is not a ray visible of Washington or even of Jackson, much less of Napoleon or Wellington. I fear the same thing may be said of us."

Mr. Adams put these reflections in a letter to his friend Richard Henry Dana, Jr., and he drew Dana's attention to "the singular effect produced upon the people of England" by the American Civil War.

"The aristocracy are decidedly against the continuance of the Union," he wrote. "The crown and the people favor it. The commercial classes are in the mean time putting in for the profits at any risk. The danger of a collision between the countries springs mainly from the action of these last."[1]

Dana could understand this point. He himself was famous because he wrote one of America's enduring literary classics, *Two Years Before the Mast,* and the ship *Alert* which his book made forever legendary had some months earlier been captured and burned by C.S.S. *Alabama,* a square-rigged, steam-powered cruiser built, armed and largely manned at Liverpool in what Mr. Adams considered a gross violation of British neutrality. Lord Russell, at the Foreign Office, had never publicly admitted that Mr. Adams' complaints had any substance. Still, *Alabama's* exploits this spring were becoming famous, and Lord Russell privately confessed that the spectacle of that cruiser "roaming the ocean with English guns and English sailors to burn, sink and destroy the ships of a friendly nation is a scandal and a reproach."[2]

The danger of a collision looked bigger than it really was. *Alabama* was a spectacular irritant but not much more than that, and Lord Lyons, the British minister in Washington, reported that although the Americans were exasperated their government did seem anxious to keep the peace; in this difficult spring he himself was "getting on pretty well again with Mr. Seward," which was an encouraging sign. He would have agreed with Mr. Adams that the desire of the commercial classes to make money was the chief problem, and he thought it would be well if London, quietly and without appearing to yield to threats, could find some way to keep British shipyards from building any more warships for the Confederacy. He warned that a good many American naval officers would actively welcome a war with Great Britain; then they could go commerce raiding themselves, winning much prize money and escaping the dull monotony of endless service on the blockading squadrons.

This feeling did exist, and it could easily get entangled with the avarice of the commercial classes mentioned by Mr. Adams. Lord Lyons' biggest single worry this winter had been a case involving both of these factors—the seizure by a United States cruiser of the British merchant ship *Peterhoff*, bound from England for the Mexican port of Matamoros on a wholly legitimate errand.

Matamoros lay on the Mexican side of the mouth of the Rio Grande, across from the Confederate port of Brownsville, Texas. Brownsville of course was under blockade, and Matamoros as a neutral port was not; and Matamoros had suddenly developed a trade ever so much greater than anything it ever had in time of peace, the inescapable deduction being that goods unloaded at Matamoros were quickly ferried across the river to Brownsville and sent on to Confederate consumers. *Peterhoff* had a mixed cargo worth 130,000 pounds sterling consigned to Mexican importers; and on February 25, 1863, she was stopped by U.S.S. *Vanderbilt* near the Virgin Islands and sent into Key West as a prize.

The case was interesting for several reasons. *Peterhoff* was seized hundreds of miles from the blockade area; furthermore, the seizure had been ordered by one American naval officer who unquestionably would welcome a war with Great Britain, Captain Charles Wilkes, the headstrong man who had brought America and England to the edge of war more than a year earlier by stopping the British steamer *Trent* in order to remove the Confederate commissioners, James Mason and John Slidell. On top of this, it developed that a large part of the trade that was moving into Matamoros these days was not British at all but came straight from New York in American-flag ships. A quick check showed that in the last four months, fifty-nine vessels bound for Matamoros had cleared from New York, carrying American-made goods that had undoubtedly been ordered by Secessionists. As Lord Russell was quick to point out, for all anyone knew the British goods were consumed in Mexico while the American goods went on into the Confederacy. Secretary Seward found the case embarrassing.

It was also dangerous, and Lord Lyons frankly warned Secretary Seward that he would consider one more seizure like this "little less than a calamity." Fortunately, the Supreme Court settled the matter by ruling that *Peterhoff's* detention was unwarranted. Admitting that Matamoros represented a serious leak in the blockade, the court held that the United States Navy could not legally do anything about it; "trade from London to Matamoros, even with intent to supply from Matamoros goods to Texas, violated no blockade and could not be declared unlawful." The tension was eased. Secretary Welles recalled Captain Wilkes for other duty, writing that the man had been sent to the West Indies to try to catch the *Alabama* and adding: "In this he totally failed, while zealous to catch blockade-runners and get prize money."[3]

Neither *Alabama* nor *Peterhoff*, then, would cause a war; yet the situation remained unquiet. The United States and the Southern Confederacy were carrying on an important fraction of their struggle on British soil, and there was always the danger that this struggle would some day produce something too big for statesmen to handle. A case in point was the activity of James D. Bulloch, correctly described by Confederate Secretary Mallory as "an intelligent and reliable officer of our Navy," who had induced the Laird shipyard, at Birkenhead, to build two ironclad rams for the Confederate service. Construction of these ships was well along: Bulloch had hoped that they could be delivered some time in the spring of 1863, but there had been delays and the ships would not be ready until late summer or early fall. If they ever got into Confederate hands all former troubles would look small, because these were regular battleships, heavily armed and armored, much more seaworthy than the sluggish monitors and far more powerful than any wooden warships afloat. Commander Bulloch believed that with them the Confederacy could break the blockade all along the Atlantic coast, and Washington was inclined to agree. Secretary Seward told Mr. Adams that the United States would probably consider their delivery cause for war with Great Britain. He also pointed out that Congress had just given President Lincoln authority to commission privateers in case of trouble.

The whole affair was intricate. Everyone knew that the rams were being built but it was hard to prove whom they were being built for because Commander Bulloch had covered his tracks with much ingenuity. He had a deal with a French firm, Messrs. Bravay of Paris, whereby Bravay appeared as the contracting party; Laird was building the rams for Bravay, who in turn was acting for the Viceroy of Egypt, and at the moment the ships bore Turkish names, *El Tousson* and *El Mounassir*. Unless Mr. Adams could offer clear proof that the work was really being done for the Confederacy the British government could not legally interfere. Thomas Haines Dudley, American consul at Liverpool, had a small army of spies at work and was collecting innumerable affidavits, and in the end he might be able to prove something. The fact that the British shipping community would look with horror on any prospect of a repetition of American privateering, 1812 style, would doubtless render his proofs more persuasive.[4]

For in the long run the British government would follow a policy of self-interest; a fact which was most discouraging to Henry Hotze, who was in England as a combined purchasing agent and propagandist for the Confederacy, and who had about concluded that Lord Russell would never help the Confederacy. The ruling Conservative party, Hotze wrote, was "all but unanimous in our favor," but that did little good because this party "has scarcely a distinctive principle except the traditional loyalty to the person of the sovereign, and as the Queen desires peace and quiet in her mourning" (Prince Albert had died a few months earlier) "and is besides a sympathizer with the North, that party is paralyzed in American policy." There had been, to be sure, a fluttering of the pulse in the previous autumn, when William E. Gladstone, Chancellor of the Exchequer, made an indiscreet speech confessing that the Confederates had created a nation and asserting that "we may anticipate with certainty the success of the Southern states so far as regards their separation from the North." This looked briefly like a sure forecast of recognition, but it was not: Lord Russell assured Mr. Adams that the cabinet disavowed the speech and that no change in policy was to be anticipated; and shortly afterward the Richmond *Whig* wrote bitterly about "the grovelling and cold-blooded selfishness of the British Ministry toward the Confederate States."[5]

Self-interest was powerful; so also was the Emancipation Proclamation, which was a factor the British cabinet had to weigh along with the threat of privateering. The threat spoke of America's power to do harm; the Proclamation, perhaps to everyone's surprise, spoke of what America was trying to become, and it had a good deal of eloquence. Benjamin Moran, an assistant secretary in the American Legation, wrote that although the Conservative party newspapers in London tried hard to argue away the Proclamation's significance they had not succeeded: there were more and more public meetings and petitions in support of emancipation, and it seemed likely that "this will go very far to prevent the Gov't here from interfering in favor of the Rebels." Gideon Welles, reflecting (as the Secretary of the Navy was bound to do) on rams and blockade runners and privateers, was struck by the same thought. He believed that if America's Civil War ever crossed the Atlantic it would become bigger and more destructive than anything the modern world had seen, because "the sympathies of the mass of mankind would be with us"; expanded thus, the war would bring "the upheaval of nations, the overthrow of governments and dynasties."[6]

It might be so. Yet proclamations, dispatches of statesmen, the postures of governments themselves, would in the end mean no more than the deeds of the soldiers in the field made them mean. On April 8—it happened to be the very day Mr. Adams wrote his letter about the need to put some general into the White House—Abraham Lincoln was a guest at headquarters of the Army of the Potomac, reviewing the troops, talking with Joe Hooker and trying to make his own estimate of what the soldiers were apt to accomplish in this third springtime of the war.

On the surface all looked well. Mr. Lincoln and his party were cordially received. They went from the wharf at Aquia Creek to army headquarters in a railroad car decked with bunting, were housed comfortably in oversized tents with wooden floors, and were attended by a cavalcade of generals, colonels, and lesser brass whenever they went about the camp. Mr. Lincoln was treated with much deference by General Hooker, who rode at the President's side when 15,000 cavalry passed in review, while Mrs. Lincoln sat in a six-horse carriage and was cheered by the soldiers. The President finished with the cavalry, saw 300 pieces of field artillery go trundling past, and reviewed three corps of infantry; the soldiers seemed in good spirits, Hooker himself was brightly confident, and a politician in the President's party felt sure that this army "will be able to march not only to Richmond but to New Orleans if necessary." A young Wisconsin staff officer agreed, and wrote hopefully: "Let Heaven give us now good weather, and smile upon the cause of the Republic, and these same boys that I saw today may do something in a few days for the country. They could do a devil of a sight of mischief if turned loose with their guns among the Rebels."[7]

Mr. Lincoln was impressed but not wholly persuaded. Something about Hooker's easy optimism seems to have worried him, and he apparently warned the man to avoid taking undue risks; much later Hooker said the President told him that the political condition of the country was shaky and that it might not be able to stand another shock like the one it received at Fredericksburg in December. Furthermore, the President had other things on his mind. On the steamboat that brought his party down the Potomac from Washington, while people chatted brightly about Hooker's army, he turned suddenly to his newspaper friend Noah Brooks to whisper: "How many of our ironclads do you suppose are at the bottom of Charleston harbor?"[8] He had to think about Charleston, where Du Pont might be overpowering Fort Sumter; about the Mississippi, where Grant was mysteriously on the move, trying a shift down the river after his other maneuvers had failed; about Louisiana, where Banks was at last beginning to make his way northward; and about central Tennessee, where Rosecrans was slowly and methodically getting ready to smite Bragg. For two years Mr. Lincoln had tried to get his generals to see that the way to defeat the Confederacy was to apply overwhelming pressure in many places at once; this spring, at last, it was going to be tried, and all in all things looked promising; things always looked promising when a campaign was beginning. The President could only wait, knowing that the force needed for victory had been assembled and hoping that it would be used. A hint of anxiety came one evening when he concluded a talk with General Hooker and Major General Darius N. Couch, commander of Hooker's II Corps, by saying earnestly: "I want to impress upon you two gentlemen, in your next fight put in all your men." General Couch considered this advice excellent. General Hooker made no comment, but in his handling of the army a few weeks later there was nothing to show that he had even been listening.[9]

As Mr. Adams said, the generals were trained for command and Mr. Lincoln was not; and it would seem odd to find this untaught civilian lecturing professional soldiers on elementary points of tactics except for the fact that many of the professionals obviously needed lecturing by somebody. The war was approaching its crisis, and everything the President hoped for would stand or fall on the way the generals did what they had been trained to do. Before April was half gone there were some ominous indications.

There was flat failure at Charleston, where the navy was unable to finish the job and the army was not ready to begin it; already the pressure on the Confederacy here had grown so much lighter that Beauregard was sending infantry off to other duty in North Carolina, and in a short time he would be instructed to send 5000 troops all the way to Mississippi. In Louisiana, General Banks had turned his back on the big river and was marching off through central Louisiana, heading for Alexandria on the Red River, fifty airline miles away from the Mississippi: which permitted the worried General Pemberton to draw much-needed reinforcements from his strong point at Port Hudson, for use against General Grant. And in central Tennessee General Rosecrans was still preparing to do something but was showing no sign that he was ready to do it. Halleck warned him, late in March, that "it is exceedingly important at the present time that you give the enemy in your front plenty of occupation," but nothing happened. Halleck also tried to appeal to the man's ambition, sending word that the first field commander who won a decisive victory would be made major general in the Regular Army—the richest prize that could be given to a professional soldier. Rosecrans was insulted, and he replied stiffly: "I feel degraded to see such auctioneering of an honor. Have we a general who would fight for his own personal benefit when he would not for honor and the country?"[10]

It was hard to tell about Rosecrans. No one ever doubted his loyalty, his energy, his courage or his freedom from political ties; yet ever since the battle of Stone's River he had held his army in camp while he plied Washington unceasingly with demands for more cavalry, more infantry, more equipment, more horses, better arms, better officers and a clearer understanding of his needs. This went on so long that Halleck at last complained about "the enormous expense to the government of your telegrams," saying that Rosecrans was on the wire more than all other army commanders combined. Meanwhile, the fact remained that General Bragg's army, which was in Rosecrans' front, got in the first half of 1863 the longest respite from action that any Confederate army had in the entire war.[11]

Rosecrans offered a number of explanations for his inaction. He did not have enough cavalry to protect his own communications and threaten Bragg's: if he drove Bragg out of Tennessee the retreating Confederates would at once go to Vicksburg and enable Pemberton to crush Grant; if Joe Johnston felt Grant's pressure he might call Bragg to him and so give Tennessee to the Federals without a struggle; furthermore, Rosecrans' army was in a sense the government's last reserve and it ought not to be committed to action until the fate of Grant's campaign could be determined. The argument is unconvincing, and apparently it reflects nothing more than Rosecrans' reluctance to start a major campaign until he had perfected all of his arrangements.[12] It is natural for a general to feel so; unfortunately, Rosecrans' caution helped the Confederacy much more than it helped the Union. One of the people it helped was Robert E. Lee.

Lee had had to play a waiting game this spring. It was not as easy as it used to be for him to learn what the Army of the Potomac was going to do; Hooker had at least created a cavalry corps, and Jeb Stuart's squadrons could no longer roam as they pleased behind the Yankee lines. Symbol of the change was a brisk battle fought in mid-March when Brigadier General W. W. Averell led a Federal cavalry division across the Rappahannock at Kelly's Ford and ran into a Confederate brigade under Brigadier General Fitzhugh Lee. Lee drove Averell back, but the mere fact that a Yankee cavalry outfit had entered Confederate territory and had fought well after it got there indicated that times were changing. In this fight the Confederates lost their incredibly daring young artillerist, Major John Pelham. Pelham was in the neighborhood on other business, and had no connection with Lee's brigade, nor did he have his battery with him; but when he heard about the fight he got a horse and hurried over to get into action, and he was gaily leading a charge when a shell burst killed him. Pelham was pure swords-and-roses, one of those irrepressible Southerners who actively liked to risk his life, and in a sense he had been living on borrowed time ever since the war began . . . Yankee cavalry taking the initiative, John Pelham dead: the war in Virginia was beginning to grow old.[13]

Lee's immediate problem of course was Hooker's army. This was problem enough, inasmuch as Hooker's army this spring was at least twice the size of Lee's and was much better equipped; yet Lee's confidence in his troops and in his own ability was so strong that the Army of the Potomac by itself did not worry him greatly. For a time it looked as if Hooker might move his army by water down to the James River as McClellan had done, but Lee was skeptical, doubting that his opponent would dare to uncover Washington. He concluded at last that when Hooker set out for Richmond he would take the direct route, which was solidly occupied by the Army of Northern Virginia, and Lee calmly told Adjutant General Samuel Cooper that if Hooker tried such an advance "I think he will find it very difficult to reach his destination." The real problem was quite different.

Lee had already had to send Longstreet and most of Longstreet's army corps down to the Virginia-North Carolina border, to counter Federal pressure there and also to gather supplies, and he probably would be unable to get Longstreet back before Hooker advanced. If the Federals now made a real combined operation out of the attack on Charleston, and at the same time mounted a strong offensive in Tennessee, the Confederacy would have to strike a heavy counterblow without delay, and the only person who could strike it was Lee himself. It would be necessary, Lee suspected, for him to take the offensive and march boldly for Maryland, because "greater relief would in this way be afforded to the armies in middle Tennessee and on the Carolina coast than by any other method." But the Virginia roads were still bad, he had neither supplies nor transportation for a forward movement, and the odds against him would be appalling. Perhaps it would be necessary to send Longstreet to the west . . . and perhaps, indeed, the problem would go beyond a solution.[14]

It did not happen so. The Lincoln administration, to be sure, was committing itself to a major offensive at Charleston, and it was arranging now to have a new admiral and a new general in charge of it, but this blow would come later. In Tennessee Rosecrans still was not ready to move, and his offensive would hardly begin until the campaign on the Mississippi was finished. Burnside and the IX Corps had been sent west, and Mr. Lincoln's old dream of an advance into eastern Tennessee would eventually be realized . . . but full co-ordination of all of these moves would not be had this spring, and it was the threat of them rather than the unbearable massed weight that bore on the Confederate strategist in Virginia. For his next fight Lee was going to be dreadfully shorthanded, but at least he would not have to be looking back over his shoulder at Tennessee and South Carolina.

Joe Hooker at last got into action. Late in April he had 130,000 men, present for duty equipped, and he put most of them on the road moving up the Rappahannock, with a powerful cavalry force going on ahead, while detachments at Falmouth feinted at making a crossing there. Lee's time of uncertainty came to an end. He had a few more than 60,000 effectives, but at last he knew what his enemies were trying to do and he told Richmond: "Their intention, I presume, is to turn our left and probably get into our rear."[15] Then, as coolly as if he had all the advantages, he set out to frustrate them.

3. *The Darkness, and Jackson, and Fear*

GOING WEST from Fredericksburg in the old days a traveler would follow the Orange Turnpike, which started out through open farming country as pleasant to see in springtime as anything east of the Blue Ridge. Eight or nine miles from Fredericksburg the countryside's mood changed, and the road went down a long slope into a gloomy second-growth forest known as the Wilderness. The Wilderness stretched west for fifteen miles or more, thinly populated, with dense timber covering irregular ravines and low hills; a year or two later a Federal soldier referred to this gloomy, shaded country, with reason, as a land of grinning ghosts. Not long after the road entered this woodland it reached an unremarkable crossroad called Chancellorsville, where a family named Chancellor had built a big house.

Chancellorsville was not important, except of course to the Chancellor family; it was just white pillars and red brickwork at an open clearing in the woods, with country roads converging in front of it. It lay four miles due south of the place where the Rapidan River flows into the Rappahannock, and from Chancellorsville a road led up to the United States Ford, a crossing-place on the Rappahannock just below the fork. Other roads went northwest from Chancellorsville, to Ely's and Germanna Fords on the Rapidan, and the turnpike itself continued through the Wilderness, going west by south and coming out at last at Orange Courthouse. All of these roads and fords and the twilight tangle about them were obscure enough, in 1863, but if General Hooker intended to fight General Lee he would have to go through this country to get at him, and sooner or later he would have to come to Chancellorsville. To Chancellorsville he came, at last, and the word has been a scar on the national memory ever since.

Perhaps Hooker's trouble was that he won his battle in anticipation, and won it too completely. What began as a simple attempt to maneuver Lee out of his impregnable lines back of Fredericksburg came before long to look like a strategic masterpiece that would win the war; as it took on this aspect it began to seem real before a shot had been fired, and Hooker's contemplated triumph kept expanding until it burst. As the campaign got under way he remarked jauntily that Lee's army now was the legitimate property of the Army of the Potomac, and on the eve of battle he formally announced to all ranks that he had maneuvered so cunningly that the enemy must either fly ingloriously or come out and submit to destruction; and after the campaign was over he confessed frankly: "What I wanted was Lee's army; with that, Richmond would have been ours, and indeed all of Virginia."[1]

Lee's army was exactly what Hooker got, but it came at him from the wrong direction when he was thinking about something else and so it was too much for him; and his real trouble was not so much his own vainglory as the fact that he was up against the wrong opponent. After all, Hooker planned very well, and although he executed poorly his advantage in numbers was large enough to rub out a good many mistakes. What he tried would have worked, against most generals. Against Lee it failed so completely that its basic excellence is too easily overlooked.

Hooker began by planning a cavalry sweep that would shear in behind the Confederate left, snip the railroads by which Lee got his supplies, and so compel him to retreat. (Once Lee was out in the open country the Army of the Potomac could doubtless attack him to advantage.) Two days after Mr. Lincoln went back to Washington, Hooker ordered his cavalry commander, Major General George Stoneman, to take his troopers across the upper Rappahannock near the line of the Orange & Alexandria Railroad and start operating in the enemy's rear, "inflicting on him every possible injury which will tend to his discomfiture and defeat." Stoneman set out, but as he began to cross the river a violent rainstorm blew up, the river rose and the unpaved roads went out of sight in mud. Stoneman considered an offensive impossible and recalled his advance guard, and the whole movement came to nothing.[2] Two weeks passed, and Hooker made a new plan, much more ambitious than the first. It was this plan that brought his army to Chancellorsville.

As before, the cavalry would cross the river and head for the Confederate rear, but this time its role would be comparatively minor. While the cavalry cut Lee's supply lines, the bigger part of the infantry of the Army of the Potomac would also march upstream, cross the Rappahannock and the Rapidan, and then march eastward behind Lee's left. In effect, this flanking column would be approaching Lee's line on Marye's Heights from the rear, and it would be only a little smaller than Lee's entire army.

This force was ordered to go first to Chancellorsville. When it moved from Chancellorsville—with Stoneman's cavalry spreading panic and destruction near Richmond, making it impossible for Lee's army to get either supplies or rein-forcements—Lee would have to get out of Fredericksburg in a hurry. If he headed for Richmond, the Federal column could strike him ruinously in the flank; if he turned to fight at Chancellorsville, the rest of the Army of the Potomac, fol-lowing hard from Fredericksburg, could pitch into him and he could be attacked in front and in rear simultaneously—which of course would be the end of him.

So went the plan. It was a good plan, and up to a point it worked well. The huge flanking column moved precisely as Hooker intended, and by the evening of April 30 he had four army corps at or near Chancellorsville. Shortly after nightfall he reached the place himself, radiating confidence, sure that he had the game in his hand.

He was sure, that is, with part of his mind, the part that he knew about: not sure, apparently, with the part that ran down out of sight in the darkness, where fears come from. Although it was at Chancellorsville that Hooker got out that strange announcement of the impending defeat of Lee's army, it was also at Chancellorsville that he ceased to look like a general who is about to win a great victory and began to resemble one who suspects that he will be beaten if he is not very cautious. He became cautious just a little too soon—a few miles and a few hours short of the victory he had talked about so much.

On the night April ended, Hooker had approximately 50,000 men at Chancellorsville, with 22,000 more on the way. Back at Falmouth, just above Fredericksburg, were 47,000 more, under Major General John Sedgwick, the com-petent commander of the VI Corps. Sedgwick and Hooker were hardly ten miles apart in a direct line, but as the roads went, roundabout on the United States Ford route, the dis-tance was more than twice that far, and it could be danger-ous to separate the two wings of an army so widely in the

presence of General Lee. However, the separation would
end very soon. On May 1 the force at Chancellorsville was
to march eastward near the river, and after a few miles this
march would uncover Banks' Ford, a river crossing hardly
four miles from Falmouth, and the separated wings would
be in touch again. Meanwhile, Sedgwick had laid pontoon
bridges below Fredericksburg and had crossed part of his
troops, hoping to convince Lee that he was about to attack.
If this worked, Lee was not likely to notice what was going
on at Chancellorsville, which would be fatal; if he did notice
he would of course retreat in haste, in which case Sedgwick
was ideally posted to pursue him and bring him to grief.[3]

The real trouble with Hooker's plan was that it was brit-
tle. It rested on the belief that Lee would react predictably
to a series of challenges; if he did not, Federal strategy might
need more flexibility than the plan allowed. It had been assumed, for instance, that when Stoneman and his cavalry
galloped south Stuart and his cavalry would gallop after; but
Stuart did nothing of the kind. The Yankee cavalry might do
damage in the unprotected rear areas but Lee's army was
the only thing that mattered now, and so Stuart kept his
cavalry on Lee's flank to give the army the protection and
the knowledge that might make the difference between victory and defeat. As a result he kept Lee posted about the advance and strength of Hooker's flanking force, and kept the
flankers from finding out very much about Lee; and by the
night of April 30 Lee knew that Sedgwick was bluffing and
that the real threat was coming out of the Wilderness at
Chancellorsville.

Then he refused to behave as expected. It seemed obvious
that if he went to Chancellorsville at all he would take his
entire force, because he was so badly outnumbered that he
could hardly do anything else, and this of course would open
the road for Sedgwick and Lee would eventually be caught
between two fires. But simply because he was so terribly outnumbered, Lee was free to take preposterous chances; the
odds against him were so long to begin with that it could not
hurt much to lengthen them a bit, and anyway an opponent
who believed that Lee would do the obvious under any circumstances was simply begging for trouble.

Stonewall Jackson wanted to smash Sedgwick before doing
anything else, and although Lee was skeptical he told Jackson

to study the ground carefully; if Jackson felt that it could be done Lee would order it. Jackson studied, concluded finally that Sedgwick was not smashable, and so reported, and Lee ordered the army over to Chancellorsville. But he did not take everybody. He detached 10,000 men, entrusted them to hard-fighting Major General Jubal Early, strengthened the contingent with extra artillery, saw that it was well posted on Marye's Heights, and instructed Early to keep Sedgwick from doing any harm.

It seemed folly to leave 10,000 men to oppose 47,000. But it would also have been folly for Lee to try to march back to Richmond with Yankee cavalry blocking the road ahead, four Yankee infantry corps on the immediate flank, and Sedgwick in hot pursuit; worse folly to let the army get pressed to death between the converging halves of the Army of the Potomac at Chancellorsville; folly in its highest form simply to do nothing, waiting at Fredericksburg for the executioner. What Lee did was risky, but it was less risky than the other options that were open . . . and anyway it was something General Hooker might not expect. And so on the night of April 30 and the morning of May 1 Lee and Jackson and everybody but Early's command marched toward Chancellorsville to meet Hooker.

Hooker gave them just time enough. Unaccountably, he lost his grip on the situation, somewhere between the afternoon of April 30 and the morning of May 1; the driving energy that had been his saving grace suddenly went out of him, and the army floundered. On this campaign it was Hooker's habit, every evening, to issue orders for the following day's movements. Yet on the night of April 30, when he proclaimed assured victory, Hooker issued no orders at all, although the advance that must be made the next day was the key to the success of the whole campaign. This advance would be short, and if made promptly it would be practically unopposed. By going forward a few miles the army would not only uncover Banks' Ford, which would end the isolation of Sedgwick's force, but would also emerge from the confusing Wilderness and reach open country where the Federal advantage in manpower and artillery could be exploited to the full. But Hooker spent most of the morning waiting at Chancellorsville. Not until eleven o'clock on May 1 was his army put in motion; then, with three corps advancing on separate roads, Hooker learned that the Confederates were not quite where he thought they were. The heads of his columns suddenly ran into Confederate skirmishers and there were bursts of rifle fire from the woods and hills that fringed the little clearings.

The opposition did not seem to be especially heavy, and the Federal commanders prepared to form lines of battle and clear the way, but Hooker's plan abruptly fell completely apart. Up from Chancellorsville came unexpected orders from headquarters: cancel the advance, break off the firing, and bring everybody back to a defensive position around the Chancellorsville crossroad.[4]

The corps commanders were dumfounded and indignant, and Darius Couch of II Corps, their senior, hurried to headquarters to protest. Hooker tried to soothe him, saying: "I have got Lee just where I want him; he must fight me on my own ground." Couch went away, convinced (as he wrote later) that "my commanding general was a whipped man,"[5] and Couch was about right. From the day of his appointment up until this moment, Hooker had been all that a general ought to be; now, in the shadows of the Wilderness, he was alone with his responsibility and it was too much for him. He had planned to destroy Lee's army: now he was hoping that Lee's army would be obliging enough to destroy itself. All that happened to Hooker at Chancellorsville—to him, and to the unlucky private soldiers who lived and died by his orders—was foreshadowed in his strange withdrawal on the afternoon of May 1.

Hooker drew his lines at Chancellorsville—long lines, and strong, with a bulging crescent on a low plateau east and south of the Chancellorsville house, one wing on the left stretching all the way up to the Rappahannock, the other drawn up along the turnpike, facing south. Here Hooker waited, his men using axes and spades to strengthen their field works, and the afternoon ended and night came. It was an uneasy night, with a big moon putting a streaky light on the landscape, Confederate patrols prowling about in front to see how things were, Stuart's squadrons sweeping all the roads and keeping the Federals from seeing anything except what the moonlight would show, a man from a rifle pit in the thickets. To Brigadier General Daniel Butterfield, his chief of staff, who had stayed at Falmouth, Hooker sent a message:

all of Stuart's cavalry was in his front, which meant that Stoneman ought to "do a land-office business" far to the south; Sedgwick was to watch the Confederates closely and keep them from doing whatever they tried to do; and at Chancellorsville "I think the enemy in his desperation will be compelled to attack me on my own ground."[6]

This meant that it was Lee's turn now; Hooker had given up the initiative and Lee had grasped it. That night, around a campfire in the woods just out of gunshot from Hooker's lines, Lee and Stonewall Jackson met to consider the best way to strike their foes.

They were not nearly strong enough to make a frontal assault, and the Federal left could not be turned, but Stuart's cavalry had learned that Hooker's right was "in the air"; the line went west from Chancellorsville for two or three miles and then simply ended, wholly unprepared for an attack from the west. If the Confederates could mass troops four or five miles west of Chancellorsville, these troops could march straight into Hooker's rear and the Federal position would collapse. Hooker had placed the bigger part of his army in position to do this to Lee but he had failed to go on and do it; as a result he had given Lee the chance to do exactly the same thing to him, and of all the soldiers in North America Lee and Jackson were the ones most likely to see and to accept this opportunity. They lost little time coming to a decision, and shortly after the sun came up on May 2 Stonewall Jackson put his army corps on the road and set off to crumple the Federal flank.[7]

Jackson was the man who would strike the blow, and much would depend on his skill and daring; but the real responsibility was Lee's, and the risk he was taking now made all his earlier risks seem mild. He had already divided his army, leaving 10,000 men to hold four times their number at Fredericksburg, and he had with him at Chancellorsville no more than 42,000 infantry. Now he was dividing this inadequate force, sending 28,000 off with Jackson on a twelve-mile flanking march that would unquestionably take most of the day. For about ten hours Lee would have just 14,000 men to oppose most of Hooker's army, 70,000 men. Ten hours could bring him to ruin if Hooker once saw what was happening.

Hooker actually did see a little of it, but he misinterpreted what he saw and in the end was worse off than if he had seen nothing at all. After Jackson moved, Lee kept his 14,000 busy, shifting men about, opening sudden bursts of artillery and infantry fire, giving indications that he was about to assault the Federal left. Hoping that such an attack would be made, Hooker accepted these indications at face value. But Jackson's march was discovered. Making his long detour to the west, Jackson at one place had to turn sharply to his left to get past a patch of open country some three miles from Hooker's right-center, and the Federal outposts saw a long column of Rebel infantry accompanied by artillery and wagons—the wagons, of course, being nothing more than Jackson's ambulances and ammunition train. For a moment Hooker was on the verge of full awareness, and he ordered Major General Oliver Otis Howard, who held the extreme right, to prepare for a flank attack.[8] Then he had a second thought, which led him to disaster.

That Confederate column, after all, was moving south, and wagon trains were with it: Did not this mean that Lee was at last making the retreat which any sensible man in his position ought to make? This seemed all the more likely because the activity on the Federal left was not actually bringing on a real fight, and Hooker accepted the welcome notion: Lee was fleeing, and it was necessary to molest him. Shortly after noon Hooker ordered Major General Daniel E. Sickles, a political general of most moderate military capacity, to take his II Corps forward and attack that moving column, and he jubilantly told General Couch: "Lee is in full retreat toward Gordonsville, and I have sent out Sickles to capture his artillery." Couch remembered afterward that it did seem odd that this momentous retreat was to be struck with only one army corps.

When Sickles advanced most of Jackson's column had passed; Jackson detailed less than one brigade to hold Sickles off and kept everybody else moving, swinging north through the concealing Wilderness to go up beyond the Federal right. Sickles got into a noisy, inconclusive fight; his own inexperience and the dense second-growth timber kept him from seeing that he was fighting no more than a detachment, and after a time he called for reinforcements. Hooker had Howard send him a brigade, and got off a message to Falmouth: Sedgwick was to seize Fredericksburg and everybody in it because Lee was in retreat and Sickles was attacking him.[9]

This was all very well; but when Hooker sent Sickles forward he created a big gap in his line and left Howard's XI Corps completely isolated, and when he reinforced Sickles he made Howard's corps still weaker. Sending away one brigade, Howard now had fewer than 10,000 men, most of them posted so that they could not possibly meet a flank attack, and the rest of the Federal army was two miles away. By three in the afternoon Jackson began to reach the position he wanted. Two hours later he had formed a battle line two miles wide and in some places three divisions deep, lined up astride of the turnpike, ready to come in from west and northwest on a Federal line that was resolutely facing to the south.

Howard's XI Corps was a hard-luck organization all the way. It included many German regiments, referred to loftily by the rest of the army as Dutchmen of unproved fighting quality, and it had previously been commanded by Franz Sigel, under whom it had won no distinction whatever. Sigel had recently resigned after a quarrel over rank, and although he was quite incompetent he was the idol of the Germans. They never warmed up to Howard, a strait-laced man famous for his unbounded piety, not at all the sort to appeal to this assemblage of ill-disciplined free-thinkers. (Abner Doubleday, who disliked Howard deeply, considered him much too other-worldly, and scoffed: "At West Point he talked nothing but religion. If a young lady was introduced to him he would ask her if she had reflected on the goodness of God during the past night.")[10] Howard was a good soldier, but he shared Hooker's idea that the Rebels this afternoon were in flight. Some of his junior officers sensed that Jackson was about to descend on them, but they could not get anyone in authority to listen to them and at five o'clock the troops were at ease, many with their arms stacked preparing supper. Over the treetops came remote echoes from Sickles' fight, but along this front all was quiet. Sunset was less than two hours away, and as far as the XI Corps was concerned an uneventful day was about to come to a close.

Then Stonewall Jackson's bugles sounded beyond the western forest, and his powerful battle line came crashing forward through the thickets, the peace and quiet of the evening ended in an uproar of Rebel yells and heavy musketry, General Hooker's delusion ended along with it, and Howard's corps was routed. Jackson's men stormed eastward through the timber, where the undergrowth was so thick some men found their uniforms ripped off entirely, and a couple of miles farther on the Chancellorsville clearing came alive with bursting shell and running men and panicky teamsters flogging frightened horses. (One trouble was that Howard's wagons and his herds of beef cattle had been parked just behind his lines: when the Rebels came all of these went east in a prodigious hurry, slicing across the immediate rear of all the rest of the army.) Night came on, and the full moon shone down through dust and smoke and bursts of flame, and the right wing of the Federal army had gone to pieces.

Say this much for Howard's Dutchmen: they fought, even if they never got credit for it, and although they were beaten they grave ground stubbornly. For proof there is their casualty list—the butcher's bill, as tough generals used to say. In about two hours of fighting, between late afternoon and night, they lost more than 2400 men in killed, wounded and missing, which means that some of them fought desperately. They could not stay very long, because there were too many Confederates; any unit that made a stand was attacked in front and on both flanks; but the thing was not the helpless runaway that is usually described. Jackson crumpled the Union right but he met some stiff opposition.

Darkness brought universal confusion. Bursts of fire kept breaking out in unexpected places, drifting smoke stained the moonlight, no one knew where anyone else was, and one Federal said it all when he wrote: "Darkness was upon us, and Jackson was on us, and fear was on us." Jackson's triumphant corps was half-disorganized itself, brigades and divisions having become all intermingled in the formless fighting. Far out in front, Sickles' men began to understand that something had gone very wrong far in the rear, and they made a shaky, unco-ordinated retreat, fighting blindly with other Federal units when they collided in the darkness. Over at Fredericksburg, Sedgwick got a peremptory order from headquarters: he was to occupy Fredericksburg and march at once along the road to Chancellorsville, being sure to "attack and destroy" any Confederate force he met.[11] Around the Chancellorsville clearing, powerful Federal artillery opened a blind fire whenever the gunners saw anything moving in the woodland in front. For the time being the Confederate attack had come to a standstill.

Then Jackson paid the penalty for being the kind of man he was. He was strange, impassioned, made of fire crossed with a belief in pre-destination, and this evening he could think of nothing except that his enemies were in trouble, so he tried with furious single-mindedness to keep the battle moving. His corps desperately needed realignment, not to mention rest, and a cautious general would have called a halt in order to get people sorted out. But Jackson knew that if he could put armed Confederates on the bank of the Rappahannock before the night ended Hooker might lose his entire army, and he had not the faintest notion of stopping. He rode on ahead of his troops, looking for the roads that might lead to his goal, and in the darkness and general mix-up he got in front of a North Carolina regiment that had been bracing itself for an expected attack by Yankee cavalry. The regiment saw Jackson and his mounted aides, moving horsemen coming out of the deep shadows, it opened fire—and Jackson was shot off his horse, bullets in him, a death wound on him. They got him back to the rear at last, and at last the night became quiet.

Most of the battle remained to be fought, and Joe Hooker could have won it, except that by now he himself had been beaten beyond recall. His troops were ready: only a few of them had fought at all, and he still had more than 70,000 men between the two halves of Lee's army. As caustic General Couch said, all he needed to do was "take a reasonable common-sense view of the state of things" in order to retrieve everything he had lost.[12] This was beyond him. When daylight of May 3 came the Confederates resumed the attack— with Jackson gone, and A. P. Hill, his ranking division commander, wounded, his corps was temporarily led by Cavalryman Jeb Stuart, who bore in mind Lee's warning that it was vital to get the two wings of the Confederate army into contact again. Stuart attacked on one side and the other wing of Lee's army attacked on the other, there was bitter fighting in the woods west of Chancellorsville, and by noon the Federals had given up more ground, Lee had his army united once more, and Hooker's men had been reduced to fortifying a rambling salient covering the approaches to United States Ford. Hooker had been stunned when a cannon ball struck a pillar of the Chancellorsville house against which he was leaning, but this made no difference because he was numb already. This was Lee's battle, all the way.

Lee went on to prove it. Sedgwick got his corps together and stormed Early's line back of Fredericksburg, and just as Lee's soldiers won the Chancellorsville clearing Lee learned that the Federal VI Corps was coming up on his rear. As coolly as if he had unlimited resources, Lee divided his army once more, keeping a fraction to bemuse Hooker while the rest went back to deal with Sedgwick. That unhappy general, whose original function had been to exploit any opening Hooker's men made and who now found himself obliged to fight his way to Hooker's rescue, was penned up next day in an uneven rectangle near Salem Church, six miles east of Chancellorsville, attacked from three sides while Hooker's 70,000 prepared to defend the Rappahannock escape route. Sedgwick had to retreat, getting his troops safely across Banks' Ford—the crossing which Hooker's maneuverings had been supposed to open in the first place—and once this had happened, Lee brought everybody back to Chancellorsville to attack Hooker's bridgehead. By any sober estimate, Lee would have ruined his army if he had tried it, attacking superior numbers in a strong, well-entrenched position . . . but he had the battle in his pocket by this time, and if he had struck Hooker once more Hooker would almost certainly have collapsed. Hooker did not wait for him. He took his army back to the north side of the Rappahannock on May 6, moved over to Falmouth, and began to argue that his woes came mostly because of the shameful flight of the XI Corps. The campaign and battle of Chancellorsville were over.

On May 10 Stonewall Jackson died of his wounds in a little cottage at Guiney Station. To the very end he was trying to move on. Just before he died he said that he wanted to cross the river—*the* river—and rest under the shade of the trees. At last he had found the road to it.

4. *Aftermath of Victory*

On May 12, in Richmond, all of the church bells were tolling, the flags were at half-mast, minute guns were fired, and government offices and places of business were closed. Thousands of people stood bareheaded in the streets to see Stonewall Jackson's coffin go past.

The coffin was covered with a Confederate flag topped by evergreen sprays and wreaths of flowers, and in the lid there was a glass plate so that when the coffin lay in state at the capitol everybody could look at the pinched waxen face; and in the tense silence there was awareness that this death meant more than the loss of a great warrior. As the devout very well knew, death was swallowed up in victory, but this all-consuming victory was personal to General Jackson; what the Confederate cause had won might not be enduring, might even mean much less than it had at first seemed to mean. When this man was cut down people were compelled to examine the hopes that had rested upon him.

The pallbearers following the hearse were all general officers. President Davis rode behind them in an open carriage, looking drawn and haggard, members of the cabinet walked after him two by two, and there was a long procession of state and city officials, government clerks, ordinary citizens, and such military detachments as were available. Men who watched remembered black plumes everywhere, the general's riderless horse led by a servant, "a common sorrow too deep for words," and the measured *thud-thud* of the minute guns; and up by the Rappahannock, on the edge of a forest reeking with unburied bodies and powdered with gray ashes from burned underbrush, General Lee sent word that unless his army could be strongly reinforced he might eventually have to retreat to the defenses of Richmond.[1]

This was disturbing, because General Lee had won the most brilliant victory of his career and a brilliant victory does not usually lead to a forced withdrawal by the victor. Yet upon examination the Chancellorsville victory looked hollow. It had been dazzling, a set piece for the instruction of students of the military art, but it had been inconclusive, winning glory and little more. It was disappointing for a reason even graver than the loss of General Jackson; it left government and army facing precisely the problems they had faced before the campaign began. Joe Hooker's pouter-pigeon strutting and circling had come to a full stop, of course, and there would be a breathing spell before the Federals moved on Richmond again, but nothing had been settled. There was not even time to take proper pride in the victory itself.

Stonewall Jackson was buried at Lexington, Virginia, and the Richmond *Dispatch* declared solemnly: "His fame will be grand and enduring as the eternal mountains at whose feet he was cradled; whose long shadows, like those of some majestic cathedral, will consecrate his grave." But by the time he was laid to rest it was the Mississippi situation that was getting top-level concern.

The victory on the Rappahannock, in fact, had been offset by bad news from General Pemberton. The end of April brought Hooker to Chancellorsville, where he grew nervous and invited a defeat that speedily came to him; but it brought U. S. Grant to the east side of the Mississippi River, where he felt vast relief because at last he had reached a place where he could fight, which he immediately began to do. While Hooker was losing the Chancellorsville clearing Grant was winning the towns of Port Gibson and Grand Gulf, and as soon as he had won them he moved relentlessly on into the interior of the state of Mississippi. Now Richmond remembered that Joe Johnston was at Tullahoma, Tennessee, theoretically commanding both Pemberton and Bragg but doing very little about it, and Richmond sent Johnston brusque orders to go to Mississippi at once, take active command there, and beat off this invasion. Meanwhile Secretary Seddon notified Lee that it might be necessary to detach at least one of Longstreet's divisions and send it to Vicksburg.[2]

This rubbed Lee where he was raw, because he had badly missed Longstreet's men at Chancellorsville and he was only now beginning to get them back; and George Pickett's division, which seemed to be the one Mr. Seddon wanted, was one of Longstreet's best. Lee replied that Pickett would of course be sent if the administration insisted, but he warned that "it becomes a question between Mississippi and Virginia." He added that Pickett could hardly reach Pemberton before June; surely, when June's hot weather struck the lower Mississippi the unacclimated Federals would have to withdraw, bringing the campaign to a close. The next day Lee told Mr. Davis that the northern newspapers, which Lee read carefully, said that Hooker was going to be reinforced, which could only mean that Virginia again was to be the theater of action. It was therefore more than ever necessary to strengthen the Army of Northern Virginia; if it could advance it might ease pressures elsewhere.[3]

Beauregard worked out a plan—elaborate, like all of Beauregard's plans, but for once not reserving the leading role for Beauregard. Hooker, he said, had been bruised and must lie quiet for at least two months. Let Longstreet's whole corps, therefore, be sent to Tennessee, and then let Lee himself go there and use Longstreet and Bragg in a quick blow to crush Rosecrans. Losing Rosecrans' army, the Federals would lose Tennessee and no doubt Kentucky as well, and if that happened Grant's campaign against Vicksburg must be abandoned. Longstreet worked out a somewhat similar plan, except that it did not involve sending Lee himself to the west, and pressed it on the Secretary of War. Lee himself, meanwhile, had a plan for Beauregard: he believed that some Confederate troops could be drawn from Georgia, Florida, and the Carolinas, and he wanted them brought to Virginia and put under Beauregard; this would help to free Lee's army for offensive operations, and would worry Washington.[4]

In the end, none of these plans was adopted. The western armies that faced Grant and Rosecrans must continue to face them alone, with such incidental reinforcements as could be scraped together. Lee's army would be kept intact, strengthened as far as possible, to face the Army of the Potomac, but it too would have to operate alone. There were too many threats, and Lee's warning that they might have to choose between Virginia and Mississippi showed the gravity of the situation. If Richmond really had to save one of these states and let the other be lost it was in profound trouble, because it could not afford to lose either; nor, for that matter, could it afford to lose Tennessee or South Carolina. The government could not weaken itself in any threatened area. It must simply go ahead and do the best it could everywhere.

Against this background Lee planned what presently became his great march into Pennsylvania. His aims were modest; he was on the defensive, this march was a defensive maneuver, and it is unlikely that he seriously thought that it would ease Grant's pressure on Pemberton.[5] If he could go to Pennsylvania, Hooker would have to follow him, and this at least would compel Mr. Lincoln's administration to think about protecting Washington rather than about capturing Richmond. On the march Hooker's army might well expose itself to an attack in detail, and although Lee did not think the South strong enough to carry on a regular war of invasion and doubted that he could force a general battle in Pennsylvania the move should at least disrupt Federal plans for the summer. Lee's army could also collect supplies north of the Potomac, and if Federal armies left Virginia more supplies could be got at home. Altogether, Lee hoped that he could spend the summer maneuvering in the north, returning in the fall in better shape than when he left.[6]

Limited objectives, in other words: yet as the campaign came nearer the objectives inevitably expanded. There was, to begin with, the state of mind of the troops. Lee had given his own army the habit of victory and he had given the opposing army the habit of defeat; if he now moved to Pennsylvania both armies must believe that the great, final showdown was at hand. There was also the state of mind of the high command. Lee came to feel that his move might be part of a peace offensive. To President Davis he wrote that "we should neglect no honorable means of dividing and weakening our enemies," and this move seemed to offer an opening. With a Southern army in Pennsylvania the Northern people might well begin to feel that they were losing the war. If, at the same time, they were gently led to believe that by making peace they could restore the Union they might stop supporting the war; "and that," wrote General Lee, "after all is what we are interested in bringing about." Once Northern will power gave way there would be time enough to disillusion people, and it would be Yankees rather than Southerners who would be hurt thereby because "the desire of our people for a distinct and independent national existence will prove as steadfast under the influence of peaceful measures as it has shown itself in the midst of war."[7]

This thinking was a trifle mixed. It assumed on the one hand that the Northern friends of peace wanted reunion so much that it would be necessary to deceive them, and on the other hand that they wanted it so little that they would readily abandon the idea once they saw that deception had been practiced on them. To believe this was to expect more of the march into Pennsylvania than was likely to be forthcoming. Men even hoped that this march might finally bring them to the pot of gold that hid at the end of the rainbow, the happy ending for all Confederate hopes . . . British recognition.

Apparently Lee retained certain reservations. He got his army into shape, and by the end of May he could record a total, present for duty, of all arms, of nearly 75,000 men. He divided this army into three corps, keeping stout Longstreet as one corps commander and giving the other two corps to newly created lieutenant generals, Richard S. Ewell (who had fought so well under Jackson in the faraway Valley campaign) and A. P. Hill, a good leader and a furious fighter; each would command some 20,000 men, and for the most part the men were veterans of high morale. Yet even as he made these arrangements Lee notified Mr. Davis that he began to fear that "the time has passed when I could have taken the offensive with advantage," saying that "there may be nothing left for me to do but fall back." He also told Secretary Seddon that Hooker apparently planned to turn the Confederate left while Federal troops on the peninsula advanced directly on Richmond. This last was a serious threat. The Federal commander at Fort Monroe, Major General John A. Dix, had some 32,000 men arrayed on both sides of the James, and to oppose him Richmond had fewer than 8000 under Major General Arnold Elzey. Richmond could get some help from Major General D. H. Hill's 20,000 in North Carolina but it probably could not get very much because Hill was under a good deal of pressure himself. A simultaneous advance by Hooker and Dix could present a most difficult problem.[8]

But anything was better than to wait idly for the storm to break, and on June 3 Lee began to move. Longstreet's corps started for the Blue Ridge, with Ewell following, while Stuart's cavalry rode off to screen the move and Hill stayed in Fredericksburg to guard the rear. The army would go through the Blue Ridge gaps and move on down the lower Shenandoah Valley for the Potomac crossings, and although for a while it would be badly strung out Lee believed that Hooker could be deceived long enough to make the march relatively safe. By June 8 Lee himself, with the two leading army corps, was in the vicinity of Culpeper Courthouse, and Stuart jauntily put on a grand review of his cavalry for the edification of the commanding general.

Perhaps the review was a mistake. It had the scent of holiday warfare, with pretty ladies applauding the gallant cavalry-men, and Stuart gave it just a little too much of his attention; the result being that on the next day Federal cavalry crossed the Rappahannock unexpectedly and brought on the biggest cavalry battle of the war on the fields and hills near Brandy Station. Yankee cavalry was no longer totally outclassed by Confederate cavalry, it knew how to ride and fight now, and this battle was a hard one. Stuart's men gave ground, and for a time seemed in danger of being driven from the field altogether, and although Stuart rallied them and at last forced the Federals back to their own side of the river he had obviously been taken by surprise, which was most hu-miliating. Also, the new Federal cavalry commander, Brig-adier General Alfred Pleasonton, had discovered what was going on, and he was able to tell Hooker that Lee's army was going north. Pleasonton got a major general's commission for his efforts, and Hooker began to suspect that Lee was mak-ing a bad move. He thought that he himself ought to march at once for Richmond.

He suggested this to President Lincoln, who shared Hook-er's suspicion but had a different idea about the proper re-sponse. He told Hooker that Lee's army, not Richmond, was the proper objective. If Lee went north of the Rappahannock, Hooker ought to follow him, stick to his flank, attack him when he could—and, "if he stays where he is, fret him and fret him."[9] Hooker took the advice, the Army of the Potomac moved up to the line of the Orange & Alexandria Railroad, and A. P. Hill got the last Confederate infantry out of Fred-ericksburg and moved on to overtake the rest of the army.

What might have happened if Hooker had marched on Richmond belongs with the might-have-beens and is subject to debate, but the President had seen one thing clearly: wherever Lee was, the center of the stage was there and not elsewhere. His army had to be looked at because it meant trouble, and now its advance was going into action. Ewell had gone past Longstreet's corps and was in the lead. He was bald, eccentric, oddly bird-like, with a nose like a hawk's beak jutting out between the bulging eyes of an affronted owl. He wore a wooden leg, carried crutches, and rode in a buggy because the Yankees had shot a leg off of him at Groveton, nine months earlier, but he was full of bounce and energy all the same. Now he took his corps down the lower

Shenandoah Valley as if the furies were on his back, and at Winchester he smashed a Federal force of 6900 men under the excitable Major General Robert Milroy. Ewell's men overwhelmed these Federals, capturing more than half of them and driving the rest off in hopeless confusion; then they crossed the Potomac and moved on, over Maryland and into Pennsylvania, and there was no longer any question about what Hooker's objective was.

A. P. Hill followed Ewell, Longstreet faded back through the mountain gaps to bring up the rear, and Hooker took his own army up close to the Potomac to look for an opening. And Jeb Stuart, who was under orders to go north and protect the army's front and flank, got permission to do it by riding clear around Hooker's army en route. (This would be spectacular, bringing shame to the Yankees and restoring the Stuart image that was so badly tarnished at Brandy Station; also, being cavalry would be fun once more, as in the old days.) But Hooker's army was not where Stuart thought it was, so Stuart got crowded off the roads he wanted and his cavalry spent eight days on a trip that should have taken two, and could not rejoin the army until July 2, which was much too late. When Lee entered Pennsylvania he moved in darkness; he had cavalry (for Stuart took only three brigades) but he had no Stuart to handle it for him, and he never knew where his enemies were until he collided with them.

Although Lee did not know it and could not have been expected to know it, his real opponent now was Abraham Lincoln, a man not trained for command but nonetheless commanding. No one on either side saw Lee's advance into Pennsylvania quite as Mr. Lincoln did. He recognized it, of course, as a dire threat, but he also saw it as a limitless opportunity for the Union cause. He had grasped a strategic point of importance: when a Confederate army left its own territory and went north it exposed itself to outright destruction. It could be cut off, forced to fight its way out of a trap, and in the end removed from the board; by the mere act of invasion it risked its very existence, and the chief responsibility of the Federal commander was to make sure that what was risked was lost.

It was hard to get generals to see it. McClellan had not seen it in Maryland, and Buell had not in Kentucky, so two armies of invasion had got away. As a civilian Mr. Lincoln could not be entirely certain that he was right and that the trained soldiers were wrong. Yet the belief grew on him, and as this invasion month of June passed the President actually seemed to grow more composed. In the middle of the month he abruptly stopped leaning over General Hooker's shoulder, anxious to counsel about every move, and turned the man over to the War Department.

Until now, Hooker had ignored Halleck and had dealt solely with the President, and although this arrangement was grossly irregular it had worked tolerably well and Mr. Lincoln obviously had liked it. Now, with Lee's vanguard about to cross the Potomac, Hooker was growing querulous. He began to complain that he was outnumbered, he alternately chafed at the orders that came from Washington and then complained because the orders were not specific enough, and at last he protested that he did not enjoy the confidence of General Halleck. At this point Mr. Lincoln cut him off.

Lee, the President told Hooker, was definitely moving north, an action which "gives you back the chance I thought McClellan lost last fall." To be sure, the President might have been wrong then and he might be wrong now, "but in the great responsibility resting upon me I cannot be entirely silent." Meanwhile, Hooker hereafter must communicate through channels: "To remove all misunderstanding I now place you in the strict military relation to Gen. Halleck, of a commander of one of the armies to the General-in-Chief of all the armies."[10] From this moment the flow of messages between Hooker and the President ceased, as the flow between McClellan and the President had ceased after Harrison's Landing, a year earlier. Hooker was a professional, and now he must answer to a professional. As far as possible (and this to be sure might be no great distance) the President would keep his hands out of it.

Washington would have been surprised, and possibly a little outraged, to know this. Living by politics, the capital had responded to Chancellorsville with the purely political assumption that a defeat so resounding was bound to create an opening for somebody, and the city had been a windy cave of rumors ever since, growing windier as Lee's army moved north. Naturally, the name of General McClellan was back in circulation; like the price of gold, his prospects rose when the country's military fortunes sank and sank when those fortunes rose. His stock was rising now, and it was impossible for anyone to speculate on Hooker's future without also speculating on McClellan's. It went so far that a good McClellan Democrat examined the pro-McClellan maneuvers and wrote in disgust that "the stinking aroma of party politics has tainted the whole concern," and a young officer in the Army of the Potomac, reflecting on the claims and counter-claims that had sprung up since that appalling battle, said that as far as he could see "the only use or purpose of all this effusion of blood is to show which is the greatest general and which has committed the more blunders, McClellan or Hooker or Burnside."[11]

Yet the President himself was not part of it. As loyal a Republican as Alexander K. McClure, the Pennsylvania publisher who often helped mend political fences for the administration, sent word from Philadelphia that McClellan must be recalled to active duty and given command in Pennsylvania, where militia levies were hastily being called to the colors; he added, sapiently, "without military success we can have no political success, no matter who commands." Governor Joel Parker of New Jersey went further, proposing that McClellan be restored to command of the Army of the Potomac forthwith.

Mr. Lincoln refused to be drawn. He quietly asked McClure, "Do we gain anything by opening one leak to stop another?" and to command militia in Pennsylvania he sent, not McClellan but General Darius Couch, who was so disgusted by Hooker's bungling at Chancellorsville that he flatly refused to serve under the man any longer. Mr. Lincoln assured Governor Parker that the whole case was much more intricate than Parker supposed. He refused to consider bringing McClellan back, and he did not bother to argue about it. It was no longer necessary to believe that the salvation of the Union depended on the political views and personal popularity of the commander of the Army of the Potomac.

The complexion of the war had changed, and so had the President's attitude. He had turned Hooker over to Halleck, and anyone could guess how that was going to come out; what was harder to see was that the President's attention now was focused largely on other matters. T. J. Barnett gave Barlow a hint of this, pointing out that Mr. Lincoln was looking westward: "He is in great spirits about Vicksburg, and looks to that as the beginning of the end of organized opposition to the war." Near the end of May Mr. Lincoln wrote to a friend in Illinois: "Whether General Grant shall or shall not consummate the capture of Vicksburg, his campaign from the beginning of this month up to the twenty-second of it is one of the most brilliant in the world."[12] The fact that Lee's army was in Pennsylvania might mean less than the fact that Grant's army was deep in Mississippi.

So the powerful support Hooker got from the radical Republicans no longer had its old value, and Hooker seems to have been aware of it. He got his army north of the Potomac shortly after Lee crossed, formed a loose concentration in the neighborhood of Frederick, Maryland, nursed the idea of moving troops over by the Harpers Ferry route to block Lee's rear and cut off Lee's tenuous communications with Virginia—and then got into a torrid row with Halleck over proper use of the Harpers Ferry garrison. The point was not nearly as important as subsequent arguments made it seem, but Hooker let it irk him, and at last—on June 27, with Lee's vanguard approaching Harrisburg—Hooker stiffly asked that he be relieved of his command.

Halleck replied that since Hooker had been appointed by the President the general-in-chief had no power to act, but he promised to see the President about it; did see him, with remarkably little delay, and found Mr. Lincoln willing to part with this general. Before the day ended the Adjutant General's office issued a formal order. Hooker had been relieved at his own request and command of the army, "by direction of the President," had been given to Major General George Gordon Meade, a regular, a Pennsylvanian, currently commander of V Corps, a good soldier who found room in his spirit for strangely contrasting qualities—a violent, often uncontrollable temper, and a streak of genuine humility not touched by cant. To a large extent he was an unknown quantity, the one certainty being that he was a man who did not scare easily.[13]

It was an odd time to make a change in command, with a battle so close; the general officers respected Meade but the rank and file had barely heard of him. The army had had leaders whom it adored and leaders whom it detested, and it had had poor luck under all of them; now, facing its su-

preme test, it must fight under a stranger, its spirit sustained
not by loyalty to a man but by loyalty to a cause. Somewhere off to the north of the sprawling camps in Maryland
it must show the full measure of its devotion . . . on its
own. Perhaps the President believed that it had at last come
of age.

5. *Mirage on the Skyline*

MARCHING INTO Pennsylvania was like entering a different
world. General Lee's men were used to Virginia, where
the country had been trampled and ravaged and fought over
until whole counties were desolate. Pennsylvania had never
been touched. Its farms looked incredibly rich, with barns
so big that the men said a whole brigade might be quartered
in each one, and all ranks were getting plenty to eat. General
Lee had issued stern orders against pillage, specifying that
supplies could be seized only by quartermaster and commissary officers, who must pay (in Confederate currency) for
everything they took; but even his massive authority could
not keep private soldiers from going about in the evening
to do some unofficial foraging. Perennially hungry, the Confederate soldier now was in a land of plenty. Also, he knew
how Yankee soldiers behaved in Virginia and he saw no
harm in a little retaliation.

In the main the invaders behaved with restraint. An
Austrian military observer was impressed to the point of
asserting, perhaps inaccurately, that "teetotalers will rejoice
to hear that none of the Confederate soldiers ever touch
spirits," and most of the citizens' complaints came because
the army methodically carried off all the livestock. A
Louisiana soldier boasted that the men now "lived on the
very fat of the land—milk, butter, eggs, chickens, turkeys,
apple butter, pear butter, cheese, honey, fresh pork, mut-
ton and every other imaginable thing that was good to eat,"
but he said the men paid for what they got, the only oddity
being that everything they bought came at a standard price
of twelve and one-half cents, whether by the pound, the
dozen, or the single portion. This, he said, happened because
"the old farmers were so awfully frightened that I believe

they forgot the denomination of any other piece of currency."

The citizens seemed to be remarkably lukewarm, as a matter of fact. It had been different in western Maryland, where Union sentiment was robust, and an army chaplain wrote scornfully that Sharpsburg was "a miserable Union hole" whose people "looked as though vinegar had been their only beverage since the battle in that neighborhood." But these Pennsylvania farmers appeared to be apathetic, and some of them said openly that they did not care much who won as long as they themselves were let alone.

The rank and file grew confident. For the first time the Army of Northern Virginia was unmistakably in enemy country. The invasion of Maryland in 1862 had not been quite the same, even though most of the citizens were Unionists, because Maryland was a slave state with a certain Southern coloration so that being there was much like being at home. This was Pennsylvania, Yankee-land incarnate, and on close inspection it seemed to be rich and naked and careless, wide open and ready to be had; confronted now by a lean and sinewy army whose spirits rose day by day. An army doctor predicted that Lee's men "will fight better than they have ever done if such a thing could be possible," and said that the Yankees were bound to be whipped when the big battle came.[1]

This reading of the case seemed logical, and as the dusty columns threaded their way east through the mountain passes an old mirage took shape on the skyline ahead—the vision of a North whose heart was not really in the war and whose people might before long give up the struggle altogether. These Pennsylvanians were too well-off, too self-centered, too anxious to save what they had; they were not at all warlike, and Federal soldiers as well as Confederates made pointed remarks about their seeming lack of patriotism.[2] Furthermore, was not this a fair representation of Northern spirit generally? Ohio was all in a ferment, with troops putting down mobs and arresting a candidate for governor, in Illinois a Federal regiment had mutinied, and the army commander at Cairo warned that "we have a population in southern Illinois ready to spring up and join any organization opposed to the government that offers itself."[3] It was easy to suppose that under all of this a true Northern peace party was rising; tilt the balance just a little more and the Lincoln administration must fail. The belief that this was so was a collateral reason for Lee's advance; also, deep in his mind, it was basic to the hope that the Confederacy could yet win despite the odds. In Richmond, Mr. Davis even now was preparing to put forth a feeler regarding peace.

Strong and confusing currents were moving in the North, and the line between stout patriotism and weary defeatism was not easily drawn. One state could contain both—one state, or one county or even (in thousands upon thousands of cases) one man. A deep desire to win the war could be married to passionate bitterness over the things that were being done to win it; if, beyond the reunion that final victory would bring, there was to be a restoration of the happy past, it followed that on the road to victory destruction should be held to a minimum. The Pennsylvania farmers, criticized by friend and by foe, were trying in their own stolid way to prevent breakage. They could easily have made their own the defiant Southern cry: *All we ask is to be let alone.*

The desire to be let alone can have explosive effects. It can also be deceptive. Pennsylvania had many things on its mind just now, but it had not lapsed into indifference. In the Army of the Potomac there were more contingents from Pennsylvania than from any other state—sixty-eight regiments of infantry, nine of cavalry, and five batteries of field artillery, volunteers to a man, many of them coming from precisely these farms whose people looked so phlegmatic. Some of them, too, came from parts of the state that apparently were on the edge of outright revolt—the anthracite fields, to which it had been necessary recently to send Federal troops to put down draft riots. It was easy to misinterpret these coal-field riotings. In the only way that was open to them, the anthracite workers were protesting— blindly, angrily, and without much hope—against woes that the war had not so much caused as emphasized: against autocratic mine bosses, against squalid company towns, against evil working conditions. In the hated enrollment officer they probably saw little more than a new reminder of the fact that their lives were hard.[4]

The currents ran both ways at once. If most of the discontent now so visible in the North came from men who had much to lose and wanted to save as much of it as possible, some of it came from men who had little to lose and might welcome a general overturn. At the moment their common protests were given unity by a new law which had gone into effect in March: the national conscription act, the cause of a great deal of dismay and some outright disorder. To men who had little to lose, this was a warning that the little they did have was likely to be taken: to the others, the men with much to save and a deep desire to save it, this law was an indication that the happy past was gone forever. Either way, the new law was highly unpopular.

Under its terms, all male citizens between twenty and forty-five were "declared to constitute the national forces," and the President could make them go into the army—the President, in faraway Washington, and not some familiar elected official of state or town or county. The measure was obviously necessary, volunteering having fallen off and the need for troops being great, and as a matter of fact the Confederacy had adopted an even stiffer measure a year earlier; yet this law had unquestionably changed the American form of government, and the President now had a power no President ever had before—the power to reach directly into the remotest township and exercise the power of life or death over the individual citizen. Senator Henry M. Rice of Minnesota, a war Democrat of unquestioned loyalty, spoke for many when he cried that this was a bill "violating the constitutions of the states"; and he warned soberly, "The moment you touch upon those rights, I say there will be a rebellion in the North."[5]

No rebellion took place; but there were scattered outbreaks of a rebellious character. In Holmes County, Ohio, for instance, in the middle of June, certain embattled farmers rose, took up arms, established themselves in a stone house on a hill near the village of Napoleon, and proclaimed defiance of the draft. Colonel William Wallace of the 15th Ohio Infantry was sent up from Columbus with 400 soldiers and a section of artillery, there was a brief exchange of shots in which two of the farmers were killed and three were wounded, and the uprising was put down; but although Colonel Wallace reported that the insurgents were "an ignorant and misguided class who hardly knew what they wanted," it was all too clear that they knew what they did not want. They had fought United States troops to make their point, and they did it while Lee's army was coming north across the Potomac.[6]

To bring matters to a head there was the excessive zeal displayed by General Ambrose E. Burnside.

After he lost command of the Army of the Potomac, Burnside was sent to Cincinnati to command the Department of the Ohio—roughly, the Middle West plus Kentucky. This was mostly peaceful country and the commanding general did not have much to do, which was why Burnside was sent there; but he arrived in this springtime of discontent, looked about him with the eyes of a frontline commander, and concluded that the Ohio country was displaying dangerous disloyalty. On April 19, with a tactical judgment no better than that of Fredericksburg, Burnside issued General Orders No. 38, announcing that "the habit of declaring sympathies for the enemy will no longer be tolerated," and threatening dire punishment for all who aided the rebellion. The order concluded: "It must be distinctly understood that treason, expressed or implied, will not be tolerated in this department."[7] Having published this the general awaited developments.

The first development was provided almost at once by Clement L. Vallandigham, who was just the man to respond to this kind of challenge and who probably was the man Burnside had chiefly in mind in the first place. Vallandigham, who was running for the Democratic nomination for the governorship (and making a good deal of headway) went to Mount Vernon, Ohio, and on May 1 addressed a large and enthusiastic audience. He voiced straight Vallandigham doctrine: the national administration did not want to make peace but was fighting to free the blacks and enslave the whites, General Orders No. 38 was a base usurpation of arbitrary power, men who meekly submitted to the conscription act did not deserve to be called free men, and "King Lincoln" must eventually be dethroned by the action of citizens at the ballot box. At this distance the speech sounds like little more than an ordinary, arm-flapping stump speech made in the heat of a lively political campaign, but to Burnside (who had an agent present, making notes) it sounded like treason, either expressed or implied. A few days later Burnside sent a company of infantry to Vallandigham's home in Dayton and the soldiers broke in the doors at midnight, caught Vallandigham in his underwear, gave him time to dress, hauled him forth despite his vigorous protests and took him to Cincinnati, where they put him in prison. Citizens of Dayton rioted vigorously to express their disapproval, burning the office of a Republican newspaper, several unoffending retail stores, and a livery stable; which helped not at all. On May 6 Vallandigham went on trial before a military commission, accused of violating Burnside's order, of expressing sympathy for the secessionists and of trying to weaken the government's efforts "to suppress an unlawful rebellion."[8]

Caught in the net, Vallandigham took on a new quality, dignity, and refused to plead. He scorned the authority of the soldiers, reading a formal statement saying that if he had violated any law he ought to be arrested by the civil authority, indicted by a regular grand jury, and tried in a civilian court; adding that he demanded his rights under the Constitution. It got him nowhere. The military commission found him guilty and ordered him imprisoned "in some fortress of the United States" for the balance of the war.

It had gone this far; for making a stump speech, a candidate for governor could be seized by the army, tried by army officers and locked up in an army prison—largely, when all was said and done, because General Burnside did not approve of what Candidate Vallandigham had been saying. In faraway Richmond, an official of the Confederate War Department made his comment: "This only was wanting to demonstrate how utterly that people" (meaning of course the lost-to-salvation Yankee race) "have lost every pretence of civil liberty. Shades of John and Samuel Adams! To what have your descendants come?" In less-faraway Albany there was a mass meeting in front of the state capitol, and people cheered when they heard a message from Governor Seymour declaring that Vallandigham's arrest "has brought dishonor upon our country" and predicting that Mr. Lincoln's handling of the case "will determine, in the minds of more than one half of the people of the loyal states, whether this war is waged to put down rebellion at the South or destroy free institutions at the North."[9]

There were formalities. Through counsel, Vallandigham appealed for a writ of habeas corpus, and the motion was heard by Judge Humphrey H. Leavitt in Federal Court.

Judge Leavitt noted that President Lincoln had suspended the right of the writ, and that General Burnside was unquestionably the President's agent. Apparently the President was trying to exercise his constitutional authority, the chief problem being that the Constitution did not say exactly what the President's authority in time of war really was. It seemed clear to the judge that "the President is guided solely by his own judgment and discretion, and is only amenable for an abuse of his authority by impeachment, prosecuted according to the requirements of the Constitution." Therefore: Burnside had not exceeded his authority, the application for a writ was denied, and Vallandigham stayed arrested.[10]

It all landed, of course, on Mr. Lincoln's desk. He had several things to think about, beginning with the cold fact that what Burnside had done was making a martyr out of Vallandigham and might make him governor of Ohio, and going on to the need to strike a balance between the ancient right of freedom of speech and the overpowering necessity to win a war. Winning the war came first. Mr. Lincoln commuted Vallandigham's sentence, ordering him sent, not to prison, but into the Confederacy. On May 25 Federal cavalry took Vallandigham through Rosecrans' lines near Murfreesboro and turned him over to surprised Confederate pickets, who hastily sought guidance from the rear and then, lacking anything better to do, accepted their charge. An unwilling exile, Vallandigham flitted across the Confederacy, got at last to a seaport, took ship for Canada, went to lower Ontario, and waited across the river from Detroit for a proper chance to get back to his constituency. He had been the victim of sharp practice, but his real trouble was that he had finally run into a middle western politician who played his own game a little faster than he himself did . . . and all without due process of law. Meanwhile, the President had a barbed answer for those who complained. To leading Democrats of New York, who had set forth their protests at length, he posed a question: "Must I shoot a simple-minded soldier boy who deserts, while I must not touch a hair of a wily agitator who induces him to desert?"[11]

Unfortunately, Burnside was not yet out of ammunition. On the night of June 2 a squad of soldiers, at his order, entered the offices of the Chicago *Times* and stopped the paper's publication.

Publisher of the *Times* was Wilbur Storey, who was admittedly a hard case. He had bought the paper early in 1861, and with skill and vigor had made it one of the most influential Democratic organs in the west. Originally, he had supported the war and called for subjugation of the South, but when the administration struck at slavery his tone changed; he denounced the Emancipation Proclamation as "the most wicked, atrocious and revolting deed recorded in the annals of civilization," and of late he had been demanding peace as the only means of saving American freedom. He wrote without restraint, and his editorials had a hard bite to them; he spoke for the Northerners who detested abolition and wanted the war taken back to its old, limited aims, but he spoke with more fury and a more bitter invective than anyone else was using, and to a man like Burnside he looked as dangerous as a Confederate army. One exasperated Union officer asserted later that Storey's *Times* was "chief among those instigators of insurrection and treason, the foul and damnable reservoir which supplied the lesser sewers with political filth, falsehood and treason." That was the tone Storey himself used and that was the tone he provoked in others, and now Federal soldiers occupied his editorial rooms and kept his presses from operating.

Naturally, the suppression of this newspaper stirred up immense trouble. The lower house of the Illinois legislature resolved that the act was "so revolutionary and despotic" that it was "equivalent to the overthrow of our government." A mass meeting of Chicagoans held that whatever the *Times* had said the remedy (if any remedy was needed) lay with the courts and not with the army, and in New York fifteen newspaper and magazine editors met, with none other than Horace Greeley presiding, and unanimously affirmed "the right of the press to criticize firmly and fearlessly the acts of those charged with the administration of the Government, also those of all their civil and military subordinates." The administration could not resist this kind of storm, and at Mr. Lincoln's direction Secretary Stanton got off a hurried message to Burnside: revoke the order of suspension, get the soldiers out of there, and in the future arrest no speakers or editors without first getting clearance from Washington. The *Times* resumed publication, jubilantly proclaiming that "the right of free speech has not passed away . . . we have, then, still a free press."[12]

The cases of orator Vallandigham and editor Storey had long echoes heard far to the south. With the Yankees in such trouble at home, might not this be a good time to suggest a peace settlement? To Vice-President Alexander Stephens it seemed that some sort of opening existed, and from his home in Georgia he wrote to President Davis about it.

The Confederate government had been wanting to make a new arrangement with the Federals regarding prisoner exchanges, and Stephens suggested that he be appointed to try it. If he could confer with President Lincoln about prisoners, he said, "I am not without hope that *indirectly* I could now turn attention to a general adjustment upon such basis as might ultimately be acceptable to both parties and stop the further effusion of blood in a contest so irrational, unchristian and so inconsistent with all recognized American principles." He admitted that the odds were against him; "but still, be assured, I am not without *some* hopes of success." (He explained that the "general adjustment" he wanted would of course be based on acceptance of the idea of Southern independence.) Mr. Davis read this letter, and promptly invited Mr. Stephens to come to Richmond. Late in June the President, the Vice-President, and the cabinet conferred on the matter.[13]

Characteristically, Stephens himself by now had lost faith in his own proposal. He felt certain that Mr. Lincoln would not see him, and he doubted that the attempt should even be made, but Mr. Davis and the cabinet saw it otherwise. Agreeing that Mr. Lincoln would not ordinarily want to talk to any Confederate emissary, they pointed out that since Stephens wrote his letter the picture had changed: the Army of Northern Virginia was in Pennsylvania now, and it probably would win a victory before long. As Stephens remembered it, they held that "the prospect of success was increased by the position and projected movements of General Lee's army." So, armed with a letter signed by Mr. Davis, Stephens went to Hampton Roads and sent a note to Rear Admiral S. P. Lee, Federal naval commander there, identifying himself as "a military commissioner" and asking permission to go to Washington under flag of truce to talk with President Lincoln.

The presidential letter Stephens carried was unusual, for in it Mr. Davis did something that he had not done before and would not do again. He identified himself, not as President of the Confederate States of America, but simply as "commander-in-chief of the land and naval forces now waging war against the United States." As all men knew, Mr. Lincoln refused to admit that there was a Confederate States of America, and he would accept no message signed by its President, because if he did he might thereby, inadvertently, recognize the existence of whatever it was that the letter-writer was president of. He could not fail to admit, however, that certain land and naval forces were making war against the United States, and to accept a letter from the commander of those forces would commit him to nothing. If flexibility would help, Mr. Davis could be flexible.[14]

It accomplished nothing. Admiral Lee notified Washington of Stephens' mission, and Mr. Lincoln discussed the matter with his cabinet; suggesting, to the statesmen's horror, that he just might go down to Fort Monroe and see what Stephens had on his mind. Secretary Seward opposed this, considering Stephens dangerous (it seems an odd epithet for Stephens, somehow) and in the end Stephens was rebuffed: if his people had anything to say about prisoner exchanges they could say it through regular military channels, but neither he nor any other person could go to Washington. Stephens went back to Georgia, and he wrote to a friend: "The prospect before us presents nothing cheering to me."[15]

He would have been no more cheerful if he had actually had that talk with Mr. Lincoln, because there was nothing the two men could have said to one another. The situation in the North offered much less than hopeful Southerners believed. What was taking shape was not a peace party at all. It only looked like one, as tipster Barnett pointed out to leading Democrat Barlow. Even Ohio's Sunset Cox, who did his best to get Vallandigham out of Burnside's grip, said that his fellow Democrats "want security at home even more than peace in the land" and reported that it would be easy to line them up in support of McClellan—who hated the Lincoln administration but as a soldier believed in keeping on with the war until the Confederacy surrendered.[16]

Northern discontent, in short, in 1863 reflected no readiness to give up the fight for the Union. It did reflect deep-seated fears—that civil liberties were being crushed, that the mere act of going on with the war was changing America permanently, that peace had become unattainable when the administration came out for emancipation—but it was not defeatist. It reflected, too, the existence of the Northerner's own mirage: the faith that Southerners did not really mean what they said about independence and would happily return to the Union once the administration suppressed the abolitionists and gave up the attempt to outlaw slavery. In the spring of 1863 there was no foundation at all for this belief, but it had a hardy life.

Conservative men believed it because they had to, for their own peace of mind. The war had changed immeasurably in two years, it had finally become what Mr. Lincoln long ago had hoped it would not become—a remorseless revolutionary struggle—and at its revolutionary heart lay precisely this decision to free the slave and so to create a new sort of America. To believe that this decision was all that stood between the old republic and a lasting peace was to do no more than make a profession of faith: the orthodox American faith, sorely beset now by diverse heresies. These conservatives were not in any real sense a peace party. They were simply a party of moderates in a revolutionary situation, faring about as moderates always fare in revolutions, ground pitilessly between two extremes. One extreme, of course, was the Lincoln administration, in the White House and in the Capitol. The other, unmistakably, was the Army of Northern Virginia, which was about to go into battle on the rolling hills surrounding the town of Gettysburg, Pennsylvania.

6. Encounter at Gettysburg

THE COMMANDING GENERALS never meant to fight at Gettysburg. The armies met there by accident, led together by the turns of the roads they followed. When they touched they began to fight, because the tension was so high that the first contact snapped it, and once begun the fight was uncontrollable. What the generals intended ceased to matter; each man had to cope with what he got, which was the most momentous battle of the war.

On June 28 Lee's army was loosely arrayed in a forty-five-mile crescent. Longstreet's corps was at Chambersburg, Hill's was eight miles to the east, and Ewell's was far in front at York and Carlisle. The army was much too dispersed to fight, but as long as Meade's army remained south of the Potomac—it must be there, because vigilant Stuart had sent no warning of any move—this dispersion could do no harm. Until the Yankees came north, Lee's army could roam across southeastern Pennsylvania at will, alarming the government at Washington and collecting the supplies whose abundance had been one of the prime reasons for invasion.

But on the night of June 28 Lee learned that things had gone terribly wrong. Somewhere, somehow, Stuart had been blocked out of the play, and the Yankees had stolen a long march; their army now was at Frederick, Maryland, nearer to the scattered pieces of Lee's army than those pieces were to each other, and for its life's sake the Army of Northern Virginia must concentrate. Lee sent off galloping couriers with orders: Ewell was to retreat, Longstreet was to advance, and the army would reunite at or near Gettysburg, which was a convenient road center. Lee was worried, but as always he seemed calm, and he remarked lightly that it was time for him to go to Gettysburg and see what Meade was up to. (The same scout who told him that the Federals were in Maryland had also brought news of the change in command.)[1]

Meade's plans as June came to an end were somewhat like Lee's: sketchy, subject to instant change, tinged strongly by wait-and-see. He had been shifting to the east, to keep Lee from crossing the Susquehanna and striking down toward Philadelphia, and when he learned about Ewell's retreat Meade felt that this part of his job had been done. Now he had to bring Lee to battle and defeat him, and it seemed that the best way to do this was to get between Lee's army and Washington and await Lee's attack. He probably would not have to wait long, because Lee was deep in hostile territory, had no real supply line, and could not remain inactive. With Meade's army in his immediate front, Lee must either fight or go back to Virginia, and the chance that he would go back without first fighting a battle was too small to think about twice.

So while Lee was concentrating Meade chose what looked

like a strong defensive position behind a stream called Pipe Creek, in northern Maryland some fifteen miles south and a little east of Gettysburg, and notified his corps commanders to prepare to go there. To mask this movement, he ordered John F. Reynolds to take his I Corps up to Gettysburg, which was lightly held by John Buford and three brigades of Federal cavalry. Behind this screen the rest of the army would have time to assemble at Pipe Creek, and if at Gettysburg Reynolds saw something that would make a different course advisable he could notify Meade without delay.

Trusting Reynolds implicitly, Meade gave him a free hand. He also gave him command of the left wing of the army, the three corps nearest Gettysburg—Reynolds' own I Corps, which was just south of the town, Howard's XI Corps a few miles to the rear, and Sickles' III Corps, east of nearby Emmitsburg. Reynolds would be strong enough to stay on the scene until he saw what the Confederates proposed to do. If attacked, he could retire slowly. Meanwhile, Meade would not definitely commit himself to the Pipe Creek plan until he heard from Reynolds in detail.[2]

Reynolds led his army corps into Gettysburg on the morning of July 1 and found that the shooting had already started. A Confederate battle line was coming in astride the Chambersburg Pike, west of town: Henry Heth's division of A. P. Hill's corps, with other troops on the road behind it. Buford had several regiments of dismounted cavalry and a few fieldpieces drawn up on a low ridge to contest this advance. There was a good deal of noise, and there was a rising cloud of smoke, but the fighting was not especially serious. Infantry could always push dismounted cavalry out of the way and everybody knew it, and Heth's men were performing a routine task in a routine way.

There was no very good reason why these Confederates had to get into Gettysburg, except that A. P. Hill was a pugnacious man who liked to fight whenever he had a chance; and there was no especial reason why Yankee cavalry should try to keep them out of Gettysburg, except that Buford felt the way Hill felt about fighting. Now Reynolds, as pugnacious as either of these two, looked at the firing lines and heard Buford's situation report: the Rebels' main body lay westward, but Ewell's corps was off to the north and east and would probably show up before long. Reynolds sent a staff officer pelting back to Meade with a message which said, in effect, that there was going to be a big fight at Gettysburg and that every Federal soldier Reynolds could lay his hands on was going to be in it. Reynolds would oppose these oncoming Confederates: "I will fight them inch by inch, and if driven into the town I will barricade the streets and hold them as long as possible."[3] He notified Howard to hurry forward with his XI Corps, and then he put his leading division into line, relieved Buford's troopers, and smashed into Heth's infantry head-on.

Nobody had told Reynolds to fight for Gettysburg, inch by inch or otherwise, any more than Hill had been told to seize the place. By his orders Reynolds would have been justified in falling back, watching the Confederates and delaying them until Meade was securely posted at Pipe Creek, and the story of the next few days would have been different if he had done this. The end result would probably have been much the same, and about the same number of men would have been killed; but they would have been killed at a different place in a different way, and the ifs and might-have-beens that seem so important today would be replaced by other ifs and might-have-beens, and there is no point in speculating about it. Reynolds did what was in character for him to do. He was an instinctive, inch-by-inch fighter, and now he rode up to the battle line to see that his men struck the blow that he wanted them to strike. As they surged forward a bullet hit him and he toppled from his saddle, dead . . . and the Battle of Gettysburg had begun, brought on without choice of Lee or Meade by the fact that the roads that crossed here brought together men possessed by a blind, driving urge to fight.[4]

The flame fed itself. The Confederate attack was beaten back, and Hill put a fresh division into action. The Federals, led now by Abner Doubleday, spread out along the crest of their ridge, facing west, to receive this new attack, and suddenly found themselves under fire from the north. Ewell's corps was coming in, exactly as Buford had predicted, and its leading division began to attack Doubleday's right and rear. Just in time, Howard's corps came into Gettysburg—sadly under strength, and in bad repute because of Chancellorsville, but most welcome in this crisis. By seniority

Howard took general command. He sent most of the XI Corps north of Gettysburg to stave off Ewell's assault, the Federal lines stiffened—and at this moment Lee himself, riding east from Chambersburg to the sound of the guns, came up in rear of Hill's battle line.

Lee was not ready for a general engagement. He had less than half of his army on the field, he still did not know where the bulk of Meade's army was, and his first impulse was to suspend the attack. But a Confederate victory was taking shape before his eyes. Off to the northeast the second of Ewell's divisions was coming into action, hitting Howard's line in flank and rear, striking the right place at the right moment entirely by accident but as effectively as if it had been planned that way. If Howard's men were driven off, which obviously was about to happen, Doubleday's men could not hold their ground in front of Hill. This was the moment of opportunity, and Lee quickly reversed himself and ordered a general advance.

For half an hour or an hour—no one counted minutes very carefully that day—there was a desperate fight on the open plain to the north and the long ridge to the west. This battle that involved only fractions of the armies grew far beyond its size, and like the war itself it became bigger and more destructive than anyone intended. The right half of the Federal line collapsed first; taken in front, flank and rear by the expanding Confederate offensive, Howard's Dutchmen finally broke and ran off, victims of sheer bad luck and of their own low morale. Brigadier General Francis C. Barlow, one of Howard's division commanders, wounded and captured in this fight, wrote a few days later that the Confederate soldiers "are more heroic, more modest and more in earnest than we are," and felt that "their whole tone is much finer than ours"[5]; and however this may have been, the right half of the Union line folded up and the downfall of the left half soon followed. The prodigious fight the Federals made on the western ridge—some regiments here lost 75 percent of their strength this afternoon—went for nothing, and by half-past three or thereabouts the survivors of the two defeated Federal corps were going helter-skelter back through Gettysburg to take refuge on the high ground south of town, where Howard had posted a brigade of infantry and some artillery to stem the rout.

The flight through town was confused and costly. Federal and Confederate regiments ran into each other unexpectedly, stray field pieces pulled up at intervals to blast canister down smoky streets, and Ewell's exultant Confederates rounded up so many Yankee prisoners that their own ranks were all disordered. A measure of the general confusion was the unhappy plight of one of Howard's brigade commanders, Brigadier General Alexander Schimmelfennig—a good man who deserved better of fate—who was trapped by armed foes, clambered over a high board fence to get away, and to avoid capture had to take refuge in a pigpen, staying there for the rest of the battle, living on what the prodigal son lived on during his dreary exile. . . . Late in the afternoon most of the Federals had reassembled in the new position. Meade had sent Major General Winfield Scott Hancock up to take charge, Hancock put a new battle line together, fresh troops began to come up, and the Confederates did not press their advantage. In killed, wounded, and captured the Federals had lost 9000 men, half of all they had put into action: the Confederates, with substantial losses of their own, had swept the field, and this first, unplanned encounter between the two armies had been a smashing victory for General Lee.[6]

But the victory meant little except that it robbed both Lee and Meade of their freedom of action. They had to finish what had been so violently begun and they had to finish it here. When darkness came on July 1 each commander accepted this fact and ordered the rest of his troops forward, Lee planning to resume the offensive as soon as possible, Meade planning to make his fight here rather than at Pipe Creek. Meade himself reached the field late that night. He found that his army had a powerful defensive position—from Culp's Hill, southeast of Gettysburg, west to Cemetery Hill and then south two miles along Cemetery Ridge to a rocky knoll called Little Round Top—and he knew that all of his army except John Sedgwick's big VI Corps would be on hand ready for action by the middle of the morning. Sedgwick, driving his men hard on a thirty-mile march, could not come up until late afternoon, but even without him Meade had enough men to hold his ground and it even seemed to him that with good management he might take the offensive himself. The qualms that had paralyzed Joe

Hooker when he found himself facing the Army of Northern Virginia had no place in Meade's makeup.[7]

Lee had won the first round, but he was under a profound handicap. None of his other battlefields had given him a problem like this one. The pressure of time and circumstance was on him, not on his opponent, and the Federal army—larger than his own, as always—was for the first time standing on the defensive on its own soil. The old equalizers were not available here. Lee could use neither the dogged defensive that had served so well at Antietam and Fredericksburg nor the dazzling shifts and feints that had won the Seven Days and Chancellorsville. He was on the offensive, but he did not quite have the initiative: this time, Lee's antagonist could not be compelled to fight Lee's kind of battle. The armies were bound together by the first day's fight, without room for maneuver, and to resume the battle— inescapable, all things considered—was simply to engage in a slugging match, the one kind of fight which when the campaign began Lee hoped to avoid.

Longstreet, to be sure, proposed that the army circle to its right to get into Meade's rear, but Lee quickly dismissed the idea. He no longer had Stonewall Jackson, the one man who could have led such a move; furthermore, in Stuart's absence he did not know just where Meade's rear was or what he might run into if he tried to go there. He answered Longstreet in the only way that was open to him: "The enemy is there and I am going to fight him there."[8] He at last knew in general terms where Stuart was—northeast, somewhere near Carlisle—but the knowledge was not helpful. Stuart and his cavalry would rejoin the army in twenty-four hours, and that would be twenty-four hours too late. Lee needed Stuart now, and because he did not have him now he had to go on with this battle where it had begun—with the odds against him.

What came out of this on July 2 was a tremendous battle that settled nothing, except for the thousands on both sides who were shot, and possibly for their next of kin. Lee's army, the incomparable instrument for finding and exploiting weak spots, struck on this day against strong points and wore itself out. It pounded the Federal left, head-on and heads-down, in a peach orchard and a wheat field and in the craggy ravines of a tumbled rock pile known as Devil's Den, and a Confederate who watched from the steeple of the Lutheran Seminary could see little but a dense fog bank of shifting gunsmoke that hid fields and woods and fighting men; a fog bank that was forever sparkling and pulsing with the sharp red flames from the muzzles of invisible cannon, whose gunners found that this fight was even worse than Antietam itself, the battle they always remembered as Artillery Hell.[9] This was one of many battles that swung up and down the long length of the Federal line, each battle desperate but each one somehow separate from the others.

The Army of Northern Virginia tried to storm Little Round Top, fought in a gloomy valley behind that hill, swept across the Emmitsburg Road to touch the crest of Cemetery Ridge, wrecking Dan Sickles' III Corps, mangling the V Corps of George Sykes, beating one division of Hancock's II Corps; and each time it came within an inch of success but had to fall back before that final inch could be gained. It took a long row of guns in the heart of the Federal position but could not hold them, and it fought once in a farm yard against massed artillery that lacked infantry support, losing at last because canister at close range could dismember foot soldiers faster than the replacements could get into action. (After the battle, men who crossed this part of the field said that war could show nothing more hideous than the human fragments that lay on the ground where infantry had been broken up by close-range artillery fire.) A division from Ewell's corps struck the Federal right on Culp's Hill, clambering up steep slopes full of young trees and fallen timber, reaching the Federal trenches, occupying parts of them, falling back down hill when the rifle fire was too heavy; hanging on in the darkness, with the sputter of musketry making flickering firefly lights in the dark woods; hanging on to renew the fight at dawn. In the evening Lee's army assaulted the sagging ridge between Culp's Hill and Cemetery Hill, broke the XI Corps line in the twilight, got into Howard's artillery, and was driven off after a furious hand-to-hand fight amid the wheels of the guns. Late at night, soldiers from the two armies went to a spring beyond the Federal right to get water, recognized one another in the shaded moonlight as enemies, and fell into a meaningless fight that went on until after midnight and did nothing but add to the casualty lists.

There was no pattern to any of this, except for the undesigned pattern that can always be traced after the event. Gettysburg was improvised, unpremeditated as a chain of lightning, searing and scarring both armies; Meade's able staff officer, G. K. Warren, summed it up when he wrote that the July 2 fight "was no display of scientific maneuver, and should never be judged like some I think vainly try to judge a battle as they would a game of chess."[10] It was a test of what men can nerve themselves to attempt and what they can compel themselves to endure, and at shattering cost it proved that the possibilities in both directions are limitless; but as Warren said it was not especially instructive otherwise.

Late that night Meade met with his corps commanders in the cramped living room of the little farmhouse he used as headquarters, heard what they had to say, and reached a simple and direct conclusion: Lee would hit him once more, and this time he would hit the center of the line because he had failed on both flanks. That would be all right; the center was held by Hancock, and he and his men could be relied on if any could be relied on. Meade was content to remain on the defensive and wait for the blow to fall.[11]

By the morning of July 3 Lee's field of choice was fatally narrow. It contained now only two elements of importance— the strength to strike one more blow and the overwhelming compulsion to strike while that strength remained. Everything Lee had planned to do north of the Potomac had been constricted by two day of immense violence here at Gettysburg, and what was left of his plans now hinged on the fact that General George Pickett of Longstreet's corps had reached the field with a fresh division—the one Secretary Seddon considered sending off to Vicksburg before he was warned about the danger of having to choose between Mississippi and Virginia. Pickett and his 5000 good soldiers were here to be used, and when Longstreet again proposed a maneuver around the Federal left Lee refused to hear him. He would strengthen Pickett with such brigades as were available to form a storming column that would hit the Yankees where they were toughest, right at the northern end of Cemetery Ridge, going uphill all the way to get at the crack combat corps of the Army of the Potomac in a prepared position of great strength. This final desperate stroke would be based on the faith that when the Army of Northern Virginia made its supreme effort it could not be stopped by anybody.[12]

The day began badly. Ewell's men had not finished their attack on Culp's Hill, and Confederate chances would obviously be improved if this attack could be renewed when Pickett's column was hitting the Federal center. But Ewell's men had spent the night on the slopes of the hill in close contact with the Federal trenches, and as soon as daylight came the fighting there flared up automatically. Meade had reinforced this position during the night, the Federals counterattacked, and after several hours of hard fighting the Confederates sullenly withdrew. By eleven o'clock they were back down on the plain below the hill, fought out, weaker by 1800 casualties. Long before the attack on the center could be made, the Federal right was out of danger.

So there was only one card left to play, and it was played so magnificently that it is not always easy to see that it probably was a losing card all along.

Lee's blow was going to be formidable, beyond question. He was putting between 10,000 and 15,000 men into this attack: Pickett's division, joined by two of Hill's divisions, Heth's and William Dorsey Pender's. (Both Heth and Pender had been wounded; Heth's division today was led by Brigadier General J. Johnston Pettigrew, Pender's by Major General Issac R. Trimble.) To prepare the way, Lee had assembled an immense rank of guns, 130 of them or more, planted almost hub to hub west of the Emmitsburg Road. These guns would pound the Yankee line with the heaviest bombardment ever seen in North America, and after they had softened it the infantry would charge. Longstreet would have additional infantry ready to go up and support the right flank of the column of assault in case of need.

But the odds were forbidding. Meade's best general, Hancock, would receive the attack, and he had more than 9000 veterans in line, fighters as good as any in either army, protected by stone walls, piled fence rails and sketchy but effective breastworks, backed by plenty of the superb Federal artillery. His men had a clear field of fire; their assailants would have to climb the slanting fields for more than half a mile without the slightest protection. Hancock's position actually was almost as strong as the famous Confederate position along Marye's Heights at Fredericksburg, where Burnside had almost ruined his army trying to do the impossible. In addition, Meade had an abundance of reserves close at hand —Sedgwick's entire army corps, rested now from its hard march, hardly used at all so far in this battle. Years afterward, Longstreet said that before the charge he pointed to the Federal position and warned Lee that "no fifteen thousand men ever arrayed for battle can take that position,"[13] and whether he actually said it or just thought later that he should have said it, his appraisal stands. The thing could not be done.

But the way it was tried still commands attention.

Somewhere around the middle of the day the noise of battle died and there was a queer, nerve-testing silence. On the far slope of Cemetery Ridge, Meade and some of his officers sat in an open field and had lunch, and Meade got off a quick note to Halleck, carefully timing it at 12:30 P.M.: "At the present moment all is quiet." Hancock's men crouched behind their barricades under the blistering July sun and peered to the west; they could see the concealing woods on the rising skyline, the ominous array of guns in front of the woods, wisps of smoke from a burning barn off to the right drifting down the breeze, nothing else moving anywhere. Hidden behind the trees, the Confederates who were going to make the charge formed their long ranks and lay down to sweat it out, knowing what was ahead of them. At last, from a fence corner at the edge of the woods, Longstreet wrote a note and gave it to a courier, the courier cantered out to the guns and gave the note to Colonel J. B. Walton, Longstreet's chief of artillery, two shots were fired as a signal, the sharp reports echoing far across the silent fields—and then the bank of guns exploded in a sudden, enormous blast of fire, driving a blizzard of bursting shell and solid shot at the rocky crest of the ridge and piling up a billow of smoke in the hollow ground west of the Emmitsburg Road. The final stage of the Battle of Gettysburg had begun.[14]

No one in either army had ever lived through anything like this bombardment. The weight of sound was obliterating, a roar as unbroken as sustained musketry-fire but infinitely louder; Hancock's artillery was firing in reply to the Confederate fire, in one square mile more than two hundred guns were in action, each one getting off two or three rounds a minute, and the racket was so prodigious that some of the gunners said afterward they could hardly hear the reports of the cannon they themselves were firing. It went on and on— half an hour, an hour, no one really knew how long—and the waiting infantry hugged the ground, each man trying to make himself as small as possible. On Cemetery Ridge the ground was rocky, and the projectiles broke the rocks and drove deadly jagged fragments into prostrate bodies; in the woods to the west waiting Confederates were killed by chunks and branches from the broken trees. One of Pickett's briga-diers, General Lewis Armistead, picked up a splinter, showed it to his men, and asked casually: "Boys, do you think you can go up under that? It is pretty hot out there." Now and then a shell would find an artillery caisson and blow it up, with a spurt of flame and black smoke. Once, during the worst of it, Hancock rode slowly from end to end of his line, risking his life to make his men feel that the danger was not quite as bad as it seemed to be. John Gibbon, commanding Han-cock's second division, strolled out in front of the Federal line with the same purpose and found himself safer there than he would have been farther to the rear; the Confederate fire was coming in a bit too high.[15]

At three o'clock or a little later the bombardment tapered off, ceased altogether, and a tense silence descended on the smoking field. Then out of the woods came General Lee's assaulting column, like actors in some unimaginable drama coming at last onto the stage—rank after rank, Pickett and Pettigrew and Trimble and their divisions and when they got into the open the men halted and dressed their ranks as carefully as if they were going on parade. They were worth looking at. Their line was a mile wide from flank to flank, Pickett's division on the right, Pettigrew's beside it, Trimble's in close support, general officers mounted, battle flags over-head, sunlight glinting off of the rifle barrels. They perfected their alignment, finally, and when the line began to roll for-ward it looked irresistible.

It was not irresistible. In point of fact it was doomed. Up on the ridge the Federal gunners were waiting and they had a perfect target—massed infantry, wide and deep, wholly unprotected, coming closer and closer, fearfully and fatally vulnerable. The gunners held their fire briefly. In the center of Hancock's line long-range ammunition had been exhausted, and some of the batteries had been all but wrecked during the bombardment, but off to the right and left all of the guns were ready and when they opened fire they tore frightful gaps in the Confederate line. Pettigrew's division, which had taken heavy losses in the first day's fight, got it first, and worst, and as the ranks went up the slope they disappeared in a rolling cloud of dust and smoke; the gunners kept firing into the heart of the cloud until at last this division could stand no more. It began to give way, hundreds of men shot down, others drifting toward the rear; and Longstreet, watching from afar with dour expectation of disaster, saw its lines crumbling and told British Colonel Fremantle, who was standing beside him, that the attack was going to be a failure.[16]

On Pickett's right things were no better. Hancock swung a brigade out into the open to deliver a punishing flanking fire, the guns on the Federal left were pounding hard, and the great attacking wave contracted, both flanks beaten in, the men who kept going crowding in toward the center. They crossed the Emmitsburg Road, went on up the last of the rising ground, and at last reached musket range and canister range and got to grips with their foes. Incredibly, a few hundred broke through the Federal line, clambering over the stone wall and getting in among the artillery, Armistead in the lead, Federal regiments running in to meet them. From his post by the western woods Lee could see little more than a swirling fog of smoke, with tossing red battle flags briefly visible here and there. One of Longstreet's brigades tried to advance to support Pickett's right, lost sight of its objective, stumbled into a terrible fire from massed artillery, and came back in fragments. Armistead died with his hand on a Federal cannon, the men who had crossed the wall with him died or were captured . . . and suddenly it was all over, and when the blinding smoke drifted away what was left of the mighty column of assault was going back to the Confederate lines. Of the men who had made the advance, just about half returned. The Battle of Gettysburg had ended.[17]

The commanding generals accepted the outcome each in his own way. Meade rode to the front as the last of the Confederate wave was draining back down the long slope, learned how completely the attack had been repulsed, made as if to swing his hat in exultation, thought better of it, and quietly said: "Thank God." When he had a chance, a little later, he got off a hasty note to his wife: "The men behaved splendidly—I really think they are becoming soldiers. . . . The army are in the highest spirits, and of course I am a great man but in my own heart I would thank God if I was relieved tomorrow and permitted to return home and live in peace and quiet." A mile to the west, Lee rode out to meet and rally the broken remnants of the three divisions, and in this backwash of defeat he had his emotions under full control. He told a disheartened general: "All this has been my fault—it is I that have lost this fight, and you must help me out of it the best you can." To Colonel Fremantle he summed it up: "This has been a sad day for us, Colonel —a sad day; but we can't expect always to gain victories." His supreme stroke as a warrior had failed, and he knew it, and there was only one thing he could do now: order a retreat, and hope that his foes had been too badly hurt to keep him from making a safe return to Virginia.

The long evening shadows came down, as the sun dropped behind the blue line of South Mountain, and except for the cries of the wounded men the field was silent. Unseen, a deeper shadow was dropping all across the Confederacy from other heights a thousand miles to the southwest. For just as the exhausted survivors of the final assault at Gettysburg were pulling themselves together, trying to find out who still lived, General Grant and General Pemberton were meeting under a flag of truce on a hill outside of Vicksburg, agreeing on the terms under which Pemberton and his army and the Vicksburg fortress and everything the Confederacy hoped for in the Mississippi Valley would next day be surrendered.

Of this, mercifully, Lee that evening knew nothing. He made arrangements for the retreat of the long ambulance train with its load of wounded, ordered Ewell's corps to withdraw to the high ground west of Gettysburg, sketched the plans by which the army would find its way back to the Potomac crossing—and finally, late at night, worn down by fatigue, he let his emotion find words. Standing by his horse in the moonlight, giving final orders to General John Imboden of the cavalry, who was to escort the ambulance train, he suddenly began to talk about the great charge his men had made. Never had he seen troops behave more magnificently, he said, than Pickett's men had behaved that day, and if they had been supported properly they would have broken the Yankee line and won the field. After a moment Lee cried out loudly: "Too bad! Too bad! *Oh—too bad!*"[18]

CHAPTER FOUR

In Letters of Blood

1. All or Nothing

THE ONLY NORTHERNER who ever expressed dissatisfaction with U. S. Grant's achievement at Vicksburg was Grant himself. When he took his army down the west side of the Mississippi in April he wanted to destroy the last trace of Confederate authority in the lower valley, and it bothered him that he had to settle for a little less than that. In the middle of June, when it was clear that both the fortress and Pemberton's army must surrender before long, he expressed his discontent in a candid note to his father: "The fall of Vicksburg now will only result in the opening of the Mississippi River and demoralization of the enemy. I intended more from it." To apply the qualifying "only" to a victory that changed the whole course of the war occurred to no one else; not even to President Lincoln, who had become a most demanding perfectionist. This general was different.[1]

Grant's basic design was simple: to reach the high ground east of the river so that he could bring on a fight to the finish. His campaign plan was so flexible that it amounted to little more than a determination to move fast, deceive the enemy and take advantage of every opening, and the flexibility was what saved it because neither the Mississippi River nor General Nathaniel P. Banks behaved quite as Grant had anticipated.

The first step was to march the army to the village of New Carthage, a steamboat landing on the Louisiana shore some twenty miles below Vicksburg. From New Carthage the army (with the aid of Porter's gunboats) could go downstream fifteen miles and capture the Confederate batteries at

185

Grand Gulf, which lay on the opposite shore below the place where the Big Black River came in from the northeast. Grand Gulf was important because here was the first place south of the fortified zone immediately around Vicksburg where the all-important high ground touched the river's edge.

At Grand Gulf, or somewhere near it, Grant proposed to leave 10,000 men, to make warlike feints from a secure position behind the Big Black and so lead General Pemberton to look for an immediate attack. With 20,000 more he would go on downstream and join forces with General Banks for an attack on Port Hudson, where Admiral Farragut's ships had taken such a pounding earlier in the spring. Once Port Hudson was pinched off there would be a clear supply line straight down to New Orleans, and Grant and Banks together could come back upstream, overwhelm Pemberton, take Vicksburg and sweep the last armed Confederates out of Mississippi once and for all.

All of this would begin with the overland march from Milliken's Bend to New Carthage—about 20 miles in an air line, more than twice that much as the roads went—and when McClernand's corps took up that line of march it found that the roads were in the highest degree abominable. This Louisiana country was half under water, and the roads went through an interminable marshland in looping semicircles along the slightly less oozy ground that fringed the bayous and swamps. To make the march at all, McClernand's men had to spend many days laying corduroy roads, building causeways and rigging up improvised bridges, and the business went so slowly that Grant privately concluded that "the enemy cannot fail to discover my plans." It was obvious that this roadway would never stand up under the day-after-day hammering it would get if the supply trains tried to make regular use of it, but the engineers managed to make a sort of waterway through the swamps by cutting channels from one sluggish backwater to another, and it seemed likely that light draft steamers could use this as a regular supply route. In mid-April Grant told Halleck that the situation was promising, and during the next two weeks he moved his army on downstream to a steamboat landing two miles above Grand Gulf, on property which some gloomy planter had named Hard Times.[2]

But at this point the water level in the Mississippi began

to fall. This was a perverse twist, because the level had been unfavorably high for weeks; now it fell, and the bayous and streams that made up the military waterway were reduced to streaky bits of marsh which not even the smallest steamer could use. Thus the waterway went entirely out of existence just when it was needed most, and although Porter did manage to run a few transports and barges past the Vicksburg batteries the supplies for an extended campaign could never be brought down that way. Neither by land nor by water could Grant maintain an adequate flow of the innumerable things his army was going to need.

Then Grant discovered that he could not cross at Grand Gulf. The Confederate engineers had emplaced heavy guns on steep bluffs there, overlooking a hairpin turn in the river where the current was strong, and this layout was more than the navy could handle. Porter took his flotilla down on April 29 and valiantly bombarded the place, but had to confess flat failure; his vessels were hurt, he had substantial casualties, he did the Confederates very little harm, and it seemed to him that in some ways the Confederate position here was stronger than the one at Vicksburg. If Grant wished, Porter could run gunboats and transports past these batteries at night, to make a crossing farther down, but to force a landing here was impossible.[3]

And finally it developed that Grant could not meet Banks at Port Hudson in any case. Banks was moving away from the big river instead of toward it. He was in excellent spirits, full of hope and energy, and on the day Porter bombarded Grand Gulf Banks wrote to his wife that the next campaign would be a success: "The atmosphere has changed in New Orleans. 'A New Man has Risen!'" On this same day he confidently assured his friend General Burnside: "Had I a few more men I would sweep the country west of the Mississippi. As it is I have hope." All of this was encouraging, but Banks' orders told him to sweep east of the river rather than west; instead of moving toward Port Hudson he was marching toward Alexandria, which lay far to the west in Louisiana, and it was precisely at this time that he composed for the administration's guidance his rhapsodic account of the limitless potential of the Red River cotton trade. He liked the idea of a joint attack on Port Hudson well enough, but the attack would have to wait because it would probably be May 10 before he could get there. When he heard this Grant correctly concluded that Banks' estimate of time was unrealistic: in the end it was a solid fortnight before the man could even leave Alexandria, and it was between three and four weeks before he actually got over to the Mississippi and established the siege of Port Hudson.[4]

By this time Grant had nothing at all to spare—not supplies, nor time, nor patience either—and being thus unencumbered he began to move fast. He pulled his army a few miles farther south, coming back to the river nearly opposite the Mississippi hamlet of Bruinsburg, eight or ten miles below Grand Gulf, and he had Porter bring his steamers down past the batteries. Then the men went piling aboard the transports, cheering mightily—they began to sense that they would be on top of the game once they crossed the river—and by April 30 Grant had his vanguard in the state of Mississippi, all of McClernand's corps either across or crossing and the head of McPherson's corps coming up behind. The profound gamble of the Vicksburg campaign was about to begin, but by his later testimony Grant felt now that the worst was over. Where so much had gone wrong the one thing that mattered had gone right: "I was on dry ground on the same side of the river with the enemy."[5] It is possible that this was about all he really cared about from the beginning.

As he moved inland from Bruinsburg, Grant was much helped by the rocketing advance, fifty miles to the east, of a slim column of Union cavalry whose movement he had ordered weeks earlier. This column was led, improbably but well, by Colonel B. F. Grierson, by profession a bandmaster, a man who disliked and distrusted all horses but who nevertheless had become a first-rate cavalryman, with a good cavalryman's eccentricities; where Jeb Stuart kept a banjo player on his staff Grierson kept a jew's-harp in his pocket, and he was doing a job now that would have been much to Stuart's taste. He had left Tennessee on April 17, and he came slicing down the eastern corridor of the state of Mississippi with some 950 Illinois and Iowa troopers, his chief mission being to stir up trouble and confuse the Rebels. He did this admirably. Pemberton was badly short of cavalry and had no way to tell what Grierson was up to, where he was going or who might be following him; one result was that a whole division of Pemberton's infantry (which would have been most useful right now at Bruinsburg) was tied up along the line of the Mobile & Ohio Railroad, and Pemberton confessed that in the general confusion it was impossible for him to get reliable information of any Yankee movements. Grierson reached the Federal lines at Baton Rouge on May 2 after a six-hundred-mile ride that had cost him no more than twenty-four men and had materially improved Grant's chances at the moment when the over-all strategic plan had to be changed in mid-air.[6]

To add to Pemberton's perplexities Grant sent special orders to Sherman, whose corps was still at Milliken's Bend; and so on April 30 and May 1 Sherman took ten regiments and some light gunboats up the Yazoo, opened a showy bombardment, put troops ashore, and acted for all the world as if he planned to attack the northern bastion of Pemberton's line at Snyder's Bluff, eight miles above Vicksburg. For the few hours that mattered, this shadow-boxing was persuasive. The harassed Pemberton knew only that there were Yankees in eastern Mississippi, Yankees downriver at Bruinsburg, and Yankees here on his own back doorstep, all of them looking for trouble, and it seemed to him that if he massed men to strike at Grant Sherman would take Vicksburg. He waited for light, and by the time he saw where the real power lay it was too late. With nearly 50,000 men at his disposal he was able to put no more than 8000 at the first point of contact, near Bruinsburg, and since Grant had 23,000 there the 8000 were not nearly enough.

The Confederate commander who had those 8000 men facing Grant, Brigadier General John S. Bowen, was one of Pemberton's best officers, and he put up a good fight. He met Grant's advance on May 1 near Port Gibson, a few miles inland from Bruinsburg, and his men fought a rugged all-day battle there in a tough country of knobby hills and deep ravines; but he was dreadfully outnumbered, he sadly missed the troops that might have been with him but were not and by evening he had to retreat. He went north of the Big Black River, heading for Vicksburg, leaving the formidable works at Grand Gulf unattended. While McClernand's men saw Bowen across the Big Black, Grant himself went into Grand Gulf long enough to get a bath and a change of clothing on one of Porter's warships and to send a message to Sherman saying that all plans had been changed.

Originally, a fragment of Grant's army was to make a
feint behind the line of the Big Black. Now the whole army
was going to go there, the feint was going to be the big blow
of the campaign, and Sherman must bring his command
downstream and join the main body as fast as he could.
Sherman protested. He had never liked this move to begin
with, it seemed to him that by marching into the middle of
Mississippi Grant was taking a fearful risk, and he pointed
out that the road from Milliken's Bend down to Hard Times
was so bad that Grant could never in the world supply his
army that way. Grant replied that he did not propose to
supply his army that way. He would bring down enough
hardtack, coffee, and salt to get by on and for everything
else he would use what his men had in their haversacks and
what they could take from the farmers of Mississippi, whose
barns and smokehouses were packed with things soldiers
could eat. For a wagon train he rounded up all of the farm
carts, carriages, buckboards, and drays he could find in the
neighborhood, impressing horses, mules, and oxen to pull
them and warning his corps commanders that the troops
might have to get along on meager rations for a while. Then,
on May 7, Sherman's corps having arrived, the army began
to move.[7]

When he moved Grant turned away from Vicksburg and
went northeast behind the line of the Big Black, heading in
the general direction of Jackson, the state capital, forty-five
miles due east of Vicksburg. He knew that if the Confederacy sent Pemberton any kind of help the help was
bound to come by way of Jackson, because the only railroad line that came into Vicksburg went through Jackson;
if Grant could break that line or occupy Jackson Pemberton would be isolated, left tied to the weighty fortress
of Vicksburg as to a millstone. There was only one problem.
Whatever Grant did must be done quickly.

It must be done quickly because the Confederacy was working desperately to build up a relieving force at Jackson. Joe
Johnston in person was hurrying to the place to take general
charge, some 6000 soldiers had already been concentrated
there and more were on the way, and before long Johnston
might make Pemberton too strong to be beaten. When the
last element of Sherman's corps came up Grant would have
a field army of rather more than 40,000 men, and he must

make his campaign with this force because he could not hope for reinforcements until he got back to the Mississippi River. In addition he faced the same factor Lee faced in Pennsylvania: an army that is mostly living off of the country must at all costs keep moving. Grant warned McPherson that "we must fight the enemy before our rations fail," told him to gather food wherever he could find it, and added: "Upon one occasion you made two days rations last seven; we may have to do the same thing again."[8] It was going to be all or nothing. If he moved fast and made no blunders, Grant could probably destroy Pemberton's army; if not he would probably lose his own.

But it was Pemberton who felt the pressure. For weeks this unhappy general had been unable to see what his enemies were trying to do. He knew only that they seemed to threaten him in half a dozen places at once. Now his lack of cavalry was a cruel handicap. Grant was moving but it was impossible to learn what his objective was; Pemberton felt obliged to keep strong forces at all the places where Grant might cross the Big Black, lest there be a sudden thrust at Vicksburg, and he also felt compelled to protect the railroad line to Jackson; it seemed necessary to keep infantry off to the north, as well, because he believed that Federal infantry was marching down from Memphis and Corinth; meanwhile, he wanted to fight Grant in the open field if he could but it was hard to assemble an adequate force. The orders from his superiors were in conflict. Johnston telegraphed him to use every man in his command to strike at Grant, even if he had to evacuate Vicksburg to do it, arguing that Vicksburg could easily be reoccupied once Grant was beaten. President Davis had telegraphed that he must hold on to Vicksburg and Port Hudson at all costs. As Pemberton cautiously moved east along the railroad line, crossing the Big Black in the vicinity of Edwards Station, he could bring with him hardly more than 18,000 men.[9]

Not enough. Grant left McClernand's corps nearby to hold Pemberton in check and marched the rest of his army off to Jackson, knocking away a Confederate brigade that tried to check him at the town of Raymond and driving on through a rainstorm on May 14 to strike the field works that protected the capital. Johnston had reached the city only the day before, his winter-long pessimism still strong in him; now he could do no more than fight a delaying action, and before the day ended he drew his inadequate force off in a retreat to the northward, sending word to Pemberton to pitch into the Federal rear if he saw a chance. Greatly pleased with themselves, Grant's soldiers marched into Jackson, seizing cannon and military stores and hoisting the United States flag over the statehouse, and that night when Grant checked in at a hotel he was given the room Johnston had just vacated.[10]

He did not linger there very long. Next day, leaving Sherman's corps to destroy bridges, railroad installations and military equipment—a task the westerners performed so vigorously that they destroyed a good part of the town as well—Grant took McPherson's corps back to rejoin McClernand, with Sherman under orders to follow as soon as adequate destruction had been accomplished.

Luckless Pemberton, meanwhile, had been edging to his right, hoping to force a Federal retreat by cutting Grant's supply line, cruelly handicapped by the fact that that line no longer existed. Now he got a new message from Johnston, telling him to circle around north of the railroad and join up with Johnston's force; but Johnston's courier had been corrupted by Yankee gold and Grant had a copy of the order, and as Pemberton tried to make the march Grant lunged at him and brought him to battle, on May 16, on an uneven plateau known as Champion's Hill, a few miles east of Edwards Station.

The battle was sharp, hard, and decisive. McClernand's leading division, under Brigadier General Alvin P. Hovey, charged across the hill, was driven back, returned to the assault, settled down to a wearing fire fight, and before the day ended lost a third of its numbers; Hovey called Champion's Hill "a hill of death" and wrote, "I never saw fighting like this." During the middle of the day the Confederates held their ground, but in the afternoon McPherson's corps came into action and stormed in hard on the Confederate left, and Pemberton's army was forced back—step by step, at first, and then in a retreat that finally became a rout. In many units organization was lost, hundreds of men left their commands and took off for Vicksburg as best they could, officers galloped frantically about trying to find their regiments, artillerists were looking for their guns, and there was so much confusion that Loring's entire division lost touch with the rest of the army, drifted off to the south, and finally circled all the way around Grant's army and stumbled off to join up with Johnston. One Confederate officer confessed that what he saw on Champion's Hill "made it look like what I have read of Bull Run," another said that dispirited soldiers chattered wildly that Yankee-born Pemberton "has sold Vicksburg," and Pemberton himself admitted that his army's morale was temporarily shattered. He got his men back to Vicksburg as best he could, leaving a shaky rear-guard to cover the crossing of the Big Black River. Not counting Loring's missing division, he had lost 3800 men and twenty-seven guns, and his force was so disorganized that it needed to sort itself out behind the fortifications.[11]

Grant's men paid for their victory with 2400 casualties of their own, and Grant had not quite done what he had hoped to do, which was to crush Pemberton's army utterly and then brush the fragments aside and take his own men into Vicksburg unopposed. At the same time, the battle had been decisive. On the day after Champion's Hill was fought Grant's vanguard came up to the Big Black River and overwhelmed Pemberton's rear-guard with little difficulty. Then, with Sherman's corps in the lead, the army marched toward Vicksburg as fast as it could, and before nightfall on May 18 it reached the stretch of ground that Grant needed more than he needed anything else in the world—the heights that ran north from Vicksburg to Haynes' Bluff overlooking the Yazoo River.

As long as Pemberton held that chain of hills, no Federal force could approach his stronghold from the upper Mississippi; indeed, it had been the Confederate grip on this area that forced Grant to make the long march by way of Hard Times, Bruinsburg, Jackson, and Champion's Hill, because everything his army had done since the end of March had really been keyed to his need to possess these few square miles. Compelled to man his trench lines on the outskirts of Vicksburg, Pemberton found that he had to evacuate Haynes' Bluff and everything that went with it, and when Sherman's troops spread out over these heights Grant's Vicksburg campaign became a success. Now he had no more worries about his line of communications; whole fleets of steamboats could come up the Yazoo and dock here in perfect security, and he could get all of the reinforcements, food, and ammunition he needed.

Among the men who realized what this would do for Grant was General Johnston, who telegraphed Pemberton to cut his losses and get out.

"If Haynes' Bluff be untenable Vicksburg is of no value and cannot be held," Johnston wrote. "If therefore you are invested in Vicksburg you must ultimately surrender. Under such circumstances, instead of losing both troops and place you must if possible save the troops. If it is not too late, evacuate Vicksburg and its dependencies and march to the northeast."[12]

It was too late. Pemberton did not think his army now was in shape for vigorous activity in the open field, and besides Grant's army blocked every road of escape. What with his battle losses, the absence of Loring's division and his growing sick list, Pemberton found that he could put no more than 18,500 muskets into line. Grant had more than twice that number facing him, with strong reinforcements on the way. Pemberton could only hold his ground and hope for the best.[13]

Meanwhile, Grant was crowding him. As soon as Sherman's corps had taken possession of the northern heights, Grant ordered it to move down on May 19 and assault the left end of the Confederate trench line, on the theory that Pemberton's shaken troops might not be in shape to resist. The theory was quite wrong. Even a badly demoralized army could recover its fighting edge quickly if it could act entirely on the defensive behind good fortifications, and the demoralization of Pemberton's soldiers had been no more than skin-deep anyway. Sherman's assault was repulsed; with more than a thousand Federal casualties.

Grant was not entirely convinced, and he hoped to avoid a long siege if possible, so he ordered a larger attack by the entire army on May 22, with careful preparation, a sharp preliminary bombardment, picked storming parties and elaborate synchronization of the general officers' watches. It went no better than Sherman's attack had gone and it was beaten back with heavy losses, many of which occurred because McClernand believed that his men had cracked the Confederate line, and called for a renewal of the offensive after it had visibly failed. When the day ended Grant had to admit that these works were too strong and too stoutly held to be carried by assault. He put his men to work with pick and shovel to develop a strong encircling line of their own (if they could not break in they could certainly keep the Confederates from breaking out) and he detached a force to the upper part of the Big Black to keep Johnston at arm's length. Not long afterward he relieved the unhappy McClernand of his command, giving his army corps to Major General E. O. C. Ord. Meanwhile he brought up heavy guns, and had the navy bring up mortars in barges, to begin a long, methodical, and relentless bombardment of the Confederate lines and the city these lines protected.

Pemberton was almost entirely helpless now; he could prolong the agony but he could do no more. His lines were so long and his numbers relatively so few that his soldiers had to stay in the trenches night and day, week after week after week, under the blistering sun and in heavy rain, without so much as a chance to get out and stretch their legs. They were locked up in their own fortress, and they had nothing to sustain them except the hope that some day Johnston would break Grant's line and rescue them.

Johnston was building up his army, battalion by battalion, but Grant's army was being built up faster; still too weak to fight, Johnston had to realize that each week increased the enemy's strength more than it increased his, and early in June he considered failure inevitable. To a brother officer he wrote: "There are odds against us here such as Napoleon never won against. The only imaginable hope is in the perpetration by Grant of some extravagant blunder, and there is no ground for such a hope."[14]

In Vicksburg soldiers and civilians settled down to endure the siege, and found that it contained unexpected elements. A Vicksburg woman discovered that her thoughts went where they had never gone before: "I have never understood before the full force of these questions—what shall we eat? what shall we drink? and wherewithal shall we be clothed?" Many people ate mule meat, and a Missouri soldier stoutly held that "if you did not know it you could hardly tell the difference, when cooked, between it and beef." An officer said that living in a besieged city was a strange experience, because it was so hard to realize that there was no way to communicate with anyone on the outside; he believed that if the affair went on much longer "a building will have to be arranged for the accommodation of maniacs," because the constant tension was driving people out of their minds.[15]

Constant tension, plus shelling: not unbroken shellfire, like that which precedes an attack on a military position, but a day-and-night business that was broken by intervals of silence but that never really let up. Some people moved into caves in the sides of cliffs, finding security amid discomfort; others discovered that it was possible to put up with anything and lived and slept at home even though a 13-inch shell might obliterate home and everyone in it at any moment. These big shells came from Porter's mortar boats, and there were two opinions regarding them. Some people considered them by far the most demoralizing weapon the Yankees had, but others said they really did little harm, and weren't even very frightening once you got used to them. One citizen who had a good vegetable garden in his back yard complained that he lost sleep, not because of shelling but because he had to stay up nights to keep hungry soldiers from stealing all he was growing. A woman reflected that the oddest thing of all was that as far as nature was concerned this was just another spring—birds were singing, building nests, and raising other birds, flower gardens were full of bright blossoms, and the air was all scented with the odor of jasmine and honeysuckle.[16] . . . People in besieged cities have talked much this way, probably, since the days of Jericho.

At Jericho the walls finally came tumbling down. Here at Vicksburg the walls held, but the people inside the walls had had all they could take. Johnston was never going to be able to break Grant's lines. Food supplies in Vicksburg were running low and the defending soldiers were close to exhaustion from unbroken days and nights in the cramped rifle pits. Grant's engineers were bringing the Federal trenches closer and closer to the Confederate works, digging tunnels and planting mines to blow up strong points, and when Pemberton polled his generals he found none who believed that his men were in shape to fight their way out of the trap. At last, on July 3, the flag of truce went out, and Pemberton stiffly conferred with Grant about terms.

Grant tried the unconditional surrender approach, found that Pemberton was not ready for it, and concluded at last to take what he could get—which unquestionably was enough. Pemberton was surrendering all he had, the sole qualification being that his soldiers would be released on parole instead of being taken north to prison camps. Reflecting that most of Pemberton's men were so disheartened that they would probably ignore their paroles and go home, and that to ship 31,000 prisoners up the river would have tied up a great deal of shipping anyway, Grant accepted this proviso, persuaded himself that it was even an advantage to the Federals, and on Independence Day marched his troops into Vicksburg.

The news went downstream to Port Hudson, where Banks for several weeks had been laying siege and making fruitless assaults, and on July 8 that place also surrendered. The Mississippi was open at last, and Banks assured Mrs. Banks that the Confederates had received a mortal wound: "We have taken from them the power to establish an independent government. It can never be done between the Mississippi and the Atlantic. You can tell your friends that the Confederacy is an impossibility."[17]

2. The Notion of Equality

FOR A FEW DAYS Richmond lived on rumors.

According to one report, Lee's army had been practically destroyed and nothing remained but disorganized fugitives trying frantically to get back to Virginia, hard-pressed by aggressive foes; which led one devoutly patriotic woman to lament that "a single day had served to crush the hopes of a speedy peace and to cloud the horizon of the future." A more welcome story asserted that it was really Meade's army that had been destroyed (as a detail it held that Lee had taken 40,000 prisoners) and a member of the home guard assured an army friend that Grant and Banks would doubtless be beaten before long and that "the beginning of the end approaches." But by the end of the second week in July most of the truth was at hand, and although neither the best nor the worst of the tall tales from Pennsylvania was verified it was painfully clear that in the west there had been genuine calamity. The last grip on the Mississippi was broken and the western Confederacy was a fragment; and to make matters worse, Federal Rosecrans was finally on the move. Bragg in fact had to retreat south of the Tennessee River, leaving all of central Tennessee in the hands of the Federals and bringing the war down to the northern border of Georgia. A War Department official called the past week "one of unexampled disaster since the war began," and confided to his diary: "We are *almost exhausted*."[1]

President Davis was not quite sure whether the ruin had been brought on by fate or by human incompetence, but he wasted little time on post-mortem investigations. Confessing privately that the losses in the west had left him "in the depths of gloom," he looked resolutely to the future. To General Edmund Kirby Smith, now commanding all Confederate forces west of the Mississippi, he sent a warning that Smith's command would have to be largely self-sufficient from now on. Smith must play a lone hand; he must develop mining and manufacturing resources, set up a rolling mill, provide his own munitions and supplies, if possible build ironclads to keep the invaders from using the western rivers; in general he must get along with little or no help from Richmond. The President believed that "we are now in the darkest hour of our political existence," and he urged Senator R. W. Johnson of Arkansas (whose people were showing a dismaying tendency to talk about making terms with the Yankees) to persuade his constituents that "it would be mad, suicidal for any state of the Confederacy to seek safety by separation from the rest."[2]

Mr. Davis believed that he had done all he could to avert the western collapse, and later in the summer he wrote frankly to an old friend: "The disasters in Mississippi were both great and unexpected to me. I had thought that the troops sent to the state, added to those already there, made a force large enough to accomplish the destruction of Grant's army. That no such result followed may have been the effect of mismanagement, or it may have been that it was unattainable." An investigation was under way, but since the disasters had already occurred "it would afford me but little satisfaction to know that they resulted from bad generalship and were not inevitable." He had to confess that many people were looking for scapegoats, criticizing the President and his generals for letting bad things happen, and he dwelt on the fact in a letter to General Lee: "Misfortune often develops secret foes and oftener still makes men complain. It is comfortable to hold some one responsible for one's discomfort."[3]

Among the discomforted was General Beauregard, against whose stronghold at Charleston the Federals were about to open a new attack, heavier than the one made earlier, with army and navy together going all-out to capture the city. At the beginning of July Beauregard wrote to Joe Johnston, complaining that the government had tried to take some more of his inadequate forces away from him and asking bluntly: "Of what earthly use is that 'raid' of Lee's army going into Maryland, in violation of all the principles of war? Is it going to end the struggle, take Washington or save the Mississippi valley?" It would have been much better, said Beauregard, if Lee had remained on the defensive in Virginia and had sent Longstreet's corps to Tennessee to enable Bragg to defeat Rosecrans.[4]

This, to be sure, had not been done, and now Rosecrans threatened to inflict another reverse as bad as the one at Vicksburg. By the loss of the Mississippi the Confederacy had been cut in half; Rosecrans' advance seemed likely to bisect what remained, and the War Department official who had been so discouraged in July grew even gloomier in August. Comparing the Confederacy of 1861 with the Confederacy of 1863, he wrote: "Nearly half of the whole area is in the hands of the enemy or outside of our lines. We have never substantially recovered any territory once lost, never retaken any important strategic point once occupied." The confirmed pessimist Colonel Lucius B. Northrop, commissary general, notified the War Department that the meat ration for troops would have to be cut to one-quarter pound daily—except for soldiers actually on the march, who could get half a pound. The reason, said Colonel Northrop, was that no more supplies could come from beyond the Mississippi, or from the states of Mississippi and Tennessee, or from parts of Alabama and Georgia, and if the army meat ration was not cut there would be no meat at all for the Negro slaves. Loss of territory was beginning to mean loss of ability to feed the fighters and the workers.[5]

Bragg did his best to get foodstuffs out of Tennessee while he could. The central part of the state was raising this year the largest crop of wheat it had ever had, although Bragg's officers had conscripted farmers so rigorously that as the grain ripened there was no one to harvest it. Rosecrans and his Yankee host were not far away, but they were quiet and as long as they remained so Bragg was willing to beat his spears into pruning hooks; so in June he detailed whole regiments for work in the wheat fields, sending them from farm to farm and encouraging the farm women to provide harvesters' dinners for them, and they brought in so much wheat that he proudly predicted that "in a little while we shall have an abundance of flour, an article of luxury for the last four months."[6] His reapers finished their work barely in time; less than a week after Bragg recorded this achievement Rosecrans began his advance.

In the opinion of General Halleck he did not begin a second too soon; an opinion heartily endorsed by Rosecrans' own chief of staff, Brigadier General James A. Garfield. All spring Rosecrans clung to his strange idea that he ought not to move against Bragg until Vicksburg fell because if he made Bragg retreat Bragg would simply go to Mississippi, join Johnston, and fall upon Grant; he seems also to have felt that his own army was the North's last reserve, to be saved until all other points were secure. Early in June he approved a detailed plan for advance, drawn up by Garfield, and then conferred with his principal generals and found that most of them did not think Bragg had sent any troops to Mississippi, doubted that he could be attacked to advantage, and considered an early Federal advance inadvisable. Approval of the advance was cancelled. Garfield gave Rosecrans his own vigorous dissent, and wrote privately that he felt "a sense of disappointment and mortification almost akin to shame"; and to his fellow Ohioan, Secretary Chase, Garfield wrote that Rosecrans' Army of the Cumberland was probably the best army the country ever had but that it lacked "that live and earnest determination to . . . make its power felt in crushing the shell of the rebellion."[7]

Two weeks later, however, on June 24, the advance did begin, and the Rosecrans who had been so inert for six months, endlessly discovering new reasons why he ought not to move, suddenly began to operate with daring, skill, and energy. His army had been resting in Murfreesboro since the beginning of the year, and a few miles to the south Bragg's troops held the gaps in the hills where the roads from Murfreesboro led south; and when the Federal army began to move there was a pelting rain that was to last the better part of a fortnight. Holding a strong numerical advantage in infantry, Rosecrans feinted with his right and then sent Thomas and Crittenden off through the hills fifteen miles to the eastward. With a minimum of fighting, this force got around Bragg's right flank and swung in behind the gaps in a way that made Bragg order a quick reconcentration at Tullahoma, a dozen miles to the rear. It developed that this was not far enough. Rosecrans kept moving, his infantry stumping manfully along roads that were deep in mud, and Bragg found that he also must move. On July 1 he left Tullahoma and headed south, and about the time Grant got into Vicksburg Bragg's army was below the Tennessee River, in and around Chattanooga, while Rosecrans halted his own army fifty miles to the northwest.

It seemed in Washington that Rosecrans might well have kept going a bit longer, and Secretary Stanton sent him a stimulating telegram: WE HAVE JUST RECEIVED INFORMATION THAT VICKSBURG IS SURRENDERED TO GRANT ON THE 4TH OF JULY. LEE'S ARMY OVERTHROWN, GRANT VICTORIOUS. YOU AND YOUR NOBLE ARMY NOW HAVE THE CHANCE TO GIVE THE FINISHING BLOW TO THE REBELLION. WILL YOU NEGLECT THE CHANCE? Rosecrans felt that the needle was being applied unjustly, and he retorted that Mr. Stanton must have failed to observe that "this noble army has driven the Rebels from middle Tennessee," adding a needle-thrust of his own: "I beg in behalf of this army that the War Department may not overlook so great an event because it is not written in letters of blood."[8]

It was true that he had won much at small cost; true, also, that he had turned a good phrase; but he was talking to the wrong people. The President and the War Department were grimly willing to have this summer's chapter written in letters of blood if it could just be the last chapter, ending the whole story of fighting and killing forever. When they talked of finishing off the rebellion they talked of what they considered a real possibility: they believed the war could be ended now, this month, if generals pressed their advantages. The elation Mr. Lincoln felt when Lee was repulsed at Gettysburg owed less to the removal of a threat than to the conviction that Lee's army was retreating with its neck in a noose. On July 7, Halleck notified Meade that Vicksburg had fallen and that the President had said: "Now, if General Meade can complete his work, so gloriously prosecuted thus far, by the literal or substantial destruction of Lee's army, the rebellion will be over." The President was in no mood to rejoice over the recovery of lost territory. He wanted Confederate armies wiped out.

The President's feeling of frustration began when he read a congratulatory order Meade issued after Gettysburg, inviting the army to keep up the good work and to "drive the invader from our soil." To Secretary John Hay Mr. Lincoln exploded angrily: "Will our generals never get that idea out of their heads? The whole country is our soil." (The Union was endangered, not because Lee's army was in Pennsylvania, but because Lee's army existed at all.) As Lee went back to the Potomac, Meade cautiously following, Mr. Lincoln grew more impatient, and when newspaperman Noah Brooks left to visit Meade's headquarters the President confessed his fear that "something would happen" to save Lee's army from annihilation. On July 14 news came that Lee's army had indeed escaped, crossing the Potomac at night on an improvised pontoon bridge and returning to Virginia bruised but alive. Brooks wrote that the President's "grief and anger were something sorrowful to behold," and Hay remembered the President saying: "We had them within our grasp. We had only to stretch forth our hands and they were ours." Mr. Lincoln wrote a sharp letter to Meade, then soberly concluded not to sign it and left it in a pigeonhole; but enough of his discontent got through, via Halleck, to make the testy Meade offer his resignation. Halleck calmed the general, the resignation was not accepted, Meade was given promotion to brigadier general in the Regular Army, and on the surface all was well. But it was not a good time for General Rosecrans to explain that he had induced Bragg to leave Tennessee without a fight.[9]

Mr. Lincoln may have wanted too much. Meade's army had had about all it could take. It had marched hard and fought hard, thousands of men lacked shoes, some of the best regiments were reduced to sixty or eighty men, and an Iron Brigade colonel said that the campaign now ending was by far the worst the Army of the Potomac ever experienced. Meade himself was living on nothing much more than a stern sense of duty. On July 8 he wrote to Mrs. Meade: "From the time I took command until today, now over ten days, I have not changed my clothes have not had a regular nights rest & many nights not a wink of sleep and for several days did not even wash my face & hands—no regular food and all the time in a state of mental anxiety. Indeed, I think I have lived as much in this time as in the last 30 years." He did not honestly feel that he had won a great victory; the most he would say was that "Lee was defeated in his efforts to destroy my army." He hoped to overtake Lee and defeat him, but in all of its career the Army of the Potomac had never yet made an energetic pursuit and it was hard to begin now. Meade was still new in command, some of his lieutenants were second-raters, the army was tired and he was tired, and almost in despair he wrote: "I *suffer* very much from anxiety & responsibility—I can get no reliable information of the enemy and have to grope my way in the dark—it is wonderful the difficulty I have in obtaining correct information— I *want Corps Comdrs*."

When Lee at last reached the Potomac near Williamsport, and dug in to await attack while his engineers were preparing a crossing, Meade found the Confederates well posted in a strong position. He consulted his corps commanders, found that hardly any of them felt that the army ought to attack, studied the situation at more length, made up his mind to attack anyway—and learned next day that Lee had crossed the river during the night and early morning, and that the last chance to strike a finishing blow was gone. On top of this came Halleck's messages indicating that the President and the general-in-chief were dissatisfied, and Meade told his wife: "It is hard after working as I have done and accomplishing as much to be found fault with for not doing impossibilities."[10]

It was hard, and probably it was unjust: the one fact that mattered was that Lee had got away. The Army of Northern Virginia had not been taken off of the board, and Mr. Lincoln was no more interested in the reasons why it had not been removed than Mr. Davis was interested in the reasons why Vicksburg had been surrendered. In point of fact, the Army of Northern Virginia had done well to get away at all. It had been hurt worse than Meade's army had been hurt and it had been weaker to begin with; all of the reasons that kept the Federal army from making a rapid pursuit rested on this army with equal weight; and yet somehow, on the march back to Virginia, Lee's army had found the extra ounce of energy that enabled it to move quickly in spite of exhaustion. (One Confederate soldier remembered, with feeling: "For 96 hours we were almost constantly on our feet, and during all that time I don't think there was an intermission of 4 hours all put together when it was not raining. Of course there was no time to cook rations & the boys went on about two biscuits and no meat a day.")[11]

Lee himself was not downcast. Before he went south across the Potomac he wrote to Mrs. Lee unemotionally: "You will have learned before this reaches you that our success at Gettysburg was not as great as reported. In fact, that we failed to drive the enemy from his position & that our army withdrew to the Potomac." Three days later he gave her a slightly more detailed appraisal of the campaign: "The army has returned to Virg., dear Mary. Its return is rather sooner than I had originally contemplated but having accomplished what I purposed on leaving the Rappk. viz: relieving the valley of the presence of the enemy & drawing his army north of the Potomac, I determined to recross the latter river." A few days later he assured her: "The army has labored hard, endured much & behaved nobly. It has accomplished all that could have been reasonably expected." To President Davis he said that the army "in my opinion achieved under the guidance of the Most High a general success, though it did not win a victory."[12]

Lee was no man to offer excuses or to gloze an unpleasant reality. He was saying nothing that was not justified by what he had said before the campaign began: he had done about what he expected to do, and although his army was coming back sooner and leaner than had been anticipated it had pushed the war out of the homeland and had disrupted all Yankee plans for the campaign in Virginia.[13] If it had not won a victory it had not suffered a shattering defeat: its losses had been desolating, but General Lee was quite as willing as Mr. Lincoln to read letters of blood so long as the record thus written was favorable. He saw the situation now, as a matter of fact, much as Mr. Lincoln saw it: whatever the Federals had won at Gettysburg might mean a good deal less than the fact that the Army of Northern Virginia remained in being, able to go on with the war.

The war was not over. It might have ended this summer, but instead it had made almost a new beginning; because it had not ended it was going to cut more deeply than ever before, plowing new forces to the surface and forcing men to deal with them as best they could. It would either create or reveal its significance as it went along, and a few days after Gettysburg Mr. Lincoln groped for a clearer understanding of it.

On July 7 a jubilant crowd, fortified by brass bands and by memories of Independence Day and military victories, came to the White House to serenade him, and he made a brief impromptu reply. It was not one of his more notable utterances. (Oddly, this veteran of political stump speaking was rarely at his best when he spoke without careful preparation.) Yet he did drop one thought that had long echoes. He said that the Declaration of Independence was worth especial remembrance this year because the Republic was coping with "a gigantic Rebellion, at the bottom of which is an effort to overthrow the principle that all men are created equal." He went on to make some homespun remarks about notable things that had happened on July 4 in other years, then returned to this theme, referring to Confederate armies as "the cohorts of those who oppose the declaration that all men are created equal."[14]

The war was growing, with a hard logic of its own. First it had been a fight to restore the Union, then it became a fight to destroy slavery, and now apparently it was a fight to establish the equality of all classes of men. This was a definition not of war but of a general overturn; a social reconstruction for the North as well as for the South, more than most men had bargained for. As a grim footnote there came, less than a week later, the draft riots in New York City.

The draft riots were based upon ignorance, misery, fear, and the inability of one class of men to understand another class; upon the fact that there really were "classes of men" in classless American society. The riots loosed war's violence on a city where violence was supposed to be a private matter between the police and the underworld. The rioters had malignant prejudice, and those rioted against had another prejudice equally malignant; if the lynchings and the burnings and the pitched battles in city streets meant anything they meant that this notion of equality was going to be hard to live with.

The draft law itself was at the root of the trouble. Built into it was a rule that a man with money could not be compelled to go into the army. All men had to register, of course, but one whose name was drawn could get release from service (at least until the next drawing) if he could pay a commutation fee of $300. He could get permanent release if, spending more than this, he hired a substitute to go soldiering for him. If he did neither of these things he must serve, under penalty of being shot as a deserter if he ran away.

To the factory hands and casual workers of New York, already pressed by a seasonal drop in employment, and by the fact that the war had raised prices much more effectively than it had raised wages, $300 was a figure from dreamland—the better part of a year's income, more money than any wage-earner ever saw or hoped to see at one time. To make matters worse, these men had been told, month after month, that the war had been basely perverted into a fight to free the Negro slave—who, once freed, would unquestionably flood the Northern cities, take any work he could find at any wages he could get, and so deprive the white worker of the little he had now.

This made a mixture as explosive as a keg of black powder, and the explosion came in the Ninth Congressional District of New York, a district filled with Irish laborers almost all of whom were Democrats. In an office at Third Avenue and 46th Street, on July 13, a dutiful army officer and some clerks fed names into a drum and began to turn it. Someone threw a paving stone through the window, this range-finding shot was followed by a regular salvo, and then a crowd of angry men came in, officer and clerks fled for their lives, the police guard was beaten half to death, the draft office was set on fire, and in another hour the entire block had been burned; and the tumult began to spread all across the city, a political protest that quickly turned into a flaming race riot.

Men made furious because they might have to serve in an army that did not seem to be fighting for anything they themselves wanted found that their fury could be vented upon the Negroes who seemed to be at the bottom of all the trouble. Policemen were killed, the mayor's house was attacked, streetcar tracks were torn up, and authority of whatever kind was derided in any way possible; then a colored orphanage was burned, business houses employing Negroes were looted, and toward evening the uproar exploded into innumerable "small mobs chasing isolated Negroes as hounds would chase a fox." Negro fugitives caught by these mobs were hanged, or burned alive, or simply kicked and beaten to death. A number of policemen and private citizens died trying to prevent such lynchings, but the police were outnumbered and the militia could not be called out at once because most of it had been sent to Pennsylvania to repel invasion, and for three days the authorities could do little more than try to set some sort of limits to the area of violence.

Finally the business was tamped down. Archbishop John J. Hughes addressed a gathering of 5000 Irishmen, urging them to "keep out of the crowd where immortal souls are launched into eternity" and reminding them that their Ireland "has been the mother of heroes and poets, but never the mother of cowards," and his words had good effect. The draft act was suspended, not to be put back into operation until combat soldiers from the Army of the Potomac reached town to restore order, and the city authorities announced that municipal funds would pay the $300 commutation fee for any drafted man too poor to pay it himself. Police estimated that a thousand people had been killed or wounded (the accuracy of this estimate is in dispute to this day and apparently the figure was badly inflated) and guesses on property damage ranged from $400,000 to $2,500,000. The violence did end, at last, and good men who loved the Union could look about them and try to understand what had happened.[15]

True understanding did not come easily. Respectability was appalled by the Irish precisely as the Irish were appalled by the freed Negro. The eminent diarist, George Templeton Strong, expressed sheer horror at what he had seen. The mobs were made up of "the lowest Irish day laborers"; they were homogeneous, "every brute in the drove was pure Celtic hod-carrier or loafer"; he was aghast at "the fury of the low Irish women"; and he wound up by crying that "Rabbledom is not yet dethroned any more than its ally and instigator, Rebeldom." *Harper's Weekly* insisted that the draft act "is in reality fair, liberal and humane," shook its head at the excesses of "the operatives of this large city, who have never been forced to realize the obligations of citizenship," and concluded that the real trouble lay in the demagoguery of Democratic politicians and editors.[16] About all anyone could be sure of was that if equality came now it was going to have an immense impact.

3. Servants of the Guns

MORRIS ISLAND looked much like any other unused part of the South Carolina coast: a long stretch of sand caught between tacky green scrub and blue water, Atlantic Ocean on the east and flat reedy marshes not far to the west. It was made an island by a chain of pools and tidal creeks that cut it off from the mainland, its width varied from one hundred to one thousand yards, and it began at the entrance to Charleston Harbor and ran south three and one-half miles to Lighthouse Inlet. Nobody in the Civil War would have paid the least attention to Morris Island except for two facts: the main ship channel to Charleston ran parallel to its length a mile offshore, and the northern tip of the island was less than a mile from Fort Sumter.

Because these things were so, Morris Island in 1863 became the deadliest sandspit on earth. It was dug up by spades and by high explosive, almost sunk by sheer weight of metal and human misery, fought for with a maximum of courage and technical capacity and a minimum of strategic understanding; a place of no real consequence, lying at the end of one of those insane chains of war-time logic in which men step from one undeniable truth to another and so come at last to a land of crippling nonsense.

The logic that brought the war to Morris Island was above reproach.

The war had begun at Charleston. To win the war the Federal power must take Charleston. It could reach the city only by water and to do that its ships must pass Fort Sumter, which mounted heavy guns. Therefore, Fort Sumter (where there was a score to settle anyway) had to be destroyed. To destroy Fort Sumter (the navy's ironclads by themselves being unable to do it) it was necessary for the Federals to plant powerful siege guns on the nearest dry land, which of course was Morris Island. But the Confederates had already built a stout fort on Morris Island, three-quarters of a mile below the extreme northern tip—a construction of palmetto logs and sand bags, known as Battery Wagner, armed with one 10-inch Columbiad, half a dozen 32-pounders, and a few ordinary fieldpieces. No Federal siege guns could accomplish anything on Morris Island until this strong point had been silenced. *Therefore*—to win the war the Federals must capture Battery Wagner.

All of this had logical coherence, and yet it ended in sound and fury. Battery Wagner was at last taken, the Federal siege guns were installed, and Fort Sumter was pounded down to a heap of broken masonry in which guns could no longer be mounted, and so it could properly be said to have been destroyed; and when all of this had been done the Federals found that they were no closer to victory than when they began. Their best warships still could not get into the harbor, their infantry could not even set foot on the rock-pile that had once been Fort Sumter, the fabulous city where the dream of secession was born was slightly battered but still lovely, defiant, and unattainable—and months of desperate effort had not brought the war one glittering minute nearer to its end. The fighting died down, at last, and the army and navy fell into bitter argument about who was supposed to have been helping whom. (Was the army, all along, trying to take the forts so that the navy could take Charleston, or was the navy simply trying to help the army besiege and capture the forts?) All that had really been proved was that Charleston would fall when and if the Confederacy fell and not before.[1]

Washington read the wrong meaning into Admiral Du Pont's repulse in the spring. Du Pont had lost hardly any men, his damaged ships had been easily repaired (except for sunken *Keokuk*, which had been a cipher to begin with) and it did seem that a sterner admiral might succeed; especially if the army reduced Fort Sumter, so that the navy could remove the mine field that clogged the harbor entrance. The sternest admiral within reach looked like Andrew Foote, who had worked so well with General Grant on the western rivers and who understood not only hard fighting but co-operation with the army, and so Foote was given Du Pont's place. At the same time the army named a new commander, Major General Quincy A. Gillmore, an engineer experienced in siege operations. He replaced Major General David Hunter, who was a hero of the abolitionists but whose other qualifications were not readily definable. This would team up a naval slugger with an army technical expert, which looked like a winning combination.

Unfortunately, Foote had never really recovered from wounds received at Fort Donelson, and he had been at home for a year trying to build up his health. Now, late in June, after the new appointment was announced, he died. In his place the navy chose Rear Admiral John A. Dahlgren, expert on naval ordnance, inventor of the big, bottle-shaped Dahlgren gun which was the navy's favorite heavy-duty weapon. Like Gillmore, he was more specialist than fighting man, and he was a square-cornered type not always easy to get along with; and in any case he hoisted his flag as commander of the South Atlantic Blockading Squadron on July 6, and the joint operation against Charleston got under way.

It began smoothly enough on July 10 when the army crossed Lighthouse Inlet at the bottom of Morris Island and moved up toward Battery Wagner. An assault was made on the fort the next day and the Confederate defenders beat it off with ease, whereupon the army planted heavy guns where they would bear on the fort and the navy brought the monitors up the ship channel, and for the better part of a week there was a noisy, intermittent and rather ineffective shelling. On July 18 Gillmore was ready for a real attack. The navy came in closer, six ironclads and five wooden gunboats, the army's batteries added their own fire, and during the afternoon Battery Wagner received a pulverizing bombardment. The defenders took to the bombproofs for safety, Wagner's guns were silent, and from the Federal lines it looked as if the fort had been overwhelmed. After dark the firing was stopped and two Federal brigades formed line and moved up the sand to make the assault.

The infantry had been called on to do the impossible. Battery Wagner ran from side to side of the island, its parapet was protected by a deep dry moat, and in front of this the island narrowed so that the assaulting column had to pull in its flanks and form a compact mass that made an ideal target. The Confederates had suffered little from the long bombardment, and when they saw the infantry advancing in the starlight they ran to the parapet and opened a blistering fire of musketry and artillery. The Federals came on bravely enough, and some of them crossed the moat and scrambled up the sandy slopes and for a time there was hard hand-to-hand fighting in the night; then, at last, the infantry was driven away, the survivors drifted back to their starting point, and of some 5200 Federals engaged more than 1500 had been lost. The Confederate loss was comparatively unimportant, Battery Wagner was as tough as ever, and if the Federals wanted the place they would have to try something else.

One thing about this attack drew special attention. Among the leading regiments in the assault wave was the 54th Massachusetts, led by a well-born young Boston colonel named Robert Gould Shaw, and what made the 54th worth looking at was the fact that it was composed of Negroes, who were down here not only to take a fort but also to prove something about themselves. They took no fort, but it appeared that they did prove something, which is to say that they got up on the fort and stayed there until they were thoroughly shot to pieces, Colonel Shaw and his Negro orderly sergeant dying side by side on the parapet. A Confederate defender wrote that Shaw was "as brave a colonel as ever lived," and said that the men he led were "as fine-looking a set as I ever saw—large, strong, muscular fellows." Anti-slavery folk in the North came to feel that the whole affair had been no more than a fight between Negro soldiers and the Southern Confederacy, which led some of Gillmore's disgruntled Federals to insist that the fort would have been taken if the 54th had not given way at the crucial moment; and in any case a great many dead men of both races were given shallow graves in the sand just outside the fort, to illustrate that distressing idea of equality. A newspaper correspondent closed his account by saying that "there was terrible fighting to get into the fort, and terrible fighting to get out of it."[2]

The assault having failed, the Federals must go by the book, and in a case like this the book called for siege warfare. So the Federals began to dig long trenches to edge nearer to the fort, setting up batteries by night, raining missiles on the fort all day long, digging more trenches after darkness came. Thousands of men cowered in shallow sand pits under hot sunlight, and sharpshooters on each side took a steady toll of men who did not crouch low enough. On the monitors, which came in day after day to hammer the fort, living conditions were all but unendurable, with hatches all closed and the foul air inside like that of an oven; Admiral Dahlgren, who insisted on leading the monitors in person, was worn almost to the point of exhaustion and wrote despairingly that "the worst of this place is that one only stops getting weaker. One does not grow stronger." Day after day, members of his crews collapsed and had to be sent away, and the admiral was especially irritated when the Navy Department chose this time to forbid further issuance of the grog ration.

Inside Battery Wagner it was worst of all. Most of the garrison spent the day in the bombproofs, ill-ventilated cellars that were even hotter and steamier than the inside of the monitors, made still worse by the fact that they also served as hospitals for all of the wounded men. (Since most casualties were caused by artillery fire, some of the wounds were fearful.) Each evening when darkness brought an end to the firing the uninjured men would come out, look at the wreckage the shells had created, and conclude that the place could not be held any longer. Then, all night, they would work with shovels and sand bags, restoring parapet and rifle pits and traverses, so that by morning the fort once more would be defensible. The unending torrent of shells tore up the shallow sand pits where the men killed in the July 18 fight had been buried, scattering horrible fragments all over everything, and the air became almost too sickening to breathe; the shallow wells that were Battery Wagner's water supply became polluted and drinking water had to be brought by night in kegs from Charleston. Each day the garrison grew weaker and the Northern siege lines came closer, each day the fort looked less and less like a fort and more like an uneven mound of earth, and it went on week after week, from July into September, the bombardment growing worse each day, as if the whole war had turned into a struggle for possession of this poor sand hill.[3]

Yet if the war had come to a focus here the focal point had been oddly chosen, for Battery Wagner ceased to matter long before it fell. As the Federal lines came nearer, Gillmore began to build new batteries for long-range Parrott rifles, arranging them so that they could fire past Wagner and strike Sumter itself, and as these came into action the lesson learned earlier at Fort Pulaski, outside of Savannah, was proved true: rifled guns of sufficient caliber could destroy any brick or stone wall ever built. Day after day the big rifles gouged into Sumter's walls, bringing the masonry down in rumbling cascades and raising a choking cloud of brick dust, pulverized mortar and powder smoke over the wreckage. Night after night Beauregard's engineers kept a working force busy making repairs, piling up tons of sand behind the rubble, taking guns ashore and filling in the casemates they had occupied, until at last the part of the fort that faced Morris Island was little more than a long rampart of earth and broken stone, forty feet high and twenty-five feet thick. There was a week of this, and then a week of bombardment by the monitors, and by the end of August Sumter had only one gun in action. Meanwhile Battery Wagner's torment continued. Gillmore mounted searchlights to play on the beaches at night so that Confederate reinforcements could be driven away. Twice the Federals tried to storm a low sandy ridge that seemed to "command" the Confederate battery, and twice they were driven back; then at last they took the ridge, all of the guns in Sumter were silenced, and the ironclads steamed up once more to pound Battery Wagner anew.

Soldiers and sailors on both sides had become servants and prisoners of their own guns. The war had come down to a routine rigorously followed as if it had some value of its own and was not expected to produce any lasting effect. By night men burrowed in the sand, brought up supplies, tried to carry their wounded to safety, and carefully nursed the guns so that firing could be resumed at dawn. By day they tended these guns, or hid in the earth while other guns were fired at them, or peered out to sea at the methodical evolutions of the fleet. From target-distance the monitors looked sluggish, almost harmless, seeming to be nothing more than round black boxes adrift on the tide; but at intervals of a few minutes fire would flash from a turret, and a 15-inch shell would come in, visible every foot of the way. If it passed overhead it sounded like an express train on the loose, and if it struck the parapet it shook the earth and sent up a high geyser of sand, and either way it was terrifying. One Confederate felt that it was even more unnerving to watch *New Ironsides,* which mounted fourteen 11-inch guns and two long-range rifles. This craft never fired by broadside but let off one gun at a time, the fire rippling along her black side as if her gunners felt that they had all the time in the world.

It was little better for the besiegers than for the besieged. The narrow trenches in the sand caught and held all the heat, the heaviest shellfire did not seem to keep Wagner's sharpshooters under cover, and Gillmore's medical inspector presently warned that unless Wagner fell very soon most of the Federal troops would become unfit for duty from sheer exhaustion; Gillmore at last made up his mind to try to carry the fort by assault in the belief that this would cost fewer lives than would be lost by one more week of siege warfare. But Beauregard concluded that Wagner had served its purpose, and on the night of September 6 he pulled the garrison out. Federal patrols crept into the ruined fort, reported that "everything but the sand was knocked to pieces," and reflected that the summer's work had cost the Union army more than 2300 men, not counting a larger number disabled by sickness.[4]

They quickly learned that they had won nothing worth getting. They had done exactly what they set out to do—that is, they had taken Battery Wagner and Morris Island, and they had reduced Fort Sumter to a shapeless wreck—but they were no nearer to Charleston than they had been six months earlier. When Beauregard took the guns out of Fort Sumter he arrayed them in new batteries all around the inner harbor; on the north side of the entrance Fort Moultrie and its satellite batteries were still intact; altogether Beauregard had fifty-eight cannon bearing on the harbor entrance, and any naval craft that came in to sweep mines and remove other obstructions from the ship channel would get extremely rough treatment. The Confederate commander also had some good infantry lurking in the Fort Sumter wreckage, and when Dahlgren sent in a naval landing party on the night of September 8 the assault was a costly failure; of 450 men in the landing party only 127 were able to go ashore at the fort, and all of these were either killed, wounded or captured.

Federal army-navy rivalry by this time had got to the point where the two services were hardly speaking to each other. The army had made up a landing party of its own to attack Fort Sumter the same night the navy tried it, but there was no co-ordination whatever; when the soldiers saw what happened to the sailors they turned around and canceled their attack. Meanwhile, even though Fort Sumter had been ground to fragments the Yankees could not have it. The Confederate flag still flew there, and the one gun that remained in the place defiantly fired a sunset salute to the colors every night.[5]

This ought to have ended it, but did not. There was a breathing spell for two or three weeks, while Dahlgren repaired his ships and Gillmore built new batteries on Morris Island, and then there were a few days of almost casual firing which accomplished nothing and apparently was not especially intended to accomplish anything; after which there were three additional weeks of idleness. Then, late in October, the army and navy together opened a tremendous bombardment that went on for twelve days; conducted, apparently, on the theory that the way to atone for a failure is to repeat the effort that has failed until sheer dogged persistence begins to make the process look admirable.

This immense bombardment, of course, was centered entirely on Fort Sumter, which had already been broken into fragments and which no longer mounted guns capable of doing anything more than salute the flag at sunset. In some ways this near-fortnight of firing was the most spectacular display Charleston had yet seen. The army had powerful Parrott rifles sited to strike what was left of Fort Sumter at almost point-blank range, and it also had a long array of immense siege mortars, and the navy came in with its biggest ships to fire 15-inch guns, and the great heap of sand and broken stones was flogged and torn apart and slammed together again, while defenders huddled in the bombproofs far down inside and waited for darkness to come so that they could go up for a whiff of air. Now and then a few of these defenders were killed. Otherwise, nothing at all was gained.

This had very little to do with winning the war. It was simply an exercise in the application of violence, as if to use the big guns and the fearful explosives had become an end in itself, owing nothing to anybody's desire for victory. It was appalling enough, and hideously impressive, and yet in a queer way not foreseen by its authors it was quite economical, at least as far as human life was concerned. For an entire summer the rivals fought here, using the most powerful weapons that had yet been invented. They threw thousands of tons of shell and solid shot at each other; they used their implements of destruction without the least restraint, trying for week after week to do the utmost that could possibly be done—and in the end, after four months of it, they had killed fewer men than died in a few July hours along Seminary Ridge at Gettysburg, where the apparatus of violence was far less impressive.

Perhaps all that was needed was for men to get used to the appalling powers they had grasped; the knowledge of the best ways to use these powers would eventually come once the will to inflict unmeasured damage became dominant, and this developed rapidly. During this eventful summer, while his engineers worked so hard to get at the forts, Gillmore had a gun emplacement built in the swamps a mile or more southwest of Battery Wagner; a cunningly engineered affair of pilings, wooden flooring, and sand bags, supporting an 8-inch Parrott rifle that fired a 200-pound shell. This gun was dubbed the Swamp Angel and it was mounted so that it could fire directly into the city of Charleston. When all was ready, Gillmore sent word that unless Sumter and Wagner were immediately evacuated he would bombard the city, and when this threat was ignored the Swamp Angel opened fire.

The firing began shortly after midnight on August 22. Most of the time the gunners used a new kind of incendiary shell, in the hope that they could set the city on fire, and Beauregard sent over a flag-of-truce message protesting against this firing into "a city taken unawares and filled with sleeping women and children." This protest was ignored and the firing continued. The incendiary shells seem to have been defective, for the city did not burn, and after thirty-six shots had been fired the Swamp Angel exploded. The bombardment of the city had been meant to be most destructive, but had not been so; once again, man's reach had exceeded his grasp, and although the sum total of fear in the world had indeed been increased for a few nights no substantial material damage had been done.[6]

It would hardly be worth mentioning, except that it showed how war had hardened men's emotions, so that things that would have been horrifying in ordinary times horrified no longer. The idea of throwing Greek fire (or, as at Vicksburg, ordinary high explosives) into homes where women and children slept did not seem dreadful at all. Good men even rejoiced in it. In the Federal army before Charleston, for instance, there was a Regular Army brigadier from Massachusetts, George H. Gordon, who heard about the Swamp Angel's work and wrote: "What a wonderful retaliation! Frightened inhabitants fleeing from the wrath of a just avenger . . . ah indeed, but this was sweet!" And far away in London another good man from Massachusetts, Minister Charles Francis Adams, noted in his diary that the latest news from America told of the destruction of Fort Sumter "and the shelling of that pestilent nest of heresy, Charleston" and felt that the effect of all of this would be good.[7]

When good men could talk so they consented to terror. A later generation might be able to make incendiaries that would really work.

4. The Road to Zion

AT THE END of July, the month when so many young men died, John J. Crittenden of Kentucky died also; an old man (older in fact than the Constitution itself) who had done his best to keep young men from having to kill each other. In 1860 he had worked for compromise, proposing that North and South agree to keep the past intact by stretching it into a tight protective film to contain the monstrous slavery issue; and when this failed and war came he tried to keep the war limited, offering (and seeing Congress accept) a resolution insisting that the war was being waged to restore the Union but not to interfere in any way with the right of strong men to own weaker men. Crittenden had opposed the confiscation act, emancipation, and the enlistment of Negro soldiers, but there had never been any question about his devotion to the Union; he simply believed that it could be saved by mutual consent if the attempt to save it could be strictly divorced from the attempt to define what it would be like afterward. He once asked, despairingly: "Is it not our duty to save our own country first and then turn around and save the Constitution?"[1]

Now he was gone, and most of what he stood for was gone with him, for there was no longer any chance of mutual consent. Mr. Lincoln had once accepted Mr. Crittenden's resolution on war aims; now he was firm in the belief that slavery and secession must be destroyed together. If there had been any doubt about it he made it clear in a brief exchange of messages with General Rosecrans, who submitted a mildly unorthodox proposal advanced by Colonel James Frazier Jaquess of the 73rd Illinois Infantry.

Colonel Jaquess had been a Methodist minister before the war, and he believed that many people in the South wanted to return to the Union. He knew many Southerners, largely through his church connections, and he believed that if he could go south and talk with them he could set in motion a genuine Southern peace movement. He had asked General Rosecrans to let him undertake this mission, and what he wanted now (aside from a presidential blessing) was some light on the peace terms Mr. Lincoln was prepared to offer.

Formal presidential blessing he could not get, but light was available. Mr. Lincoln was interested in this slightly fantastic plan; he had always believed, despite much evidence to the contrary, that there was a deep Union sentiment in the South, and this might be a good way to test it. He pointed out that Jaquess could not go south with any government authority whatever, and warned that if he went without it the Confederates might shoot him as a spy. However, if the man wanted to take his chances and go on his own hook, and if General Rosecrans cared to give him a furlough so that he could get away from his regiment, the President would rather like to see him try it. As to terms: the South must of course return to the Union, and it must accept universal emancipation, and the Federal war debt must be shared by all of the states in the restored Union. In return the Federal government would offer general amnesty, with no enforcement of the confiscation act "except as against the leaders."[2]

Whatever else these terms meant, they certainly did not mean compromise. If the Confederacy wanted peace it must begin by consenting to its own dissolution, and in the spring of 1863 (the President formulated these terms more than a month before the victories at Vicksburg and Gettysburg) few things seemed less likely. What Mr. Lincoln had been willing to subscribe to in 1861—the simple statement that the Federal government was fighting solely "to preserve the Union with all the dignity, equality, and rights of the several states unimpaired"—he subscribed to no longer. He would undo nothing that had happened in the last two years. Such words as dignity, equality, and rights had grown larger than they used to be; they no longer applied just to states but had begun to attach themselves to people who had not previously known anything about them, and this had to be accepted even if its implications were still unfathomable. What the President really was saying was that if there was to be a peace conference, Southerners would have to take the future on faith—believing (as the abolitionist poet Whittier would have said) where they could not prove. A peace conference so conceived was apt to be hard to arrange.

Nevertheless, Mr. Lincoln was trying to give faith something to stand on. By promising general amnesty he was indicating that although the Confederacy must be destroyed the states that had supported it could return to the Union as regular members of the American family. Accepting reunion and emancipation, they could resume their old places; a victorious government would exact neither revenge nor punishment. Here Mr. Lincoln was expressing his own faith, which included the belief that he could control the radical Republicans, whose support was essential to him and who were beginning to articulate a murky faith of their own. This faith was based on the argument that secession had been effective even though it was both illegal and short-lived. The act of secession (they held) had destroyed the states that subscribed to it; once beaten, these states would simply be conquered territory, to be disposed of as the victors saw fit, and they could not resume their old places because those places no longer existed.

Out of this faith could come nothing better than a peace of desolation, which was unlikely to be worth as much as it would cost. Mr. Lincoln was trying to head it off, and S. L. M. Barlow's correspondent Barnett got a foggy glimpse of his purpose and wrote, after Gettysburg, that "the President has *words* for the ultras and *acts* for the more conservative." To a limited extent, Barnett was right. The ultras were dreaming of vengeance, and a few months later (when the likelihood of Southern defeat was beginning to be clearer) Attorney General Bates wrote to Francis Lieber, the émigré German political scientist, to denounce their "pestilent doctrines" and to confess his dismay: "When the public cauldron is heated into violent ebullition, it is sure to throw up from the bottom of society some of its dirtiest dregs, which, but for the heat and agitation, would have lain embedded in congenital filth in the lowest stratum of society. But once boiled up to the top they expand into foam and froth, dance frantically before the gaping crowd, often concealing for a time the whole surface of the agitated mass. . . . It is wonderful how, in times like these, the minds of men are made dizzy and their imaginations are wrought up to frenzy by the whirl of events."[3]

What was agitating the cauldron was the fact that the war could not now be ended by negotiation. Peace must follow victory, and although it was likely to take its shape from the things that were done in order to win victory, the victory nevertheless had to be gained; this was what stimulated the radicals, distressed Bates, and confused Barnett, who felt that the President was a conservative at heart. Late in August Mr. Lincoln tried to explain the situation in a letter prepared to be read at a Union mass meeting in Springfield, Illinois: a letter ostensibly addressed to the discontented Northern conservatives.

"You desire peace; and you blame me that we do not have it," Mr. Lincoln wrote. "But how can we attain it? There are but three conceivable ways. First, to suppress the rebellion by force of arms. This I am trying to do. Are you for it? If you are, so far we are agreed. If you are not for it, a second way is to give up the Union. I am against this. Are you for it? If you are, you should say so plainly. If you are not for *force,* nor yet for *dissolution,* there only remains some imaginable *compromise.* I do not believe any compromise, embracing the maintenance of the Union, is now possible. All I learn leads to a directly opposite belief."

The trouble of course was that the use of force had led to the Emancipation Proclamation, and many conservative men willing to fight for re-union were not willing to fight for the Negro. For such men the President had this answer:

"I issued the proclamation on purpose to aid you in saving the Union. Whenever you shall have conquered all resistance to the Union, if I shall urge you to continue fighting, it will be an apt time, then, for you to declare that you will not fight to free Negroes." Meanwhile: "Peace does not appear so distant as it did. I hope it will come soon, and come to stay; and so come as to be worth the keeping in all future time."[4]

Here of course was the rub. In order to win, Mr. Lincoln needed the help of the very men who were calling for the kind of peace that might not be worth keeping in all future time: they at least were willing to fight for the Negro, and Mr. Lincoln's conviction that this was his fight too was the point Barnett had missed. Later in the fall, when he was preparing to tell the Congress just what he meant about amnesty and reconstruction, Mr. Lincoln expressed himself in a letter to General Schofield in Missouri, where it seemed likely that the radical Republicans would win the next election. The President remarked that he was willing to see the radicals win, going on to explain: "They are nearer to me than the other side, in thought and sentiment, though bitterly hostile personally. They are utterly lawless—the unhandiest devils in the world to deal with—but after all their faces are set Zion-wards."[5]

The road to Zion was unmapped and poorly lighted, and to follow it with the utterly lawless was perhaps to take a long chance. But the President was determined to go there, and if these lawless ones were the only available companions he would go with them. They at least kept moving. They had undying energy, and they shared with their enemies to the south the belief that it was essential to fight without a let-up until the foe was broken. They were unhandy devils, earning hatred and distrust and giving hatred and distrust in return, but they were also most useful and in the end their help would be essential. The Federal war effort tended to go spasmodically, with fatigue and indecision enforcing long pauses between strokes; it was pausing now, in the wake of the Vicksburg-Gettysburg victories, and it actually seemed to be the Confederates who had the true spirit of war.

There was some sort of significance, for instance, in the startling exploit of a young Southern naval officer, Lieutenant Charles W. Read, who put to sea in the spring commanding the armed brig *Clarence*, with 120 men and one gun, to go commerce raiding off the Virginia capes. In three weeks he took twenty-one Yankee merchantmen, including one vessel carrying arms and clothing from New York to that famous source of Confederate supplies, the Mexican port of Matamoros. The shipping community cried out in agony and the United States Navy took off in pursuit, fatally handicapped by the fact that it did not know what it was looking for. Lieutenant Read had a way of shifting his command from one vessel to another; he transferred to the captured bark *Tacony*, burning his own brig, and after a time he burned

Tacony and resumed his cruise in the captured schooner *Archer*, and he sailed north to the New England coast with Mr. Welles' cruisers utterly baffled. Presently Lieutenant Read sailed boldly into the harbor of Portland, Maine, and at night he boarded and captured the revenue cutter *Caleb Cushing*, in which he put to sea for more adventures. He was at last caught and overpowered by a makeshift Federal squadron out of Portland, being unable to stand and fight because he could not find where *Cushing's* former crew had stored the cutter's ammunition; and although his whole venture had really brought the South no closer to final victory it had been highly embarrassing to the United States Navy and to Mr. Lincoln's administration. It was not exactly important, but it was significant.[6]

Much more to the point was a fiasco at Sabine Pass, Texas, where the Federal power displayed a fumbling incompetence that would have been hard to explain away even in the early, amateurish days of the war.

Federal soldiers and sailors went to Sabine Pass because French soldiers had gone to Mexico. Napoleon III, Emperor of France, who had built his career by taking advantage of turmoil wherever it existed, was trying to set up a French-controlled empire in Mexico. He had chosen the luckless Habsburg prince, Maximilian, to be his puppet emperor there, and in June of 1863 he sent a French army into Mexico City, thereby fracturing the Monroe Doctrine in a way no American government could approve but which the government at this moment could not effectively resent. It seemed to Washington to be necessary to establish a Federal army in Texas, both as a warning of the wrath to come and as a hedge against the chance that Napoleon, having occupied Mexico, would go on to occupy Texas as well. So, early in the summer, General Banks was ordered to make immediate preparation to send a powerful expedition into Texas.

Here the Lincoln administration made a substantial error. The way to checkmate Napoleon was to win the war at home; once that was done, the French could be driven out of the New World without difficulty. To send an army to Texas now would not help much; indeed, it was a move in the wrong direction, a dispersion of force that cost more than it was worth. The Mississippi Valley had just been won, and the massive force that won it could have moved eastward across the cotton South, cutting the last supports out from under the Confederacy; both General Grant and General Banks wanted to do this, and they had been planning a descent on Mobile, Alabama, as a first step. The Texas expedition made this impossible. Grant was able to send Sherman out to drive General Johnston away from the city of Jackson, but he could do no more; he was immobilized for the summer, his army split into detachments, and in effect the entire Federal force in the great valley stood by to guard the rear while Banks invaded Texas.

Unhappily but dutifully, Banks worked out a plan. Giving up his earlier idea that the Red River offered the best way into Texas—the summer drought had made that stream too shallow for transports—he elected to go along the Gulf Coast to the mouth of the Sabine River, the dividing line between Texas and Louisiana. Sabine Pass, where the river reached the Gulf, was lightly defended, and Banks believed he could move inland from that point and occupy Houston with 15,000 men; this would give him control of the Texas railroad network and the most populous part of the state, and his mission would be accomplished. (If accomplished smartly, there might still be time and strength enough to turn east and attack Mobile.) So on September 5 the advance guard of the expedition, a division of 4000 men under Major General William B. Franklin, got under way for Sabine Pass, escorted by lightdraft gunboats.[7]

It should have been automatic. At Sabine Pass the Confederates had an unfinished fort mounting six light guns, manned by forty-odd members of the 1st Texas heavy artillery, commanded by Lieutenant Richard Dowling, and Banks had told Franklin to land along the coast and flank this force out of there. But Franklin, who had been so reluctant to use his troops at Fredericksburg, was equally reluctant now. He felt that it would be simpler to let the navy pound the fort into submission, and on the afternoon of September 8 the gunboats *Clifton*, *Sachem*, *Arizona*, and *Granite City* steamed in across the bar and opened fire.

They did not fire very long, and they did Lieutenant Dowling's little force no harm. *Sachem* was disabled by a shot through her boilers, lost steerage-way and could bring no guns to bear. *Clifton* ran aground and also got shot through the boilers. Both ships surrendered, *Arizona* grounded, got free and retired, *Granite City* never got into action at all, and after forty-five minutes Franklin considered the attack a flat failure, abandoned it, and sailed back to his starting point in Louisiana. A captured Federal officer went up to Lieutenant Dowling, found him "a modest, retiring, boyish-looking Irish lad," and blurted out his embarrassed tribute: "You and your forty-three men, in your miserable little mud fort in the rushes, have captured two gunboats, a goodly number of prisoners, many stands of small arms and plenty of good ammunition—and all that you have done with six pop-guns. . . . And that is not the worst of your boyish tricks. You have sent three Yankee gunboats, 6000 troops and a general out to sea in the dark."[8]

Ignominious failure, in other words, followed by the exchange of bitter words between the army and navy; damaging the Confederacy not at all, conveying no warning to the French, proving only that although the President of the United States was demanding all-out war he was not getting it. If the help of the radicals looked essential perhaps there was reason for it.

Perhaps . . . and yet the appearance was deceptive. Dark shadows were rising around the Confederacy, and neither Yankee failure at Charleston nor Yankee bungling in Texas altered the fact. Surveying the scene with cold realism, Jefferson Davis in mid-summer conceded that one of the South's fundamental hopes was gone forever: Great Britain was not going to help the Confederacy win its independence, neither directly with its fleet nor indirectly with a benevolent neutrality. To James Mason, who had so brightly gone to London two years earlier to plead the Southern cause, went a letter from Secretary of State Judah P. Benjamin, who notified Mr. Mason that President Davis had concluded that "the Government of Her Majesty has determined to decline the overtures made through you for establishing friendly treaty relations between the two Governments and entertains no intention of receiving you as the accredited Minister of the Government near the British court. Under these circumstances your continued residence in London is neither conducive to the interests nor consistent with the dignity of this Government, and the President therefore requests that you consider your mission at an end and that you withdraw with your secretary from London."[9]

Mr. Davis was saying that King Cotton was dead. The dream that King Cotton would compel the outside world to make the new nation permanent had been basic at Montgomery, when the man and the hour met under bright flags and secession looked like a logical step toward a destined goal. Now the dream was gone forever. Her Majesty's Government was acting upon the belief that the North was going to win the war, and it gave the soberest proof of this before Mason even got Secretary Benjamin's letter: it sent a gunboat and a detachment of marines to the Laird's building yard at Birkenhead and announced that the famous ironclad rams, now almost completed, would not be allowed to sail.

These rams had given United States Minister Adams a distracting summer. No one over the age of ten doubted that they were being built for the Confederacy, but to prove it was another matter. Commander James Bulloch, the Confederate agent who had arranged for their construction, had acted with skill, and the legal record still showed they were being built for Messrs. Bravay of France. Mr. Adams had been bombarding Lord Russell with affidavits, his Bostonian inflexibility stiffened by the grimmest instructions from Secretary Seward. If the cruisers sailed, said Mr. Seward, the United States Navy would go after them, pursuing them if necessary into neutral ports—obviously, though the Secretary did not say so, into British ports—and this would inevitably lead to shooting. "If," wrote the Secretary, "through the necessary employment of our means of national defense, such a partial war shall become a general one between the two nations, the President thinks that the responsibility for that painful result will not fall upon the United States."[10]

It did not seem to Mr. Adams that the British government was going to stop the rams. On September 5 he sent a sober dispatch to Lord Russell, who was then in Scotland, reciting his case against the rams and climaxing his argument with a sentence which became famous: "It would be superfluous in me to point out to your lordship that this is war." He wrote this, he privately confessed, in "utter dreariness of spirit," and concluded that his only hope was to play for time by letting it be known that he must await further instructions from Washington.[11]

In point of fact Mr. Adams had already won his battle, although he did not then know it, and his famous sentence was sent to a man who had already backed down. On September 1 the British Under Secretary for Foreign Affairs wrote to the Treasury that "so much suspicion attaches to the iron-clad vessels at Birkenhead, that if sufficient evidence can be obtained to lead to the belief that they are intended for the Confederate States Lord Russell thinks the vessels ought to be detained until further examination can be made." Two days later, on September 3, Lord Russell wired to the Under Secretary to stop the ironclads AS SOON AS THERE IS REASON TO BELIEVE THAT THEY ARE ACTUALLY ABOUT TO PUT TO SEA, AND TO DETAIN THEM UNTIL FURTHER ORDERS. On the same day he wrote to the Prime Minister, Lord Palmerston: "I have thought it necessary to direct that they should be detained. The solicitor-general has been consulted and concurs in the measure as one of policy though not of strict law." Lord Palmerston approved. He had felt all along that Britain would be playing "a suicidal game" if it let the Confederacy have these ships, and by now he wanted to avoid "even a diplomatic wrangle" with Washington. He did have reservations about Mr. Adams' language—after all, semi-colonial types from beyond the seas ought not to talk as Mr. Adams had talked to a British Foreign Minister—and late in September, after the crisis was over, he told Lord Russell: "It seems to me that we cannot allow to remain unnoticed his repeated and I must say somewhat insolent threats of war. We ought I think to say to him, in civil terms, 'You be damned,' and I endeavored to express that sentiment to him in measured terms."[12]

Mr. Adams could bear up under this. The big point was that the rams never crossed the Atlantic. They had looked like doom itself, and Mr. Adams had had dreadful visions of the Federal blockade crumbling before them, but in the end the British put the broad arrow on them and they became two more warships in the British Navy, H.M.S. *Wivern* and *Scorpion*, obsolescent when commissioned, wholly obsolete shortly thereafter because warship design then was moving ahead with great speed. A few years later Mr. Adams saw a naval review at Portsmouth, studied one of these precious ironclads, and reflected: "As I looked on the mean little thing I could not help a doubt whether she was really worth all of the anxiety she had cost us."[13]

Probably not. Yet what the British government did about these rams closed an iron door on the Confederacy, and when he addressed the Congress at Richmond at the end of the year Mr. Davis took note of it. Great Britain, he said, was not really neutral at all. It was siding with the Yankees. It showed partiality "in favor of our enemies," and he explained what this meant:

"This Confederacy is either independent or it is a dependency of the United States: for no other earthly power claims the right to govern it. Without one historic fact on which the pretension can rest, without one word of treaty or covenant which can give color to title, the United States have asserted, and the British government has chosen to concede, that these sovereign States are dependencies of the Government which is administered at Washington. Great Britain has accordingly entertained with that Government the closest and most intimate relations, while refusing, on its demands, ordinary amicable intercourse with us, and has, under arrangements made with the other nations of Europe, not only denied our just claim of admission into the family of nations, but interposed a passive though effectual bar to the knowledge of our rights by other powers. . . . I am well aware that we are unfortunately without adequate remedy for the injustice under which we have suffered at the hands of a powerful nation."[14]

5. A Mad Irregular Battle

THE FINAL significance of the loss of the Laird rams could be analyzed at leisure, if the Confederacy ever found the time to draw up a proper balance sheet; in the late summer of 1863 Mr. Davis had something far more serious to worry about. The spasmodic Federal war machine, swinging from stolid inertia to furious energy, was at last starting to invade the heart of the South.

After maneuvering Bragg out of central Tennessee, General Rosecrans had gone into camp halfway between Murfreesboro and Chattanooga, staying there for six weeks while he repaired a railroad line, collected supplies and argued tirelessly with General Halleck about everything from high strategy to the cavalry's need for more horses. Now he was on the march again, coming southeast across the Cumberland Plateau with nearly twice Bragg's numbers, handling his sprawling columns so smartly that his adversary could never bring him to battle; if Old Rosey's superiors found it impossible to make him move before he felt entirely ready to move they could find no fault with him once he got under way. He came down to the Tennessee River at the end of August, crossed without opposition, and then pushed one army corps toward Chattanooga and moved two more farther south and sent them eastward across the mountains straight into Bragg's unprotected rear. Bragg would obviously have to evacuate Chattanooga without a struggle, and if this Yankee advance could not speedily be thrown back the Confederacy was likely to be split beyond repair.[1]

Here, in short, was the ultimate threat, and Mr. Davis resorted to the ultimate answer; that is, he took men from Lee's army and sent them west to help Bragg. What he would not do in June he did do in September; the war that could not be settled and must not be lost was exerting irresistible pressure, and for a time the President even thought of the unthinkable and considered sending Lee west in person. This he did not do, but on September 9 General James Longstreet and 12,000 of the best soldiers in Lee's army left their camp along the Rapidan and made their way to the railroad trains that would take them to a destination not marked on any timetable—the field of Chickamauga.[2]

It would have been better if they could have started earlier. The President had called Lee to Richmond on August 24, to discuss the western crisis, and the conference had gone on for the better part of a fortnight. By the time it was over, and the commitment to transfer troops had been reached, the government's physical ability to make the transfer had deteriorated badly.

The direct route from Richmond to Chattanooga was the Confederacy's one real railroad trunk line, the line that went by way of Lynchburg, Bristol, and Knoxville, a five-hundred-mile haul; Longstreet, perhaps a bit optimistically, had figured the move could be made in four days. But while the conference was going on another spasm of energy possessed the Federals, and General Ambrose E. Burnside brought a small army down across the mountains from Kentucky and did what Mr. Lincoln had desperately wanted some general to do from the earliest days of the war: he occupied Knoxville, liberating much of the strongly Unionist area of eastern Tennessee and taking possession of a long stretch of that all-important railroad. As a result, Longstreet's soldiers had to make a huge detour, traveling in a long circle down through the Carolinas to Augusta and Atlanta. The distance was nearly twice as far and the going was more than twice as bad, because the separate railroads involved had different track gauges so that men and equipment had to change cars over and over, with much loss of time. The roads themselves were in bad shape, lightly built to begin with and badly run down because of the demands of war and the impossibility of replacing worn-out equipment, and one of Longstreet's staff officers remarked in disgust: "Never before were so many troops moved over such worn-out railways . . . Never before were such crazy cars used for hauling good soldiers." The move could not have been made at all if quartermaster officers and railroad men had not done prodigies of planning and organization; but it did take a solid ten days, nearly half of the men reached the battlefield only after the fighting had ended, and the artillery came in even later. An earlier start could have made a substantial difference.[3]

Chickamauga, which was a resounding Southern victory, might have been even more resounding—would have been so, possibly, if those missing men had all been there—and because it was not it was finally wasted. For this battle marked the appearance of the Confederacy's last great opportunity. In the gloomy thickets above Chickamauga Creek the Confederates, for the last time east of the Mississippi River, were able to strike back at a foe who made war without co-ordination. Never again, after Rosecrans' defeat, did any major Federal army operate independently, as if neither the actions of other Federal armies nor the logic of the whole military situation were anything its leader needed to consider; and never again was a major Federal army exposed to outright annihilation. Never again could a Southern commander east of the Mississippi really hope to destroy the opposing army: after this his only valid target had to be the will-to-resist of the opposing general, and after much trial and many errors the government at Washington was finding generals in whom that quality was powerfully developed. Bragg had the last big chance. He got a victory out of it, but he did not get the great, shattering victory that was briefly possible. This was partly his own fault, and it was also partly the fault of some of his subordinates, but it must be said that the 6000 shock troops who did not arrive on time would have helped.

Perhaps there was something a little fated about what happened in Tennessee, anyway. Neither government had ever been able to lay a really firm hand on the war in that state; it was too far from the centers of control, and nothing that took place looked the same to the governments as to the soldiers on the spot. Once, after trying in vain to get an offensive started there, Mr. Davis consoled himself with the sensible reflection: "However desirable a movement may be, it is never safe to do more than suggest it to a commanding general, and it would be unwise to order its execution by one who foretold failure."[4] This was entirely correct; the trouble was that it seemed to apply to Tennessee so often, on both sides.

Mr. Lincoln and General Halleck had both suggested and ordered various movements, without the slightest effect. All of their authority this spring had been insufficient to get their Tennessee army into action while the campaign against Vicksburg was going on, and honest bumbling Burnside was the first general who ever paid effective attention to the call for an advance on Knoxville. Mr. Davis had had no better luck. During the last winter he had been unable even to make a change in army commanders, and when he sent a general to the west to make one cause out of the defense of Tennessee and the defense of Vicksburg, Vicksburg went off to ruin as incontinently as if the general had never gone beyond the Blue Ridge. The most Mr. Davis could do now, with the very life of the nation at stake, was to scrape troops from here and there, send them off to Bragg, and hope for the best.

The best might turn out to be very good indeed, because the reinforcements stiffened Bragg's naturally pugnacious instincts and during the second week in September he unexpectedly reversed the flow of the campaign, passing from defense to offense so quickly that Rosecrans nearly lost his army.

In the middle of August when the campaign began Bragg had an over-all strength of some 44,000 men, as compared to slightly less than 80,000 under Rosecrans. Then he began to get additions. Simon Bolivar Buckner brought 8000 men down from Knoxville (evacuated perforce as Burnside drew nigh) and from Joe Johnston in Mississippi came 900 under John C. Breckinridge and W. H. T. Walker, followed shortly afterward by 2500 more; and of course Longstreet and his 12,000 were coming down from Virginia. (The contingents from Mississippi and Virginia of course would not have been present at all if the Federal advance had taken place while the Vicksburg and Gettysburg campaigns were in progress.) Inasmuch as a fair number of Rosecrans' men were on duty in the rear and would not be present in battle, Bragg faced the prospect, unheard-of for a Confederate, of going into action with the numerical odds equal if not indeed slightly in his favor.[5] He shaped his plans accordingly, and suddenly he had Rosecrans in serious trouble.

Rosecrans got Crittenden's corps into Chattanooga on September 9, after Bragg evacuated the city, and as far as he could see the Confederates were running away and needed only to be caught. His army was well placed to catch them. The largest corps, that of Pap Thomas, 22,000 or more, was twenty miles southwest of Chattanooga at Stevens Gap in the long ridge of Lookout Mountain, with its leading elements thrust forward into a valley known as McLemore's Cove; and a third corps, McCook's, was twenty miles southwest of Thomas', moving through another gap in the Lookout ridge and heading toward the town of Alpine, just east of the Georgia-Alabama line. Bragg seemed to be making for Rome, Georgia, which was more than fifty miles south of Chattanooga. A loyal Tennesseean who got to Federal headquarters that day assured Rosecrans that if the retreating Confederates were pressed hard "they will not stop short of Atlanta," and one of Crittenden's brigadiers wrote afterward that the commanding general "expected to drive Bragg to the sea." Rosecrans sent a wire to Halleck saying that "our move on the enemy's flank and rear progresses, while the tail of his retreating column will not escape unnoticed." This message, breathing the true spirit of the offensive, was most welcome in Washington, but the general who wrote it had lost touch with reality.[6]

For Bragg was not retreating, and the Federals who thought they were chasing him were marching straight into trouble. Bragg was concentrating his army at Lafayette, less than twenty-five miles south of Chattanooga; far from running away, he was preparing to strike the nearest part of the invading army as soon as he could organize columns of assault. He could hardly have asked for a better opportunity. He could attack the three Federal corps one at a time; all of them were within his reach, but they were so widely separated that no one of them could easily come to the rescue of either of the others. On the evening of the day Rosecrans sent his confident dispatch to Halleck, Bragg issued orders for a counterattack.

His most obvious target was Thomas' corps, nearly half of which had been sent forward from Stevens Gap into McLemore's Cove, with scouts and skirmishing parties thrown on ahead to prepare for an advance to Lafayette, where the sensitive flank of the retreating foe could doubtless be assailed. Thomas' corps was dangerously exposed, with its nearest friends two days' march away; with proper handling, Bragg's army could crush it, and if this happened the Federal center would be destroyed and there would be a forty-mile gap between the Federal right and left wings . . . which meant, of course, that Rosecrans' entire army would be mortally wounded and that the war itself would look very different.

Bragg devised a good plan: one Confederate column would march southwest, following Chickamauga Creek into McLemore's Cove, while another drove west from Lafayette, and Thomas' isolated troops would be hit in front, flank, and rear all at once and so of course would be overwhelmed. It could have been done . . . but nothing ever worked out right for Braxton Bragg. Sometimes the fault was his and sometimes it was not, but in the long run the man wore failure as a habit; and now, during the time when Rosecrans' army might have been destroyed, Bragg could do no more than alarm it.

The column that was to strike the Federals from the northeast was led by Major T. C. Hindman, lately of Arkansas, and the column from Lafayette was under Lieutenant General D. H. Hill, veteran of the Virginia wars, sent west by Mr. Davis in the belief that the army in Tennessee needed hard-fighting generals; and these two men were good soldiers but difficult, tenacious of their own opinions, ready to interpret orders in the light of their own judgment. On September 10, the day appointed for their attack, they did not attack. Hill, as senior officer, explained that the roads in his front had been obstructed, that his best division commander was ill, and that the move, all in all, was not practicable . . . Balked here, Bragg ordered a similar attack for the next day, with Hindman and General Buckner leading the columns. Buckner too could be difficult; he and Hindman conferred, disliked the plan, and asked Bragg to change it, and when he refused and told them to go ahead as originally ordered they remained passive, making no attack. And at last Thomas' advance guard took alarm and marched back out of danger.

Two mis-fires, and the Federal center was no longer vulnerable. Now Bragg tried to hit Crittenden's corps, which was coming south on the road from Chattanooga to Lafayette, with one division crossing the Chickamauga at Lee and Gordon's Mills and the other two extended eastward toward Ringgold and Dalton. General Polk, commanding the nearest Confederate corps, was told to attack at Lee and Gordon's Mills at daylight on September 13.

Polk was both a lieutenant general and an Episcopal bishop, and in his own upright way he was even more difficult than the other generals. He found that the Federals who had gone off eastward had rejoined the division on Chickamauga Creek, and instead of attacking he sent back word that he had taken a strong defensive position and thought he could hold his ground if he were properly supported. Bragg angrily insisted that Polk was to attack, and told him that Buckner's troops would help him, but the bishop was convinced that he was right and his commanding general was wrong. Firm in this faith, he stayed where he was, no attack was made, and once again the Federals were unharmed . . . and at last Rosecrans began to understand his position, and hastily ordered his widely separated units to concentrate in the area occupied by Crittenden. Bragg in turn pulled his own army together on the opposite side of the creek, holding the crossing at Lee and Gordon's and extending his lines several miles downstream, and he sent a hopeful telegram to Richmond: ENEMY HAS RETIRED BEFORE US AT ALL POINTS. WE SHALL NOW TURN ON HIM IN THE DIRECTION OF CHATTANOOGA.[7]

It took time to make all of the necessary movements, and

time was what Rosecrans desperately needed for survival.
After Bishop Polk overrode Bragg's orders for an attack on
September 13, five days went by, and as the Federal corps
drew closer together the chance that Rosecrans' army might
be destroyed by piecemeal vanished. Even so, it was still in
danger. Longstreet's leading brigades came into Bragg's
camp on September 18, and on the following morning Bragg
at last began to fight the battle which he had three times tried
unsuccessfully to open. In place of the somewhat intricate
maneuvers which his lieutenants had considered unworkable,
his plan now was simple. He would turn the Federal left, cutting Rosecrans off from Chattanooga and driving him back
into the blind alley of McLemore's Cove; that is, he would
put his right wing across the Chickamauga a few miles below the Federal position and march upstream on the Yankee
side, holding the upper crossings with his left and moving the
left over to join in the fight as opportunity offered. Rosecrans
was facing south, and Bragg would attack him from the east.
If the advancing Confederates could get past the Federal left
and seize the north–south road that ran from Lafayette to
Chattanooga, Rosecrans' army would be done for.

That was what Bragg planned, and he probably would have
got it if he had been able to start the fighting twenty-four
hours earlier. On September 18 the Federal left rested at Lee
and Gordon's Mills, where the Lafayette road crossed the
Chickamauga, and nobody but Crittenden was there to hold
it. The country off to the northeast, downstream, across
which Bragg proposed to attack, was empty except for cavalry, Thomas and McCook were still coming in from the distant right, and Confederate infantry could have marched
straight to the Lafayette road, deep in the Federal rear. But
on September 18, while this balky Confederate army was moving down its side of the river, driving Yankee cavalry away
from the crossings and getting itself properly organized,
Thomas' four divisions were making a prodigious hike. They
left their camp in the afternoon and they kept on marching
all night, setting fences on fire to light the way, infantry
stumbling with fatigue but plowing on regardless; and by
the morning of September 19, when Bragg's army at last
opened its offensive, Thomas had most of his people in line
east of the Lafayette road several miles north of Crittenden,

drawn up squarely in the path of the Confederate divisions that were coming west from the river.

So the Yankee army was not where Bragg thought it was. It was still highly vulnerable, to be sure; if the left ever gave way the whole army would be lost, and Bragg's army had shown at Stone's River that when it struck a blow it struck with bone-crushing power. But Bragg's army could no longer win by maneuver. It would have to fight for everything it got, and although at last it got a good deal it did not get what it needed most. The battle of Chickamauga went by nobody's plan, once the first shots were fired. A Federal brigadier summed it up perfectly when he wrote that it was "a mad, irregular battle, very much resembling guerrilla warfare on a vast scale, in which one army was bushwhacking the other, and wherein all the science and the art of war went for nothing." The Confederate Senator G. A. Henry of Tennessee called the turn before the battle began when he told President Davis that the Army of Tennessee needed better leadership and warned him: "As sure as you are born, that army is better than its commanders."[8] Both armies were.

It began a little west of the Chickamauga on that morning of September 19, when Bedford Forrest's cavalry—advancing dismounted, as competent foot-soldiers as any infantry—collided with one of Thomas' brigades near Reed's bridge. Confederate infantry moved up to help, and before long both armies were heavily engaged. Rosecrans brought McCook's weary corps in on Thomas' right and pulled Crittenden back from Lee and Gordon's, and all day long his army fought desperately to keep the Confederates away from the Lafayette road, with Thomas' corps drawn up in a long shallow crescent and taking most of the pressure. The country was full of trees and underbrush, with little clearings here and there; nobody could see much of his enemy's position, it was almost impossible to move artillery along the narrow country lanes, both armies were sodden with weariness, drinking water was hard to find, casualties were extremely heavy, and by nightfall all anyone could be sure of was that there had been a terrible fight and that it would be worse tomorrow.

That night there was a full moon, lighting the smoky fields and woods where lay so many thousands of dead and wounded men. In each army, generals who went to headquarters to report and compare notes felt a pervading air of depression and uncertainty; it was the hard fighting men, John B. Hood and Phil Sheridan, who were most struck by it.[9] Rosecrans got a dozen of his chief lieutenants into a cramped log cabin owned by a lady who comes down in history simply as "the Widow Glenn"; there was a cot for the commanding general to rest on, and a camp chair for General Thomas, but everyone else sat on the floor or lounged against the wall. A fire flickered in the fireplace, and some aide lit a candle, with an inverted bayonet for a candle-holder. The generals were subdued, and the innumerable small noises of the surrounding camp could be heard in the little room; for some reason, when men spoke they spoke in low tones or even in whispers. Thomas was practically torpid for want of sleep. He kept dozing in his chair, rousing himself now and then to say, "I would strengthen the left," and then drowsing again.[10]

His advice was sound. The Federal army held a long, irregular line facing eastward, in front of the Lafayette road. The Confederates had tried all day to crush the northern end of that line—the left, held by Thomas—so that they could get in between Rosecrans and Chattanooga, and they were certain to renew the pressure in the morning. Rosecrans had some thought of shifting his troops into a position from which he could make a counterattack, but he felt that the men were too exhausted to be disturbed. The most he could do was to tell McCook and Crittenden to contract their lines in the morning so that they could send additional help over to Thomas in case he needed it.[11]

A few miles away, on the Confederate side of this most dismal of battlefields, in a country so tangled that a general could get lost making a simple trip to his superior officer's headquarters, Bragg was revising his command arrangements. It was natural that he should do this, in view of the way some of his generals had performed, although it was a risky thing to do in the middle of a big battle; one suspects that he was trying to find a way to make full use of the talents of General Longstreet, who reached the scene that evening, ready for action even though only five of his brigades were on hand. At any rate, Bragg divided his army into two wings, giving the right wing to Polk and the left to Longstreet. Polk was to make an all-out assault on Thomas at daybreak, and Longstreet was to apply pressure at the other end of the

Federal line, making a full-scale attack of his own as soon as Polk's offensive showed progress.[12]

As usual, there was a hitch. Polk's attack did not get under way until somewhere around nine o'clock in the morning, for reasons now indecipherable: Bragg blamed Polk, Polk blamed D. H. Hill, Hill proclaimed his utter innocence, and probably the real trouble was simply that the chain of command was distressingly loose and that the units of this unhappy army moved with a timelag much like the one that was habitual in the Army of the Potomac.[13] At any rate, the attack on Thomas was badly delayed, and the delay may have saved the life of the Union army because when at last Polk's troops attacked they struck with enormous force and if they had come in before Rosecrans could send reinforcements from his right Thomas' corps would probably have been overpowered.

The attack flamed all along his front, overlapping his left as he had feared, and men from McCook's and Crittenden's corps were sent to the left, where Thomas already had more than half of the Union army under his command. Thomas touched the edge of final disaster, once, when John Breckinridge broke past his flank with his division and put two brigades squarely on the vital Lafayette road; these brigades swung around, astride that fateful sandy highway, and came charging south straight into the Union rear, and for a time part of Thomas' line was under attack from two sides at once. By a prodigious effort, the Federals broke these brigades and drove them away, mangling them so badly that they had to be taken out of action altogether; but after they were gone another Confederate corps came in in their place, and the fight had to be made all over again, and Thomas notified Rosecrans that he had to have more help.

The unexpected result of this pressure on the Union left was that the Union right collapsed. In the hot confusion of battle, army headquarters at last lost track of the shifting and counter-marching that had been ordered, and Rosecrans finally pulled the division of Major General Thomas J. Wood out of Crittenden's line and sent it off to the left. This left a big gap in the line, and before anyone could fill it Longstreet made his own attack, striking with five divisions at the precise spot that had just been vacated, handling his men with the cold professional competence that prevailed in Lee's army.[14] A third of Rosecrans' army was crumpled and driven off to the west, Sheridan's entire division and most of Jeff Davis', with elements from other commands, going all the way beyond the lower end of Missionary Ridge and shambling in disorganized rout toward the crossroads of Rossville, five miles north of the battlefield. With them went Rosecrans himself and two of his corps commanders, McCook and Crittenden. Since the last word the unhappy Rosecrans had from Thomas indicated that the left was in dire straits, Rosecrans seems to have assumed now that the entire army had been broken up, and he himself went all the way to Chattanooga in the belief that the commander of a beaten army ought to return to his base and make arrangements for a last-ditch stand.[15]

That left Thomas to pick up the pieces and save the army, and Thomas did all any soldier could have done. He contracted his original lines and formed a long extension on Snodgrass Hill to the west, getting his men into a huge horseshoe-shaped formation, determined to hold on until dusk and make the final withdrawal an orderly one. He was powerfully helped by two circumstances: Polk's wing had been so roughly handled in the morning's fighting that it was unable to renew the assault until late in the day, and a Federal reserve corps under Major General Gordon Granger, three brigades that had been stationed east of Rossville, came hurrying down to buttress the lines on Snodgrass Hill. Longstreet pressed his attack with grim energy, Polk renewed his own attack, and some of the most terrible fighting of the entire battle came shortly before sunset. The Federal lines never broke, and for the stand his men made Thomas was known ever after as "the Rock of Chickamauga," but the most that can be said is that he staved off complete catastrophe. At the end of the day he managed to get his tired soldiers out of line and everybody began to march north toward Chattanooga.

Federal morale was far down. Ambrose Bierce, serving that afternoon on Thomas' staff, recalled the mood that came on at twilight: "Away to our left and rear some of Bragg's people set up the 'rebel yell.' It was taken up successively and passed round to our front, along our right and in behind us again until it seemed almost to have got to the point whence it started. It was the ugliest sound that any mortal ever heard—even a mortal exhausted and unnerved by two days of hard fighting, without sleep, without rest, without food, and without hope. There was, however, a space somewhere at the back of us across which that horrible yell did not prolong itself—and through that we finally retired in profound silence and dejection, unmolested."[16]

From Chattanooga, at about the time Thomas was retiring from the field, Rosecrans sent a wire to Halleck: WE HAVE MET WITH A SERIOUS DISASTER; EXTENT NOT YET ASCERTAINED. ENEMY OVERWHELMED US, DROVE OUR RIGHT, PIERCED OUR CENTER, AND SCATTERED TROOPS THERE. THOMAS, WHO HAD SEVEN DIVISIONS, REMAINED INTACT AT LAST NEWS. GRANGER, WITH TWO BRIGADES, HAD GONE TO SUPPORT THOMAS ON THE LEFT. EVERY AVAILABLE RESERVE WAS USED WHEN THE MEN STAMPEDED. And Charles A. Dana, the Assistant Secretary of War who stayed with Rosecrans as Secretary Stanton's observer, sent a dark message of his own: MY REPORT TODAY IS OF DEPLORABLE IMPORTANCE. CHICKAMAUGA IS AS FATAL A NAME IN OUR HISTORY AS BULL RUN.[17]

Meanwhile, General Bragg had a singular fact to reflect on at his convenience. He had fought to the limit of his army's capacity for two days in an attempt to drive Rosecrans away from Chattanooga, and he had at last driven him straight into it. He had won a victory that he could not use.

6. 37,000 Plus One

THE REASON why the victory at Chickamauga could not really be used appears in the bare account of the steps the opposing governments took as a result of the battle. The Union government sent 37,000 soldiers to Tennessee: the Confederacy sent Jefferson Davis. The contrast does not reflect different ideas about what was needed; it simply measures the extent of the resources at hand. Each government did the most it could do.

The commanding generals came in for bitter criticism. Bragg had failed to win as much as might have been won, and Rosecrans had failed to win anything at all, and each man had subordinates zealous to prove that much more ought to have been done. The case against Rosecrans, of course, was self-opening. He had passed too quickly from triumph to disaster. After proudly boasting that his strategy did not need to be written in letters of blood he had plunged into one of the bloodiest battles of the war, and his period of brilliant maneuvering that got the Confederates out of Tennessee began to look like nothing better than a happy moment of calm between the miseries of Stone's River and Chickamauga. Worst of all, he had left the field before the fighting stopped, and his army's finest feat of arms came after he himself had ridden to the rear in the belief that all was lost. No one could ever question his physical courage, and yet it seemed clear that the fury of Longstreet's attack had given him some sort of numbing shock.

Bragg in his turn suffered from the contrast between what was and what might have been. The victory he won had been an opening rather than a final achievement, and the opening had not been seized. Longstreet wrote after the war that "our last opportunity was lost when we failed to follow the success at Chickamauga and capture or disperse the Union army." This to be sure was an afterthought, formulated when it was easy to see how the lost cause had been lost, but even at the time Longstreet was bitter. Less than a week after the battle he assured Secretary of War Seddon (not bothering to forward the letter through channels; that is, through Bragg, his commanding officer) that having won the most complete victory of the war, except perhaps for Bull Run, Bragg was unable to follow it up. Longstreet concluded dolefully: "I am convinced that nothing but the hand of God can save us or help us as long as we have our present commander." His opinion was shared by two other lieutenant generals, Polk and Hill—both of whom Bragg summarily relieved of their commands shortly after the battle—and some of the division commanders got together and drew up a sort of round robin as a public avowal of their utter lack of confidence.[1]

The trouble of course was that Rosecrans' army had got off alive. Bragg might have made a more vigorous pursuit, while the Federal rout was still on; later, he might have taken his own army across the Tennessee, past one or another of the Yankee flanks, to cut Rosecrans' supply line and force him to surrender. To the argument that he should have done these things Bragg had fairly good answers, but hardly anyone was in a mood to listen to them.

Chickamauga had hurt his army dreadfully, putting more than 18,000 men out of action. This amounted to about a third of his effective infantry total—a genuinely crippling loss, by ordinary standards—and although Rosecrans' own loss of 16,000 was in about the same proportion it was undoubtedly true that on the morning after the battle Bragg's army was in poor shape for brisk movement. During the forty-eight hours following the Federal flight into Chattanooga, Bragg was informed by his frontline commanders that Rosecrans' army was itself going north of the Tennessee—Bedford Forrest watched Yankee wagon trains snaking west past the foot of Lookout Mountain and sent back word, "I think they are evacuating as hard as they can go"—and perhaps it was good to leave well enough alone.[2] Besides, Bragg felt that it was physically impossible for him to go north of the Tennessee just then. He lacked the wagons and horses for a long cross-country march, and so he was tied to the railroad line that came up from Atlanta. All of the railroad bridges over the Tennessee had been destroyed. He had no pontoon trains, and any Confederates who crossed the river would have to wade, which meant that a sudden rise in the stream (it could happen at any time, following a thunderstorm in the mountains) would make it impossible for them to get back.[3]

It was hard to refute this, and it was equally hard to deny that Bragg apparently had this Yankee army locked up in its city of refuge. Rosecrans was too weak to fight his way out, his line of supply was at Bragg's mercy, and it seemed likely that he must eventually be starved into surrender. Yet the atmosphere around Bragg's headquarters was murky with fault-finding, and the hard things Bragg was saying about his principal lieutenants were matched, if not somewhat surpassed, by the hard things they were saying about him. There was enough back-biting going on, in short, to paralyze any army, and Mr. Davis faced just about what Mr. Lincoln faced after the battle of Fredericksburg. He had to go west and set things straight.

He reached Bragg's camp on October 9, and presently he had Bragg and his chief generals in for a round-table discussion of everybody's errors. His handling of the situation, admittedly, was incredibly clumsy, although things had reached a point where no conceivable deftness would be of much service; and presently Mr. Davis asked the assembled generals, one by one, whether they thought the army needed a new commander. One after another, in Bragg's presence, they said that they did think so, giving reasons, which boiled down to an almost universal feeling that Bragg was not up to his job. Regardless of where the fault lay, it was obvious that Bragg did not have the confidence of the men who were working for him.

Time to replace him, then? Possibly; yet—with whom? To appoint one of the lieutenant generals who had been leading the chorus against Bragg was more than Mr. Davis would do. Joe Johnston was available, but after all he had been top man in the west when both Tennessee and Mississippi were lost and Mr. Davis would have none of him; Longstreet got a snub for his pains when he advanced the man's name. Beauregard was busy at Charleston, and anyway Mr. Davis felt that the Confederacy's troubles in this part of the country had really begun when Beauregard led the Army of Tennessee and he wanted him in command no more than he wanted Johnston. The President did have a good deal of faith in Pemberton, who as a matter of fact had accompanied him on this trip, but judicious soundings revealed that the army would probably mutiny if Pemberton came in; his northern birth and the failure at Vicksburg weighed heavily against him. In the end there seemed to be nothing for it but to retain Bragg and support him, and this Mr. Davis did. He confirmed the removal of Polk and Hill, brought the absent Hardee back to take Polk's place, and returned to Richmond. The end of the Chickamauga chapter, like the beginning, would be Bragg's responsibility.[4]

Then and later, Mr. Davis was blamed for making a bad decision. Yet what the Army of Tennessee really needed was not only a new commander but also new muscle—more manpower, more transportation, more of all of the sinews of war so that it could surge forward and destroy the stubborn Federal army that had lost a battle but still clung to life. Mr. Davis limited himself to dealing with the command situation because there was nothing else he could do. He had given this army all the added strength there was to give, weeks earlier, and the victory at Chickamauga had followed. That victory had opened a gateway for the Confederate nation, but to go on through the gateway to independence achieved and full realization of the impelling dream—that needed more than Mr. Davis could provide. The armies could never be made substantially stronger than they were now. No losses, whether of men or of material resources or of faith itself, could ever again be made good. If the war was to be won it would have to be won with what was already in use. Chickamauga was a cruel hint that the Confederate horizon was immovable.

In shattering contrast there was what the battle meant to the North.

Here it showed what could be done rather than what could not be done. By demanding a greater effort it compelled men to see that a greater effort could in fact be made. It called on the President to do something that was physically within his power and the power of the nation; if there was to be failure it would be failure of will rather than of means. Responding to this defeat, the Federal government began to find the road to ultimate victory.

The first panicky messages from Chattanooga, indicating that all (including fortitude) had perhaps been lost, quickly gave way to more hopeful advices, both from General Rosecrans and from Mr. Dana. There was no more talk about continued retreat, and on September 23 Dana told Secretary Stanton that the general "has determined to fight it out here at all hazards"; he had 35,000 effectives, said Dana, and could probably hold out for two or three weeks without help, but for safety he ought to get 25,000 men as reinforcements.[5]

After weeks of ineffectual fretting about the situation in Tennessee the government at last had something it could get its teeth into, and the President held a conference with Secretary Stanton and General Halleck and got quick action. On the Rapidan, General Meade was ordered to pack up two army corps and send them to Washington at once. Being human, Meade chose two slightly sub-standard outfits, Howard's XI Corps and Slocum's XII Corps, both of which were understrength and somewhat looked down upon by the rest of the army. But they did have man-power and an unrealized potential, and Joe Hooker was taken off the shelf and put in charge of them, and they began to move without delay. General Slocum, to be sure, had so low an opinion of Hooker, as a soldier and as a human being, that he protested against serving under him, saying that it would be degrading and that he would like to resign; the War Department refused to accept his resignation and he stayed on the job, apparently with an unwritten understanding that his personal contacts with Hooker could be held to a minimum. Stanton assembled railroad presidents, state governors, War Department functionaries, and quartermaster officers, and the movement went with a rush. The first troop trains left Washington on September 25 forty-eight hours after Dana's message arrived, four days later the head of the column reached Louisville, and in just under twelve days 20,000 soldiers, ten batteries of field artillery, and a hundred cars of baggage had been put down in Bridgeport, Alabama, thirty miles west of Chattanooga.[6]

It was quite an achievement. In a way it was less remarkable than the Confederate transfer of Longstreet's men, because the Confederacy had so much less to work with, but as a demonstration of the power of the North it was most impressive; it showed a smoothly running machine, directed by able technicians, delivering what was needed promptly and without lost motion. It was supplemented by another troop movement which went more slowly but was perhaps even more important; from Mississippi Grant sent Sherman and four divisions of the veterans who had taken Vicksburg, 17,000 men in all, and they left Vicksburg by steamer on October 3, went up the river to Memphis, and then headed east along the line of the Memphis & Charleston, repairing that badly battered railroad as they went. The repairs delayed them, and it was six weeks before they got to Bridgeport, but the delay did no real harm. Long before they reached the scene the gate that the Confederacy had opened at Chickamauga had been slammed shut, once and for all, and the hour of crisis had passed.[7]

In the first weeks of October the danger that Rosecrans might be starved into surrender was perfectly genuine. When he retired into his defensive lines at Chattanooga the general incautiously withdrew a brigade that had been holding the northern end of Lookout Mountain, a massive height that looked down on the Tennessee River a few miles below the city, and when Bragg's army came up Longstreet was promptly sent to occupy this point. As a result the Federal army was effectively besieged even though it was by no means surrounded. All of its supplies came down from Nashville by rail, and the railroad from Nashville joined the Memphis & Charleston at Stevenson, Alabama, ten miles southwest of Bridgeport. From Stevenson and Bridgeport the supplies could be moved to Chattanooga by rail, by river, or by road; but all three routes were commanded now by Longstreet's guns on Lookout Mountain so that it was impossible to use any of them, and Rosecrans' army was slowly but surely being strangled.

It was barely possible, of course, for wagon trains to make a long detour from Bridgeport, moving up the Sequatchie Valley on the north side of the Tennessee and then crossing the barren plateau of Walden's Ridge to the riverbank opposite Chattanooga, but the army could not really be supplied this way. The route was sixty miles in length, the roads were all but completely impassable, there was no forage for horses or mules anywhere along the way, and a loaded wagon needed eight days to make a one-way trip. No wagon could take a full load because it had to carry the hay and grain its own team needed. (For a modern parallel: a long truck route wholly devoid of filling stations, with each truck obliged to carry fuel for the round trip.) Since the army needed several hundred tons of freight every day, this route was totally inadequate. To make matters worse, Confederate Joe Wheeler took his cavalry across the river early in October, caught one of the toiling wagon trains, and destroyed three hundred wagons before Federal cavalry drove him away. Ten days later a civilian who crossed Walden's Ridge saw five hundred army wagons stalled, horses and mules all too weak from hunger to move. For a final note of gloom: if the army ever had to retreat its only escape route would be this terrible road over Walden's Ridge, on which it would almost certainly disintegrate.[8]

Mr. Dana kept Washington posted on all of this, and he was growing more and more pessimistic. He said that Rosecrans seemed to be in a daze, lacked administrative capacity, and could neither see the impending catastrophe nor do anything to prevent it. Dana at last predicted that the army would have to retreat within a fortnight unless it got the river route open, and he asserted that Rosecrans was doing nothing to open it. The War Department had posted Dana at this army's headquarters to keep it informed, as it had sent him to report on Grant a few months earlier, and this was the information it was getting. Rosecrans' standing sank to zero when, on top of all of this, his own chief of staff, Brigadier General James A. Garfield, quietly told various important people (including Secretary Chase and a reporter for the New York *Tribune*) that Rosecrans had fled from the field at Chickamauga in a panic, hurrying off to Chattanooga while Garfield, more heroically, rode back to join Thomas and share the glory of that last stand on Snodgrass Hill. The *Tribune* printed the gist of the story, Mr. Chase ceased to be a heart-and-soul supporter of General Rosecrans, and the administration had had enough.[9] In the middle of October it acted. Having sent 37,000 men to Chattanooga it now sent one more—U. S. Grant.

Grant had had a difficult summer. Ever since Vicksburg he and his army had been wasted; Washington had not let him make the campaign he thought he ought to make, sending him instead to New Orleans to see what General Banks needed from him in connection with the unfortunate Sabine Pass expedition. In New Orleans, Grant's disgust with this way of making war exploded, before witnesses. Banks gave him his fastest and most spirited horse to ride, Grant rode so hard that he and the horse took a fall, injuring Grant's leg so badly that he had to go about on crutches for weeks afterward; and Banks in pious shock wrote to Mrs. Banks: "I am frightened when I think that he is a drunkard."[10] Presumably Washington heard about this and ignored it: needing the best Federal general to repair the damage at Chattanooga, it unhesitatingly sent Grant, crutches and all.

It sent him clothed with full authority. The day when the right hand did not know what the left hand did was over. Grant was given command over everything between the Alleghenies and the Mississippi, except for Banks' preserve around New Orleans. Secretary Stanton, who met him at Indianapolis and rode down to Louisville with him, told him that the War Department, if Grant wished, would when it announced his appointment announce also that Rosecrans had been replaced by Thomas. Grant did wish, and Rosecrans got the news next day, October 19, a month after the fateful battle opened. He left at once for his home in Ohio, getting first an effusive farewell from his troops; he might have lost caste with his generals but the enlisted men were for him all the way. They were hardcase veterans, quick to disown any officer whose nerve failed him, and they simply refused to blame Rosecrans for anything he did or did not do at Chickamauga; they remembered his amazing personal bravery at Stone's River, and the encouragement he had given them there, and the way he had somehow been on the private soldier's side ever since he took command of the army, and now they were genuinely sorry to see him go. They liked Pap Thomas and they respected Grant . . . but Old Rosey had the touch.

On October 23 Grant reached Chattanooga. Less than a week later the river route to Bridgeport was open, supplies were coming in freely, all danger of starvation was over, and the Federal army had regained the initiative and Bragg was back on the defensive. The only question remaining was when Grant would drive Bragg away.[11]

There had been a military miracle, in short, and it must be said that not all of it was Grant's doing by any means. Plans for opening the river route—the Cracker Line, the soldiers called it, because it brought the hardtack crackers that were the army's stand-by—had been drawn, at Rosecrans' direction, by the army's chief engineer, General William F. Smith: Baldy Smith himself, who had so notably lost faith in Burnside after Fredericksburg, and had helped others to lose faith; working now with unworried efficiency. Thomas had ordered Smith's plan put into effect as soon as he took command, and Grant simply approved Thomas' order and saw to it that people got busy. It is possible that the siege would have been broken even if Grant had stayed in Vicksburg. He was more a symbol than a moving cause; the government was going to apply every needed resource to the job at hand, and Grant's arrival testified to that fact.

But it was also true, here as elsewhere, that when Grant showed up things began to happen. People got busy; if new resources were available, he was the man who saw to it that they were used, and he wasted little time writing to Washington about it. There was a different atmosphere at Chattanooga now, and after the war an officer who was there tried to describe the change that came in with Grant: "We began to see things move. We felt that everything came from a plan. He came into the army quietly, no splendor, no airs, no staff. He used to go about alone. He began the campaign the moment he reached the field. Everything was done like music, everything was in harmony."[12]

Opening the Cracker Line turned out to be quite simple. Bragg's grip on the army's windpipe was much weaker than had been supposed, and it was quickly broken.

Opposite Chattanooga the Tennessee River turns left and flows south for two miles. Striking the northern end of Lookout Mountain (where Longstreet had his forbidding guns) it makes a 180-degree turn and goes north again, and in the big loop thus formed there is a long finger of land known as Moccasin Point. Across the base of this point there was in 1863 a little road, going west from Chattanooga to the riverbank opposite a place called Brown's Ferry, which was five miles from Chattanooga by water, but less than two miles by this road. From Brown's Ferry it was easy to get to Bridgeport, by road or by river, and although the Confederates had infantry at the ferry the guns on Lookout could not reach the place. So the Federals could break the blockade wide open if they could occupy Brown's Ferry and build a pontoon bridge there.

This they presently did, very neatly, floating pontoons down the river past the Confederate pickets by night, sending troops across at Brown's Ferry to rush the infantry out of there, and bringing Hooker's troops up from Bridgeport to occupy Lookout Valley. Neither Bragg nor Longstreet diagnosed the move until too late, and anyway nearly all of Longstreet's men were around on the eastern side of the mountain, with only one brigade to cover the country between the riverside batteries and Brown's Ferry. This brigade tried hard to hold its ground, and Longstreet sent three more brigades to help it, but Hooker sent in all of Howard's corps and half of Slocum's and after a bruising fight the Confederates were driven away. By October 29 the mopping-up was over. Now the Unionists held everything west of Lookout Mountain, Chattanooga was entirely out of danger, and the only surprise was the discovery that the great threat to the Federal army's life had really been applied very weakly.[13]

This weakness having been exposed and exploited, General Bragg went on to make a substantial mistake, inspired thereto by a dispatch from Mr. Davis, driven (as Mr. Davis was driven) by the fact that the necessities of the case compelled him to try to do more than he had means to do. It was essential to beat this Yankee army at Chattanooga, essential also to recover Knoxville, held by Burnside; and at the end of October Mr. Davis wrote to Bragg to suggest that "you might advantageously assign General Longstreet with his two divisions to the task of expelling Burnside." Bragg told Longstreet to make the move, and Longstreet took his men out of the lines and set off for east Tennessee on November 4, protesting gloomily (and correctly) that his force was not big enough to do the job. Working for Bragg did not seem to be the same as working for Lee, and to General Buckner Longstreet muttered that he could see that "this was to be the fate of our army—to wait till all good opportunities had passed, and then in desperation to seize upon the least favorable one."[14]

. . . all the good opportunities were gone forever, and now for three weeks Bragg's army waited, in meaningless expectation of nobody knew just what, inexplicably weakening itself while its enemy grew stronger; looking down from the encircling heights on Chattanooga in a queer, almost trance-like state, seeing too much but unable to profit by what it saw. There was an uncanny beauty in the spectacle, and Bragg told about it in a letter to his wife: "Just underneath my H D Qtrs are the lines of the two armies, and beyond with their outposts and signal stations are the Lookout, Raccoon and Walden mountains. At night all are brilliantly lit up in the most gorgeous manner by the miriads of camp fires. No scene in the most splendid theater ever approached it."[15] The moon was near the full, and there was an eclipse, putting a cold running shadow on the mountains and the plain and the men who were going to fight there—an omen, beyond doubt, if anyone could figure out what it meant. Bragg sent Buckner and his division away to help Longstreet, and Sherman and his tough western divisions reached the Federals, who by now were nearly twice as strong as the army that was trying to besige them. And at last, on November 24, Grant struck.

The battle of Chattanooga was both a solid achievement and an incredible bit of military melodrama. The whole battlefield was the amphitheater, and the soldiers were spectators and actors at the same time, which had something to do with the way the battle came out. It did not go at all as Grant had planned it, and yet in a strange way he was dominant throughout. In a place where the spectacular was commonplace the picture that lasts the longest is the glimpse of Grant standing on a hill and watching his men break the Confederate line with a charge he had not ordered . . . clamping his jaw on a cigar and remarking that somebody was going to catch it if this charge did not succeed.

The original battle plan was dictated by the shape of the ground. Bragg's army faced Chattanooga in a long crescent, one horn of the crescent touching the Tennessee above town, the other touching it below. Upstream the Confederates held Tunnel Hill, an uneven wooded knob standing a little way back from the water's edge, and downstream they held Lookout Mountain; and the long center of the crescent rested on Missionary Ridge, three hundred feet high, with steep sides, a line of infantry dug in at the base and another, supported strongly by artillery, all along the crest. The whole position was tough but the center was toughest of all, so Grant elected to hit at the flanks: Sherman was to attack above the city and Hooker was to strike at Lookout, leaving Thomas to face Missionary Ridge and to put on enough pressure to keep Bragg from taking troops away from his center to reinforce his flanks.

Hooker's job was easier than had been anticipated, and it produced a fragrant legend. Where the northern end of Lookout Mountain reaches the Tennessee there is a low fore-shore, wide enough for a highway and a railroad right of way, and then there is a long slope, rocky and timbered but not unendurably steep, rising to the base of the great Lookout Mountain precipice. This goes a thousand feet above the river, jutting against the sky like the prow of some fabulous ship out of Valhalla—magnificent to see, but without military significance. The Confederates had a flag and a signal station up there, but their real defensive position was on the lower slope, and it was on the slope that Hooker's men attacked them. The Federals swung around the mountain with their left on the river and their right touching the base of the precipice; they were not so much fighting uphill as fighting along the side of a hill, and as they advanced they found that Bragg had not put enough men in this position to hold it. The Confederates made a good fight but they were badly outnumbered and Hooker's men swept the field clean, knocked Bragg's left entirely away from the mountainside

. . . and during the night sent details up the tall cliffs to raise the flag on the crest. And in the morning the sun burned away the early mists and the whole army saw the flag there, and talked fatuously about "the battle above the clouds"; and Hooker's exiles from the Army of the Potomac found that they were heroes, and did nothing whatever to dilute the fable.

Sherman's luck was just the opposite of Hooker's. Under Grant, pre-battle reconnaissance was not left to staff engineer officers, but was made by the top brass in person, and Grant and Thomas and Sherman had carefully studied Bragg's right before the battle began—and, with the bad luck that sometimes ironically besets the diligent, had unanimously fallen into error. They believed that the high ground held by Bragg's right was the northern end of Missionary Ridge, and that if it could be taken the whole line would collapse. Actually, Tunnel Hill was separate, isolated from the ridge by deep ravines and a tangle of rocky broken country: as powerful a defensive position as any army could hope to find. Bragg's right was commanded by Polk's replacement, General Hardee, and Hardee had entrusted Tunnel Hill to the division led by Irish-born General Pat Cleburne, a crack combat outfit under one of the Confederacy's best soldiers. Altogether Sherman's men had an impossible assignment. They found this out when they attacked on November 24, and although they took the northern tip of the ridge they could not carry Tunnel Hill. Next day, while Hooker's people mopped up at the other end of the line, Sherman's soldiers renewed the attack and got nowhere.

Looking down the whole length of the Confederate line, Grant and Sherman and other Federal officers saw powerful reinforcements moving from the center to reinforce Cleburne; or, at any rate, they thought they did, although they apparently were under some sort of hallucination, because nothing of the kind was really happening. What mattered, however, was what Grant thought he saw, and shortly after noon on November 25 he told Thomas to have his men carry the Confederate trenches at the base of Missionary Ridge. A full-dress assault on the ridge itself might come later, but for the moment this move was simply a battlefield maneuver designed to keep Bragg from strengthening his right.[16]

And so—acting on faulty knowledge his own eyes had given him, trying to balk a move his opponent was not really making—Grant launched the blow that won the battle.

It made a fabulous spectacle: four divisions in a line two miles wide, flags flying, ranks carefully dressed (the Army of the Cumberland had always been a bit particular about infantry drill), moving toward the base of the great mountain wall whose crest was all white with gunsmoke; both armies watching an advance as dramatic as Pickett's charge, and to all appearances as hopeless. Thomas' men reached the base of the ridge, took the trenches there, and then found that they could not stay there because the Confederates on top of the ridge had the whole line under a murderous plunging fire which the Federals could neither hide from nor silence. Grant and Thomas were a mile in the rear, there was no time to wait for new instructions, the only way out of this box was straight ahead—and that way, suddenly, the four divisions took. By regiments and brigades, tentatively at first and then in a desperate all-embracing rush, swept forward by battlefield madness and by the impromptu orders of their own officers, the Federals went scrambling up the side of Missionary Ridge.[17]

Far in the rear Grant looked on, impassive once he realized that nobody near him had ordered this incredible attack and that the only thing to do was to watch and wait for victory or disaster.[18] Beside him was Thomas, equally impassive but more majestic about it; and on top of Missionary Ridge Bragg's soldiers also watched, hardly believing what they saw, sensing finally that what was coming up the mountain was defeat. Perhaps their worst handicap was that they could see all of the enemy's strength and none of their own; each infantryman could see no more of his army than his own platoon or regiment, but out in front he could see 20,000 Federals all of whom seemed to be coming straight at him. All at once it was too much to take, and some of the best soldiers in the Confederacy broke and ran for the rear, abandoning a position which the furious Bragg insisted could have been held by a skirmish line. Long afterward, one of Bragg's veterans told a Union officer: "You Yanks had got too far into our inwards," and Bragg himself felt that his men had been able to see too much.[19]

However it came about, Bragg's line broke in half, the

center of it all gone, Missionary Ridge gone with it, the battle irretrievably lost; and the Army of Tennessee drew off southeastward to the Georgia railroad town of Dalton, with Cleburne's division fighting a stiff rear-guard action to keep the catastrophe from becoming complete. On the crest of Missionary Ridge victorious Federal soldiers capered and yelled, flourishing captured battle flags, straddling captured cannon, "completely and frantically drunk with excitement." Grant wanted to press forward in full pursuit, believing that "an army was never whipped as badly as Bragg was" and that he could push this one clear out of the Confederacy; but he did not think he had enough rations or wagons for a long march across a harsh mountain country, and Washington was ordering him to send help to Burnside, who was believed to be in dire peril, besieged at Knoxville by Longstreet.[20] Anyway, the memory of Chickamauga was a powerful reminder of the trouble a Yankee general could get into, making too impetuous a pursuit in this part of the country. Vigorous pursuit was not made, and it really did not matter much. The Confederate grip on Chattanooga had been broken. Now the North could get on with the war.

CHAPTER FIVE

The Impossibilities

1. The Impassable Gulf

AFTER THE FALL of 1863 their paths divided sharply. The two Presidents had been implacable foes all along, but so far they had gone on parallel courses. They met similar problems with similar expedients, faced the same sort of men in Cabinet, in Congress and in uniform, and if they had different thoughts they at least thought in the same way and related the items thought about to the same basic values. The government at Richmond in the first two and one-half years of war was simply the government at Washington transposed to a different key.

But now the war itself changed. The Presidents after all were its creatures. It imprisoned them even as they shaped it; requiring greatness of them, it determined the form this greatness could take. After this fateful autumn the parts these men had to play became very different. Mr. Lincoln was compelled to look in one direction and Mr. Davis was compelled to look in another direction entirely. It became necessary, in short, for Mr. Lincoln to think about what was going to happen after the war ended; Mr. Davis had to concentrate on ways and means by which the war could be kept from ending. For one man the horizon was expanding, for the other it was growing fatefully narrower, and each man had to do what he could.

For Mr. Davis, it was immediately necessary to pick up the pieces after the disaster in Tennessee. General Bragg asked to be relieved of his command, there being nothing else he could possibly do. He blamed his defeat on "the bad conduct of veteran troops who had never before failed in any duty," and considered this partly due to "the effect produced by the treasonable act of Longstreet, Hill, and Polk in sacrificing the army in their effort to degrade and remove me for personal ends." He also blamed "drunkenness, most flagrant, during the whole three days of our trials"; General Breckinridge and Major General B. F. Cheatham could not be counted on in time of adversity because "they take to the bottle at once, and drown their cares by becoming stupid and unfit for any duty." Then, coming down to the real difficulty, he told the President frankly: "I fear we both erred in the conclusion for me to retain command here after the clamor against me."[1] For Bragg to keep his command any longer was of course out of the question, and Mr. Davis reluctantly removed him, putting Hardee in his place temporarily while he looked for a permanent successor.

Once again he looked first at General Lee, and for a time it seemed likely that Lee would be sent west. In the War Department some men argued that Lee and most of his army ought to go, leaving in Virginia just enough force to garrison Richmond, and striving to recover Tennessee at all costs: this idea arising after the Commissary General, Colonel Northrop (who was gloomy even in the best of times), reported that with Tennessee gone the Confederacy could not possibly get enough meat to feed both the army and the civilian population. Bragg told Mr. Davis that a counterstroke ought to be built up with the Army of Tennessee as a nucleus, so that "with our greatest leader at the head—yourself if practicable" the inspired host could strike the Yankee invader "and crush him in his power and glory." Lee tactfully suggested that if the President would like to put Beauregard in Bragg's place it would be easy to find another competent man for the defense of Charleston. Lee agreed that the situation was desperate, remarking that "upon the defense of the country threatened by General Grant depends the safety of the points now held by us on the Atlantic and they are in as great danger from his successful advance as by the attacks to which they are at present directly subjected."

Beauregard, in turn, called for "a sudden and rapid concentration upon some selected, decisive, strategic point." Such a point, he believed, lay in the Tennessee-Georgia area, and Beauregard wanted 40,000 men drawn from other parts of the Confederacy and added to Hardee's army, believing that it would then be able to drive Grant back to the Ohio River. He doubted that the administration would accept any plan that came from him direct, so he sent his proposal to his Louisiana friend, Pierre Soulé, suggesting that he pass it around in Richmond wherever he thought it might have effect. He added: "I am filled with intense anxiety lest golden opportunities shall be lost—lost forever."

At one point Lee took it for granted that he himself would be sent to Georgia, and he told Jeb Stuart that the most he hoped was that he could some day come back to Virginia. He did not want to go at all, and he offered quiet but firm resistance. He could do little, he told the President, if sent west as a temporary commander; if he got the job as a permanent assignment he did not think he would get cordial co-operation, it would be necessary to find somebody to command the Army of Northern Virginia, and "I have not that confidence either in my strength or ability as would lead me of my own option to undertake the command in question."[2]

Lee was always most deferential when he wrote to Mr. Davis, and these mild remonstrances coming from him were the equivalent of another man's slamming his hat on the floor and stamping his feet; the idea that Lee might be sent to Georgia was abandoned, and in the middle of December Mr. Davis did what he had rebuked Longstreet for suggesting after Chickamauga: that is, he gave the job to Joe Johnston. He disliked this prickly little general as much as ever and he distrusted his fighting capacity, but the man still looked like a good one to call on in a crisis. Besides, it seemed likely that the long-suffering Army of Tennessee would not accept anybody else.

The President gave Johnston the army but he could give him nothing more. Neither he nor anyone else doubted that the price of Confederate salvation might be the defeat of Grant's army, but Johnston's army was much too weak to inflict such a defeat—Hardee had just warned that it would have to retreat if Grant made a serious advance—and how it was to be reinforced substantially was more than Mr. Davis could say. The available figures gave him no comfort whatever.

Before the battle of Chattanooga a War Department functionary tried to discover exactly how many soldiers the Confederacy had under arms in that fall of 1863. Counting every unit in existence—Lee's army and Beauregard's and Bragg's, troops in the Virginia and Carolina mountains, garrisons of coastal fortifications, men guarding the innumerable openings along the Carolina sounds and in Florida, troops in Alabama and along the Gulf Coast, and finally the faraway soldiers in Arkansas, Texas, and other lands beyond the Mississippi—he came up with a tabulation showing a total effective strength of 227,000. Forty thousand of these were in Edmund Kirby Smith's domain beyond the river, and they might as well be in the moon for all the direct use Richmond could make of them. Ten thousand more were in various partisan units that were often useful for plaguing the Yankees but could not be counted on for combat duty; and 26,000 of the remainder were cavalrymen. Thus east of the Mississippi and available for line-of-battle service Mr. Davis had slightly more than 150,000 men, infantry and artillery. Johnston already had upwards of 50,000 of these; which meant that there were in existence, outside of his own force and responsive to Richmond's orders, not quite 100,000 Confederate soldiers. Beauregard had talked hopefully of giving Johnston 40,000 reinforcements, which would seem to be a minimum if Johnston were to take the offensive, although by the December troop returns even this would have left Johnston's army smaller than Grant's. But those 40,000 would have to come out of the less-than-100,000 total, and to perform such subtraction without wrecking the Confederacy's defense elsewhere called for an extremely special kind of arithmetic. Mr. Davis did not try it.[3]

So Johnston got about what Bragg had left him, along with a cheerful letter from Secretary Seddon bidding him restore "the discipline, confidence, and prestige of the army," to build up its numbers and to do all he could to strengthen its ordnance and transportation departments. As soon as possible Johnston was to take the offensive; a point also emphasized by the President, who strongly hoped that "you will soon be able to commence active operations against the enemy." Johnston had no such hopes. He privately told Senator Wigfall "We cannot take the offensive," adding that in consequence "I may fairly expect, in a month or two, such denunciations as have been heaped upon my predecessor." He did his best to increase the size of his army, and the return of absentees and the recovery of sick and wounded men presently made good the losses incurred on Lookout Mountain and Missionary Ridge. In addition, Johnston tried to increase his combat strength by getting slaves to do all of the army's "extra duty" work—the jobs ordinarily done by cooks, engineer laborers, pioneers and so on. Even for an army no larger than his, he told Senator Wigfall, such details normally kept 10,000 men away from the firing line.[4]

Johnston was going to have to make the best of it with an inadequate force, and the same thing was true of Lee. Lee had escaped being torn away from his Army of Northern Virginia, but he had to get through the autumn with that army sadly understrength. Longstreet's corps had been detached in the hope that it would quickly return once a western victory had been won. The victory had been won but the missing corps had not returned; after sharing in the long failure to exploit the victory it had been sent off toward Knoxville to destroy Burnside, and this move had accomplished nothing better than to worry Mr. Lincoln and to alarm the East Tennessee Unionists, who feared that the Secessionist power might re-establish itself among them and inflict horrid indignities. Longstreet did make Burnside withdraw inside his fortified lines at Knoxville, but when he attacked those lines he was repulsed and not long afterward Sherman came on the scene with a powerful relieving column from Chattanooga. Longstreet had to withdraw, and now he was marooned in the mountainous border country along the Tennessee-Virginia line. He would rejoin Lee in the spring, lighter by the loss of various illusions. Meanwhile, it was necessary to realize that Tennessee probably had been lost for good.[5]

Lee's army had been active enough all summer and fall, but the most that could be said was that it had avoided disaster and had kept the Federals from mounting a real offensive.

When Lee crossed the Potomac on his way south from Gettysburg Meade followed, going east of the Blue Ridge and planning to strike Lee's flank when the Confederate army came through the mountain passes. Meade maneuvered skillfully, and late in July he found the opening he wanted at Manassas Gap, with almost half of Lee's army east of the Blue Ridge and the rest of it still trying to get out of the Shenandoah Valley. The opportunity was glittering, but

Meade tripped over the same thing that had tripped Bragg—inability to get a subordinate to execute a good battle plan. He ordered the new commander of his III Corps, Major General William H. French, to go through the gap and attack, and a vigorous blow might very well have disposed of Ewell's corps and possibly a good part of A. P. Hill's; and this, coming on the heels of the terrible losses at Gettysburg, would almost certainly have brought the curtain down on the Army of Northern Virginia. But French skirmished weakly with one brigade when he should have struck with his entire corps, backed by all the rest of the army, which was coming up fast, and the opportunity quickly vanished. Lee brought his separated corps together safely and took up a good defensive position south of the Rapidan River. And here, halfway between the two capitals, separated by a river that had seen much campaigning and would see much more, the two armies caught their breath and waited to see what would happen next.[6]

As they waited, Mr. Lincoln noted an oddity in the military art and raised an interesting question: a civilian's question, awkward and somewhat innocent, but hard to answer.

Meade had asked Halleck whether the government wanted him to take the offensive; he thought the risk would be substantial and he did not think he could accomplish much, but he would move forward if Washington wanted him to. Lincoln told Halleck he had neither orders nor advice to give, but he said there was this one point that bothered him: Lee had with him, and available at Richmond, of all arms, counting extra-duty men, probably 60,000 soldiers; Meade, estimating numbers in the same way, had about 90,000, for a good three-to-two advantage. But apparently to stand on the defensive on ground of one's own choosing (as Lee would do, if Meade moved against him) gave such an advantage that three could not safely attack two, and so when the two went on the defensive the three were immobilized.

"If the enemy's sixty thousand," said the President, "are sufficient to keep our ninety thousand away from Richmond, why, by the same rule, may not forty thousand of ours keep their sixty thousand away from Washington, leaving us fifty thousand to put to some other use? Having practically come to the mere defensive, it seems to be no economy at all to employ twice as many men for that object as are needed.

With no object, certainly, to mislead myself, I can perceive no fault in this statement, unless we admit that we are not the equal of the enemy man for man. I hope you will consider it."[7]

By a singular chance, Mr. Lincoln wrote this letter the day the Battle of Chickamauga began. Before the week was out he provided his own answer; that is, he had Stanton and Halleck take two army corps away from Meade and send them to Tennessee.

It may be interesting to speculate on the reply he would have got if he had been able to ask his question of General Lee. Lee had no intention of going on the defensive, even though he had the two and the other man had the three; early in October he boldly marched up the Rapidan, crossed the river and swung northeast around Meade's flank, looking for a chance to use his smaller army to beat the larger one. He had done it before, and he was trying it now even though Longstreet's corps was gone. But Meade was more alert than the other Federal generals had been and he handled his army better; Lee could neither interpose between him and Washington nor compel him to stand and fight, and the one solid contact between the two armies came when Lee's advance struck incautiously at the Federal rear guard at Bristoe Station, near Broad Run, not a great way from the historic Bull Run battlefield. A. P. Hill's corps was repulsed here, with substantial loss, Meade drew his army together at Centreville, and Lee realized that a further advance would simply cause the Federals to get into the fortified lines around Washington, where it would be impossible to attack them.

In a somewhat similar situation in the fall of 1862, Lee had crossed the Potomac and invaded the North, pulling the Yankee army after him. He wanted to do the same thing now but he finally concluded that he could not, and he told Secretary Seddon why: the move would take him a long way from Richmond, "and the condition of the roads and the stage of the streams at this season of the year are so uncertain that I think it would be hazardous"; besides, his soldiers were too miserably shod and clothed for an invasion. The sublimest sight of the war, Lee said, "was the cheerfulness and alacrity exhibited by this army in the pursuit of the enemy under all the trials and privations to which it was exposed," but this sublimity should not be tried too far. In a letter to Mrs.

Lee he revealed that he had ruled out a further advance entirely because of his feeling for the soldiers: "If they had been properly provided with clothes I would certainly have endeavored to have thrown them north of the Potomac. But thousands were *barefooted,* thousands with fragments of shoes, and all without overcoats, blankets or warm clothing. I could not bear to expose them to certain suffering on an uncertain issue."[8]

In short, 1863 was not 1862 . . . Lee could not advance, and it was pointless to stay where he was, and so he brought his army back, skirmishing and sparring along the way. He made a stand on the Rappahannock River, at last, planning to remain there, but the aggressive Federals wrenched a bridgehead away from him, and finally he returned to the old position behind the Rapidan. The campaign had lasted a month, and at its close things were about as they had been when it began—except that Lee had been compelled to realize that his army now was too weak to carry the war to the enemy. Nobody knew it then, but the Army of Northern Virginia had made its last offensive campaign.

If not the offensive, then the defensive. Late in November Meade moved out to try what three could do against two, and he got down past Lee's right, crossed the Rapidan and went on into the eastern fringe of the Wilderness in the hope that he could crush Ewell's corps before the rest of Lee's army could come to its rescue. Meade's general plan was excellent, but it called for movement by several columns, and one of these was headed by French and the III Corps. French took a wrong turn at a crossroads, and then let one of Ewell's divisions delay him for a day, and the whole movement was thrown off schedule. Lee moved over to meet this thrust and posted his army behind a little brook known as Mine Run. Meade ordered an assault on the center of this line, but he quickly changed his mind when Major General G. K. Warren of the II Corps assured him that it would be possible, on Warren's front, to overwhelm the Confederate right. Meade gave Warren powerful reinforcements and told him to make the assault. But he got no fight at all because Warren, after a day's delay, took a fresh look in the cold dawn of November 30, considered Lee's lines too strong and canceled the attack. No other openings appeared, and the Army of the Potomac, humiliated but not hurt very much, went back to its old camp; and presently both armies went into winter quarters.[9]

By putting on blinders and looking resolutely at nothing but the area between Richmond and Washington, it was possible to argue that the Confederacy was as well off at the year's end as it had been at the beginning. The rival armies had neither advanced nor retreated: all the might the Federals could bring to bear here had gained nothing at all, and the fiasco at Mine Run was significant—"Forward to Richmond" always meant either a bloody beating or a shameful fumble for the invaders.

But nobody could wear blinders now, neither the President nor the ordinary thoughtful citizen. The war was not just what happened between Richmond and Washington, and although no Southerner was ready to think of the awful word, Defeat, it was impossible to deny that the sky was getting darker. Looking back after the war, a Richmond woman remembered that fall as a time when "gloom pervaded our hearts," and said that there was no way to dispel it: "The fine weather, the bracing atmosphere, the delicious, dreamy influence of the Indian summer, could not chase from our doors the dread phantom that lurked on the threshold—could not drive from the dark closet the skeleton of the house."[10] When Mr. Davis addressed the Congress on December 7 he tried, as in duty bound, to put a good face on things, but his speech was somber.

It could hardly be anything else. The government was almost bankrupt, with an inflated currency and a grossly inadequate tax system; it had no foreign affairs worth mentioning, the kingdoms of the earth having apparently concluded that this was no nation but simply a revolted province that would eventually be brought back to its old condition; and during the year cities, states, rivers, and armies had been lost, so that in the time just ahead a larger burden would have to be borne by a strength that had been diminished. To meet this, Mr. Davis called on his people to be steadfast, and to realize that the men who controlled the government at Washington were demanding nothing short of complete submission.

"They refused," he cried, "even to listen to proposals for the only peace possible between us—a peace which, recognizing the impassable gulf which divides us, may leave the two peoples separately to recover from the injuries inflicted on both by the causeless war now being waged against us." It was necessary therefore to talk the one language that could be understood, the language of military force: "We now know that the only reliable hope for peace is in the vigor of our resistance."

The Richmond *Examiner,* which rarely found itself on Mr. Davis' side, was with him all the way when it came to demanding bitter-end defiance of the malevolent Yankee, and its editor shaped one sentence that summed up the world which Confederate President and people had to live in at the close of 1863: "Our sole policy and cunningest diplomacy is fighting; our most insinuating negotiator is the Confederate army in line of battle."[11]

This stated the case accurately, but it was also a cruel statement of ruinous limitations. A later generation would criticize Mr. Davis for being too engrossed by purely military problems, but he was a man beset. The terrible gulf he was talking about did exist, because men believed that it did, and the Confederate nation was alone on the far side of it. To build a bridge that would reach across the gulf to the future was beyond him. There was only the army, drawn up in line of battle; the army, and the hope that out of dwindling resources it could be made strong enough to keep the battle line from breaking.

2. Eloquence at Gettysburg

MR. DAVIS believed that the gulf was impassable; Mr. Lincoln believed that it did not really exist. His refusal to admit that there were two countries was as firm as Mr. Davis' insistence that there could never be anything but two, and although the war was a fearful destroyer—of young men, of wealth, of the certainties the nation used to live by—Mr. Lincoln was compelled to see it as an instrument of continued growth. It was necessary for him to believe that when the war ended there would be one country, big enough now both for those who had fought to save it and those who had fought to divide it. Believing this, and trying to make victory certain, he had greatly raised the stakes; unless what he had done was to be disowned, the nation must eventually be big enough for everybody who lived in it, for master and servant as well as for friend and foe, claiming the loyalty of all men because it recognized all men as equals. Political unity based on acceptance of the fundamental unity of human beings would be unbreakable; it was also, at the moment, almost unimaginable.

The dread of equality was one of the things that had destroyed unity in the first place. When the President proclaimed the emancipation of slaves he had made it impossible for the Southern leadership to accept reunion, and he had disturbed many people in the North as well. The proclamation was a commitment to the future, of almost unlimited scope. In the war that had called it forth the past was breaking up, and a thing done to win the war had to be at the same time a thing done to help shape the future.

It was useless for the President to insist—as he did insist, over and over—that everything he did was done solely to bring military victory. When Secretary Chase urged him to broaden the Emancipation Proclamation he refused, saying that the proclamation "has no constitutional or legal justification except as a military measure," and that to extend it without direct military necessity would put him "in the boundless field of absolutism"; and yet the proclamation meant much more than battles won and everybody knew it, and Mr. Chase voiced the belief that unless people recovered from their infatuated confidence in Mr. Lincoln the country was done for.[1] One of the first men to discover where the President's thinking was taking him was General Banks, in New Orleans.

Mr. Lincoln was going to try an experiment. He wanted to begin to rebuild the Union before the fighting stopped, and he had a plan that would be tested in Louisiana. Under this plan, if one-tenth of the qualified voters in the state would take the loyalty oath, abjuring secession and all of its works and specifically accepting the death of slavery, any state government they formed would be recognized and defended in Washington; legally, Louisiana would be back in the Union, with its own executive, courts and Congressional representation, and there would be amnesty (with certain stipulated exceptions) for all, including the non-jurant majority.[2]

The first question to arise, naturally, was what this new, war-born state government would be expected to do about emancipation, and when he wrote about this to Banks the

President ranged far ahead of military victory and reflected on the distant future. It would be best, he said, if Louisiana would draft a constitution recognizing the Emancipation Proclamation, and adopting emancipation in those parts of the state not covered by the proclamation; but there was more to it than that, and he tried to make it clear.

"And while she is at it," wrote Mr. Lincoln, "I think it would not be objectionable for her to adopt some practical system by which the two races could gradually live themselves out of their old relation to each other, and both come out better prepared for the new."

Apparently it was hard to define it better than that—as a matter of fact, in a century to come a better definition would not be found—and Mr. Lincoln felt strongly that "education for the young blacks" ought to be included in the plan. He considered, too, that the self-interest of the owning class might be appealed to: "As an anti-slavery man I have a motive to desire emancipation which pro-slavery men do not have; but even they have strong enough reason to thus place themselves under the shield of the Union . . . to hedge against the recurrence of the scenes through which we are now passing."

As an old-time statehouse politician Mr. Lincoln knew the tricks political conventions are capable of, and later in the fall he warned General Banks (an old-time statehouse man himself) that no sharp practices would be allowed: "If a few professedly loyal men shall draw the disloyal about them and colorably set up a state government, repudiating the Emancipation Proclamation and re-establishing slavery, I cannot recognize or sustain their work." There could be no return to the Union, in other words, without the destruction of slavery; yet the President was prepared to be reasonable in regard to gradual emancipation provided always that the gradualists were honest.

"I have said and say again," he wrote, "that if a new state government, acting in harmony with this government and consistently with general freedom, shall think best to adopt a reasonable temporary arrangement in relation to the landless and homeless freed people, I do not object; but my word is out to be *for* and not *against* them on the question of their permanent freedom."[3]

Embedded in the thinking of many Americans was the

conviction that these landless and homeless ones were nat-
ural inferiors who would always need guidance and restraint.
Almost everyone had a little of this feeling; some were full
of it, and showed prejudice in its most graceless form. Early
in August one John McMahon, from the north woods of
Pennsylvania, sent President Lincoln a telegram of protest:
EQUAL RIGHTS & JUSTICE TO ALL MEN IN THE UNITED STATES
FOREVER. WHITE MEN IS IN CLASS NUMBER ONE & BLACK MEN
IS IN CLASS NUMBER TWO & MUST BE GOVERNED BY WHITE
MEN FOREVER. Secretary John Nicolay wrote a reply whose
phrasing clearly came from Mr. Lincoln. After reporting that
the President had received this telegram and was meditating
on it, Nicolay wrote: "As it is my business to assist him
whenever I can, I will thank you to inform me, for his use,
whether you are either a white man or a black one, because
in either case you cannot be regarded as an entirely impartial
judge. It may be that you belong to a third or fourth class
of *yellow* or *red* men, in which case the impartiality of your
judgment would be more apparent."[4]

How this sat with John McMahon is not recorded, but the
man had merely said bluntly what other men put in smoother
terms. Belief in the inevitability of emancipation was growing, but many of the believers refused to admit that the death
of slavery should mean any genuine change in the levels on
which the two races lived. Near the end of the year Montgomery Blair, Postmaster General and a faithful leader of
border state Republicans, wrote to Democrat Barlow insisting
that no such change was necessary. It was absurd, Blair said,
for Barlow or any other man to think that the war could possibly end without the destruction of slavery; but there was
abundant room for Republicans and Democrats (including
the presently embattled Democrats of the deep South) to
join hands against the abolitionists "in sustaining this exclusive right of government in the white race." This was
little less than John McMahon had been rebuked for saying,
but no Presidential secretary asked Blair if he happened to be
Chinese or Indian; after all, he was a member of the cabinet,
and of The Blair Family to boot, and besides he was stoutly
insistent that men who still thought slavery could be kept
alive were fools. A few days later he sent Barlow an edged
warning for conservative Democrats: "Carlyle tracing the
growing disorders of the French Revolution to the obstinate

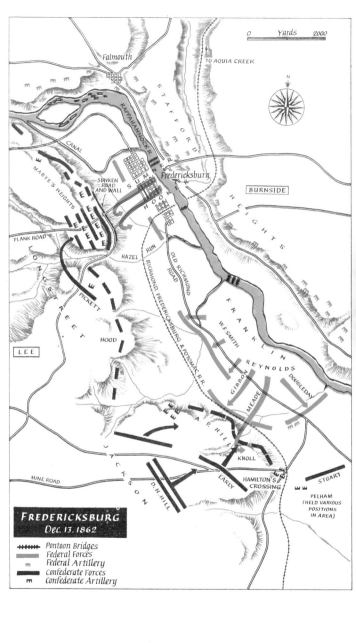

FREDERICKSBURG
Dec. 13, 1862

+++++++ Pontoon Bridges
▬▬▬▬ Federal Forces
▥ Federal Artillery
▬ ▬ ▬ Confederate Forces
▥ Confederate Artillery

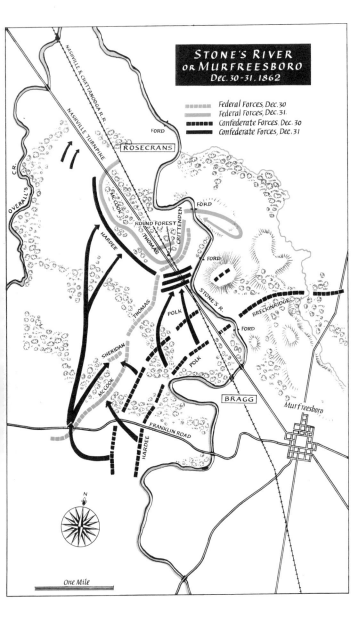

STONE'S RIVER
OR MURFREESBORO
Dec. 30-31. 1862

Federal Forces, Dec. 30
Federal Forces, Dec. 31.
Confederate Forces, Dec. 30
Confederate Forces, Dec. 31

NASHVILLE K CHATTANOOGA R.R.
NASHVILLE TURNPIKE

FORD
ROSECRANS
FORD

O.R.
OVERALL'S C.R.

McCOOK
ROUND FOREST
THOMAS
HARDEE
CRITTENDEN

FORD

FORD

POLK
THOMAS
STONE'S R.
BRECKINRIDGE

SHERIDAN

POLK

FORD

McCOOK

BRAGG

Murfreesboro

FRANKLIN ROAD

HARDEE

N

One Mile

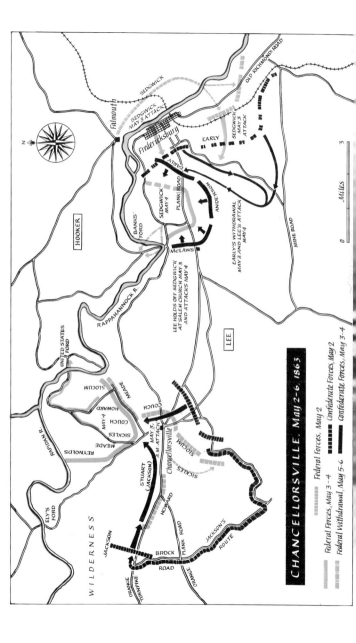

CHANCELLORSVILLE May 2-6, 1863

Federal Forces, May 2
Federal Forces, May 3-4
Federal Withdrawal, May 5-6
Confederate Forces, May 2
Confederate Forces, May 3-4

FALMOUTH
Fredericksburg
SEDGWICK MAY 3 ATTACK
SEDGWICK MAY 3 ATTACK
SEDGWICK MAY 3 ATTACK
OLD RICHMOND ROAD
EARLY
SEDGWICK MAY 4
BANKS' FORD
PLANK ROAD
ANDERSON
EARLY'S WITHDRAWAL MAY 3 AND LEE'S ATTACK MAY 4
MINE ROAD
McLAWS
LEE HOLDS OFF SEDGWICK AT SALEM CHURCH MAY 3 AND ATTACKS MAY 4
RAPPAHANNOCK R.
HOOKER
LEE

UNITED STATES FORD
RAPIDAN R.
SLOCUM
MEADE
HOWARD
COUCH
SICKLES
COUCH
SICKLES
MAY 3, A.M. ATTACK
Chancellorsville
STUART (JACKSON)
HOWARD
SICKLES
ELY'S FORD
REYNOLDS
MEADE
WILDERNESS
JACKSON
ORANGE TURNPIKE
BROCK ROAD
PLANK ROAD
ORANGE PLANK ROAD
JACKSON'S ROUTE

Miles
0   3

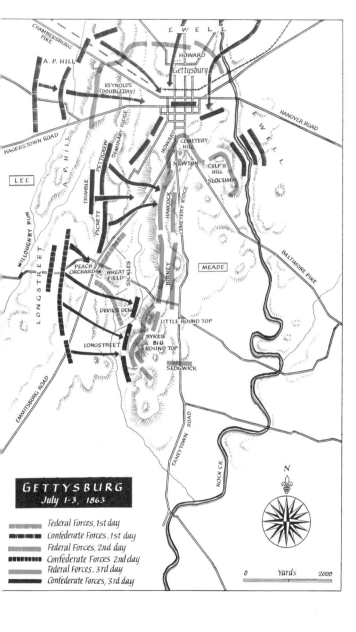

GETTYSBURG
July 1-3, 1863

▓▓▓ Federal Forces, 1st day
▬▬▬ Confederate Forces, 1st day
▓▓▓ Federal Forces, 2nd day
▬▬▬ Confederate Forces 2nd day
▓▓▓ Federal Forces, 3rd day
▬▬▬ Confederate Forces, 3rd day

0   Yards   2000

N

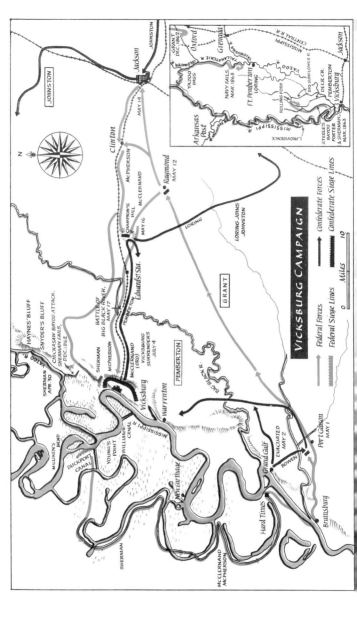

VICKSBURG CAMPAIGN

Federal Forces
Confederate Forces
Federal Siege Lines
Confederate Siege Lines

Miles
0   10

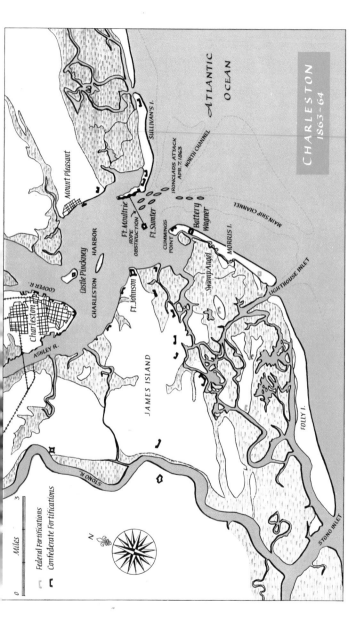

CHARLESTON
1863-64

ATLANTIC OCEAN

Federal Fortifications
Confederate Fortifications

Miles
0   3

N

SULLIVAN'S I.

Mount Pleasant

Castle Pinckney

Charleston

ASHLEY R.

COOPER R.

CHARLESTON HARBOR

Ft. Moultrie
ROPE OBSTRUCTION
Ft. Sumter

IRONCLADS ATTACK
APR. 7, 1863

NORTH CHANNEL

Battery Wagner

CUMMINGS POINT

MORRIS I.

MAIN SHIP CHANNEL

Ft. Johnson

JAMES ISLAND

Swamp Angel

LIGHTHOUSE INLET

STONO R.

FOLLY I.

STONO INLET

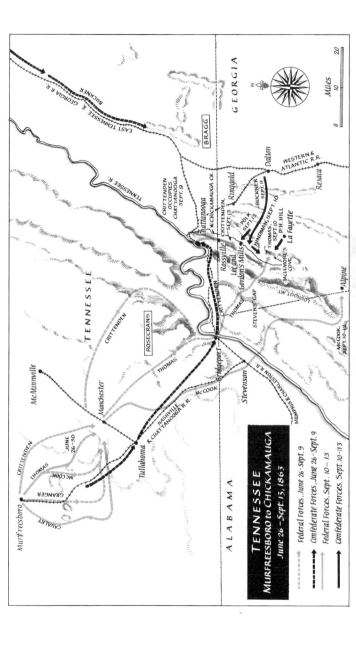

TENNESSEE
MURFREESBORO to CHICKAMAUGA
June 26–Sept. 15, 1863

Federal Forces, June 26–Sept. 9
Confederate Forces, June 26–Sept. 9
Federal Forces, Sept. 10–13
Confederate Forces, Sept. 10–13

GEORGIA

TENNESSEE

ALABAMA

Miles
0   10   20

GEORGIA & TENNESSEE R.R.
EAST TENNESSEE & GEORGIA R.R.
BUCKNER
BRAGG

TENNESSEE R.

CRITTENDEN OCCUPIES CHATTANOOGA SEPT. 9

WESTERN & ATLANTIC R.R.

Dalton
Resaca
Ringgold
BUCKNER SEPT. 11
POLK SEPT. 13
HINDMAN, SEPT. 10
D. H. HILL
La Fayette
THOMAS, SEPT. 10
McLEMORE'S COVE
Alpine

W. CHICKAMAUGA CR.
Chattanooga
CRITTENDEN SEPT. 13
Rossville
Lee and Gordon's Mills
CRITTENDEN
THOMAS
STEVENS GAP
McCOOK, SEPT. 10–13
LOOKOUT MT.

ROSECRANS
CRITTENDEN
THOMAS
Bridgeport
Stevenson
McCOOK

NASHVILLE & CHATTANOOGA R.R.
MEMPHIS & CHARLESTON R.R.

McMinnville
Manchester
THOMAS
Tullahoma

Murfreesboro

GRANGER
CRITTENDEN
THOMAS
McCOOK
SYMOW
JUNE 26–30
CAVALRY

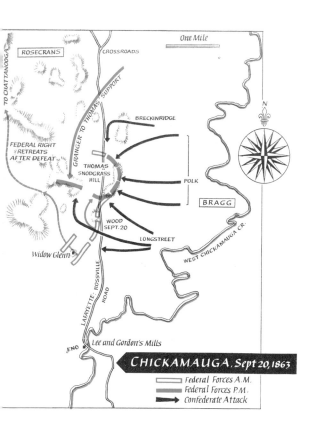

One Mile

ROSECRANS   CROSSROADS

TO CHATTANOOGA

BRECKINRIDGE

FEDERAL RIGHT
RETREATS
AFTER DEFEAT

GRANGER TO THOMAS' SUPPORT

THOMAS
SNODGRASS
HILL

POLK

BRAGG

N

WOOD
SEPT. 20

LONGSTREET

Widow Glenn

WEST CHICKAMAUGA CR.

LAFAYETTE-ROSSVILLE ROAD

ENO   Lee and Gordon's Mills

CHICKAMAUGA, Sept. 20, 1863

☐ Federal Forces A.M.
▬ Federal Forces P.M.
➤ Confederate Attack

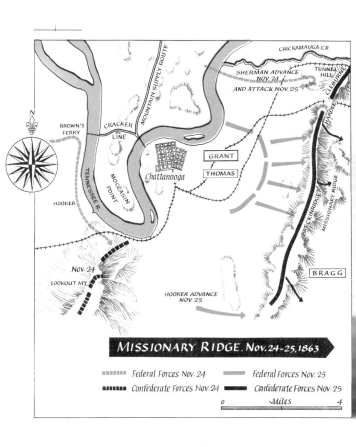

MISSIONARY RIDGE, Nov. 24-25, 1863

Federal Forces Nov. 24 ········ Federal Forces Nov. 25 ━━━━
Confederate Forces Nov. 24 ▪▪▪▪ Confederate Forces Nov. 25 ━━━━

0   Miles   4

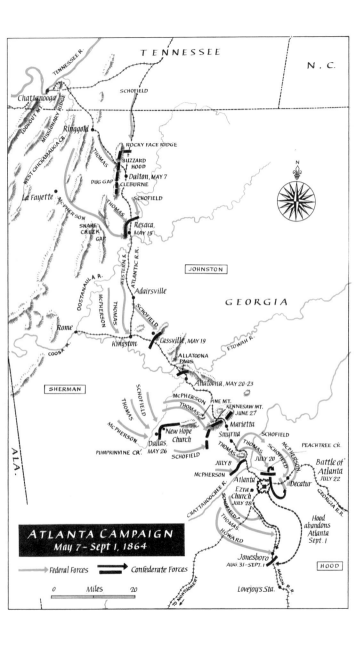

ATLANTA CAMPAIGN
May 7 – Sept 1, 1864

→ Federal Forces ➤ Confederate Forces

0   Miles   20

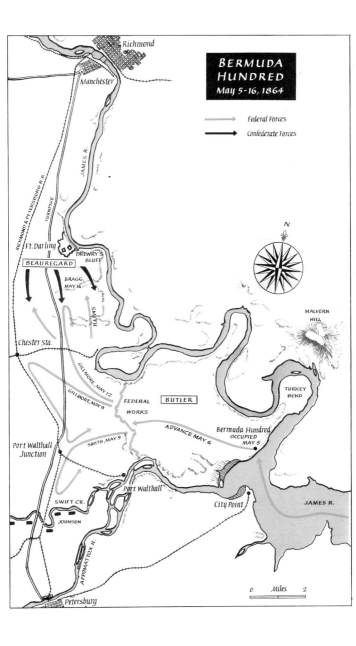

BERMUDA
HUNDRED
May 5-16, 1864

Federal Forces

Confederate Forces

Richmond

Manchester

JAMES R.

RICHMOND & PETERSBURG R.R.

TURNPIKE

Ft. Darling

BEAUREGARD

DREWRY'S BLUFF

BRAGG, MAY 16

HAGOOD

N

MALVERN HILL

Chester Sta.

GILLMORE, MAY 12

GILLMORE, MAY 9

FEDERAL WORKS

BUTLER

ADVANCE MAY 6

TURKEY BEND

SMITH, MAY 9

Bermuda Hundred
OCCUPIED MAY 5

Port Walthall
Junction

SWIFT CR.

Port Walthall

City Point

JAMES R.

JOHNSON

APPOMATTOX R.

Petersburg

0   Miles   2

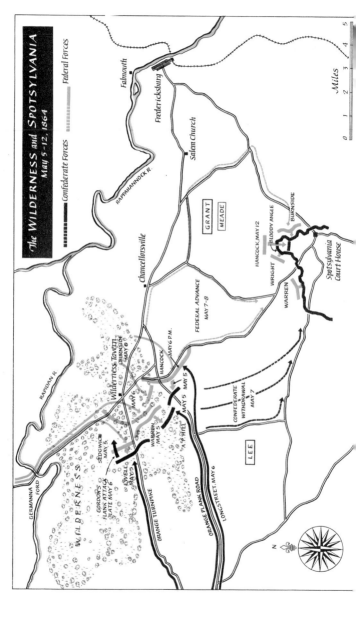

The Wilderness and Spotsylvania
May 5–12, 1864

Confederate Forces   Federal Forces

Miles
0 1 2 3 4 5

GERMANNA FORD
RAPIDAN R.
RAPPAHANNOCK R.
Falmouth
Fredericksburg
Salem Church
Chancellorsville
Wilderness Tavern
WILDERNESS
GORDON'S FLANK ATTACK LATE MAY 6
SEDGWICK MAY 5
EWELL MAY 5
WARREN MAY 5
A.P. HILL
ORANGE TURNPIKE
ORANGE PLANK ROAD
LONGSTREET, MAY 6
MAY 5
MAY 5
MAY 5
HANCOCK
MAY 6 P.M.
BURNSIDE MAY 6
CONFEDERATE WITHDRAWAL MAY 7
LEE
GRANT
MEADE
FEDERAL ADVANCE MAY 7–8
HANCOCK, MAY 12
BLOODY ANGLE
WRIGHT
WARREN
BURNSIDE
Spotsylvania Court House

N

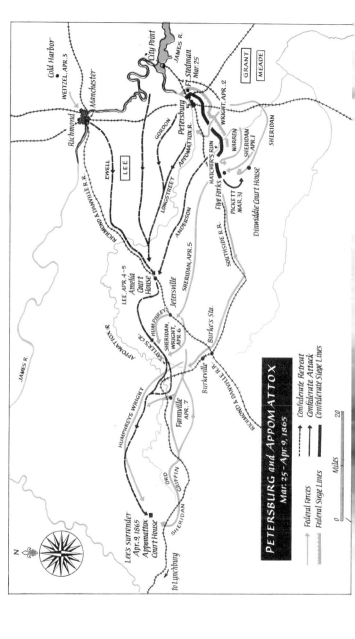

PETERSBURG and APPOMATTOX
Mar. 25–Apr. 9, 1865

Federal Forces
Confederate Retreat
Confederate Attack
Federal Siege Lines
Confederate Siege Lines

0   10   20
Miles

N

Lee's surrender Apr. 9, 1865
Appomattox Court House

to Lynchburg

JAMES R.

APPOMATTOX R.

Richmond & Danville R.R.

Richmond

Manchester

Cold Harbor

WEITZEL, APR. 3

Cold Harbor

JAMES R.

City Point

GRANT
MEADE

Ft. Stedman
Mar. 25

WRIGHT, APR. 2

Petersburg

APPOMATTOX R.

GORDON

LONGSTREET

ANDERSON

EWELL

LEE

SAYLER'S CR.

HUMPHREYS

Amelia Court House

LEE, APR. 4–5

SHERIDAN, APR. 5

WRIGHT, APR. 6

Jetersville

SHERIDAN, APR. 6

HATCHER'S RUN

WARREN

SHERIDAN, APR. 1

Five Forks

PICKETT MAR. 31

SHERIDAN

Dinwiddie Court House

SOUTHSIDE R.R.

Burke's Sta.

Burkeville

RICHMOND & DANVILLE R.R.

Farmville APR. 7

HUMPHREYS, WRIGHT

HUMPHREYS WRIGHT

ORD

GRIFFIN

SHERIDAN

VIRGINIA, 1863–65

0   Miles   30

palacios

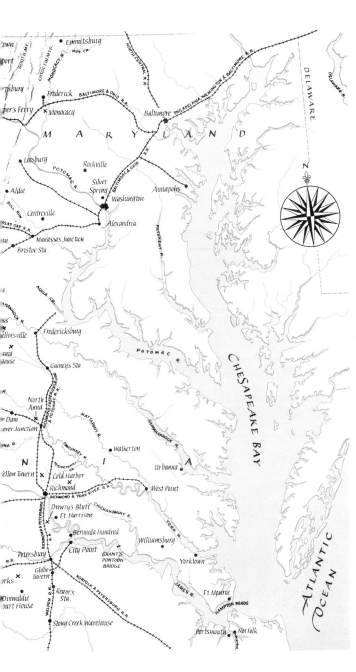

adherence to the past which characterized the noblesse who surrounded poor Louis—says in his quaint way, 'A political party that knows not *when it is beaten* may become one of the fatalest things to itself & to all.' "⁵ Change was coming down the wind, as Blair saw it, but if moderate men rallied it need not be revolutionary change.

It was going to look revolutionary, simply because so many people took it for granted that the Negro was different— a man against whom one could of course commit a crime but on whom it was hardly possible to inflict a real injustice inasmuch as injustice was his natural lot. There was, for example, a young Union cavalryman whose squadron this fall was sent out on a foraging expedition near Brandy Station, Virginia, to collect lumber, cattle and other items. He wrote to his wife, telling how they had looted a fine plantation house, and he was disturbed by what had been done: "Bureaus were overhauled, and all they contained stolen or destroyed. Book cases were pillaged or tipped over; furniture smashed or stolen; crockery broken to pieces; mirrors stolen or broken . . . it sickened me to look on." Then, virtuously, he added: "I did nothing in the way of sacking the house. I was busy tearing down Negro huts to get the lumber. That was not destroying property needlessly; it was only getting stuff to make officers comfortable."⁶

Yet some sort of progress was being made—in the mind of the President if nowhere else. His letter to General Banks gave quiet burial to the old project of colonization—the proposal that the country transplant the liberated Negroes in some place beyond the seas. That was simply a plan to evade the problem of racial equality, and he had supported it for a long time. Less than a year earlier he had met with Negro leaders and had pleaded with them to accept colonization, pointing out sadly that "there is an unwillingness on the part of our people, harsh as it may be, for you free colored people to remain with us."⁷ The unwillingness remained, but now he was hoping to soften it, and he was searching for ways by which the American people could (as he put it) live themselves out of it. In their watch-night services at Philadelphia at the beginning of the year, when they met to pray and sing because the great proclamation was at last being issued, jubilant Negroes had said that the President would never really insist on colonization, and they gave "God's in his heart!" as ground for their belief[8]; and although he was following his head rather than his heart, he was justifying their confidence.

He would face up to the problem rather than run from it; and at the year's end he was stronger politically than he had been for a long time. The by-elections had gone heavily in his favor. The Republicans—Unionist Party, technically, since temporary alliances had been made with war Democrats—had carried all the Northern states except New Jersey, good Republican governors like John A. Andrew of Massachusetts and Andrew G. Curtin of Pennsylvania had been re-elected —and Clement Vallandigham had been badly beaten in Ohio.

Vallandigham had survived his Southern exile and had made his way into Canada, and at Windsor in Ontario he had campaigned, in absentia, as Democratic candidate for governor of Ohio; looking formidable as summer began, looking much less so as autumn approached, losing finally to the Unionist John Brough by a record-breaking 100,000 votes. Fate had not been kind to Vallandigham. He was the candidate of despair, and when the people voted most of them had ceased despairing. After Gettysburg and Vicksburg his appeal was blunted, and it became even blunter when John Hunt Morgan, the dashing Confederate cavalryman, led 2400 troopers north of the Ohio River on an unauthorized and wholly meaningless raid. Morgan got into Indiana about the time Lee got into Pennsylvania, and he moved over into Ohio, apparently with some idea of riding eastward to join forces, rallying the Ohio Copperheads as he went; but his men harried the farmers and small-town businessmen so relentlessly that many Copperheads were converted to Republicanism on the spot, and the raid at last flickered out in southeastern Ohio, with Morgan and most of his men taken prisoner. All that had been done was to take votes from Vallandigham.[9]

Thus Mr. Lincoln had won some sort of endorsement at the polls. So had the Republican radicals, and although for the moment there was happy harmony between the President and the radicals it was unlikely to endure. At bottom they all wanted the same thing—a restored Union and an end to slavery—but the very fact that the election improved their chances of getting it meant that there must soon be a trial of strength because they saw it in such different ways. As Mr. Lincoln had said, the radicals wanted to go to Zion and so did he; but they disagreed with him, both on the best way to get there and on what Zion ought to look like after it had been reached. They were already sniffing suspiciously at the ten percent plan that had been entrusted to General Banks, and when these men had suspicions they neither suppressed them nor kept quiet about them.

What all of this meant was that the President himself and the Northerners who disagreed with him—those who thought he was going much too far, and those who thought he was not going far enough—were looking ahead now to the end of the war, looking with blind hope and tormenting anxiety. Victory was almost being taken for granted, and everyone was trying to prepare for its consequences; the war had grown so far beyond its original dimensions that it was time to define it anew. As they groped for a definition people found themselves looking intently at the war's most terrible single aspect, as if from their own grief and agony they could extract a meaning that would be worth remembering when more grief and agony were demanded of them. On a hilltop at Gettysburg they were about to dedicate a cemetery.

The cemetery had been planned by the governors of the states (the Northern states, that is) whose men had fought at Gettysburg. There was a park-like place across the road from the spot where Southern infantry had broken into Howard's artillery in the hot twilight of the second day, a few rods north of the clump of trees where the battle reached its climax the next afternoon; and in this little park the Union dead were laid to rest. In the fall of 1863 the work had not ended. Re-interments were still taking place, sixty or more every day when the weather permitted, and it would be spring before all was finished. But the dreadful wreckage that littered the field had mostly been cleared away, there was green sod on some of the graves, and it was time for the ceremonies. These would take place on November 19, and a Gettysburg citizen named David Wills, who had charge of the arrangements, wrote to Mr. Lincoln about it. There would be a parade, the sacred soil would be consecrated, the famous Edward Everett would deliver a suitable oration, the governors would be present, and it was hoped that the President himself might attend and "formally set apart these grounds to their sacred use by a few appropriate remarks . . . and perform this last but solemn act to the soldier dead on this battlefield."[10]

Mr. Everett would speak at length because that was his function; he was an orator, and the occasion called for an oration. Mr. Lincoln would act the part of President, receiving and dedicating ground that was to be a national shrine, intoning suitable words as he did so. To the arrangements committee both men were simply items on the program; the occasion was a day of mourning, and the graves themselves were what mattered.

More than 12,000 people crowded into the little town on the appointed day, and they had a hard time because neither transportation nor accommodation was adequate. They had not come to Gettysburg to hear anyone make a speech. A great many of them were relatives of men who had been killed in the battle, and they wanted to see where these men were buried, or at least where they had died, as if some sort of healing and understanding would come that way. A reporter listened to their stories, and wrote down two remarks as typical of all: *I have a son who fell in the first day's fight and I have come to take back his body, for his mother's heart is breaking and she will not be satisfied until it is brought home to her. . . . My brother was killed in the charge of the Pennsylvania Reserves on the enemy when they were driven from Little Round Top, but we don't know where his remains are. . . .* From all over the country these people had come to spend a few hours with their feelings of loss; as the President surmised, they would little note nor long remember any fine speeches that might be made.

There were hundreds of unmarked Confederate graves in fields where new wheat was growing, and hardly anyone noticed them, although the reporter was moved to rhapsodize: "So swift does the plowshare of Peace cover up, and the emerald mantle of kindly Nature conceal, the wrath and destruction of war." An officer who fought by the little clump of trees felt that it would have been better if all of the dead had been treated so, with no new graves for anyone. A soldier (he argued) ought to be left in the grave his comrades dug for him, at the place where he fell, and if all of the burial mounds finally vanished altogether under grass or grain or trees the dead would rest just as well. To this veteran (who himself was to die in action at Cold Harbor, half a year later) there was something grotesque about making this showplace cemetery: "The skeletons of these brave men must be handled like the bones of so many horses, for a price, and wedged in like herrings in a box on a spot where there was no fighting—where there was no fighting—where none of them fell! It may be all right, but I do not see it."[11]

November 19 came in clear and pleasant. Judge Wills had everything organized and the procession moved promptly at ten o'clock. The parade marshals were brightly done up in straw-colored satin sashes fastened at the shoulder with mourning rosettes, each man wearing a red-white-and-blue rosette on his breast, his saddle-cloth made of white cambric edged in black; minute guns pounded away as the parade moved, and a "national salute" was fired when the head of the column reached the cemetery. When Mr. Everett at last arose to deliver the address of the day he was a figure to catch the eye. He was tall, white-haired, trim in a closely buttoned frock coat, worth looking at although (as a reporter confessed) not a tenth of the audience could hear what he was saying. His speech ran to 13,000 words and took the better part of two hours to deliver; incredibly, he had memorized every word of it and never referred to notes or manuscript, and although few people could hear him everyone could feel him. The reporter wrote with awe of "the gesture, once observed never to be forgotten, when the orator rises to some climax and, the arms outspread, the fingers, quivering and fluttering, as one said, like the pinions of an eagle, seem to rain down upon the audience the emotions with which they vibrate." Mr. Everett was a professional, at the top of his form, and although another reporter considered the audience "most orderly, but phlegmatic and undemonstrative" the men and women who went to the cemetery unquestionably got what they had gone there to get.[12]

Which is to say that they got a performance. They got all that an oration could give them. They had come to Gettysburg to remember their dead, and this was part of the ritual, just as the minute guns and the military bands were part of it. Beyond that there were only the graves, those marked and those unmarked and those lost beneath the new grain, and the day began and ended with them. Their presence was what counted, and the fact that the men buried in them had spent themselves here was what would be remembered so long.

The graves had their own terrible eloquence, saying that

victory by itself was not enough; saying this to a land whose millions, in the North and in the South, had come to believe the exact opposite. The more sensitive and devoted a man was, the more likely he was to feel that the war and the lives it consumed would lose all meaning if *his* cause did not win; and if this was so, half of the dead men here had been hideously deluded, along with all who mourned for them, and there was nothing to dedicate except the dust that covered the thousands of lifeless bodies. The people watched Mr. Everett's persuasive fingertips, while the wind carried his words away, and presently a choir sang an ode composed especially for this occasion. And at last Mr. Lincoln arose to make the appropriate remarks he had been asked to make.

He was very brief; perhaps what had to be said here was phrasing itself in men's hearts and needed only to be touched lightly in order to be brought alive. He spoke of liberty and equality instead of victory, as if these words alone could give meaning to what had been done here, and instead of dedicating the ground he called upon those who stood there to dedicate themselves to something that might justify all that Gettysburg had cost them; and after two minutes he had done with it, and the Associated Press man wrote that there was "long-continued applause." Then the crowd broke up and people began their long journeys home, and by eight o'clock that night Gettysburg was quiet again.

Secretary John Hay, who had spent a pleasant twenty-four hours in the town, put an entry in his diary: "Mr. Everett spoke as he always does, perfectly—and the President, in a fine, free way, with more grace than is his wont, said his half-dozen words of consecration, and the music wailed and we went home through crowded and cheering streets. And all the particulars are in the daily papers."[13]

3. Amnesty and Suffrage

ALTHOUGH THE 38th Congress had mostly been chosen in the fall of 1862, when the Republicans did poorly in the elections, it had a safe Unionist majority when it convened on December 8, 1863. In the House of Representatives Republican Schuyler Colfax of Indiana was elected speaker, with 101 votes; his principal opponent, the mellifluous Sunset Cox of Ohio, an unmitigated Democrat, got 42, and 39 votes were scattered to the winds among six candidates who had no hope of winning anything. In the Senate only five members voted against seating two Senators from one of the administration's newest creations, the state of West Virginia.[1] Once organized, the two houses heard and applauded a message from the President of the United States.

The message was long, unemotional, and dutifully optimistic, routine except for one point: it included the text of a general Proclamation of Amnesty and Reconstruction which the President had that day issued.

The important word, of course, was "reconstruction." The most sustained fighting of the war lay ahead, but the President had already begun to put the country together again. The proclamation explained how he was going about it; essentially, it was a careful exposition of the ten percent plan which even now was being presented to the people of Louisiana and Arkansas.

Amnesty, it said, would go to residents of seceded states who took a solemn oath, and the wording of the oath showed what Mr. Lincoln expected in the way of a changed mind and heart. The oath taker was called upon to swear "that I will henceforth faithfully support, protect, and defend the Constitution of the United States, and the Union of the States thereunder; and that I will, in like manner, abide by and faithfully support all acts of Congress passed during the existing rebellion with reference to slaves, so long and so far as not repealed, modified or held void by Congress, or by decision of the Supreme Court; and that I will, in like manner, abide by and faithfully support all proclamations of the President made during the existing rebellion having reference to slaves, so long and so far as not modified or declared void by decision of the Supreme Court."

Certain people would not be allowed to take this oath—officials of the Confederate government; colonels and generals in the Confederate army, and naval officers with or above the rank of lieutenant; men who had left United States judicial posts, seats in Congress or commissions in the army and navy in order to join the Confederacy; and any persons who treated white or colored prisoners "otherwise than lawfully as prisoners of war." All others could take the oath, and when ten percent of a state's electorate had done so, any state government they set up would be recognized in Washington and would come under the Constitutional provision guaranteeing to each state a republican form of government and protection against invasion or domestic violence. As Mr. Lincoln had told General Banks, there would be some leeway in regard to emancipation, or at least in regard to the speed with which emancipation was made effective: "Any provision which may be adopted by such State government in relation to the freed people of such State, which shall recognize and declare their permanent freedom, provide for their education and which may yet be consistent, as a temporary arrangement, with their present condition as a laboring, landless and homeless class, will not be objected to by the National Executive."[2]

On the Republican side there was general approval. John Hay wrote (perhaps overstating things a little) that he had never seen such an effect produced by a public document, and said that "men acted as if the millenium had come." Here, it seemed, was the final death sentence for slavery, and slavery's bitter enemies could not for the moment hear anything else. Radicals like Zach Chandler and Henry Wilson were among those made jubilant. Owen Lovejoy exulted that "I shall live to see slavery ended in America," and although Senator Sumner showed displeasure while the message was being read, flapping books and papers about on his desk and ostentatiously not listening to the reading, he called at the White House to offer his congratulations.[3]

As everyone anticipated, the Democrats were much less happy, and their case was promptly stated on the floor of the House by Sunset Cox, who drew attention to an oddity. The Emancipation Proclamation had been based (inadequately, in Mr. Cox's opinion) on the President's war powers; this reconstruction plan, which logically was a derivative of that proclamation, was even less adequately based on his power to pardon, and Cox spoke bitterly of the President "assuming to pardon crime without conviction, and revivify dead States which are indestructible." Of the oath itself he was contemptuous: "As the Emancipation Proclamation . . . can never be reconciled with the normal control of the states over their domestic institutions, so all oaths to sustain the same are oaths to subvert the old governments, Federal and State. The oath required both of loyal and disloyal men in the South is an oath of infidelity to the very genius of our federative system, for it is an oath to aid anarchy, and out of anarchy create a new nation."[4]

Yet the Democrats in Congress could do little more than conduct sniping fire at long-range, and build up a record for the next presidential election. Earlier, Fernando Wood of New York had moved that the President be requested to name three commissioners to open negotiations with the authorities at Richmond so that "this bloody, destructive and inhuman war shall cease and the Union be restored on terms of equity, fraternity, and equality under the Constitution." The House tabled this resolution, 98 to 59; whereupon Joseph Edgerton of Indiana moved to censure the administration, denouncing as "among the gravest of crimes" the use of armed force to induce a state to modify its position on slavery, and contrasting the Emancipation Proclamation with Mr. Lincoln's earlier disclaimer of any intent to interfere with slavery. This motion also was tabled, 90 to 66, and the two actions meant little except that the House contained about sixty men who would support extreme pro-slavery and anti-war positions.[5]

For the time being the President could ignore the Democrats. The real fight was going to be with the radical Republicans, who soon found that they liked his proclamation of amnesty and reconstruction much less than they had supposed. They felt that it built up the presidency at the expense of Congress, which was bad; much worse, they considered it dangerously soft on secession. Senator Jacob Collamer of Vermont proclaimed the need to protect the government from "the keeping of men who avow their enmity to its existence," and this expressed the radical viewpoint. Detesting the doctrine of states' rights, they sought to destroy it by insisting that secession destroyed the states that attempted it. As fervently as Jefferson Davis himself, they argued that an impassable gulf existed; they simply went on to say that the seceding states had fallen into it and were lost forever, and they considered Mr. Lincoln's argument that the states were indestructible no better than a restatement of the position taken by Sunset Cox.

The Democrats detected a logical flaw in their argument, and W. S. Holman of Indiana submitted a resolution that the radicals' position "ought to be rebuked and condemned

as manifestly unjust . . . tending to prolong the war and
to confirm the treasonable theory of secession," but the resolution was quietly tabled.[6] Eventually, implacable Thaddeus
Stevens raised questions. If the seceding states were still in
the Union, he inquired, where were their representatives on
the floor of Congress? "Every one of the United States is
entitled to have members here and Senators in the other
branch. Where are these evidences of existing states? They
are at Richmond, where the Congress of the Union does not
sit. . . . It is said that the Constitution does not allow them
to go out of the Union. That is true, and in going out they
committed a crime for which we are now punishing them
with fire and sword. What are we making war upon them
for? For seceding, for going out of the Union against law."[7]

What the radicals wanted to do became clear, after the
first of the new year, when Congressman Henry Winter Davis
of Maryland presented a bill—sponsored in the Senate by
Ben Wade of Ohio, and known to history as the Wade-Davis
bill—offering a new plan for reconstruction.

Davis was a bitter-ender: a border state man who was a
flaming Unionist and anti-slavery man. In 1859 he had voted
for a Republican for Speaker of the House, which led the
Maryland legislature to assert that he had misrepresented his
state and had forfeited its confidence; he retorted that the
legislators ought to take that message back to their masters,
the people, for he would reply only to the people. He
was slim, pale, with a tangled mop of black hair, and a
biographer put the case mildly by remarking that "he sel-
dom permitted the opinions of friends to influence his own
resolutions." Now he was trying to set forth the terms on
which beaten states might be brought back into the Union:

First, the President would name a provisional governor
for each Confederate state as soon as military resistance in
that state had been suppressed. That governor would then enroll all white male citizens of voting age and require each
one to take the oath to support the Constitution of the
United States. If those taking the oath amounted to a majority of all those enrolled, they would be invited to elect
delegates to a convention to re-establish a state government;
but no one could either be a delegate or vote in this election
unless he took an additional, "ironclad" oath that he had
never held office under the Confederacy or voluntarily

borne arms against the Union. The convention in turn was obliged to amend the state constitution so as to abolish slavery, outlaw Confederate war debts and disfranchise all those who held important civil or military office under the Confederacy. The new constitution had to be approved by the voters, with the franchise again limited to those who took the ironclad oath. Then, if the Federal Congress approved, the President could announce that this state was duly back in the Union—after which it could elect Senators and Congressmen as of old.[8]

The contrast between this plan and the President's plan was striking. Instead of ten percent the Wade-Davis plan demanded an outright majority, which was likely to be unattainable since so much of the male population would be disfranchised. It offered no amnesty at all, and left the future of the secessionists entirely up to Washington, with the secessionists barred from the capitol while Washington made up its mind. About all the two plans had in common was that both demanded the end of slavery and the outlawing of Confederate war debts.

Mr. Lincoln had stretched the doctrine of presidential war powers and pardoning powers to its extreme limit: Congressman Davis was doing the same with the constitutional provision guaranteeing to each state a republican form of government. "That monster of political wrong which is called secession," said Davis, was simply a usurpation of power. This usurpation had brought about "the erection of governments which do not recognize the Constitution of the United States, which the Constitution does not recognize, and therefore not republican governments of the states in rebellion. . . . We are engaged in suppressing a military usurpation of the authority of the state government. When that shall have been accomplished there will be no form of state authority in existence which Congress can recognize. Our success will be the overthrow of *all* semblance of government in the Rebel states. The government of the United States is then, in fact, the *only* government existing in those states, and it is there charged to guarantee them republican governments."[9]

This logic was sound enough, but it was the logic of revolution, not of ordinary politics; applied to a question which was basically simple but which in this third winter of the war was taking on some extraordinary convolutions.

Ben Wade stated the question, for the Senate: "The Union is to be preserved; but upon what principle will you permit these people to come back into the Union?"

The 38th Congress was being given its choice of three principles. The conservative Democrats offered one: nothing really had changed, and These People would come back willingly once Washington stopped insisting on change. The President offered another: there was enormous change, present and still to come, but These People could and must be brought to accept it because it could not endure unless they did. Now the radicals presented the third: the enormous change would be imposed whether These People liked it or not. As Wade put it: "Majorities must rule, and until majorities can be found loyal and trustworthy for state government they must be governed by a stronger hand."[10] Three principles: two of them implying the acceptance of revolution.

Mr. Lincoln is usually pictured as occupying a middle role between opposing extremes in this situation, but actually he was not. He was at one of the extremes himself, and he disagreed with the radicals only on the method by which the change was to come. He and Wade and Davis agreed on the essentials: the Union must be restored and the slave must be freed. This was what made the revolution—not the details of the restoration but the consequences of the freedom. Abolition of slavery was not a point at which anyone could stop. It was just a momentous beginning.

The President was perfectly clear about this. It struck him that whether certain states were technically in or out of the Union was "a merely metaphysical question and one unnecessary to be forced into discussion."[11] The real problem involved the next step. Was the Negro to get complete civil and political equality when slavery died? Did freedom logically carry with it the right to vote? Must amnesty for the owner be accompanied by suffrage for the man who had been owned?

This involved the most fundamental question of all, and the case was odd. There was only one way to give a negative answer: say No, once and for all, and be done with it. But there were many ways to say Yes, and one or another of them was bound to follow a simple refusal to say No the first time the question came up. Qualifying clauses that might accompany the affirmative meant nothing. Unless the idea was immediately rejected it would finally be accepted, carrying its own imperatives.

To say now that the Negro should get the vote as well as freedom was to get out on the very front line of the radical position, and Mr. Lincoln was not yet prepared to go that far.[12] But even to admit that some Negroes ought to vote now was to agree that all ought to vote sometime; and although the President this spring was feeling his way carefully, letting his mind make itself up as he had done on emancipation itself, he had already refused to say No. On March 13 he wrote, most cautiously, to Michael Hahn, his new ten percent governor of Louisiana:

"You are about to have a convention which, among other things, will probably define the elective franchise. I barely suggest for your private consideration whether some of the colored people may not be let in—as, for instance, the very intelligent, and especially those who have fought gallantly in our ranks. They would probably help, in some trying time to come, to keep the jewel of liberty within the family of freedom. But this is only a suggestion, not to the public but to you alone."

He was considering the question, partly on a basis of high principle and partly as a matter of practical politics. He was not entirely a free agent. The current set in motion by the war was now and then irresistible, and it was at about this time that Mr. Lincoln wrote candidly: "I claim not to have controlled events, but confess plainly that events had got into a condition no man had planned or foreseen; the most the President could say now was "Whither it is tending seems plain," but there was no certainty anywhere.[13]

Yet the drift of things could be seen. The President had put emancipated Negroes into the army—100,000 of them, he told the Congress, with at least half in combat assignments —and most diverse effects came of it. The army got soldiers, of course, and at Port Hudson and Battery Wagner it found them useful under fire. The administration, possibly to its surprise, got a political dividend also; by putting the freedmen into the army it kept them out of the labor force, relieved pressure on the labor market in the North, and reduced an irritant that had been largely responsible for the New York draft riots. (Democratic Congressman Henry Stebbins of

New York pointed this out in an irascible what-can-we-do-about-it letter to Party Statesman Barlow.)[14] But if the use of black regiments was helping both the army and the administration, it was also doing something, the extent of it not wholly predictable, to the Negro himself. A Massachusetts officer in one of the new colored regiments in Louisiana tried to explain what he saw happening, in a letter to his mother:

"You would be much interested in the teaching of our soldiers. It seems very queer to see grown men & women learning their a b ab's & making great staggering letters on their slates with great muscular exertion & a grin of satisfaction at producing one less drunk than the rest. Almost every regiment now has its school house & in some the first sergeants already make out their morning reports without assistance. This afternoon I observed a relief marching off guard at the parapet, and the last man lagging behind. I rode up intending to blow him sky high, but when I got there found that he had his gun in his right hand & his spelling book in his left & was so intent on the latter that he didn't see where he was going. I considered a moment & rode back to my place with a merciful wink at the neglect of duty."[15]

Perhaps it mattered little if the President talked boldly to one man and cautiously to another when he discussed Negro suffrage. A Negro who went soldiering with a gun in one hand and a spelling book in the other plainly was on his way to some place where he had never been before, and if all men had to accept that prodigious fact the difference between ten percent and Wade-Davis was not as big as men thought it was. Curious things began to happen. The House of Representatives, which had mustered 101 votes for the administration in the speakership contest, presently passed Davis' harsh bill, 73 to 59. No one opposed the measure except the hard core that opposed the administration on everything, at least fifty members did not vote at all, and if the President made the least effort to rally his supporters to defeat this bill there was no evidence of it. A little later the bill passed the Senate in a way equally curious, 26 to 3, with twenty Senators absent. And then Mr. Lincoln killed the bill with a pocket veto—that is, he simply refrained from

signing it—and he issued a public statement which was the
most curious part of the whole business.

He was unprepared, he said, by a formal approval of the
Wade-Davis bill, to commit himself inflexibly to any single
plan of reconstruction; he was also unprepared to destroy
the ten percent governments already set up in Arkansas and
Louisiana, or to assert that Congress was competent under
the Constitution to abolish slavery in the states. At the same
time, he hoped that a constitutional amendment killing
slavery would soon be adopted, he was satisfied that the
Wade-Davis plan was "very proper" for the loyal people
of any state that chose to adopt it, and he was ready to go
ahead with the Wade-Davis program in all such cases . . .
all in all, he would not sign this bill but he would more or
less go along with it if that was what people wanted.

This aroused Wade, Davis, and other radicals to a fine
pitch of fury, showed that the President was not ready for
a showdown on whether Congress or the executive would finally call the turn on reconstruction, and left the deep question of political rights for the former slave open for future
determination; very far in the future, possibly. And it led
Attorney General Bates to conclude that the friends of the
Negro in Congress had gone quite mad.

"The Negro is ever uppermost in their thoughts, and is
sure to give a sable tinge to every subject of legislation that
comes before either house," he wrote. "And yet, strange to
say, there has not been a single proposition calculated in the
smallest degree to give any substantial advantage to the *freedmen,* by establishing their *status,* and giving them locality,
stability and consistent social relations. The subject is used
only as a topic (very sensitive) for electioneering—not at all
for the good of the Negro."[16]

4. Solitary in a Crowd

BITTERLY OPPOSED on all other matters, Thaddeus Stevens
and Sunset Cox did have one thing in common. Each man
had reservations about Ulysses S. Grant.

How men felt about Grant became important, as 1864
began. Everyone was looking ahead to reconstruction, but it
was necessary to remember that the war had not yet been

won; to find a soldier who could win it was not really a function of Congress, but it was nevertheless a matter of concern. Grant looked more like a winner than anybody else, and after Bragg's beaten army drifted down the far slope of Missionary Ridge it was as certain as anything could be that Grant was going to be given the top command. Congress now had before it a bill to revive the old rank of lieutenant general in the army, and if the bill passed Grant would unquestionably get the job, which meant that he would rank every other Union soldier from Halleck on down; and both Stevens and Cox were opposed.

Neither man had anything in particular against Grant, but neither wanted to see him get this promotion. Cox had been disillusioned about him. As a good party man Cox had known moments, in the fall, when Grant looked like the answer to Democratic prayer: he was one of the most non-political of army officers, but he had voted for Buchanan in 1856 and if he was anything at all politically he must be a Democrat, so after Chattanooga there was a good deal of talk of making him the party's candidate for President in 1864. But before 1863 ended Cox wrote to Barlow that this would not do. Grant had gone on record—in a letter to a Republican Congressman—as saying that slavery was dead beyond hope of resurrection, and had declared flatly that although he wanted peace restored he would not "be willing to see any settlement until this question is forever settled." No one who talked that way could hope to get the Democratic nomination, and Cox told Barlow: "I regard the above expose of Gen. Grant's position as ending his chances for any Democratic support & as rendering Gen. McClellan a political 'necessity'—as our candidate."[1]

Grant was not enough of a Democrat for Cox, and at the same time he may have been a little too much of one for Stevens. It was hard to tell, because although Stevens was most outspoken it was not always easy to know what his outspoken words really meant. All that was clear now was that he was quibbling. He could see no point in reviving the rank of lieutenant general; the existing law gave the President power to put any major general in command of all of the armies, and "I think that we had better wait before we decorate this hero until the war is over." Stevens shared this position with James A. Garfield, who had ceased to be chief of staff of the Army of the Cumberland and had become instead a Congressman from Ohio. Garfield pointed out that "the President already has full power to select any major general from the regular or volunteer service to serve as General-in-Chief," and he felt that if the legislation was meant to honor a distinguished soldier for services rendered "I argue against its propriety at this time when the great race for the prizes of the war is not yet ended."[2]

To make Grant a lieutenant general was automatically to make him some sort of presidential candidate. Nobody especially wanted it that way, but nobody could prevent it because this was after all a political war and the principal military command was a political post no matter how hard everyone tried to pretend that it was not. Grant himself was highly disturbed by the prospect. He insisted that to become President was "the last thing in the world I desire," and said that it would be "highly unfortunate for myself, if not for the country." He said this in a letter to a friend in Illinois, and he went on to make it most explicit: "I am not a politician, never was and hope never to be, and could not write a political letter. My only desire is to serve the country in her present trials. To do this efficiently it is necessary to have the confidence of the Army and the people. I know no way to better secure this end than by a faithful performance of my duties. So long as I hold my present position I do not believe that I have the right to criticize the policy or orders of those above me, or to give utterance to views of my own except to the authorities at Washington, through the General-in-Chief of the Army. In this respect I know I have proven myself a good soldier. . . . I infinitely prefer my present position to that of any civil office within the gift of the people."[3]

Neither quibbles nor disclaimers made any difference. The general mood now was to turn the entire military problem over to Grant and hope that he could handle it, and to give him increased rank was to serve notice on all other generals that this man was going to be boss. Congressman Elihu B. Washburne of Illinois, who had been Grant's political sponsor ever since the early summer of 1861, was backing this bill, and he really had little trouble with it. It was passed on February 26 and President Lincoln signed it on February 29. On the next day the President appointed Grant lieutenant general, the Senate confirmed the appointment within twenty-four hours, and on March 8 in obedience to orders Grant reached Washington and presented himself at the White House.

Waiting for him was the lieutenant general's commission—and a universal curiosity. Nobody knew very much about this man. Most people, including the President himself, had never set eyes on him, and although his record as a soldier spoke for itself the man who had made the record had never actually become visible. Through some mix-up, nobody met Grant's train when he reached Washington, and he made his way to Willard's Hotel unescorted; registered, went to the dining room for dinner, and was no sooner seated there than everyone present recognized him. People stood up, craning their necks to see, and inevitably some man got up on a chair and cried: "Three cheers for Lieutenant General Grant!" There was much yelling and pounding on tables, and Grant, highly embarrassed, stood up, fumbled with his napkin, bowed all-inclusively, and then sat down and tried to go on with his meal. Presumably he did manage to eat something, but before long a Pennsylvania Congressman took him in tow, introduced him to everyone who could get within shouting distance, and then carried him off to the White House, where a weekly reception was in progress.

Here there was another mob scene. Grant met the President and Mrs. Lincoln, and learned that he was to come in next day for the formal presentation and acceptance of his new commission; then he was surrounded, and at last he found himself hoisted up on a crimson sofa where he had to stand so that everybody could see him. Reporter Noah Brooks called the crowd "the only real mob I ever saw in the White House," and described a wild disorder in which women suffered torn laces and crinolines and climbed on tables and chairs, partly to escape further damage and partly to get a better look at the general. Gideon Welles considered the whole business "rowdy and unseemly," and the general at last escaped, "flushed, heated and perspiring with the unwonted exertion."[4]

The people who were so eager to see Grant did not quite know what they were looking at. There was something baffling about him. Richard Henry Dana, Jr., looked him over and concluded that he "had no gait, no station, no manner."

There was a scrubby look about him, said Dana, "rather the look of a man who did, or once did, take a little too much to drink," and Dana felt that except for the hard look in the clear blue eyes Grant looked like a half-pay character who had nothing to do but hang around the entrance to Willard's, cigar in mouth. There was a certain air of resolution about him, to be sure, but one can see Dana shaking his head disapprovingly as he finished the comment: "To see him talking and smoking in the lower entry of Willard's, in that crowd, in such linen, the general in chief of our armies on whom the destiny of empire seems to hang!"[5]

Men who were much less supercilious than Dana were equally puzzled. After the war a man who had served with Grant in the west talked about the relationship between Grant and the soldiers: "He was a man in whom the men had confidence, but they did not love him. He'd ride past without their knowing it. A few of the army knew him by sight. Logan, Smith, McPherson would raise a ripple of applause every time they went by; Grant never did." This man agreed with General Banks that the soldiers who took Vicksburg were a tough lot—"entirely cowhands, western men, fierce-fighting western men in for work and in for the war," Banks called them—and he could sum up their feeling toward Grant only by saying: "They knew him and trusted him and he knew them. He could stand any hardship they could stand and do their thinking besides."

A woman who saw Grant frequently in Washington noted that even in a crowd he always seemed to be alone. He was friendly and approachable, but he had "a peculiar aloofness," and she felt that a mysterious atmosphere surrounded him; "He walked through a crowd as though solitary."[6] The crowds would always be about him, from now to the end of his life, and it would be his fate to go through them alone. Probably he never was more alone than he was on March 10, when he finished his ceremonial chores at the White House and went down to Brandy Station to visit headquarters of the Army of the Potomac.

This army had been in the back of everybody's mind all through the debate on the bill to have a lieutenant general. If Grant's promotion made people see him as a presidential candidate it also made them see him as a new broom. There was a feeling that a new broom was needed; a suspicion, right or wrong, that this army was never used to its full potential. Its officer corps complained bitterly that the administration played politics with military matters, and the administration in turn complained that the officers' own political bias sapped the army's will to win, and there was a good deal of truth in both complaints. Months earlier, when Gideon Welles suggested that it might be well to put someone in Meade's place, the President burst out: "What can I do with such generals as we have? Who among them is any better than Meade? To sweep away the whole of them from the chief command and substitute a new man would cause a shock and be likely to lead to combinations and troubles greater than we have now." As a matter of fact, shortly after Vicksburg the War Department did plan to replace Meade with Grant, and Grant protested vigorously, saying that "my going would do no possible good" and pointing out that officers of the Army of the Potomac would certainly resent having an outsider brought in to take command. Now he was here, the outsider, and as Grant left for Brandy Station Mr. Lincoln told John Nicolay that he hoped the new lieutenant general could "do something with the unfortunate Army of the Potomac."[7]

Under such circumstances, the reception at headquarters was bound to see everyone stalking around stiff-legged. Major General Andrew A. Humphreys, Meade's capable chief of staff, wrote that Grant's reception was "of the simple frankness which high-toned soldiers give each other, yet there could be perceived something (arising chiefly from his own manner) that indicated that it was the visit of a rival commander of a rival army." Colonel Charles S. Wainwright, chief of artillery in the V Corps, and a good reflector of the state of mind of the army's old-line officers, wrote of Grant with disdain touched with a faint, cynical hope that things might turn out for the best: "It is hard for those who knew him when formerly in the army to believe that he is a great man; then he was only distinguished for the mediocrity of his mind, his great good nature and his insatiable love of whiskey. He will doubtless now be placed in supreme command of all the armies; and as the radicals must see that they have nothing more to gain by prolonging the war, we shall probably have matters pushed with great energy in the coming campaign." A few days later, after he had actually looked at the man, Wainwright conceded that he was "not so hard-looking a man as his photographs make him out to be," but felt that he was "stumpy, unmilitary, slouchy and western-looking; very ordinary, in fact."[8]

When Humphreys wrote of high-toned soldiers and their simple frankness he was undoubtedly thinking of Meade. Of all the officers at headquarters Meade was the one with whom Grant had no trouble at all. A meeting that must have been an immense strain for both men passed off well. Meade opened by saying he supposed Grant might want some westerner—Sherman, perhaps—to command the Army of the Potomac, and he said that if this was the case Grant should not hesitate to make the change; he, Meade, would understand, would give up his place without a murmur, and would serve to the best of his ability in any post the general-in-chief chose for him. Grant replied that he had no intention of putting anyone in Meade's place, and when he wrote his *Memoirs*, long afterward, he said that "this incident gave me even a more favorable opinion of Meade than did his great victory at Gettysburg." Meade told his wife that he was "very much pleased with General Grant," and said Grant "showed much more capacity and character than I had expected." It was settled, then, that Meade would continue as he was; but it was settled, too, that Grant as commander of all the armies would make his headquarters with the Army of the Potomac, moving where that army moved, keeping Halleck in Washington as chief of staff to handle paper work and housekeeping details. Meade could make no objection to this, but he did write Mrs. Meade that "you may now look for the Army of the Potomac putting laurels on the brows of another rather than your husband."[9]

The laurels went where Meade thought they would go, especially after the newspaper correspondents—who were not fond of Meade anyway—took to referring to the Army of the Potomac, casually, as "Grant's army." The command arrangement was clumsy, it inevitably produced friction, and only the fact that Grant and Meade were dedicated men kept the friction from becoming ruinous. Everybody felt that Grant's constant presence betrayed a feeling (notoriously shared by the White House and the War Department) that someone had to ride herd on this army. Its officers would have been more than human if they had not resented it.

Grant's responsibility, however, went far beyond the

Army of the Potomac. Every soldier the country had was his to command. It was reported (a little inaccurately) that he was being given an absolutely free hand. The President said that he neither knew nor wanted to know his military plans. Grant's fundamental concern was grand strategy. It was up to him to devise and execute the broad design that would destroy the Southern Confederacy.

Early in the winter, before he knew that he would soon be made general-in-chief, Grant had tried his hand at over-all planning. He limited himself at first to affairs in his own sphere, the west, and on January 15 he sent Halleck a plan for bisecting the cotton South. He wanted to begin by having Sherman march east from Vicksburg to the railroad center of Meridian, under orders to destroy the railroads along the Mississippi-Alabama line so completely "that the enemy will not attempt to rebuild them during the rebellion." Then Grant would take Mobile, that ripe plum which he and Banks and Farragut had been wanting to pluck ever since the fall of Vicksburg. This done, he would strike with two powerful armies, one going from Chattanooga to take Atlanta and the other coming up from Mobile to take Montgomery. He considered Sherman and McPherson the proper commanders for these armies.

Less than a week later he submitted a supplementary plan involving the war in the east. He began by coolly asking whether "an abandonment of all previously attempted lines to Richmond is not advisable, and in lieu of these one be taken farther south." Specifically, he suggested that an army of 60,000 men go inland from Suffolk, Virginia, near the great Federal base at Hampton Roads, and head for Raleigh; and as soon as Raleigh was taken this army could move on Wilmington. All of this "would virtually force an evacuation of Virginia and indirectly of East Tennessee"; it would pull Lee's army down into the Carolinas, and "it would draw the enemy from campaigns of their own choosing, and for which they are prepared, to new lines of operations never expected to become necessary." He outlined the same plan to Thomas, saying that these movements would threaten the Confederacy's lines of interior communications so sharply that they could no longer bring large armies against the main Federal forces in the field; and he warned that before any of this could be done Longstreet and his troops must be driven out of East Tennessee.[10]

Thus Grant planned before he had authority, and the plan does not much resemble what he finally did. He talks here about paralyzing the Confederacy by isolating its different areas, crippling its communications and forcing its armies to operate where they would not; essentially, the design is to translate the quick movements of the Vicksburg campaign into continental terms. It is a *western* plan, based on a truth westerners had discovered—that Confederate geography is too big for Confederate resources. Coming east, talking with the President and Secretary of War and taking a firsthand look at Meade's army, Grant learned that his planning had to be adjusted to certain realities.

The first of these was that "forward to Richmond" was still a compelling slogan. A presidential election was approaching, and politically it was out of the question to abandon the offensive in Virginia, as it had been out of the question a year earlier to abandon the Mississippi River campaign, return to Memphis, and go down to Vicksburg overland, east of the river. Like it or not, the attempt that had been too much for McDowell, McClellan, Pope, Burnside, and Hooker must be made again, and Grant's announcement that he would travel with Meade's army indicated that he knew it. Incidentally, he found that Meade's army was a better instrument than he had supposed, and before the spring was over he frankly admitted this in a letter to Halleck: "The Army of the Potomac is in splendid condition and evidently feels like whipping some body; I feel much better with this command than I did before seeing it."[11]

In addition, he discovered that his plan for the two-pronged offensive in the west would not work because the administration had committed itself to Banks' old dream of a lucrative campaign up the Red River. This snapped off one of the prongs; the troops that would have moved against Mobile were going to be tied up indefinitely in a floundering march through cotton toward Texas. Sherman, to be sure, began his Meridian campaign early in February, tearing up mile after mile of railroad and displaying a sinister zeal for destroying Southern property; in his report he boasted that "Meridian, with its depots, store-houses, arsenal, hospitals, offices, hotels and cantonments, no longer exists." The Confederates believed that he intended to go on and seize Mobile but he did not, possibly because his cavalry failed him. He had 7000 horsemen led by an unfortunate brigadier named W. Sooy Smith, and these, coming down from Corinth to help him, ran into Bedford Forrest and 2500 Confederates near Okolona and were roundly whipped, and Sherman presently marched his men back to Vicksburg, smoke lying across the land where he had been.[12] Mobile was neither taken nor threatened, and the general-in-chief had to make a new plan.

The plan he at last evolved was based on a simple idea: the Federal power must strike wherever it could with all the force it had, and it must make certain that all of its blows were co-ordinated. This was fairly elementary, but it had never been tried before, and Grant drily summed up the past by saying that heretofore "the armies in the East and West acted independently and without concert, like a balky team, no two pulling together." What he proposed now was precisely what Mr. Lincoln had been urging (without the least success) for two years and more: to keep pressure on the Confederacy on many points at once in the knowledge that some of the pressure points were bound to collapse.[13]

On April 9 Grant gave Meade a letter marked FOR YOUR PERUSAL ALONE, setting forth the details.

When the campaign opened, Meade was to march south from the Rapidan with a directive of Biblical simplicity: "Lee's army will be your objective point. Wherever Lee goes, there you will go also." At the same moment, Sherman was to move south from Chattanooga with a similar directive, "Joe Johnston's army being his objective point and the heart of Georgia his ultimate aim." Grant hoped that Banks could disentangle himself from whatever he was getting into on the Red River in time to mount an offensive from New Orleans toward Mobile, but apparently he was not really counting on this; the principal offensives were to be those of Meade and Sherman.

Everything else the Federal forces did would be related to these two campaigns. Even purely defensive responsibilities would be discharged in such a way as to contribute to the offensive; an important point, because a great handicap for Federal commanders had always been the need to guard vital areas from Confederate counterstrokes. The Army of the

Potomac itself had always been obliged to cover Washington even while it was trying to capture Richmond. It had been considered necessary to keep a fairly strong force in the lower Shenandoah Valley, in case someone tried to repeat Stonewall Jackson's game, and a substantial number of troops was kept in comparative idleness around Norfolk and Fort Monroe, guarding the lower Chesapeake and the tip of the Virginia peninsula.

Grant believed that these defensive duties could be performed just as well by armies that were advancing as by armies that were sitting still, and he issued orders accordingly. Ben Butler—by no means Grant's choice, but he was a presidential dispensation, and untouchable—was to make up a field army of 33,000 or more from the occupation troops around Norfolk and from South Carolina, and move up the James River toward Richmond; eventually, Grant hoped, Meade's army and Butler's could join hands south of the James and advance together. In the Shenandoah, Franz Sigel (another Presidential dispensation, unfortunately) was to advance toward the head of the valley, and a Federal force of cavalry and infantry was to cut eastward from West Virginia to join him. Altogether, the Confederacy would have to meet five offensives at once—in central Virginia, in northern Georgia, along the James, in the Shenandoah Valley, and (once Banks had made himself available) in front of Mobile.[14]

Nothing was going to work out as Grant had planned, but one thing was certain. The President at last had found the general he wanted, and if he could not win the war with him he could never win it with anybody. They saw the military problem in the same way, Grant's over-all design was exactly what Mr. Lincoln had long hoped to see put into effect . . . and the two men talked the same language. When Grant explained that an army with a defensive role must do its job in a way that would contribute to the offensive elsewhere, Mr. Lincoln nodded and said: "As we say out west, if a man can't skin he must hold a leg while somebody else does." This remark would have puzzled Meade, it probably would not have been made to Hooker, and it undoubtedly would have made McClellan wince; as the son of a tanner, Grant understood it. The President had a general-in-chief he could talk to.

But the general would walk solitary, alone with the weight of command. Shortly before the campaign opened Grant sent Mr. Lincoln a letter:

". . . since the promotion which has placed me in command of all the armies, and in view of the great responsibility and the importance of success, I have been astonished at the readiness with which everything asked for has been yielded, without even an explanation being asked. Should my success be less than I desire and expect, the least I can say is, the fault is not with you."[15]

5. The General and the Statesman

HOWELL COBB had a talent the Confederacy never quite knew how to use. He was meant to be a statesman. He looked like one, he acted like one when he had a chance, and he was fitted for the part both by experience and by natural endowments; and yet in this fourth winter of his necessitous country's independence he was limited to the command of state troops in Georgia, which offered him nothing much better than a vantage point from which to discuss the mistakes that were being made in Richmond.

A good many people were discussing the subject these days, because the times had grown hard and the war was not being won. Mostly, the critics centered their fire on Jefferson Davis, taking the traditional American view that if anything goes wrong the President must be at fault. As a member of the intimate circle surrounding that wan perfectionist, Vice-President Alexander Stephens, who criticized Mr. Davis with a sad but tireless persistence, Cobb knew all about that kind of talk; but as the new year began he felt that at least part of the trouble lay with Congress. After a visit to the capital he wrote candidly to Stephens: "What is wanting in Richmond is *brains*. I did not find the temper and disposition of Congress as bad as I expected, but there is a lamentable want of brains and good sound common sense."[1]

Stephens probably would have agreed—he felt that the times were so far out of joint that hardly anyone was behaving intelligently—but at the moment he believed national disaster was taking shape at the direct urging of the President, and it was hard for him to talk about anything else. Mr.

Davis was calling on the Confederate Congress to pass an act suspending the privilege of the writ of habeas corpus.

Mr. Davis liked this no better than any other old-line Democrat would like it, but his hand was forced.

His armies were being crippled by absenteeism—by the desertion of men already in service and by the failure of drafted men to report for duty—and six months ago he had said bitterly that there were so many of these absentees that if they all came into camp they would create something like a military millennium: that is, there would be "numerical equality between our force and that of the invaders." Since then, the situation had grown worse; yet when an unwilling man was conscripted, or an absentee was plucked from an imperfectly exempt job and ordered back to the army, some judge could almost always be found to release him on a writ. This had gone so far that Mr. Davis feared lest "desertion, already a frightful evil, will become the order of the day." He asked Congress much the same question Mr. Lincoln had raised in the Vallandigham case: "Who will arrest the deserter when most of those at home are engaged with him in the common cause of setting the government at defiance?"

There was increasing war-weariness. As Mr. Davis carefully put it, "it can no longer be doubted that the zeal with which the people sprang to arms at the beginning of the contest has, in some parts of the Confederacy, been impaired by the long continuance and magnitude of the struggle." Confederate society was supposed to be harmonious, but it unquestionably contained secret organizations through which misguided citizens worked actively for submission, reunion, and abolition. Spies kept coming and going, citizens in areas near the enemy lines were notoriously in touch with the Federal authorities, and Ben Butler was believed to be plotting with certain disloyalists in Richmond to bring about a slave insurrection. There was little jury-proof evidence, however. If suspected persons were arrested they speedily went free, as the draftees and absentees went free, on writs, and Mr. Davis felt compelled to inquire: "Must the independence for which we are contending . . . be put in peril for the sake of conformity to the technicalities of the law of treason?"[2]

As far as Stephens was concerned, something much more important was in peril: the sacred principle that led to secession in the first place. He not only marched to the beat of a different drum but felt that keeping in step meant more than the final destination of the march, and so he wrote dolefully: "If the pending proposition before Congress passes, to put the whole country under martial law, with the suspension of the writ of habeas corpus, and the President signs and enforces it, and the people submit to it, constitutional liberty will go down, never to rise again on this continent, I fear. This is the worst that can befall us. Far better that our country should be over-run by the enemy, our cities sacked and burned and our land laid desolate, than that the people should thus suffer the citadel of their liberties to be entered and taken by their professed friends."[3]

Congress at last did pass the pending proposition and the President did enforce it, and to an extent the people submitted; and Stephens looked on, the doctrinaire liberal in full bloom, preferring to fail and to come to ruin rather than to try to win by inadmissible means. He brooded, and in the spring he assured Senator Herschel V. Johnson of Georgia that although he did not really hate Mr. Davis he had begun to doubt his good intentions. The President had given up too many states' rights principles, all he did was consistent with the belief that he wanted absolute power, and "My hostility and wrath (and I have enough of it to burst ten thousand bottles) is not against him or any man or men, but against the thing—the measures, and the policy which I see is leading us to despotism."[4]

This meant little, except that what had happened in the North was also happening in the South: criticism of the President increased when military fortunes declined. Robert Toombs, who had been Secretary of State and then served for a time as a hard-to-manage brigadier general, said that real control over practically everything was falling into the hands of the President and the "old army" crowd, predicted "the entire surrender of the country, executive, legislative and judicial departments, to Mr. Davis," and said that when that happened "the cause will collapse."[5] The Confederate tide had for one reason and another left Toombs on the beach, which naturally irked him; equally irksome was his suspicion that the Congress seemed to be going on the beach also. It gave Mr. Davis most of the legislation he needed, but it exerted little actual power, and it broke out every so often in sharp criticism which helped neither the cause nor the status of the critics.

Typical was the effervescence of Congressman Henry S. Foote of Tennessee, whom a Richmond editor considered "a voluble debater, but afflicted with extravagance and a colicky delivery." Foote was making the rafters quiver with his denunciations of the President. He blamed Mr. Davis for the defeat at Chattanooga, and demanded a Congressional investigation of it; demanded also an investigation of the causes of the loss of Vicksburg, and an investigation of the fraud and corruption which seemed to taint the quartermaster and commissary departments; he also called upon Congress to demand the retirement of all generals who lacked the confidence of the army and the people. What he demanded, Foote did not get, one reason being that he himself unmistakably lacked stature. The House remembered an encounter he had had with Edward S. Dargan, a member from Alabama. While Dargan was speaking, Foote called out that he was a damned rascal, on which Dargan drew a bowie knife and rushed at him. Other members overpowered Dargan, wrestling him to the floor and taking away his knife; seeing which, Foote struck an attitude, smote his breast dramatically, and cried: "I defy the steel of the assassin!"[6]

A critic of this sort could do little harm, and in the main Mr. Davis got about as much co-operation from Congress as any President is likely to get—more, in some respects, than Mr. Lincoln got in Washington. Toward the end of the war, and for that matter long afterward as well, there was a good deal of talk about an anti-Davis coalition or cabal, but the opposition in Congress was not organized and although it harassed him sorely it never seriously handicapped him. The state governors were another matter. They were jealous of their prerogatives, alert to every last paragraph of the states' rights creed, and they were not going to be stranded on any beach; when they spoke up Mr. Davis had to listen.

One who spoke sharply as 1863 closed was Zebulon Vance of North Carolina, who told the President he ought to try to make terms with the enemy.

North Carolina had done as well as any state in sending good fighting men into the Confederate armies, but before the war it had never belonged to the "Gulf Squadron," hot for secession and noisy about King Cotton, and it contained now a number of honest patriots who were both confused and tired—along with a certain number of the kind of people Mr. Davis was thinking about when he asked for suspension of the privilege of the writ. Governor Vance said that there was much discontent in the state, and he believed it probably could not be removed "except by making some effort at negotiation with the enemy." He was by no means calling for submission. He simply argued that "if fair terms are rejected" (by Washington) "it will tend greatly to strengthen and intensify the war feeling, and will rally all classes to a more cordial support of the government." If the Confederacy publicly offered to negotiate, Vance said, it would at least "convince the humblest of our citizens—who sometimes forget the actual situation—that the government is tender of their lives and would not prolong their sufferings unnecessarily one moment." He added a sentence containing a small drop of acid: "Though statesmen might regard this as useless, the people will not, and I think our cause will be strengthened thereby."

What Governor Vance proposed was entirely logical; the difficulty, as Mr. Davis promptly pointed out, was that there was nothing that the President could do about it. Offers to negotiate had in fact been made, the most recent having won Vice-President Stephens a rebuff at Hampton Roads, six months ago. The Confederacy could not make peace proposals in the ordinary way of a warring nation because the Federals simply refused to receive its envoys. The only other course Mr. Davis could think of was for the President to announce his country's desire to make peace in his messages to Congress, and this he had done from the beginning: "I cannot recall at this time one instance in which I have failed to announce that our only desire was peace, and the only terms which found a *sine qua non* were precisely those that you suggest, namely, 'a demand to be let alone.'" None of this had had any effect.

Furthermore, the Northern President had made his own position clear, as Mr. Davis pointed out: "Have we not been apprised by that despot that we can only expect his gracious pardon by emancipating all our slaves, swearing allegiance and obedience to him and his proclamations, and becoming in point of fact the slaves of our own Negroes? Can there be in North Carolina one citizen so fallen beneath the dignity of his ancestors as to accept, or to enter into conference on the basis of these terms? . . . It is with Lincoln alone that we ever could confer, and his own partisans at the North avow unequivocally that his purpose in his message and proclamation was to shut out all hope that he would *ever* treat with us, on *any* terms." The only possible course, Mr. Davis concluded, was to go on fighting until the enemy was willing to admit complete defeat: "Then and not till then will it be possible to treat of peace."[7]

It was impossible to quarrel with what Mr. Davis said; impossible, as well, to see in it anything less than the confession of a fatal handicap on statesmanship. The only negotiators now were the men with guns in their hands, because there was no longer anything for anyone else to negotiate. The very least Mr. Davis would accept was precisely the thing his opponent would not concede at any price, and if the two men had met face to face they would have had nothing to say to one another; in a sense, each man now was fighting for an unconditional surrender by the other. There was nothing to do with this war but fight it out.

The men with guns would do their best. From his camp below the Rapidan General Lee contemplated the future with hope, even though the immediate present depressed him. His army was wretchedly fed and clothed; the meat ration had been reduced again, there seemed to be no reserve stocks on hand, and the general tartly reminded Colonel Northrop that when food supplies ran short "this was the only army in which it is found necessary to reduce the rations." Joe Johnston's army, Lee found, was getting the full allowance of everything, although General Johnston was complaining that it was impossible for him to accumulate the extra stocks that would enable him to take the offensive; and the best Colonel Northrop could say was that "for months we have been living from hand to mouth." There was meat in Virginia's border counties, but the farmers refused to take Confederate money for it, and Lee suggested that the government get it by barter, sending cotton in and taking meat out. The dire nature of his need was illustrated by his comment: "I do not consider the objection that some of this cotton would find its way to the enemy as worthy of being weighed against the benefits that we would derive from adequate supplies of articles of prime necessity to the army." There was a serious

shortage of shoes, blankets and clothing also, because these
items were wearing out (even in the comparative inactivity
of a winter camp) faster than they were being replaced. The
chief trouble, of course, was the collapsing railroad system,
whose condition was not improved by the railroads' inability
to get repair and maintenance men detailed from the army.
Service to Lee's camp was bad, and Lee warned Secretary
Seddon that if it got much worse "it will be impossible for
me to keep the army in its present position."[8]

Despite these problems, when he looked to the spring
Lee thought in terms of the offensive; a limited offensive,
designed to avert disaster rather than to gain a victory
that might win the war, but an offensive nonetheless. Early in
February Lee told the President he saw two possibilities. If
Longstreet's force could be reinforced and given greater mobility, Longstreet might be able to get up into Kentucky and
force the Federals to recall their troops from the Chattanooga-
Knoxville area. Alternatively, if Longstreet could be secretly
returned to Lee, "I might succeed in forcing Gen. Meade
back to Washington," which would disrupt any designs the
Federals might have for an advance in Virginia. Each of
these plans was modest; what Lee was thinking about was
the need to put the invaders off balance. "If we could take
the initiative, fall upon them unsuspectedly," he wrote, "we
might damage their plans & embarrass them the whole summer." It was idle to think of anything much more substantial than this: "We are not in a condition, & never have been
in my opinion, to invade the enemy's country with a prospect of permanent benefit. But we can alarm & embarrass
him to some extent, & thus prevent his undertaking anything of magnitude against us."[9]

Lee's letter to Mr. Davis, set beside Mr. Davis' letter to
Governor Vance, showed what the Confederacy was up
against. In a military sense it was impossible to win an unlimited victory; in a political sense it was impossible to consider anything less. It was going to be extremely hard to fit
these two impossibilities together, and perhaps neither the
soldier nor the statesman at that moment fully grasped the
implications of the terrible divergence in their appraisals.
There was only one favorable factor, and its importance
would be realized only gradually—would be seen most clear-

ly, apparently, by Joe Johnston: in November the people of the North were going to have a presidential election.

This offered the South some reason for hope. If, by November, the Northern people had been made to feel that the war was too painful and discouraging to carry on any longer, they would vote Mr. Lincoln out of the White House. Then there might be an independent Confederacy. With other avenues to victory closed, the Confederacy might yet win by hanging on until the enemy got tired. A military program based simply on the necessity to stay alive through the autumn could gain what more ambitious programs had missed. The chance was slim, but the moral of what the two men had said was that it might be the only chance remaining.

As he looked ahead to the new year's activity, Lee did not at first think that the Federals would begin with a large-scale attempt to take Richmond. He had seen newspaper reports that the new Federal general-in-chief would make his headquarters with the Army of the Potomac, but he suspected the Federals of trying to conceal their real purpose. Their main offensive, he thought, might be a blow at General Johnston, with a thrust at Richmond coming later. It was necessary to make preparation on every front, but "should a movement be made against Richmond in large force, its preparation will no doubt be indicated by the withdrawal of troops from other quarters, particularly the Atlantic Coast and the West." If that happened the Confederacy could attack the weakened points, and "energy and activity on our part, with a constant readiness to seize any opportunity to strike a blow, will embarrass if not entirely thwart the enemy in concentrating his different armies, and compel him to conform his movements to our own."[10]

Lee did not then realize that the Federals were strong enough to take the offensive in great strength both in Virginia and in Georgia, and he did not yet conceive of a massive Federal attack all along the line. However, he was on the alert, and less than a week later he warned Richmond that there probably would be a heavy attack on his own front, with Grant present in person to direct it. If some Confederate blow could be struck in the west so as to disarrange Federal plans, all might be well; if not, Longstreet and his troops should be brought back to Virginia, either to operate in the Shenandoah or to rejoin the main army below the Rapidan. Lee still felt that if the Federals made an all-out attack on his front they would have to weaken their forces somewhere else, but as the time to begin the new campaign drew nearer he thought more and more in terms of what was going to happen in Virginia. He urged the Secretary of War to build up reserve supplies in Richmond, suggested that all of the residents of the capital whose presence there was not essential be forced to go elsewhere, and he bluntly told the President that if anything interrupted the flow of rations to the Army of Northern Virginia he might have to retreat all the way to North Carolina.[11] In the middle of April he was pessimistic, and he told the War Department: "My hands are tied. If I was able to move, with the aid of Longstreet & Pickett, the enemy might be driven from the Rappahannock and be obliged to look to the safety of his own capital, instead of the assault upon us." Lee could not even draw in his own cavalry and artillery, for want of forage, although "the season has arrived when I may be attacked any day." The survival of his army apparently depended on the state of its supplies, and Lee asserted that all railroad travel should be suspended until his army's mobility had been restored.[12]

The War Department official to whom this gloomy note was addressed was General Braxton Bragg. Mr. Davis had removed him from command of the Army of Tennessee, but he still felt that the only thing wrong was Bragg's inability to get along with his fellow officers, and he believed that in a Richmond office this failing would not matter so much. Accordingly, he called him to his side and made him general-in-chief of Confederate armies. This title meant less than it said: Bragg was Mr. Davis' chief military adviser and little more, and as always final authority over everybody in uniform rested in the hands of the President. The anti-Davis contingent in Congress derided Bragg and denounced Mr. Davis for promoting him, but the move was sensible enough, and when Lee had problems there was at least a fellow-soldier in Richmond with whom he could discuss them.

At the end of the first week in April, Longstreet was ordered to come east and rejoin the Army of Northern Virginia. By April 22 he had his men in camp near Mechanicsburg, not far from the railroad junction town of Gordonsville; and while the men rested there Lee came down, to talk to Longstreet and to look at the troops. Longstreet's veterans had not enjoyed their western adventure. They were proud of what had been won at Chickamauga, but after that everything had gone downhill, the whole east Tennessee expedition left a feeling of frustration, Longstreet and some of his chief lieutenants had quarreled bitterly, and when all was added together the winter had been unhappy. Now they were back in Virginia where they belonged, and it was like coming home; and they were drawn up on an open field in spring sunlight, long ranks motionless, ragged men precisely aligned . . . and then there was a bugle call, and the crash of artillery firing a salute, and Robert E. Lee rode out in front of them, brought his war-horse to a stand, took off his hat and looked at these soldiers who had come back to him. The men cheered, all of the emotions born of hard battles and bleak campaigning breaking out in the echoing cry of the Rebel yell; and a man who was there remembered, forty years later, and said that "the effect was as of a military sacrament."

A chaplain in Longstreet's corps, riding with the officers who followed the commanding general, turned to Colonel C. S. Venable, of Lee's staff, and asked: "Does it not make the general proud to see how these men love him?"

Venable shook his head.

"Not proud. It awes him."[13]

CHAPTER SIX

Act of Faith

1. The Last Barrier

DESIGNED TO BE IDENTICAL, the two campaigns quickly became very different.

In Virginia it finally seemed that there was just one unending battle, measuring from the Rapidan to the Appomattox in one dimension and from May to April in another. In Georgia there were many separate battles, along with sieges and skirmishes and constant raids, tied together by prodigious marching to make at last a campaign that went all across the Confederacy. Utterly dissimilar, the two campaigns nevertheless ran parallel. They took the war to its climax and then to its end, and to this day no one is quite sure what either one cost or what the two together bought.

Grant was one sort of soldier and Sherman was another; equally important, Lee was a different sort than Johnston. Each campaign was the result of a grim collaboration between enemies, taking its shape from the man who lost quite as much as from the man who won; which is to say that Grant-plus-Lee gives one total and Sherman-plus-Johnston gives another. Four concepts of strategy were at work, and not just two.

Grant and Sherman were on the offensive, but they instinctively interpreted the offensive task in different ways. Grant always thought in terms of the opposing army, and Sherman thought geographically. If one man wanted to come to grips with the enemy's soldiers, the other wanted to possess the enemy's land, cities and farms and rivers and hills. One man would drive his foe and the other would be more likely to go around him; curiously enough, Grant saw the human beings beyond the rival army as people who would some day be his fellow citizens again, and Sherman saw them as the ultimate targets of his military wrath and would reach past the opposing army to get at them.

Lee and Johnston also saw their roles differently. Lee was offensive-minded even when he was on the defensive; he was born to make the attack, and his idea of the way to parry a blow was to strike before the blow could be delivered. Any Federal general who began a "forward to Richmond" campaign was apt to learn, before much time had passed, that his chief concern had suddenly become the defense of Washington. Given the slightest opening—a pause between attacks, a breathing spell during which his antagonist waited for supplies or reinforcements—Lee would seize the initiative. He wanted to use his army rather than protect it, and he thought about victory rather than about the fear that victory might cost more than he could afford to pay.

Johnston was more passive; in an odd way, more courtly, as if the formalities that came down from seventeenth-century warfare had not yet been eradicated from the military art. The defensive seemed to fit him. He made war like an overmatched fencer, moving rapidly to meet every thrust and shift, always conscious that his opponent was the stronger, delaying his own riposte until some of that strength had been spent. At times it seemed that he fought for points rather than to draw blood, but he was pugnacious enough; he would let his counterstroke wait until his opponent had finished his maneuver. Like Lee, Johnston had the complete affection and confidence of his soldiers, and this thought sustained him when he reflected that the administration disliked him. With mingled pride and bitterness, he told a friend this spring that "if this army thought of me & felt toward me as some of our high civil functionaries do it would be necessary for me to leave the military service, but thank heaven it is my true friend."

Richmond had been impatient all winter, urging him to take the offensive and fretting because he did not. He believed he was not nearly strong enough—when May came he had about 55,000 men, and Sherman had nearly twice that many—and he thought the administration could have reinforced him if it had tried: there were plenty of idle troops in the deep South, he said, but Richmond would not send them to him. As spring came he feared that "Grant's arrival on the Potomac will turn the eyes of our authorities too strongly in that direction to let them see in this." Doubting that the Confederacy ever had the power to invade the North successfully, he still felt that it had one advantage; its soldiers believed they were defending their homes, and so had higher morale than their foes. (One reason he wanted to delay action as long as possible was the fact that the term of service of Sherman's veteran regiments would expire in May and June. Johnston did not think many of these men would re-enlist.) He was not enthusiastic about some of his general officers, among whom jealousies and rivalries remained from the Chickamauga and Chattanooga campaigns, and he told a friend: "If I were President I'd distribute the generals of this army over the Confederacy."[1]

He was at least satisfied with the generals who commanded his two army corps. One was Hardee, stolid, unspectacular, and reliable, who had been given temporary command of the army after Bragg's removal but who refused to keep it because he thought the place belonged to Johnston. The other was a transfer from Lee's army, John B. Hood, one of the most famous combat commanders in all the Confederacy.

Johnston was glad to get Hood, although physically the man was almost a wreck—at thirty-two years of age—with one arm permanently disabled by a Gettysburg wound and one leg gone entirely from a wound at Chickamauga. Hood clumped about on crutches, when he rode he had to be strapped in the saddle, and the stump of his amputated thigh gave him much pain; but he remained the perfect picture of a warrior. He still had the long, tawny beard everyone recognized, and the sad drowsy eyes that had an uncanny way of lighting up when he rode into battle, and he was obviously an asset for any army. Not until much later did Johnston learn that Hood bore a watching brief for the administration. Hood kept sending confidential letters to the President, the Secretary of War, and General Bragg, and these letters steadily and methodically undercut Johnston's own reports. Hood assured Richmond that Johnston's army was in better shape than Johnston said, and had better prospects, and Mr. Davis' dark suspicion that Johnston was more defensive-minded than he needed to be got constant confirmation.[2]

Later on this would lead to catastrophe, but for the moment all was serene. When Joe Wheeler's cavalry sent back word on May 5 that the huge Federal host was advancing, Johnston and his army were ready.

Sherman was leading three armies: one army, to all practical purposes, broken into three operating units, but technically three separate armies. Largest was the sturdy Army of the Cumberland, under Thomas, 60,000 men, veterans of everything since Shiloh, devoted to Pap Thomas and full of self-confidence. Next came the Army of the Tennessee, once Grant's and later Sherman's, led now by a curly-haired young major general who was a particular favorite of these two soldiers, James B. McPherson; in this army were 30,000 men, with more to join up later. Finally there was the Army of the Ohio, really no more than an army corps but denominated an army for administrative reasons; it contained slightly more than 17,000 men and was commanded by John M. Schofield, who had held the prickly Missouri command until Rosecrans was sent there in the shake-up that followed Chickamauga. Altogether, Sherman had about 112,000 men present for duty, although he reported that his effective marching strength would be around 100,000. Of this total, perhaps 15,000 were cavalry.[3]

These men were full of bounce, and Johnston's belief that they would refuse to re-enlist was wrong. In Thomas' army alone, seventy-one regiments—more than 30,000 men in all —had signed up for another three-year hitch; a larger number than the entire Army of the Potomac could show. The proportion was about the same in the other armies. In one of McPherson's corps it was proudly reported that every regiment from Ohio, Indiana, and Wisconsin and nearly all of those from Illinois and Iowa had re-enlisted. These westerners thought that they were winning and they wanted to be around for the finish.[4]

Now Sherman was taking them down to attack Joe Johnston, his drum beats echoing those that took the far-off Army of the Potomac across the Rapidan; and this one time, at the start of the campaign, Sherman tried for a battle of annihilation and a quick ending to everything.

It looked like a bad place to try to make a finish fight. Johnston had his men arrayed in front of Dalton, Georgia, a junction point on the railroad to Atlanta, thirty miles southeast of Chattanooga. West of Dalton, extending several miles to the north and south of the town, there was a craggy mountain called Rocky Face Ridge, coming almost to a knife-edge at its crest, with its western wall almost perpendicular. The main approach from Chattanooga came down through an opening near the northern end of this ridge, a gap with the ominous name of Buzzard Roost, held by Hood's corps. This position was so tough and had been fortified with such care that Sherman (always a man for the picturesque word or phrase) called it "the terrible door of death." A few miles to the south there was a narrower opening, Dug Gap, where the prospects were even worse. A stronger defensive position could hardly have been invented, and Confederate Pat Cleburne was conservative when he said that if Sherman tried to fight his way through here Johnston could hold him off for months, perhaps even until winter, killing numerous Yankees the while.

Sherman believed he knew what to do about this. Thirteen miles south of Dalton the railroad that came up from Atlanta ran through a town called Resaca, and a few miles west of Resaca was the opening of a long shallow valley, Snake Creek Gap, which angled off to the northwest toward the old Chickamauga battlefield. Snake Creek Gap thus was an avenue leading straight to Joe Johnston's lifeline, and by some flaw in Confederate arrangements—Cleburne blamed disobedience of orders by the cavalry—the gap had been left unprotected. So Sherman planned to have Thomas and Schofield press ostentatiously against Rocky Face Ridge while McPherson slipped in through Snake Creek Gap to break the railroad at Resaca. Johnston would have to make a disastrous retreat; attacked in front and in rear, and cut off from supplies, his army might well have to surrender or disperse.

It was a good plan, and as a matter of fact George Thomas had worked it out, and had asked permission to execute it, away back in February. In the general reshuffling of Federal command arrangements his proposal had been lost to view; now Sherman was reviving it, and he might have won the war with it if his insight and his luck had been a little better.

Believing that McPherson would move faster than Thomas, Sherman used Thomas for the holding operation and McPherson for the stroke at the rear, and his orders to McPherson were a little too mild: McPherson was to break the railroad at Resaca and then dig in at the mouth of the gap and prepare to smite the Rebels when they took off in flight. In other words, Sherman was using his most powerful unit for a feint that a smaller force could have made, and was striking his main blow with much less than his full strength; and, arranging things so, he gave the commander of his striking force orders that had a fatally defensive overtone. In addition, the situation at Resaca was not at all as Sherman had supposed it would be. Added together, these factors brought frustration.

The armies moved as ordered. Schofield and Thomas demonstrated around the terrible door of death, at considerable cost in casualties, and McPherson moved down Snake Creek Gap, came out at Resaca on May 9—and found the place strongly held by Confederate infantry and artillery. He advanced tentatively, drew a heavy fire, considered that if he moved on to break the railroad he would expose himself to a ruinous flank attack, and went back to the mouth of the gap, dug in, and awaited developments. Sherman ruefully said later that McPherson had had the sort of opportunity that a soldier gets only once in a lifetime—he could have walked right through Resaca, he said, overstating the case slightly—but he confessed that McPherson was entirely justified in what he did by the orders he had received.[5] So McPherson stayed there, and both armies regrouped at Resaca, Johnston moving down east of Rocky Face Ridge and Sherman coming down in McPherson's trail—and the big trap was not sprung.

One reason for McPherson's trouble was the fact that a thousand miles to the west General Banks had got entangled along the Red River in a campaign he could neither break off nor win. His projected advance against Mobile—the "main feature" of the whole western operation, according to Sherman—was neither made nor threatened, and Richmond ordered Bishop Polk to come to Johnston's aid with an army corps that should have been fully occupied in southern Alabama. As a result, a division of 5000 of Polk's soldiers under Brigadier General James Cantey got to Resaca on May 7. If Thomas and his 60,000 Cumberlands had come down through Snake Creek Gap they could have shouldered this force out of the way and Johnston would have been caught, but Cantey was just strong enough to make Mc-Pherson wait.[6]

Beginning on May 13 there was sharp fighting at Resaca, and after three days of it Sherman had lost 6800 men and Johnston's position remained intact. Johnston had lost nearly as many men, but Bishop Polk had come into camp with another division, Loring's, and his army was stronger than it had been when the campaign began. Sherman had clearly been foiled in his effort to destroy the force that opposed him.[7]

Then the campaign began to fall into the pattern that it followed all the way to Atlanta.

Keeping most of his army in front of Johnston at Resaca, Sherman sent infantry and cavalry on a long swing beyond his right, striking south to hit the railroad in Johnston's rear. Heavily outnumbered, Johnston could do nothing but shift his own army to meet this threat. He evacuated Resaca, ordering things so deftly that the Federals confessed he left behind not so much as a solitary wagon or a disabled cannon, and he marched down across the Oostenaula River and halted at Adairsville, fifteen miles to the south. Again Sherman skirmished in his front and sent out a flanking column beyond the Confederate left, and again Johnston quickly shifted his army to meet him, going ten miles south to Cassville, where he posted his troops north and north-east of the town.

Sherman's advance elements came out, a long spray of skirmishers in their front, there was a hard rear-guard action, and Johnston rode forward to study the situation. He realized, presently, that a good half of the Federal army was off to the west, at a town called Kingston—beginning, apparently, another of those flanking maneuvers—and it struck him that he had a fine chance to crush the half that was in his immediate front. Posting Hardee's corps off to the left, to guard against the Federals at Kingston, he ordered Hood and Polk to make the attack.

First and last, Hood complained that Johnston would rather retreat than fight, and he lodged these complaints in the highest quarters. But now, on May 19, when Johnston ordered a fight, Hood found reasons why a fight should not be made. He advanced a mile or so, reported that Federal troops were menacing his right and rear—a delusion, for there were no Federals in that vicinity—and took up a defensive position. Johnston then pulled back to a ridge south of Cassville and, after dark, Hood and Polk—who had not been especially co-operative when Bragg tried to go on the offensive—went to Johnston and told him he must retreat, arguing that they could not hold their ground next day because the Federals held a strong position and had artillery posted so that it could blast the whole Confederate line. Johnston thought they were wrong, and when he was able to get in touch with Hardee he found that Hardee thought so too; still, he did not see how he could attack if two of his three corps commanders were convinced that they were going to be defeated, and so, reluctantly, he ordered another retreat. This time he took his army south of the Etowah River and posted it around Allatoona Pass, where the Atlanta railroad passed through a defile in a forbidding rocky ridge.[8]

This was no place for a frontal attack, and Sherman did not dream of making one. He relied again on the flanking operation, this one on a large scale. Twenty-five miles south and slightly east of his headquarters at Kingston there was a little nowhere of a place called Dallas, notable because it was the center for a modest network of country roads and also because it was a dozen miles behind Johnston's position at Allatoona Pass. If Sherman could reach Dallas quickly he might get behind Johnston and cut him off from Atlanta, and so he sent McPherson off on a wide arc, marching for Dallas, and brought Thomas and Schofield down farther eastward, where they could keep Johnston from breaking into the Federal rear.

Johnston recognized the move and marched his men over to meet it, and on May 25 the armies began a round of vicious engagements near Dallas, the Federals trying to brush past the Confederate left and failing. The roads were bad, the country was inexpressibly dreary with scattered farms making lonely clearings in the spiky forests, there was heavy rain, and the soldiers floundered into a series of battles with homespun names like New Hope Church, Pumpkin Vine Creek, and Pickett's Mills. By the Chickamauga standard these were not large battles; mostly they were fought by divisions or brigades, each fight isolated from the others but all developing a singular characteristic—it was almost impossible to win one of them, in the ordinary sense, because no attack could really succeed. The smallest knoll or ravine or stand of dense underbrush could become a place where determined men might hold on as long as they had ammunition, and even when the fighting stopped the battle lines were so close together that the shooting would flare up savagely if either side tried to move.

It was here that the soldiers learned the value of entrenchments. Sherman called it "a big Indian war," and said that in this wooded country an enterprising foe could, in a remarkably short time, make an almost impassable barrier of felled trees and earth parapets; the Confederates used spade and ax so fast, he said, that they could build new works as fast as he could dislodge them from the old ones, they were always protected by these barricades, and they were so obscured by branches and underbrush that "we cannot see them until we receive a sudden and deadly fire."[9]

The campaign became a queer blend of rapid movement and utter immobility. Johnston had slaves dig trenches in advance, and his army had ready-made protection almost everywhere it went; when it did not, the men in the ranks dug themselves in without delay whenever they came to what looked like a place to fight. Federal soldiers did the same, on the sound theory that an unprotected man could not fight a man who had protection, and the interconnected trench systems became intricate and elaborate and sometimes seemed to cover half of north Georgia. A Federal soldier asserted that one area measuring roughly ten by twenty miles "was cut up by earthworks almost as thick as furrows in a ploughed field," said there was hardly half a square mile that was not so marked, and estimated that between 400 and 500 miles of earthworks had been built by the two armies in the six weeks following their arrival at Dallas. There was no end to the skirmishing, picket-line sniping and general volleying that went on from these trenches, and for a time the Army of the Cumberland was expending 200,000 rounds of small arms ammunition every day. Veteran soldiers grew very canny when it came to attacking trenches, and some ardent generals thought they were losing their fighting edge. General Schofield saw it otherwise, saying that reluctance to make hopeless assaults simply showed that the men had good sense. He added a remark that applied to both sides: "The veteran American soldier fights very much as he has been accustomed to work his farm or run his sawmill; he wants to see a fair prospect that it is going to pay."[10]

It soon became clear that the effort to beat Joe Johnston in this area was never going to pay, and Sherman put his troops on the road again; moving this time northeast toward the railroad line, and then striking southeast in an attempt to get past Johnston's right. Federal cavalry managed to compel the Confederates to evacuate the works at Allatoona Pass, thus clearing Sherman's own line of supply back to Chattanooga, but Sherman could not get past Johnston; that officer once more saw what was coming and moved to meet it, so that Sherman presently found his men facing a long line of trenches that ran across mountainous country a few miles in front of the town of Marietta. Once more the business of shifting, feinting, and probing began, the weather became worse—one man recalled that there were three weeks of rain during the month of June—and Sherman grew edgy. His temper flared up once with singular results; examining the lines opposite a height called Pine Mountain on June 14, he saw on that eminence a group of Confederate officers with field glasses studying his position, and he irritably told General Howard to have his artillery throw a few shells to drive them away. A Federal battery went into action, and the second shell it sent over struck Bishop Polk and killed him instantly. (The legend grew that Sherman with his own hands had sighted the gun that fired this shell, but that was not so, and Sherman did not until some time later know that Polk had even been present.)[11]

If the commanding general was developing a temper there was some reason for it. His line of supply was growing longer, and the need to protect it kept men away from the firing line; early in June he told Halleck that he had garrisons at Dalton, Resaca, Rome, Kingston, and Allatoona Pass, and although reinforcements made up for these detachments and for battle losses the fact remained that after a month of hard campaigning he still had not really come to grips with Joe Johnston. He briefly fell victim to the suspicion that all of these trenches had done something to army morale, and he wrote to Grant that Thomas' army was dreadfully slow. "A fresh furrow in a ploughed field will stop the whole column, and all begin to entrench," he wrote. "I have again and again tried to impress on Thomas that we must assail and not defend."[12]

The enemy was there to be assailed, and late in June Sherman made up his mind to try it. Conditions were unfavorable. Johnston held a strong line, with the center solidly posted on the wooded slopes of Kennesaw Mountain, Little Kennesaw to the south, and a rise now known as Cheatham Hill. The defense had all the advantages. But the long rains had raised the creeks and soaked the dirt roads so badly that flanking movements were impossible, stalemate here was intolerable, Atlanta was little more than twenty miles away if one measured the distance in an air line—and it is possible that Sherman remembered how Thomas' soldiers had stormed an even worse position on Missionary Ridge, seven months ago. Anyway, on June 27 his guns opened a furious cannonade, and in the middle of the morning Thomas and McPherson sent three divisions forward in a driving, headlong assault up the mountainside.

This was not Missionary Ridge. Instead of taking panic and running away Johnston's men coolly waited in their trenches and sent down a storm of fire that broke the Federal lines to pieces. Johnston paid a soldier's tribute to the Federals' courage, remarking that "the characteristic fortitude of the northwestern soldiers held them under a close and destructive fire long after reasonable hope of success was gone," but the courage only increased the casualty list. The attack barely dented Johnston's line, the Confederates shot down more than 3000 Yankees while losing fewer than 500 of their own men, and by the middle of the afternoon Thomas sent a warning to Sherman: "We have already lost heavily today without gaining any material advantage; one or two more such assaults would use up this army." This was a little strong, perhaps, because by the grim economics of 1864 a loss of 3000 men in battle was by no means excessive, but Thomas was entirely right in the belief that the position in front of him could not be carried. Sherman accepted the fact and called off the offensive, giving Thomas the cold comfort of a philosophic remark, "At times assaults are necessary and inevitable. At Arkansas Post we succeeded; at Vicksburg we failed." General Howard was less philosophical but more to the point: "We realized now, as never before, the futility of direct assaults upon entrenched lines already well prepared and well manned."[13]

There was nothing for it, obviously, but to start maneuvering again. The long rains had stopped, the roads dried, and Sherman returned to the old formula: pin Johnston's army in position with Thomas' massive host, and use the others to reach out beyond the Confederate flanks. So the Federal host began to sidle to the right, Schofield and McPherson fading back and then going south, and by July 1 their advance elements were beyond Johnston's left, actually closer to Atlanta than he was. Johnston took the alarm at once, and on July 3 Sherman found the terrible Kennesaw Mountain lines empty, with Johnston occupying new works (prepared well ahead of time) around the hamlet of Smyrna, five miles to the southeast. Sherman tapped these lines, found them substantial, and again sent his right out past the Confederate left. Once more Johnston saw his danger and retreated—going this time to the last barrier before Atlanta, the Chattahoochee River.

At first Sherman was jubilant, citing the military axiom that a wise general does not offer battle when a wide river flows across his immediate rear. This case, however, was somewhat special. On the west side of the Chattahoochee Johnston had had constructed what one Federal officer considered the strongest defensive works encountered in the entire campaign: an entrenched line six miles long, covering the railroad bridge and the principal highway crossings, with cavalry screens extending upstream and downstream to guard more remote crossings. Johnston got his army into these works and awaited developments. The memory of Kennesaw Mountain being fresh, Sherman made no attack. He kept on maneuvering, did it skillfully, and was blessed by a stroke of good luck.

Ranging upstream several miles above Johnston's right, Schofield found a gap in the Confederate cavalry screen, got down to the river, laid pontoon bridges, and put two infantry divisions across before Johnston knew what was happening.

Now the last barrier was broken. With Yankee infantry on the Atlanta side of the river Johnston had to retreat in a hurry. He did so, burning the bridges behind him, and as he entered the fortified lines about Atlanta he considered what was going to happen next. His army was on high ground be-

hind Peachtree Creek, a few miles north of the city. When
Sherman got across the Chattahoochee he would have to
find some place to cross this creek, which was just enough of
a stream to be an obstacle to a smooth military movement,
and it seemed likely that when he crossed it, with Johnston
on his flank, he would expose himself to attack. Johnston believed that he might be able to hold the Atlanta lines with
Georgia militia and, with his own army as a mobile striking
force, make at last the hard counterblow that he had not seen
a chance for since that day at Cassville.[14]

Sherman spent several days repairing bridges and amassing
supplies, then made the move across the Chattahoochee. On
the night of July 17 his entire combat force went into bivouac
east of the river, almost on the doorsteps of Atlanta. And
on the same night Johnston got a telegram from Richmond
ordering him to turn command of his army over to General
John B. Hood.

2. Sideshows

IT IS EASY NOW to see that the removal of General Johnston
was a mistake, but Mr. Davis was operating under a fatal
limitation. His narrowing horizon left him little chance to see
anything but the purely military problem—the maps, the
tracks made by the moving armies, the things done on fields
of battle—and he made a wrong choice that arose from his
own faulty concept of his responsibilities. The Federal government was applying an unendurable pressure, and if it was
not quite using all of its strength—Mr. Lincoln too had made
a mistake, and his armies were paying for it—it was nevertheless beginning to win. To play for time, risking all on
the chance that victory deferred would make the North give
up the struggle, might conceivably have worked, but Mr.
Davis did not have much time to spare.

Removing the general, Mr. Davis was supported both by
his natural impulses and by his most trusted advisers, and
as a result he saw a picture that was oversimplified and hence
distorted. He had to remember the past. Johnston had retreated up the Virginia peninsula before McClellan in 1862,
and the Yankees had been checked only when Lee came in
and took the offensive. A year later, in Mississippi, Johnston

had felt unable to attack Grant, and Vicksburg had been lost; this winter he had felt unable to strike toward Chattanooga, and now Sherman had driven him down to the suburbs of Atlanta. To argue from all of this that the man could do nothing but retreat was grossly unfair, but it was perfectly natural: when Secretary of State Judah Benjamin argued (as he was arguing now, incessantly) that "Johnston is determined not to fight, it is of no use to re-enforce him, he is not going to fight," the President was apt to listen. By the time Johnston retired across the Chattahoochee the entire cabinet was urging his removal, and when the general told Secretary Seddon that he would use militia to guard Atlanta while he maneuvered against Sherman with his main army, the President misread this as indicating a fixed intent to abandon the city entirely.[1]

This prospect was wholly unacceptable. Not only was it painful to consider what such Georgians as Alexander Stephens and Robert Toombs would say, in public and in unguarded privacy; Atlanta had in fact become a center of war industries which the Confederacy could not afford to lose. Equally important was the transportation network that centered there; after the war, Mr. Davis testified to "our dependence on the system of Georgia railroads for the food with which we were holding the field in Virginia."[2] The plain fact was that the presence of a powerful Federal army on the edge of Atlanta was intolerable.

At the last minute, Mr. Davis sent the discredited General Bragg, of all people, to Atlanta for a confidential report, and after he got there and looked things over Bragg pointed out that it might be the Yankees who would play for time now. Sherman might not even try to capture Atlanta outright; he could elect to paralyze the place, and the central Confederacy along with it, and his position east of the Chattahoochee made it possible for him to do so. Bragg explained: "You will readily see the advantage the enemy has gained, and that it may not be his policy to strike on this side of the river unless he sees his success assured. Alabama and Mississippi will be devastated and our army will melt away. Our railroad communication with Montgomery is now at the mercy of the enemy, and a mere raid may destroy Montgomery." (The point here was that the railroad through Montgomery was the eastern Confederacy's last remaining link with Alabama,

Mississippi, and the whole western country.) Bragg concluded: "There is but one remedy—offensive action."[3]

There was one adviser who lacked enthusiasm for the change. On July 12 Mr. Davis notified Lee that it was necessary to relieve Johnston "at once," and asked: "Who should succeed him? What think you of Hood for the position?" Lee immediately wired his reply: I REGRET THE FACT STATED. IT IS A BAD TIME TO RELEASE THE COMMANDER OF AN ARMY SITUATED AS THAT OF TENNESSEE. WE MAY LOSE ATLANTA AND THE ARMY TOO. HOOD IS A BOLD FIGHTER. I AM DOUBTFUL AS TO OTHER QUALITIES NECESSARY. In a letter written a few hours after this, Lee enlarged upon these points: "It is a grievous thing to change commander of an army situated as is that of the Tennessee. Still if necessary it ought to be done. I know nothing of the necessity. I had hoped that Johnston was strong enough to deliver battle. We must risk much to save Alabama, Mobile and communication with the Trans Mississippi. It would be better to concentrate all the cavalry in Mississippi and Tennessee on Sherman's communications. . . . Hood is a good fighter, very industrious on the battle field, careless off, and I have had no opportunity of judging his action when the whole responsibility rested upon him. I have a high opinion of his gallantry, earnestness and zeal. Genl. Hardee has more experience in managing an army."[4]

Lee picked his words carefully when he wrote to the President, and Hood had been one of his most prized division commanders in the Army of Northern Virginia; altogether, Lee must have had powerful misgivings if that was the best recommendation he could write for Hood. But although he was thus warning that this choice would be a mistake, his advice was disregarded; inevitably so, probably, because Hood had been the heir apparent to the command ever since the campaign began. He had been in touch, all along, drawing attention to his commander's errors; much of what Richmond believed about Johnston's failure to accept good chances to bring Sherman to battle came direct from Hood. When Bragg visited Atlanta, Hood gave him a letter asserting that since leaving Dalton the army had lost 20,000 men without having fought a decisive battle, although chances to strike a blow had several times been offered. Atlanta, said Hood, should in no circumstances be given up, and he closed with the same note of diffident self-advancement that had been sounded for Mr. Lincoln under other circumstances by Secretary Seward and General McClellan: "I have, general, so often urged that we should force the enemy to give us battle as to almost be regarded as reckless by the officers high in rank in this army, since their views have been so directly opposite. I regard it as a great misfortune to our country that we failed to give battle to the enemy many miles north of our present position. Please say to the President that I shall continue to do my duty cheerfully and faithfully, and strive to do what I think is best for our country, as my constant prayer is for our success."[5]

With one point in General Lee's letter practically everybody agreed. The best way to stop Sherman was to turn the cavalry loose on his line of communications—and, specifically, not just any cavalry, but the cavalry commanded by Bedford Forrest, the one Confederate horseman who would be absolutely certain to concentrate on hurting the Yankees without having distracting thoughts about his own fame or the glamour of a dashing cavalry raid.

The railroad operation by which Sherman kept a steady stream of supplies coming all the way down from Nashville, via Chattanooga, was at the same time the gaudiest and the most vulnerable aspect of his entire campaign. It was wartime railroading of a kind never seen before and not often seen since, with everything subordinated to the need to get the required amounts of rations, forage, and ammunition laid down at the advanced depots on time. It was said that engineers on this railroad did not especially need to know much about operating locomotives but they did have to be daring and energetic, and few of them got any sleep to speak of. Trains came down without timetables or regular schedules, going when the dispatchers told them to go, and whenever there was a wreck or any kind of disabling accident the locomotive and cars were simply tumbled off the track to make room for the next train. It was asserted—with a degree of exaggeration impossible to assess properly, at this distance—that beside a long embankment, somewhere below Chattanooga, there was so much wreckage that a man could walk five miles on the debris, without once setting foot on the ground. Repair gangs were of fabulous speed and competence; the railroad bridge over the Chattahoochee, 900 feet long

(including the approaches) and 90 feet high, was rebuilt in
four and one-half days, although all of the timbers used in
the construction were living trees when the job began.[6] Repairs were made so quickly that Johnston's soldiers used to
say it did no good to destroy track behind Sherman because
he carried spare tunnels. When Sherman called this campaign
a big Indian war he used the wrong word; it was really a big
railroad war.

Joe Wheeler had operated against this road all the way
down from Chattanooga, but Sherman had his own cavalry
protecting it, with infantry detachments at frequent intervals
in blockhouses, and the damage Wheeler's men inflicted was
an annoyance rather than a problem. As a matter of fact—
and before he was much older Sherman would find that the
same thing was true of his own troopers—cavalry in the Civil
War was not very efficient when it came to railroad destruction. The job involved a little too much plain drudgery.
Simply to remove a few rails and burn a bridge or two would
not answer; that sort of damage could be made good before
the cavalry raiders had got away far enough to start bragging
properly.

But Forrest was different. One of his admiring troopers put
the essence of him in one sentence: "Forrest never did anything as anyone else would have done or even thought of doing in regard to a fight." Forrest and his men were not recog-
nizable as the romantic sabreurs of misty tradition; they were
matter-of-fact people who believed that the object of all they
did was to bring harm to their foes, and they went about
their jobs with single-minded energy. When Forrest struck
the Federal rear it took a real fight to keep him off; not just
skirmish-line firing between galloping patrols but a grinding,
man-killing battle in which everybody played for keeps. The
admiring trooper told how, in action, Forrest "would curse,
then praise, then threaten to shoot us himself if we were
afraid the Yankees might hit us," and he remembered that
the general was always telling people to hurry.[7] When Forrest hit a railroad line with evil intent that line was obliter-
ated, with as much care and effort devoted to its destruction
as had gone into its original building. If Forrest ever got on
Sherman's railroad line Sherman was likely to be in serious
trouble.

Johnston had several times asked that Forrest (who was

not under his command) be sent against Sherman's communications. So had Governor Joseph E. Brown of Georgia, a tireless mouthpiece for the Georgia dissenters. When Mr. Davis told Brown that Forrest had in fact spent weeks operating deep in Sherman's rear areas, although not on his railroad, and that he was kept very busy on important assignments far to the west of Georgia, Brown replied: "If your mistake should result in loss of Atlanta and the occupation of other strong points in this state by the enemy, the blow may be fatal to our cause and remote posterity may have reason to mourn over the error."[8]

This was somewhat unjust, because Forrest had been busy and effective. In March and April he had raided in western Tennessee and Kentucky, getting all the way to the Ohio River, occupying Paducah briefly, collecting recruits and horses and food and weapons and returning to his base in Mississippi stronger than when he started out.

On this raid he stormed Fort Pillow, on the Mississippi in Tennessee some forty miles above Memphis, held by approximately six hundred Federals, half of them Negro soldiers, the other half Tennessee whites whom the Confederates contemptuously called "homemade Yankees." The defense was poorly directed, no one seemed sure whether the fort was actually surrendered or was simply overrun, and a number of white and colored soldiers were killed after effective defense had ended. Radical Republicans in Washington charged that there had been an outright massacre, after Forrest went back to Mississippi the Committee on the Conduct of the War collected a hair-raising set of atrocity stories, and there were demands for stern retaliation. The retaliation never took place, but a new note of bitterness entered Northern war propaganda and the affair testified to the grimness of the fighting in the disputed border country.

Early in June, Forrest started north to do more damage, but learned that Sherman had ordered Major General S. D. Sturgis with 8000 men to come down from Memphis and destroy him. He turned to meet Sturgis, caught him on June 10 at Brice's Crossroads, Mississippi, where the Federals were all strung out on a muddy road with a mired wagon train blocking the path for the infantry, and inflicted on this luckless command one of the most startling defeats of the war. In this battle Forrest caused more than 2200 Union casual-

ties and lost fewer than 500 of his own men, seizing sixteen
guns and two hundred wagons and leaving the routed Federals, as Sturgis confessed, "in no condition to offer determined resistance." Sturgis was glad enough to get his
bedraggled men back to Memphis, where he reported that he
had been attacked by a force numbering somewhere between
15,000 and 20,000 men. In reality, Forrest had taken no more
than 3500 into action.[9]

Forrest in short had been accomplishing a great deal; yet
as far as the outcome of the war was concerned his efforts
had been wasted. This man, who better than anyone else in
the Confederacy could create chaos in the rear of an invading army, had not been used for that purpose when an invasion was threatening the Confederacy's very life. He had
compelled the Federal government to waste money and manpower on what it had supposed was a thoroughly conquered
area, and he had driven Sherman to cry angrily that there
would never be peace in western Tennessee until Forrest was
dead: but he had not made Sherman turn about and go north
instead of south, and that was all that really mattered. He
was a priceless resource and he had been used on a sideshow.

This was tragic, because Mr. Davis had no margin for error. His military resources were so limited that he dared not
misuse any of them. Here Mr. Lincoln held an increasing
advantage. In a military sense he had almost unlimited funds;
he might lose the war by making political mistakes, but his
military mistakes could be made good. This was an enormous
point in his favor. Mr. Davis made the Federal invasion of
Georgia easier by what he did with Johnston and Forrest,
and Mr. Lincoln made it harder by what he did with General
Banks; the difference was that the Northern President had
something to spare and the Southern President did not.

When Mr. Lincoln authorized the Red River expedition he
tried to do several things at once. He wound up by doing
none of them, yet the big trouble was not that the expedition
failed but that it was made at all. Like Forrest, Banks was
put to work in the wrong place and he represented wasted
effort. He carried out his assignment miserably, but the basic
idea was bad to begin with.

The idea dated away back to the early days of the war, beginning to take active shape when General Banks got to

Louisiana and sent back that glowing report about the enormous amount of cotton that could be had if the Federals controlled the Red River Valley. As the war grew older the Federal appetite for cotton increased, along with the price of cotton, and the profits that could be made by traders who laid their hands on it; and other events made that distant river valley look even more important.

The Red River came down from the country where Texas, Arkansas, and Louisiana touched corners, and the city of Shreveport, three hundred tangled miles from the place where the Red River reached the Mississippi, was several things at once. It was the temporary capital of Confederate Louisiana, and it was also headquarters of General Edmund Kirby Smith and so, in a way, the capital of the trans-Mississippi Confederacy. It was a big supply depot, and a first-rate gateway to Texas. If the Federals held Shreveport and the river they could frustrate all of Smith's plans, protect their own control of the Mississippi and states like Missouri, and invade Texas whenever they pleased; also, the insecure ten percent governments set up in Louisiana and Arkansas would be strengthened. Shreveport looked like a place worth taking, and early in January Halleck told Banks that he was to go ahead and take it.

The stated objectives were simple: occupy Shreveport and drive the Rebels away from the Red River. Banks would have help. From Arkansas Major General Frederick Steele was to march down to join him with 15,000 men; Sherman was ordered to send 10,000 more under Major General A. J. Smith, and Admiral Porter would take a powerful flotilla up the Red River, convoying transports and supply steamers. All in all Banks would command between 40,000 and 50,000 men. He had lost much of his early enthusiasm for the venture, but he considered its objectives good and he assured Halleck that "the occupation of Shreveport will be to the country west of the Mississippi what that of Chattanooga is to the east."[10]

This might well be so, although the precise value of a triumph gained west of the river at a time when the war was to be won or lost east of the river was never thoroughly examined. Military and political considerations were so mixed that it was hard to say what the basic idea back of the expedition really was, and when Congressional investigators later asked Admiral Porter what the operation was intended to do the admiral replied: "I never understood."[11] At the time he testified, Porter was on the most hostile terms imaginable with Banks, and this may have colored his answer; but it must be admitted that the thing was a jumble.

Whatever was meant, the expedition never came close to success. Banks himself was late, being held in New Orleans by ceremonies connected with the installation of the new loyalist government of Louisiana, but his troops took off on March 13 under General Franklin and ten days later they got to Alexandria, sixty miles up the Red River, where they met Smith's contingent and Porter's fleet. Banks overtook them there on March 24, and found waiting for him a dispatch from General Grant.

Grant had taken the top command intending Banks to join a combined movement of all the armies east of the Mississippi, and one of his first discoveries was that it was too late to cancel this Red River foray. He wrote his dispatch to Banks on March 15, immediately after his exploratory visit to Meade's army, saying frankly that he saw little point to this expedition and that the destruction of Confederate armies was "of vastly more importance than the mere acquisition of territory." If Shreveport fell, Banks and most of his men must return to New Orleans at once to mount an offensive toward Mobile; further—and this Banks found really troublesome—whatever happened, Smith and his 10,000 must go back to Sherman by April 25 at the latest, even if this wrecked the entire operation.[12]

Handicaps piled up so fast that this one made no difference. Coming down from Arkansas on bad roads swarming with hostile cavalry under General Sterling Price, Steele found it impossible either to drive Price away or to carry adequate supplies, and presently he had to beat a laborious retreat, giving Banks no help whatever. Water in the Red River was abnormally low, and it was April 3 before Porter could get his fleet past the rapids just above Alexandria. The army plodded on, two-thirds of the way from Alexandria to Shreveport, and on April 8 it encountered 8000 Confederates under Major General Richard Taylor, son of old Zachary and a good fighter in his own right. Taylor caught Franklin's column much as Forrest had caught Sturgis—strung out on a narrow road, with a wagon train stalled just where it would do the most harm—and at a place called Sabine Crossroads, south of Mansfield, he struck this column, mangled it and drove it back in confused retreat. Banks got things in hand, next day, and in a fight at Pleasant Hill A. J. Smith's men routed Taylor in a battle made odd by the fact that as soon as it ended both armies retreated as fast as they could go.

Kirby Smith took part of Taylor's force north to aid Price in driving back Steele, while Taylor, greatly depleted, managed an able harassing campaign against the gunboats and Banks. The Federal general wanted to confer with the navy and take stock, and he put his army in camp around the steamboat landing of Grand Ecore, where low water had brought the fleet's advance to a halt. What he learned here gave him scant comfort. The navy's luck had been worse than the army's, the river was falling so fast that if the fleet did not get out soon it could not get out at all, and under Grant's orders it was time to send Smith east. It had already been necessary to send away 3000 men who properly belonged to McPherson, 4000 more had been battle casualties, Steele and his 15,000 had never arrived at all, and without Smith's troops Banks felt that he would be forced to go back to New Orleans. He wired Grant that "this campaign cannot be abandoned without abandoning the navy and permitting the invasion of Missouri," and Porter sent an anxious message to Sherman saying that the safety of both the fleet and the army depended on keeping Smith: "He is the only part of the army that was not demoralized, and if he was to leave there would be a most disastrous result."[13]

In the end both the army and the navy escaped, but the thing was such a crashing failure that the mere fact that Porter's gunboats were saved came to look almost like a victory and was about the only point of the campaign the people in the North ever cared to remember. Low water made it impossible to get the gunboats down past the Alexandria rapids; the Confederates were bringing up sharpshooters and field artillery to harass them, Porter had already lost one light gunboat and two auxiliaries, and if the army retreated he must destroy all the rest. To blow up ten good gunboats was unthinkable, but to let the enemy have them would be far worse: give the Confederates a solid fleet of ironclads on the Mississippi and the war in the west might as well be started all over again.

The boats probably would have been lost if it had not been for Lieutenant Colonel Joseph Bailey of the 4th Wisconsin Infantry, chief engineer for Franklin's XIX Corps. Bailey had worked on western rivers and he saved the navy with a western river trick: when the water was too low the westerners simply built dams to make it higher. Banks gave Bailey two or three Maine regiments composed mostly of lumberjacks, handy with axes and used to riverside work, and Bailey put them to work building dams to create a suitable head of water. The river rose and hid the rocks, Porter's gunboats came bumping and grating over the shallows, and then the flood waters were released and the ungainly ironclads went careening downstream, all smoke and steam and spray, everybody whooping, army bands on the banks playing to cheer them along. On this gratifying but negative achievement the campaign came to an end, and by May 21 army and navy were back on the Mississippi.[14]

The campaign had been a blunder, not because it failed but because it was made at all. It prevented the Mobile offensive, kept 10,000 good men away from Sherman when he needed them most and enabled Mr. Davis to send Bishop Polk's corps to help Joe Johnston, and it would have had all of these effects even if Banks had been successful. It was an offensive that pointed in the wrong direction.

Also it was tainted. Nobody ever forgot about that Red River cotton, and although the campaign's basic objectives were clean enough the cotton business stained it. Washington wanted cotton and it also wanted to make good Unionists out of Southern planters: natural desires, both of them, but not compatible with purely military aims. In January the Treasury had issued new rules for the cotton trade: any Southerner who brought cotton inside the Union lines and took an oath of loyalty would be paid 25 percent of the cotton's market value in cash and could get a receipt for the balance, and at the end of the war, if he could show that his loyalty had remained firm after he made this deal, he could cash the receipt. In theory, this gave him a financial motive for wishing to see the Union restored; in practice it raised a whole mare's nest of problems, and later in the summer the Federal Major General E. R. S. Canby dilated upon these in a letter to President Lincoln.

When a Federal army entered a cotton-growing area, said

General Canby, Confederate officers were supposed to burn cotton and Union officers were supposed to confiscate it. The cotton traders wanted neither thing to happen, and so they tried to make such invasions fail, tipping off the Confederate authorities whenever a move was being planned. Much worse, they swarmed all over everybody, trying to buy cotton before it could be either burned or seized, and they did this because the government's rules gave them a direct incentive. The government was actively promoting trade with the enemy at the very moment when it was trying its best to destroy him.

The ins and outs of it were most complicated, and Mr. Lincoln tried to explain them in a somewhat labored letter to General Canby. The blockade, he said, had made the price of cotton six times as high as it used to be, and in spite of the blockade the enemy managed to export at least a sixth as much cotton as he ever did, so that he got a normal income for a fraction of the normal effort. "The effect, in substance," wrote Mr. Lincoln, "is that we give him six ordinary crops, without the trouble of producing any but the first; and at the same time leave his fields and his laborers free to produce provisions. You know how this keeps up his armies at home and procures supplies from abroad. . . . We cannot give up the blockade, and hence it becomes immensely important to us to get the cotton away from him. Better give guns for it than let him, as now, get both guns and ammunition for it."[15]

Wherever this kind of logic might take a man, cotton certainly gave the Red River expedition a peculiar coloration. Relying on the new Treasury rule, many planters brought cotton to the river as the expedition moved upstream, ready to take the oath and sell the stuff. Porter's naval officers promptly confiscated as much of this as they could get and sent it north as naval prize; they were far from the high seas, but the old high seas prize rule applied and naval officers got a certain percentage of the value of enemy goods seized. Considering this a gross breach of faith, the planters took thought of their innate Southern loyalty and began to burn their cotton. The army managed to buy some of it, turning it over to the quartermasters for shipment north and ultimate transfer to the Treasury; and the ever-present traders (two of them bearing passes signed by Abraham Lincoln) came along and bought whatever cotton had been missed by the navy, the army, and the flames of the indignant planters. An army officer remembered with glee that most of the bales the traders got were piled up at Alexandria and were at last seized by Colonel Bailey and used to build dams.

One thing the operation did accomplish; it created bitter friction between army and navy officers, and it may be that interservice antagonism reached its all-time peak on the Red River. Porter, who used language somewhat loosely, said that "the whole affair was a cotton speculation," and asserted that Banks came upstream in a steamer loaded down with speculators, with ice and champagne, and with bagging and ropes for the baling of cotton. Banks retorted that at Alexandria the navy sent marines inland with wagon trains to get cotton at the source, taking along engine room mechanics to put the cotton gins in operation. Army officers were furious because naval officers collected prize money (and bragged about it) and naval officers held that they almost lost their fleet because the army failed to do its job properly. Banks insisted, doubtless truthfully, that nothing in the way of a military operation was subordinated to a desire to get cotton, and one of his staff officers, Brigadier General William Dwight, said that only a few thousand bales were ever sent north although from 200,000 to 300,000 might have been had if that had been a genuine objective.[16]

An uncommonly bad odor was created, in other words; yet the trouble had little to do with cotton. The assistant medical director on Banks' staff rendered an indisputable verdict: "It seemed to me that any life lost in battle west of the Mississippi River after January, 1864, was an unnecessary sacrifice, and that the real theater of war was east of the river and the operations west of it only a sideshow."[17]

3. The Cork in the Bottle

THE TRANSPORTS floated up Hampton Roads to the James River in a line ten miles long, sending up more than two hundred pillars of smoke to make a great cloudbank against the clear sky of a May morning. The navy led the way with five ironclads and a swarm of lesser craft, and on the transports there were more than 30,000 soldiers: veterans, armed and equipped with the best their country could provide, moving directly toward a Richmond that was hardly a day's journey away and that was defended now by no more than a totally inadequate handful. The spring breeze was warm and easy, and the air was bright with promise; the soldiers looked on the picture they were making, took pride in it, and saw in their own moving column a display of the Republic's armed might.

The commanding general felt as they felt. His steamer moved at the head of the line, but around mid-day it swung out, turned and went ranging downstream, and the general stood bareheaded on the upper deck and as each transport came abreast he swung his hat in an imperious full-arm gesture toward the west, lunging with his body, as he did so, to give the gesture added emphasis. On transport after transport the soldiers lined the rails and cheered with high enthusiasm. At this moment they believed in this general implicitly, and believing in him they believed also in themselves, and they had never a doubt that he was leading them to a triumph that would win the war and turn all of them into heroes.[1]

The commanding general was Benjamin F. Butler.

In a war where the pressures of politics were always strong and at times irresistible, Butler was getting a final, dazzling chance to win the military distinction which he always wanted and never got. Of military capacity, to be sure, he possessed not a trace, but he was a lifelong Democrat who had wholeheartedly defected to the radicals, and so in this election year he had to be used; and it was sheer bad luck that he held a spot that was pivotal to Grant's whole Virginia campaign. Compelled to use him in a role that demanded a first-rater, Grant was trying to make the best of him; he had at least been able to encase him between two solid professional subordinates, on the hopeful theory that these lieutenants could steer him into competent behavior. Anyway, the odds favored this expedition so powerfully that ordinary incompetence could hardly spoil it.

Butler's expedition up the James was in fact a blow at the almost unguarded rear of Lee's army. It was the vitally important other half of the Federal campaign in Virginia, and the plans for Meade's army had been drawn up on the assumption that Meade's job would be made easier by what was done on the James.

On the afternoon of May 5, while Butler was sending hand-signals to fame from the hurricane deck of a steamboat, Grant and Meade were taking 120,000 men across the Rapidan to attack Lee's 65,000. Meade's army and Butler's were a hundred miles apart, but they were engaged in one operation. To Halleck, before the campaign opened, Grant was explicit: "Should Lee fall back within his fortifications at Richmond, either before or after giving battle, I will form a junction with Butler and the two forces will draw supplies from the James River. My own notions about our line of march are entirely made up, but as circumstances beyond our control may change them I will only state that my effort will be to bring Butler's and Meade's forces together." To Butler he was equally definite: "That Richmond is to be your chief objective point, and that there is to be co-operation between your force and the Army of the Potomac, must be your guide." Grant hoped that Butler could invest Richmond on the south side, with the left of his army touching the James just above the city; in that case, Grant would bring Meade's army down so that its right could join hands with Butler's left across the river. He emphasized that Butler was to "use every exertion to secure footing as far up the south side of the river as you can, and as soon as you can."[1]

If Butler did what he was supposed to do Meade's success would be almost certain, because if Richmond were closely invested from the south Lee's army would face quick starvation. The capital city produced quantities of munitions, but the food it sent to the Army of Northern Virginia came from the west and south, and the approach Grant called for would cut the railroads by which this food came to Richmond. At sunset on May 5, when the head of the line of transports drew up at the Bermuda Hundred landing on the James, Butler's opportunity was as bright as any general could wish.

Coming down from Richmond to the sea, the James goes due south for seven miles, swings east past the height of Drewry's Bluff, where the Confederates had built Fort Darling, drifts southeast in a series of aimless hairpin turns, makes a final loop at Turkey Bend, with Malvern Hill lying a mile to the north, and then flows south past Bermuda Hundred. Here the river broadens, beginning to look more like an arm of the sea than a river, and two miles below Bermuda Hundred it is joined by the Appomattox River, which comes in from the west and south. The flat country enclosed by the two rivers is irregularly shaped, from west to east it is seven or eight miles long, and its western neck measures three miles, north and south, from one river to the other.

Once he landed at Bermuda Hundred, Butler's immediate job was to march straight west for about ten miles. Doing this, he would strike both the railroad and the turnpike that connected Richmond with the city of Petersburg, which lay on the south side of the Appomattox ten miles upstream from the James. Then he would have two options: turn right, as his orders directed him to do, and move on Richmond, or turn left and move on Petersburg. It did not matter much which he did, because if he took Petersburg either he or Meade would inevitably get Richmond shortly afterward. Of the railroads that connected the capital with the south, all but one came up to Petersburg, and the capital could not be held without them.[3]

The way was all but wide open, because the Confederate authorities had been deceived. All spring it had been known that Burnside's army corps, brought east from Tennessee, was being built up at Annapolis, and it was believed that the Federals planned to invade North Carolina with this force as a nucleus—exactly the move, as a matter of fact, that Grant had proposed early in the winter, before he became lieutenant general. Beauregard had been detached from Charleston and given command of Confederate forces in North Carolina and in Virginia below the James, and he had his headquarters and most of his troops in North Carolina. Butler had kept his cards well concealed, and not until May 3 was Lee able to warn the War Department that in his belief this Federal force was preparing to move against Richmond. To defend Richmond south of the James there was Fort Darling, at Drewry's Bluff, manned by heavy artillerists, and several thousand War Department clerks and munitions workers could be called up in an emergency to hold the fortifications immediately around the city; but of regular field troops to come out in the open and prevent the kind of investment

Grant was demanding there were at that moment only two brigades of infantry, perhaps 3000 men in all. To defend Petersburg there were at most 2000 more. Against these, Butler (who detached a division of 5000 men to hold City Point, at the mouth of the Appomattox) could put at least 25,000 men into action. In addition he had sent 3000 cavalry on a long swing to the southwest to cut the railroads below Petersburg, and he had half as many more riding up the north side of the James. For a few days there was no way on earth for the Confederates to keep him from carrying out his orders.

On the night of May 5 Butler seems to have had an awareness of this fact, and as his troops began to disembark at Bermuda Hundred he called in his two corps commanders and proposed that they take the men who had already gone ashore and march forthwith on Richmond, midnight or no.

These corps commanders were the professional soldiers on whom Grant relied to keep Butler from folly. As far as Grant could see they were well chosen. The commander of Butler's X Corps was Major General Quincy A. Gillmore, who had conducted the siege of Charleston. He had failed there through no especial fault of his own. The experience had left him highly distrustful of any operation that involved attacking entrenched Confederates, but there was no way to know that it had left him very reluctant to make any attack at all. The other man, leading the XVIII Corps, was Major General William F. Smith, who had greatly impressed Grant by his handling of the engineering assignment at Chattanooga. Like Bragg's lieutenants at Chickamauga, Smith was capable but difficult: difficult in an erratic way that finally became altogether incomprehensible. At the beginning of May, Grant thought him one of the best generals in the army; by July, he considered him one of the worst.[4]

Anyway, these two professionals naturally advised Butler to curb his enthusiasm. To march that night would be to take no more than 10,000 men off through unfamiliar country, in pitch darkness, against no one knew how many Confederates; better wait for daylight and move with everybody. This advice was good, and Butler accepted it, and yet it seems a pity, somehow: this was the last time in the campaign that Butler showed a spark of initiative, and it was the only time these two generals gave him the kind of help

Grant expected them to give. Immediately after this the expedition ran hard aground.

On May 6 the troops were ready and the march began, Gillmore's corps on the right and Smith's on the left. At noon the men reached the base of the Bermuda Hundred peninsula, where instead of going on with the advance they stacked arms and began to entrench. As good engineers, Gillmore and Smith laid out an excellent defensive line three miles long, facing west, right flank touching the James, left flank on the Appomattox; a good idea, no doubt, except that the army was supposed to be on the offensive. From the middle of this line the advance guards could just see the spires of Petersburg, seven miles to the south. Richmond lay fifteen miles to the north; two or three miles directly west of the Federal line were the turnpike and the railroad that linked those cities; and within fifty miles there were fewer than 10,000 armed Confederates, counting everybody. While his 25,000 industriously dug in, Butler forwarded orders: let each corps commander advance a brigade to seize the railroad and the turnpike.

To do even this might have insured success, as it would have broken Richmond's principal railroad connection with the south, but that did not happen. Gillmore for some reason made no advance at all. Smith dutifully sent one brigade forward; it marched two miles, sparred lightly with a thin Confederate skirmish line, and presently went back to its starting point. Smith reported that to try to carry the railroad would have risked loss of his entire force (which was opposed that day by no more than nine companies of infantry); and Butler, the commanding general, instead of riding to the front to see to it that his orders were carried out, followed his political orientation and wrote an indignant letter to Senator Henry Wilson of Massachusetts, demanding that Gillmore's recent nomination to the grade of major general be rejected.

Next day, May 7, the army had been ashore for thirty-six hours, and Butler tried again. This time he managed to get 8000 men sent forward, but these men accomplished nothing; they ran into 2600 Confederates under a determined general named Bushrod Johnson, skirmished until they had 339 casualties, held the railroad briefly without harming it, and before sunset were recalled to their entrenchments. That night the Federal soldiers began to circulate a wry joke: How long will it take to get to Richmond if you advance two miles every day and come back to your starting point every night?

At this distance it all seems rather unbelievable, but the surface of the incredible had barely been scratched. On May 9 Butler at last came to the front in person, and this time he got most of his army in motion. On the right Gillmore reached the railroad at Chester Station and actually tore up a little of the track. Four miles to the south of him Smith marched on Port Walthall Junction, but his skirmishers ran into a spatter of musket fire before they got there and Smith immediately called a halt and sent couriers off to Gillmore with an urgent request: if Gillmore would at once march south along the turnpike, his force and Smith's together, could pinch off and capture the Confederates who held the junction. Gillmore complied, suspending most of his railroad-destroying activities, and the whole thing was quite logical except for the fact that there were hardly any Confederates at the junction to be captured. Johnson had moved out the night before, and today he was dug in two miles to the south, behind an inconsequential stream known as Swift Creek; he had left no more than a few platoons behind to annoy the Yankees.

In the end, 14,000 Federal soldiers spent the afternoon trying to capture a hundred Confederates, who got away; and eventually Smith and Gillmore learned where Johnson was, made as if to attack his position, concluded that it was too strong to be taken by storm, and advised Butler that he had better attack Petersburg, if at all, from the east. Unhappily, they who so advised him were then due north of the place, unable to get at Petersburg from the east unless they went all the way back to Bermuda Hundred and got on the steamboats or bridged the Appomattox with pontoons.

Butler was furious, a fatal quality when it is blended with complete impotence. Undeniably, he had been poorly served by his lieutenants; but he was in addition utterly lacking in any military insight of his own, and so he never realized that he ought at least to keep his army on the Richmond & Petersburg Railroad, now that he had it there. He climaxed this day of errors by ordering everybody to come back once more to the fortified lines between the James and the Appomattox.

The blind were being led by the blind, and because nothing at all had been accomplished so far the unlimited opportunity that had been so obvious on May 5 was beginning to disappear entirely. During the next forty-eight hours some quiver of concern about this fact seems to have disturbed Butler, and on May 12 he got his army on the road once again, turning north this time to move up to Fort Darling and Drewry's Bluff and the immediate approaches to Richmond. The first part of the movement was unopposed, but it was made with great caution, and two days saw a total advance of approximately four miles; and at last the army entrenched, facing north, a mile short of the Confederate works that ran west from Fort Darling. Some dim premonition of on-coming trouble led Smith on May 15 to bring up a bale of telegraph wire and weave a cunning network of it, from stump to fence-post to felled timber, a foot off the ground, along the front of his corps.[5]

Among them, the leaders of this army had given away altogether too much time, and they had given it to men who knew how to use it—chiefly to General P. G. T. Beauregard, who was given to bombast but who underneath it all was an extremely able general. By the end of the second week in May Beauregard had had just time to get to the scene himself, and, with the aid of Braxton Bragg, to assemble close to 20,000 Confederate soldiers. He conferred hastily with President Davis and then, on May 16, he struck savagely at Butler's advance, trying to break Butler's right loose from the bank of the James, drive the Federal force inland, and capture it entire. Ten days after Butler had disembarked the tale of lost opportunities had come down to this: he no longer had any chance to do what he was supposed to do, and the only question remaining was whether his army would simply be defeated or would be destroyed outright.[6]

The Confederate attack came on a foggy dawn in a wet gray twilight that hid the rival lines from each other until they were at point-blank range. It struck Smith's corps, drove his right brigade away from the James, and seemed likely to crumple the whole line; but Smith partly atoned for his wretched performance down to date by handling his part of the battle with unflustered competence, and his network of

telegraph wire threw the Confederate attack into confusion
at the right moment. Men running forward through the fog
never saw the wires until they fell over them, and when
they got up and tried to get realigned the Federals shot them
down; in Smith's expressive phrase, the attacking Southerners "were slaughtered like partridges." However, this did no
more than stave off disaster. After half a day of hard fighting
the Federal army had to retreat, and by late afternoon it was
back in those entrenched lines on Bermuda Hundred neck
once more. It had lost more than 4100 men, killed, wounded
and missing, and although Beauregard's own losses had been
severe the one fact that mattered was that the Yankee blow
at Lee's rear had been completely frustrated. Beauregard felt
that his victory would have been complete if a division which
he had ordered up from Petersburg had pitched vigorously
into Butler's rear, as instructed, while everybody else was
assailing him in front, and he wrote that "we could and
should have captured Butler's entire army." Considering the
way Butler's army was commanded, this was probably correct, but even so Beauregard had accomplished a good deal.
Half of Grant's plan for the Virginia campaign had been disrupted, and something like ten additional months of life had
been won for the Confederacy. Generals have fought larger
battles to win less.[7]

Butler's lines on the Bermuda Hundred neck were strong,
and once he got his army back in them he was safe. Reflecting on this he felt that he had done all that could have
been expected of him, and he revealed his glassy inability
to understand either his responsibilities or the fate that had
befallen him by assuring Secretary Stanton that "we can hold
out against the whole of Lee's army," adding that "Grant will
not be troubled with any further reinforcements to Lee from
Beauregard's force." Half of this statement was irrelevant, inasmuch as Lee's army never had any intention of attacking Butler, and the other half of it was dead wrong, because
Beauregard did reinforce Lee, promptly and substantially. If
the Confederates could not break through Butler's lines, he
could not now break out of them: it was simple enough for
Beauregard to entrench an opposing line as invulnerable as
Butler's, and Grant described the situation perfectly by remarking that as soon as Butler's army had withdrawn to the
Bermuda Hundred position "it was as completely shut off

from further operations directly against Richmond as if it had been in a bottle strongly corked." Shortly after the battle of Drewry's Bluff a good 6000 of Beauregard's troops joined Lee, who needed more troops desperately just then, on the dismal battlefields around Spotsylvania Courthouse.[8]

As a matter of fact, these 6000 were not the only reinforcements Lee received. He also got 2500 from the Shenandoah Valley, where Major General Franz Sigel became involved in a fiasco fully as humiliating as Butler's, although it was on a smaller scale. Like Butler, Sigel was politically important, because he had a devoted following among the German-Americans, who if left to themselves had a tendency to line up with the Democrats. Unlike Butler, he had had solid military training, in Germany, although it does not seem to have done him much good; he was a fretful, intellectually wizened sort who knew war by the books but could not handle it when he met it in person. Sigel took 6500 men up the Shenandoah early in May, intending to capture the town of Staunton and break the Virginia Central Railroad, and nothing went right. There were heavy rains, his little force got stretched out along fourteen miles of muddy roads, and at New Market on May 15 his advance guard met some 5000 Confederates led by Major General John C. Breckinridge, who had once run for President of the United States against Abraham Lincoln.

Breckinridge had brought 2500 veterans in from the western mountain country, had picked up such other units as were available in the upper valley, and from Lexington had drawn a spirited battalion that won part of the battle and almost all of the headlines—the corps of cadets from Virginia Military Institute, spruce and trim in parade-ground uniforms.

The cadets are about all many people remember of the battle of New Market, and some accounts make it appear that they beat Sigel all by themselves, with the rest of the army looking on in admiration. It was not quite that way—after all, there were only 247 of them, and Sigel probably would have been beaten if they had stayed at the Institute—but they did fight extremely well, and more than fifty of them got shot, making their ratio of casualties to numbers engaged something any combat outfit could be proud of; and they earned their right to the praise they got. When they

joined Breckinridge's troops before the battle the veterans
greeted them with tolerant derision. Some band struck up a
tune which a cadet remembered as sounding like "Rockabye
Baby," one lean foot soldier came around with a pair of scis-
sors offering to cut off lovelocks, to be forwarded to next-
of-kin after the battle, and others inquired whether the boys
wanted their remains sent home in rosewood coffins lined with
satin; and the muddy roads soon turned the trim uniforms
into something that would never be tolerated on any parade
ground. After the battle the cadets were made much of, and
ever since then the anniversary of New Market has been a
great day at the Institute.[9]

Sigel rode to the front when the firing began, and unwisely
accepted battle without waiting for all of his troops to come
up. He became boisterous, under fire, and rode about snapping his fingers at shell-bursts and shouting orders to his staff
in German—unfortunate, since most of the staff spoke nothing but English—and Breckinridge drove back the advance,
pounded the supporting regiments with artillery, and finally
swept the Federals away in complete rout, capturing six guns
and a number of prisoners, and compelling Sigel to retreat
to Strasburg, twenty-five miles to the north.

Grant did not get the news for two or three days, and before it reached him he asked Washington to urge Sigel to
speed up his advance on Staunton, pointing out that Lee was
drawing supplies from that point and saying that "if Sigel
can destroy the road there it will be of vast importance to
us." Halleck replied that Sigel was in full retreat, adding: "He
will do nothing but run. He never did anything else." Years
afterward Douglas Southall Freeman summed it up: "Sel-
dom did a small victory have so large an effect. Had Sigel
not been driven back when he was, the Valley of Virginia
might have been occupied by the Federals before the wheat
crop was harvested. Hunger would have come sooner."[10]

About all that can be said for Sigel is that he spent little
time afterward trying to explain away the disaster. Butler
did. Butler came to see, at last, that his expedition might
perhaps have done more than it did do, but he never could
see that he himself was at fault in the least degree. He
pointed out that Grant, after all, did not get Meade's army
down to the James promptly so that the two armies could
co-operate in an assault on Richmond, and he had bitter

words for his subordinates. Smith and Gillmore, he asserted,
"agreed upon but one thing and that was how they could
thwart and interfere with me," and he went on to say that
when they were not thwarting him they were trying to thwart
each other, because "neither . . . really desired that the
other should succeed."[11] Neither failure is worth extended
study: Sigel's defeat is self-explanatory, and Butler's military
operations defy rational analysis. All that matters is that a
great opportunity had been missed.

4. However Bold We Might Be

THE WILDERNESS was lonely, with few roads and fewer clearings, lying under a shadow so heavy that most of its unproductive acres never saw sunlight. Armies operating here
moved blindly and took their fighting where they found it,
and in the spring of 1863 Lee and Stonewall Jackson came
into the eastern fringe of this area to defeat Joe Hooker in
a savage and confused battle around the weedy Chancellorsville crossroads. In May of 1864, exactly a year later, Lee's
army was drawn up near Orange Court House, west of the
Wilderness, astride the turnpike that went east to Fredericksburg, and eighteen miles to the northeast Grant and Meade
had their host in camp above the Rapidan. On May 5 the
rival armies marched into the heart of the Wilderness and
began a fight that lasted until the end of the war. Except
for part of a week in June, when there was a short break in
contact, these two armies remained at close quarters for
eleven months, with men killed every day—a great many of
them on some days, only a few on others, but some every day,
month after month, all the way to the end.

When May began Lee had probably 65,000 effectives, of
all arms. The corps led by Ewell and Hill were on the turnpike, and Longstreet with two divisions was ten miles southwest, near Gordonsville. (Longstreet's third division, Pickett's,
had been sent to North Carolina in the fall, when Longstreet
went to Chickamauga, and had not yet been brought back.)
Lee suspected that the Federals were likely to try to move
past his right flank, and by May 3 he became virtually certain. His patrols reported smoke clouds by day and bon-
fires by night all along the Federal front—sure sign that the

men were burning the winter's accumulation of wood and "fixings," always an army's last act when it broke up a winter camp; and then there were moving banks of dust beyond the forests, and occasional glimpses of white wagon tops and the glint of sunlight on musket barrels, to show that Grant's force was marching down to the lower fords of the Rapidan.[1]

Grant had 120,000 men; probably close to 100,000 foot soldiers, of whom 84,000 were in the Army of the Potomac, which Meade had recently regrouped into three corps—II Corps under Hancock, V Corps under Warren, and VI Corps under Sedgwick. Attached to this army, but answerable then to Grant rather than to Meade, was Burnside with the IX Corps, perhaps 15,000 infantry. On May 4 this vast array crossed the Rapidan and headed south, and Grant telegraphed Halleck that FORTY-EIGHT HOURS NOW WILL DEMONSTRATE WHETHER THE ENEMY INTENDS GIVING BATTLE THIS SIDE OF RICHMOND.[2]

It took much less than forty-eight hours, and the demonstration was conclusive: Lee intended to fight as far "this side of Richmond" as he could possibly manage it. His army moved at noon on May 4, with Ewell going east along the Orange Turnpike and Hill marching on the Plank Road two or three miles to the south. Longstreet had much farther to go, and it would be close to forty-eight hours before he could come up into line with the others, but Lee refused to wait. He wanted to strike this Federal army while it was entangled in the Wilderness, with its inadequate roads and almost impenetrable thickets. Grant's advantage in numbers would count for less here, his superiority in artillery would be nullified because there were few places where guns could be used, and the 4000 wagons that moved with his army would be a cumbersome handicap. So the armies rapidly drew closer, the Federals going south and the Confederates moving east.

Collision point was reached promptly on May 5. The advancing Confederates met Yankee skirmishers on both the Turnpike and the Plank Road, drove them away, and brought on an expanding fight whose battle lines grew longer and longer until they ran beyond vision in the trackless woods. Lee had told Ewell he wanted to bring the enemy to battle as soon as possible, and he had his wish. By noon his two corps were fighting what seemed to be most of Meade's army, and now Lee wanted to wait for Longstreet before he made this fight any bigger. But the Wilderness battle was hard to control. The Federals had been flanked, but by mid-afternoon they were forcing the fighting and the Confederates could only hold on, dig in and take advantage of the fact that in this woodland the odds were all in favor of the defense.[3]

Grant's men were learning what Sherman's men learned in similar country around Dallas and New Hope Church— that it was almost impossible for any attack to succeed in a tangle like this. Warren and Sedgwick sent their brigades in against Hill and Ewell, and late in the day Hancock got some of his men into action, and the disjointed Federal lines were driving westward, trying to sweep the Confederates away by sheer force of numbers; but in woods like these men fought blindfolded, and a historian of the Army of the Potomac said that this was one of the strangest battles ever fought—"a battle which no man could see." Hancock said that men who tried to make a charge could not tell where their enemies were until they ran full tilt into them, and generals knew where the battle lines were only by listening to the roar of musketry—which was not much of a guide because it was everywhere, unbroken, always getting louder, a wall of sound that seemed to trap the battle smoke and turn the forest twilight into a choking fog full of unseen dangers. One Confederate infantryman reported that although everybody was fighting at close quarters, men hardly ever saw their enemies. The smoke was too heavy and the saplings and underbrush were too dense; one could only crouch and shoot at spurts of flame in the twilight. Men lost all sense of direction. At times whole divisions went astray, ran into flanking fire and were broken up before they knew what had hit them. Gaps in opposing lines went unexploited because nobody saw them; contrariwise, advancing reinforcements sometimes lost their way and fetched up behind units that needed no help. Toward evening the dead leaves and dry branches took fire, and there were spreading pools of flame running along hillsides and into ravines, trapping helpless wounded men and burning them alive. On most battlefields, the wounded tried to be stoical, and suffered in silence; here they kept screaming for help, and their cries echoed through the night. It was hard for men in either army to rescue them, for anyone who stood up and moved about in the firing zone was likely to get shot.[4]

Next day, May 6, was a series of climaxes muffled by fire and darkness. Hill's corps, badly mauled in the first day's fighting, was hit at dawn by Hancock's corps; wavered, fell back, and came to the verge of destruction. Just in time the head of Longstreet's corps arrived, reaching a little clearing where Lee himself was trying to restore his battle line.

Altogether, a legendary moment. Lee rode hat in hand to greet these stout fighting men, who had been on the march since midnight: found the famous Texas brigade, once Hood's, and tried to lead it against the Yankees in person. The Texans refused to budge unless he stayed behind, and their cry of "Lee to the rear!" sounded across the clearing above the clatter of musketry. Lee submitted, at last, and the Texans swept past him, struck the Federal advance and broke it, giving Hill's men a chance to rally. Burly Longstreet rode to the front, found an opening on the left of Hancock's line, sent troops there in a swift flanking attack, and compelled Hancock's entire line to beat a panicky retreat which was all the worse because most of the men who fled could see no enemies and knew only that something up in front had gone wrong.

Now, abruptly, the obstacles to a decisive offensive in the Wilderness began to work for the Federals. Longstreet tried to press the advantage his men had won, but the Confederates could see no farther into the smoky woods than the Yankees could see. Two of Longstreet's units moved at right angles to each other, collided, opened fire—and Longstreet was critically wounded, Brigadier General Micah Jenkins was killed, and the assault fell into a confusion that gave Hancock ample time to rally his men behind log breastworks a mile or so to the rear. When the Confederate counterattack at last was renewed the men had to advance through what amounted almost to a forest fire, and the Federals drove them back.

At the close of the day opportunity opened, briefly, at the other end of the Confederate line, on Ewell's front, where it was found that Sedgwick's right flank was exposed. John B. Gordon's brigade struck this flank in the twilight, drove it back, captured several hundred prisoners, and then met stiffening resistance that could not be overcome before night ended the fighting. After the war Gordon argued that if his attack had been ordered earlier the whole Federal right would have been crumpled and Grant would have been soundly defeated. Perhaps the lost chance looked larger than life-size, as the years passed, and perhaps the whole episode was simply one more proof that in this woodland fighting the brightest opportunities could go unseen until it was too late; whatever the truth of it, the two-day battle ended at last, the armies grimly facing each other at close range on a field fearfully littered with dead and wounded. Casualty lists had been prodigious. The Federals had lost more than 17,000 men, of whom more than 2200 had been killed outright; Lee's losses had been smaller but bore about the same relation to the numbers engaged; neither side had won anything worth mentioning.[5]

One thing was clear: Grant and Lee did not make war in the style of Sherman and Johnston, sparring cautiously and looking for openings. They simply looked for each other, and as soon as they found each other they began to fight. Neither man had yet met anyone like the other. Trying to go around his opponent's flank, Grant got nothing but a head-on engagement out of it, and his army received a tactical setback nearly as severe as the one Hooker got at Chancellorsville; yet the Chancellorsville pattern did not repeat itself and the setback lost its meaning—if Grant was not Sherman he was not Hooker, either. Having seized the initiative, Lee could not hold it because the Federals had both the will and the power to make him fight a continuous battle in which he could do no more than follow their lead. On the evening of May 7, after a day in which the tired armies faced each other across a dull smolder of skirmish-line firing, Grant put his men on the road and moved off in the night—not back toward the river crossings, but on toward the southeast, heading for the crossroads of Spotsylvania Courthouse, beyond Lee's right.

Lee recognized the move as soon as it began, and countered it with great skill, getting infantry down to the crossroads barely ahead of the Federals and turning this blow at his flank into another head-on engagement. Both armies swarmed up to the firing line, and the battlefield expanded as it had done in the Wilderness, spreading out across farms and woodlots, division after division coming into action on each side under directives which amounted to little more than the stern imperative: Find the enemy as soon as you can and fight him where you find him. There was no subtlety in this battle, and no let-up either. It went on and on, day after day, for almost two weeks, the whole ponderous engagement revolving slowly, like a clumsy hurricane, as the Federals tried in vain to force their way past Lee's right. Among the many Federals who died in this fighting was one irreplaceable: Major General John Sedgwick, commander of the VI Corps, killed on May 9.

It was hard for anyone to tell what was happening. In Washington, Secretary Stanton reflected that at least this fight was not going as previous fights had gone. Before, he said, "the enemy's strength has always been most felt in his first blows"; here Lee's first blows had been heavy but they had failed, instead of retreating Grant was continuing to advance, and perhaps complete success was in sight. Grant believed that the result of the Wilderness fight was "decidedly in our favor," but he confessed that it had been "impossible to inflict the heavy blow on Lee's army I had hoped"; significantly he added that the exact route he would follow to reach the James River was "not yet definitely marked out." Lee told Mr. Davis that every Federal attack had been repelled and that his own army was still on the front and flank of its opponent, and he closed stoutly: "With the blessing of God I trust we shall be able to prevent Gen. Grant from reaching Richmond."[6]

There was reason for Lee's assurance. He had proved that the Federal host could neither slip past him nor overpower him; whatever happened, there was not going to be the helter-skelter "race for Richmond" which Grant had looked forward to when he marched toward Spotsylvania.[7] Yet Lee was paying a high price for this. He was accepting the defensive. His genius was for the dazzling maneuver that could cancel the weight of numbers and give his own army the initiative, and this continuous all-out fighting gave that genius insufficient scope. He had compelled McClellan and Pope and Hooker to give up their own plans and fight defensively to escape destruction, but the most he could say now was that he believed he could keep Grant from getting to Richmond. He could interfere with Grant's plans, but he could not impose plans of his own.

Originally the crossroads at Spotsylvania seemed important

because it lay behind Lee's right flank. As the armies moved that ceased to be true, but the crossroads still drew the fighting: to possess it, or to destroy each other, or perhaps just to explore the grim potentials of modern war, the armies struggled and pounded each other, day after day, all about a vast semicircle west and north and east of the road center. The fighting taught certain lessons, at a remarkably high price. In the Wilderness it showed the futility of trying to win a significant victory in an untracked forest; at Spotsylvania it proved that trench warfare was even more constrictive—with both sides well dug in, a breakthrough meant little because the defenders could repair the break faster than the attackers could exploit it, and the only sure result would be an immense loss of life under conditions more than ordinarily abominable. If there could be a climax to a battle of this kind it came on May 12, in a heavy rainstorm, when Grant and Meade ordered a frontal assault on a bulging crescent of Confederate trenches and brought on one of the most terrible fights of the entire war—a close-range struggle in the mud that began before dawn and lasted until nearly midnight, the worst of it centering about a little angle in a trench line remembered ever afterward as the *bloody* angle. Here Hancock's corps broke Lee's line, capturing an infantry division and twenty guns, and by the old standards the Federals had won the day—except that actually they had won no more than a pen-full of prisoners and a quarter section of splintered groves and pastures, crisscrossed by rifle pits where dead bodies had been trampled out of sight in the mud. Next day the fighting went on as if nothing had happened, except that for a time the tempo was rather subdued.

Before the bloody angle offensive, Grant had told Halleck that he intended to "fight it out on this line if it takes all summer," and this blunt vow greatly pleased Northern patriots—few of whom noticed that in little more than a week Grant abandoned "this line" entirely and went off to find another one. In effect, he had said that he would make Lee fight here until the end came, but this abruptly ceased to be a good idea because the things that should have happened far in Lee's rear, which would have made this a ruinous fight for the Confederacy, did not happen.[8]

Butler and Sigel had failed, one man bottled up, the other driven off, both men utterly thwarted: hollow men, punctured

by their betters. Even Phil Sheridan had done less than was
expected. Sheridan had been given the Army of the Potomac
cavalry, on the ground that he was enough of a driver to get
some effective work out of it, and on May 9 he had ridden
off with 10,000 troopers to threaten Richmond, which was
supposed to be under attack by Butler. Stuart met him and
fought him, two days later, at Yellow Tavern; Stuart himself
was mortally wounded and his cavalry was beaten, but the
Richmond defenses were too strong to penetrate, Butler's
people were nowhere in sight, and Sheridan could do no
more than ride down the peninsula to refit under protection
of Federal gunboats. He had made a spectacular raid and he
had ended the career of one of the Confederacy's most famous soldiers, but he had not shaken Lee's grip on Spotsylvania.

Because of these failures—most especially, because of Butler's failure—Spotsylvania was no longer an impossible place
for Lee to make an extended stand. Grant's promise to fight
here if the fight lasted all summer was based on the expectation—fully justified, at the time he voiced the promise—that
the subsidiary offensives on the Shenandoah and the James
would compel Lee to use part of his inadequate resources to
defend his rear. Overnight, these offensives had evaporated;
instead of having to look out for his rear, Lee was drawing
new strength from it—the reinforcements Richmond sent him,
once Butler and Sigel had been disposed of, made up for the
total he had lost in the Wilderness. Lee wanted to keep Grant
away from Richmond, and after the middle of May Spotsylvania was a perfectly good place for him to do it.

For that matter it was a perfectly good place for Grant
to fight, if Grant sought nothing more than the war of attrition which is sometimes written down as the basis of his
strategy. A good deal of attrition had already taken place
at Spotsylvania, and there could be as much more as anybody needed; the armies were locked together, and the remorseless, two-men-for-one kind of killing such a program
demanded could take place there as well as anywhere else.
Actually, Grant wanted something different. He wanted precisely what Lee hoped to deny him—to get close to Richmond, attacking the geographical rear of the Army of Northern Virginia, pinning that army in a tight circle on the James
River so that it must either counterattack against long odds

or submit to a siege that would deprive it of all mobility. With the Butler-Sigel moves canceled he could not hope to do this by continuing to fight within fifteen miles of the Rapidan crossings. So he re-cast his plans in the middle of the campaign and on the night of May 20 he began to move again.

His army was large and Lee's army touched it everywhere, and to move it was a ponderous business. Bit by bit, Grant shifted strength to his left, heading southeast again as he had done after the Wilderness, trying to establish himself beyond and behind the Confederate right. Once again, Lee understood the move and shifted to meet it. The armies were never wholly out of contact, there were incessant stabbing fights between cavalry and infantry patrols, and after three days the armies faced each other once more at the crossings of the North Anna River, twenty miles from Spotsylvania. Lee got there first and chose his ground here with care, and after several days of unrewarding fighting Grant shifted again, moving once more by his left, the armies striking sparks as they brushed against each other. They got below the Pamunkey River, and as May came to an end they confronted each other along Totopotomoy Creek, eighteen miles below the North Anna battlefield and hardly ten miles northeast of Richmond. Here again they sparred and struck at one another, looking for openings and finding none; then the Federals side-slipped once more, bringing up on June 1 at the desolate crossroads of Cold Harbor, out on the fringe of the Gaines' Mill field where Lee's men and McClellan's had fought so desperately two years earlier.

By now the armies were running out of space. They had covered more than fifty miles in the unmanageable, rolling series of battles that began in the Wilderness, and now they could roll no farther. Beyond the Federal left at Cold Harbor was the Chickahominy River, a swampy barrier to additional maneuvering; behind Lee's army was Richmond itself, less than a day's march away. Now battle line faced battle line, with tangled abatis to protect the hastily dug trenches, and with field guns sited to cover all of the approaches. Grant had summoned W. F. Smith's corps from its bottled-up idleness at Bermuda Hundred to help in the assault, and Lee had his entire strength in line, with virtually no reserves. When the fighting began it would be head-on because there was no other way to fight here.

The armies had reached this spot after unending fighting and appalling losses; yet in the week just before this battle the high command on each side was hopeful. Grant told Halleck that Lee's army "is really whipped" and would not fight outside of entrenchments; Meade assured his wife that "we undoubtedly have the morale over them," and G. K. Warren wrote that "the Rebs are getting dispirited" and predicted that "they would fall back if they had any place to go to." At the same time, Lee wrote Mr. Davis that Grant's army "has been very much shaken" and said that the spirit of his own army was never better; "I fear no injury to it from any retrograde move that may be dictated by sound military policy." In the same vein, Colonel Venable of Lee's staff wrote that the Federals were "dispirited by the bloody repulse of repeated attacks on our lines." Actually, there is little to show that the rank and file on either side was discouraged. The average soldier remained ready to try to do whatever he was ordered to do, although every man would doubtless have agreed with a remark made by one of Lee's veterans: "There has never been such fighting, I reckon, in the history of war."[9]

Late on the afternoon of June 1 Federal infantry attacked at Cold Harbor, won minor successes, and led Grant to feel that a hard blow at daylight on June 2 might break the line. The idea was good, in a way, because the Confederates at Cold Harbor were not ready to meet an all-out attack; unhappily, the Federals were not ready to make one. Massing the troops took much longer than had been anticipated, twenty-four hours were lost, the big assault could not be made until June 3, and when it was made a storm of Confederate rifle fire tore the Federal columns and inflicted a resounding defeat—the most unrelieved and tragically costly one the Army of the Potomac had suffered since it crossed the Rapidan. The assault was made by three army corps—Hancock's, Smith's, and Sedgwick's old VI Corps, now led by Horatio G. Wright. Wright's men took some out-works but were pinned down by rifle fire before they could make an effective penetration, and they had to give up after suffering severe losses. Hancock attacked with two divisions and Smith with one, and these three divisions were wrecked. Altogether, the

Federals lost close to 7000 men in less than an hour. Even Burnside's hopeless attack on the stone wall at Fredericksburg had not been more brutally smashed.[10]

Here was final proof of the truth that had been emerging for the past month: the rifle and the trench now dominated the battlefield, so that good field works adequately manned by determined men could not be taken at any price. (Fifty years later, in the First World War, European generals would have to learn this lesson all over again.) As Thomas had said at Kennesaw Mountain, an army fighting thus could literally use itself up. For a week after the battle, both sides perfected their defenses, and the armies faced each other along miles of intricate entrenchments, enduring agonies of heat and thirst and weariness, and daily losses from fitful bombardments and unending sniper fire; and General Grant had to make new plans.

From the beginning he had hoped to strike Lee's vulnerable rear along the James River. He could not roll to the left here, because he had run out of space, and yet if he could not somehow get past Lee's flank his whole campaign was a failure and the Confederacy was substantially nearer to independence. Two possibilities were open, and he undertook to use both of them at once.

For one thing, he would try again to break Lee's important supply line to the Shenandoah Valley. Sigel had failed ignominiously, but his troops had been pulled together and entrusted to Major General David Hunter, strengthened by a solid body of infantry under Brigadier General George Crook that had come eastward from the West Virginia mountains. Early in June Hunter was moving up the Shenandoah Valley, defeating Confederate forces that tried to stop him and showing a marked talent for burning homes and spreading destruction and bitterness among the civil population as he advanced. Now Hunter was striking toward Lynchburg: Grant concluded to send Sheridan off, with two divisions of cavalry, to join Hunter and destroy the line of the Virginia General Railroad some distance west of Richmond, and Sheridan started on June 7.

Simultaneously, Grant would take a leaf from the book written at Vicksburg: break off contact with Lee entirely, move fast, get his army clear over to the other side of the James and strike directly into the rear area before Lee knew what was happening. This would be a move unlike any Grant had tried in Virginia—harder and riskier, with disaster as penalty for failure—but there was no other good card to play. Grant played it; and while Sheridan's troopers set out for Charlottesville, Warren's V Corps left the trenches, crossed the Chickahominy by the old Long Bridge Road, and took position on the edge of White Oak Swamp, for all the world as if the Federal army planned to march on Richmond between the Chickahominy and the James.[11]

The risk of course was that when Lee's army was left to itself its commander had a way of doing unexpected things, and one of Grant's prime responsibilities from the day the campaign began had been to grip that army so tightly that it could not move off on an offensive of its own. So far he had done this, at substantial cost; now he was letting go, and the armies were moving out of contact. Yet the risk was smaller than it seemed. Lee was restricted, not because Grant's army was immediately in front of him but because Richmond was immediately behind him. Maneuvers that might have been possible fifty miles north were impossible here. At all costs Lee had to wait and counter whatever move his opponent might be making now.

The thrust was made deftly. The Federals left Cold Harbor on the night of June 12, and next morning the long chain of trenches was empty. The Yankee army had gone off the map, and while Confederate patrols located Warren's corps, and reported that Smith's corps had gone back to the Pamunkey and embarked on transports, it was hard to tell what this meant. Lee could only shift his army down below the Chickahominy to await developments; meanwhile, the Federal army went all the way to the James, where monitors cruised back and forth to protect the engineers who were laying a long pontoon bridge. Then Warren's corps withdrew, all the road crossings were held by Federal cavalry, and Lee was in the dark. To make matters much worse, the threat posed by General Hunter became so grave that Lee had to detach troops to meet it—8000 men, or thereabouts, under General Early, sent off at a time when Lee needed every man he could get. A few days earlier Lee had told Secretary Seddon: "If we can defeat Grant here the valley can easily be recovered, but if we cannot defeat Grant I am afraid we will be unable to hold the valley."[12] It was more than the valley that was in danger now, however. If Hunter took Lynchburg, came east and joined Sheridan the pressure on the capital and on Lee's army would be overwhelming.

Grant's plan worked perfectly up to the point where it was about to win the war. Then it did not work at all. For one thing, Grant left altogether too much to his lieutenants; for another, some of them did not measure up properly. In addition, it was easier to deceive Lee for a few days than to beat him permanently; and for a climax David Hunter was no match for Jubal Early.

But it did begin well. On June 15 Grant was squarely in Lee's rear. He was south of the James and Lee was north of it, and a column of 15,000 Federals led by Baldy Smith was marching up to Petersburg, the railroad center whose fall would mean the fall of Richmond. Beauregard, defending Petersburg, had 9000 men, but 7000 of them were holding the lines at Bermuda Hundred, keeping the cork in the bottle that held Ben Butler. To meet Smith, Beauregard had hardly more than 2000 men, including cavalry and home guards, and that evening Smith broke the Petersburg line and the road into the little city was wide open. Beauregard testified after the war that "Petersburg at that hour was clearly at the mercy of the Federal commander, who had all but captured it,"[13] but Smith served Grant now as he had served Butler a few weeks earlier; he saw risks rather than opportunity, went on the defensive, and made no further advance. By noon of the next day, June 16, three Federal army corps were present—Smith's, Hancock's, and Burnside's, a total of more than 50,000 men—and Beauregard was forced to withdraw the force that had been watching Butler (taking the cork out of the bottle, at last) and bring it down for a last-ditch defense of Petersburg.

By all the odds, Grant's troops should have won a shattering victory, but they did not. Butler could do nothing with his own opportunity, and by the time he was ready to try something Pickett's division had come down and reoccupied the empty Confederate lines at Bermuda Hundred. The 50,000 Yankees at Petersburg somehow did not attack until evening, and Beauregard was just able to throw them back. Next day, June 17, most of Meade's army was on hand and most of Lee's was not, but the Federal assault was miserably co-ordinated and although it finally broke the Confederate line Beauregard managed to draw a new line and hold it until darkness ended the fighting. On June 18 Meade's command arrangements seemed to come apart altogether, and the blow he wanted to strike was halting, disjointed, and ineffective; Lee's army reached the scene, the Federal offensive ground to a standstill, and by the end of the day Petersburg was wholly secure, Lee was on hand and in charge, and Grant had concluded that it was time to give up frontal assaults and resort to siege warfare.

The stroke that had taken the Federal army across the James, brilliantly begun, ended in fumbling futility. When the leading elements of the army most needed skillful and aggressive leadership they were left to themselves. Grant unfortunately devoted himself largely to rear-area operations during this expedition, and while that ordinarily was proper enough for a commander-in-chief it did assume that competent lieutenants up front knew what to do and would do it quickly; but Butler did nothing, Smith failed abjectly, and Meade himself put on the weakest performance he made in all the war.[14] To round out the picture, Early defeated Hunter at Lynchburg on June 18 and drove him off in full retreat, Sheridan fought an inconclusive battle with Wade Hampton's cavalry at Trevilian Station, near Gordonsville, and withdrew after failing to do any substantial harm to the Virginia Central Railroad, and the dire threat to Lee's line of supplies was ended.

So the campaign that began on the Rapidan on May 4 ended, six weeks later, in the trenches around Petersburg. In those weeks the Federals had lost between 60,000 and 70,000 men, Lee's army was still undefeated, and it seemed —in the North, and also in the South—that Grant's massive campaign had been wasted effort. On the one side there was profound discouragement and on the other there was extravagant hope, and each condition took shape so quickly that men were bewildered. Appraising what had taken place in the light of what had been anticipated, men could not at once understand that the war in Virginia had permanently changed: that the two armies had gone south of the James River under circumstances which meant that they would stay there, intimately embraced, until the war ended. Never again would either of these armies see the area for which it was named—Northern Virginia, the Potomac River. Although Lee's army was safe enough, in Petersburg, it could not get out. Never again would it take the offensive, threatening to win the war by sheer aggressive brilliance. Already it was under dominance: it was pinned down, and it could only fight for time. As one Confederate general remarked, afterward: "However bold we might be, however desperately we might fight, we were sure in the end to be worn out. It was only a question of a few months, more or less."[15]

5. *Vested Interest in Failure*

THE WAR WAS an exercise in violence bounded by two presidential elections; one had brought it on, and another would help to end it. The election of 1860 indicated that great change was coming to a society that could endure no change, and there had been an appeal to arms from that finding; now, in 1864, there was going to be a new election to determine whether the appeal should be sustained or denied. No matter what the election said, the mere fact that it was being held was significant. It was an act of faith, an affirmation that even war itself must at last be subject to a decision reached at the polls. Perhaps the strangest thing about this strangest of all elections was that it never occurred to anyone not to have it. Whether any nation so conceived and so dedicated could long endure . . . well, they would vote.

How they would vote was unpredictable because the appeal to war had wondrously clouded all matters of politics.

By mid-summer it was clear that the opposing candidates would be Abraham Lincoln and General George B. McClellan, with Pathfinder John Charles Frémont hovering on the fringe as a third-party candidate. The issues were mixed. The war was an issue, and the way to win the war, and the course to be taken in respect to the Negro. Also there was a point Mr. Lincoln had raised in his first inaugural, more pressing now than when he said it: "Suppose you go to war, you cannot fight always; and when, after much loss on both sides, and no gain on either, you cease fighting, the identical old questions as to terms of intercourse are again upon you." These identical old questions were an issue, their weight resting on every voter; the nation must presently face what it tried to avoid four years earlier.

Confederates of course could not vote in this election. Yet it was everlastingly to their interest that the election be held, because this proved that constitutional government still functioned; and the future offered them no other safeguard. Grim General Sherman had recently warned them that when they appealed to war they put themselves utterly at the mercy of the rules of war—which, he asserted (and he was a rising authority on the subject), were altogether merciless. When the Southern states seceded, he said, they made it possible for the Federal government to do literally anything it wanted to do with them because "war is simply power unrestrained by constitution or compact."

Sherman put these thoughts in a letter to his brother, Senator John Sherman of Ohio, suggesting that to publish the letter "would do no harm except turn the Richmond press against me as the prince of barbarians." He did not understand democracy, he had nothing against slavery, and he certainly belonged to no political faction; he was, in fact, that most unpredictable of persons, a completely radical arch-conservative, and his footnote to the pending election deserved attention. It was almost as if this election was an appeal from war back to the ballot. As Sherman said, war was power unrestrained; here was the restraint coming back into play again—a restraint which unhappily could be applied only in the atmosphere created by war.[1]

This disturbed Governor Horatio Seymour of New York, a devout Democrat whose appeals for restraint were so unrestrained that some Republicans considered him a Copperhead. Seymour now was raising a perfectly valid point. "The rights of the states were reserved, and the powers of the general government were limited, to protect the people in their persons, property and consciences in time of danger and civil commotion."[2] Yet because the war had been fought so long and so hard, neither the rights of the states nor the powers of the general government would ever again look quite as they had looked in 1860, and with an election approaching this colored everything men did. Congress discovered this early in the spring when it found that it could not provide a temporary government for the new territory of Montana without first arguing hotly about the Dred Scott decision.

Montana was empty and faraway, and so was the Dred

Scott case, but the two were fused by the heat of an election year. It began when the House sent to the Senate a territorial bill providing in a routine way that "any white male inhabitant" could vote in Montana; whereupon Senator Morton S. Wilkinson of Minnesota moved to amend the bill by giving the vote to "any male citizen of the United States." This was an avowed attempt to let Negroes vote in Montana, and Senator Reverdy Johnson of Maryland protested that in the Dred Scott case Chief Justice Taney had held that a Negro was not a citizen. But the Senate liked Wilkinson's amendment, and after Senator Sumner cried that Congress should no longer "wear the strait-jacket of the Dred Scott decision" the amendment was adopted.

When the amended bill went back to the House it was quickly apparent that in this chamber the radicals were not in control. The Ohio Democrat, George H. Pendleton, asserted that the amendment was nothing less than an attempt to reverse a ruling of the Supreme Court, and he pointed out that in addition it was a bold leap into the dark. He wanted everyone to understand "that now, for the first time in the history of the government, one of the branches of Congress has attempted to establish Negro political equality." A majority felt as he did, and by a vote of 75 to 67 the House refused to accept the amendment and instructed its conferees to agree to no bill that did not limit the franchise to white men.

The whole business was somewhat unreal, inasmuch as Montana then contained no Negroes at all and it seemed unlikely that it would ever have very many. Yet the war itself was based on a similar bit of unreality, because it had developed out of a furious demand for a slave code for territories almost equally devoid of Negroes; possibly the abstract principle governing the granting of human rights ran roughly parallel to the one that governed their denial. At the moment, however, the question hardly seemed worth developing, and Senator James Doolittle of Wisconsin protested earnestly against interjecting this disturbing element— "I mean the issue of Negro suffrage"—into an election campaign. The Senate finally backed down, saving face slightly by agreeing that the government in Montana should be organized by the class of persons previously authorized to organize the territory of Idaho: that is, by white male citizens.

Ben Wade, one of the toughest of the radicals, said that this was all right because the non-existence of Negroes in Montana made the case inconsequential; but he served notice that "whenever this question shall be raised in such sort as to affect the rights of any man, I shall take the broad principle of right and stand by it as firmly as anyone else."[3]

The Dred Scott decision had been controlling, once, and it had helped to create the conditions that brought on a war, but now it was nearing the end of its existence. So was its author, Chief Justice Taney, a frail man living out the summer, sere and shrunken as an oak leaf in February. Senator Wade made a rough joke about him, and General Halleck, who loved to collect bits of Washington gossip, passed it along in a chatty letter to his friend Francis Lieber:

"You speak of Chief Justice Taney's health. Did you ever hear of Ben Wade's joke about the Chief Justice? Ben (who is probably the most profane man in Congress) says that he used to pray for Taney every night during Buchanan's administration, that his life might be spared till a new president could appoint his successor; but he over-did the business & his prayers were likely to carry him through this administration also! 'If the Lord will forgive me this time, I will never pray for a Chief Justice again!' "[4]

Wade had stopped praying—possibly the exercise was unfamiliar and exhausting—and in mid-July he was denouncing the President in a fine fury. Mr. Lincoln had applied a pocket veto to the Wade-Davis bill, which held that Congress rather than the President must control the process of reconstruction, but he had refused to make an issue of it and had said that any Southern state wishing to be rebuilt by the Wade-Davis formula, which was most restrictive, could have its way. Now Wade and Davis were out with an angry manifesto, making the issue Mr. Lincoln had refused to make, warning the President that "if he wishes our support he must confine himself to his executive duties—to obey and execute, not make, the laws—to suppress by arms armed rebellion and leave political reorganization to Congress." The manifesto sounded ferocious, and it led Mr. Lincoln to remark that "to be wounded in the house of one's friends is perhaps the most grievous affliction that can befall a man"; yet it was a warning for the future rather than a real and present danger.[5]

Proof of this lies in what did not happen in connection with the presidential candidacy of General Frémont.

Frémont was nominated at the end of May by a group styling itself the party of the Radical Democracy, meeting in Cleveland and drawing some four hundred delegates of whom a scant handful had national reputations. It listened to oratory, received a letter from Abolitionist Wendell Phillips denouncing the President's ten percent plan, "which puts all power in the hands of the unchanged white race, soured by defeat, hating the laboring classes, plotting constantly for aristocratic institutions"; and after nominating Frémont it adopted a platform which seemed to express the fullest desires of the Republican radicals. The platform called for reunion, a Constitutional amendment to end slavery, limitation of presidential tenure to one term, Congressional control of reconstruction, and confiscation and redistribution of all lands held by Rebels. This caused rejoicing among Democrats, who were delighted to see a split in the opposition, but it failed to win the support of the principal radicals, including the impassioned Senator Wade and Congressman Davis.[6]

One reason may have been that Frémont failed to be as fierce as he was expected to be. He quickly disavowed the plank on confiscation, saying that such a program was neither practical nor wise and that "in the adjustments that are to follow peace no considerations of vengeance can consistently be admitted." A bigger reason was that if the radicals defeated Mr. Lincoln by throwing their strength to Frémont they would certainly cause the election of a Democrat, which was the last thing on earth they wanted. After all, they could live with President Lincoln. What he wanted most, they wanted: reunion on terms imposed in Washington, and abolition of slavery by constitutional amendment. They were just warning him.

For that matter Mr. Lincoln could issue warnings of his own. He issued one on June 30 when he abruptly dropped Salmon P. Chase from his cabinet, replacing him as Secretary of the Treasury with Senator William P. Fessenden of Maine.

Chase was a radical, tried and true; the senatorial bloc considered him too erratic and too self-righteous, but he was unquestionably thoroughly sound on the essentials. For months he had done all he could do to win the presidential

nomination, and when at last he failed—his political inepti-
tude was almost as unlimited as his political ambition—Mr.
Lincoln quietly waited for an opening. It came when the two
men differed about a Treasury appointment. Chase sent in a
resignation, as he had done several times before, meaning
only to put on a little heat, and immediately got a starchy
note accepting the resignation. . . "you and I have reached
a point of mutual embarrassment in our official relation
which it seems cannot be overcome, or longer sustained, consistently with the public service."[7] Chase was out.

For the moment Mr. Lincoln was leading from strength. In
the winter and spring there had been sporadic attempts to
find another nominee, but the hard fact was that the Republicans had no other man of comparable stature, and by
the time the party convention opened in Baltimore—officially
it was the National Union Party now, to prove that it welcomed war Democrats—the opposition was helpless. David
Davis, who had managed Mr. Lincoln's candidacy at the
Wigwam in Chicago in 1860, did not even bother to attend,
and he wrote to Mr. Lincoln to explain his course: "If there
had been a speck of opposition I would have gone to Baltimore. But the opposition is utterly beaten. The fight is not
even interesting, and the services of no one is necessary."[8]
Davis was correct. Mr. Lincoln was renominated on June 8
without trouble, and although the Missouri delegation did
vote for U. S. Grant it swung into line as soon as the ballot
ended and successfully moved that a unanimous vote for
Mr. Lincoln be recorded. Without visible guidance from the
White House, the convention discarded Vice-President Han-
nibal Hamlin in favor of an anti-slavery war Democrat from
the South, nominating Andrew Johnson, military governor
of Tennessee, for the vice-presidency.[9] Mr. Lincoln warmly
endorsed the party platform, emphasizing his support of the
plank that called for a constitutional amendment to end
slavery, and for the moment the party was in harmony.[10]

The platform was straight war-party doctrine. It was not,
actually, very different from the one the Cleveland convention had given Frémont. It endorsed the President, whereas
the Clevelanders wanted him out, and instead of demanding
confiscation of Rebel lands it recommended undefined "punishment"; and where the Cleveland platform specifically asserted that reconstruction was a matter for Congress, the

Baltimore platform avoided this issue and simply called on the administration to demand unconditional surrender, without compromise. At Cleveland the radicals had laid their demands on the line; at Baltimore they had been flexible, accepting harmony in the belief that they could control what would follow. They risked little, for if the President grew soft on secession during the summer they could swing over to Frémont; Frémont's candidacy was, in effect, the fine type buried in the contract reached at Baltimore.

The platform had one plank that seemed pointless but was not: a declaration that harmony must prevail in national councils and that "we regard as worthy of public confidence and official trust only those who cordially endorse the principles proclaimed in these resolutions, and which should characterize the administration of the government." This shaft was aimed at Montgomery Blair, the Postmaster General—at him, at the Blair family in general, and through them at all of the conservative Republicans who might backslide from the true faith. The radicals wanted Blair out of the cabinet and this was their way of saying so.[11]

Montgomery Blair was trying to make a deal with the Democrats. He wanted Mr. Lincoln re-elected and he wanted slavery destroyed, but he also most passionately wanted the radicals beaten. He was trying to put together a conservative coalition that would accept emancipation and yet keep America a white man's country, and if his proposal was somewhat Byzantine it would be copied (now with success and now without it) for a century or more. He put it bluntly in a letter to S. L. M. Barlow: "By giving up the past, conceding slavery to be extinct, you can make an issue upon which not only the Democrats of the North and South may unite against the Republicans, but on which the larger portion of the Republicans will join in sustaining this exclusive right of Government in the white race."[12]

Blair had a specific plan. Believing McClellan the strongest candidate the Democrats could name, he wanted him out of the way, and all through the winter and spring he had been calling for action: let McClellan take himself out of the presidential race, make his peace with President Lincoln, and accept once more some command in the army. For McClellan, Blair confessed, this might be a wrench: "He is young and there is a great future opening to one of his genius and antecedents. But you must bear with me when I tell you that it does not lie in the direction of waging a war against the chief magistrate, who is waging a war for the liberties of this continent at home and also will soon have to do it against despots abroad." The renunciation need not be permanent: "You must not understand that when I object to his being a candidate for the presidency that I would call upon him to remove such pretensions for all time. I mean only that *now* is not the proper time for indulging such thoughts—we have on hand a Rebellion."[13]

It was a curious proposal, all in all, and it was supported not long after the Baltimore convention when Francis P. Blair, Sr.—redoubtable Old Man Blair, in person—went to New York to talk to General McClellan. The Old Man repeated what Montgomery had said, urging McClellan to ask President Lincoln for reassignment to the army with the express proviso that this was not a step toward the Democratic nomination; and he added, "In case the President should refuse this request he would then be responsible for the consequences." McClellan listened courteously, nodded, said he would let him know—and that was that.[14]

McClellan was unmoved, and so was Barlow, who told Montgomery Blair that although a hot election campaign probably would be bad, its evils would be nothing compared to those that would follow a victory for President Lincoln, "whose re-election will be claimed to be, and will in fact be, an endorsement by the people of every fallacy and monstrosity which the folly and fanaticism of the radicals may invent, including miscegenation, Negro equality, territorial organization and subjugation, all to end in bankruptcy, dishonor and disunion." But Barlow's recital of the catalog of horrors showed that he had not got Blair's point—which was that it really ought not to matter much, either to Northern Democrats or to actually embattled Confederates, if Mr. Lincoln won both the war and the election, so long as nothing more than slavery died. Unadorned emancipation, all naked and defenseless, need not be feared because it could be handled. Blair believed that what had frightened Congressman Pendleton was the phantom that had driven Southerners to war in the first place, and in another letter he became most explicit:

"The people of the South have not been aroused against

the people of the North by the love of slavery. I am to the manner born and know whereof I speak—it is Negro equality, not slavery, that they are fighting about, and it is necessary to demonstrate that the North is not fighting for Negro equality. The late vote on the Montana question in the House of Representatives, on which the Democrats voted in the majority for the first and only time this winter, shows how important it is to get rid of the slavery question in order that we may get at the Negro question which lies immediately behind it. My object is, if possible, to make this the Presidential issue, with a view to a restoration of the Union. If we can dispose of the slave question, and not without, we shall have the miscegenators in a party to themselves and can beat them easily, but whilst they can cover themselves behind the slave question they will prevail."[15]

. . . Dig down far enough and one always found it: the old terror, coiling and uncoiling in the dark, demanding an everlasting wall to protect one race from intimacy with another. The only wall so far devised was slavery, and it was high enough but so fragile that it had begun to crumble on the plains of Kansas where it did not even exist; and now its final fall was certain. What Blair was saying was that another barrier could be built if men who dreaded equality were appealed to properly. It was merely necessary to understand where the real issue lay.

One man who understood this more and more clearly, although he did not hear what Blair was saying, was the very executive who in Blair's opinion needed to be re-elected and neutralized: Abraham Lincoln. Mr. Lincoln was beginning to see and say that a barrier built against one is built against all, and that freedom has the magical property of being indivisible. Not long ago he had told a group of politically minded New York working men "that the existing rebellion means more, and tends to more, than the perpetuation of African slavery—that it is in fact a war upon the rights of all working men." More recently, when a new Ohio regiment stopped at the White House for a word of encouragement, he remarked that in free America "every man has a right to be equal with every other man," and he went on to say that in this war "every form of human right is endangered if our enemies succeed . . . There is involved in this struggle the question whether your children and my children shall enjoy the privileges we have enjoyed."[16]

Blair's argument was undoubtedly persuasive, but the Democrats ignored it. They believed they were going to win the election without making a deal with anyone. To them, as to almost everyone in the North, the war itself had become the dominant factor. It would determine how the election came out, and the Democrats were becoming more and more convinced that it would drive the election their way.

As far back as February, Barlow told his Washington aide, Barnett: "We shall nominate McClellan unless events bring up some new man. In any case we mean to run the strongest candidate, and unless there are greater successes in the field than now seem probable we shall win." He had already told Reverdy Johnson that "if the war drags its slow length along another summer I have no doubt of the success of the opposition"—that is, of the Democrats. He appraised Republican prospects by confessing that "if Grant wins, all will go well" —go well, that is, for the Republicans—and he played on the same theme by telling Blair: "If the Army of the Potomac is strong enough to defeat Lee without McClellan, all is well. If it should prove otherwise, is there anyone who will forgive Mr. Lincoln for the monstrous crime in permitting the great fight of the war to take place without the benefit of his personality?"[17] Barlow to be sure was not the Democratic party, but he was McClellan's closest confidant and he unquestionably spoke for the conservative party leaders—the men who were not Copperheads, and who sincerely wanted the Union restored, but who felt certain that Mr. Lincoln could never restore it and who shuddered to think what might happen if he did. They had given the party a vested interest in military failure, and if this was a risky position for a political party to take it can only be said that by mid-summer military failure seemed very real.

The war was in its fourth year, death and agony were familiar shapes, casualty lists were reaching out to every city and village in the land, day after heartbreaking day, all spring and all summer, and it was hard to see that victory was any nearer now than it had been in the spring. Grant had indeed forced Lee all the way from the Rapidan to the Petersburg trenches, and Sherman had driven Johnston from the Tennessee line to the suburbs of Atlanta; but the cities did not

fall, the armies defending them had not been overpowered
. . . and Grant and Sherman between them had lost more
than 90,000 men in less than four months. Never before had
the North had to bear anything like this, and when in the
middle of July the President signed a call for 500,000 more
men it looked as if it might go on and on forever.

To make it worse, there was General Jubal Early, whose
muscular Confederate army had driven David Hunter away
from Lynchburg. Forced to retreat, Hunter felt himself compelled to flee westward across the mountains, leaving the old
Stonewall Jackson trail down the Shenandoah Valley wholly
undefended. Early promptly marched on that trail in the old
Jackson style, crossed the Potomac, knocked aside a hastily
collected Federal force that tried to stop him, and moved
boldly toward Washington. He got to Silver Spring, half a
dozen miles north of the capitol dome, and his soldiers un-
feelingly burned the home of Montgomery Blair; for a haunting moment on July 12 it looked as if he might upset everything by capturing Washington. This was a little beyond him;
Grant sent General Horatio Wright and the VI Corps up
just in time, after a brief skirmish Early withdrew, and by
the end of July he was back below the Potomac again. He
was not far below it, to be sure; he lingered in the northern
end of the Shenandoah Valley, ready to strike again if he saw
an opening, but at least he was no longer tapping at the back
door of Washington.

He had made a raid, not an outright invasion, and although
it was done in the old Jackson manner it did not have the
old effect. President Lincoln and Secretary Stanton were not
as ready to take alarm now as they used to be, and it had not
been possible for Lee to give Early enough force to turn
this fencer's thrust into a hard blow. But the operation greatly damaged the administration's prestige. After the high hopes
of the spring, when men told one another that Grant would
soon march into Richmond, to find Lee still able to send off
a detachment that apparently could come within inches of
seizing the Federal capital was more than anyone cared to
think about.

An unrelated setback intensified the gloom. Late in July
Grant's army got its one chance to break the Petersburg lines
when a regiment of Pennsylvania coal miners in Burnside's
corps dug a long tunnel and planted four tons of black

powder beneath a Confederate fort. Exploded at dawn on
July 30, this mine blew a huge gap in the otherwise impregnable trench system, and for about one hour the way was
open for the Army of the Potomac to march straight through
and bring Lee's army to destruction. But Burnside, who had
arranged this stratagem with intelligence, was incredibly
clumsy in his attempt to execute it. He entrusted the all-
important assaulting column to a division commander who
turned out to be a drunken coward and who huddled in a
dugout and let his soldiers lead themselves. Nobody could
ever beat Robert E. Lee fighting that way; the Confederates
repaired their line before Burnside's men could apply heavy
pressure, and the Federal attack failed, with substantial loss.
There was of course a court of inquiry, and Burnside's corps
got some new officers, starting at the top; but about the most
anyone in the North could see was that Grant had lost nearly
3800 more men in another meaningless head-on attack.[18]

These episodes had not actually changed the military picture materially, but they helped to create massive war-
weariness in the North. Republican leaders fell into a panic,
scurrying to and fro to see if they could not call a new convention and find a new nominee. Secretary Seward's political
mentor, canny Thurlow Weed of New York, told Lincoln
early in August that his re-election was an impossibility, and
a little later he wrote to Seward: "Nobody here doubts it;
nor do I see anybody from other states who authorizes the
slightest hope of success. . . . The people are wild for peace."
Henry Raymond of the New York *Times*, chairman of the
Republican National Committee, told Mr. Lincoln that "the
tide is setting strongly against us." Made desperate by the
rising argument that peace could never be had under Mr.
Lincoln because of his inflexible stand against slavery, Raymond made a desperate proposal, urging the President to
appoint a commission "to make distinct proffers of peace to
Davis as the head of the Rebel armies, on the sole question
of acknowledging the supremacy of the Constitution—all
other questions to be settled in a convention of the people of
all the states." David Davis, who had been so perky at the
time of the Baltimore convention, wrote unhappily: "There
is no disguising the fact that people are getting tired of the
war. Some of them can't see a ray of light. I am speaking
of good men."[19]

This pessimism briefly infected Mr. Lincoln himself, and on August 23 he wrote a memorandum, folded and sealed it, asked his cabinet members to sign their names on the outside so that it could be identified later, and put it in his desk. Opened after the election, the memorandum read: "This morning, as for some days past, it seems exceedingly probable that this Administration will not be re-elected. Then it will be my duty to so co-operate with the President-elect as to save the Union between the election and the inauguration; as he will have secured his election on such ground that he cannot possibly save it afterward." The somber final clause reflected his analysis of the problem that confronted the Democrats, and Mr. Lincoln bluntly stated the case to the reporter, Noah Brooks: "They must nominate a Peace Democrat on a war platform, or a War Democrat on a peace platform; and I personally can't say that I care much which they do." The day after he wrote the memorandum, when Brooks came to say goodbye before leaving for Chicago to cover the Democratic convention, the President shook his hand and said: "Don't be discouraged. I don't believe that God has forsaken us yet."[20]

The President's prediction about the inevitable contrast between the party's nominee and its platform was accurate. The Democratic convention, which opened on August 29, was unquestionably going to nominate General McClellan; equally without question it was going to take the rest of its tone from Clement Vallandigham, who was on hand as a delegate, avoiding the limelight but most effectively busy behind the scenes. (McClellan saw the problem as clearly as the President did, and before the convention he wrote: "I wish they had left Vallandigham down south when they had him there!")[21] Vallandigham had his way, and the only part of the platform anyone remembered was a plank he himself wrote and shepherded through to adoption: "After four years of failure to restore the Union by the experiment of war, during which, under the pretense of a military necessity, or war power higher than the Constitution, the Constitution itself has been disregarded in every part, and public liberty and private right alike trodden down and the material prosperity of the country essentially impaired—justice, humanity, liberty and the public welfare demand that immediate efforts be made for a cessation of hostilities, with a view to an ultimate convention of the states, or other peaceable means, to the end that at the earliest practicable moment peace may be restored on the basis of the Federal Union of the States."[22]

Having swallowed this the convention went on to nominate McClellan, and when the ballots had been cast Vallandigham himself went to the platform to move that the nomination be made unanimous. He got "a whirlwind of applause," and he stood there, basking in it, "bland, smiling and rosy"—for all the world the way William L. Yancey stood and basked and smiled at Charleston four years earlier when he succeeded in splitting the party. (Yancey was dead now, his passing almost unnoticed; the war he had done so much to bring on had never quite had a place for him.) Having nominated McClellan, the convention made another concession to the peace wing by naming Congressman Pendleton of Ohio for Vice-President. Reporter Brooks noted, as an oddity, that the convention always cheered when the band played "Dixie" but cheered no Northern patriotic airs; and a friend of Jefferson Davis who attended the convention hastened to send a letter to Mr. Davis: "I'm glad to assure you, McClellan is pledged to *peace*. . . . It *all means peace*—let the South go, So they all understand it."[23]

However they all understood it, the delegates had done as Mr. Lincoln expected: they had named a War Democrat on a peace platform . . . tying the two together with the assertion that the war was a failure. And two days after the convention adjourned, General Sherman captured Atlanta.

6. A Grand Simplicity of Purpose

JOHN B. HOOD was uncomplicated, and when they gave him Joe Johnston's army he assumed that he was expected to go out and fight. This he did, and as a result the South lost 20,000 good soldiers, Atlanta, the presidential election, and most of what remained of the war. Hood can be blamed too much, because when he applied simple pugnacity to a situation that required finesse he was in the grand tradition; after all, that was how the independence of the Confederacy had been asserted in the first place, and perhaps it was only natural that it should be lost in the same way. The black mark against Hood is that after he overtried his army and broke it he complained that his soldiers had let him down.

Hood took over the Army of Tennessee on July 18, and he had it in battle inside of forty-eight hours. He could have used more time, for administrative reasons if for no other; he had more than 60,000 men, but fully a sixth of them were on the "extra duty" list and could not be used in battle, and he wanted to devise a better system.[1] But Sherman, whose success in crossing the Chattahoochee River had led to Johnston's removal, was pressing him.

The Federal advance led by McPherson was about to enter Decatur, five miles east of Atlanta, and the rear, commanded by unhurried George Thomas, was crossing Peachtree Creek, four miles north of the city. Sherman was threatening encirclement but his column was extended and probably there were gaps in it. Hood believed that it was impossible to defend Atlanta without stirring up a fight, and Thomas made a likely target; he represented Sherman's grip on the vital railroad back to Tennessee, and if he could be struck while his men were still getting across the creek he could be caught at a ruinous disadvantage. Crush him, and then go after the Yankees over by Decatur: Hood made up his mind, and on the afternoon of July 20 he struck at Thomas with two army corps, Hardee's and the one formerly led by Bishop Polk, now under Lieutenant General Alexander Stewart.[2]

Hood acted on defective information and his timing was off. Thomas had finished crossing the creek hours earlier, Hood was unable to get his attack moving promptly, and when the Confederate lines advanced Thomas was waiting for them, most of his men entrenched, with plenty of artillery in support. The rule that men in trenches could repel almost any imaginable frontal assault held good. Federal fire power was devastating—delivered so enthusiastically that some units kept on volleying away long after their assailants had retreated out of range—and Hardee and Stewart lost 5000 men and got nowhere. Grumbling that the failure was Hardee's fault, Hood immediately went on to execute the second part of his plan and launched a blow at McPherson.[3]

His plan was bold. Sherman was using McPherson to flank the Confederate right; Hood now divided his army in order to flank McPherson, and on July 21, while half of his army

drew a new defensive line closer to Atlanta, to hold off
Thomas and Schofield, he ordered a reinforced Hardee to
come back through the city, march east, get around Mc-
Pherson's left and attack him in the rear. He was asking too
much. Hardee's men were tired from the fight of the day
before, and in oppressive July heat they had to make an
all-night march of fifteen miles on congested roads deep in
dust, with unskilled guides, to attack a foe whose position was
changing. The effort almost exhausted them, but late in the
morning of July 22 they got behind McPherson's flank near
the Decatur road, swung into line, and made a furious attack
which brought on the heaviest battle of the entire campaign.

It nearly worked. McPherson was killed, part of his line
was under fire from front and rear at the same time, and
there was violent hand-to-hand fighting along a plateau
known as Leggett's Hill. John A. Logan, an old Douglas
Democrat from Illinois, a "political general" in the strictest
sense of the word, temporarily succeeded to McPherson's
command and turned out to be an able combat commander,
and his men held their ground. Hood's army did its best,
but when the day ended the Federals were still in position
and Hood had lost between 7000 and 8000 men (against a
Federal loss about half that size). Not until some time afterward did men see that Sherman may have missed a bright
opportunity. Hood had used most of his strength to attack
the Federal left, and Thomas and Schofield could possibly
have overwhelmed the force in their front and gone on into
Atlanta. Somewhat oddly, Sherman explained that he wanted
McPherson's troops—the old Army of the Tennessee, which
he himself formerly commanded—to win their battle un-
aided.[4]

Surprisingly, Sherman after the battle gave command of
McPherson's troops to Major General Oliver Otis Howard,
the one-armed transplant from the Army of the Potomac,
whose dignified sobriety made him seem a little out of place
in this carefree army of westerners. Logan seemed to have
earned the job, but Sherman distrusted political generals and
when Pap Thomas protested that he and Logan could not
work well together Sherman concluded that he had to have
harmony in the upper levels of command. Deeply disappointed, Logan made no protest, and remained in command
of the XV Corps; but Joe Hooker, who ranked Howard and

had a high opinion of his own merits, and blamed Howard for the defeat at Chancellorsville, announced that the appointment was "an insult to my rank and services" and sent in his resignation. Sherman, who disliked Hooker anyway, accepted the resignation without the least delay, Hooker went north to a quiet assignment far from the combat zone, and when the campaign was resumed Howard led the Army of the Tennessee.[5]

The campaign was resumed quickly. Sherman saw that he could not cut off Atlanta on the east without getting too far from his railroad line, so he had Howard move back and swing far to the Federal right, passing behind the rest of the army to get west of the city, while Schofield and Thomas kept up the pressure by opening a bombardment—on Hood's lines and on the city beyond. Hood believed that Howard's move offered an opening, and on July 28 he attacked in a featureless woodland near a country chapel called Ezra Church. The opening was not as good as he thought it was, the attack was poorly co-ordinated, and by nightfall Hood had lost another 5000 men. The Federal advance was unchecked.[6]

After that it was only a question of time—a couple of days more than a month, to be exact, seeming longer to Northern impatience. Having fought three big battles in nine days, failing each time and suffering ruinous losses, Hood was too weak to stop Sherman, who kept shifting to the right, moving slowly but steadily to cut the railroads that came to Atlanta from the southwest and south. The bombardment went on and on, and while Henry Slocum and the XX Corps stayed to watch the beleaguered city the rest of the Federals moved farther and farther toward Hood's rear. At the end of August, when Vallandigham was persuading the Democrats to proclaim the war a failure, Hood realized that the Federals were about to complete their encirclement. He struck desperately at the Federal right, at Jonesboro, fifteen miles due south of the city, failed to drive it away, and then took the only course that was left to him and evacuated Atlanta.

Slocum's men saw it first. They were the old kid gloves and paper collar soldiers from the Army of the Potomac, sent west when Rosecrans was trapped in Chattanooga, at first derided by the westerners but finally accepted as good fighting men; and they crouched, half-stunned and unbelieving, in their trenches facing Atlanta on the night of September 1, while great lights flashed across the sky and the ground quivered underfoot as Hood's rear guard blew up carloads of ammunition that could not be removed. Next morning the easterners marched into Atlanta, bands playing, and while the soldiers looked curiously at the buildings that had been wrecked during the long bombardment, anxious women set buckets of drinking water along the streets as propitiatory offerings. The Federals hoisted their colors over the city hall, and Slocum sent a telegram to Secretary Stanton: GENERAL SHERMAN HAS TAKEN ATLANTA. Hood wrote to Richmond to explain what had happened, pointing out that it was not his fault: "It seems the troops had been so long confined to trenches, and had been taught to believe that intrenchments cannot be taken, so that they attacked without spirit and retired without proper effort." The spirit and the effort had been there in abundance, according to the casualty lists: after all, a good 20,000 of his men had been lost since he took command.[7]

As a matter of fact Sherman had done less than he set out to do. Hood's army had escaped, slipping south to the town of Lovejoy, and after following it for a few miles Sherman let it go and took his own army into Atlanta to rest and refit. He had been told to destroy the Confederate army and he had not done it, and the capture of Atlanta had been no more than incidental to his plans. But now Sherman was part of a political campaign. All across the North, Atlanta had become a symbol. While it held out, the war was a failure; when it fell, the war was visibly on the way to success. Little more than a week earlier Mr. Lincoln had soberly confessed that he was likely to lose the election. Now, as people digested Sherman's exultant telegram—SO ATLANTA IS OURS, AND FAIRLY WON—the President's prospects suddenly grew better. Sherman, who despised politics, had brought about a stunning political change.

Then another Federal general, who also had done less than he was supposed to do, won a victory that accelerated the change. On September 19 Phil Sheridan sent a telegram to Grant from the Shenandoah Valley: . . . I ATTACKED THE FORCES OF GENERAL EARLY ON THE BERRYVILLE PIKE AT THE CROSSING OF OPEQUON CREEK, AND AFTER A MOST STUBBORN

AND SANGUINARY ENGAGEMENT, WHICH LASTED FROM EARLY
IN THE MORNING UNTIL 5 O'CLOCK IN THE EVENING, COM-
PLETELY DEFEATED HIM, AND DRIVING HIM THROUGH WIN-
CHESTER CAPTURED ABOUT 2500 PRISONERS, FIVE PIECES OF
ARTILLERY, NINE ARMY FLAGS AND MOST OF THEIR WOUNDED.
Here was a new note: not merely victory, but victory announced with a chesty arrogance which seemed to say that
anything but further victory was unthinkable. The North
responded with high enthusiasm, Washington fired a 100-gun
salute to celebrate, and James A. Garfield wrote that "Phil
Sheridan has made a speech in the Shenandoah Valley more
powerful and valuable to the Union cause than all the stump-
ers in the Republic can make—our prospects are everywhere heightening."[8]

Like Sherman, Sheridan had struck at a symbol. Jubal
Early's long presence in the lower Shenandoah Valley, close
to the Potomac, right at the gateway to the heart of the
North, had been one of the big reasons why so many
Northerners considered the war a failure, and although he
looked more dangerous than he was it was because he had
done a remarkable job with inadequate means. First he had
driven General Hunter away from Lynchburg, thereby removing an essential piece from Grant's strategic plan. Then
he marched on Washington, and thereafter he threatened the
whole Potomac border country, and with an army that apparently never included more than 15,000 men he had forced
the Federals to divert 40,000 soldiers who could have been
used elsewhere.[9] He had sent a cavalry column into Pennsylvania, burning Chambersburg in reprisal for the places
Hunter had burned in Virginia, he had broken service on
the important Baltimore & Ohio railroad line, and he had
reduced the United States War Department to the same
frantic shuffling of troops and proliferation of ineffective
orders that Stonewall Jackson had evoked two years earlier.
Clearly, the North would not be getting on with the war
properly until it did something about General Early.

Early was a hard man for anyone to do anything about.
He was "Old Jube" to his troops, a sardonic man twisted
by arthritis, caustic and provoking and profane, always riding in a queer hunched-over manner, "solemn as a country
coroner going to his first inquest": respected by all but liked
by hardly anybody. He had no patience with any human

shortcoming, and once when an infantry regiment failed to
protect a wagon train the way he thought it should have
done he rode up, all steaming, and swore loudly that he
would put this regiment in the very front of the next fight
that came up, "where he hoped every one of them would
get killed and burn through all eternity." He was as good
as his word, too, and the regiment had a bad time in the
next battle; yet the men mixed a grudging admiration in with
their dislike, and one veteran who survived this affair wrote
that Early was "a queer fish . . . but no humbug." If it was
hard for his own men to get along with him it was even
harder for the enemy, and Early deserved more credit from
his fellow Southerners than he ever got.[10]

Immediately after Early made his thrust at Washington
in July the Federal troops assembled along the Potomac
were under Hunter's command, but Hunter was unable to
use them effectively and Grant removed him and sent Sheridan up to take charge. Sheridan had the furious driving
energy Grant wanted, but for a time he seemed lost in this
assignment. He shared the War Department belief that Early's
army was more than twice as big as it really was, he spent
a good deal of time getting his army organized, and Early's
feints and excursions confused him; for six weeks after he
took command, Sheridan did little more than hold his
ground at the lower end of the Shenandoah Valley, and
at last Grant came up from Petersburg, talked to him, and
ordered him to strike.

Grant's idea about what ought to be done in the valley
was the same now as it had always been. He wanted the
valley used for a blow at Lee's rear, with a Federal army
going all the way to Staunton, coming east to Charlottesville
and breaking the Virginia Central Railroad between that
place and Gordonsville so that the fertile valley could send
no more supplies to Lee. Sigel tried it and failed, Hunter
tried it and failed even more disastrously, and now Sheridan
seemed unable to do it. To clear the lower valley was not
enough; Grant was afraid that Early might retreat, just out
of reach, returning when Federal forces were withdrawn,
and he concluded that it would be necessary to devastate
the valley so thoroughly that it could not again be used as a
military highway or granary. Late in August he grimly told
Sheridan: "If the war is to last another year, we want the

Shenandoah Valley to remain a barren waste." But the plan to strike down the whole length of the valley in such a way as to force Lee to evacuate Petersburg and Richmond was always his goal.[11]

Sheridan attacked Early and roundly defeated him on September 19. As he said, the battle was long and hard. He got his troops into action clumsily, so that when the battle began half of them were struggling up the Opequon Creek ravine, their way blocked by another of those misplaced wagon trains, and in the first part of the action the Federals were in danger of being beaten by fewer than half of their numbers. But during the afternoon Sheridan got everybody into action, his own talents as an inspirational battlefield leader came into full play, and by nightfall Early was in retreat, his army badly battered. Sheridan pursued, and struck him again three days later at Fisher's Hill, twenty miles to the south, sending him flying in a retreat so headlong that Sheridan assured Grant: "I do not think there ever was an army so badly routed."[12] This was an overstatement, as Sheridan learned a few weeks later, but the two triumphs were spectacular. Sheridan methodically began the work of devastation, turning a garden spot into a smoking desert, and the campaign to re-elect Abraham Lincoln took on increased momentum.

Sheridan and Sherman had provided powerful arguments, and another one came from Admiral Farragut. From the moment New Orleans fell, the old admiral had wanted to run the forts at the entrance to Mobile Bay and seal off that port permanently, and early in August he got his wish. With his fleet of wooden warships stiffened by four monitors, he steamed into the bay on August 5, pounded his way past the forts, took the formidable Confederate ironclad *Tennessee*, overwhelmed the few wooden gunboats that were its consorts, and made it possible for the army to come in and capture the forts shortly afterward. It was a hard fight, Farragut lost the monitor *Tecumseh*, his fleet suffered more than three hundred casualties, and in the general Northern depression of mid-summer the victory somehow did not seem as impressive as it did a month or two later. By the middle of the autumn it was bracketed with Atlanta and the Opequon, and Republican orators jeered that Sherman, Sheridan, and

Farragut had knocked the bottom out of the Democratic platform.

The platform had already been somewhat damaged by General McClellan. As a war Democrat running on a peace platform, McClellan was not happy, and when he sat down to draft his formal acceptance of the nomination he found the going difficult. He finally produced a letter saying that although he believed in reconciliation and compromise (qualities which in his opinion the administration notably lacked) there could be no peace without full reunion: "I could not look in the face my gallant comrades . . . who have survived so many bloody battles, and tell them that their labors and the sacrifice of so many of our slain and wounded brothers had been in vain—that we had abandoned the Union for which we have so often periled our lives." McClellan, in short, believed in going on with the war until it was won, despite the platform's demand for an armistice and a peaceful settlement. This outraged Vallandigham, who announced that the Democratic party was still a peace party and that its platform was binding on one and all, including the head of the ticket; and the Democrats began to bicker among themselves as the Republicans had been doing a month earlier.[13]

Meanwhile, the Republicans got their own house in order. In August there had been a strong, not wholly invisible movement to call a new convention and nominate someone in Lincoln's place, and Ben Butler appears to have maneuvered quietly in the hope that he might get that nomination. He would have been a formidable opponent, a former Democrat with a large following but also a hard-war man perfectly acceptable to the radicals; the potential threat he always represented may help to explain why the administration kept him in a top army command despite his notorious incompetence as a soldier. But the change in the military climate made everything look different, and before September ended the party had closed its ranks. The movement for a new convention ended. Frémont, waited upon by a committee of party leaders, announced on September 22 that in the interest of party harmony he was withdrawing from the race—and on the next day Mr. Lincoln, who had a fairly good line on all of the things that had been happening, asked for and got the resignation of Montgomery Blair.[14] The radicals came back to the fold and they went out and stumped for the party ticket—as did Blair, for that matter—and if Mr. Lincoln had any further thoughts about the gloomy memorandum he had written predicting his own defeat he said nothing about them. Down at Petersburg General Humphreys, chief of staff of the Army of the Potomac, meditated on the campaign and wrote a letter: "What an extraordinary fortune McClellan has had. Extolled to the skies by the newspapers in the first place, in the summer and fall of 1861, having a reputation affixed to him *by them* of being one of the greatest generals of any age, without having done more than a general of division may do every day without notice; —exhibiting in his campaigns no more ability or skill than scores of other officers of the old Army would have done, abused by one set of newspapers and extolled by others only because he was displaced, and now made the candidate for the Presidency of the United States! For myself, I would rather be a Major Genl. in the regular army than President of the United States, and I think McClellan would also."[15]

A tide was flowing now. It had its springs in many things, ranging all the way from the solemnity of the Gettysburg Address to the extreme heat which the Lincoln administration put on everyone from war contractors to private soldiers who were going to be allowed to vote, compounded like the war and like the nation of the noble and the ignoble and an odd intangible. From England, John Bright wrote to Horace Greeley that Englishmen like himself hoped for the re-election of Abraham Lincoln, "not because they believe Mr. Lincoln to be wiser or better than all other men on your continent, but because they think they have observed in his career a grand simplicity of purpose and a patriotism which knows no change and which does not falter."[16]

As the tide flowed, Sheridan got into it once more. By the middle of October (state elections in the North were going Republican, and it was harder and harder to believe in failure) Sheridan had the lovely Shenandoah Valley pretty well burned out. In his matter-of-fact way he reported that "I have destroyed over 2000 barns filled with wheat, hay and farming implements; over 70 mills, filled with flour and wheat; have driven in front of the army over 4000 head of stock, and have killed and issued to the troops not less than 3000 sheep. . . . The people here are getting sick of the war." He had not gone on down to strike at Lee's railroad because, all in all, he felt that it would be too difficult, and he concluded that "the best policy will be to let the burning of the crops of the valley be the end of this campaign."

That might have been all right, except that General Early did not propose to let it end there. He and his beaten army had more resilience than Sheridan suspected, and when the Federals moved northward to rest from destruction and to consider what ought to happen next Early followed them; and on the morning of October 19, while Sheridan's army lay in camp behind Cedar Creek, not far from the old Fisher's Hill battlefield, and while Sheridan was far in the rear having a top-level conference on strategy, Early attacked this army in its tents and sent half of it flying north along the valley pike, capturing camp, guns, and a varied assortment of prisoners.

There were Southerners who argued that he might have done even more. Sometime before the middle of the day the impetus went out of the Confederate attack. Early said that his men left their ranks to loot the Federal camps, one of his officers declared that the general simply sat down and waited for the half-routed Federal army to become entirely routed and go away without further pushing, and the truth may be that his men had done all they could do against a stronger foe and that a complete victory was beyond them. Anyway, Sheridan came riding back from Winchester, a red-faced man on a horse all flecked with foam, and as he charged into the backwash of defeated stragglers the men cheered with sudden rebirth of valor and he cursed them with a mighty anger: "God *damn* you, don't cheer me! If you love your country, come up to the front! God *damn* you, don't cheer me! There's lots of fight in you men yet! Come up, God damn you! Come up!"[17] They swung up into line beside the men who had not run away, Sheridan suddenly cooled off and saw to it that everything was in order, and then he drove them forward in an irresistible, storybook charge. Early's army was defeated, routed, broken—all of the overworked words were at last made good—and the Republican orators had one more item to put in their speeches.

From a properly grateful government Sheridan got official

congratulations and a commission as a major general in the Regular Army. From General Grant he got a telegram: IF IT IS POSSIBLE TO FOLLOW UP YOUR GREAT VICTORY UNTIL YOU CAN REACH THE CENTRAL ROAD (that is, the Virginia Central between Charlottesville and Gordonsville: Lee's lifeline, Grant's goal all the way) DO IT, EVEN IF YOU HAVE TO LIVE ON HALF-RATIONS. IF THE ARMY AT RICHMOND COULD BE CUT OFF FROM SOUTHWEST VIRGINIA IT WOULD BE OF GREAT IMPORTANCE TO US.[18]

Sheridan found this impractical and he did not do it, but it no longer made much difference. The war had got to that point now: if Sherman settled for less than the destruction of Hood's army, or if Sheridan beat Early but failed to carry out Grant's design, it did not actually matter very much. To do these things would have made the end come more quickly, but the end was coming now in any case and the people of the North could see it. And so on November 8 they went to the polls, and Mr. Lincoln got 212 electoral votes against 21 for General McClellan. The popular vote, as usual, was much closer, but it was still emphatic; the President had a margin of nearly half a million votes out of slightly more than 4,000,000 cast. For the first time he had a vote of confidence, and it came to him with a decisive margin.

For McClellan, who three years earlier had entered Washington as the destined savior of his country, hearing men say that he could be a dictator then or President later at his choice, there was nothing now but the unhappy consolation that comes to a valiant loser. Sam Barlow wrote to him, saying that by being defeated he had escaped terrible trials: the next administration would face an almost impossible task, and to take office in March "with an empty treasury, a wasted army and a defiant and apparently united people in rebellion is enough to appall anyone." . . . One of the things that re-elected Mr. Lincoln was the fact that his political opponents were unable to see what was going on in the world. They made a political asset out of military failure, and when the asset proved inadequate they had to go on believing in the failure. In November of 1864, when the last long night of the Confederacy was so obviously beginning, they could still see Federal prospects as all but hopeless.

McClellan agreed that he was well out of it. He deplored

the result of the election for his country's sake, but he himself had been prepared for defeat and he was not disheartened. He had one sobering thought: "God grant that our poor country may not be mired in the course of finding that we were right."[19]

CHAPTER SEVEN

His Almost Chosen People

1. *Appeal Against the Thunderstorm*

FOR THE THIRD TIME in three years Jefferson Davis left Richmond to place his own rigid figure, with its gray face and the cold fire in its veins, between the Confederacy and disaster. In the fall of 1862 he had visited Tennessee and Mississippi to inspire a firmer grip on the great valley. Tennessee and Mississippi had been lost, and the great valley along with them, and at the bleak end of 1863 he had gone to northern Georgia in a vain effort to repair the damage. Now Georgia itself was being broken, and with Sherman in Atlanta further damage was imminent, so Mr. Davis left the capital again to make one last attempt to give other men a share of his own limitless tenacity of purpose.

Beyond tenacity he had little to offer, other resources having run thin. On his earlier trips he had talked to generals, trying to meet a problem of command. Now he had to talk to the people themselves, because this military crisis arose out of a failure of the spirit: the rolls of the Confederate armies by the fall of 1864 showed that between 100,000 and 200,000 soldiers were no longer present for duty.[1] The Confederacy was being overwhelmed by superior numbers but it was not getting nearly all of its own manpower into action. Unless these absentees returned to the ranks the cause was going to be lost.

People needed to be touched with fire, and Mr. Davis' logic was clear but cold. At Macon, he assured a crowd that "if one-half the men now absent without leave will return to duty, we can defeat the enemy." By occupying Atlanta, Sherman had thrust his army into a trap, and the trap could

377

be sprung: "Sherman cannot keep up his long line of communication, and retreat, sooner or later, he must. And when that day comes, the fate that befell the army of the French Empire in its retreat from Moscow will be re-enacted. Our cavalry and our people will harass and destroy his army as did the Cossacks that of Napoleon, and the Yankee general, like him, will escape with only a body-guard. . . . Let us with one arm and one effort endeavor to crush Sherman."[2]

When U. S. Grant heard about this he remarked that "Mr. Davis has not made it quite plain who is to furnish the snow for this Moscow retreat," but he read the accounts of Mr. Davis' speeches attentively, for with a remarkable lack of discretion they contained broad hints on strategic planning. At Augusta and at Columbia the President declared that General Hood would strike a powerful blow far in the Federal rear if the people supported him properly: "If but a half, nay, one fourth, of the men to whom the service has a right will give him their strength, I see no chance for Sherman to escape from a defeat or a disgraceful retreat." The military plans were being made, Hood would engage in a vigorous counteroffensive, he would gain thousands of recruits in Tennessee, and "it is in the power of the Confederacy to plant our banners on the banks of the Ohio." Materially, the Confederacy was stronger than ever before: "Once we had no arms, and could receive no soldiers but those who came to us armed. Now we have arms for all, and are begging for men to bear them."

Appealing for a rebirth of the war spirit, Mr. Davis remained what he had always been, faithful to the defiant warcry he had given the first Confederate Congress: "All we ask is to be let alone." What he said now was bounded by those limits. The Confederate program had not been changed by four years of war. Mr. Davis addressed himself to men who had much to lose and who were beset by malignant foes in a changing world. "Ours is not a revolution," he insisted. "We are not engaged in a Quixotic fight for the rights of man; our struggle is for inherited rights; and who would surrender them?" It was idle to talk about making a compromise peace, because the Northern President demanded outright submission: "If you will acknowledge your crime, lay down your arms, emancipate your slaves and turn over your leaders—as they call your humble servant—to be punished, then you will have permission to vote, together with your Negroes, upon the terms upon which Mr. Lincoln will be graciously pleased to allow you to live as a part of the nation over which he presides."[3]

This was eloquent, if planter-aristocrats were the only people who mattered, but by now Mr. Davis was facing enemies who had bowels of iron. General Sherman saw things just as he did; he knew that before long he would have to move and that when he moved he must risk everything. Before he moved, Sherman wanted to neutralize Atlanta, and on September 8 he announced that "the city of Atlanta, being exclusively required for warlike purposes, will at once be evacuated by all except the armies of the United States." The civilian inhabitants, in short, must get out, and the most Sherman would do was arrange a ten-day truce with General Hood so that the refugees could be transported across the Confederate lines. Accepting the truce, Hood protested that "the unprecedented measure you propose transcends, in studied and ingenious cruelty, all acts ever before brought to my attention in the dark history of war," and the mayor of Atlanta, James M. Calhoun, pointed out that sick, aged and helpless people would have to be moved and that their suffering would be "appalling and heart-rending." Sherman agreed that this was probably true but insisted that the orders must stand, "because my orders are not designed to meet the humanities of the case but to prepare for the future struggles. . . . War is cruelty, and you cannot refine it. . . . You might as well appeal against the thunder storm as against these terrible hardships of war." The appeal failed, and the exodus took place.[4]

Sherman knew that while he stayed in Atlanta his position was potentially dangerous; he was deep in a hostile country, bad things could happen if he made any mistakes, and he told a friend, "I've got my wedge pretty deep, and must look out that I don't get my fingers pinched." However, he did not propose to withdraw the wedge. He was in the Georgia uplands, with pines and sandy fields and mountains all about him, but he was beginning to scent a salt breeze from the sea, two hundred and twenty airline miles off to the southeast, and while he was exiling the civilians he was thinking about a march to the coast. This, he believed, was the road to final victory, and he assured Grant that the Confederates "may stand the fall of Richmond but not of Georgia." Yet he could not just get up and go. He needed a fixed objective and a solution to the supply problem, because "otherwise I would risk our whole army by getting too far from Atlanta." He urged Grant to seize and provision a seacoast base, possibly Savannah; then Sherman could "sweep the whole state of Georgia," and if he did that while Grant was taking care of Lee, "I think Uncle Abe will give us a twenty days leave of absence to see the young folks."[5]

Before he could do these attractive things Sherman had to attend to General Hood. Hood's army had by no means been put out of action. It still contained 34,000 infantry and 12,000 cavalry, and if Hood felt that it had lost its fighting capacity by standing on the defensive in trenches no Federal soldier could ever be found to agree with him. Hood had all of his old aggressive energy, and a few weeks after he evacuated Atlanta he marched north and west to strike Sherman where he was vulnerable, along the railroad line that led back to Chattanooga. Sherman could do no more than leave Slocum's corps to hold Atlanta and take everybody else north to fight Hood, and for the better part of a month the two armies maneuvered and sparred up and down the north Georgia country, going at one time almost up to the Tennessee line.

Hood was never strong enough to strike effectively, but he was so elusive that Sherman could not make him stand and fight. Exasperated beyond endurance to find that six weeks after the fall of Atlanta he was still campaigning over ground he had covered early in the summer, Sherman at last came to a radical conclusion. He would cut loose from everything. If Hood wanted that railroad he could have it, and Atlanta along with it: both would be thoroughly wrecked, and Sherman would not need either because he was going to go to the Atlantic. He would send enough men back to Tennessee to keep Hood from doing anything too destructive in the Federal rear, and then he would ignore the army that had been his stated objective when the campaign began, marching directly away from it and heading for salt water.[6]

In a sense, Hood provoked him into this action; in another sense he made the action easier. Late in October he drew off into northern Alabama, preparing to make the strike into Tennessee that President Davis had hinted at so broadly in his excellent speeches, working on the theory that, if he marched on Nashville, Sherman would be compelled to come north to meet him. Sherman simply sent George Thomas back to Tennessee, telling him to take part of his Army of the Cumberland and reinforce it with levies that would be made available after he got north of the Tennessee River; meanwhile, Sherman would organize 60,000 men for a march to the coast.

Thomas obeyed, unprotesting but slightly unhappy. He was the Rock, the man who could not be beaten, and so now he must go back to handle Hood's veterans while Sherman marched to glory against Georgia militia. Thomas may have reflected that he himself had been the first man to think about the march to the sea. He was supposed to be a stolid defensive fighter, and yet he had a way of seeing the sharp offensive blows ahead of other people. He had wanted to march into east Tennessee two years earlier, while Rosecrans was cautiously approaching Murfreesboro, and before the Georgia campaign even began it was Thomas who proposed a hard smash at Resaca and Joe Johnston's rear; and immediately after the fall of Atlanta he had suggested that while Sherman held the city and looked after Hood, Thomas' army be sent off on a march to the sea.[7] Now he had to go back to Nashville and stand the hammering while somebody else made the big march. He went back, uncomplaining, while Sherman sought final approval from Grant.

This he got. But Grant could not spare the force to take Savannah and establish a base there; he could only send supplies and transports down to Hilton Head, South Carolina, to stand by and provision Savannah after Sherman took it, and he warned that "your movements therefore will be independent of mine, at least until the fall of Richmond takes place." Sherman himself had doubts, and while Grant was making up his mind Sherman wrote to his brother that "Mobile or Savannah should be taken before I venture further." But he believed that the rich Georgia farm country could support his army, he believed he would be strong enough to break his way into Savannah once the march was made, and he had Grant's full confidence. (Grant told Secretary Stanton, who was most skeptical about the whole performance, "Such an army as Sherman has—and with such a commander —is hard to corner or capture.") It was settled at last, and early in November Grant sent Sherman his final word: "I say, then, go as you propose."[8]

The point of all of this was that Sherman's campaign could not be made—could not be tried, or even thought of rationally—except against a foe who was in the process of collapse. To abandon communications and march 60,000 men some three hundred miles through enemy territory, with nothing ahead except the prospect of storming a fortified city to keep the 60,000 from starvation, was an idea that was wholly insane from a military standpoint: except that the enemy had become powerless. The walls of Jericho were coming down, falling before the sound of the trumpets that would never call retreat, and Grant and Sherman knew it. They acted accordingly.

Probably Jefferson Davis knew it, too. On November 7, the day before the Northern election—the last day on which there was a light of hope in the Southern sky—Mr. Davis sent a message to the Congress voicing the grimmest of resolves: "There are no vital points on the preservation of which the continued existence of the Confederacy depends. There is no military success of the enemy which can accomplish its destruction. Not the fall of Richmond, nor Wilmington, nor Savannah, nor Mobile, nor of all combined, can save the enemy from the constant and exhaustive drain of blood and treasure which must continue until he shall discover that no peace is attainable unless based on the recognition of our indefeasible rights."[9] This was magnificent, but it was a rallying-cry from the last ditch; and it was also an evocation of the very revolution which Mr. Davis had always disavowed. A Confederacy that abandoned its cities and no longer relied on any fixed bases would survive (if it survived at all) only by guerrilla warfare, counting military coup in terms of crossroads ambushes and the shooting of traitors, living in the desperate hope that the victors would eventually be poisoned by hatred and terror. This had nothing to do with the nation created at Montgomery, which prized its legitimacy above all else, and that the President should even take a step in this direction hinted at dreadful stress and tension.

The step was more easily taken, perhaps, because Mr. Davis' government had already dabbled in various revolutionary stratagems. Early in the spring it had set up in Canada a sort of conspiratorial headquarters, under the direction of

Jacob Thompson of Mississippi, who had been James Buchanan's Secretary of the Interior, and Clement C. Clay, Jr., of Alabama. From this place there had come an elaborate plan to organize a midwestern revolution with the aid of native Copperheads, and at one point a date was set for a general uprising to carry Illinois, Indiana, and Ohio out of the Union. The uprising never took place, largely, when all was said and done, because the Copperheads wanted to vote against their government but had no intention of taking arms against it. There was also a plan to seize U.S.S. *Michigan*, the one warship on the Great Lakes, and lay Detroit and Cleveland and Buffalo under contribution. This plot resulted in nothing better than the temporary capture of a side-wheel excursion steamer on Lake Erie; and a plan to harry the northern border brought a raid on the Vermont town of St. Albans which wound up simply as a well-publicized bank robbery. One set of conspirators tried to burn the city of New York by planting fire bombs in hotel bedrooms, but their bombs were ineffective and neither New York nor the separate hotels were burned. Although nothing ever quite worked the Richmond government showed that it was at least ready to fight in most unorthodox ways if it had to.[10]

Warfare in its more orthodox forms offered the thinnest hope, as autumn passed. During the summer it had been believed that Grant's campaign in Virginia was a bloody failure, and optimism in Richmond had run high; but now, with the Northern election killing all hope for a peace administration in Washington, it began to be clear that Grant had not failed at all and optimism turned into bleak pessimism. Grant had a firm grip on the army that defended Richmond; Lee was pinned in his lines, growing weaker month by month, his task always growing harder. During summer and fall the Federals had tried to edge past his flanks without much success, although the lines had been considerably extended; they had been repulsed at Ream's Station and Hatcher's Run, and they had been unable to exploit gains made at Globe Tavern and Fort Harrison—but they were still there, playing a game in which they had all of the advantages. Early in September, Lee pointed out that "we have no troops disposable to meet movements of the enemy or strike when opportunity presents without taking them from the trenches and exposing some important point";

the only immediate remedy he could see was to restore to the ranks all soldiers serving as cooks, mechanics, teamsters, and laborers, replacing them with Negro slaves.[11] Meanwhile, he had more and more ground to hold, and always fewer men to hold it with.

It seemed impossible to bring the armies up to strength. As far back as the spring, Secretary Seddon had complained of "the decadence of the volunteering spirit." Many men who were liable to conscription were claiming exemption, and often enough were getting it. Major General J. L. Kemper, in charge of reserve forces in Virginia, estimated during the summer that Virginia contained 40,000 men between the ages of eighteen and forty-five who were not in the army, and he pointed out that partial returns in the Bureau of Conscription on September 1 showed more than 28,000 Virginians of military age were exempted or on detail. The commandant of conscripts in Alabama said that although more than half of 7994 deserters from Alabama regiments had been rounded up and returned to duty during the summer, there had been 6000 additional desertions from Alabama regiments in October and November, and in many counties it was impossible to enforce the conscription law because the absentees were armed and defiant. In December Howell Cobb urged a return to the old volunteer system, saying that "it would require the whole army to enforce the conscript law if the same state of things exists throughout the Confederacy as I know is the case in Georgia and Alabama, and I may add Tennessee."[12]

Some of the state authorities were of no help. Governor Joe Brown of Georgia insisted that the Confederate authorities had no power to draft men whom a state governor declared exempt, and he granted exemptions liberally; by autumn he had made 1350 justices of the peace exempt, along with an equal number of constables, not to mention 2751 officers in the state militia. Brown took an all-out states' rights position: if the central government could draft some state officials it could draft all of them—governor, legislators, judges, and everybody—and if it could do that it had the power to destroy any state government whenever it wanted to, in which case the cherished principle of states' rights was a nullity. This probably was entirely true, but clinging to this belief brought no recruits to the armies of

Lee and Hood, and involved a complete failure to understand that the immediate threat to states' rights, as far as Georgia was concerned, came not from the government at Richmond but from General Sherman. In December Mr. Davis wrote wearily to a friend that some state officials were "hindering the action of this government, obstructing the execution of its laws, denouncing its necessary policy, impairing its hold on the confidence of the people, and dealing with it rather as if it were the public enemy than the government which they themselves had established for the common defence and which was their only hope of safety from the untold horrors of Yankee despotism."[13]

The problems were interlocking. One thing that made it impossible to enlarge the armies was the number of men exempt and on detail; one thing that made it impossible to feed and clothe the armies properly was the fact that not enough men were exempt and on detail, so that railroads and wagon lines and processing plants and mills operated badly; and one thing that caused desertions was the fact that the armies were poorly fed and clothed. There were not enough men behind the lines to round up and restore to service the men who had run away, but there were so many that their absence from the fighting front was sorely felt. (A wrathful War Department inspector found a host of skulkers at innumerable scattered commands in Mississippi: "Each little town in the state has its commandant of post, its conscript officer, its adjutants, its guards, in a word its little army around it. One of these officers could perform the duty of the whole.")[14]

From the beginning the Confederacy had had too much to do and not enough to do it with, and although it could not bring requirements into line with resources, it clung to the simple faith that Southern valor would overcome all obstacles. Now the machinery that had been overtaxed so long was breaking down, but what could be understood with the mind could not be accepted with the heart; and so there was a blind, unavailing hunt for the person, institution or practice that had been at fault. The trouble no doubt lay in the failure to conscript more vigorously, or possibly in the attempt to conscript at all; in too rigid observance of the principle of states' rights, or in the scandalous flouting of that principle; in some mysterious inability, by President or by Congress or by someone else, to give the Southern cause a greater dimension than the Founding Fathers had specified. A discouraged Senator from Texas noted that although the administration was constantly asking Congress for more men, Congress had long since placed at its disposal every able-bodied man in the Confederacy, and he went on to reflect: "It is true that they were not in the ranks, but it was not because Congress had not passed the laws desired by our military authorities to put them there." To attend the fall session of Congress, this Senator had come across the whole of the Confederacy, all the way from Texas, talking to people, listening to them, coming to his own conclusion about the failure of the laws to bring men into the army, and he quietly recorded a somber verdict: "Confidence was gone, and hope was almost extinguished."[15]

One by one the little flags that had flown so brightly were coming down. That famous sea raider, C.S.S. *Alabama*, which had ranged the seven seas to take more than threescore Yankee merchant ships, was at the bottom of the English Channel now, sunk by U.S.S. *Kearsarge* after a fight off Cherbourg breakwater on June 19; a romantic cruiser, gone from a war that no longer had romantic overtones. John Hunt Morgan, the cavalryman who had ridden Federal troopers off their horses in forays along the middle border, was dead, killed in an outpost clash at Greeneville, Tennessee, on September 4. Worst of all, the old hope that a bold stroke into Missouri would restore vitality to the dying war west of the Mississippi had flickered out in a meaningless cavalry raid.

The story of the raid was eloquent. After Banks' Red River campaign came to grief, General Edmund Kirby Smith had been moved to strike at Missouri, but he never managed to put any real weight into it. When his force at last moved from Arkansas into Missouri late in September it was strictly a cavalry expedition, 8000 men or more, led by valiant General Sterling Price. Price hoped to reclaim Missouri for the Confederacy, but he was not strong enough; desperately needing the infantry Smith had not given him, he won minor victories, briefly threatened St. Louis, rode off to the northwestern part of the state, and ran into an overpowering array of Federals under such competent generals as A. J. Smith, Samuel R. Curtis, and Alfred Pleason-

ton. The odds were too great. There were several days of
fighting, climaxed by a hard battle at Westport on October
23, and Price was routed. He went off in a confused retreat,
marked by sharp rear-guard actions, and rode desperately
south through eastern Kansas and western Missouri, shaking
off his pursuers but going on all the way to Texas. He proudly reported that he had made a 1400-mile march, capturing
many guns and prisoners, seizing abundant supplies and giving the Yankees cause for alarm, but the hard fact was that
the campaign had failed. For its supreme effort the trans-
Mississippi Confederacy had been able to do no more than
make a spectacular but ineffective cavalry raid. . . . Hope
in truth was almost extinguished.[16]

On October 4—more than a month before the re-election
of Abraham Lincoln sent its warning across the South: not
long after General Sherman had spoken of men's inability to
appeal against the thunderstorm—General Lee wrote to Secretary Seddon to ask if there was any chance at all to increase the army.

"If we can get out our entire arms-bearing population in
Virginia and North Carolina," he wrote, "and relieve all detailed men with Negroes, we may be able, with the blessing
of God, to keep the enemy in check to the beginning of winter. If we fail to do this the result may be calamitous."[17]

2. What Have You Done?

IN A WAY, Mr. Lincoln's message to Congress was routine.
He spoke of fair harvests, of growth in the western territories,
of the prospect for a Pacific railroad, and of a treasury whose
condition was good despite a public debt that was rising toward two billion dollars. He avoided eloquence, talking quietly as a man might who was at the head of a strong nation
with an assured future, and he drew especial attention to the
temporary disappearance of General Sherman.

Sherman and his army had gone off the board. On November 15 the army left Atlanta and marched southeast into
darkness, beyond the reach of telegraph wires and newspaper correspondents. Sherman sent back no reports, nobody
in the North knew exactly where he was or what was happening to him, and the President invited Congress to reflect

on the significance of this fact. "It tends to show a great increase in our relative strength," he said, "that our General-in-Chief should feel able to confront and hold in check every active force of the enemy and yet to detach a well-appointed army to move on such an expedition." What looked like a risky venture was, in short, nothing less than a move to sweep in the chips.[1]

It was made easier by the fact that General Hood committed a great blunder.

Late in October Hood had gone into northern Alabama, hoping that Sherman would follow and that he could be defeated in detail while doing so. Instead Sherman returned to Atlanta, wrecked the railroad he had been guarding so long, and prepared to march off to the sea; and now Hood was too far away to stop him. Mr. Davis had talked hopefully of a Confederate army going to the banks of the Ohio, a river as remote as the Ganges, but he insisted that Sherman must be beaten first. When it became apparent that an unbeaten Sherman was going to march southeast Mr. Davis urged Hood to come across Georgia with all speed and at least beat the Federals to Augusta; but the odd fatality that had always kept the President from getting a firm grip on the western war was still at work, and now Hood was convincing himself that he must go into Tennessee at once, no matter what Sherman did.

Hood's reasoning was somewhat glib: if he moved from northern Alabama to southeastern Georgia his men would think he was in retreat, and because of their low morale (which Hood had been talking about for weeks) the army would probably come apart. The only hope was to march north. If Hood could not reach the Ohio he could at least get into western Tennessee, and if he did this smartly he could defeat Thomas and capture Nashville. This surely would call Sherman back, and if it did not Hood could turn eastward, march to Virginia, and help Lee defeat Grant.[2]

This was the strategy of despair, verging on the wholly fantastic, based on the belief that the way to counter Sherman's thrust into the deepest South was to march off in the opposite direction. Hood discussed the move with his new superior, General Beauregard, who had been given the same kind of supervision over western operations that Joe Johnston had found so impractical two years earlier. Beauregard gave reluctant approval, feeling that the plan might work if it were executed immediately. He specified that Joe Wheeler and his cavalry must be sent down to oppose Sherman—a move that did Sherman no harm but that helped Hood substantially, because to take Wheeler's place on the march of invasion Hood got Forrest.

Unfortunately the speedy action Beauregard demanded was not forthcoming. The long spell of railroad-wrecking the Yankees had inflicted on the Alabama-Mississippi country made it hard to concentrate troops and collect supplies, and for some reason Hood was strangely irresolute. Beauregard kept prodding him, but not until November 21 did Hood begin to move. It was too late now, or nearly so. Sherman had already gone beyond the reach of anything Hood might conceivably do in Tennessee, and Pap Thomas had been given the extra days he needed.

Thomas would be safe enough if he could have a little time. He had a field army of 22,000 infantry and 7700 cavalry, which had not yet been assembled in one place. Grant had ordered General A. J. Smith to bring 10,000 veterans over from Missouri, but Smith was delayed by Price's raid and his men had not yet arrived. Thomas also had 27,000 soldiers in permanent garrisons, but this figure was deceptive. It included 16,000 infantry, much of it wholly untrained, 3000 gunners manning heavy artillery in fixed forts, and more than 8000 dismounted cavalry which properly considered itself useless, and these men were scattered all over the state guarding bridges and supply depots. To make an army out of all of these elements was going to take time; with more than 35,000 seasoned combat soldiers ready to go, Hood had an immediate advantage if he used it immediately. If he did not he must face the old, insoluble problem of trying to make an offensive campaign against an enemy who greatly outnumbered him.[3]

When he finally moved, Hood moved fast, and he almost began with a smart victory. The Federal General Schofield was Thomas' outpost; he had 23,000 infantry and 5000 cavalry at Columbia, 40-odd miles south of Nashville on the Duck River, squarely in Hood's path, and he intended to impose delay. Hood marched up to his front, studied the situation, deftly moved upstream, crossed the river far beyond Schofield's left, and by the afternoon of November 29 had his army in position at Spring Hill, ten miles in Schofield's rear. By everything in the books, Hood now had a winning advantage. Schofield had to retreat, his escape route ran right past Hood's front, and one hard blow might obliterate him. The oddest tactical mystery of the war lies in the fact that Hood, a hard hitter if nothing else, was unable to strike him.

Hood had set the stage skillfully. His troops were in a winning position, he issued the proper orders, the Confederacy's last chance for a significant victory was bright on the skyline—and all Hood got out of it was some brisk but unproductive fighting and an unending controversy. From early afternoon until long after midnight the Federals marched the length of the Confederate battle line, within gunshot, and although they had to fight to hold the road their way was never blocked, as it could have been. Inexplicably, Hood's army did not make a serious attack. Hood blamed his generals, they blamed him, and all anyone knew for certain was that Schofield escaped. By morning the chance was gone, and Hood wrote bitterly: "The best move in my career as a soldier I was thus destined to behold come to naught."[4] Wherever the fault lay, the command system in his army had failed dismally.

By noon of the next day, November 30, Schofield's army reached Franklin, on the Harpeth River, a dozen miles to the north. Finding no pontoons to make a crossing, Schofield entrenched his men at the top of a long rise on the south side of the river, put details to work building temporary bridges, made preparations to continue the retreat and waited for his opponents to come up.

They came up fast, driven by Hood's fury, and when Hood saw the Federal battle line he ordered an immediate assault: a wild, reckless order, born of anger over the failure at Spring Hill. With Forrest to lead the march, Hood could have repeated the flanking maneuver that had eased Schofield out of the way earlier. As an alternative, if he had simply waited a few hours the Federals would have been gone: Schofield was in telegraphic communication with Thomas and learned that he could retire to Nashville, eighteen miles away, whenever his trains were safe, and he was prepared to leave Franklin that evening.[5] In addition, the Federal position here was as powerful as the one Meade held at Gettysburg against Pickett, and to attack it was to invite

a repetition of Pickett's fate. But Hood had a score to settle—
with the Yankees, with his own men, probably with himself
—and so he lined his men up in a broad front and sent them
straight on to the Federal line.

The field was a long treeless slope, with tough westerners
dug in at the crest, taking everything in over the sights of
their rifles, quietly waiting; and two miles away 20,000 soldiers as good as any in the country dressed their ranks, took
a last speculative look to right and left, and marched up
under the cold autumn sun. For months their commander
had complained that they were too defensive-minded to fight
out in the open, and now they were in the open for General
Hood to see. They made their charge, reached and briefly
cracked the Yankee line, got into desperate hand-to-hand
fighting in back yards and gardens around a big cotton-gin
house, were driven off by a shattering counterattack—and at
last had to give it up, after they had done all that any soldiers could have done and more than any ought to have been
asked to do; a survivor wrote that "the enemy's line was
crossed in one or two places, but no man who went over was
ever known to return." In fighting that began late in the afternoon and lasted until after dark, nearly 6500 Confederates
were lost, among them twelve general officers. One of the
dead was General Pat Cleburne, who tried to talk Hood out
of this attack and went into action remarking: "If we are
to die, let us die like men." Another general killed was a
South Carolina brigadier named States Rights Gist. In the
fall of 1860 he had gone across the cotton belt as an emissary from his state, trying to concert united action in the
face of a Black Republican's election; his mission ending now
in a Federal trench.[6]

The fighting continued far into the evening, but the Federal position was unshaken. Hood's army was half-wrecked,
and for whatever it was worth to him General Hood had
learned that his men still had the heart to fight. During the
night Schofield got his men out of their trenches and went
on back to Nashville, and Hood's shattered army followed,
to take position on the hills a few miles south of that city
and await further developments.

There was nothing much to wait for except disaster, because by now Hood was strategically bankrupt. He was far
too weak to storm Thomas' lines: Nashville was the most

strongly fortified city in America, A. J. Smith and his troops were on hand, and Thomas was building up an army that would soon number 55,000 men or more, most of them veterans who had learned their way around many battlefields. To swing out past this host and head for the Ohio was a vain dream, to sidestep and march for Virginia was equally vain, and to turn about and go back south would be to confess total defeat; and so the Confederates waited, expecting nothing, while Thomas methodically got ready to hit them. And that was how things were on December 6 when Abraham Lincoln assured the Congress that even with Sherman off in the darkness the Federal power now was strong enough "to confront and hold in check every active force of the enemy."

If this was true, as it unquestionably was, the war was about to be won, and Mr. Lincoln was looking to the future, which was still plastic. Americans at that moment had a strange, terrifying power. Not only could they shape the future; they had conquered time, so that what they did now could send the future's meaning backward, putting significance into the insensate killings that ran from Franklin all the way back to Shiloh and Bull Run. Out of pain and horror already endured they could light a beacon fire. Mr. Lincoln invited the Congress to adopt and submit to the states a constitutional amendment that would outlaw slavery forever.

Here was the final step. The President had come to it slowly, with many heart-searchings. When the war began he had endorsed a statement of war aims confessing that the peculiar institution was not to be touched, and when he proclaimed emancipation he did it hesitantly, freeing slaves only partially and where the invocation of freedom looked convenient to those who had never worn chains. Even now, two years after the Emancipation Proclamation, most of America's slaves were still slaves by any law anyone could call to mind. Only the amendment would strike off all the chains, and it was the amendment that the President was demanding now.

He had been groping his way to this point all along. The light to guide his feet had been there from the first, but it had been hard to know when to follow it. In the faraway winter of 1861, when he was on his way to Washington to become

President of a dissolving Union, he had spoken broodingly to the New Jersey Senate about the meaning of an earlier revolution. It always seemed to him (he said then) that George Washington's army at Trenton had been struggling "for something more than common . . . something that held out a great promise to all the people of the world, to all time to come." He had gone on to say that he hoped himself to become an instrument in the hands of the Almighty "and of this, His almost chosen people, for perpetuating the object of that great struggle."[7] Now the instrument was ready to act, offering opportunity to the almost chosen people who had paid a terrible price to reach this moment.

This was fair enough; but Mr. Lincoln faced a problem in arithmetic. The Congress he was talking to had been elected in the fall of 1862, when many Republicans were defeated. In the spring of 1864 the amendment had passed the Senate, but the House of Representatives had turned it down. (Actually, the House had approved the bill by 93 votes against 65, with 23 absent or not voting; but this was not enough because a resolution sending a constitutional amendment to the states needed a two-thirds majority.) The same House would handle it now, and the case was unchanged . . . except that the war was visibly nearing its end, Mr. Lincoln had won re-election, and things began to look different. The President was going to try it.

He might have waited. In 1865 there would be a new Congress, elected in the Republican landslide of 1864, and the lower House then would unquestionably have a two-thirds majority for the 13th Amendment. But Mr. Lincoln refused to wait. Under the idealism that had seen something more than common beyond the blood-stained snows at Trenton he had the objective eye of a tactician, and he saw the amendment now as he had seen the Emancipation Proclamation: as a means to help win the war. Rightly or wrongly, he believed that with the destruction of slavery written into the Federal constitution—and, most particularly, written in with the support of the slave-holding border states that had never left the Union—the South would realize that it was useless to prolong a losing fight in the hope of winning some slavery-saving concession. He made this clear when he wrote to Congressman James S. Rollins of Missouri, urging him to support the amendment: "This is my chief hope and main

reliance to bring the war to a speedy close. . . . The passage
of this amendment will clinch the whole subject; it will bring
the war, I have no doubt, rapidly to a close."[8]

As a matter of practical fact this tactical stroke was not
really needed. The war was indeed moving rapidly to a close,
not because of anything Congress did but because of things
done by the soldiers commanded by General Thomas and
General Sherman, and this was obvious long before the
amendment came to a vote.

On December 15, a fortnight after Hood had appeared in
front of Nashville, Thomas completed his preparations,
marched out of the city, and struck Hood's army with overwhelming force. Hood retreated a few miles, drew a new
line, tried to make a fresh stand, and was struck again on
the next day, and this time his army was completely routed.
It went streaming south to the Tennessee River and beyond,
hopelessly beaten, saved from total destruction only by Forrest's skillful handling of the rear guard. It reassembled, at
last, far down in Tupelo, Mississippi, out of the war. Hood
was relieved of his command, and although some of his soldiers were used later in other fields this army was no longer
a factor in anybody's calculations. Thomas had won one of
the decisive victories of the entire war.

It seems strange, but the one man who had really worried
about Hood was the soldier who ordinarily did not worry
about anything: Ulysses S. Grant.

The fortnight Hood spent facing Thomas at Nashville was
the only time when Grant's nerves got the better of him.
Grant apparently overestimated both Hood's numbers and the
strategic possibilities open to him. He also felt that Thomas,
the solid rock of defensive fighting, might not move smartly
enough to meet this threat and he entirely ignored the fact
that a December ice storm made it impossible for Thomas
to move at all for a few days. In a most uncharacteristic way
Grant became obsessed briefly with the thought of the calamity that would come if Hood by some mischance got away
and made that march to the Ohio. He harassed Thomas with
demands for immediate action; signed an order relieving
the man in favor of Schofield; suspended the order before it
was sent, then ordered John A. Logan west to take charge—
and, at last, made up his mind to go to Nashville himself
and take personal command. Logan had got as far as Louis-

ville and Grant had reached Washington when news of Thomas' sweeping victory arrived. Logan came back east, and Grant sent Thomas his congratulations and returned to his own lines in front of Petersburg. This one time, if never before or afterward, General Grant had had the jitters.[9]

While the welcome news from Nashville was still being digested, Sherman came up out of the darkness and captured Savannah. He had marched 60,000 men through the heart of the South, leaving a blackened desolation behind him and proving once and for all that the final hours were arriving. His march had been practically unopposed. The Confederacy had been able to send some most distinguished generals to Georgia—Beauregard, Bragg, Hardee, enough top brass for a host—but in this hour of supreme crisis it could not provide enough enlisted men to make an effective fight. Sherman went where he pleased and did what he pleased because the Confederacy simply was not strong enough to stop him. His march to the sea was not so much a military campaign as a convincing demonstration of the Federal power to smash things.

That power was used relentlessly. Sherman began by burning Atlanta, and when his army moved out the XX Corps was rear guard; it marched through smoke clouds, with bands playing, the soldiers singing "John Brown's Body." The army went down to the sea like a prairie fire forty miles wide, living on the supplies it took from plantation barns and smokehouses and pantries, looting where it did not burn, making war with the lid off as if the whole business had come down to a wild Halloween brawl. What the regular foraging parties did not take was seized by a swarm of uncontrolled stragglers, and what these men missed was often enough despoiled by Confederate deserters and by casuals from Wheeler's cavalry, and all in all the rich Georgia farming country got a heavy scar. One of Slocum's New Yorkers confessed that "we had a gay old campaign," and he defined it thus: "Destroyed all we could not eat, stole their niggers, burned their cotton & gins, spilled their sorghum, burned & twisted their R. Roads and raised Hell generally." A Confederate officer estimated that at least 10,000 slaves ran away to follow the army, and said that hundreds of these died of hunger, disease, or exposure along the way; he added that the Federals killed so many cattle, hogs, mules, and horses that "the whole re-

gion stunk with putrefying carcasses, and earth and air were
filled with innumerable turkey buzzards battening upon their
thickly strewn death feasts." Sherman himself wrote that his
army had inflicted $100,000,000 worth of damage. Of this,
he said, about one fifth "inured to our advantage" while "the
remainder is simple waste and destruction."[10]

The army came up to Savannah in mid-December. It
stormed Fort McAllister, on the Ogeechee River, thus getting in touch with the Federal fleet and establishing a secure
supply line, and Sherman occupied the land approaches and
prepared to capture the city. He was careless, so that General
Hardee and the 10,000 Confederates who held the place
found an opening and slipped out, escaping into South Carolina, but Sherman was unabashed; he wanted Savannah as
a place where he could rest and refit and prepare for a new
campaign, and he seems to have cared very little what happened to Hardee. He marched into the city, his troops suddenly stopped looting and went on their good behavior,
and on December 22 Sherman sent a jaunty telegram to
President Lincoln announcing that he was presenting him
with the city of Savannah as a Christmas gift. From Savannah, in due time, his army could go anywhere—clear across
the Carolinas to Richmond, if Grant wanted it that way—
and the fact was clear to the blindest. In Richmond the Assistant Secretary of War, John A. Campbell, wrote to his
former colleague, Justice Samuel Nelson of the United States
Supreme Court, offering to confer about means of ending the
war; to a friend Campbell confessed that "it will all end in
reconstruction and that the only question now is the manner
of it."[11]

For a climax, the Federals captured Fort Fisher. This fort,
at the mouth of the Cape Fear River, protected Wilmington,
North Carolina, the last haven for blockade runners, and
General Lee had written that he could not subsist his army
if Fort Fisher fell. The Federals had tried to take the place
in December with a fleet under Rear Admiral Porter and
an army under Ben Butler, but the venture failed wretchedly
when Butler, having landed his troops, concluded that the
fort was too strong to be taken, re-embarked his men, and
sailed back to Hampton Roads. . . . Butler had pressed his
luck too far, at last. The presidential election was over, he
no longer had to be handled with tongs, and after Porter

told Grant that the fort could be taken any time a real soldier was sent down to take it, Butler was relieved of his command and sent home so that his singular blend of arrogance and military incompetence could no longer hamper the war effort. On January 12 a new expedition came down —Porter's fleet again, and an 8000-man army under General A. H. Terry—and now things went differently. The fleet bombarded the fort for two days, Terry got his men ashore and made ready to assault, on January 15 the fort's land face was carried by storm, and that night Fort Fisher was surrendered. The Anaconda coil dreamed of so long ago by old Winfield Scott was complete now, and the four-year blockade had become airtight, save for minor leakage caused by the corrupting Yankee lust for cotton. The Confederacy was finally isolated.[12]

Matters stood so while the House of Representatives debated the 13th Amendment, and the argument that this act was needed in order to bring the war to a close began to look very thin. The war was being won anyway, at an accelerating rate as all men could see, and the Congress was really debating a consequence of victory rather than a probable cause of it. To kill slavery now was to prepare to step out of the war and enter the future, and although passage of the amendment would not exactly define that future it unquestionably would make a new definition inevitable: would mean, in short, that the future would be totally unlike the past. Essentially, the question before the House and the nation was simply: Having won this victory, what are you going to do with it?

Montgomery Blair tried in vain to get Barlow to line up Democrats in support of the amendment. He spoke from the same platform he had been using a year earlier—give up slavery in order to save the master race—and he pleaded that to speed the amendment to passage "would obviously be to reconstruct parties on the Negro question, as contra-distinguished from the slave question." If this could be done, the radicals could be beaten forever: "It is not slavery or independence which the South is fighting for. They are fighting against 'Negro equality'—I speak of the fighting men, not the Snobbery. If the northern Democracy could now be rallied to the support of the President and ignore the slavery question, we can soon bring back the South."

Less subtle—if indeed Blair's argument had any especial subtlety—was the argument made on the floor of the House by the New York Democrat Fernando Wood. He had been mayor of New York in 1861 and when one after another the Southern states announced that they were leaving the Union he proposed that New York City should somehow detach itself and maintain a happy and profitable neutrality; which led Mr. Lincoln to remark that he had never before heard of the front porch trying to set up in business for itself. Now former Mayor Wood had a timeless word of warning that would echo down the years from his own particular tower of darkness: "We may amend the constitution; we may by superior military force overrun and conquer the South; we may lay waste their lands and destroy their property; we may free their slaves. But there is one thing we cannot do: we cannot violate with impunity or alter the laws of God. The Almighty has fixed the distinction of the races; the Almighty has made the black man inferior, and sir, by no legislation, no partisan success, by no revolution, by no military power, can you wipe out this distinction. You may make the black man free, but when you have done that what have you done?"[13]

The search for an answer might take many generations, but the vote itself could not be delayed. On the afternoon of January 31, before a crowded House and packed galleries, the hours of argument came to a close, and in a tense quiet the voice of Speaker Schuyler Colfax put the question: "Shall the Joint Resolution pass?" The clerk called the roll; it was found that ten Democrats had joined the Republicans in support of the amendment, and that eight other Democrats (who presumably would have opposed the measure) had found it convenient to be absent; and in short the amendment passed the House, by 119 votes to 56. As the total was announced there was a moment of dazed silence, then a wild explosion of cheers "the like of which" (said a slightly partisan reporter) "probably no Congress of the United States ever heard before." In all of the jubilation hardly anyone recalled that only four years had passed since the Congress passed, and Abraham Lincoln accepted, a proposed amendment specifying that the Constitution could never, in all time, be changed in such a way as to permit interference with the institution of slavery.[14]

3. Too Late

GENERAL SHERMAN intended to start north from Savannah by
the middle of January, but heavy rains delayed him. They
came down day after cold gray day, unbroken, so that the
Savannah River finally went over its banks and became three
miles wide where General Slocum had put a pontoon bridge.
The bridge tugged at its moorings in mid-stream isolation,
and it had to be spliced at each end with long trestle works
before any soldiers could walk on it. Beyond, the South
Carolina low country turned into an immense swamp and
the Confederate authorities considered it impossible for the
Yankees to make a campaign now. This seemed reasonable:
as a sample of the problems, the Salkehatchie River at Buford's Bridge was so swollen that it offered fifteen separate
channels, all of which must be bridged before an army could
get across. Sherman had put some units in motion early in
January, but he confessed that in the end "the real march
began on the first of February."[1] Then his 60,000 veterans
went tramping and splashing up into South Carolina to begin
the climactic campaign of the war, heading north and expressing a desire to get even with the state that had started all
of this trouble.

Two days later, Abraham Lincoln and Secretary Seward
sat down in the cabin of a steamboat at Hampton Roads to
discuss terms of peace with three representatives of the Confederate government.

This conference was taking place for a number of reasons. For one, the hour after all was getting late; for another, old Francis P. Blair was a great busybody; for still
another, possibly most important of all, General U. S. Grant
felt that if the Confederates really wanted to talk peace somebody at the highest level ought to come down and listen.

Peace feelers had been put out many times in the past
year. None had brought any results, because each side used
them chiefly to show that its opponent was so unyielding that
negotiations would be pointless. This, as it happened, was
about the case. Mr. Lincoln would talk peace only if reunion
and emancipation were accepted, and Mr. Davis would talk
peace only if Confederate independence were accepted, and

no one had ever been able to think of a bridge that would cross that kind of gap.

No one, that is, except the elder Blair, who had his family's ability to believe that a Blair could do anything. Bearing a pass from President Lincoln, Blair went to Richmond at the end of 1864 and early in January he had two long chats with President Davis, whom he had known in the old days. It seemed that he had come all this way to propose that North and South should stop fighting each other and join hands to drive the French out of Mexico; Blair felt that this would restore the Monroe Doctrine and create a fraternal feeling under which reunion might take place. Mr. Davis was not drawn by this gambit, but he reflected that what Blair said was much less important than the fact that he had been allowed to come to Richmond to say it; he would not be here if the Lincoln administration did not have some sort of desire to talk peace. So Mr. Davis named Vice-President Stephens, Assistant Secretary of War Campbell, and Senator R. M. T. Hunter commissioners to discuss peace terms, and at the end of January these three crossed the lines under flag of truce and presented themselves at the headquarters of General Grant.

It seemed unlikely that they would get any farther. Their written instructions told them to seek peace between "the two countries," and Mr. Lincoln would negotiate on no such basis. But Grant knew how bad the Confederacy's military situation was, and he sensed that this move meant business. (After all, Mr. Davis had appointed moderates, not bitter-enders, and this could hardly be accidental.) Grant talked with Senator Hunter and with Vice-President Stephens (whom Grant, as an old Douglas Democrat, had long admired from afar) and he became convinced that they were ready to accept reunion. So the general sent a rather diffident telegraph to Washington, saying that these men were sincere, that it would be too bad to dismiss them without a hearing, and that while he himself did not know what to recommend he did wish Mr. Lincoln would at least talk with them.

. . . Once before Mr. Lincoln had received political advice from a general who faced Lee's army along the James River. In the summer of 1862 McClellan, fresh from the disaster of the Seven Days, wrote a long letter explaining that only by following a thoroughly conservative course with respect to slavery could the North hope to win the war; Mr. Lincoln thanked him, pocketed the letter, and went his way as if the letter had never been written. Now there was this advice from Grant, the tone of it slightly different, received by a President who had just seen the 13th Amendment through the Congress; and it got an immediate response. Back to Grant came a telegram from the President: SAY TO THE GENTLEMEN THAT I WILL MEET THEM PERSONALLY AT FORTRESS MONROE AS SOON AS I CAN GET THERE. And the next morning the Confederate commissioners had their talk with the President of the United States.[2]

Unfortunately, when the commissioners talked they did not say much, possibly because they were in a state of shock. They had been expecting from this meeting much more than they had the remotest chance to get, and when this was made clear to them they were outraged. They seem to have anticipated the sort of give-and-take negotiations that come when two parties talk from positions of relatively equal strength—a concession here met by a concession there, each side receding bit by bit from its announced position until at last there is a suitable compromise halfway between extremes—and the first thing they learned was that this was not that kind of meeting. The parties here were not talking from positions of equal strength: one of them was talking from the edge of extinction, and it had almost no bargaining strength at all. The conference had been called a trifle too late.

Indignantly, Senator Hunter wrote that the Northern President "distinctly affirmed that he would not treat except on the basis of reunion and the abolition of slavery," and after the war the Senator voiced his protest: "Neither Lincoln nor Seward showed any wise or considerate regard for the whole country, or any desire to make the war as little disastrous to the whole country as possible. If they entertained any such desires they made no exhibition. Their whole object seemed to be to force a reunion and an abolition of slavery. If this could be done they seemed to feel little care for the distress and suffering of the beaten party." Vice-President Stephens picked up Blair's idea and proposed an armistice so that the French could be expelled from Mexico, but Mr. Lincoln made it clear there would be no armistice under any circumstances, and Stephens noted that "the only

basis on which he would entertain a proposition for a settlement was the recognition and re-establishment of the National authority throughout the land."[3]

Senator Hunter's indignation was natural but illogical. The
whole object of the war, as far as the Northern government
was concerned, was indeed precisely what the Senator said
it was—to force a reunion and the abolition of slavery—
and by this time it was as certain as anything could be that
this object would speedily be won no matter what anybody
said at Hampton Roads. To suppose that the President would
abandon his objective just when he was finally winning it was
to take a long flight from reality. The result was tragic, because the commissioners tried so hard to get the President
to yield points on which he was bound to be unyielding that
they neglected to bring up subsidiary points on which he was
prepared to be flexible. That they might conceivably have won
concessions that would make the time of defeat "as little disastrous to the whole country as possible" seems not to have
occurred to them, except for the suggestion that an armistice
and a joint war against the French might somehow lead to
reconstruction, as Justice Campbell remarked, or at least to
a harmonious and intimate alliance between two independent
nations, as Senator Hunter proposed. In the end the conference ended with no agreement on anything, and Senator
Hunter offered a gloomy summary: as far as he could see
there could be no treaty between the Confederacy and the
United States, and "there was nothing left for them but unconditional submission."[4]

So the conference closed, and the commissioners went
back to Richmond. Mr. Lincoln stopped off to visit General
Grant, and gave him an account which Grant summarized
in these words: "He spoke of his having met the commissioners, and said he had told them that there would be no use
in entering into any negotiations unless they would recognize, first; that the Union as a whole must be forever preserved, and second; that slavery must be abolished. If they
were willing to concede these two points, then he was ready
to enter into negotiations and was almost willing to hand
them a blank sheet of paper with his signature attached for
them to fill in the terms on which they were willing to live
with us in the Union and be one people." In more guarded
terms, the President told the Congress that the Confederate

commissioners did not say that, "in any event, or on any condition, they *ever* would consent to reunion, and they equally omitted to declare that they *never* would so consent. They seemed to desire a postponement of that question and the adoption of some other course first, which, as some of them seemed to argue, might, or might not, lead to reunion, but which course we thought would amount to an indefinite postponement." Secretary Seward told Mrs. Seward that "the condition of the South is pitiable, but it is not yet fully realized there."[5]

The Confederate commissioners missed something. Mr. Lincoln was ready to make concessions; some time later he told Justice Campbell that "it seems useless for me to be more specific with those who will not say that they are ready for the indispensable terms even on conditions to be named by themselves"—a fair indication that he meant what he told General Grant.

Insisting on emancipation, for instance, he nevertheless thought that the Federal government should ease the economic shock by appropriating at least $400,000,000 to pay for the loss of property in slaves. He wanted civil government in the occupied Southern states restored as quickly as possible and he was willing under certain conditions to see the former Confederate legislatures used in this connection. Agreeing that Congress could accept or reject any Senators or Congressmen the Southern states might select, he insisted that the recognition of state governments was strictly a matter for the executive and that Congress properly had no control over it. Secretary Welles paraphrased the President's general attitude in these sentences: "We must extinguish our resentments if we expected harmony and union. There was too much of a desire on the part of some of our very good friends to interfere and dictate to those states—too little respect for their rights. He did not sympathize with that feeling." Mr. Lincoln hoped, in short, that when the new Congress convened in the autumn it could be presented with a fully restored Union, with courts and local governments functioning, and if he was inflexible in the demand for reunion and emancipation he was ready to be highly flexible on the details by which these would be made effective.[6]

All of this, to be sure, would have involved Mr. Lincoln in a hard struggle with his cabinet and with the Republican leadership. Two days after the Hampton Roads conference he drafted a bill providing $400,000,000 compensation for the loss of slaves, only to drop it when he found the entire cabinet opposed to the idea, and it is generally assumed that he would have been beaten all along the line if he had ever embodied his ideas in a formal action program. But if he had been able to return to Washington with a concrete proposal —The war will end at once, with immediate dissolution of the Confederacy and full acceptance of reunion and emancipation, provided that we do this and this and this—he might have been able to carry the day. The Confederate commissioners had given him nothing to bargain with. As Secretary Seward remarked, they did not quite realize the South's true condition.

Or perhaps, recognizing it full well, they were simply caught up in the desperate emotional current of the war. If Mr. Lincoln seemed unyielding, Mr. Davis was granite itself. He could do anything but accept defeat. His government still lived, and it clung to life with all his own doggedness. Even the Confederate Congress, which nourished a good deal of hostility toward the President, accepted his view that simple survival was all that mattered now. By a supreme irony, this winter the Congress was wrestling with the last problem the Confederacy cared to attack—the matter of emancipation.

This grapple had been reached by indirection, but it was going on. A year earlier, General Pat Cleburne, dismayed by the increasing shortage of manpower, presented a paper to the general officers of the Army of Tennessee arguing that the nation ought to free some of its slaves and turn them into soldiers. A few of the generals had agreed with him, but most of them had been shocked and the whole matter had been hushed up lest it scandalize the faithful. Now Cleburne was in his grave, but his idea had a certain vitality and it came back to life in this final session of Congress.

For some time there had been a law empowering the Confederate government to requisition a limited number of slaves to do non-military work for the army—to dig trenches, build roads and bridges, drive wagons and in other ways release soldiers for combat duty. Many slaves had been used in this way but the government had never been able to get enough of them because the men who owned slaves were most reluctant to have them used in this way; so in Novem-

ber the administration brought in a stiff new bill by which
the army could get at least 40,000 Negro laborers. This, inevitably, made people think of what Cleburne had thought
about, and when he sent the measure to Congress Mr. Davis
touched on the subject: "Until our white population shall
prove insufficient for the armies we require and can afford
to keep in the field, to employ as a soldier the Negro . . .
would scarcely be deemed wise or advantageous. . . . But
should the alternative ever be presented of subjugation or
the employment of the slave as a soldier, there seems no reason to doubt what would then be our decision."[7] The alternative now was being presented with overpowering force,
and Congress found itself discussing a bill whereby a number of slaves would be taken out of bondage, put into uniform, and sent to the front to fight for the South.

The bill proposed that "in order to provide additional
forces to repel invasion, maintain the rightful possession of
the Confederate states, secure their independence and preserve their institutions, the President be, and he is hereby,
authorized to ask for and accept from the owners of slaves
the services of such number of able-bodied Negro men as
he may deem expedient, for and during the war, to perform
military service in whatever capacity he may direct." There
were qualifying clauses, carefully drawn. The consent of both
the slave and his owner must be obtained, nothing in the act
could "be construed to authorize a change in the relation
which the said slaves shall bear toward their owners, except
by the consent of the owners and of the states in which they
may reside," and officers were instructed to treat these new
soldiers kindly and with proper humanity. It was as mild as
anything could be . . . except that it did propose to turn
slaves into soldiers, it implied that they would not go back
to slavery after the war was over, and it opened a mile-wide
fissure in the monolithic slave nation that had been created
four years earlier.[8]

It was strong medicine, and it got a convulsive response.
Senator Louis Trezevant Wigfall of Texas, the burly duelist
who used to lounge about the Senate chamber in the capitol
building at Washington, taunting the impotent anti-slavery
Republicans, arose to say that it was time to determine
"whether this was to be a free Negro free country, or a free
white man's free country." To make the Negro a soldier was

just the first step toward emancipation, and when emancipation came what would become of the white man? It was being said that half of the army was absent from its duty, but the missing men would come back if the armies were led by men who inspired confidence; the evil of the times was incompetence in command, and to make soldiers out of slaves was not the remedy. Senator Wigfall would never consent to have the Southland turned into Santo Domingo.

Senator Hunter, late of the peace commission, took up the refrain. The Virginia legislature had instructed him to vote for this bill, and he believed a state legislature had a right to tell its Senators what to do, but he thought this project was utterly wrong and before he voted for it he was going to speak against it. He had supposed that secession had got rid of the slavery question forever, but here the question was back again, full-blown, more troublesome than ever before; if the government could arm the slaves it could also free them, and it would have to do this because "when they come out scarred from this conflict they must be free." He urged one and all to consider the error they were about to make: "If we are right in passing this measure we were wrong in denying to the old government the right to interfere with the institution of slavery and to emancipate slaves."[9]

From Georgia, Howell Cobb sent his protest: "Use all the Negroes you can get, for the purposes for which you need them"—that is, as hewers of wood and drawers of water—"but don't arm them. The day you make soldiers of them is the beginning of the end of the revolution. If slaves will make good soldiers our whole theory of slavery is wrong." Secretary of War Seddon, to be sure, favored the bill. He felt that although it would be better to "leave the subordinate labors of society to the Negro, and to impose the highest, as now existing, on the superior class," no Southerner should hesitate to use the Negro as a soldier because the Negro was even more vitally concerned than the Southern white man in repelling the Yankees. The friendship of a people "so selfish, cruel and remorseless as our foes" would be fatal to the poor colored man; Negroes would be faithful to the Southern cause because they had "the homes they value, the families they love and the masters they respect and depend on, to defend and protect against the savagery and devastation of the enemy."[10]

There was in short much writhing on a cruel hook, along with a belief in never-never land—the land in which better generals would revive the old volunteering spirit and in which the devoted slave would happily die to defend the plantation cabin and the master who had put him in it. But although Howell Cobb might be right in crying that this proposal went against fundamental Confederate theory, Mr. Davis refused to be doctrinaire. He spent much time trying to convert members of Congress, now and then growing heated. To one man, who seems to have followed Cobb's line, he burst out: "If the Confederacy falls, there should be written on its tombstone, 'Died of a theory.'" He was not at his best in these attempts to persuade individuals. Secretary Mallory, who said that no man was more pleasant, genial, or engaging than Mr. Davis when he was relaxed among friends, felt that the President's approach on these occasions was unfortunate. It was not in the man to "sacrifice a smile, an inflexion of the voice or a demonstration of attention to flatter the self-love of those who did not stand well in his esteem"—the problem here being that by the winter of 1864 few Congressmen did stand well in his esteem. When he tried to persuade recalcitrant lawmakers "he rarely satisfied or convinced them, simply because in his manner and language there was just an indescribable something which offended their self esteem and left their judgments room to find fault with him." Knowing as well as any man could know how desperate the Confederacy's situation was, Mr. Davis had no patience with men who were unwilling to adopt a desperate remedy.[11]

In the end, reluctantly and with profound misgivings, Congress did pass the bill; largely, when all is said and done, because the measure was wholeheartedly supported by Robert E. Lee, the one man whom patriotic Southerners were willing to follow blindfolded.

General Lee did not have to reverse himself when he subscribed to this bill. He had never been fighting for slavery; he had fought for the South, most especially for Virginia, and he had all of the born fighter's distaste for quitting a fight when he still was on his feet with a weapon in his hand. The most he ever said in favor of slavery was that the relation between master and slave, "controlled by humane laws and influenced by Christianity and an enlightened public sentiment," was probably the best that could be devised considering the present situation of the two races, and he confessed that he "would deprecate any sudden disturbance of that relation unless it be necessary to avert a greater calamity to both." It seemed to him now that it was most decidedly necessary, and in a letter designed for Congressional consumption he stated his position:

"We must decide whether slavery shall be extinguished by our enemies and the slaves be used against us, or use them ourselves at the risk of the effects which may be produced upon our social institutions. My own opinion is that we should employ them without delay. I believe that with proper regulations they can be made efficient soldiers."

They could be made into good soldiers, he continued, if they were convinced that they themselves had an interest in Confederate victory, and he went on to talk about this aspect of it: "Such an interest we can give our Negroes by giving immediate freedom to all who enlist, and freedom at the end of the war to the families of those who discharge their duties faithfully (whether they survive or not), together with the privilege of residing at the South. To this might be added a bounty for faithful service." This to be sure involved fundamental, far-reaching change, but General Lee was prepared to face it: "The reasons that induce me to recommend the employment of Negro troops at all render the effect of the measures I have suggested upon slavery immaterial, and in my opinion the best means of securing the efficiency and fidelity of this auxiliary force would be to accompany the measure with a well-digested plan of gradual and general emancipation. As that will be the result of the continuance of the war, and will certainly occur if the enemy succeed, it seems to me most advisable to adopt it at once, and thereby obtain all the benefits that will accrue to our cause."

Above all, the matter was urgent: "I can only say in conclusion that whatever measures are to be adopted should be adopted at once. Every day's delay increases the difficulty. Much time will be required to organize and discipline the men, and action may be deferred until it is too late."[12]

In a way, this quietly stated argument by General Lee was the most revolutionary of all of the proposals anyone put forward regarding the future of the Negro. Lee was not

merely suggesting that the Negro be freed: he was saying
in addition that once freed the Negro ought to be treated as
a Southerner.

. . . It was too late; or perhaps, considering the final implications of General Lee's remark, it was several generations
too early. Congress finally passed the act in March, when
the Confederate government had a scant month to live, and
a War Department official who considered the bill "a colossal
blunder, a dislocation of the foundations of society," correctly predicted that it would bring no practical benefits.[13]
The machinery to enroll, uniform, and drill Negro recruits
was set up, Lee saw to it that trusted General Richard
Ewell was put in charge of the operation, a company or two
of Negro recruits appeared briefly on the streets of Richmond
—and then the darkness came, and nobody ever found out
what would happen if Negroes tried to fight for their freedom
in Confederate gray.

4. None Shall Be Weary

INAUGURATION DAY in 1861 had seen riflemen alert in the
windows of the capitol, cavalry with drawn sabers riding
close to the presidential carriage, other troops posted in
side streets; the nation that installed its new President was
not sure that he would survive the day or that the nation itself
would survive his term of office, and it waited, all tense, to
hear what he had to say. Abraham Lincoln took the oath and
made a speech that was both an appeal for peace and a
challenge to the warlike. The appeal failed and the challenge was taken up, and in the war that followed more than
600,000 men lost their lives and a long era came to an end.
Now it was March 4, 1865—rainy, with deep mud in the
streets of Washington, and a huge bedraggled crowd waiting
in the open space east of the capitol—and there would be
another oath-taking and another speech.

As Mr. Lincoln pointed out, this was not the occasion
for a long address. The four years had delivered their own
terrible message, and interpretation must come later. Now
he could only say that men had done infinitely more than
they intended. They had made a war when they wanted
peace, the result had been more "fundamental and astound-

ing" than any had foreseen, and perhaps Northerners and Southerners alike had been instruments used by a power greater than themselves; now they must accept the result and go into the future with dedication and without hatred. The speech was well received, although the President did not think it would be immediately popular. As he told Thurlow Weed, "Men are not flattered by being shown that there has been a difference of purpose between the Almighty and them." If the last four years had shown nothing else, in all conscience they had at least shown that much.[1]

Inauguration Day had been oddly stage-managed. First, Vice-President Johnson took the oath in the Senate chamber. He had been most unwell, just before entering the chamber he took whiskey to fortify himself, the dosage was too heavy, and after he was sworn in he made clumsy, rambling remarks that were a five-day scandal. (The scandal faded after a while, when men came to realize that whatever other faults he might have Andrew Johnson was no drunkard.) Then, when Mr. Lincoln came on the platform in the open air to deliver his address, the drizzle stopped and the clouds parted, the sun shone down, and a bright star was visible in the blue sky near the sun. Lounging in the background not far from where the President stood was a pale, sardonic spectator, the young actor John Wilkes Booth.

The oath of office was administered by the Chief Justice of the United States, Salmon P. Chase—Chase, who tried so hard to put himself in Mr. Lincoln's place, who was dropped from the cabinet, and who after the election was nonetheless made Chief Justice: doing today what Taney had done four years earlier, his appearance as Taney's successor a visible sign that this was not the world of 1861. When the oath was given, Mr. Lincoln bent, as by ancient custom, and kissed the open pages of the Bible. Chase noted the precise spot the lips had touched, marked the place, and later gave the Bible to Mrs. Lincoln. The marked verses were the 27th and 28th verses of the fifth chapter of Isaiah:

"None shall be weary nor stumble among them; none shall slumber nor sleep; neither shall the girdle of their loins be loosed, nor the latchet of their shoes be broken;

"Whose arrows are sharp, and all their bows are bent, their horses' hoofs shall be counted like flint, their wheels like a whirlwind."[2]

The text was apt; Mr. Lincoln was most alert this spring to guard against weariness and stumbling, and he wanted his armies to keep driving. In January Secretary Stanton showed him a dispatch from Sherman, who planned to "get a good ready" before invading the Carolinas. Mr. Lincoln told Stanton that this was fine but that *"time, now that the enemy is wavering, is more important than ever before. Being on the down-hill, and somewhat confused, keep him going. Please say so much to General S."* Early in March the President wrote a stiff telegram which Stanton signed and sent to General Grant, who had just received from General Lee a note proposing a meeting to discuss "the possibility of arriving at a satisfactory adjustment of the present unhappy difficulties by means of a military convention." The wire Stanton signed was firm: THE PRESIDENT DIRECTS ME TO SAY TO YOU THAT HE WISHES YOU TO HAVE NO CONFERENCE WITH GENERAL LEE UNLESS IT BE FOR THE CAPITULATION OF GEN. LEE'S ARMY, OR ON SOME MINOR AND PURELY MILITARY MATTER. HE INSTRUCTS ME TO SAY THAT YOU ARE NOT TO DECIDE, DISCUSS OR CONFER UPON ANY POLITICAL QUESTION. SUCH QUESTIONS THE PRESIDENT HOLDS IN HIS OWN HANDS; AND WILL SUBMIT THEM TO NO MILITARY CONFERENCES OR CONVENTIONS. MEANWHILE YOU ARE TO PRESS TO THE UTMOST YOUR MILITARY ADVANTAGES.[3]

Get on with the war, in other words: and this Grant was doing. While Sherman was coming north from Savannah, Schofield and 20,000 of Thomas' veterans were brought east and sent down to North Carolina. After picking up General Terry and the men who had taken Fort Fisher, they occupied Wilmington and established a garrison there; then they moved up the coast to New Berne and started to march inland, preparing for an eventual meeting with Sherman at Goldsboro, one hundred miles from the coast and not much farther than that from Grant's lines at Petersburg. When he reached this point, Sherman would have a secure seacoast base, all of the supplies he could need, and a field army of more than 80,000 men for the final stage of his campaign.

Another part of Thomas' army, 16,000 men under General A. J. Smith, was sent to the Gulf Coast to join General E. R. S. Canby, who at last was moving against Mobile as Grant and Farragut had wished in 1863. On Smith's arrival, Canby would have a field army of 45,000 men, to operate against a foe who could hardly muster a fourth of that number. Grant wanted everybody to hurry, and Halleck late in February sent Canby a brief warning: "I hope your expedition will be off before this reaches you, for Genl Grant is very impatient at delays & too ponderous preparations. He says that nearly all our generals are too late in starting & carry too much with them."[4]

Thomas was getting his cavalry into action, not to raid but to cripple. Striking east through the Great Smokies came General George Stoneman with three brigades of troopers, aiming to disrupt Confederate supply and transportation arrangements in the area where Virginia, Tennessee, and North Carolina met, and to end the last chance that Lee could get any sort of help from the west. (Stoneman had led Hooker's cavalry unsuccessfully during the Chancellorsville campaign, and had gone into temporary eclipse; now, operating under a better general, he was a better cavalryman.) Meanwhile, Thomas' top cavalry commander, the youthful General James H. Wilson, was putting together the strongest mounted striking force seen in all the war—13,000 troopers armed with repeating carbines, trained to move as cavalry but to fight as infantry, carrying more fire power than the ordinary army corps; taking no part in the romantic cavalry tradition, using horses only because the man who rode to work could get there more quickly than the man who walked. Wilson was preparing to move down into Alabama, to destroy the important munitions center at Selma and then to occupy Montgomery, where Jefferson Davis once stood under the flags to meet the tragic hour.[5]

The Confederacy was being torn up by the roots, including the ones that went deepest. Charleston fell before Mr. Lincoln was sworn in for his second term. For four years it had been proof against bombarding fleets, storming parties and the long blockade, but it went down forever when Sherman's marching army tramped across its supply lines fifty miles inland. This drowsy, haunted, passionate city, where first the Democratic party and then the Federal Union had been gloriously broken amid a tossing foam of palmetto flags and brave cadets in shining gray-and-gold, surrendered without dramatics on February 18. Hardee's troops hastily marched away, on orders from Charleston's own Beauregard, with rear-guard patrols setting fire to warehouses, ammunition dumps, warships, and stacked cotton bales; then the mayor sent a deputation down to a wharf and formally turned the city over to a Yankee colonel, who had just come up the harbor in a transport's lifeboat. Presently the Federal fleet came steaming in, and the ugly grim ships that had been kept out so long anchored close to the Battery. That evening a Federal brigade marched through Charleston to go on provost guard duty. One regiment in this brigade was the 5th Massachusetts, colored troops, some of the men once held to service in this very city, going in proudly now with their forage caps held aloft on fixed bayonets, fife-and-drum corps playing "John Brown's Body."[6]

Sherman had been the cause of this, although neither he nor his soldiers got within many miles of Charleston. He was marching north without a pause, crossing the flooded low country as if it were dry land, corduroying roads and building bridges as he came; Joe Johnston, who had supposed nobody could make a campaign in that land in winter, remarked that there had been no army like Sherman's since the days of Julius Caesar. The army came up to Columbia, went into it (which was when Charleston had to be given up) and presently marched on again, leaving behind it the dying flames and charred timbers of a burned-out city; leaving behind, also, an unending argument about the responsibility for the fire. Sherman himself did not order Columbia burned, and he argued later that the city was destroyed because retreating Confederate cavalrymen set fire to much cotton and because a high wind made these flames uncontrollable. It is permissible, though difficult, to accept this explanation; but it is also necessary to realize that if the fire had not started so it would quickly have been started in some other way, because, as the capital of the first state to secede, Columbia was certain to go up in flames as soon as these soldiers reached it. One of Sherman's veterans came close to the truth when he wrote to his wife, not long after the army entered North Carolina: "The army burned everything it came near in the state of South Carolina, not under orders but in spite of orders. The men 'had it in' for the State, and they took it out in their own way. Our track through the state is a desert waste." Perhaps all that needs to be understood is that Columbia began to burn when Sherman's soldiers arrived, and stopped burning when they left. All their bows were bent, and their wheels were like a whirlwind.[7]

The one fixed point in a dissolving Confederate world was Lee's army, which held the lines around Petersburg and Richmond as it had been doing for nine months and more. The lines were longer now, and the army was smaller: with thirty-seven miles of works to hold, Lee by March had no more than 50,000 men at his disposal; the Federals in his immediate presence had more than 120,000, with reinforcements available in case of need. Day after day, in summer and autumn and winter, there had been firing along the battle lines, with a steady wastage of manpower. Visiting Grant at City Point, Abraham Lincoln got a distant glimpse of this, once, in March, when a furious cannonade broke out late at night. It was dark—"as dark as a rainy night without a moon could be," the President said—and the firing went on for two hours and more, the bright flashes from the guns lighting up the black underside of the heavy clouds. The President told Stanton: "It seemed to me a great battle, but the older hands here scarcely noticed it, and, sure enough, this morning it was found that very little had been done."[8] Little had been done—but men died under such cannonades, and for an army like Lee's, which found replacements almost impossible to get, the unending attrition was crippling.

Even worse, now, was the fact that so many men were losing heart. Late in February, Lee drew the War Department's attention to "the alarming number of desertions that are now occurring in this army," pointing out that in the last fortnight four hundred men had run away from two of A. P. Hill's famous divisions, with other men leaving other commands. During a nine-day period in March more than a thousand men disappeared from Longstreet's corps, and Lee made a bleak report: "The number is very large and gives rise to painful apprehensions. . . . I do not know what can be done to put a stop to it." General R. H. Anderson, a highly reliable corps commander, did not think anything could be done, and he explained later: "The depressed and destitute condition of the soldiers' families was one of the prime causes of desertion, but the chief and prevailing reason was a conviction among them that our cause was hopeless and that further sacrifices were useless." One of the stoutest fighting men in the army, General John B.

Gordon, remarked that "Everything was exhausted except devotion and valor." General John S. Preston, head of the Bureau of Conscription, who had reported that more than 100,000 deserters were scattered all over the Confederacy, asserted: "So common is the crime that it has, in popular estimation, lost the stigma that justly pertains to it, and therefore the criminals are everywhere shielded by their families and by the sympathies of many communities. They form the numerical majorities in many places."[9]

As spring came the net was drawn more tightly. Early in March, Phil Sheridan led 10,000 troopers up the Shenandoah, and at Waynesboro where the road from Staunton came east to tidewater he destroyed the meager army with which Jubal Early was maintaining a shadow of Confederate sovereignty west of the Blue Ridge. Almost all of Early's infantry had long since been called back to Lee's army, so that his total force amounted to no more than 2000 men; these were overwhelmed, half of them captured and the rest routed, and Early himself barely got away with fewer than a hundred men as the remnant of an army that had taken the war to the gates of Washington in the summer of 1864. Now the valley of Virginia was locked up, and Sheridan was coming east to join Grant, destroying railroads and the James River canal as he came. Upon his arrival, Grant would have a powerful mobile force to reach out around the right of Lee's entrenchments and strike at the last railroad lines that enabled Lee's army to stay alive.

Unable to increase Lee's resources, the Confederate government had at least increased his authority. After a long wrangle with Congress, Mr. Davis early in February named Lee general-in-chief of all Confederate armies. About all Lee was able to do with this new authority was bring Joe Johnston back into service; on February 22 he put Johnston in over-all command of Confederate forces in the Carolinas, hoping desperately that the jaunty little Game-Cock could somehow rally enough strength to beat Sherman before Schofield reached Goldsboro. Somewhat reluctantly, Johnston accepted. He explained later that "we could have no other object, in continuing the war, than to obtain fair terms of peace; for the Southern cause must have appeared hopeless then to all intelligent and dispassionate Southern men." He found that he could muster about 17,000 infantry and

6000 cavalry, counting the fragments that were coming in from Hood's army; even without Schofield, Sherman commanded 60,000 veterans. Johnston told Lee: "I can do no more than annoy him."[10]

Obviously, Richmond could not be held much longer. Lee could beat off any frontal assault, because the long defensive works were all but completely invulnerable; months earlier Grant had told Meade that under existing conditions of warfare "fortifications come near holding themselves without troops," and estimated that with plenty of artillery, and one infantryman to every six feet of trenches, "either party could hold their lines against a direct attack of the other." But a direct attack was not what the Confederates had to fear now, and Lee explained the problem in a note to Johnston. If he held his lines the Federals could cut the railroads, and Richmond would soon be starved into surrender; if he moved out to protect the railroads he must evacuate his trenches, and Richmond would fall at once. The only chance was to abandon everything, march down to join forces with Johnston somewhere in North Carolina, defeat Sherman with the united armies, and then turn to meet Grant. It was an extremely thin chance—considered soberly, it was next to no chance at all—but it would at least keep the armies alive for a time, and Lee told Mr. Davis that nothing else mattered now: "The greatest calamity that can befall us is the destruction of our armies. If they can be maintained we may recover from our reverses, but if lost we have no resource."[11]

It was easier to plan the move than to make it. Grant's left was solidly posted, miles southwest of Petersburg, and it probably would be impossible to slip past it for the march to North Carolina. The only hope was that a quick, hard blow at the Federal right might compel Grant to shorten his lines. It was of course useless to suppose that Grant's host could actually be driven off in defeat, after the old Chancellorsville pattern, but if he could be made to pull in his left the Army of Northern Virginia might have the room and time to make its escape. The problem of supplies for a moving army had been temporarily solved. Mr. Davis had at last removed the incompetent commissary general, Colonel Northrop, replacing him with General I. M. St. John, and this officer had been energetically piling up a surplus of meat and bread and forage from areas where Northrop had been able to find nothing. For a short time—time enough, probably, to fight one battle and make one long march—the army could have plenty to eat. And so, for the last time in the war, Lee ordered an attack.

He entrusted the attack to General Gordon and he gave him about half of the army. Gordon made a careful study and elected to strike at Fort Stedman, due east of Petersburg, a run-down box of a fort which a Federal engineer called "one of the weakest and most ill-constructed works of the line." A mile or two behind it was the military railroad that ran out from the Federal base at City Point to supply the long Federal line, and if this could be broken the whole Federal left would have to withdraw. Gordon made his plans, massed his troops, took the defense by surprise, and in the shadowed half-light of early morning on March 25 made his assault. His men swarmed across the picket lines, captured Fort Stedman, occupied several hundred yards of trenches on either side, drove on toward the Federal rear—and then ran into trouble. The Federals drew a new line, all of the artillery in the world seemed to be hammering at the assailants, there were hard counterattacks by fresh troops, the Federal left was wholly unshaken, and before the morning was half gone it was clear that the attack had failed. Lee ordered the surivors back into the Confederate lines; they returned, with a loss of 4000 men. A Virginia lieutenant, captured in the front wave of the assault, realized how badly his army had been overmatched when, on his way to the Federal rear, he saw that the Yankees were having a review, back of the combat zone, with General Grant and President Lincoln himself looking at parading troops "seemingly not in the least concerned and as if nothing had happened."[12]

Now the next move was up to Grant, and it was not long in coming. The day before Gordon attacked, in fact, Grant had issued his orders. He would build up a powerful force of infantry on his extreme left, somewhere in the neighborhood of Dinwiddie Courthouse, and he would put Sheridan's cavalry there as well, and as soon as the wretched unpaved roads were dry enough he would strike hard at Lee's right flank. If all went well he could break the flank, curl in behind the Confederate army and win everything in one swoop; if this failed he could at least send Sheridan ranging far into the rear, to cut the last railroads and then perhaps to ride on down cross-country and join Sherman, and if Lee thinned his skimpy lines in front of Petersburg to meet this threat Grant would attack his trenches regardless of their fabulous strength. Even if nothing worked as planned, this ought to pin Lee in position and keep him from going down to North Carolina. The big move was set for March 29.[13]

First, however, there was a top-level conference, held in the cabin of the steamer *River Queen*, which was tied up at City Point. This was the Presidential steamer, the floating White House where Abraham Lincoln was living for a few days while he escaped the plague of officeseekers in Washington and visited with General Grant. Strictly speaking, it was not really necessary for Mr. Lincoln to be here at all; Grant could be relied on to press the war to a conclusion without further prompting from the President. Apparently, with everything coming to a final climax, Mr. Lincoln just could not stay away.

The conference was highly informal—a long chat, rather than a council of war—and it brought together three men who had worked closely as a team but who had never before sat down together: President Lincoln, General Grant, and a lean, red-haired soldier who had made a hurried trip up from North Carolina, General Sherman. Sherman's army had at last reached Goldsboro and had been joined by Schofield, and while the troops drew new uniforms and fresh supplies Sherman had gone to the seacoast and had taken a fast steamer to this anchorage on the James River, drawn by the same magnet that had pulled the President. During four years of war, Abraham Lincoln had talked with many generals. This was probably the first time that he had talked with two in whom he had unlimited confidence and to whom he could speak his mind without reservation.

When Grant first came east, a year earlier, Mr. Lincoln found that he had not before seen a general quite like him. Now he was seeing another one who was unique; Sherman, grim, hard, full of proud talk about his ruthless "bummers" —he liked to say that his army was "dirty, ragged and saucy," stained by the smoke of many fires—confident that if Grant held Lee in Petersburg a little longer his own inexorable advance could come up and stamp out the last of secession. The President was happy to have the military situation explained, but he insisted that Sherman ought to get back to his army: in his absence something might go wrong. Sherman assured him that Schofield was perfectly competent to handle things, and said that his army could take care of itself no matter what happened, but the President was slightly uneasy, and brought the matter up several times. He also hoped that the war could be ended without another big battle, and over and over he asked: "Must more blood be shed?" The generals believed there must be at least one more big fight. As Sherman explained later: "We had to presume that General Lee was a real general, that he must see that Johnston alone was no barrier to my progress . . . that he would not await the inevitable conclusion but would make one more desperate effort." With this the President had to be content. He seemed relieved when Sherman said he would start back to North Carolina as soon as the conference ended; Admiral Porter had a fast steamer, all fueled, waiting for him.

Before he left, Sherman asked what was going to happen after the Confederate armies surrendered, and he learned more than the peace commissioners had learned, or had tried to learn, in the famous meeting at Hampton Roads.

The President wanted an easy peace, with no hangings and no reprisals: a real peace in which the shattered country could grow together again. He hinted broadly that he would be very well pleased if—"unbeknownst to me"—Jefferson Davis somehow managed to escape from the country, going to some foreign land where no scheme of vengeance could ever reach him. He hoped to see the disarmed Confederate soldiers going back to their homes, picking up the threads of life as peaceful citizens of a reunited nation, he looked for early re-establishment of civil government in the Southern states, and he made such an impression on Sherman that the general wrote afterward: "I know I left his presence with the conviction that he had in his mind, or that his cabinet had, some plan of settlement, ready for application the moment Lee and Johnston were defeated."[14]

The conference ended, Sherman went back to his army, Grant's troops began to move—and President Lincoln stayed where he was, to watch and to wait and to let his presence exert whatever influence it might have. He consulted Secretary Stanton by telegraph and was urged to remain with

Grant: THERE IS IN FACT NOTHING TO BE DONE HERE BUT
PETTY PRIVATE ENDS THAT YOU SHOULD NOT BE ANNOYED
WITH. A PAUSE BY THE ARMY NOW WOULD DO HARM; BUT IF
YOU ARE ON THE GROUND THERE WILL BE NO PAUSE.[15]

There was no pause. By the evening of March 29 Grant
had 50,000 men massed on his extreme left, behind a stream
called Hatcher's Run. Sheridan was a few miles to the
southwest at Dinwiddie Courthouse, with 10,000 cavalry; and
General Lee, getting wind of all of this, drew on his last
reserves to post General Pickett with 11,000 men at the
crossroads of Five Forks, half a dozen miles beyond the
Confederate right and an equal distance north of Sheridan.
Pickett's instructions were clear: "Hold Five Forks at all
hazards." To Mr. Davis, Lee reported that Grant's move
"seriously threatens our position and diminishes our ability
to maintain our present line." It was necessary, he said, to
prepare at once for a retreat from the James River.[16]

The case was clear. Except for the line to Richmond, the
Confederacy now controlled only one railroad out of Petersburg, the South Side line that ran west to the Tennessee border. Fifty miles out, at the junction town of Burkeville, this
line crossed the Richmond & Danville, Richmond's one remaining link with the South. Any supplies Lee's army or the
capital itself got had to come by these railroads; if Lee wanted
to go to North Carolina his only good course was to follow
the South Side line to Burkeville and then turn south. If the
Federals broke the South Side line, Lee could neither stay
in Petersburg nor join Johnston: he could only make a desperate retreat westward, hoping against hope that some
Federal error would enable him to slip south and keep his
army alive. As Lee told Pickett, this railroad had to be held
at all hazards.

There was a brief respite. Beginning on the night of March
29 there were thirty-six hours of heavy rain, putting every
creek over its banks and turning roads and fields into quag-
mires. Then, at last, on March 31, the skies cleared and the
Federals began to move, Sheridan edging up toward Five
Forks while Grant's left-flank force, the V Corps under
General Warren, attacked Lee's right. Neither move went
well that day. Pickett struck Sheridan and drove him back
to Dinwiddie; Warren's attack failed, and until late in the
afternoon he could do no more than hold his ground. Never-

theless, the Federal advantage was so great that minor reverses did not matter. Grant ordered Warren to move over and join Sheridan, and told Sheridan to take this infantry and his cavalry and go up to Five Forks and defeat Pickett. Other troops would side-slip to the left, to keep up the pressure along Hatcher's Run; meanwhile, everybody else would be alert, ready to assault Lee's center if there were any signs that he was weakening his entrenched line to reinforce his right.

April 1 was another day when things went wrong, and good generals in each army lost reputation because of it. To begin with, the orders Warren received were confusing, the obstacles in his way were worse than the high command supposed, and instead of reaching Sheridan at dawn he did not get his men to the scene until mid-afternoon. Sheridan met him in a fury of impatience, and when the infantry advance—made, at last, late in the day, with cavalry moving forward on the left—was slightly misdirected, and two of Warren's divisions lunged off into an area where there were no foes to fight, Sheridan removed Warren from command, sending him back to City Point in disgrace and turning his corps over to the senior division commander, General Charles Griffin. It was hard going for the soldier who had been the hero of Gettysburg, but there was no help for it. The President was at headquarters, Grant was insistent on fast action, and this was the day when nobody was allowed to stumble.

Pickett's fate was even more dismal. He put his men in light field works at Five Forks, and then—assuming that the Yankees would not attack today—he went to the rear with the cavalry leaders, Fitzhugh Lee and Thomas Rosser, to enjoy a pleasant shad bake. When Sheridan's attack finally came, Pickett did not even know that the battle had started (some acoustical quirk apparently kept the sound of the firing from reaching him) and by the time he got the news his line had been completely broken. Sheridan took 5000 prisoners, the survivors went streaming off beyond rallying, and Lee's last chance to keep the Federals away from the South Side railroad was gone beyond recall. Pickett's men unquestionably would have been beaten, even if Pickett had been present, because Sheridan's advantage was overwhelming, but Lee was unforgiving. It had been no day to go to a fish fry; a bad day, altogether, for Gettysburg heroes.[17]

Trying to bolster up his right, Lee had done what Grant supposed he might be compelled to do—he had drawn three brigades from the center of his line, already stretched thin past the point of safety. Late in the afternoon of April 1, Grant ordered an attack. Sometime after midnight there was a heavy bombardment, and then Meade sent his troops forward against the main Confederate position. Wright's VI Corps charged, lost 2000 men in a wild, confused early dawn assault where the Confederate trenches could be made out only by the flickering sputter of rifle-flashes along the parapet, broke through, and went triumphantly all the way to the edge of the Appomattox River. The long Petersburg campaign was over at last. Altogether, from the middle of June to the end of March, it had cost the two armies something like 75,000 casualties; this, finally, was the day of catastrophe. As the Federal patrols advanced toward the river they killed one more of Lee's legendary fighting men, the famous General A. P. Hill.

The most Lee could hope for now was to hold what was left of his position until night came and then make a desperate effort to get to Burkeville. He notified Richmond that the government must get out of the capital at once. Federal troops would enter the capital next day. Somehow, with the house coming down about his ears, Lee found time on April 2 to tell Mr. Davis that he was sending in the names of officers who were willing to help organize the new Negro troops.[18]

5. As in the Old Days

RICHMOND PEOPLE remembered how that last Sunday came in as a special sort of day. It was warm, with a mild breeze stirring the early blossoms on the capitol grounds; the city's churches were crowded, not because national affairs were at crisis but simply because it was a good day to go to church, with high spring in the air and Easter only two weeks away. One woman recalled it as "one of those unusually lovely days that the spring sometimes brings, when delicate silks that look too fine at other times seem just to suit." A Massa-

chusetts soldier out in the siege lines confessed that spring
reaches Virginia "with greater splendor" than New England
ever sees, and felt that there had not been a finer day than
this one since the creation. Secretary of the Navy Mallory
wrote that in all the war the city had never looked more
serene and quiet, and the woman who had put on her best
silk said that she never saw a calmer Sunday morning—or a
more thoroughly confused and alarming Sunday evening.[1]

The news from Petersburg came up shortly after the eleven
o'clock services had begun, and an aide with a telegram from
General Lee extracted President Davis from St. Paul's just
as Dr. Minnigerode intoned the words: "The Lord is in His
holy temple: let all the earth keep silence before Him." The
congregation took Mr. Davis' departure calmly enough—after
all, the President might get called out of church at any time,
by almost anything—but other dignitaries were called out
later, from this church and from others, and by early afternoon the tidings had gone all across the city: Lee was going
to retreat, the government was to move out tonight, the
Yankees would take over in the morning. Those who could
leave the city were comparatively few; for most people there
could be nothing now but a restless, fruitless stirring-about in
the face of approaching catastrophe.[2]

Richmond's fate was strange. Other cities, like Atlanta
and Columbia, were burned and sacked by their enemies;
Richmond was burned and sacked by her own people, and
when the hated conquerors at last entered they came in as
rescuers and protectors.

Ancient military protocol requires a retreating army to
burn the supplies it cannot carry off, lest they be of use to
the enemy. The army that had to leave Richmond now was
taking the shortest road to extinction and it was leaving behind nothing that the Yankees especially needed, but the old
ritual prevailed: possibly, for somebody, it eased the agony
of dissolution. President and cabinet, clerks and servants and
others of more or less consequence—all of these, amid much
confusion, much jostling and running about, and gabble of
frantic orders on gas-lit station platforms, got on the last
trains of the Richmond & Danville line and went south out of
Richmond. By midnight their exodus was over. Then the
Richmond defense troops began to come back through the
city, the men who had been holding the fortifications so long,

going across the James now to meet, as they hoped, General
Lee's troops from Petersburg somewhere on the road to
Burkeville. As they left, dutiful officers went about setting
fire to the rations and warehouses and warships and bridges
that could not be taken along, and when the last of the
cavalry patrols went out of the city Richmond was in flames,
with all of its defenders bound elsewhere.

When the sun came up on April 3 it was a red ball, shining
dully through heavy layers of smoke. In the murky streets
there were thousands of men and women, breaking into army
depots to get the bacon and flour and other things the army
could not carry away, following this before long by breaking into stores and residences to take anything else of value;
consuming barrels of whiskey that had not been dumped
in the gutters soon enough. There was no chance to control
the flames, and no chance to control the mob, which gleefully
disabled the few fire engines that appeared. Like all wartime
capitals, Richmond had drawn to itself much human refuse,
including, at an estimate that will do until someone makes a
better one, at least 5000 deserters from the now-absent armies.
Until today these had been kept under restraint, because
the city authorities could always call on the military; but now,
with calamity dawning, the military was gone, all restraint
had been removed, and the lawless had a field day. The day
was frightening enough even without them. Just after dawn
a new ironclad at the builders' dock, C.S.S. *Richmond*, blew
up with a noise like the sky cracking open; then a government arsenal took fire, and when the flames reached its
magazines the air was full of exploding shells, the crackle
of the spreading fire blended with the crackle of thousands of
rounds of small-arms ammunition, and a dense cloud of
black smoke hung over the center of the city.

Somewhere around eight in the morning the United States
Army came in—combat patrols, conquerors-on-parade and
life-saving fire brigades arriving all at once. First, scattered
cavalry details trotted into Capitol Square, with bright officers
running into public buildings to hoist flags; then came more
cavalry, followed by rank upon rank of infantry, whose bands
played "The Girl I Left Behind Me" and "Dixie." Smoke
from burning buildings lay across their shoulders, and the
looters went scurrying at last for cover. Presently there came
regiments of Negro soldiers, and men and women who had

been slaves until this moment ran out to greet them with hysterical cries, seeing the substance of things hoped for in these black men who wore Federal blue. (The officer in command of these occupation forces was General Godfrey Weitzel, the same man who two years earlier in New Orleans had told Ben Butler that no good would ever come of putting Negroes into the army uniform.) Some of the soldiers stood guard over homes and stores, and others stacked their arms and went to work to fight the fire, blowing up buildings that stood where the flames were going so as to make gaps the flames could not cross. Some time that night the city became comparatively quiet. Most of the fires were out, although smoldering ruins still sent wispy smoke into the April night. The streets were crowded, but the looting had been stopped, and Capitol Square was piled with bundles of things the Federal soldiers had taken away from marauders on the chance the proper owners could some day claim them.[3]

The next morning—Tuesday, April 4—Abraham Lincoln came to Richmond.

It was not really necessary for him to be here, and the way his visit was handled would have given a modern security officer the vapors. He came upstream in the *River Queen*, with Admiral Porter cruising just ahead in his flagship, U.S.S. *Malvern*, and the narrow river had not yet been swept clear of mines. Some distance below the landing, obstructions in the river kept the steamers from going farther, so Admiral Porter's 12-oared barge came alongside and President, Admiral, and three or four army and navy officers got in it and finished the trip that way. A tug carrying a guard of marines to escort the President through the city went astray en route, and when the party at last got ashore there were no guards except for ten sailors carrying carbines. For a mile and a half the President walked up the streets to the Confederate White House, where General Weitzel had his headquarters, his way obstructed by ecstatic crowds of colored people shouting "Glory, Glory, Glory!" and striving to get close enough to touch the hand or the garments of the man who was the embodiment of their freedom. Somehow the trip was made without mishap, and at last Abraham Lincoln sat down to rest in the office where Jefferson Davis had worked so long.[4]

Resting here, he presently had a caller; Justice John A.

Campbell, Assistant Secretary of War, last seen by Mr. Lincoln at the Hampton Roads conference. Campbell had not joined in the flight from Richmond, and he came now to urge the President to talk to the leading men of Virginia "as to the restoration of peace, civil order and the renewal of her relations as a member of the Union." This Mr. Lincoln was willing to do, although he was disappointed to learn that Campbell was present, not as an emissary of the government but simply as a private citizen anxious to make peace. (Somewhat bitterly, Campbell wrote later that the Confederate government seemed to have "a superstitious dread of any approach to the one important question of settlement by negotiation." Mr. Davis, he said, held that "his personal honor did not permit him to take any steps to make such a settlement," and as a result Campbell felt that "he became in the closing part of the war an incubus and a mischief.") In any case, Mr. Lincoln replied that his terms were as previously stated: no armistice, full restoration of national authority, and acceptance of emancipation. He gave Campbell a letter saying "If there be any who are ready for those indispensable terms, on any conditions whatever, let them say so and state their conditions, so that such conditions can be distinctly known and considered." After Justice Campbell left, Mr. Lincoln gave General Weitzel a specific order:

"It has been intimated to me that the gentlemen who have acted as the Legislature of Virginia, in support of the rebellion, may now desire to assemble at Richmond and take measures to withdraw the Virginia troops and other support from resistance to the General government. If they attempt it, give them permission and protection until, if at all, they attempt some action hostile to the United States, in which case you will notify them and give them reasonable time to leave; and at the end of which time, arrest any who remain. Allow Judge Campbell to see this, but do not make it public."[5]

Two days later Mr. Lincoln wrote to General Grant, telling him what was afoot and adding, "I do not think it very probable that anything will come of this." He had told Justice Campbell, he said, that "if the war be now further persisted in by the rebels" the rigors of the confiscation act would be applied, but that these penalties would be remitted "to the people of any state which will now promptly, and in good faith, withdraw its troops and other support from resistance to the government."[6] The case was intricate. He would make no treaty with the Confederate government, partly because he held that that government did not legally exist and partly because Mr. Davis showed no disposition to treat in any case. But he did want the war closed out quickly, and he was willing to make a temporary, limited use of "the gentlemen who had been acting as the Virginia legislature" if that would help. Perhaps it would be worth while to put one formal touch into a situation where all the ordinary formalities of peace-making were ruled out.

Justice Campbell was enthusiastic, and he may have read more into this than Mr. Lincoln meant to put there. Campbell agreed that the Federal government had the South in its grip, but he believed that the Southern spirit had not been broken and that "a prolonged and embarrassing war might still be continued." To use the state legislatures might bring something resembling treaties of peace; he had been assured that the North Carolina legislature was ready to act, and in the President's highly qualified proposal he appears to have seen a readiness to deal with a state legislature to settle all differences between the state and the United States. The President had suggested an expedient for a limited end, and Justice Campbell was looking for a pattern that would be applied everywhere to bring "a speedy and effectual pacification of the country."[7]

Mr. Lincoln's suspicion that nothing would come of this was quickly borne out, largely because the collapse of the Confederacy was proceeding so rapidly that negotiators could not catch up with it. He had hoped that certain Virginia gentlemen would remove Virginia's troops from the Confederate army, but before these gentlemen could do anything about it Grant and Lee settled the matter forever. On Palm Sunday, April 9, Lee surrendered the Army of Northern Virginia at Appomattox Courthouse.

Lee's attempt to take his army south for further battles was never much more than a flight from the inevitable. The defeat at Five Forks compelled him to make a wide detour. To escape from Petersburg he had to go north of the Appomattox River, march northwest for twenty-five miles, recross the river, and go ten miles west to Amelia Courthouse, which was on the Richmond & Danville railroad. Here Lee was to

meet the troops from Richmond, and here he had ordered
rations delivered. Once his forces were assembled and supplied, he must then move down the railroad toward Burkeville, twenty miles away—at which point his march to join
forces with Joe Johnston would really begin. The trouble
was that Grant had the shorter route; he was nearer to Johnston than Lee was, and he was also nearer to Burkeville. Instead of pursuing his retreating foe, Grant moved due west to
get ahead of him, his van led by Sheridan, who was exactly
the man for a hard-driving operation of this kind. The armies
were running a race in which the Federals had all of the
advantages. If Lee met the least delay his army was bound
to lose.

Delay came in less than forty-eight hours. Lee reached
Amelia Courthouse on April 4, to find that the Richmond
troops would not arrive until next day. Worse yet, the expected rations had not been delivered. Whether Lee's orders
had never been received, or had been ignored in the monu-
mental confusion attending the government's flight from Richmond, made no difference; the result was simple calamity,
because the army had nothing at all to eat, and twenty-four
hours were lost while details combed the neighborhood in a
largely unsuccessful attempt to find supplies. The result of all
of this was that when Lee at last was able to resume the
march, late on the afternoon of April 5, Sheridan and his
cavalry and 50,000 of Meade's infantry were squarely across
the railroad at Jetersville, halfway between Amelia and
Burkeville. The Federals had won the race. Lee's only hope
now was to make another wide detour, much longer than the
first one, swinging far to the westward in a desperate attempt
to get around the Federal flank. The chance that this could
be done was too small to be seen with the naked eye; the
men could neither be fed nor rested, and every mile the army
moved took it farther away from Johnston.

To make matters worse, the march had to be made with
energetic Federals on the flank, and on April 6 this brought
new disaster. In the dreary low country by a stream known
as Sayler's Creek, Sheridan's cavalry, Wright's VI Corps and
other infantry elements struck the stumbling column, overwhelmed the rear guard, put 7500 Confederates out of action
and destroyed a good part of Lee's wagon train. The rest
of the Army of Northern Virginia managed to keep going—

it had been marching and fighting, wholly unfed, for a solid twenty-four hours—and that night it got to the town of Farmville, where there was a small depot of supplies, crossed to the north side of the Appomattox River once more, and burned the bridge behind it. When it continued its march the river would at least protect it from any more flank attacks.

But by this time the army was not really marching toward anything. Its only possible course now was westward, to Lynchburg and the mountain country. If it went far enough, and if Sheridan was unable to get around in front of it again, it could perhaps find supplies and stay alive a little longer, but it could do no more than that. That night Sheridan sent Grant a telegram describing the situation and concluding: IF THE THING IS PRESSED I THINK LEE WILL SURRENDER. A copy of this reached Mr. Lincoln next morning, and he sent Grant a telegram of his own, quoting Sheridan's final sentence and adding: LET THE THING BE PRESSED.[8]

The Army of Northern Virginia kept moving, one heavy foot after another, marching through a trance. Hour by hour it diminished. Its line of march now was marked as it had never been marked before—by hundreds and hundreds of abandoned muskets, some just dropped by the roadside, others standing butt-upward, bayonets thrust in the ground: weapons discarded by men who had given up and drifted out of the ranks. Many of these men, beaten and weaponless, continued to tramp along with the army, staying where Lee was because he was the only man they could be sure about in their disintegrating world. Sooner or later, armed or unarmed, the soldiers would have to recross the Appomattox River—they were approaching its headwaters, and it was not much of a stream now—exposing themselves again to the constant thrusts of the hard-riding Yankee cavalry. It was believed that at Appomattox Station, where the line of march would once more touch the South Side railroad, there would be freight cars full of rations sent east from Lynchburg, and perhaps this was as good a reason as any to keep going. A week after the departure from Petersburg, Lee was informed that he had fewer than 8000 organized, effective infantrymen, armed and ready for combat.[9]

Time to end it, in short. On April 7 a note from Grant came through the lines, calling on Lee to surrender. Lee sent a reply asking what terms Grant had in mind, Grant wrote in return that he simply wanted Lee's army to lay down its arms and accept disqualification from further combat, and then Lee tried to broaden the scope of the inevitable meeting by writing that although he did not think that "the emergency has arisen to call for the surrender of this army" he would like to talk about the general subject of restoring peace between North and South.

Grant was bound by his orders from Stanton, and he also had Mr. Lincoln's curt "Let the thing be pressed," and he was unresponsive. He notified Lee that he could not engage in any such conversation and that the kind of meeting Lee proposed would do no good; the only thing to talk about was the surrender of Lee's army. Still: Grant believed that this surrender would mean surrender everywhere, and he hoped that "all of our difficulties may be settled without the loss of another life." . . . Then, on April 9, Sheridan forced the showdown. His cavalry won the race to Appomattox Station, capturing the supplies that represented Lee's last thin hope, and with two corps of infantry that came up after a hard all-night march the Federals drew an unbreakable battle line across the road to the west, the only road on earth that meant anything now to General Lee. The Army of Northern Virginia was at bay, at last, helpless, surrounded; Sheridan was in front and on the flank, Meade was close in the rear and coming up fast, no possible escape route was open to the north, and Lee sent Grant a flag-of-truce message saying that he was ready to talk surrender.[10]

The two men met that day in a house at Appomattox Courthouse, a few miles from the station. But before he went to this meeting Lee quietly spoke a few words that were both a judgment on the past and an omen for the future. To him, as he prepared to meet Grant, came a trusted lieutenant who urged him not to surrender but simply to tell his army to disperse, each man taking to the hills with his rifle in his hand: let the Yankees handle guerrilla warfare for a while and see what they could make of that. Lee replied that he would have none of it. It would create a state of things in the South from which it would take years to recover, Federal cavalry would harry the length and breadth of the land for no one knew how long, and he himself was "too old to go bushwhacking"; even if the army did break up into die-hard bands of irreconcilables, "the only course for me to pursue would be to surrender myself to General Grant." This was the last anybody heard about taking to the hills. The officer who suggested this course wrote that Lee "showed me the situation from a plane to which I had not risen, and when he finished speaking I had not a word to say."[11]

The unquenchable guerrilla warfare this officer had been hinting at was perhaps the one thing that would have ruined America forever. It was precisely what Federal soldiers like Grant and Sherman dreaded most—the long, slow-burning, formless uprising that goes on and on after the field armies have been broken up, with desperate men using violence to provoke more violence, harassing the victor and their own people with a sullen fury no dragoons can quite put down.[12] The Civil War was not going to end that way (although it was natural to suppose that it might, because civil wars often do end so) and the conquered South was not going to become another Ireland or Poland, with generation after generation learning hatred and the arts of back-alley fighting. General Lee ruled it out, not only because he was General Lee but also because he had never seen this war as the kind of struggle that could go on that way. He understood the cause he served with complete clarity. His South had meant neither revolution nor rebellion; it simply desired to detach itself and live in its own chosen part of an unchanging past, and Mr. Davis had defined it perfectly when he said that all his people wanted was to be let alone. Borne up by that desire, the Confederacy had endured four years of war, and it was breaking up now because this potential for inspiring the human spirit had been exhausted. With unlimited confidence the Confederacy had fought an unlimited war for a strictly limited end. To go on fighting from the woods and the lanes and the swamps might indeed plague the Yankees and infect a deep wound beyond healing, but the one thing on earth it could not do was give the South a chance to be left alone with what used to be.

Yet men have to live by their memories, and the memory of death and defeat is bitter enough to keep unforgiving men carrying their rifles across the hills for generations. Lee made it possible for men to turn this memory into a strange source of strength, a tragic and moving remembering that provided a base on which the present could be accepted and the future could be faced. Because of what happened when he and

Grant at last met, Lee when he left Appomattox—a paroled soldier without an army—rode straight into legend, and he took his people with him. The legend became a saving grace. The cause that had failed became The Lost Cause, larger than life, taking on color and romance as the years passed, remembered with pride and with heart-ache but never again leading to bloodshed. Civil wars have had worse endings than this.

A little of it is due to Grant. It was not grim old Unconditional Surrender with whom Lee sat down to talk terms. Instead it was a sensitive man who angrily stopped his own soldiers when they began firing salutes in loud celebration of their victory, reminding them that the late members of the Army of Northern Virginia were their fellow citizens now, and calling on them to send rations into the Confederate camp. His terms were generous: Lee's soldiers were to lay down their arms, accept paroles, and then go to their homes, the officers keeping their side-arms, the men taking their horses so that they could do the spring plowing. Beaten men were not to be paraded through Northern cities and then held in prison camps while the government made up its mind how it might punish men taken in rebellion. Grant in fact made punishment impossible, inserting a clause specifying that these men were never to be disturbed by Federal authority as long as they observed their paroles and obeyed the laws. Some time later, this kept vengeance-minded officials in Washington from putting Lee on trial for treason.

Counting men without arms, innumerable stragglers, and stray details that came in when they learned what had happened, Lee surrendered approximately 27,000 men at Appomattox. The contrast between that figure and the 8000-and-odd who could actually have stood in line of battle on April 9 tells all anyone needs to know about the way his army had been worn down on its long retreat. Lee returned to his camp, making his way through broken ranks of men trying numbly to adjust themselves to the blow that had fallen, and after a conversation with some of his officers around a campfire he told an aide to draft a farewell order to the army that was about to disband. The first version of this order did not suit him, and he struck out a few lines that seemed likely to keep hard feelings alive. At last he had what he wanted, and the next day it was published to the troops:

"After four years of arduous service, marked by unsurpassed courage and fortitude, the Army of Northern Virginia has been compelled to yield to overwhelming numbers and resources. I need not tell the brave survivors of so many hard-fought battles, who have remained steadfast to the last, that I have consented to the result from no distrust of them. But, feeling that valor and devotion could accomplish nothing that could compensate for the loss that must have attended the continuance of the contest, I determined to avoid the useless sacrifice of those whose past services have endeared them to their countrymen.

"By the terms of the agreement officers and men can return to their homes and remain until exchanged. You will take with you the satisfaction that proceeds from the consciousness of duty faithfully performed; and I earnestly pray that a merciful God will extend to you His blessing and protection.

"With an increasing admiration of your constancy and devotion to your country, and a grateful remembrance of your kind and generous consideration for myself, I bid you all an affectionate farewell."[13]

That was the end of it. Lee himself returned to Richmond, Grant started back for Washington, and a day or so later the Confederates formally paraded and gave up their arms and their flags, receiving a salute from the waiting Federals, giving a salute in return. Then the men who had been paroled broke ranks, and the Army of Northern Virginia went away from its last parade ground.

It would of course be easy to make too much of the general air of reconciliation. Lee's soldiers were hard, passionate fighters, they did not enjoy defeat, they were not ready to start loving their enemies with sentimental fondness, and there were wounds that would be a long time healing. And yet by any standard this was an almost unbelievable way to end a civil war, which by all tradition is the worst kind of war there is. Living for the rest of their lives in the long gray shadow of the Lost Cause, these men were nevertheless going on toward the future. General Lee, who had set the pattern, had given them the right words: ". . . unsurpassed courage and fortitude . . . steadfast to the last . . . the consciousness of duty faithfully performed." Pride in what they had done would grow with the years, but it would turn them into a romantic army of legend and not into a sullen battalion of death.

Here is how the legend worked. Fifteen years after the surrender, one of Lee's veterans—a soldier from South Carolina, who had been in the worst of it from beginning to end—sat down to write his memoirs, a little job of writing that did not get published until many years after its writer was dead. Looking back, he seemed to see something that was worth everything it had cost him, something indeed that a man would almost like to get back to if he only could. He wrote, remember, as one who had been through the mill and not as a starry-eyed recruit, and this is how he put it:

"Who knows but it may be given to us, after this life, to meet again in the old quarters, to play chess and draughts, to get up soon to answer the morning roll call, to fall in at the tap of the drum for drill and dress parade, and again to hastily don our war gear while the monotonous patter of the long roll summons to battle? Who knows but again the old flags, ragged and torn, snapping in the wind, may face each other and flutter, pursuing and pursued, while the cries of victory fill a summer day? And after the battle, then the slain and wounded will arise, and all will meet together under the two flags, all sound and well, and there will be talking and laughter and cheers, and all will say: Did it not seem real? Was it not as in the old days?"[14]

The worst experience on earth could be remembered that way, with a still-youthful veteran dreaming about foes meeting under two flags and one all-embracing sky. No civil war ever ended quite like this. The men who lost at the Boyne or at Culloden did not write memoirs in this vein.

6. To the Dark Indefinite Shore

IT BEGAN WITH one act of madness and it ended with another. John Brown heard history's clock strike in the night and tried to hurry the dawn along with gunfire; now John Wilkes Booth heard the clock strike, and he tried with gunfire to restore the darkness. Each man stood outside the human community, directed by voices the sane do not hear, and each kept history from going logically. Brown, the Old Testament prophet gone wrong, wrote that the crimes of a guilty land must be washed out with blood, and in the bloodshed he evoked the nation learned that some things cannot be washed out that way. Booth, the actor who played for an audience that lived far back in the shadows, wrote that America was forever ordained to be the white man's country, leaving his fellows to reflect that the Negro also had become an American. The line from Harper's Ferry to Ford's Theater is a red thread binding the immense disorder of the Civil War into an irrational sort of coherence.

On Good Friday, April 14, Abraham Lincoln told his cabinet a haunting story. Something big was about to happen, he said, because he had a dream that always came just before some great event. He had had it before the firing on Fort Sumter, before the battles of Bull Run, before Antietam and Stone's River and Gettysburg and Vicksburg; once in a while, for this man, the sky failed to touch the horizon and he saw moving shapes, off beyond.

Naturally enough, the ministers asked what the dream was, and Gideon Welles wrote it down. Mr. Lincoln said that "he seemed to be in a singular, indescribable vessel . . . and that he was moving with great rapidity toward a dark and indefinite shore." No one could read this riddle, but the President was sure it meant good news: doubtless Joe Johnston was about to surrender to General Sherman. General Grant, who attended this meeting, remarked tartly that as far as he could see Stone's River had not been good news for anybody, but the President was undisturbed; this dream was an omen and it must mean news from Sherman because he could think of no other place big news was apt to come from right now.[1]

That night Mr. Lincoln went to see *Our American Cousin* at Ford's Theater, and Booth shot him to death.

He died, as they say, in his hour of triumph; an accurate saying, if triumph on the battlefield expresses the whole meaning of the Civil War. He had returned to Washington in time to hear the city come crashing awake on the morning of April 10, when a 500-gun salute announced Lee's surrender, broke windows in Lafayette Square and sent government clerks and everybody else out to parade and sing and cheer in the rain. That night a crowd came to the White House with brass bands, demanding some word from the President. When at last he came to the window to make a bow he said that tonight he could say nothing—except to ask that the

bands play "Dixie," which he considered a good tune, a fair
prize of war—but he suggested that if people wanted to come
back the next evening he might make a speech. So on the
night of April 11 a crowd gathered on the White House
lawn. It was misty, with candles burning in every window,
transparencies shining along the avenues, the white dome
of the capitol all illuminated, gleaming in the wet darkness
like a high cloud touched by faraway sunrise. When the
President at last appeared there was a tremendous cheer, and
Correspondent Noah Brooks felt that "there was something
terrible" in the enthusiasm the people displayed.[2]

They did not get the kind of speech they wanted. This was
a night for celebration; the people who had come here
wanted to fire guns, and shout, and hear the eagle scream, so
that they could spend themselves in the happy thought that
the rebellion had been put down and all troubles were over.
What they got was a sober, unemotional talk about the job
that lay ahead of them—the job of building a new union and
a new freedom that would be great enough for all the generations of men. They wanted to hear about victory, and the
President made them attend a seminar on reconstruction.

Specifically, Mr. Lincoln talked about Louisiana.

Here the fabulous ten percent plan was being tried. Twelve
thousand citizens had adopted a new state government and
a new constitution, and the state thus rebuilt wanted to resume its place in the Union. Congress had refused to seat
the new Louisiana legislators, and Mr. Lincoln felt that Congress was making a mistake. He did not think that the program adopted in Louisiana was the only possible plan for
reconstruction, nor did he think it was necessarily the best
plan, but at least it was a start, and he enumerated its advantages:

"Some twelve thousand voters in the heretofore slave state
of Louisiana have sworn allegiance to the Union, assumed to
be the rightful political power of the state, held elections, organized a state government, adopted a free-state constitution,
giving the benefit of public schools equally to black and
white and empowering the Legislature to confer the elective
franchise upon the colored man. Their Legislature has already voted to ratify the Constitutional amendment recently
passed by Congress, abolishing slavery throughout the nation.
These twelve thousand persons are thus fully committed to

the Union, and to perpetual freedom in the state—committed to the very things, and nearly all the things, the nation wants —and they ask the nation's recognition and its assistance to make good their committal."

Admittedly there were flaws in the plan. It would be better if many times 12,000 had supported the new organization; better too if the franchise had been given outright to at least some former slaves—to "the very intelligent," and to those who had served in the army. But to reject the plan would be risky: "We in effect say to the white man, 'You are·worthless, or worse—we will neither help you nor be helped by you.' To the blacks we say, 'This cup of liberty which these, your old masters, hold to your lips, we will dash from you, and leave you to the chances of gathering the spilled and scattered contents in some vague and undefined when, where and how.' If this course, discouraging and paralyzing both white and black, has any tendency to bring Louisiana into proper practical relations with the Union, I have so far been unable to perceive it."[3]

It was Abraham Lincoln's last speech, and it struck no sparks; and yet under his labored exposition of the uninspiring Louisiana plan his vision of the future was clear enough if men made giddy by victory achieved could stop to think about it. He wanted to do two things at once, each of them extraordinarily difficult. The millions of Southerners who had tried so hard to leave the Union must somehow be brought back into the old relationship, welcomed rather than coerced, themselves rebuilding the shattered house until reconciliation was complete. Along with this, the Negro must have complete freedom and membership in the American community, he must be brought along as fast as possible to full citizenship, and—hardest of all—much of this must be done by the very society that had formerly held him in slavery, with the understanding and approval of the people who had beaten that society into helplessness. Both reunion and liberty were to be total and indivisible. Mr. Lincoln was proposing reconstruction, not just of the broken South but of America itself.

Characteristically, he was making tentative approaches, and his first experiments had not gone well. The Louisiana plan was in trouble, the cabinet had refused to agree that the South should be paid for its loss of human property, and shortly before his death he saw that his plan for making limited and informal use of the Virginia legislature was not going to work. Not only was the cabinet opposed; in Richmond, Justice Campbell was pushing the plan in a way neither the Republican leadership nor Mr. Lincoln himself could accept. Campbell was saying that there could be an armistice while the Federal government and the Southern state legislatures held "a very grave, important and patient inquiry" into the terms of reunion; among the things to be inquired into, as Campbell saw it, was the basic question of whether anything in particular needed to be done about slavery. This was too much for the President, and it would certainly be a great deal too much for the cabinet and Congress, and so on April 12 Mr. Lincoln ordered General Weitzel not to permit the proposed meeting of the gentlemen who had been acting as the Virginia legislature.[4]

He would have to make a new approach; and as he always did in such cases Mr. Lincoln sparred for time. At the haunted cabinet meeting on Good Friday he listened to a proposal from Secretary Stanton, providing for military government in the Southern states with a methodical re-establishment of post offices, Federal courts, revenue and customs offices and the like; self-government would follow afterward, and the whole question of Negro suffrage was left for later consideration. To this plan Mr. Lincoln expressed a guarded, tentative approval, and he asked the cabinet members to study the matter and present their comments at the next cabinet meeting—Tuesday, April 18. He indicated that it would be well to get some plan into operation fairly soon, so that the reconstructed state governments could be in full operation when Congress convened in December. As Secretary Welles remembered it, the President said that there were men in Congress whose motives were good but who "had a feeling of hate and vindictiveness in which he could not participate." These, to be sure, were the radical Republicans—the men who, as he had said, were most unhandy devils to deal with, but still men whose faces were set toward Zion: "nearer to me than the other side, in thought and sentiment, though bitterly hostile personally."[5]

That was the point. The radicals would attack him but they would also work with him—in the end because he and they wanted to reach the same goal. (People bound for Zion almost always have trouble with their fellows along the way.) It had been so during the war, and it could have been so after the war. The fury with which the radicals eventually destroyed Andrew Johnson came chiefly because Johnson was interested in just half of the Lincoln program, the half that the radicals would accept only if a new deal for the Negro came with it. They had their full share of hate and vindictiveness, to be sure, but they were also passionately interested in freedom, sharing with Edward Bates the belief that if the Negro was freed at all he was freed completely and must share in all of the safeguards which the Constitution provides for free Americans.[6] This spring they were watching Abraham Lincoln with much suspicion, tormented by the old myth that he was too weak to take a firm stand, fearful lest the Negro be sacrificed in the interests of an easy peace; and yet there was no impassable gulf between their position and his. In thought and sentiment they were near to him.

No one will ever know what Abraham Lincoln would have done—with Stanton's scheme for military government, with radicals like Wade and Sumner and Stevens, with any of the separate aspects of the intricate problem that lay ahead—because it was at this delicate moment (about half-past ten on the night of April 14) that Booth came on stage with his derringer. Booth pulled the trigger, and the mind that held somewhere in cloudy solution the elements that might some day have crystallized into an answer for the nation's most profound riddle disintegrated under the impact of a one-ounce pellet of lead: the heaviest bullet, all things considered, ever fired in America. Thinking to destroy a tyrant, Booth managed to destroy a man who was trying to create a broader freedom for all men; with him, he destroyed also the chance for a transcendent peace made without malice and with charity for all. Over the years, many people paid a high price for this moment of violence.

With Lincoln gone, other men had to go about the job of closing out the war and creating a peace. One of these was Andrew Johnson, unluckiest of politicians, still living down the sorry spectacle born of ill health and whiskey when he took the oath of office; somewhat dazed, now, able for the immediate present to do no more than assure callers that treason must be made odious and that the martyred President's program would be carried out, while Secretary

Stanton reigned as temporary dictator. Another was General Sherman, who tried earnestly to do what Lincoln would have wanted him to do, misunderstood what that might be, and blundered into a short-lived peace treaty with Joe Johnston that aroused the worst suspicions of all of the radicals.

It was strange, about Sherman. He was the worst the South had to fear, the man who had burned his way across Georgia and South Carolina exulting in destruction, brutal and ruthless and wholly without compassion: emerging suddenly as an advocate of the softest peace, giving to the defeated Confederates so much more than Lincoln himself was willing to give that he almost wrecked his own career. Grant was praised for magnanimity because he let Lee's soldiers keep their side-arms and their horses: Sherman seemed willing to let the men who surrendered to him—all Confederate soldiers from Carolina to the Rio Grande, as he and Johnston set it up—keep everything but complete independence. Stanton's anger when he heard about it was matched only by Sherman's anger when he learned what Stanton was saying about him.

From the day he took command in North Carolina, Joe Johnston felt that his principal duty was to make a decent peace. He fought his last battle on March 19, attacking a wing of Sherman's army at Bentonville in a vain attempt to win a victory before Schofield came up, and after this fight he found himself obliged to withdraw to the region of Raleigh and await developments. By the first week in April he had about 18,000 effective infantry; Sherman and Schofield, united now, had more than 80,000, and when he learned of Lee's surrender Johnston was convinced that it was time to quit. On April 12 he saw President Davis at Greensboro and told him frankly that "it would be the greatest of human crimes for us to continue the war," adding that the President should "exercise at once the only function of government still in his possession and open negotiations for peace." When the harassed President explained that the Federals would not recognize his authority to negotiate Johnston blandly pointed out that his military commanders could do it for him . . . and won permission to write to General Sherman.[7]

So Johnston and Sherman met in a little cabin near Durham Station, North Carolina, on April 17. As soldiers, they respected each other—they had indeed developed an odd sort of mutual liking, although they had not met before—and when Johnston admitted that his military position was hopeless, Sherman confessed that "to push an army whose commander had so frankly and honestly confessed his inability to cope with me were cowardly and unworthy the brave men I led." Both generals were worried that the end of organized Confederate resistance would bring guerrilla warfare and general disorder, and instead of talking about Johnston's surrender they presently began to discuss an all-embracing settlement that would cover every armed Confederate everywhere. Sherman observed that Johnston had no authority over any army but his own, but Johnston said that could be fixed; not far away was General John C. Breckinridge, who two months earlier had replaced James A. Seddon as Confederate Secretary of War, and Breckinridge had power over all the armies. So the men met again on April 18, this time with Breckinridge present, and out of this came a strange document that undertook to settle everything.[8]

This document was entitled "A Memorandum or Basis of Agreement," and it contained several interesting items.

All Confederate armies (it said) were to go to their state capitals, disband, deposit their weapons in state arsenals and agree to cease from all acts of war and submit to Federal authority; the deposited weapons, pending action by the United States Congress, could be used "to maintain peace and order within the borders of the states." (This would take care of guerrillas and marauders.) State governments would be recognized as soon as state officers took the oath of allegiance to the Constitution of the United States, Federal courts would be re-established, and Southerners would be guaranteed "their political rights and franchises, as well as their rights of person and property, as defined by the Constitution of the United States and of the states, respectively." There would be amnesty for everyone, with an armistice while the word got around; and as a final note Johnston and Sherman admitted that they had not been empowered to sign any such agreement as this but promised "to promptly obtain the necessary authority and to carry out the above program."

Thus the generals, inept but well-intentioned, tried to arrange things so that the nation could live at peace; fighting men have made worse mistakes, and have shown less humanity making them. . . . Sherman sent the document to

Grant by courier, with a letter explaining that this was total victory: it made peace, restored the Union and settled the problem of guerrilla warfare, and "if you can get the President to simply indorse the copy and commission me to carry out the terms, I will follow them to the conclusion."[9]

Sherman is rarely called an innocent, but no other word applies here. Rushing in where no reasonably sophisticated angel would dare to tread, he had composed and signed something that practically recognized the Confederacy, took reconstruction entirely out of the hands of President and Congress, left the South fully armed and cast grave doubt on the validity of emancipation; every line of it written with the purest motives a man could have. Grant realized that it was all wrong the moment he saw it, and hurried to show it to Secretary Stanton; and on the night of April 21 President Johnson and the cabinet unhesitatingly rejected the agreement and sent Grant off to Raleigh to break the news to Sherman. The armistice must be canceled and Johnston must be called on to surrender on exactly the terms that had been given Lee.

Sherman was not badly surprised, some remnant of practical judgment having warned him, apparently, that what he and Johnston had done would be too much for the War Department. Grant was tactful, keeping his visit as nearly secret as possible so that Sherman's soldiers would not realize that their general had been overruled by the general-in-chief in person; Sherman obeyed orders cheerfully, Johnston was summoned to a new conference, and on April 26 he and Sherman signed terms duplicating those signed at Appomattox. What infuriated Sherman was his discovery, shortly after this, that Stanton had made a merciless public attack on him, saying that Sherman had willfully violated President Lincoln's orders, implying that he had granted an armistice in order to let Jefferson Davis escape, and stopping just short of accusing him of actual disloyalty. With public statements and an unofficial prodding of news correspondents, Stanton had opened a campaign that seemed designed to drive Sherman out of public life altogether.[10]

This, as a matter of fact, it never came close to doing, and it was not what Stanton really had in mind. The Northern public had no sooner digested this attack than it learned that Joe Johnston had surrendered all over again, giving up

39,000 soldiers and closing out the war everywhere except along the Gulf Coast and beyond the Mississippi, and it was hard to feel hostile toward the soldier who had forced this development. Sherman was a popular hero in the North anyway, and although Stanton's attack aroused Sherman's undying hatred it accomplished no more . . . except that it served notice on one and all that reconstruction was not to be hurried for the sake of an easy solution, which probably is just what it was meant to do in the first place.

Sherman had stumbled onto a fact that was basic to everything that happened in the reconstruction period.

Once such soldiers as Lee and Johnston formally accepted military defeat, there would be amazingly little trouble in getting the seceded states to reaccept the Union—provided that these states were allowed to interpret emancipation and Negro rights in their own way. The dream of an independent Southern nation was fading rapidly, and what was left of it could spiral off into Lost Cause romanticism without ever again being a real problem to anyone; what remained, however, touched with no romanticism whatever, was the determination that the Negro, slave or free, must stay just about where he was and must on no account be given any real control over his own destiny. On this point the reserves of resistance were all but inexhaustible. Sherman warned Chief Justice Chase that to assert political equality for the Negro might "rekindle the war" on a bloodier and more destructive basis than ever. At about this time General Oliver Otis Howard was made head of the new Freedman's Bureau, which was supposed to see to it that the former slave got fair treatment all along the line, and Sherman advised him that there was no sense in going to extremes about it. To provide votes for the Negro, for instance, was to court grave danger: "If that be attempted, we arouse a new and dangerous element, prejudice, which, right or wrong, does exist and should be consulted. . . . As we have just emerged from one attempted revolution it would be wrong to begin another."[11]

. . . possibly wrong; and unquestionably much more trouble than most people were prepared to take now. There was not going to be a second revolution. Practical men were going to agree that although prejudice must be deplored it must also be consulted, and as Montgomery Blair had predicted a year earlier, once good conservatives everywhere recognized their common interests the high fever of radicalism would subside. Lincoln was dead, and no one else could arouse the terrible enthusiasm that he aroused, or make sensible use of what remained of it. For that matter, Lee was a soldier no longer and the terrible enthusiasm he had evoked was not transferable, either; perhaps men everywhere had used all of the enthusiasm they had, for a time, and instead of trying to think what the war meant were content simply to know that it had stopped.

It came to its close swiftly, once the Northern President and the two great Southern armies died. Mr. Davis clung valiantly to what remained of his position, and even after Johnston's surrender he hoped that somewhere to the west a formal center of organized resistance to Federal conquest could be kept alive. As long as he and his cabinet were together, the Confederacy had a capital: if only it could be planted somewhere. It could not; and as the presidential party flitted south, across the Carolinas and down into Georgia, the most anyone dared to hope was that President Davis could get to some safe place where Federal vengeance could not reach him. It was probably just as well that Secretary Stanton never heard the story that was current around Mr. Davis' headquarters just now. At the conference with Johnston, it was said, Sherman had quietly told Secretary Breckinridge that he would provide a ship if Mr. Davis wanted to leave the country, guaranteeing safe passage to some foreign land for Mr. Davis and his family and their effects. Postmaster General John Reagan said long afterward that Mr. Davis rejected the offer, both because he did not want to be under obligations to any Yankee and because he refused to leave "Confederate soil" while a single Confederate regiment remained under arms.[12]

But Confederate soil had shrunk to almost nothing, and by the end of the first week in May there was not an armed Confederate regiment within six hundred miles. No valid reason for flight existed, except the desire to leave the stage with dignity, which Mr. Davis tried his best to do. Fate was unkind to him, when Yankee cavalry at last overtook him and captured him near Irwinville, Georgia, on May 10. The cavalry swooped down on his camp in a rainy dawn, Mr. Davis snatched up a waterproof and a shawl as he left his tent, when he was taken the garments turned out to be his wife's, and unfeeling Northerners chuckled over the story that the Confederate President had tried to escape disguised as a woman—much as they had chuckled four years earlier over the story that Abraham Lincoln had sneaked into Washington disguised in a Scotch cape and tam-o'-shanter. Sherman, by the way, had nothing to do with the capture. He never forgot how President Lincoln had said that he would be happy if Mr. Davis could get out of the country "unbeknownst to me," and he said contemptuously that if Stanton wanted this fugitive arrested he ought to turn the job over to some sheriff or bailiff because the United States Army had better things to do.[18]

Actually, Mr. Davis was taken by men who were technically under Sherman's command—James H. Wilson's men, outriders of the great cavalry corps George Thomas had sent swinging down from Tennessee early in the spring. They had beaten Bedford Forrest (at last!), had taken Selma and Montgomery in Alabama, and then had galloped eastward almost to the Atlantic, scooping up the Confederate President as their last act of war. Even before they did this, General Canby in southern Alabama had received the surrender of the last organized Confederate army east of the Mississippi, that of General Richard Taylor, and at the moment of Mr. Davis' capture nothing remained but the inert, unmanageable lost province of trans-Mississippi.

That did not last much longer. There was a final, lonely, meaningless little spatter of a fight on May 13, when a few hundred white and colored soldiers fought a handful of Confederates at Palmito Ranch on the Rio Grande near Brownsville, Texas, in the Civil War's last useless battle. Then Edmund Kirby Smith, frustrated viceroy of the trans-Mississippi, made the final act of surrender. On paper he had 40,000 soldiers, but in actual fact he had hardly anyone he could use for an effective campaign, he wrote that "I feel powerless to do good for my country, and humiliated by the acts of a people I was striving to benefit," and on May 26 he surrendered and the war was over.[14]

All over, finished forever, ready to be done up in veterans'-reunion music and oratory and lilacs-on-gravestones in a thousand village cemeteries, if it had been nothing more than tragedy and shared agony. Jefferson Davis was a prisoner in a casemate at Fort Monroe, dignity returning to him as he endured the malice of captors who still looked on him as a dangerous man. Sherman was in Washington for the grand review and the muster-out of the armies, regaining his own dignity by giving a ferocious public snub to Stanton. (General and Secretary were sworn enemies, each man believing that he knew how to carry out Lincoln's dream of an enduring peace, their enmity testifying to the fact that nobody knew how to do it.) At various places in the South there were occupation troops whose generals looked vainly for guidance, seeing their duties in different ways. In Raleigh, General Schofield protested that it was neither politic nor just to let the Negro advance too rapidly toward full citizenship; and, in Savannah, General Gillmore (who had had so much trouble trying to make a campaign under Ben Butler) notified the city authorities that if they proposed to reopen their schools they must provide classes, teachers and equal facilities for children who had been born in slavery.[15] It began to seem that there had been neither clear-cut victory nor defeat, but that governors and governed were simply trying to live their way through a problem that was confusingly unsettled.

Something had been won; but it was nothing more, and at the same time nothing less, than a chance to make a new approach toward a goal that had to be reached if the war and the nation that had endured it had final meaning. The ship was moving through Lincoln's dream, toward a dark indefinite shore, it had a long way to go, and the sky contained no stars the ordinary mortal could see. All that was certain was that the voyage was under way.

Notes

Chapter One: IN THE RAPIDS
1. Castles in the Air

1. Richmond *Dispatch* for Dec. 31, 1862. The correspondent failed to note that Mr. Davis was accompanied by a military aide, Gen. G. W. C. Lee, son of Robert E. Lee.

2. Edward Younger, ed., *Inside the Confederate Government: the Diary of Robert Garlick Hill Kean,* 28; William E. Dodd, Jr., *Jefferson Davis,* 294-95; *The War of the Rebellion: a Compilation of Official Records of the Union and Confederate Armies,* Vol. XX, Part Two, 421-22. (This is cited hereafter as O.R. Unless otherwise indicated, the volume referred to is from Series One.)

3. William E. Polk, *Leonidas Polk, Bishop and General,* Vol. II, 177; Stanley Horn, *The Army of Tennessee,* 195; Isabella D. Martin and Myrta Lockett Avary, eds., *A Diary from Dixie,* by Mary Boykin Chesnut, 242-43. Incidentally, Mattie Ready's last name was pronounced "Reedy."

4. Troop strengths are Pemberton's estimates; draft of an unfinished letter, apparently to Maj. W. T. Walthall, in the J. C. Pemberton Papers, Manuscript Department, New York Public Library.

5. Dunbar Rowland, *Jefferson Davis, Constitutionalist* (cited hereafter as Rowland), Vol. V, 384, 386; Diary of Robert Kean, 33.

6. Senator Phelan's long, despairing letter to Davis is in O.R., Vol. XVII, Part Two, 788-92.

7. Robert Hartje, *Van Dorn Conducts a Raid on Holly Springs and Enters Tennessee,* Tennessee Historical Quarterly, Vol. XVIII, No. Two, 120-22; O.R., Vol. LII, Part Two, 371.

8. John C. Pemberton, *Pemberton, Defender of Vicksburg,* 22,

43-48; Major R. W. Memminger, *The Surrender of Vicksburg—a Defense of Gen. Pemberton,* Southern Historical Society Papers (a compilation cited hereafter as SHSP), Vol. XII, 352-53; O.R., Vol. XXIV, Part One, 287-88.

9. Phelan to Davis, as cited in footnote 6, above; O.R., Vol. XIII, 888.

10. Col. Thomas L. Snead, *The Conquest of Arkansas,* Battles and Leaders of the Civil War (cited hereafter as B. & L.), Vol. III, 441-50; O.R., Vol. XIII, 918.

11. O.R., Vol. XIII, 906-7, 914; Vol. XVII, Part Two, 728; Vol. XX, Part Two, 423-24; Rowland, Vol. V, 356, 371-72; Earl S. Miers, ed., J. B. Jones, *A Rebel War Clerk's Diary,* 118, 120; Diary of Robert Kean, 28-31.

12. O.R., Vol. XX, Part Two, 424, 435, 436; Vol. XVII, Part Two, 766; Joseph E. Johnston, *Jefferson Davis and the Mississippi Campaign,* B. & L., Vol. III, 472-75. Davis' letter of Dec. 21 to Holmes (Rowland, Vol. V, 386-88) is a very clear analysis of the Mississippi valley situation at that time. Attention should be called here to Frank Vandiver's persuasive argument that Davis fully recognized the need for on-the-spot direction and coordination of army movements in the west and meant Johnston to have real authority in that theater. Johnston, Vandiver suggests, did not quite understand how much power was being given to him, doubted that the President meant him to act with firmness, and failed to grasp an opportunity that was actually extremely broad. (Vandiver, *Rebel Brass,* 33-35, 57-59.)

13. O.R., Vol. XVII, Part Two, 783-84.

14. Rowland, Vol. V, 31-32; letter of Johnston to Senator Wigfall dated Dec. 15, 1862, in the Wigfall Family Papers, Library of Congress.

2. Battle without Logic

1. Jefferson Davis to Varina Davis dated Dec. 15, 1862, in the Davis Letters, Confederate Memorial Literary Society, Richmond; letter of Gen. Johnston to Senator Wigfall, same date, in the Wigfall Family Papers, Library of Congress.

2. Shortly after he took command Burnside wrote to his friend, the Rev. Augustus Woodbury: "The responsibility is so great that at times I tremble at the thought of assuming that I am able to exercise so large a command. Yet when I think that I have made no such assumption, that I have shunned the responsibility, and only accepted it when I was ordered to do it, and when it

would have been disloyal and unfriendly to our government not to do it, then I take courage, and I approach our Heavenly Father with freedom and trustfulness, confident that if I can act honestly and industriously, constantly asking His protection and assistance, all will be well." (Ben: Perley Poore, *The Life and Public Services of Ambrose E. Burnside, Soldier—Citizen—Statesman*, 182-83.)

3. There is little reason to suppose that Lee would have been in serious trouble if McClellan had carried out the plan he was following when relieved of his command. Lee put Jackson in the Valley, with half of the army, to operate against the flank, rear and communications of the Army of the Potomac if it advanced along the line of the Orange & Alexandria Railroad, and there is no doubt that Jackson would have done so effectively. Lee wrote President Davis that he believed Jackson's presence in the Valley deranged the Federals' plans "and defeated their purpose of advancing upon Gordonsville and Charlottesville." O.R., Vol. XXI, 1029.

4. Ibid., 84, 1014-15.

5. Letter of Daniel Reed Larned to his sister dated Nov. 27, 1862, in the Daniel Reed Larned Correspondence, Library of Congress. The dreary tale of the bureaucratic bungling which delayed the pontoons is well set forth in K. P. Williams, *Lincoln Finds a General*, Vol. II, 479-505.

6. Daniel Larned's complaint, on Nov. 22, "We are actually helpless until our pontoon trains arrive" (Larned Correspondence, Library of Congress), is an overstatement. Burnside could have had Sumner's Right Grand Division ford the Rappahannock (as Sumner wanted to do) letting its engineers find in Fredericksburg material for makeshift bridges to carry artillery and wagon trains. He might also have posted a force in the Warrenton-Culpeper area to keep Lee from concentrating his entire army at Fredericksburg; after all, in the XI and XII Corps Burnside had 30,000 men whom he did not use at all. His reasons for clinging to the original program despite the delay are set forth in his report on the campaign. O.R., Vol. XXI, 84-86.

7. *Personal Recollections of the First Battle of Fredericksburg*, by an unidentified Confederate artillerist, typescript in the Littlefield Collection, the Eugene C. Barker Texas History Center, University of Texas; Reminiscences of George W. Shreve of Stuart's Horse Artillery, in the Virginia State Libary, Richmond; Moore's *Rebellion Record*, Vol. VI, 105, citing a dispatch in the Richmond *Enquirer;* Gen. James Longstreet, *The Battle of Fredericksburg*, B. & L., Vol. III, 79.

8. Longstreet, op. cit., 81.

9. Undated memorandum on the battle of Fredericksburg by Daniel Larned, in the Library of Congress; letter written by Gen. Humphrey's son, Harry, dated Dec. 18, 1862, in the A. A. Humphreys Papers, Historical Society of Pennsylvania, Philadelphia; Hooker's testimony in the *Report of the Joint Committee on the Conduct of the War* (cited hereafter as *CCW Report*) 1863, Part One, 668.

10. *CCW Report, 1863,* Part One, 658, 671; George H. Washburn, *A Complete History and Record of the 108th Regiment New York Volunteers,* 36-37; Maj. Gen. W. F. Smith, *Franklin's Left Grand Division,* B. & L., Vol. III, 138.

11. O.R., Vol. XXI, 71, 89-92. The George G. Meade Papers, in the Historical Society of Pennsylvania, have an interesting exchange of letters between Franklin and Meade regarding the orders Burnside wrote. On March 28, 1863, Meade wrote to Franklin: "I have always told Genl. Burnside . . . that I did not think you were impressed with the importance he attached to the attack ordered on the left. Of course he maintained his orders admitted no other construction." Franklin told the Committee on the Conduct of the War that he was not sure that "the mere carrying of the heights" would have won the day because he did not know how much of a force Lee had concealed there. He added the old, old complaint of Army of the Potomac generals: "I know that wherever we appeared we found a great many more men than we had." (*CCW Report, 1863,* Part One, 662.)

12. Letter to Mrs. Meade dated Dec. 20, 1862, in *The Life and Letters of George Gordon Meade,* Vol. I, 340. Meade told the Committee on the Conduct of the War that if he had been supported "by an advance of the whole line" he could have held his ground. His immediate superior, Maj. Gen. John F. Reynolds, agreed with him. (*CCW Report, 1863,* Part One, 691, 700.)

13. Burnside's order to Sumner was like his order to Franklin: it told Sumner to advance "a column of a division or more . . . with a view to seizing the heights in the rear of the town." O.R., Vol. XXI, 71, 90.

14. D. Watson Rowe, *On the Field of Fredericksburg,* in *Annals of the War Written by Leading Participants, North and South* (cited hereafter as *Annals of the War*), 261-63.

15. Letter of William Noland Berkeley to his wife dated Dec. 17, 1862, in the Alderman Library, University of Virginia; diary of Henry Robinson Berkeley, entry for Dec. 18, in the Virginia

State Historical Society; letter of J. E. B. Stuart dated Dec. 18, in the Duke University Library.

3. The Politics of War

1. Letter of Congressman Wadsworth to "My Dear Mitchell" dated Dec. 16, 1862, in the S. L. M. Barlow Papers, Huntington Library, San Marino, Calif.; letter of Senator Chandler to Mrs. Chandler dated Dec. 18, in the Zachariah Chandler Papers, Library of Congress; letter of Joseph Medill to Elihu Washburne, in the Washburne Papers, Library of Congress.

2. O.R., Vol. XXI, 67; Albert D. Richardson, *The Secret Service, the Field, the Dungeon and the Escape,* 306.

3. Letter of Bancroft to Lieber dated Oct. 29, 1862, in the Francis Lieber Collection, Huntington Library.

4. Basler, Vol. V, 527-30, 534;; Albert Gallatin Riddle, *Recollections of War Times,* 207-8.

5. Letter of T. J. Barnett to Barlow dated Nov. 30, and an undated letter, Barnett to Barlow, telling of a conversation with President Lincoln; both in the Barlow Papers, Huntington Library.

6. Basler, Vol. VI, 48-49.

7. Unpublished manuscript biography of McClernand, possibly written by Major Adolph Schwartz, McClernand's chief of staff in the XIII Army Corps, in the Illinois State Historical Library, Springfield; K. P. Williams, *Lincoln Finds a General,* Vol. IV, 147-48. McClernand's orders are in O.R., Vol. XVII, Part Two, 282.

8. O.R., Vol. XVII, Part One, 468-69, 601; Williams, op. cit., 157 ff; *Personal Memoirs of U. S. Grant,* Vol. I, 426-28.

9. O.R., Vol. XVII, Part Two, 400-2; Williams, 187. McClernand's command was the XIII Corps, Sherman's the XV Corps. Maj. Gen. Stephen Hurlbut was named commander of the XVI corps and Maj. Gen. James B. McPherson of the XVII Corps.

10. O.R., Vol. XVII, Part Two, 425.

11. Francis Vinton Greene, *The Mississippi,* 67; O.R., Vol. XX, Part Two, 415, 422.

12. Greene, op. cit., 68-70; O.R., Vol. XVII, Part One, 546-99; Robert Selph Henry, *First with the Most: Forrest,* 107-21; James R. Chalmers, *Forrest and His Campaigns,* SHSP, Vol. VII, No. Nine, 460.

13. Mss. biography of McClernand as cited in Note 7, above.

14. Greene, 70-71; O.R., Vol. XVII, Part One, 503; news story in the Mobile *Register and Advertiser* for Jan. 7, 1863, reprinted

in the Richmond *Dispatch,* Moore's *Rebellion Record,* Vol. VI, Document 79, 281-82. Grant's orders announcing the raid are in O.R., op. cit., 515-16.

15. O.R., Vol. XVII, Part One, 605-10, 625, 666-68; George W. Morgan, *The Assault on Chickasaw Bluff,* B. & L., Vol. III, 462-70.

4. In the Mists at Stone's River

1. William D. Bickham, *Rosecrans' Campaign with the Four-teenth Army Corps of the Army of the Cumberland; a Narrative of Personal Observations,* 12; O.R., Vol. XX, Part Two, 422, 453; Stanley Horn, *The Army of Tennessee,* 192-93.

2. O.R., Vol. XX, Part One, 189; Part Two, 6-7, 49, 57, 59; Bickham, op. cit., 13-14.

3. O.R., Vol. XX, Part Two, 117, 118, 123-24.

4. Bickham, 28-30, 83; O.R., Vol. XX, Part Two, 6-7, 49.

5. O.R., Vol. XX, Part Two, 457, 458; War Letters of C. I. Walker, in the Eugene C. Barker Texas History Center, University of Texas; Stanley Horn, 195-96.

6. Bickham, 137-39.

7. Edwin C. Bearss, *Cavalry Operations in the Battle of Stone's River,* Tennessee Historical Quarterly, Vol. XIX, No. One, 53; letter of Bragg to President Davis dated Jan. 17, 1863, typescript in the J. Stoddard Johnston Papers, Filson Club, Louisville; Horn, 203; O.R., Vol. XX, Part One, 663.

8. Excellent accounts of the battle are in Horn, 190-208, and G. C. Kniffin, *The Battle of Stone's River,* B. & L., Vol. III, 612-32. See also Bickham, 203-365, passim; Wilbur F. Hinman, *The Story of the Sherman Brigade,* 355; diary of Charles C. Hood, entry for Dec. 31, 1862, in the Library of Congress.

9. There is a graphic account of the swarm of Federal stragglers in the manuscript diary of Capt. John D. Inskeep of the 17th Ohio, Ohio Historical Society, Columbus. Bragg's telegrams are in O.R., Vol. LII, Part Two, 402, and Vol. XX, Part One, 662.

10. Journal of Capt. W. L. Trask, Confederate courier at Murfreesboro, in possession of Mr. and Mrs. Gordon W. Trask, Oak Park, Ill.; letter of John W. Rabb of the Texas Rangers, in the Eugene C. Barker Texas History Center; letter of E. John Ellis, in the Department of Archives, Louisiana State University; W. L. Gammage, *The Camp, the Bivouac and the Battlefield,* 69.

11. Thomas B. Van Horne, *The Life of Major General George H. Thomas,* 97; John Lee Yaryan, *Stone's River,* in War Papers

Read before the Indiana Commandery, Military Order of the Loyal Legion of the United States, Vol. I, 173-74. (Hereafter, when these Loyal Legion papers are referred to, they will be cited simply as MOLLUS Papers, with the State Commandery added.)

12. Thomas L. Livermore, *Numbers and Losses in the Civil War,* 97, puts the Federal effective strength at 41,400, with total casualties of 12,906. He credits Bragg with 34,732 effectives and puts his losses at 11,739. In all the story of the Civil War there is nothing much more appalling than these Stone's River casualty lists.

13. Bragg gives his reasons for retreat in O.R., Vol. XX, Part One, 669.

14. Basler, Vol. VI, 424-25.

5. Paralysis of Command

1. Rowland, Vol. V, 390-95, citing an account in the Richmond *Enquirer* for Jan. 7, 1863.

2. Ibid., 409, 411.

3. Edward A. Pollard, *Life of Jefferson Davis,* 254-55.

4. Richard Malcolm Johnston and William H. Browne, *Life of Alexander H. Stephens,* 431-32, 435, citing letters from Stephens to his brother Linton dated Jan. 18, Jan. 22 and Jan. 29, 1863.

5. Johnston, *Narrative of Military Operations,* 161-62. The interesting point here is that the darling of President Davis' contemporary critics was Johnston himself.

6. O.R., Vol. XX, Part One, 669, 682-84; Stanley Horn, 222-23.

7. Letter of Bragg to Clement C. Clay, dated Jan. 10, 1863, in the C. C. Clay Papers, Manuscript Department, Duke University Library; letter of Bragg to President Davis dated Jan. 17, in the J. Stoddard Johnston Papers, the Filson Club, Louisville; Rowland, Vol. V, 434.

8. Letter of Johnston to Wigfall dated March 8, 1863, in the L. T. Wigfall Papers, Library of Congress; Johnston to President Davis dated Feb. 3 and Feb. 12, in O.R., Vol. XXIII, Part Two, 624, 632-33.

9. O.R., op. cit., 626-27, 640-41, 658-59. The relationship between Johnston and Bragg proposed by Secretary Seddon was precisely the one that existed between Grant and Meade during the 1864 campaign in Virginia.

10 Ibid., 674, 684-85, 708; letter of Johnston to Davis dated April 10, 1863, in the Johnston Papers, Duke University Library.

11. Letters of Johnston to Wigfall dated March 4 and March 8, 1863, in the Wigfall Papers, Library of Congress.

12. O.R., Vol. XXIII, Part Two, 761.

13. Frank Vandiver, ed., *The Civil War Diary of General Josiah Gorgas,* 26; Rowland, Vol. V, 460-62.

14. Johnston and Browne, *Life of Alexander H. Stephens,* 440, 441.

6. A Question of Control

1. Letter of Bates to Winthrop dated Jan. 5, 1863, in the Robert C. Winthrop Papers, Massachusetts Historical Society, Boston.

2. Lincoln to Green Adams of Kentucky, Jan. 7, in Basler, Vol. VI, 42; O.R., Vol. XX, Part Two, 282, 308; New York *Tribune* for Feb. 11, 1863.

3. Letter of Nicolay to his wife Therena, dated Jan. 15, in the John G. Nicolay Papers, Library of Congress; letter of Medill to Elihu B. Washburne dated Jan. 16, in the Washburne Papers, Library of Congress; Congressional Globe, 3rd Session, 37th Congress, Part One, 284-90; diary of John A. Dahlgren, entry for Dec. 22, 1862, cited in *Manuscripts from Goodspeed's,* Catalog 510.

4. It has been said that Lincoln did read Clausewitz, but this writer has been unable to confirm it. The records of the Library of Congress do not show that he ever drew the book from that library. This of course is not conclusive. It does seem obvious that the Clausewitz dictum is one that as good a politician as Lincoln would have understood instinctively.

5. On Dec. 18 Senator Zachariah Chandler of Michigan wrote to his wife that "The President is a weak man, too weak for the occasion," and he told her: "The Senate has in caucus commenced the warfare upon Gov. Seward and I think he will have to leave the cabinet before it is over. Seward as you are aware has been the bane of Mr. Lincoln's administration." (Zachariah Chandler Papers, Library of Congress.) It was right at this time that T. J. Barnett was warning S. L. M. Barlow: "So much does he" (the President) "seem influenced by men of will that I feel it a duty to urge Conservatives to storm his mind & carry it if possible." (Letter dated Dec. 22, in the Barlow Papers, Huntington Library.)

6. For a judicious appraisal of this affair see Allan Nevins, *The War for the Union,* Vol. II, 350-65. Gideon Welles left a full account of the proceedings in his *Diary,* Vol. I, 194-202.

7. Letter of Franklin and Smith to Lincoln dated Dec. 21, in

the W. F. Smith Papers, courtesy of Walter Wilgus; with a supplementary letter by Franklin dated Dec. 26.

8. Basler, Vol. VI, 31; John G. Nicolay and John Hay: *Abraham Lincoln, a History*, Vol. VI, 213-14. (Cited hereafter as Nicolay & Hay.)

9. Nicolay & Hay, Vol. VI, 211, 213-14; letters of G. K. Warren to his brother dated Dec. 18, 1862, and Jan. 5, 1863, in the G. K. Warren Papers, Manuscript and Historical Section, New York State Library, Albany.

10. Allan Nevins, ed., *A Diary of Battle*, by Col. Charles S. Wainwright, 157-59; *The Life and Letters of George Gordon Meade*, Vol. I, 349; Darius N. Couch, *Sumner's Right Grand Division*, B. & L., Vol. III, 119. It should be borne in mind that Wainwright was a conservative Democrat, a bitter critic of Abraham Lincoln and a devout supporter of McClellan.

The common assumption that Burnside's march never had a chance may need revision. At the time, some competent critics commended the plan. Meade wrote (loc. cit.) "I believe but for the storm we would have succeeded," and Maj. Gen. A. A. Humphreys assured his wife: "If we had only marched a day earlier, and could have attacked the enemy's entrenchments in that storm, we should have carried them." (Letter dated Jan. 24, in the Humphreys Papers, Historical Society of Pennsylvania.) Wainwright said that Gen. Henry Hunt, chief of artillery of the Army of the Potomac, "thinks our chances of success were good had there been no disaffection in the ranks." Wainwright added that he understood that Gen. John F. Reynolds, commander of the I Corps, felt the same way. (*A Diary of Battle*, 161.)

11. O.R., Vol XXI, 998-99, 1004-5; *CCW Report, 1863*, Part One, 720. Sumner had no part in the anti-Burnside cabal. He did, however, rank Hooker and it seemed advisable not to make him serve under a junior. In addition, he was an old man, stout-hearted but rather antiquated, hardly fitted for high command in an army that needed vigorous rebuilding.

12. Basler, Vol. VI, 78-79.

13. The literature on the Porter case is voluminous. For a brief review of the affair, see Richard B. Irwin, *The Case of Fitz John Porter*, B. & L., Vol. II, 695-97. For a stout defense of Porter and McClellan, see Otto Eisenschiml, *The Celebrated Case of Fitz John Porter*.

Chapter Two: PARTING OF THE RED SEA WAVES

1. The Land of Cotton

1. Cecil D. Eby, ed., *A Virginia Yankee in the Civil War; the Diaries of David Hunter Strother*, 134-36; John W. De Forest, *A Volunteer's Adventures*, 44, 48, 50.

2. O.R., Vol. XV, 639; Strother, *A Virginia Yankee in the Civil War*, 145-46.

3. Ibid., 144; letter of Gen. Banks to "My Dearest Mary," dated Jan. 15, 1863, in the N. P. Banks Papers, Essex Institute Library, Salem, Mass.

4. O.R., Vol. XV, 590-91; John C. Palfrey, *Port Hudson*, in Papers of the Military Historical Society of Massachusetts, Vol. VIII, 24-25. (When this collection is cited hereafter it is referred to as MHSM Papers.)

5. Letter of Barnett to Barlow dated Dec. 30, 1862, in the Barlow Papers, Huntington Library.

6. O.R., Vol. XV, 164, 171, 440-41, 486-87, 535. In April 1861, when he commanded Federal troops in Maryland, Butler assured Gov. Thomas H. Hicks that if necessary he would use his troops to put down any slave uprising. O.R., Vol. II, 593.

7. O.R., Vol. XV, 623, 640; Fred Harvey Harrington, *Fighting Politician: Major General N. P. Banks*, 93; letter of Banks to Mrs. Banks dated Feb. 5, 1863, in the N. P. Banks Papers, Essex Institute Library.

8. Harrington, op. cit., 91; O.R., Vol. XV, 667; *A Virginia Yankee in the Civil War*, 148-50.

9. For Federal and Confederate strengths at this time see O.R., Vol. XV, 627, 965; Vol. XXVI, Part One, 7-8.

10. In west Louisiana Maj. Gen. Richard Taylor had some 3500 Confederate soldiers, present for duty, equipped; at Mobile there were 7600 under Brig. Gen. W. W. Mackall. O.R., Vol. XV, 240-43, 888, 903; Vol. XXVI, Part One, 8.

11. Letter of Banks to Halleck dated May 4, 1863, in the N. P. Banks Papers, Essex Institute Library.

12. Farragut to Admiral B. T. Bailey dated April 22, 1863, in the Farragut Papers, David H. Annan Collection; Loyall Farragut, *The Life of David Glasgow Farragut*, 307.

13. Farragut to Commander H. H. Bell, dated March 5, 1863, in the Farragut Papers, Annan Collection.

14. *Official Records of the Union and Confederate Navies in the War of the Rebellion*, Vol. XXIV, 385-96 (cited hereafter as N.O.R.); Edwin C. Bearss, *Federal Attempts to Cut Supply Lines*, an excellent series of articles in the Vicksburg *Sunday Post*, February-April, 1961.

15. Strother, *A Virginia Yankee in the Civil War*, 161.

16. N.O.R., Vol. XIX, 665-68; letter of Farragut to Maj. Gen. Augur dated April 16, 1863, in the C. C. Augur Collection, Illinois State Historical Library, Springfield.

2. In Motion in All Directions

1. Johnston to Davis dated Jan. 2, 1863, in the J. E. Johnston Papers, Manuscript Department, Duke University Library.

2. O.R., Vol. XVII, Part One, 700.

3. O.R., Vol. XVII, Part Two, 546-47, 553-55; *Memoirs of Gen. W. T. Sherman*, Vol. I, 296.

4. O.R., Vol. XVII, Part One, 710, 719; Part Two, 563. In his *Memoirs* (Vol. I, 301) Sherman has McClernand exulting over his victory with the words: "Glorious! Glorious! My star is ever in the ascendant. . . . I'll make a splendid report!" In his personal copy of the published book, however, Sherman marked this passage for deletion and wrote: "I was not justified in reproducing it in the 1st Edition. His exclamation was natural and proper enough." (Sherman's copy with his pencilled annotations is in the Northwestern University Library, Evanston, Ill.)

5. O.R., Vol. XVII, Part Two, 573.

6. Ibid., 551-52.

7. Letter of F. P. Blair, Jr., to Mrs. Blair, in the Francis P. Blair Papers, Library of Congress; letters of C. C. Washburn to Congressman Elihu B. Washburne (the men were brothers but they gave the family name different spellings) in the Washburne Papers, Library of Congress. The letter is dated March 16, 1863. There is a more detailed account of the army's activities this winter in *Grant Moves South*, 366-87.

8. Letter of Capt. Delos Van Deusen, 6th Missouri Volunteers, dated Feb. 22, 1863, in the Huntington Library; letter of Lucian B. Chase from Young's Point dated Feb. 11, in the Chicago Historical Society.

9. O.R., Vol. XVII, Part Two, 833, 835-36; Vol. XXIV, Part Three, 596-97.

10. O.R., Vol. XXIV, Part Three, 593, 597, 599-600.

11. Ibid., 631-32, 650, 663, 677.

12. Ibid., 670-730, passim. In a long letter to Maj. W. T. Walthall, written in 1878, now in the New York Public Library, Pemberton argued with a good deal of logic that the withdrawal of his cavalry in January "was not only a remote but a great proximate cause of all our misfortunes." Because of this, he said, he had "the greatest difficulty . . . in obtaining any reliable information of (Grant's) strength, movements or disposition of his troops."

13. O.R., Vol. XXIV, Part One, 44-48; Part Three, 709-38, passim.

14. Ibid., 745, 747.

3. The Needs of Two Armies

1. E. P. Alexander, *Military Memoirs of a Confederate*, 318; O.R., Vol. XXI, 1110.

2. Letter of Lieut. Henry Ropes to John Codman Ropes dated April 17, 1863, in the Ropes Letter Book, Rare Book Room, Boston Public Library; letter of August Augur to S. L. M. Barlow dated Jan. 17, in the Barlow Papers, Huntington Library; diary of Marsena Patrick, entry for Jan. 29, in the Library of Congress.

3. *CCW Report, 1865*, Vol. I, 112-13; letter of Frank A. Haskell dated March 31, 1863, in the Haskell Papers, State Historical Society of Wisconsin, Madison; J. H. Stine, *History of the Army of the Potomac*, 312.

4. There is a good summary of Hooker's achievements as an administrator in Walter H. Hebert, *Fighting Joe Hooker*, 164-91. K. P. Williams is sharply critical of the abolition of the Grand Divisions in *Lincoln Finds a General*, Vol. II, 560-61.

5. Gen. William E. Doster, *Lincoln and the Episodes of the Civil War*, cited in *Glory Road*, 148-49.

6. Noah Brooks, *Washington in Lincoln's Time*, 56; John Bigelow, Jr., *The Campaign of Chancellorsville: a Strategical and Tactical Study*, 31.

7. Augustus Buell, *The Cannoneer: Recollections of Service in the Army of the Potomac*, 48-49.

8. Stine, *History of the Army of the Potomac*, 313.

9. Lee to G. W. C. Lee dated Feb. 28, 1863, in the R. E. Lee Papers, Manuscript Department, Duke University Library; Lee to Davis dated Feb. 16, in the André de Coppet Collection, Princeton University Library; O.R., Vol. XXV, Part Two, 631-32.

10. Charles W. Ramsdell, *General Robert E. Lee's Horse Sup-

ply, American Historical Review, Vol. XXXV, 758-60; O.R., Vol. XXV, Part Two, 604, 681-82; Series Four, Vol. II, 615-16.

11. Edward Younger, ed., *Inside the Confederate Government: the Diary of Robert Garlick Hill Kean,* 47; O.R., Series Four, Vol. II, 881-83; Robert C. Black, *Railroads of the Confederacy,* 294-95.

12. Seddon to Lee, Feb. 10, 1863, in O.R., Vol. XXV, Part Two, 609-10; Lee to Seddon, Feb. 21, ibid., 638-39.

13. J. B. Jones, *A Rebel War Clerk's Diary,* 152, 174, 188.

14. Varina Howell Davis, *Jefferson Davis: A Memoir by His Wife,* Vol. II, 373-76; *A Rebel War Clerk's Diary,* 183-84.

15. Clifford Dowdey, ed., *The Wartime Papers of R. E. Lee,* 430, 433, 435; Jed. Hotchkiss, *Confederate Military History,* Vol. III, *Virginia,* 375-76.

16. *The Wartime Papers of R. E. Lee,* 400, 427; letters to Mrs. Lee dated March 6 and March 9 in the R. E. Lee Papers, Library of Congress.

17. Letter to Mrs. Lee dated April 19, in the R. E. Lee Papers, Library of Congress.

4. A Bridge for the Moderates

1. Congressional Globe, 37th Congress, Third Session, Appendix, 53-60.

2. It seems to be impossible to get a solid figure for the number of political arrests during the war. Both James Ford Rhodes (*History of the United States, 1850-1877,* Vol. IV, 230-32) and James G. Randall (*Constitutional Problems Under Lincoln,* 152) delved into the question and could come up with nothing better than estimates that the total was somewhere between 13,535 and 38,000. Randall felt that the latter figure was much too high; Rhodes could only conclude that the arrests must be counted in the thousands.

3. Cox to Marble dated March 11, 1863, in the Manton Marble Papers, Library of Congress.

4. Letters of Barnett to Barlow dated Dec. 20 and Dec. 22, 1862, and May 15 and May 16, 1863, in the Barlow Papers, Huntington Library.

5. Lincoln to Seymour dated March 23, in Basler, Vol. VI, 145-46; Seymour to Lincoln dated April 14, in the Robert Todd Lincoln Papers, Library of Congress.

6. Letter of Bates to James B. Eads dated March 23, 1863, in the Eads Papers, Missouri Historical Society; Basler, Vol. VI, 234.

7. Ibid., 291.

5. The Way of the Liberated

1. Congressional Globe, 37th Congress, Third Session, Appendix, 55-56.

2. Letter of T. J. Barnett to Barlow dated Nov. 30, 1862, detailing a conversation with President Lincoln, in the Barlow Papers, Huntington Library.

3. Letter of Plumly to Lincoln dated Jan. 1, 1863, in the Robert Todd Lincoln Papers, Library of Congress.

4. Appleton's American Annual Cyclopaedia for 1863, 428.

5. John Eaton, Grant, Lincoln and the Freedman, cited in Grant Moves South, 357.

6. Letter of Grant to Halleck dated Feb. 18, 1863, in the New York Historical Society. There is an extensive discussion of the refugee camps in Appleton's American Annual Cyclopaedia for 1863, 428-29.

7. Letters from Maria R. Mann at Helena, Ark., dated Feb. 10 and April 19, 1863, in the Manuscript Division, Library of Congress.

8. Many of these findings are from Appleton's Cyclopaedia, as noted in Note 6, above; much of the material there apparently is based on a report by James E. Yeatman, president of the Western Sanitary Commission. See also a report to Secretary Stanton by Brig. Gen. R. Saxton in O.R., Series Three, Vol. IV, 1028-29.

9. Letter of Grant to Washburne dated Aug. 30, 1863, in the Illinois State Historical Library, Springfield.

10. Basler, Vol. VI, 56, 149-50.

11. Letter of Halleck to Grant dated March 31, 1863, in the Lieber Collection, Huntington Library.

12. Letter of Nicolay to his wife dated March 8, 1863, in the John G. Nicolay Papers, Library of Congress.

13. Letter of Bragg to Mrs. Bragg dated June 13, 1863, in the Edward S. Bragg Papers, State Historical Society of Wisconsin Library.

14. Saxton to Stanton, as in Note 8, above. Frederick Douglass' statement is quoted in Benjamin Quarles, The Negro in the Civil War, 184.

Chapter Three:
REMORSELESS REVOLUTIONARY STRUGGLE

1. Ironclads at Charleston

1. N.O.R., Vol. XIII, 543, 549-50, 697-98; Daniel Ammen, *The Atlantic Coast*, 83, 87; Col. Allen P. Julian, *Historic Fort McAllister*, pamphlet.

2. Mary Chesnut, *A Diary from Dixie*, 247; Appleton's *American Annual Cyclopaedia for 1863*, 741.

3. Beauregard, *The Defense of Charleston*, B. & L., Vol. IV, 1-5; letter of Lee to President Davis dated Feb. 5, 1863, in the André de Coppet Collection, Princeton University Library; Frank M. Bennett, *The Steam Navy of the United States*, Vol. I, 367-77.

4. Bennett, op. cit., 369-72; N.O.R., Vol. XIII, 579-82, 605-7, 617; *Naval Letters of Capt. Percival Drayton*, Bulletin of the New York Public Library, Vol. X, Number Eleven, 615, quoting a letter dated Feb. 28, 1863.

5. *Confidential Correspondence of Gustavus Vasa Fox*, Vol. I, 179-80, 197; O.R., Vol. XIV, 436.

6. Beauregard, op. cit., 4-5.

7. Samuel Jones, *The Siege of Charleston*, 170-71.

8. Ibid., 167 ff. There is a good description of the scene inside Fort Sumter in John Johnson, *The Defense of Charleston Harbor, Including Fort Sumter and the Adjacent Island*, 50-56.

9. Du Pont's report of April 8, in N.O.R., Vol. XIV, 3-4.

10. Ibid., 11-25, passim; Jones, *The Siege of Charleston*, 172-77.

11. Letter of Rodgers to Welles dated May 2, 1863, in the Welles Papers, Huntington Library.

12. N.O.R., Vol. XIV, 75-78; John Johnson, op. cit., 58. For a statement by six of the monitor captains agreeing that the ironclads could not subdue the forts, see N.O.R., Vol. XIV, 45-48.

13. *Diary of Gideon Welles*, Vol. I, 259; N.O.R., Vol. XIV, 41-43, 59-60; Basler, Vol. VI, 170. In the fall of 1863 a naval court of inquiry cleared Stimers of Du Pont's charges.

14. *A Virginia Yankee in the Civil War*, 139; *Harper's Weekly*, issue of April 25, 1863.

2. Men Trained for Command

1. Letter of Adams to Dana dated April 8, 1863, in the R. H. Dana Papers, Massachusetts Historical Society.

2. Lord Newton, *Lord Lyons: a Record of British Diplomacy,* Vol. I, 99-100, quoting a letter from Lord Russell dated March 28, 1863.

3. Ibid., 102, 104-5; Montague Bernard, *A Historical Account of the Neutrality of Great Britain during the American Civil War,* 314-16; N.O.R., Vol. II, 97-98; *Diary of Gideon Welles,* Vol. I, 266-67, 304-5.

4. N.O.R., Series Two, Vol. II, 131, 151, 309; C. F. Adams, *Charles Francis Adams, by His Son,* 316, 319; William W. Wade, *The Man Who Stopped the Rams,* American Heritage, Vol. XIV, No. Three, 80-81.

5. N.O.R., Series Two, Vol. III, 505-6; Sarah Agnes Wallace and Frances Elma Gillespie, eds., *The Journal of Benjamin Moran,* Vol. II, 1083; editorial from the Richmond *Whig,* quoted in the *Manchester Guardian* for Jan. 16, 1863.

6. *The Journal of Benjamin Moran,* Vol. II, 1106-7; *Diary of Gideon Welles,* Vol. I, 259.

7. Letter of Anson G. Henry of Oregon, dated April 12, 1863, in the Anson G. Henry Papers, Illinois State Historical Society; letter of Frank A. Haskell dated April 8, in the Haskell Papers, State Historical Society of Wisconsin.

8. Memoirs of Captain William G. LeDuc, quoting a postwar letter to the editor of the *National Tribune* setting forth Hooker's version of Lincoln's warning, in the Huntington Library; Noah Brooks, *Washington in Lincoln's Time,* 51-56. Brooks remarks that during this visit Lincoln anxiously read Southern newspapers that came in through the picket lines, hoping to get news about Du Pont's attack.

9. Darius N. Couch, *The Chancellorsville Campaign,* B. & L., Vol. III, 155.

10. O.R., Vol. XXIII, Part Two, 111, 171.

11. Ibid., 255-56; Stanley Horn, *The Army of Tennessee,* 231.

12. Rosecrans explained his reasoning in testimony before the Committee on the Conduct of the War (*CCW Report, 1865,* Vol. III, Rosecrans' Campaigns, 26-27). See also O.R., Vol. XXIII, Part One, 9, 403-4. Anyone who cares to leaf through his long exchange of messages with Halleck can find plenty of material in O.R., Vol. XXIII, Part Two, 9-383, passim.

13. A good account of the action at Kelly's Ford is in H. B. McClellan's *I Rode with Jeb Stuart*, 202-17.

14. Lee's appraisal of the possibilities is set forth in his dispatches to Cooper, to Seddon and to President Davis during April. O.R., Vol. XXV, Part Two, 713-14, 724-25, 745.

15. Ibid, 756-57.

3. The Darkness, and Jackson, and Fear

1. William Swinton, *Campaigns of the Army of the Potomac*, 275; *CCW Report, 1865*, Vol. I, *Army of the Potomac*, 139-40.

2. Ibid., 114-16; O.R., Vol. XXV, Part One, 1057-65, 1066.

3. Walter H. Hebert, *Fighting Joe Hooker*, 195-98; O.R., Vol. XXV, Part One, 171; Part Two, 306-7.

4. Chancellorsville has been exhaustively analyzed by highly competent critics. To this writer the best study is John Bigelow's massive *The Campaign of Chancellorsville;* it should be supplemented by Douglas Southall Freeman's material in *R. E. Lee* and *Lee's Lieutenants*. A good brief account of Federal maneuvers is Darius N. Couch, *The Chancellorsville Campaign*, B. & L., Vol. III, 154-71. Also useful is Edward J. Stackpole, *Chancellorsville; Lee's Greatest Battle*.

5. Couch, op. cit. 161.

6. O.R., Vol. XXV, Part Two, 330.

7. Col. William Allan, manuscript account of postwar conversations with Lee, in the Southern Historical Collection, University of North Carolina Library; Lee's report on Chancellorsville, O.R., Vol. XXV, Part One, 797-98; Freeman, *R. E. Lee*, Vol. II, 520 ff.

8. O.R., Vol. XXV, Part Two, 360-61. General Howard insisted that this order never reached him. Carl Schurz, one of his division commanders, said that he himself received the order and read it to Howard. Schurz said Howard told him that Hooker did not anticipate a flank attack, citing as proof Hooker's detachment of an XI Corps brigade to go to Sickles' aid. (Carl Schurz, *Reminiscences*, Vol. II, 416-20; Howard, *The Eleventh Corps at Chancellorsville*, B. & L., Vol. II, 196.)

9. Couch, op. cit., 163; O.R., Vol. XXV, Part Two, 363. The order to Sedgwick was timed 4:10 P.M., shortly before Jackson was completing the formation of his column of assault.

10. Letter of Abner Doubleday to Samuel P. Bates dated Oct. 19, 1875, in the Bates Collection, Pennsylvania Historical and Museum Commission, Division of Public Records, Harrisburg.

11. O.R., Vol. XXV, Part Two, 365. The message to Sedgwick was sent at 9 P.M. Headquarters apparently misunderstood Sedg-

wick's position; he had crossed below the town and he needed time to get back into position to carry the sunken road and Marye's Heights. For an analysis of the fight put up by the XI Corps see Augustus Choate Hamlin, *The Battle of Chancellorsville*, 125-28. The soldier's comment quoted here is from the Civil War Diary of Thomas Evans, Manuscript Division, Library of Congress.

12. Couch, op. cit., 164-65.

4. Aftermath of Victory

1. *A Rebel War Clerk's Diary*, 205-7; T. C. De Leon, *Four Years in Rebel Capitals*, 251-52; Richmond *Daily Dispatch*, issues dated May 12 and 13, 1863; Lee to Seddon dated May 10, in O.R., Vol. XXV, Part Two, 790.

2. O.R., Vol. XXIV, Part One, 215; Vol. XXV, Part Two, loc. cit.

3. O.R., Vol. XXV, Part Two, 790-92.

4. Thomas Jordan, *Notes of Projected Operations on the Confederate Side Immediately Following the Battle of Chancellorsville*, in B. & L., extra-illustrated, Vol. XIII, at the Huntington Library. Written in 1877, Jordan's notes were corrected by Beauregard himself. See also O.R., Vol. XXV, Part Two, 791-92; *Lee's Lieutenants*, Vol. III, 42-45.

5. As late as June 23 Lee wrote Davis that if his campaign succeeded "we might even hope to compel the recall of some of the enemy's troops from the west." O.R., Vol. XXVII, Part Three, 924-25.

6. Lee's own postwar explanation of his plans is in Col. William Allan's manuscript notes of a conversation at Lexington, Va., in 1870, now in the Southern Historical Collection, University of North Carolina Library. Maj. Gen. Harry Heth said that Lee told him: "The question of food for this army gives me more trouble and uneasiness than everything else combined; the absence of the army from Virginia gives our people an opportunity to collect supplies ahead." SHSP, Vol. IV, 153.

7. E. P. Alexander, in SHSP, Vol. IV, 98; Lee to Davis, June 10, in O.R., Vol. XXVII, Part Three, 881-82.

8. O.R., Vol. XXV, Part Two, 833-34, 846; Vol. XXVII, Part Three, 453-54, 909, 947; Freeman, *R. E. Lee*, Vol. III, 12-28; Clifford Dowdey, *Experiment in Rebellion*, 277-86.

9. O.R., Vol. XXVII, Part One, 34-35; Basler, Vol. VI, 257.

10. O.R., Vol. XXVII, Part One, 45; Basler, Vol. VI, 281-82. On the eve of the Battle of Gettysburg the President wrote to Gov.

Joel Parker of New Jersey: "I really think the attitude of the enemy's army in Pennsylvania presents us the best opportunity we have had since the war began." O.R., Vol. XXVII, Part Three, 436-37.

11. Letter of T. J. Barnett to Barlow dated May 18, 1863, in the Barlow Papers, Huntington Library; letter of Frank Haskell to his brother dated May 12, in the Haskell Papers, State Historical Society of Wisconsin.

12. Letter of Barnett to Barlow dated June 10, in the Barlow Papers; letter of Lincoln to Isaac Arnold dated May 23, in the Lincoln Collection, Chicago Historical Society. For the exchange of views on McClellan, see O.R., Vol. XXVII, Part Three, 429, 436; also Basler, Vol. VI, 311-12.

13. The assumption that the administration nagged Hooker into resigning does not seem entirely justified by the record. The dispute over Harper's Ferry simply was not big enough to bring a resignation from a general who was not ready to quit anyway. The decisive factor appears to have been Lincoln's order putting Hooker under Halleck; the two men cordially disliked and distrusted each other. For the "forced resignation" theory, see Charles F. Benjamin, *Hooker's Appointment and Removal*, B. & L., Vol. III, 239-43; a very different analysis is in K. P. Williams, *Lincoln Finds a General*, Vol. II, 646-53. Hooker's own version is in *CCW Report, 1865*, Vol. I, *Army of the Potomac*, 163-78, passim.

5. Mirage on the Skyline

1. Diary of Francis Middleton Kennedy, chaplain, entries for June 25 and June 29, 1863, in the Southern Historical Collection, University of North Carolina Library; letter of Major William Noland Berkeley to his wife dated June 28, in the Alderman Library, University of Virginia; Fitzgerald Ross, *Cities and Camps of the Confederate States*, 34, 39; letter of Edward McGehee Burrus dated July 27, in the John C. Burrus Family Papers, Department of Archives, Louisiana State University; James Arthur Lyon Fremantle, *The Fremantle Diary*, 195; Spencer Glasgow Welch, *A Confederate Surgeon's Letters to His Wife*, 56-57. Both Chaplain Kennedy and Major Berkeley testified that despite Lee's orders the Confederate private managed to do a good deal of effective free-lance foraging.

2. Cf. Col. Charles F. Wainwright, *A Diary of Battle*, 229-30: "The Pennsylvanians do not give us an over-warm welcome; they

are much more greedy than the Marylanders. . . . They fully maintain their reputation for meanness."

3. Letter of Gen. N. B. Buford dated June 4, 1863, in the Jacob Ammen Papers, Illinois State Historical Library. For the mutiny of the 109th Illinois regiment, see the New York *Tribune* for Feb. 7, 1863.

4. There is a slightly more detailed discussion of the coal field disturbances in *Glory Road*, 239-44.

5. Congressional Globe, 37th Congress, Third Session, Appendix, 209-10; Part Two, 998. See also O.R., Series Three, Vol. V, 611-12.

6. O.R., Vol. XXIII, Part One, 395-96. There is an engaging retelling of the story in the Cleveland *Plain Dealer* for August 27, 1933.

7. Appleton's *American Annual Cyclopaedia for 1863*, 473.

8. Nicolay & Hay, Vol. VII, 331; *American Annual Cyclopaedia for 1863*, 473-74; Journal of D. R. Larned, entry for May 5, 1863, in the Library of Congress; Dayton dispatch in the Cincinnati *Daily Commercial* for May 7, 1863; O.R., Series Two, Vol. V, 634-35.

9. Ibid., 635-38, 645; Kean, *Inside the Confederate Government*, 63; Cincinnati *Daily Enquirer*, issue of May 25, 1863.

10. *American Annual Cyclopaedia for 1863*, 482.

11. Nicolay & Hay, Vol. VII, 338-39; Basler, Vol. VI, 260-69.

12. There is an excellent account of this case in Mrs. L. E. Ellis, *The Chicago Times During the Civil War*, Illinois State Historical Society's *Transactions for the Year 1932*, 135-69. See also the Chicago *Times*, issues for Jan. 3 and June 5, 1863; *American Annual Cyclopaedia for 1863*, 423-25; O.R., Series Two, Vol. V, 724, and Series Three, Vol. V, 837-38. It seems clear that Burnside's actions against both Vallandigham and Storey were taken without consultation with Washington.

13. Rowland, Vol. V, 513-15; Alexander H. Stephens, *A Constitutional View of the Late War Between the States*, Vol. II, 563-64.

14. Ibid., 565-66; O.R., Series Two, Vol. VI, 74-76.

15. *Diary of Gideon Welles*, Vol. I, 359-61; Johnston and Browne, *Life of Alexander H. Stephens*, 444-45.

16. Letter of Barnett to Barlow dated May 28, 1863, declaring that the political opposition to President Lincoln "is so mixed up that it, as much as anything, presents the spectacle of a peace party"; letter of S. S. Cox to Barlow dated Nov. 21, 1863; both in the Barlow Papers, Huntington Library.

6. Encounter at Gettysburg

1. To follow Lee from June 28 to the beginning of the battle see Freeman, *R. E. Lee,* Vol. III, 60 ff.

2. O.R., Vol. XXVII, Part One, 70-71; Part Three, 458; testimony of Gen. W. S. Hancock, *CCW Report, 1865,* Vol. I, *Army of the Potomac,* 404.

3. Col. George Meade, *The Life and Letters of George Gordon Meade,* Vol. II, 35-36; Col. Thomas L. Livermore, *The Gettysburg Campaign,* MHSM Papers, Vol. XIII, 524-26, 528-29.

4. Abner Doubleday, who was Reynolds' ranking division commander, said that in conversations en route to Gettysburg Reynolds "was clearly of opinion that it was necessary to bring the enemy to battle as soon as possible . . . He was really eager to get at them." (Letter of Doubleday to Samuel Bates dated April 3, 1874, in the Bates Collection, Pennsylvania Historical and Museum Commission, Division of Public Records, Harrisburg.) The orderly who was with Reynolds when the battle began wrote that he had seen many men killed in action but that he never saw one die as quickly as Reynolds did. (Letter of Charles H. Veil to "Mr. McConaughy," dated April 7, 1864, in the Civil War Institute, Gettysburg College.)

5. Letter of Gen. Barlow dated July 7, 1863, in the Francis Channing Barlow Papers, Massachusetts Historical Society. The XI Corps did some hard fighting before it retreated. Its Gettysburg losses included 369 men killed and 1922 wounded, and the great bulk of these losses came on July 1. It listed fewer men as "missing" than did the I Corps.

6. *Reminiscences of Carl Schurz,* Vol. III, 34-37; Ewell's report, O.R., Vol. XXVII, Part Two, 444-46; Jubal Early, *Causes of Lee's Defeat at Gettysburg,* SHSP, Vol. IV, 253-61; A. L. Long, *Memoirs of Robert E. Lee,* 276-78. Ewell has probably been too much blamed for the Confederate failure to seize the heights south of Gettysburg on July 1. His troops were temporarily disorganized by their victory and by the large number of Federal prisoners they had taken; one of the two divisions on the scene, Rodes', had lost 2500 men, and Howard's artillery was laying down a sharp fire. Lee's orders—to take the high ground but not to bring on a general engagement—were vague, and Ewell's decision to wait until Johnson's division arrived is quite understandable. By the time that division was ready to go into action the Federal grip on the new defensive line was probably too firm to be broken.

7. At 6 P.M. on July 1 Meade wrote to Hancock and Double-day: "It seems to me we have so concentrated that a battle at Gettysburg is now forced on us, and that, if we get up all our people and attack with our whole force tomorrow, we ought to defeat the force the enemy has." O.R., Vol. XXVII, Part Three, 466.

8. Longstreet, *Lee's Right Wing at Gettysburg*, B. & L., Vol. III, 339.

9. Diary of Henry Robinson Berkeley, entry dated July 2, in the Virginia State Historical Library, Richmond; letter of E. P. Alexander to his brother dated July 17, in the E. P. Alexander Papers, Southern Historical Collection, University of North Carolina Library.

10. Notes by Gen. Warren commenting on Samuel P. Bates' *The Battle of Gettysburg,* in the G. K. Warren Papers, New York State Library, Albany.

11. The theory that Meade on the night of July 2 wanted to order a retreat to the Pipe Creek line hardly needs to be taken seriously. The Hooker contingent in the Army of the Potomac officer corps argued this at length, and was supported by members of the Committee on the Conduct of the War, and the dreary record of this back-biting is available in the Committee's 1865 report, but the alleged evidence hardly merits detailed consideration.

12. Cf. Gen. Heth, Vol. IV, SHSP, 160: "The fact is, General Lee believed the Army of Northern Virginia, as it then existed, could accomplish anything."

13. Longstreet, *Lee in Pennsylvania,* in *Annals of the War,* 429.

14. O.R., Vol. XXVII, Part One, 74; Col. J. B. Walton, in SHSP, Vol. V, 47-52.

15. John Gibbon, *Personal Recollections of the Civil War,* 147-48; report of Col. Joseph Mayo, Jr., of the 3rd Virginia Infantry, in the George Pickett Papers, Manuscript Department, Duke University Library; diary of Henry Robinson Berkeley, entry for July 3, in the Virginia State Historical Society; Freeman, *R. E. Lee,* Vol. III, 120; memoirs of Gen. Henry H. Bingham, in the Palmer Collection, Western Reserve Historical Society, Cleveland.

16. Longstreet, *Lee's Right Wing at Gettysburg,* B. & L., Vol. III, 346-47.

17. All estimates of numbers and losses in this attack are conjectural, and it is hard to feel sure that one knows how many men made the advance. The figures in the text simply represent

the best guess this writer can make. A good study of the subject is George R. Stewart, *Pickett's Charge.*

It might be emphasized that only a third of "Pickett's charge" was actually Pickett's, since he was not formally in command of either Pettigrew or Trimble. In fact, the command situation was extremely odd. Most of the men belonged to A. P. Hill, but Longstreet was in general control, and he used his control hardly at all—possibly because of his profound premonition of disaster—to direct or guide the operation. Once the advance began the separate divisions were more or less on their own.

18. Frank A. Haskell, *The Battle of Gettysburg,* 118; letter of Meade to "Dear Margaret" dated July 5, in the George G. Meade Papers, the Historical Society of Pennsylvania, Philadelphia; Walter Lord, ed., *The Fremantle Diary,* 213-15; John D. Imboden, *The Confederate Retreat from Gettysburg,* B. & L., Vol. III, 421.

Chapter Four: IN LETTERS OF BLOOD

1. All or Nothing

1. Letter of Grant to his father dated June 15, 1863, in the Philip H. and A. S. W. Rosenbach Foundation, Philadelphia. In this letter Grant said that if his May 22 assault had succeeded, "I could by this time have made a campaign that would have made this state of Mississippi almost safe for a solitary horseman to ride over."

2. For a glimpse of Grant's plans in the early stages, see his letter to Banks, dated March 22, in O.R., Vol. XXIV, Part Three, 125; his April 12 message to Halleck, in the Illinois State Historical Library; message from Charles A. Dana to Secretary Stanton dated April 12, in the Charles A. Dana Papers, Library of Congress; and an incomplete letter by Grant to his father dated April 21, in the Civil War Collection, G. A. R. Room, Chicago Public Library.

3. N.O.R., Vol. XXIV, 610-12, 632-33. The intensity of the fire is indicated by the Confederate estimate that Porter's ships got off more than 3000 rounds in this engagement.

4. Letter of Banks to Mrs. Banks dated April 29, in the N. P. Banks Papers, Essex Institute Library: letter to Burnside, same

date, B. & L., extra-illustrated, Vol. XI, Huntington Library; O.R., Vol. XXVI, Part One, 12.

5. *Personal Memoirs of U. S. Grant*, Vol. I, 480-81.

6. O.R., Vol. XVII, Part One, 252-53, 521-29; study of the Vicksburg campaign in the J. C. Pemberton Letters, New York Public Library. For an excellent account of the cavalry exploit see D. Alexander Brown, *Grierson's Raid.*

7. *Memoirs of W. T. Sherman*, Vol. I, 319; letter of Grant to Sherman dated May 7, in the Illinois State Historical Library, Springfield; O.R., Vol. XXIV, Part One, 576-78. For a recital of Pemberton's problems see his report, ibid., 257-59.

8. Letter of Grant to McPherson dated May 11, in the Rutgers University Library.

9. O.R., Vol. XXIV, Part Three, 815, 842, 859-60.

10. Adam Badeau, *Military History of U. S. Grant*, Vol. I, 249. Edwin C. Bearss, Research Historian at the Vicksburg National Military Park, and one of the most thorough students of the Vicksburg campaign, has argued (in the Vicksburg Sunday *Post* for April 7, 1957) that Pemberton's only real chance was to attack McClernand's corps vigorously on May 13. Grant's army was divided at that time, and Bearss suggests that if Pemberton had been alert and aggressive, "Grant probably would have suffered a humiliating defeat."

11. *Grant Moves South*, 443-45; letter of Maj. William Augustus Drennan, 27th Mississippi infantry, to his wife, dated May 30, in the Mississippi State Department of Archives and History, Jackson; diary of Joseph Dill Alison, in the Southern Historical Collection, University of North Carolina Library; O.R., Vol. XXIV, Part One, 268-69.

12. O.R., Vol. XXIV, Part One, 241.

13. Ibid., 272-73. Pemberton's sick list, and the number of detailed men, must have been high. When Vicksburg finally surrendered more than 31,000 Confederates were paroled.

14. Letter of Gen. Johnston to Gen. W. W. Mackall dated June 7, from the Mackall Papers, Southern Historical Collection.

15. Peter F. Walker, *Vicksburg: A People at War*, 156; letter of Sgt. Thomas Hogan, 5th Missouri infantry, dated July 5, in the Civil War Papers of the Missouri Historical Society; letters of Maj. William Augustus Drennan dated May 30 and June 2, as cited in Note 11, above.

16. Maj. J. T. Hogane, *Reminiscences of the Siege of Vicksburg*, SHSP, Vol. XI, 296; Edward S. Gregory, *Vicksburg During the Siege*, in *Annals of the War*, 116; diary of Rowland Chambers, entries for June 9 and June 14, in the Department of Archives,

Louisiana State University; diary of "Miss Balfour," owned by Mrs. J. W. Collier of Vicksburg, copy in the Mississippi Department of Archives and History.

17. Letter of Banks to Mrs. Banks dated July 8, in the N. P. Banks Papers, Essex Institute Library.

2. *The Notion of Equality*

1. Sallie A. Putnam, *In Richmond During the Confederacy,* 242-43; letter of F. Sorrel, Jr., to Col. Henry Innes Thornton dated July 8, 1863, in the Henry Innes Thornton Papers, California Historical Society, San Francisco; Kean, *Inside the Confederate Government,* 79-81, quoting Robert Garlick Hill Kean's diary entry for July 12.

2. Rowland, Vol. V, 548-49, 552-54.

3. Letter of Jefferson Davis to Judge James H. Howry dated Aug. 27, 1863, in the Howry Family Papers, Library of Congress, the Davis letter having been presented to the Library by Mary Harris Howry and Elizabeth Butler Howry; Rowland, Vol. V, 578-80.

4. O.R., Vol. XXVIII, Part Two, 173. On June 25 Davis had written to Beauregard urging him to send more troops west if he could do so without losing Charleston, adding: "I need not state to you that the issue is vital to the Confederacy." Ibid., 162.

5. *Inside the Confederate Government,* 100; *A Rebel War Clerk's Diary,* 246. Col. Northrop, a Job's comforter if ever there was one, brightly pointed out that even if people had to go without meat they might remember that European peasants rarely ate meat and that peasants in Hindustan never had any.

6. Letter of Bragg to Mrs. Bragg dated June 20; photostat in the Library of Congress.

7. O.R., Vol. XXIII, Part One, 8; Part Two, 420-24; *CCW Report, 1865,* Vol. III, 27; letter of Garfield to his brother dated June 11, in the James A. Garfield Papers, Library of Congress; letter of Garfield to Secretary Chase dated July 27, reprinted after the war in the New York *Sun,* clipping in the Garfield Papers.

8. Stanton to Rosecrans, in the Rosecrans Papers, Library of the University of California at Los Angeles; O.R., Vol. XXIII, Part Two, 518. Rosecrans' losses for the Tullahoma campaign are listed at 570. O.R., Vol. XXIII, Part One, 424.

9. O.R., Vol. XXVII, Part One, 83, 92-94; Nicolay & Hay, Vol. VII, 278; *Lincoln and the Civil War in the Diaries and Letters of John Hay,* 66-67; Noah Brooks, *Washington in Lincoln's Time,* 91-92, 94; Basler, Vol. VI, 327-28.

10. Letter of Rufus Dawes to Mary Gates dated July 14, in the Rufus Dawes Papers, courtesy of Rufus D. Beach and Ralph G. Newman; letter of Frank Haskell dated July 17, in the Frank Haskell Papers, State Historical Society of Wisconsin; letters of Meade to Mrs. Meade dated July 8, July 12 and July 14, in the George G. Meade Papers, Historical Society of Pennsylvania. It should be noted that Meade did not carry his complaints to the press or Congress, but confined them to letters to his wife.

11. Letter of Edward Burrus dated July 27, in the Department of Archives, Louisiana State University.

12. Letters of Lee to Mrs. Lee dated July 12 and July 15, in the R. E. Lee Papers, Library of Congress; Clifford Dowdey, ed., *The Wartime Papers of R. E. Lee*, 560, 564-65.

13. Supra, 188-89.

14. Basler, Vol. VI, 319-20. This short, rambling speech is worth looking at as a first approach to the line of thought that ultimately found expression in the Gettysburg address.

15. *American Annual Cyclopaedia for 1863*, 811-16; Morgan Dix, *Memoirs of John Adams Dix*, Vol. II, 72-75; O.R., Vol. XXVII, Part Two, 878-81, 886-89; diary of Mrs. Gustavus V. Fox, entries for July 13-15, in the Blair Family Papers, Library of Congress.

16. George Templeton Strong, *Diary of the Civil War, 1860-1865*, edited by Allan Nevins, 335-39; editorial in *Harper's Weekly* for July 25, 1863.

3. Servants of the Guns

1. The reader who enjoys drawing historical parallels might reflect on the odd similarity between the Federal operation at Charleston in 1863 and the British attack on the Dardanelles in 1915. In each case, extensive and unsuccessful trench warfare grew out of a simple attempt to open a way for warships. A key feature in each case was naval inability to remove floating mines until the guns which protected the mine fields were silenced; the army came in to help the navy and presently found itself bearing most of the load with the navy in support.

2. Alfred P. Rockwell, *The Operations Against Charleston*, MHSM Papers, Vol. IX, 167-75; Col. Charles H. Olmstead, *Reminiscences of Service in Charleston Harbor in 1863*, SHSP, Vol. XI, 120-21; Maj. Gen. Q. A. Gillmore, *The Army Before Charleston in 1863*, B. & L., Vol. IV, 58-60; Lieut. Iredell Jones, *Letters from Fort Sumter in 1862 and 1863*, SHSP, Vol. XII, 137-39; Gen. W. W. H. Davis, *The Siege of Morris Island*, in *Annals*

of the War, 95-99; dispatch in the New York *Tribune* dated July 19, 1863, reprinted in Moore's *Rebellion Record,* Vol. VII, Documents, 211-14.

3. Journal of Admiral Dahlgren, entries for Aug. 9 and Aug. 13, quoted in *Memoir of John A. Dahlgren,* by Madeleine Vinton Dahlgren, 407; Charles H. Olmstead, op. cit., 164-65.

4. Gen. W. W. H. Davis, op. cit., 104-5; Olmstead, 158-59; O.R., Vol. XXVIII, Part One, 210.

5. Capt. Justus Scheibert, *Seven Months in the Rebel States During the North American War,* 135-36; Maj. Gen. Samuel Jones, *The Siege of Charleston,* 255-59, 278-84; Brig. Gen. George H. Gordon, *A War Diary of Events in the War of the Great Rebellion,* 183-92.

6. William H. Stryker, *The Swamp Angel,* B. & L., Vol. IV, 72-74.

7. Gordon, *War Diary,* 194; C. F. Adams, *Charles Francis Adams, by His Son,* 342.

4. The Road to Zion

1. *American Annual Cyclopaedia for 1863,* 332-33. Crittenden, a Senator in 1860, was a Representative in 1863. His 1860 compromise plan involved chiefly a permanent restoration of the old Missouri Compromise line, with slavery forever prohibited north of it and permitted, at the option of the inhabitants, south of it. This was to be written into the Constitution, with a specific proviso that Congress lacked power to interfere with slavery where it then existed.

2. Letter of James Roberts Gilmore to Rosecrans on May 28, 1863, in the Rosecrans Papers, Library of the University of California at Los Angeles. Gilmore had talked to Lincoln and said his peace terms "will be something as follows." See also Lincoln's telegrams to Rosecrans dated May 21 and May 28, in Basler, Vol. VI, 225, 236.

3. Letter of T. J. Barnett to Barlow dated July 9, in the Barlow Papers, Huntington Library; letter of Attorney General Bates to Francis Lieber dated Oct. 8, in the Lieber Collection, also at the Huntington Library.

4. Basler, Vol. VI, 406-10.

5. Lincoln to Schofield dated Oct. 28, in John Hay, *Lincoln and the Civil War,* 108.

6. N.O.R., Vol. II, 322-25, 655-57.

7. Banks discusses his general plan, his orders to Franklin and the failure of the expedition in O.R., Vol. XXVI, Part One, 18-20.

8. Col. O. M. Roberts in *Confederate Military History*, Vol. XI, *Texas*, 106-7, 111.

9. Montague Bernard, *Neutrality of Great Britain During the American Civil War*, 471-72; *Messages and Papers of the Confederacy*, Vol. II, 539-40. Benjamin's letttter was dated Aug. 4, 1863.

10. Frederick W. Seward, *Seward at Washington as Senator and Secretary of State*, Vol. III, 180.

11. C. F. Adams, *Charles Francis Adams, by His Son*, 342-43.

12. Spencer Walpole, *The Life of Lord John Russell*, Vol. II, 359; Rhodes, Vol. VI, 381-83; Herbert C. F. Bell, *Lord Palmerston*, Vol. II, 354-55.

13. *Charles Francis Adams, by His Son*, 317.

14. Rowland, Vol. VI, 103-5.

5. A Mad Irregular Battle

1. O.R., Vol. XXX, Part One, 47-53. For a cogent defense of Rosecrans' delay, see W. M. Lamers, *Edge of Glory*, 292-300.

2. Freeman, *R. E. Lee*, Vol. III, 163-67; O.R., Vol. XXIX, Part Two, 700-2.

3. George Edgar Turner, *Victory Rode the Rails*, 282-83; Robert C. Black, *The Railroads of the Confederacy*, 185-91; James Longstreet, *From Manassas to Appomattox*, 436-37; G. Moxley Sorrel, *Recollections of a Staff Officer*, 180-82; E. P. Alexander, *Military Memoirs of a Confederate*, 448-49.

4. O.R., Vol. XXIII, Part Two, 953.

5. The difficulty of getting a satisfactory count of Civil War numbers is especially acute in the Chickamauga campaign. The figures available do not necessarily mean what they seem to mean. Rosecrans' Aug. 10 return shows just under 80,000 men present for duty in his command. An undetermined number must be subtracted for duty in the rear, and it seems likely that the effective total for the field army was somewhere between 60,000 and 65,000. Bragg's present-for-duty total includes a much higher proportion of cavalry than Rosecrans' total includes, and ordinarily cavalry had only a very minor role in a major battle; but a good part of Bragg's cavalry belonged to Forrest and could fight dismounted, on equal terms, against any infantry in the land. The returns are in O.R., Vol. XXIII, Part Two, 607, 957.

6. O.R., Vol. XXX, Part Three, 479, 481; letter of Gen. W. B. Hazen to Benson H. Lossing dated Aug. 23, 1866, in the Palmer Collection, Western Reserve Historical Society, Cleveland.

7. Original in the Braxton Bragg Papers, Manuscript Depart-

ment, Duke University Library. Bragg's recital of all of this is in O.R., Vol. XXX, Part Two, 26-31; Hindman's defense is in the same volume, 292-96. See also D. H. Hill, *Chickamauga, the Great Battle of the West*, B. & L., Vol. III, 638-47; Capt. W. N. Polk, *Leonidas Polk, Bishop and General*, Vol. II, 240-44, and *The Battle of Chickamauga*, SHSP, Vol. X, 5-7. Careful study of all this material bears out the remark in the text; Bragg unquestionably was served by some very difficult generals. (One is tempted to add that although the Confederacy seemed to have more of these difficult generals the Federals had more who were not so much difficult as downright impossible.)

8. John B. Turchin, *Chickamauga*, 95; O.R., Vol. LI, Part Two, 760-61. Stanley Horn calls Bragg's plan "a masterpiece of strategy which, if successful, would have driven the whole Federal army into McLemore's cove, and never could they have scaled those precipitate walls in time to escape butchery or capture. . . . If one overlooks the fact that Rosecrans had changed the position of his army from where Bragg thought it was, one can find no fault with Bragg's basic strategy." (*The Army of Tennessee*, 255.)

9. On the Federal side, Sheridan wrote: "Nearly all the superior officers of the army were at headquarters, and it struck me that much depression prevailed." (*Personal Reminiscences*, Vol. I, 279.) For the Confederates, Hood said that he met the principal officers of Bragg's army that night, "and to my surprise not one spoke in a sanguine tone regarding the result of the battle in which we were then engaged." (*Advance and Retreat*, 62-63.)

10. Charles A. Dana, *Recollections of the Civil War*, 113; L. W. Mulhane, *Memorial of Major General William Stark Rosecrans*, 68-70.

11. Letter of Rosecrans to George B. Pearson dated Nov. 1, 1863, in the Rosecrans Papers, UCLA Library; Dana, op. cit., 113-14.

12. O.R., Vol. XXX, Part Two, 33.

13. Shortly after the battle Bragg told his wife that at seven in the morning a member of his staff found Polk sitting in a rocking chair on the porch at his headquarters, waiting for breakfast and explaining that he really did not know why his attack had not begun. A few days later Bragg wrote another letter, placing the incident at eight o'clock and declaring: "I shall say candidly to the President that he must relieve Genl. Polk or myself." (Letters dated Sept. 22 and 27, in the Braxton Bragg Papers, Missouri Historical Society.) Polk issued orders for the attack before midnight on Sept. 19; he asserted that in the morning, learning that the

order had not reached Hill, he rode to the front to get things moving. O.R., Vol. XXX, Part Two, 47.

14. The fatal element in the disaster was of course the withdrawal of Wood's division, and Rosecrans and Wood argued furiously afterward, each blaming the other. Inasmuch as Wood did precisely what Rosecrans' written order told him to do it is hard to feel that Rosecrans could blame anyone but himself. For details, see O.R., Vol. XXX, Part One, 58-59, 102-4, 634-37, 645-47. Excellent recent treatments are in Lamers' *The Edge of Glory*, 336-48, and in Glenn Tucker's *Chickamauga, Bloody Battle in the West*, 251-59.

15. That at least is the only conclusion this writer can draw. Rosecrans was an appealing character, and most of the time he was a first-rate general, but he does seem to have lost his grip—certainly on the battle, and probably on himself as well—once he left the field. The post-battle claim that Chickamauga actually was a Union triumph—expressed most strongly by H. V. Boynton in the assertion: "It was not a forced withdrawal . . . it was an advance toward Chattanooga"—is hardly worth serious consideration. (Boynton, *The Chickamauga Campaign*, MHSM Papers, Vol. VII, 362-63.)

16. *Ambrose Bierce's Civil War*, 37.

17. O.R., Vol. XXX, Part One, 142, 192.

6. 37,000 Plus One

1. Longstreet, *From Manassas to Appomattox*, 466; O.R., Vol. XXX, Part Two, 65-66; Part Four, 706. Bragg put Polk under arrest and prepared to file charges against him, but President Davis —who retained confidence in both men—talked him out of it. Ibid., 734-36; Rowland, Vol. VI, 54-56.

2. O.R., Vol. XXX, Part Four, 681, 691, 695, 701; Livermore, *Numbers and Losses*, 105-6; Alexander, *Military Memoirs of a Confederate*, 452.

3. Bragg's argument is in O.R., Vol. XXX, Part Two, 36-37. He said that nearly half of his army consisted of reinforcements that came in just before the battle, bringing no transportation whatever, and he added that nearly a third of his artillery horses were battle casualties.

4. Capt. Irving A. Buck, *Cleburne and His Command*, 158-59; *From Manassas to Appomattox*, 465-67; Armand Beauregard to his brother, Gen. Beauregard, in O.R., Vol. XXX, Part Four, 746; letter of Davis to Bragg dated June 29, 1872, reviewing the

situation in respect to Pemberton, in the Lincoln National Life Foundation, Fort Wayne, Ind.

5. O.R., Vol. XXX, Part One, 197-98.

6. Thomas Weber, *The Northern Railroads in the Civil War*, 180-86; Nicolay & Hay, Vol. VIII, 236-37; George Turner, *Victory Rode the Rails*, 286-96; O.R., Vol. XXIX, Part One, 146-95, passim; David Homer Bates, *Lincoln in the Telegraph Office*, 174-79. Slocum's protest is in O.R., Vol. XXIX, Part One, 156. See also D.A.B., Vol. XVII, 217.

7. *Memoirs of W. T. Sherman*, Vol. I, 347-58; James R. Sullivan, *Chickamauga and Chattanooga Battlefields*, 27. Halleck ordered these reinforcements before the battle of Chickamauga, realizing that Rosecrans was going to need help, but the orders did not reach Grant until Sept. 22.

8. Thomas B. Van Horne, *History of the Army of the Cumberland*, Vol. I, 386-88; O.R., Vol. XXX, Part One, 214-21, passim.

9. O.R., op. cit., 218-19. For a more cheerful view see H. V. Boynton, *The Battles Around Chattanooga*, MHSM Papers, Vol. VII, 379-81; see also Henry Villard, *Memoirs*, Vol. II, 157, 185. The Rosecrans Papers at the UCLA Library contain an interesting memorandum, *Recollection of Circumstances Surrounding the Removal of Rosecrans from Command of the Army of the Cumberland*, which includes letters from Dana and from Montgomery Blair confirming the story of Garfield's indiscretions. Secretary Chase had always been a strong supporter of Rosecrans; according to this memorandum, a letter from Garfield caused him to withdraw his support.

10. Letter of Banks to Mrs. Banks dated Sept. 5, 1863, in the N. P. Banks Papers, Essex Institute Library. Somewhat later, Gen. Franklin wrote to Gen. W. F. Smith that Grant was lucky to have fallen: "Grant had commenced a frolic that would have ruined him in body and reputation in a week. For two days he had been on a continued bender." (Letter dated Dec. 28, 1863, in the papers of William Farrar Smith, private collection of Walter Wilgus.)

11. O.R., Vol. XXX, Part Two, 27; Van Horne, op. cit., 393-94, 401, 405.

12. Interview by Hamlin Garland with Col. L. B. Eaton, in the Hamlin Garland Papers, University of Southern California Library.

13. There is a good study of the operation in T. L. Livermore, *The Siege and Relief of Chattanooga*, MHSM Papers, Vol. VIII, 319-23.

14. Rowland, Vol. VI, 69-71; O.R., Vol. LII, Part Two, 559-60.

15. Letter to Mrs. Bragg dated Nov. 14, 1863, in the Braxton Bragg Papers, Missouri Historical Society.

16. Maj. Gen. Thomas J. Wood said Grant told him that if the Confederate line at the foot of the ridge could be taken "it would so threaten Bragg's center that he would draw enough troops from his right . . . to ensure the success of General Sherman's attack." (Wood, *The Battle of Missionary Ridge*, in *Sketches of War History*, Ohio Commandery Papers, MOLLUS, Vol. IV, 34.)

17. It is clear that various generals, notably Sheridan and Wood, ordered their men up the mountainside; equally clear that the men got the idea independently. Wood wrote: "I frankly confess that I was simply one of the boys on that occasion. I was infected by the prevailing enthusiasm." (Wood, op. cit., 37.) Brig. Gen. William B. Hazen of Wood's division said flatly that the battle "was fought by the men of the army and not by the generals." (Hazen's account of Missionary Ridge, in the Palmer Collection, Western Reserve Historical Society.)

18. Montgomery Meigs, who was with Grant during the battle, wrote: "General Grant said that it was contrary to orders, it was not his plan—he meant to form the lines and then prepare and launch columns of assault, but as the men carried away by their enthusiasm had gone so far he would not order them back." (Mss. *Journal of the Battle of Chattanooga*, in the M. C. Meigs Papers, Library of Congress.) Grant's behavior during the battle is described by Joseph Fullerton, *The Army of the Cumberland at Chattanooga*, B. & L., Vol. III, 725.

19. O.R., Vol. XXXI, Part Two, 664-67; Wood, op. cit., 38.

20. James A. Connolly, *Three Years in the Army of the Cumberland*, 158; letter of U. S. Grant to "Dear James" dated Dec. 3, 1863, in the Grant Papers, Chicago Historical Society.

Chapter Five: THE IMPOSSIBILITIES

1. An Impassable Gulf

1. O.R., Vol. XXXI, Part Two, 664-67; post-war letter to Major G. T. Sykes, quoted in W. M. Polk, *Leonidas Polk*, Vol.

II, 308; letters to Davis dated Nov. 30 and Dec. 10, in the Palmer Collection, Western Reserve Historical Society; letter to Davis dated Dec. 8, in the Jefferson Davis Papers, Manuscript Department, Duke University Library.

2. Kean, *Inside the Confederate Government*, 116-17, 119; letter of Bragg to Davis dated Dec. 2, in the Palmer Collection; Lee to Davis dated Dec. 3, in the André de Coppet Collection, Manuscripts Division, Princeton University Library; private letter, Lee to Jeb Stuart, dated Dec. 9, in the H. B. McClellan Papers, Virginia State Historical Society; O.R., Vol. XXXI, Part Three, 792, 813-16.

3. The tabulation was made by Robert Garlick Hill Kean, head of the War Department's "Bureau of War," and is found in *Inside the Confederate Government*, 120-21. A return for the Confederate army on or about Dec. 31, 1863, gives a present for duty total of 233,586. O.R., Series Four, Vol. II, 1073.

4. O.R., Vol. XXXI, Part Three, 842-43, 856-57; Johnston to Wigfall, letters dated Dec. 27, 1863, and Jan. 6, 1864, in the Louis T. Wigfall Papers, Library of Congress.

5. Burnside's account of his operation gives a convincing explanation of his inability to come to Rosecrans' aid at Chattanooga; O.R., Vol. XXX, Part One, 272-79, and Part Three, 904-5.

6. *CCW Report, 1865*, Vol. I, *Army of the Potomac*, 339-40, 381; Swinton, *Campaigns of the Army of the Potomac*, 373-75.

7. Basler, Vol. VI, 466-67.

8. O.R., Vol. XXIX, Part One, 407-9; letter to Mrs. Lee dated Oct. 19, in the R. E. Lee Papers, Library of Congress.

9. Meade's report on the Mine Run campaign is in O.R., Vol. XXIX, Part One, 12-18. There is a good treatment of the affair in Thomas L. Livermore, *The Mine Run Campaign*, November 1863, MHSM Papers, Vol. XIV, 45-53.

10. Sallie A. Putnam, *In Richmond During the Confederacy*, 262.

11. Rowland, Vol. VI, 127-28; editorial in the Richmond *Examiner*, issue of Nov. 24, 1863.

2. Eloquence at Gettysburg

1. Basler, Vol. VI, 428; diary of William T. Coggeshall, military secretary to Gov. Dennison of Ohio, entry for Nov. 26, 1863, in the Illinois State Historical Library; the gift of Mrs. Foreman M. Lebold.

2. This was the famous "ten percent plan," set forth in Lin-

coln's Proclamation of Amnesty and Reconstruction dated Dec. 8, in Basler, Vol. VII, 53-56.

3. The letters to Banks are dated Aug. 5 and Nov. 5, 1863; Basler, Vol. VI, 364-65, and Vol. VII, 1-2.

4. Telegram dated Aug. 5 and draft of reply dated Aug. 6, in the John G. Nicolay Papers, Library of Congress.

5. Letters of Blair to Barlow dated Dec. 23 and Dec. 29, 1863, in the Barlow Papers, Huntington Library.

6. Letter to "My dear Wife" dated Dec. 16, in the Edwin Oberlin Wentworth letters, Library of Congress.

7. *Terrible Swift Sword*, 370-71.

8. Supra, 134. Lincoln occasionally gave lip service to the idea of colonization after this, but to all intents and purposes he had abandoned it.

9. O.R., Vol. XXIII, Part One, 632-818, passim. Morgan's orders from Joe Wheeler, dated June 18, were to operate in Kentucky against Federal railroad lines and supply depots, and to fall on Rosecrans' rear if Rosecrans moved against Bragg.

10. Clifford D. Owsley, *Genesis of the World's Greatest Speech*, in the *Lincoln Herald*, Fall 1962, 136.

11. Cincinnati *Daily Commercial* for Nov. 23, 1863, photostats from Lincoln National Life Foundation, courtesy of Dr. R. Gerald McMurtry; letter of Frank Haskell to his brother dated Nov. 20, in the Haskell Papers, State Historical Society of Wisconsin. The estimate of the number of visitors is from the Washington *Daily Chronicle* for Nov. 20.

12. Cincinnati *Daily Commercial*, as cited in Note 11, above; Fred Stripp, *The Other Gettysburg Address*, in *Civil War History*, June 1955, 164; Boston *Journal* for Nov. 23, 1863. Excellent coverage of the day at Gettysburg can be found in Louis A. Warren, *Lincoln's Gettysburg Declaration: A New Birth of Freedom*, and David C. Mearns and Lloyd A. Dunlap, *Long Remembered*.

13. Associated Press text, photostat from the Lincoln National Life Foundation; John Hay, *Lincoln and the Civil War*, 121.

3. Amnesty and Suffrage

1. *American Annual Cyclopaedia for 1864*, 219.

2. Basler, Vol. VII, 53-56.

3. John Hay, *Lincoln and the Civil War*, 131-32; Noah Brooks, *Washington in Lincoln's Time*, 150-51.

4. Congressional Globe, 38th Congress, First Session, Part III, 2095-96.

5. Ibid., Part I, 21, 45.

6. *American Annual Cyclopaedia for 1864,* 227; Congressional Globe, 38th Congress, First Session, Part I, 22.

7. Ibid., Part III, 2041-45.

8. Congressional Globe, 38th Congress, First Session, Part IV, 3448-49. For a brief sketch of Davis, see the *American Annual Cyclopaedia for 1865,* 305-6.

9. Congressional Globe, 38th Congress, First Session, Part IV, Appendix, 82-85.

10. Ibid., Part III, 3449-51.

11. John Hay, op. cit., 205.

12. A supposed letter from Lincoln to Gen. James Wadsworth, vaguely dated "January 1864" and stating the President's readiness to accept universal suffrage (Basler, Vol. VII, 101-2), would be most useful if its authenticity could be accepted. Unfortunately, it seems to be a shaky bit of evidence. The original of the letter has not been found; the text comes from a story in the New York *Tribune* for Sept. 26, 1865, quoting a story supposed to have appeared in the *Southern Advocate*—and, as Editor Basler points out, the original copy of that paper has not been found, either. That the document may state Lincoln's private position is of course quite possible, but by itself it is not convincing. On top of other objections, it contains sentences that just do not sound like Lincoln.

13. Basler, Vol. VII, 243, 281-82.

14. Letter of H. G. Stebbins dated Jan. 20, 1864, in the Barlow Papers.

15. Letter of Lt. Col. Samuel M. Quincy dated March 12, 1864, in the Samuel M. Quincy Papers, Massachusetts Historical Society.

16. Basler, Vol. VII, 433-34; Noah Brooks, op. cit., 154-55; John Hay, 204-5; Diary of Edward Bates, 382-83.

4. Solitary in a Crowd

1. Letter of Cox to Barlow dated Dec. 13, 1863, in the Barlow Papers.

2. Congressional Globe, 38th Congress, First Session, Part I, 428-29.

3. Grant to J. N. Morris of Quincy, Ill., dated Jan. 21, 1864; from the U. S. Grant Association, original in the Illinois State Historical Library.

4. Helen Nicolay, *Lincoln's Secretary: a Biography of John G.*

Nicolay, 194-95; Noah Brooks, *Washington in Lincoln's Time,* 134-35; *Diary of Gideon Welles,* Vol. I, 538-39.

5. R. H. Dana, Jr., to his wife, dated April 21, 1864, in the Dana Papers, Massachusetts Historical Society.

6. Hamlin Garland's notes on an interview with Judge J. H. Robinson, in the Hamlin Garland Papers, University of Southern California Library; letter of Banks to Mrs. Banks dated Aug. 1, 1863, in the N. P. Banks Papers, Essex Institute Library; typescript, *Note by Mrs. Dr. Baker,* in the Garland Papers.

7. *Diary of Gideon Welles,* Vol. I, 440; letter of Grant to C. A. Dana dated Aug. 5, 1863, thanking Dana for "your timely intercession in saving me from going to the Army of the Potomac," from the U. S. Grant Association, original in the Library of Congress; letter of Grant to Congressman Elihu B. Washburne, in the Illinois State Historical Library; Helen Nicolay, op. cit., 196.

8. Letter of Gen. Humphreys to Mrs. Humphreys dated March 10, in the A. A. Humphreys Papers, the Historical Society of Pennsylvania; Wainwright, *A Diary of Battle,* 329, 338.

9. *Personal Memoirs of U. S. Grant,* Vol. II, 116-17; *The Life and Letters of George Gordon Meade,* Vol. II, 177-78.

10. O.R., Vol. XXXII, Part Two, 99-101, 142-43; Vol. XXXIII, 394-95.

11. Letter of Grant to Halleck dated April 26, 1864, in the Illinois State Historical Library.

12. O.R., Vol. XXXII, Part One, 173-79.

13. O.R., Vol. XXXVI, Part One, 12-18. The President's unavailing attempt to get Don Carlos Buell to see this point is set forth in *Terrible Swift Sword,* 472-73.

14. O.R., Vol. XXXIII, 827-28.

15. U. S. Grant, *Preparing for the Campaigns of 1864,* B. & L., Vol. IV, 112. Grant apparently liked Lincoln's expression; a little later, telling Sherman about his plans for a move up the Shenandoah Valley, he remarked that "if Sigel can't skin himself he can hold a leg whilst someone else skins." O.R., Vol. XXXII, Part Three, 246.

5. The General and the Statesman

1. Ulrich Bonnell Phillips, ed., *The Correspondence of Robert Toombs, Alexander H. Stephens and Howell Cobb;* Annual Report of the American Historical Association for the Year 1911, Vol. II, 631.

2. Richardson, *Messages and Papers of the Confederacy,* Vol.

I, 329-31; Rowland, Vol. VI, 164-69. See also E. Merton Coulter, *The Confederate States of America, 1861-65,* 392-93.

3. Richard Malcolm Johnson and William H. Browne, *Life of Alexander H. Stephens,* 452-53.

4. From the André de Coppet Collection, Princeton University Library: letter in the handwriting of W. T. Sherman, copied by him from an original loaned to him after the war by a former soldier who picked it up at Johnson's home, Sandy Green, Ga., in 1864.

5. Ulrich Bonnell Phillips, op. cit., 628.

6. Edward A. Pollard, *Life of Jefferson Davis,* 309, 312-13; Frank Vandiver, ed., *Proceedings of the First Confederate Congress, Fourth Session,* SHSP, Vol. L, 21-22, 37, 49.

7. Rowland, Vol. VI, 141-46.

8. O.R., Vol. XXXIII, 1064-65, 1073, 1076-77, 1094-95; *The Wartime Papers of R. E. Lee,* 672-73.

9. Letter of Lee to Davis dated Feb. 3, in the André de Coppet Collection, Princeton University Library.

10. Lee to Davis dated March 25, in *The Wartime Papers of R. E. Lee,* 682-84.

11. Letter to G. W. C. Lee dated March 29, in the R. E. Lee Papers, Manuscript Department, Duke University Library; letters to Davis dated March 30 and April 12, in the André de Coppet Collection; O.R., Vol. XXXIII, 1260-61, 1276-77; Vol. XXXII, Part Three, 156.

12. Lee to Bragg dated April 16, in the Eldridge Collection, Huntington Library; O.R., Vol. XXXVI, Part Two, 1054.

13. *Military Memoirs of a Confederate,* 493-94.

Chapter Six: ACT OF FAITH

1. The Last Barrier

1. Letters of Johnston to Senator Wigfall dated Jan. 6, Jan. 9, March 6, April 5, and April 30, in the Louis Wigfall Papers, Library of Congress; letter to J. E. B. Stuart dated Jan. 21, in the Huntington Library.

2. For a discussion of Hood's role, see Gilbert E. Govan and James W. Livingood, *A Different Valor,* 249-57.

3. O.R., Vol. XXXII, Part Three, 468-69. Note that the Federals named their armies for rivers while the Confederates named theirs for states. Thus Johnston's command was the Army of Tennessee and McPherson's was the Army of *the* Tennessee.

4. Henry Stone, *The Atlanta Campaign; Part One, the Opening of the Campaign*, MHSM Papers, Vol. VIII, 347.

5. M. A. DeWolfe Howe, *Home Letters of Gen. Sherman*, 291-94; *CCW Report, 1865*, Supplement, Part One, *Report of Maj. Gen. George H. Thomas*, 198, 201-2; O.R., Vol. XXXVIII, Part One, 61-65; Part Three, 721; *Memoirs of Gen. W. T. Sherman*, Vol. II, 34; Govan and Livingood, *A Different Valor*, 263-67.

6. *The Sherman Letters: Correspondence between General and Senator Sherman from* VRCG *to 1891*, edited by R. S. Thorndike, 235-36; Joseph E. Johnston, *Opposing Sherman's March to Atlanta*, B. & L., Vol. IV, 262-65.

7. The estimate of casualties is in Stone, op. cit., 390.

8. Johnston, *Opposing Sherman's March to Atlanta*, 268-69, and *Narrative of Military Operations*, 321-24; O.R., Vol. XXXVIII, Part Three, 615-16. Hood's account of this, so unlike Johnston's that the two simply cannot be reconciled, is in his *Advance and Retreat*, 98-101, 104-9.

9. *The Sherman Letters*, 235-36; letter of Sherman to Silas F. Miller of Louisville; photostat in the Filson Club, Louisville, from original owned by John Mason Brown of New York.

10. Stone, op. cit., 412-13; John M. Schofield, *Forty-six Years in the Army*, 145.

11. *Memoirs of Gen. W. T. Sherman*, Vol. II, 51-53.

12. Sherman's report from Acworth, Ga., dated June 8, in B. & L., extra-illustrated, Vol. XIII, Huntington Library; Sherman to Grant dated June 18, in the Sherman Papers, also at the Huntington Library.

13. O.R., Vol. XXXVIII, Part Four, 610-11; Johnston, *Narrative of Military Operations*, 341; O. O. Howard, *The Struggle for Atlanta*, B. & L., Vol. IV, 311. The estimate of 3000 Union casualties is Sherman's; Livermore (*Numbers and Losses*, 120-21) puts it at 2051 and says that slightly more than 16,000 Federals were engaged. Johnston insisted that Union losses were far above Sherman's estimate.

14. Johnston discussed his plans in a letter to Senator Wigfall dated Aug. 27, in the Wigfall Papers, Library of Congress. Good accounts of Sherman's operations from Kennesaw Mountain to the crossing of the Chattahoochee are in Stone, 422-35, and Jacob Cox, *Military Reminiscences of the Civil War*, Vol. II, 262-77.

2. Sideshows

1. Diary of S. R. Mallory, in the Southern Historical Collection, University of North Carolina Library; letter of Secretary Seddon, in Rowland, Vol. VIII, 349-54. Mallory believed that Benjamin's constant criticisms of Johnston had much to do with Mr. Davis' action.

2. Davis, *Rise and Fall of the Confederate Government*, Vol. II, 555-56; postwar letter to James Lyons of Richmond, dated Aug. 13, 1876, in the Virginia State Historical Society.

3. Bragg to Davis, dated July 15, sent from Atlanta to Richmond by special messenger, in Vol. XIII of the extra-illustrated edition of B. & L., at the Huntington Library. A staff officer in Hardee's corps may have appraised the situation accurately when he wrote: "The fact is that Pres. Davis is influenced by political as well as military considerations." (Letter of W. W. Gordon, an officer on the staff of Brig. Gen. H. W. Mercer, dated July 17, in the Gordon Family Papers, Georgia Historical Society.)

4. *The Wartime Papers of R. E. Lee*, 821-22; Rowland, Vol. VI, 293-94.

5. O.R., Vol. XXXVIII, Part Five, 879-80. Hood's estimate of the army's losses appears to have been a good deal too high.

6. Henry Stone, *The Atlanta Campaign*, MHSM Papers, Vol. VIII, 433-34.

7. William Witherspoon, *Tishomingo Creek, or Brice's Cross Roads*, 113.

8. Rowland, Vol. VI, 278-80. Johnston's appeals for Forrest are in O.R., Vol. XXXVIII, Part Four, 772, 777, 792, 796.

9. Robert Selph Henry, *First with the Most: Forrest*, 235 ff; O.R., Vol. XXXII, Part One, 611-13; Vol. XXXIX, Part One, 89-96, 221-28. The literature on Fort Pillow is extensive, and it is almost impossible to be sure that one knows exactly what happened. Two studies that struck this writer as especially useful are Henry, op. cit., 248-68, and Albert Castel, *The Fort Pillow Massacre: a Fresh Examination of the Evidence*, in *Civil War History*, Vol. IV, Number One, March 1958, 37-50.

10. O.R., Vol. XXXIV, Part Two, 15-16, 55-56, 133.

11. *CCW Report, 1865*, Vol. II, *Red River Expedition*, 273. The Committee on the Conduct of the War developed much interesting testimony regarding the Red River expedition. Because of the Committee's bias against Banks and the ten percent plan, its material needs to be handled with some caution; from first

to last, this body was more a propaganda agency than a fact-finding committee.

12. O.R., Vol. XXXIV, Part One, 196-97; Part Two, 610-11; Richard B. Irwin, *The Red River Campaign*, B. & L., Vol. IV, 349-50.

13. John Homans, *The Red River Expedition*, MHSM Papers, Vol. VIII, 77-82; E. Kirby Smith, *The Defense of the Red River*, B. & L., Vol. IV, 372; O.R., Vol. XXXIV, Part Two, 181-87; N.O.R., Vol. XXVI, 56.

14. A. T. Mahan, *The Gulf and Inland Waters*, 198-207; Thomas O. Selfridge, *The Navy in the Red River*, B. & L., Vol. IV, 364-65.

15. E. Merton Coulter, *Commercial Intercourse with the Confederacy in the Mississippi Valley, 1861-65*, in the Mississippi Valley Historical Review, Vol. V, No. Four, 387-95; O.R., Vol. XLI, Part Four, 785-87; Basler, Vol. VIII, 163-64.

16. Thirty-eighth Congress, Second Session, House of Representatives Report No. 24, *Trade with Rebellious States*, 84; *CCW Report, 1865*, Vol. II, *Red River Expedition*, 18-19, 27, 81, 244, 270-71.

17. John Homans, op. cit., 71.

3. The Cork in the Bottle

1. Lieut. Col. George Bruce, *General Butler's Bermuda Campaign*, MHSM Papers, Vol. IX, 310-11; dispatch of Gen. George Pickett to Bragg and Beauregard, dated May 6, in the Palmer Collection, Western Reserve Historical Society.

2. O.R., Vol. XXXIII, 794-95, 904, 1017-18.

3. In 1864 Richmond had two railroad connections with the deep South—the Richmond & Danville line, which intersected the broken trunk line across Tennessee, and the Richmond & Petersburg road, tying in at Petersburg with the principal routes across the Carolinas to Georgia and the Gulf. The line to Petersburg was vital, and in the spring of 1865 the loss of Petersburg brought about the immediate evacuation of Richmond.

4. After the battle of Chattanooga, Smith was promoted to major general, largely on Grant's recommendation. There was strong opposition in the Senate, but confirmation was voted on Grant's insistence. After the war, Grant wrote that "I was not long in finding out that the objections to Smith's promotion were well founded." (Grant, *Preparing for the Campaigns of 1864*, B. & L., Vol. IV, 104.)

5. Barbed wire did not exist in 1864, but this use of telegraph

wire foreshadowed the way barbed wire would eventually be
used. The telegraph wire, of course, was intended simply to trip
the advancing soldiers rather than to entangle them. There was
a similar use of it by Burnside's engineers during the siege of
Knoxville. Butler's letter to Senator Wilson is in O.R., Vol.
XXXVI, Part Two, 518.

6. The best account of Butler's adventures before the battle of
Drewry's Bluff is that of Col. Bruce, cited in Note 1, above. There
is also a good account by Alfred P. Rockwell, *The Tenth Army
Corps in Virginia, May, 1864,* MHSM Papers, Vol. IX, 294 ff.

7. Beauregard, *The Defense of Drewry's Bluff,* B. & L., Vol.
IV, 195-205; W. F. Smith, *Butler's Attack on Drewry's Bluff,* in
the same volume, 206-11; Livermore, *Numbers and Losses,* 113;
Martin A. Haynes, *A History of the Second Regiment, New
Hampshire Volunteer Infantry,* 224-26.

8. O.R., Vol. XXXVI, Part One, 20-21; Part Two, 10-11;
Freeman, *R. E. Lee,* Vol. III, 356.

9. Edward Raymond Turner, *The New Market Campaign,
1864,* ix, 98-100; Gen. John D. Imboden, *The Battle of New
Market,* B. & L., Vol. IV, 480-86; Gen. Franz Sigel, *Sigel in the
Shenandoah Valley in 1864,* in the same volume, 487-91; William
Couper, *Virginia Military Institute Seventy-fifth Anniversary of
the Battle of New Market,* 8-14; John S. Wise, *The West Point of
the Confederacy Boys in Battle at New Market, Virginia,* in an
unidentified magazine in the files of E. B. Long; Cecil D. Eby, Jr.,
With Sigel at New Market: the Diary of Col. D. H. Strother,
Civil War History, Vol. VI, No. One, 75-82. The veteran's
memory as to "Rockabye Baby" may have deceived him: apparently this tune was written after the war.

10. O.R., Vol. XXXVI, Part Two, 840-41; Freeman, *Lee's
Lieutenants,* Vol. III, 515.

11. Benjamin F. Butler, *Ben Butler's Book,* 649, 651, 656-57,
664.

4. However Bold We Might Be

1. McHenry Howard, *Notes on Opening of Campaign of 1864,*
MHSM Papers, Vol. IV, 94-95.

2. O.R., Vol. XXXVI, Part One, 1, 18, 198, 915; Livermore,
Numbers and Losses, 110.

3. Jed. Hotchkiss, *Virginia,* in *Confederate Military History,*
Vol. III, 433-36.

4. O.R., Vol. XXXVI, Part One, 325; William Swinton, *Campaigns of the Army of the Potomac,* 439; Reminiscences of Berry

G. Benson, 1st S.C. Volunteers, in the Southern Historical Collection, University of North Carolina Library; McHenry Howard, op. cit., 101-2; G. Moxley Sorrel, *Recollections of a Confederate Staff Officer*, 239-40.

5. A. A. Humphreys, *The Virginia Campaign of 1864 and 1865*, 136-59; Col. C. S. Venable, *The Campaign from the Wilderness to Petersburg*, SHSP, Vol. XIV, 522-26; Maj. Gen. C. W. Field, *The Campaign of 1864 and 1865*, in the same volume, 542-46; Sorrel, op. cit., 230-35; Gen. John B. Gordon, *Reminiscences of the Civil War*, 242-52. Federal casualties are from O.R., Vol. XXXVI, Part One, 133. To get a satisfactory figure for the Confederates is impossible, since returns for most of the regiments in this battle no longer exist. Freeman (*R. E. Lee*, Vol. III, 297) estimates Lee's losses at approximately 7600. *The Medical and Surgical History of the War of the Rebellion*, Part One, Vol. II, cvi, gives an estimate of 11,400, which seems too high.

6. O.R., Vol. XXXVII, Part One, 411; Vol. XXXVI, Part Two, 526; *Lee's Dispatches*, 176-77.

7. *Personal Memoirs of U. S. Grant*, Vol. II, 211-12.

8. Grant to Halleck dated May 11, the U. S. Grant Association from the New York Historical Society. There is a good general account of the Spotsylvania fighting in Humphreys, op. cit., 55-90. A detailed list of sources for the fighting in the Wilderness and at Spotsylvania can be found in *A Stillness at Appomattox*, 399-406.

9. O.R., Vol. XXXVI, Part Three, 206-7; *Life and Letters of George Gordon Meade*, Vol. II, 198; letter of G. K. Warren dated May 20, in the G. K. Warren Papers, New York State Library; *Wartime Papers of R. E. Lee*, 747-48; C. S. Venable, *The Campaign from the Wilderness to Petersburg*, SHSP, Vol. XIV, 533-34; letter from "Frank" to his mother dated May 17, in the Southern Historical Collection, University of North Carolina Library; from the Confederate letters loaned, through Bell Wiley, by Mrs. E. K. Atkinson of Baltimore.

10. There is a good summary of the Cold Harbor action in Joseph P. Cullen, *Richmond Battlefields*, National Park Service Historical Handbook Series, No. XXXIII, 29-34. The armies were in contact along a six-mile front, and the June 3 engagement covered about two and one-half miles of it. Apparently, fewer than 50,000 Federals attacked some 30,000 Confederates. Cold Harbor casualty figures usually include totals for all of the June 1-3 fighting, and it is hard to get a firm figure for the June 3 attack by itself. Cullen (op. cit.) accepts 7000; Humphreys, *The Virginia Campaign*, 191, estimates the loss at 6617. It may be

worth noting that on June 4 Meade wrote to his wife: "I had immediate and entire command on the battlefield all day, the Lieutenant-General honoring the field with his presence only about one hour in the middle of the day." (*Life and Letters*, Vol. II, 200.)

11. On June 5 Charles F. Adams, Jr., wrote from the Army of the Potomac: "I think Grant will be forced to adopt his Vicksburg tactics—he will have to uncover Washington, cross the James, move up the south bank and then throw himself on the Confederate line of communications and supplies." (Letter to R. H. Dana, Jr., in the Dana Papers, Massachusetts Historical Society.) Grant explains his reasoning in O.R., Vol. XXXVI, Part One, 22-23.

12. Lee to Seddon dated June 6, in the Robert E. Lee Papers, Chicago Historical Society.

13. Beauregard, *Four Days of Battle at Petersburg*, B. & L., Vol. IV, 541.

14. On June 21 Meade wrote to his wife regarding the effort to take Petersburg: "In all this fighting and these operations I had exclusive command, Grant being all the time at City Point and coming on the field for only half an hour on the 17th." (*Life and Letters*, Vol. II, 205-6.)

15. E. P. Alexander, *Military Memoirs of a Confederate*, 557-58.

5. Vested Interest in Failure

1. Rachael Sherman Thorndike, ed., *The Sherman Letters: Correspondence between General and Senator Sherman from 1837 to 1891*, 227-33.

2. Note by Horatio Seymour dated April 28, 1864, in the Miscellaneous File, Barlow Papers, Huntington Library.

3. *American Annual Cyclopaedia for 1864*, 237-40.

4. Letter of Halleck to Lieber dated Jan. 11, 1864, in the Lieber Collection, Huntington Library.

5. *American Annual Cyclopaedia for 1864*, 306-10; Brooks, *Washington in Lincoln's Time*, 155-56.

6. Edward McPherson, *The Political History of the United States of America During the Great Rebellion*, 411-14; Allan Nevins, *Frémont, Pathmarker of the West*, 573-74. The Barlow Papers fairly sparkle with expressions of hope that the Frémont candidacy would mean Lincoln's defeat.

7. Basler, Vol. VII, 419.

8. Davis to Lincoln, June 2, in the David Davis Papers, Chicago Historical Society.

9. Noah Brooks (op. cit., 141-42, 148) insisted that Lincoln took no position at all on the vice-presidential contest, and so did John Nicolay (Helen Nicolay, *Lincoln's Secretary: A Biography of John G. Nicolay,* 207-8). The Pennsylvania politician A. K. McClure, on the other hand, said flatly that "Lincoln conceived and executed the scheme to nominate Andrew Johnson"; a statement whose credibility is slightly flawed by McClure's vigorous attempt to show that he was a prime insider at the convention. (*Abraham Lincoln and Men of War Times,* 115-29.) For a temperate analysis, see James F. Glonek, *Lincoln, Johnson and the Baltimore Ticket,* in the *Abraham Lincoln Quarterly,* Vol. VI, No. Five, 255-59.

10. Basler, Vol. VII, 380-83.

11. McPherson, op. cit., 406-7.

12. Letter of Montgomery Blair to Barlow dated Dec. 25, 1863; in the Barlow Papers, Huntington Library.

13. Blair to Barlow, letters dated May 1 and May 4, in the Barlow Papers.

14. Nicolay & Hay, Vol. IX, 247-49, citing a letter of the elder Blair in the *National Intelligencer* Oct. 5, 1864.

15. Barlow to Blair, dated May 10; Blair to Barlow, dated May 11 and May 27; in the Barlow Papers.

16. Basler, Vol. VII, 259, 504-5.

17. Barlow to Johnson, Jan. 19; to Barnett, Feb. 18 and April 15; to Blair, May 3; in the Barlow Papers.

18. Records of the court of inquiry on the mine fiasco are in O.R., Vol. XL, Part One, 42-129.

19. Thurlow Weed to Seward, letter dated Aug. 22, and Henry Raymond to Lincoln, also dated Aug. 22, both in the Robert Todd Lincoln Papers, Library of Congress; David Davis to his brother Rockwell, dated Aug. 4, in the David Davis Papers, Chicago Historical Society.

20. Basler, Vol. VII, 514; Noah Brooks, *Two War-Time Conventions, Century Magazine,* Vol. XXVII, April 1895, 732-35.

21. Letter of McClellan to Barlow, apparently of June 17, in the Barlow Papers.

22. McPherson, op. cit., 419, 423.

23. Brooks, *Two War-Time Conventions,* 734; letter of Noah Brooks to John G. Nicolay, for Lincoln, dated Aug. 29, in the Robert Todd Lincoln Papers; letter of J. Ditzler to Jefferson Davis dated Sept. 15, in the Davis Papers, Duke University Library.

6. A Grand Simplicity of Purpose

1. Letter of Braxton Bragg to President Davis dated July 27, in the Braxton Bragg Papers, Duke University Library: "The return of 10th July will show 50,000 men for duty, and over 10,000 men on extra duty—all able-bodied, and as a general rule the best men in the army. This will in a few days be reduced by at least half."

2. O.R., Vol. XXXVIII, Part Three, 630.

3. John B. Hood, *The Defense of Atlanta*, B. & L., Vol. IV, 336-38; Stanley Horn, *The Army of Tennessee*, 352-54; L. G. Bennett and W. M. Haigh, *History of the 36th Regiment, Illinois Volunteers*, 614-15; James Cooper Nisbet, *Four Years on the Firing Line*, 209-11.

4. There is a detailed account of the Confederate attack in Col. T. B. Roy, *General Hardee and the Military Operations around Atlanta*, SHSP, Vol. VIII, Nos. Eight and Nine, 340-66. Also good is Horn, op. cit., 354-59. For Sherman's missed opportunity, see Maj. Gen. Grenville Dodge, *Personal Recollections of President Abraham Lincoln, General Ulysses S. Grant and General William T. Sherman*, 156; Gen. John M. Schofield, *Forty-six Years in the Army*, 148, and *Memoirs of Gen. W. T. Sherman*, Vol. II, 82.

5. Dodge, op. cit., 159-60, 162-66; letter of Hooker to Logan dated July 27, in the Logan Family Papers, Yale University Library.

6. There is a brief summary of the Ezra Church affair in William Key, *The Battle of Atlanta and the Georgia Campaign*, 65-68.

7. Lloyd Lewis, *Sherman: Fighting Prophet*, 407-9; Brig. Gen. Alpheus S. Williams, *From the Cannon's Mouth*, 340-42; O.R., Vol. XXXVIII, Part Three, 635, 992; Lt. Col. William F. Fox, *Slocum and His Men*, 271-72; Julian Wisner Hinkley, *A Narrative of Service with the 3rd Wisconsin Infantry*, 141; letter of Hood to Bragg dated Sept. 4, in the Jefferson Davis Papers, Duke University Library.

8. O.R., Vol. XLIII, Part Two, 110, 117; letter of Garfield to his wife dated Sept. 23, in the James A. Garfield Papers, Library of Congress.

9. The difficulty of getting a reasonably close count on Civil War numbers once more arises. Early himself consistently understated his numbers, and the Federals wildly exaggerated them— Halleck assured Grant that "Early's force is now about 40,000, perhaps a little more" (Halleck to Grant dated Aug. 3, in the

Sheridan Papers, Library of Congress). Early's strength at the Opequon is given by Freeman (*Lee's Lieutenants,* Vol. II, 577) as 12,150; by Livermore (*Numbers and Losses,* 127) as 18,131. The only real certainty is that Early was very heavily outnumbered.

10. *Recollections of Jubal Early, by One Who Followed Him,* Century Magazine, Vol. LXX, 311-13. For a somewhat less emotional sketch see John Esten Cooke, *Wearing of the Gray,* edited by Philip Van Doren Stern, 99-100.

11. O.R., Vol. XLIII, Part Two, 202. Grant's desire to strike at the Virginia Central was expressed many times, and he continued to call for such a move even after the victory on the Opequon. See O.R., Vol. XXXVII, Part Two, 300, 408, 413,14, 426, 558, for messages July 14, July 21, July 22 and Aug. 1; and Vol. XLIII, Part Two, 345.

12. O.R., Vol. XLIII, Part Two, 152.

13. Three drafts of McClellan's letter of acceptance are preserved in the Barlow Papers at the Huntington Library. One draft, whose language is somewhat cloudy, seems to favor the idea of an armistice, but also asserts that restoration of the Union must be the basis for any settlement. For Vallandigham's comment, see McPherson, 422.

14. Butler's operations can be glimpsed in a letter William Dennison of Ohio wrote to Lincoln on Sept. 2, citing widespread rumors about Butler's desire for the nomination (in the Robert Todd Lincoln Papers, Library of Congress), and in Thurlow Weed's assertion that Butler asked him for his support on a new ticket (John Hay, *Lincoln and the Civil War in the Diaries and Letters of John Hay,* 220-21). Frémont wrote that his only consideration in withdrawing was "the welfare of the Republican party" (correction in Frémont's hand on a manuscript written by his wife and son; in the Frémont Papers, Bancroft Library, University of California).

15. Letter of Humphreys to his wife, undated but obviously written in August or September 1864, in the A. A. Humphreys Papers, the Historical Society of Pennsylvania.

16. Letter of John Bright to Horace Greeley dated Oct. 1, in the A. Conger Goodyear Collection, Historical Manuscripts Division, Yale University Library. For a revealing letter about the business of getting campaign contributions from war contractors, see Henry J. Raymond to Secretary of the Treasury Fessenden, dated Aug. 11, in the same collection.

17. Letter of Dr. H. C. Parry, a Union army surgeon, dated

Oct. 19, to his father, made available by Dr. Edward Owen Parry of Devon, Pa.

18. O.R., Vol. XLIII, Part Two, 249, 307-8, 436. The literature on Cedar Creek is of course voluminous. For contrasting Confederate accounts, see Early's *Autobiographical Sketch and Narrative of the War Between the States,* 440-58, and John B. Gordon, *Reminiscences of the Civil War,* 337-65. An interesting Federal account, strongly colored in Sheridan's favor, is George A. Forsyth, *Thrilling Days in Army Life,* 126-66.

19. Barlow to McClellan, dated Nov. 9, and McClellan to Barlow, dated Nov. 10, in the Barlow Papers, Huntington Library.

Chapter Seven: HIS ALMOST CHOSEN PEOPLE

1. Appeal Against the Thunderstorm

1. O.R., Series Four, Vol. III, 520, with June 30 returns showing 121,000 absentees; 989, where an end-of-the-year return shows an "aggregate present" of 196,016, as against an "aggregate present and absent" of 400,787. At the close of 1864, accordingly, there were at least 200,000 absentees.

2. Rowland, Vol. VI, 341-44.

3. Horace Porter, *Campaigning with Grant,* 313; Rowland, op. cit., 353-61, passim.

4. O.R., Vol. XXXVIII, Part Five, 837-38; Vol. XXXIX, Part Two, 415; petition of the Mayor of Atlanta dated Sept. 11, and Sherman's reply dated Sept. 12, in the Dearborn Collection, Houghton Library, Harvard University.

5. Letter of Sherman dated Sept. 22, in the Silas F. Miller Papers, originals owned by John Mason Brown, photostats in the Filson Club, Louisville; O.R., Vol. XXXIX, Part Two, 411-13.

6. For excellent accounts of Hood's and Sherman's maneuvers in this period see Jacob D. Cox, *Atlanta,* 218-39, and Horn, *The Army of Tennessee,* 369-83.

7. Thomas B. Van Horne, *The Life of Major General George H. Thomas,* 255; O.R., Vol. XX, Part Two, 128-29.

8. O.R., Vol. XXXIX, Part Three, 202, 324, 594; letter of Grant to Stanton dated Oct. 13, in the Ulysses S. Grant Letters and Papers, Illinois State Historical Library; letter of Sherman

to Senator John Sherman dated Oct. 11, in R. S. Thorndike, ed., *The Sherman Letters*, 240.

9. Rowland, Vol. VI, 386-87.

10. Jacob Thompson's report is in O.R., Vol. XLIII, Part Two, 930-36. There is a vast literature on this fifth column movement, most of it rather uncritical, and a sober re-examination of the entire picture is much needed. For a participant's story, see John W. Headley, *Confederate Operations in Canada and New York.* A recent treatment of the daring Confederate operative Capt. Thomas Hines is James D. Horan, *Confederate Agent.*

11. Lee to Davis, Sept. 11, in Rowland, Vol. VI, 327-29.

12. O.R., Series Four, Vol. III, 324-44, 855-56, 880-81, 964.

13. Ibid., 869-70; Rowland, Vol. VI, 421.

14. O.R., Series Four, Vol. III, 976-77.

15. Manuscript memoirs of Senator Williamson Simpson Oldham, in the Eugene C. Barker Texas History Center, University of Texas. For a moving discussion of the dawning awareness of defeat, see George Cary Eggleston, *A Rebel's Recollections*, 172-77.

16. For excellent articles on Price's Missouri campaign, see Howard N. Monnett: *The Confederate Invasion of Missouri*, Missouri Historical Society Bulletin, October 1951; *The Battle of Westport*, Kansas City *Star*, April 23, 1961; *Retreat from Westport*, in The Trail Guide, Kansas City Posse, The Westerners, Vol. VII, No. 3, September 1962. Pertinent reports are in O.R., Vol. XLI, Part One, 313-17, 341-43, 491-519, 636-40.

17. O.R., Vol. XLII, Part Three, 1134.

2. What Have You Done?

1. Basler, Vol. VIII, 136-53.

2. Hood sets forth his plans in *Advance and Retreat*, 263-69, 271-73. In a postwar letter to his friend Lucius B. Northrop, Davis wrote that "I certainly did not contemplate a movement into Tenn. as the means which would cause Sherman to countermarch," and said that the projected march to the Ohio "was to be subsequent to the defeat of Sherman's army." When Davis learned where Hood was going he telegraphed Beauregard, warning him that Grant and Sherman would "regard the occupation of Tennessee as of minor importance." (Letter dated Sept. 25, 1879, in the Goodyear Collection, Historical Manuscripts Division, Yale University Library; telegram to Beauregard dated Nov. 30, 1864, copy in the Eugene C. Barker Texas History Center, University of Texas.)

3. T. Harry Williams, *Beauregard: Napoleon in Gray*, 243-45; Alfred Roman, *Military Operations of General Beauregard*, Vol. II, 293-94, 299-300; Henry Stone, *The Battle of Franklin*, MHSM Papers, Vol. VII, 436-42; O.R., Vol. XXXIX, Part One, 590; Vol. XLV, Part One, 663, 678.

4. Hood, *The Invasion of Tennessee*, B. & L., Vol. IV, 425-32; O.R., Vol. XLV, Part One, 652-53. The reasons for Hood's failure to strike at Spring Hill are by no means clear even now. Hood laid the blame on General Cheatham, one of his corps commanders, but his account of the affair differs so sharply from other accounts—notably Cheatham's—and is so infused with Hood's constant effort to show that his army had let him down, that it is quite unconvincing. In a careful analysis of the whole situation (*The Army of Tennessee*, 386-93), Stanley Horn seems inclined to put most of the blame on Hood. Henry Stone, one of Thomas' staff officers, asserts that there "were queer doings in the Rebel lines among some of the leading officers," and implies that some heavy drinking had taken place. Op. cit., 462.

5. Thomas B. Van Horne, *History of the Army of the Cumberland*, Vol. II, 198, 204, 219.

6. Letter of William D. Gale dated Jan. 14, 1865, in the Gale-Polk Papers, Southern Historical Collection, University of North Carolina; Capt. Irving A. Buck, *Cleburne and His Command*, 280-90; Stone, op. cit., 464-77.

7. Basler, Vol. IV, 235-36; Vol. VIII, 149-50.

8. Isaac N. Arnold, *The Life of Abraham Lincoln*, 359.

9. O.R., Vol. XLV, Part Two, 114-16, 118, 295-96; *Personal Memoirs of U. S. Grant*, Vol. II, 379-80, 382-83.

10. Letter of J. H. Everett of the 143rd New York Volunteers, dated Dec. 19, 1864, in the J. H. Everett Papers, Georgia Historical Society; Lt. Col. Charles C. Jones, Jr., *The Siege of Savannah*, 169, 173-74; Sherman's report, O.R., Vol. XLIV, 13.

11. Kean, *Inside the Confederate Government*, 182; O.R., Vol. XLIV, 783. A copy of Campbell's letter is in the Campbell-Colston Papers, Southern Historical Collection.

12. Col. William Lamb, *The Defense of Fort Fisher*, B. & L., Vol. IV, 642-54; Admiral David Porter, *Incidents and Anecdotes of the Civil War*, 273.

13. Letters of Blair to Barlow dated Jan. 7, Jan. 12, and Feb. 9, 1865, in the Barlow Papers, Huntington Library; speech of Fernando Wood, Jan. 10, in the Congressional Globe, 38th Congress, Second Session, Part One, 194.

14. Brooks, *Washington in Lincoln's Time*, 185-87; Nicolay & Hay, Vol. X, 88-90.

3. Too Late

1. Jacob Cox, *The March to the Sea—Franklin and Nashville*, 165-71; O.R., Vol. XLVII, Part One, 17-19.

2. O.R., Vol. XLVI, Part Two, 511; Davis, *Rise and Fall*, Vol. II, 612-17; Nicolay & Hay, Vol. X, 93-110.

3. R. M. T. Hunter, *The Peace Commission of 1865*, SHSP, Vol. III, 173-74; Alexander Stephens, *Constitutional View of the War Between the States*, Vol. II, 602.

4. No minutes were made at the conference. A detailed summary of the discussion, written shortly afterward by Justice Campbell, is in the Campbell-Colston Papers in the Southern Historical Collection, at the University of North Carolina, and a copy of this, apparently made by Mrs. Hunter, is in the R. M. T. Hunter Papers in the Alderman Library, University of Virginia.

5. *Personal Memoirs of U. S. Grant*, Vol. II, 421-22; Basler, Vol. VIII, 284-85; Frederick Seward, *Seward at Washington*, Vol. III, 261.

6. Letter of Justice Campbell to Horace Greeley dated April 26, 1865, quoting a memorandum given him by Lincoln after the fall of Richmond, in the Southern Historical Collection, University of North Carolina; Basler, Vol. VIII, 260-61; manuscript by Gideon Welles setting forth Lincoln's plans for reconstruction, in the John Hay Library, Brown University.

7. Rowland, Vol. VI, 396.

8. O.R., Series Four, Vol. III, 1161-62.

9. SHSP, New Series No. XIV, Old Series No. LII, 282-83, 454-55.

10. O.R., Series Four, Vol. III, 761-62, 1009.

11. Davis, *Rise and Fall*, Vol. I, 518; manuscript diary of Secretary Mallory, in the Southern Historical Collection, University of North Carolina.

12. Letter of Lee to Andrew Hunter, in O.R., Series Four, Vol. III, 1012-13.

13. Kean, *Inside the Confederate Government*, 204.

4. None Shall Be Weary

1. Brooks, *Washington in Lincoln's Time*, 210; letter of Lincoln to Thurlow Weed dated March 15, in Basler, Vol. VIII, 356.

2. *Washington in Lincoln's Time*, 211-12, 214; diary of Michael Shiner, a free colored man of Washington, who was

greatly impressed by the appearance of the star, in the manuscript division of the Library of Congress.

3. Basler, Vol. VIII, 201, 330-31; O.R., Vol. XLIV, 842. Lee's proposal to Grant grew out of a flag of truce interview between General Longstreet and his "old army" friend, Gen. E. O. C. Ord, who had succeeded Ben Butler in command of the Federal Army of the James; *The Wartime Papers of R. E. Lee*, 911-12.

4. Halleck to Canby dated Feb. 25, in B. & L., extra-illustrated, Vol. III, at the Huntington Library.

5. Jacob Cox, *The March to the Sea—Franklin and Nashville*, 147-62, 199-203; James H. Wilson, *Under the Old Flag*, Vol. II, 160-89.

6. O.R., Vol. XLVII, Part One, 1018-21; Charles Carleton Coffin, *The Boys of '61*, 462-66, 481-82.

7. Sherman's disavowal of blame, and his explanation of the origin of the fire, are set forth both in his official report (O.R., Vol. XLVII, Part One, 21-22) and in his *Memoirs* (Vol. II, 268-88). The veteran's letter cited in the text is quoted in the diary of Major James Austin Connolly, *Transactions of the Illinois State Historical Society for the Year 1938*, 379. One of the darkest pictures of the army's behavior in Columbia is that of a Federal officer, Capt. David P. Conyngham, in *Sherman's March Through the South*, 331-32. The remark of Gen. Johnston is in Jacob Cox, op. cit., 168.

8. O.R., Vol. XLVI, Part One, 62-63, 389-90; Series Four, Vol. III, 1161; Basler, Vol. VIII, 377.

9. *The Wartime Papers of R. E. Lee*, 910; O.R., Vol. XLVI, Part Three, 1353-54; Anderson's account of his operations from October, 1864, to April 8, 1865, in the Lee Headquarters Papers, Virginia State Historical Society; John B. Gordon, *Reminiscences of the Civil War*, 397. Preston's report is O.R., Series Four, Vol. III, 1119-20.

10. Freeman, *R. E. Lee*, Vol. III, 533-35; O.R., Vol. XLVII, Part One, 1050-51, 1055; Johnston, *Narrative of Military Operations*, 372.

11. O.R., Vol. XL, Part Three, 638-39; Vol. XLVII, Part Two, 1395-96; *The Wartime Papers of R. E. Lee*, 914-15.

12. O.R., Vol. XLVI, Part One, 173, 382; R. D. Funkhouser, *The Storming of Fort Steadman on Hare's Hill, Front of Petersburg, Va.*, in E. R. Hutchins, *The War of the Sixties*, 224-25. Gordon has a good account of the battle in his *Reminiscences of the Civil War*, 397-412.

13. Grant's orders of March 24 and his account of what followed are in O.R., Vol. XLVI, Part One, 50-54.

14. Letter of Sherman to I. N. Arnold dated Nov. 28, 1872, photostat in the Chicago Historical Society; *Memoirs of Gen. W. T. Sherman,* Vol. II, 325-28; Nicolay & Hay, Vol. X, 215; *Home Letters of General Sherman,* 336.

15. O.R., Vol. XLVI, Part Three, 332.

16. LaSalle Corbell Pickett, *Pickett and His Men,* 386; *The Wartime Papers of R. E. Lee,* 922-23.

17. There is a good summary of this operation in one of the best of the National Park Service's excellent handbooks, Richard Wayne Lykes' *Petersburg.* The orders to Warren, and the reports dealing with his movement, are in O.R., Vol. XLVI, Part Three, 336 ff; Warren's defense is detailed in the G. K. Warren Papers, New York State Library, Albany, Rosser's story of the shad bake is in his postwar letter to A. S. Perham, in the Alexander Stewart Webb Collection, Historical Manuscripts Division, Yale University Library. For the findings of the Court of Inquiry which at last cleared Warren, see B. & L., Vol. IV, 723-24.

18. Lee to Davis dated April 2, in the Lee Headquarters Papers, Virginia State Historical Society.

5. As in the Old Days

1. Diary of S. R. Mallory, in the Southern Historical Collection, University of North Carolina Library; letter of Mrs. Mary A. Fontaine to Mrs. Marie Burrows Sayre dated April 30, 1865, in the Confederate Memorial Literary Society, Richmond; Col. George A. Bruce, *The Capture and Occupation of Richmond,* MHSM Papers, Vol. XIV, 125.

2. Longstreet, *From Manassas to Appomattox,* 607; Varina Davis, *Jefferson Davis: a Memoir, by His Wife,* Vol. II, 582-84; H. W. Bruce, *Some Reminiscences of the Second of April, 1865,* SHSP, Vol. IX, No. Five, 206-7.

3. Edward M. Boykin, *The Falling Flag: Evacuation of Richmond, Retreat, and Surrender at Appomattox,* 10-16; Diary of S. R. Mallory, as cited in Note 1, above; Clement Sulivane and Thomas Thatcher Graves, *The Fall of Richmond,* B. & L., Vol. IV, 725-27; Eunice Crump Lightfoot, *Papers Relating Personal Experiences in and Around Richmond during the Last Days of the Confederacy,* Confederate Memorial Literary Society, Richmond; letter of Mary A. Fontaine, cited in Note 1, above; diary of Miss Lelian M. Cook, in the Virginia State Historical Society, Richmond, original loaned by Mrs. J. C. Pettit of Blackstone, Va.; letter of Miss Emma Mordecai to "a Confederate officer" dated April 5, 1865, in the Confederate Memorial Literary So-

ciety; Mrs. LaSalle Corbell Pickett, *The First United States Flag Raised in Richmond after the War*, in Rossiter Johnson, *Campfire and Battlefield*, 453-54.

4. Nicolay & Hay, Vol. X, 216-19; Major Charles B. Penrose, *Lincoln's Visit to Richmond*, from *The Century*, May-October 1890, 306-7; Charles Carleton Coffin, *The Boys of '61*, 510-12.

5. Henry G. Connor, *John Archibald Cambell*, 175-76; Basler, Vol. VIII, 386-87, 389; Campbell, *A View of the Confederacy from the Inside, Century Magazine*, October 1889, 952.

6. Basler, Vol. VIII, 388.

7. Letter of Campbell to Horace Greeley dated April 26, 1865, in the Campbell-Colston Papers, Southern Historical Collection, University of North Carolina. Lincoln's appraisal of Campbell's misconception of the situation is in Basler, Vol. VIII, 406-7.

8. Basler, Vol. VIII, 389, 392. For an excellent study of operations between the fall of Petersburg and the final scene at Appomattox see Col. Thomas L. Livermore, *The Generalship of the Appomattox Campaign*, MHSM Papers, Vol. VI, 489-501.

9. Dr. John Herbert Claiborne, *Last Days of Lee and His Paladins*, in George S. Bernard, *War Talks of Confederate Veterans*, 255-56; *The Wartime Papers of R. E. Lee*, 938-39.

10. The exchange of notes between Grant and Lee is in O. R., Vol. XLVI, Part One, 56-57.

11. E. P. Alexander, *Lee at Appomattox: Personal Recollections of the Break-up of the Confederacy, Century Magazine*, April 1902, 921-26.

12. Note Sherman's remark in a letter to Mrs. Sherman at this time: "There is a class of young men who will never live at peace. Long after Lee's and Johnston's armies are beaten and scattered they will band together as highwaymen and keep the country in a fever, begetting a guerilla war." (*Home Letters of General Sherman*, 342.)

13. Col. Charles Marshall, *An Aide-de-Camp of Lee*, 269-78; O.R., Vol. XLVI, Part One, 1267.

14. From the Reminiscences of Berry Benson, in the Southern Historical Collection, University of North Carolina.

6. To the Dark Indefinite Shore

1. Gideon Welles, *Lincoln on Reconstruction*, typed manuscript in the John Hay Library, Brown University.

2. Noah Brooks, *Washington in Lincoln's Time*, 222-27.

3. Basler, Vol. VIII, 399-405.

4. The assumption that the cabinet forced Lincoln to abandon

his Virginia plan seems unjustified. On the morning of April 12—after he had learned the full extent of his cabinet's opposition to the plan—Lincoln telegraphed Weitzel to ask whether there were any visible indications that the legislators were actually going to meet; not until six o'clock that evening did he order Weitzel to forbid the meeting, and he prefaced this order by saying that he had just seen a letter from Campbell to Weitzel giving Campbell's free interpretation of the program that was to be followed. O.R., Vol. XLVI, Part Three, 723-35; Basler, Vol. VIII, 405-8; Benjamin P. Thomas and Harold M. Hyman, *Stanton: the Life and Times of Lincoln's Secretary of War*, 355-56.

5. *Supra*, 271; Thomas and Hyman, *Stanton*, 357-58; Welles, *Lincoln on Reconstruction*, mss. cited in Note 1, above.

6. At the beginning of 1863 Bates wrote that once the slaves were freed they were not just partly free: "In the language of the Constitution they will be 'free persons.' . . . The Constitution was made as it is for the very purpose of securing to every citizen common and equal rights all over the nation, and to prevent local prejudice and captious legislation in the states." (See supra, 67.) Incidentally, Bates left the cabinet late in 1864, and James Speed took his place as attorney general.

7. Johnston, *Narrative of Military Operations*, 372, 385-89, 396-99; O.R., Vol. XLVII, Part One, 43, 1059; Part Three, 73-74. For Bentonville, see Jay Luvaas, *Johnston's Last Stand: Bentonville*, North Carolina Historical Review, Vol. XXXIII, No. Three, 333-54.

8. Sherman's report, O.R., Vol. XLVII, Part One, 31-33.

9. The text of the Sherman-Johnston "memorandum," and Sherman's covering letter to Grant, are in O.R., Vol. XLVII, Part Three, 243-44.

10. Ibid., 293; letter of Grant to Sherman dated April 21, 1865, in the J. P. Morgan Library, New York; Thomas and Hyman, *Stanton*, 406-14; Lloyd Lewis, *Sherman: Fighting Prophet*, 544-60.

11. O.R., Vol. XLVII, Part Three, 410-11, 515.

12. In a postwar letter to Reagan, Davis wrote that "The offer of Sherman to furnish a ship on which I might leave the country with family & personal effects was communicated to me by Breckinridge, after you and he returned from Raleigh." (Letter dated Aug. 9, 1877, in the Davis-Reagan Papers, Dallas Historical Society, Dallas.) Reagan refers to the offer in *The Flight and Capture of Jefferson Davis*, in *Annals of the War*, 150.

13. James H. Wilson, *Under the Old Flag*, Vol. II, 328-33;

Burton Harrison, *Capture of Jefferson Davis, Century Magazine,* November 1893, 142-43; O.R., Vol. XLVII, Part Three, 345-46.

14. O.R., Vol. XLVIII, Part One, 193-94, 265-67; Part Two, 600-1.

15. O.R., Vol. XLVII, Part Three, 461-67, 493.

Bibliography

The following bibliography for *Never Call Retreat,* Volume III, The Centennial History of the Civil War, has been condensed from the list of research materials used in writing this volume. Only entries not in the bibliography of Vol. I, *The Coming Fury,* or Vol. II, *Terrible Swift Sword,* have been included. Space has permitted the listing of about 40 percent of the new titles specifically consulted for this volume. Many hundreds of additional manuscripts, books, articles, and newspapers contributed to the research notes for the Centennial History. The bibliography consists of four parts: I. Resources. II. Primary manuscript collections consulted. III. Principal newspapers. IV. Books, pamphlets, and periodicals from which substantial material has been extracted or items used as major reference.

SECTION I: *Resources*

In addition to the institutions listed in the first two volumes of the Centennial History, the following were consulted for *Never Call Retreat.* All the major battlefields and many of the secondary ones pertaining to this volume have been visited. Appreciation is extended to all those who so generously aided in the research.

Champion, Sid, Edwards, Miss., private family collection.
Civil War Collection, G. A. R. Room, Chicago Public Library, Harold Teitelbaum, and others.
Evans, Robert P., Camerillo, Calif., private collection.
Filson Club, Louisville, Ky., Richard H. Hill, Mrs. Dorothy Cullen, Miss Evelyn Dale.
Giannitrapani, Duilio, Oak Park, Ill., private collection.

Grant, Ulysses S., Association, formerly Ohio State Museum now at Southern Illinois University, Carbondale, Ill., John Y. Simon, Executive Director; Ralph Newman, President; Ulysses S. Grant III.

Herzog, William, Santa Barbara, Calif., private collection.

McWhiney, Grady, Evanston, Ill., research notes.

Merryweather, John, Chicago, private collection.

Morgan, J. P., Library, New York.

Ohio Historical Society, Ohio State Museum, Columbus, O., Erwin C. Zepp, Kenneth W. Duckett.

Parry, Dr. Edward Owen, Devon, Pa., private collection.

Stern, Alfred, Collection, Rare Book Room, Library of Congress.

Underwood, Elmer, Forest Park, Ill., private collection.

Williams, Ray, Cleveland, private collection.

SECTION II: *Manuscript Collections*

This lists only a portion of the major manuscript collections consulted:

Abbott, A. T., Diary, Library of Congress.

Abbott, L., Letters, Massachusetts Commandery, MOLLUS, Houghton Library, Harvard University.

Affeld, C. E., Notes, Vicksburg National Military Park.

Affleck Papers, Department of Archives, Louisiana State University.

Agnew, Samuel Andrew, Diary, Southern Historical Collection, University of North Carolina.

Alexander, E. P., Papers and Letters, Western Reserve Historical Society and Library of Congress.

Alison, Joseph Dill, Diary, Southern Historical Collection, University of North Carolina.

Allen, Isaac Jackson, Papers and Autobiography, Library of Congress.

Alvord, Augustus, Letters, Library of Congress.

Ammen, Jacob, Papers, Illinois State Historical Library.

Anderson, E. C., Papers, Georgia Historical Society.

Arnold, Isaac N., Papers, Chicago Historical Society.

Atkinson, Mrs. E. K., Letters, Southern Historical Collection, University of North Carolina.

Atwater, M. B., Reminiscences, State Historical Society of Wisconsin.

Augur, C. C., Collection, Illinois State Historical Library.

Babcock, Orville E., Papers, Chicago Historical Society.

Badeau, Adam, Letters, Princeton University Library; Western Reserve Historical Society; and Huntington Library.

Bailey Family Letters, Stanford University Libraries.

Balfour, Miss, Diary, Mississippi Department of Archives and History.

Bate, William, Letter, B. & L. Extra-illustrated, Huntington Library.

Bateman, Warner M., Papers, Western Reserve Historical Society.

Bates, David Homer, Stern Collection, Library of Congress.

Bates, Edward, Expression of Patriotism, Huntington Library; and File, Chicago Historical Society.

Bates, Samuel Penniman, Collection, Pennsylvania Historical and Museum Commission.

Beauregard, P. G. T., Letters and Papers, Huntington Library and Virginia State Library.

Bennett, James Gordon, Papers, Library of Congress.

Berkeley, William Noland, Letters, Alderman Library, University of Virginia.

Bingham, Henry H., Memoirs, Western Reserve Historical Society.

Biondi, Eugene N., Reminiscences, Bancroft Library, University of California.

Bonsell, Mrs. Rebecca Wright, Houghton Library, Harvard University.

Boykin Papers, Southern Historical Collection, University of North Carolina.

Boynton, H. V., Papers, New York Public Library.

Bragg, Braxton, Papers, Missouri Historical Society.

Breckinridge, John C., Papers, Filson Club, Louisville, Ky.

Bright, John, Letter, Goodyear Collection, Yale University Library.

Brown, Campbell, Papers, Southern Historical Collection, University of North Carolina.

Burgess, William Wallace, Papers, Alderman Library, University of Virginia.

Burt, Elizabeth Johnston, Papers, Library of Congress.

Butler, B. F., Letters and Papers, Library of Congress and Alderman Library, University of Virginia.

Cadwallader, Sylvanus, Papers, Illinois State Historical Library.

Calhoun, James M., Petition of Mayor of Atlanta, Dearborn Collection, Houghton Library, Harvard University.

Campbell, Given, Narrative of Last March of J. Davis, Library of Congress.

Carter Brothers, Papers and Manuscripts, Huntington Library.

Chambers, Rowland, Diaries, Louisiana State University Department of Archives.

Chancellor, Sue M., Personal Recollections, Alderman Library, University of Virginia.

Chase, Lucian B., Letters, Chicago Historical Society.

Chase, Salmon P., Papers, New York Historical Society and New York Public Library.

Cobb, Howell, Papers, Duke University Library.

Cobbett, J. P., Scrapbook, annotated, E. B. Long Collection.

Conlee, Alexander W., Letters, Huntington Library.

Cook, Lelian M., Diary, Virginia State Historical Society.

Cook, John Esten, Papers and Diary, Virginia State Historical Society and Alderman Library, University of Virginia.

Cox, Jacob D., Collection, Library of Congress.

Dahlgren, John A., Letters, Newberry Library, and *Manuscripts from Goodspeed's,* 1962.

Davis, David, Papers, Chicago Historical Society.

Davis, Jefferson, Letters, Philip D. and Elsie O. Sang Collection, River Forest, Ill.; Yale University Library; Lincoln National Life Foundation, Fort Wayne, Ind.; Confederate Memorial Literary Society; Eugene C. Barker Texas History Center, University of Texas; Virginia State Historical Society; National Archives; Chicago Historical Society; Louisiana Historical Association; New York Historical Society; and Dallas Historical Society.

Dawes, Rufus, Papers, Courtesy of Rufus D. Beach and Ralph G. Newman.

Dodge, Theodore A., Letters, Library of Congress.

Doubleday, Abner, Letters, Western Reserve Historical Society.

Drennan, William Augustus, Diary, Mississippi State Department of Archives and History.

Duke-Morgan Papers, Southern Historical Collection, University of North Carolina.

Early, Jubal A., Letters, Virginia State Historical Society and Huntington Library.

Evans, Thomas, Diary, Library of Congress.

Everett, J. H., Papers, Georgia Historical Society.

Fessenden, William Pitt, Papers, Western Reserve Historical Society.

Fontaine, Mary A., Letters, Confederate Memorial Literary Society.

Fredericksburg, Personal Recollection of, no author, Littlefield

Collection, Eugene C. Barker Texas History Center, University of Texas.

Gale, William D., Papers, Southern Historical Collection, University of North Carolina.

Garfield, James, Letters and Papers, Library of Congress and Huntington Library.

Garland, Hamlin, Papers, University of Southern California Library.

Gay, Sydney Howard, Papers, Columbia University Library.

Gettysburg Address, Text by Associated Press, Lincoln National Life Foundation.

Gilpin, Samuel J. B. V., Diary, Library of Congress.

Grant, Ulysses S., Papers and Letters, U. S. Grant Association; California Historical Society; J. P. Morgan Library; Princeton University Library; Rosenbach Foundation; John Hay Library, Brown University; Massachusetts Historical Society; Western Reserve Historical Society; Library of Congress; New York Historical Society; and Illinois State Historical Library.

Groner, J. A., Papers, Southern Historical Collection, University of North Carolina.

Hancock, Winfield S., Letters, Massachusetts Commandery, MOLLUS, Houghton Library, Harvard University.

Harrison, Benjamin, Papers, Library of Congress.

Hayes, Rutherford B., Diary, Ohio State Museum.

Hazen, W. B., Account of the Battle of Chickamauga and Missionary Ridge, Western Reserve Historical Society.

Holt, Joseph, Papers, Library of Congress.

Hood, Charles C., Diary, Library of Congress.

Hood, John Bell, Letters, Western Reserve Historical Society and Huntington Library.

Hooker, Joseph, Papers and Letters, Huntington Library; Civil War Institute, Gettysburg College; and National Archives.

Hotchkiss, Jed., Papers, Library of Congress.

Howry Family Papers, Library of Congress.

Inskeep, John D., Diary, Ohio State Museum.

Jackman, John S., Journal, Library of Congress.

Johnston, J. Stoddard, Papers, Filson Club, Louisville, Ky.

Johnston, Joseph E., Letters and Papers, Western Reserve Historical Society; Chicago Historical Society; and Huntington Library.

Jordan, Thomas, Memorandum, Huntington Library.

Keifer, Joseph Warren, Letters, Library of Congress.

Kelaher, James, Papers, Huntington Library.

Larned, Daniel Reed, Correspondence, Library of Congress.

Latta, James W., Diaries, Library of Congress.

LeDuc, William Gates, Memoirs, Huntington Library.

Lee, R. E., Letters and Papers, Huntington Library; Lincoln National Life Foundation; Philip D. and Elsie O. Sang Collection; Eugene S. Barker Texas History Center, University of Texas; Chicago Historical Society; Missouri Historical Society; New York Historical Society; and New York Public Library.

Letcher, John, Papers, Library of Congress.

Lightfoot, Emmie Crump, Papers, Confederate Memorial Literary Society.

Lincoln, Abraham, Letters, Huntington Library and New/Not in Collected Works File, Illinois State Historical Library.

Logan Family Papers, Yale University Library.

Longstreet, James, Letters, courtesy Ralph G. Newman.

Lord, Mrs. W. W., Journal Kept During the Siege of Vicksburg, Library of Congress.

McClellan, George B., Papers, New York Historical Society.

McClellan, Henry Brainerd, Papers, Virginia State Historical Society.

McLaws, Lafayette, Letters and Papers, Western Reserve Historical Society and Southern Historical Collection, University of North Carolina.

Mackall, W. W., Papers, Southern Historical Collection, University of North Carolina.

Mann, Maria R., Letters, Library of Congress.

Meade, George G., Letters, Rosenbach Foundation and Huntington Library.

Meigs, Montgomery C., Papers, Library of Congress.

Mercer, George A., Diary, Southern Historical Collection, University of North Carolina.

Merryweather, George, Letters, John Merryweather Collection, Chicago.

Mordecai, Emma, Diary, Southern Historical Collection, University of North Carolina, and Letters, Confederate Memorial Literary Society.

Mosby, John S., Papers, Duke University Library.

Motley, John Lothrop, Letters, Massachusetts Historical Society.

Munford, Thomas T., Five Forks—The Waterloo of the Confederacy, Virginia State Historical Society, and Papers at Duke University Library.

Olmstead, Charles Hart, Reminiscences, Georgia Historical Society.

Parker, Ely S., Narrative of Appomattox, Benjamin Harrison Papers, Library of Congress.

Parry, D. H. C., Letters, Dr. Edward Owen Parry Collection, Devon, Pa.

Pemberton, John C., Letters and Papers, New York Public Library; Huntington Library; Southern Historical Collection, University of North Carolina.

Perham, Aurestus S., Papers, Library of Congress.

Phillips, Wendell, Papers, Library of Congress.

Pickett, George E., Letters and Papers, Western Reserve Historical Society; Duke University Library; and Huntington Library.

Pleasonton, Alfred, Papers, Pleasonton Family collection, courtesy Ralph G. Newman.

Porter, Albert Quincy, Diaries, Library of Congress and Mississippi Department of Archives and History.

Quincy, Samuel M., Papers, Massachusetts Historical Society.

Rabb Family Papers, Eugene C. Barker Texas History Center, University of Texas.

Rawlins, John A., Letters and Papers, Chicago Historical Society; and Western Reserve Historical Society.

Reichhelm, E. Paul, Journal, Library of Congress.

Riddle, Albert G., Papers, Western Reserve Historical Society.

Roman, Alfred, Papers, Library of Congress.

Ropes, Henry, Letters, Boston Public Library.

Ross, Levi Adolphus, Papers, Illinois State Historical Library.

Schurz, Carl, Papers, State Historical Society of Wisconsin.

Seward, Fanny, Papers, Rush Rhees Library, University of Rochester.

Shellenberger, John K., Papers, Library of Congress.

Sherman, W. T., Letters and Papers, Huntington Library; Mississippi Department of Archives and History; Princeton University Library; Houghton Library, Harvard University; Rosenbach Foundation; Duke University Library; Filson Club; Illinois State Historical Library; Library of Congress; and Ohio State Museum.

Shreve, George W., Reminiscences, Virginia State Library.

Stewart, William H., The Charge of the Crater, Personal Statements, Confederate Memorial Literary Society.

Stiles, Joseph Clay, Papers, Huntington Library.

Stout, S. H., Reminiscences, Western Reserve Historical Society.

Stuart, J. E. B., Letters and Papers, Huntington Library; Chicago Historical Society; and State Historical Society of Wisconsin.

Sublett, Emmie, Letters, Confederate Memorial Literary Society.

Synopsis of the Agreement Between Generals Johnston and Sherman, Western Reserve Historical Society.

Thomas, George H., Letter, Huntington Library.

Thomson, Archibald H., Recollections of the Pursuit of Jefferson Davis, Western Reserve Historical Society.

Thornton, Henry Innes, Papers, California Historical Society.

Tod, Governor, Collection, Ohio State Museum.

Towle, George W., Personal Recollections, Bancroft Library, University of California.

Van Deusen, Delos, Letters, Huntington Library.

Veil, Charles H., Letter, Civil War Institute, Gettysburg College.

Wallace, Frances W., Diary, Southern Historical Collection, University of North Carolina.

Walthall, William T., Papers, Mississippi State Department of Archives and History.

Waring, Joseph Frederick, Diary, Southern Historical Collection, University of North Carolina.

Washburne, C. C., Papers, Library of Congress.

Welles, Gideon, "Lincoln and Reconstruction," John Hay Library, Brown University.

Wentworth, Edwin Oberlin, Correspondence, Library of Congress.

Wigfall Family and Louis T. Wigfall, Papers, Library of Congress.

Williams, Alpheus, Letters, Huntington Library.

Williams, George, Letters, Ray Williams Collection, Cleveland.

Winslow, John A., Papers, New York Historical Society.

Wood, John Taylor, Diary, Southern Historical Collection, University of North Carolina.

Young, A. P., Papers, courtesy of Robert P. Evans and Ralph G. Newman.

SECTION III: *Newspapers*

Extensive use has been made of newspapers and among them are the following not previously listed:

Atlanta *Daily Herald;* Carlisle (Penn.) *Evening Herald;* Chicago *Morning Post;* Chicago *Times;* Cincinnati *Daily Inquirer;* Cleveland *Plain Dealer;* Dallas *Morning News;* Hartford *Courant;* Houston *Post-Dispatch;* Indianapolis *Star; Irish Times;* Jackson (Miss.) *State Times;* Kansas City *Star;* Kansas City *Times;* Lexington (Va.) *Gazette; London Press; Manchester Examiner; Manchester Guardian;* Philadelphia *Public Ledger;* Richmond *Sentinel; Sheffield Daily Telegraph;* Vicksburg *Post;* Washington *Daily Chronicle;* Wooster (Ohio) *Republican.*

SECTION IV: *Books, Pamphlets, and Periodicals*

Many articles were also used that appeared in collections, listed previously, such as government publications, Battles and Leaders, Papers of the Military Historical Society of Massachusetts, Southern Historical Society Papers, Annals of the War, and other compilations. Space precluded listing many important secondary sources. Short title form has been used.

Adams, Brooks, The Seizure of the Laird Rams, Proceedings, Massachusetts Historical Society, Vol. XLV, Dec. 1911.

Alexander, E. P., Lee at Appomattox; Personal Recollections, *Century Magazine*, Vol. LXIII, No. 6, April 1902.

Allen, Charles J., Some Accounts and Recollections of the Operations Against the City of Mobile, Glimpses of the Nation's Struggle, I, Minnesota Commandery, MOLLUS, St. Paul, 1887.

Andrews, C. C., History of the Campaign of Mobile, New York, 1867.

Andrews, Eliza Frances, War-Time Journal of a Georgia Girl 1864-65, New York, 1908.

Arnold, Isaac N., The Life of Abraham Lincoln, Chicago, 1885.

As They Saw Forrest, edited by Robert S. Henry, Jackson, Tenn., 1956.

Atkinson, J. H., Forty Days of Disaster, Arkansas Democrat, Dec. 29, 1958.

Ayer, I. Winslow, The Great Treason Plot, Chicago, 1895.

Ayers, James T., The Diary of, edited by John Hope Franklin, Springfield, Ill., 1947.

Bache, Richard Meade, Life of General George Gordon Meade, Philadelphia, 1897.

Barnard, J. G., A Report on the Defenses of Washington, Washington, 1871.

Barrett, John G., Civil War in North Carolina, Chapel Hill, 1961, and Sherman's March Through the Carolinas, Chapel Hill, 1956.

Bates, Samuel P., Battle of Chancellorsville, Meadville, Pa., 1882.

Battine, Cecil, The Crisis of the Confederacy, London, 1905.

Bearss, Edwin C., Battle of Chickasaw Bayou, Vicksburg Sunday *Post*, Nov. 13, 1960-Jan. 29, 1961; Cavalry Operations in the Battle of Stone River, Tennessee Historical Quarterly, Vol. XIX, No. 1-2, March and June, 1960; Decision in Mississippi, Jackson, Miss., 1962; Destruction of the Cairo, Vicksburg Sunday *Post*, Sept. 19 and 25, 1960; Federal Attempts to Cut Supply

Lines, Vicksburg Sunday *Post,* Feb.-April, 1961; Jackson Campaign, Jackson, Miss., *State Times,* July 21-Aug. 21, 1960.

Belknap, Geo. E., The 'New Ironsides' Off Charleston, United Service, Vol. I, No. 1, Jan. 1879.

Bell, Herbert C. H., Lord Palmerston, two vols., London, 1936.

Benjamin, L. N., The St. Albans Raid, Montreal, 1865.

Bickman, Wm. D., "W.D.B.," Rosecrans' Campaign with the Fourteenth Army Corps, Cincinnati, 1863.

Bigelow, John, Jr., The Campaign of Chancellorsville, New Haven, Conn., 1910.

Bloodgood, J. D., Personal Reminiscences of the War, New York, 1893.

Bolles, Charles E., General Grant and the News of Mr. Lincoln's Death, *Century Magazine,* Vol. XL, No. 2, June 1890.

Booth, Edwin, Edwin Booth and Lincoln, *Century Magazine,* Vol. LXXVII, No. 6, April 1909.

Boykin, Edward M., The Falling Flag, New York, 1874.

Boynton, H. V., compiler, Dedication of the Chickamauga and Chattanooga National Military Park, Washington, 1896.

Brooks, Noah, Castine Letters, Sacramento Union, 1862-1863; and Washington in Lincoln's Time, edited by Herbert Mitgang, New York, 1958.

Brown, D. Alexander, Grierson's Raid, Urbana, Ill., 1954.

Buck, Irving A., Cleburne and His Command, and Thomas Robson Hay, Pat Cleburne, Jackson, Tenn., 1959.

Bulloch, James D., The Secret Service of the Confederate States of America, two vols., New York, 1959.

Cadwallader, Sylvanus, Three Years With Grant, edited by Benjamin P. Thomas, New York, 1955.

Campbell, John A., A View of the Confederacy from the Inside, *Century Magazine,* Vol. XXXVIII, No. 6, Oct. 1889.

Carman, E. A., General Hardee's Escape from Savannah, District of Columbia Commandery, MOLLUS, Washington, 1895.

Castel, Albert, The Fort Pillow Massacre, Civil War History, Vol. Four, No. One, March 1958.

Chamberlain, Joshua L., Military Operations on the White Oak Road, Virginia, March 31, 1865, Portland, Maine, 1897; and The Passing of the Armies, New York, 1915.

Chandler, Albert, Military Telegraph Under Lincoln, Sunday Magazine, June 17, 1906.

The Chicago Copperhead Convention, n.p., n.d.

Claiborne, John Herbert, Last Days of Lee and His Paladins, in Bernard, George S., War Talks of Confederate Veterans, Petersburg, Va., 1892.

Cleaves, Freeman, Meade of Gettysburg, Norman, Okla., 1960.

Cocke, Preston, The Battle of New Market, n.p., 1914.

Coffin, Charles Carleton, The Boys of '61, Boston, 1881.

Connolly, James Austin, Major Connolly's Letters to His Wife, 1862-1865, Transactions of the Illinois State Historical Society, Springfield, Ill., 1928.

Conyngham, David P., Sherman's March Through the South, New York, 1865.

Cooke, John Esten, Wearing of the Gray, edited by Philip Van Doren Stern, Bloomington, 1959.

The Copperheads & Lake Erie Conspiracy, Ohio Handbook of the Civil War, Columbus, 1961.

Corruptions and Frauds of Lincoln's Administration, New York, 1864.

Coulter, E. Merton, Commercial Intercourse in the Mississippi Valley 1861-65, Mississippi Valley Historical Review, Vol. V, No. 4.

Couper, William, Virginia Military Institute Seventy-fifth Anniversary of the Battle of New Market, May 15, 1939, n.p., n.d.

Cox, Jacob D., Atlanta, Campaigns of the Civil War, New York, 1882; and The March to the Sea, Franklin and Nashville, Campaigns of the Civil War, New York, 1913.

Cox, Samuel S., Three Decades of Federal Legislation, San Francisco, 1885.

Crawford, W. T., The Mystery of Spring Hill, Civil War History, Vol. One, No. II, June 1955.

Crook, George, General George Crook, His Autobiography, edited and annotated by Martin F. Schmitt, Norman, Okla., 1946.

Crotty, D. G., Four Years Campaigning in the Army of the Potomac, Grand Rapids, Mich., 1874.

Crownover, Sims, The Battle of Franklin, Tennessee Historical Quarterly, Vol. XIV, No. 4, Dec. 1955.

Cullen, Joseph P., Richmond National Battlefield Park, Virginia, National Park Service Historical Handbook Series No. 33, Washington, 1963.

Cunningham, Edward, The Port Hudson Campaign 1862-1863, Baton Rouge, 1963.

Dahlgren, John A., Memoir of, Boston, 1882.

Dalzell, George W., The Flight from the Flag, Chapel Hill, 1940.

Davis, Jefferson, The Peace Conference of 1865, Century Magazine, Vol. LXXVII, No. 1, Nov. 1908.

Davis, Robert Stewart, Three Months Around Charleston Bar, United Service Magazine, Vol. I, No. 2, Feb. 1864.

Dawes, Rufus, Service with the Sixth Wisconsin Volunteers, Marietta, Ohio, 1890.

DeForest, John William, A Volunteer's Adventures, edited by James H. Croushore, New Haven, 1946.

Dodd, William E., Jefferson Davis, Philadelphia, 1907.

Dodge, Grenville M., The Battle of Atlanta and Other Campaigns, Council Bluffs, Iowa, 1910; and Personal Recollections of President Abraham Lincoln, General Ulysses S. Grant and General William T. Sherman, Council Bluffs, Iowa, 1914.

Dodge, Wm. Sumner, History of the Old Second Division, Army of the Cumberland, Chicago, 1864.

Doubleday, Abner, Chancellorsville and Gettysburg, Campaigns of the Civil War, New York, 1882.

Dowdey, Clifford, Death of a Nation, New York, 1958; and Lee's Last Campaign, Boston, 1960.

Downey, Fairfax, Storming of the Gateway, Chattanooga, 1960, New York, 1860.

Drayton, Percival, Naval Letters from Captain Percival Drayton, Bulletin of the New York Public Library, Vol. X, No. 11, Nov. 1906.

Duke, Basil W., A History of Morgan's Cavalry, Bloomington, Ind., 1961.

DuPont, H. A., The Campaign of 1864 in the Valley of Virginia, New York, 1925.

Early, Jubal, Recollections of, By One Who Followed Him, *Century Magazine,* Vol. LXX, May-Oct. 1905.

Edwards, John N., Shelby and His Men, Cincinnati, 1867.

Ellis, Mrs. L. E., The Chicago Times During the Civil War, Transactions for the year 1932, Illinois State Historical Society, Springfield.

An English Merchant, Two Months in the Confederate States, London, 1863.

Feight, Henry B., When Ohioans Rebelled Against Draft Act of 1863, Cleveland *Plain Dealer,* Aug. 27, 1933.

Fitch, Michael Henrick, The Chattanooga Campaign, Madison, Wis., 1911.

Fitzhugh, Lester N., Saluria, Fort Esperanza, and Military Operations on the Texas Coast, Southwestern Historical Quarterly, Vol. LXI, No. 1, July, 1957.

Fletcher, William Andrew, Rebel Private Front and Rear, preface by Bell Irvin Wiley, Austin, 1954.

Forsyth, George A., Thrilling Days in Army Life, New York, 1900.

Fox, William F., Slocum and His Men, Albany, 1904.

Fremantle, James Arthur Lyon, The Fremantle Diary, edited by Walter Lord, Boston, 1954.

Funkhouser, R. D., Storming of Fort Steadman, in E. R. Hutchins, The War of the 'Sixties, New York, 1912.

Gardner, Asa Bird, Argument on Behalf of Lieut. Gen. Philip H. Sheridan, U.S.A., Chicago, 1881.

Gladstone and Palmerston, being the Correspondence of Lord Palmerston with Mr. Gladstone 1851-1865, edited by Philip Guedalla, New York, 1928.

Glonek, James F., Lincoln, Johnson, and the Baltimore Ticket, Abraham Lincoln Quarterly, Vol. VI, No. 5, March 1951.

Gordon, George H., A War Diary of Events in the War of the Great Rebellion, 1863-1865, Boston, 1885.

Gorgas, Josiah, The Civil War Diary of, edited by Frank Vandiver, University, Ala., 1947.

Gracie, Archibald, The Truth About Chickamauga, Boston, 1911.

Grant, Frederick Dent, With Grant at Vicksburg, Outlook, July 2, 1898.

Green, Anna Maclay, Civil War Public Opinion of General Grant, Journal of the Illinois State Historical Society, Vol. 22, No. 1, April 1929.

Greene, Jacob L., Franklin at Fredericksburg 1862, Hartford, 1900.

Haight, Theron Wilber, Three Wisconsin Cushings, Madison, 1910.

Hamlin, August Choate, The Battle of Chancellorsville, Bangor, Maine, 1896.

Hanna, A. J., Flight into Oblivion, Richmond, 1938.

Hansard's Parliamentary Debates, various issues.

Hardin, Martin D., The Defence of Washington Against Early's Attack, Military Essays and Recollections, II, Illinois Commandery, MOLLUS, Chicago, 1894.

Harkness, Edson J., The Expeditions Against Fort Fisher and Wilmington, Military Essays and Recollections, II, Illinois Commandery, MOLLUS, Chicago, 1894.

Harrison, Burton N., The Capture of Jefferson Davis, Century Magazine, Vol. XXVII, No. 1, Nov. 1883.

Hartje, Robert, Van Dorn Conducts a Raid on Holly Springs and Enters Tennessee, Tennessee Historical Quarterly, Vol. XVIII, No. 2, June 1959.

Hascall, Milo S., Personal Recollections and Experiences at Stone River, Military Essays and Recollections, IV, Illinois Commandery, MOLLUS, Chicago, 1899.

Haskell, Frank Aretas, The Battle of Gettysburg, edited by Bruce Catton, Boston, 1958.

Haskell, John, The Haskell Memoirs, edited by Gilbert E. Govan and James W. Livingood, New York, 1960.

Hay, Thomas Robson, Hood's Tennessee Campaign, New York, 1929.

Hazen, W. B., A Narrative of Military Service, Boston, 1885.

Headley, John W., Confederate Operations In Canada and New York, New York, 1906.

Heaton, H., Personal Reminiscences of Sherman's March to the Sea, E. R. Hutchins, The War of the 'Sixties.

Hebert, Walter H., Fighting Joe Hooker, Indianapolis, 1944.

Hedley, F. Y., Marching Through Georgia, Chicago, 1890.

Henry, Robert Selph, As They Saw Forrest, Jackson, Tenn., 1965; and "First with the Most" Forrest, Indianapolis, 1944.

Hesseltine, William B., Lincoln's Plan of Reconstruction, Tuscaloosa, Ala., 1960.

Hinkley, Julian Wisner, A Narrative of Service with the Third Wisconsin, Madison, 1912.

Hitchcock, Henry, Marching with Sherman, edited by M. A. DeWolfe Howe, New Haven, Conn., 1927.

Hoke, Jacob, The Great Invasion of 1863, New York, 1959.

Hood, J. B., Advance and Retreat, New Orleans, 1880.

Horan, James D., Confederate Agent, New York, 1954.

Horn, Stanley, The Decisive Battle of Nashville, Baton Rouge, 1959.

Hosea, Lewis M., Campaign of Selma, Sketches of War History, I, Ohio Commandery, MOLLUS, Cincinnati, 1888.

Hotchkiss, Jed., and William Allan, The Battle-Fields of Virginia, Chancellorsville, New York, 1867.

Howard, O. O., Autobiography, two vols., New York, 1907.

Hughes, N. C., Jr., Hardee's Defense of Savannah, Georgia Historical Quarterly, Vol. XLVII, No. 1, March 1963.

Humphreys, Andrew A., The Virginia Campaign of '64 and '65, Campaigns of the Civil War, New York, 1883.

Hutchins, E. R., The War of the 'Sixties, New York, 1912.

Issues of the Campaign, Chicago Tribune Campaign Document, No. 2, 1864.

Jackson, Huntington W., The Battle of Chancellorsville, Military Essays and Recollections, II, Illinois Commandery, MOLLUS, Chicago, 1894.

Johnson, Richard W., Memoir of Maj. Gen. George H. Thomas, Philadelphia, 1881.

Jones, Archer, Confederate Strategy from Shiloh to Vicksburg, Baton Rouge, 1961; and The Gettysburg Decision, Virginia Magazine of History and Biography, June 1960.

Jones, Charles C., The Siege of Savannah, Albany, N.Y., 1874.

Jones, Jenkin Lloyd, An Artilleryman's Diary, Madison, 1914.

Julian, Allen P., Historic Fort McAllister, Savannah, 1958.

Kellogg, J. H., War Experiences and the Story of the Vicksburg Campaign, n.p., 1913.

Kay, William, The Battle of Atlanta and the Georgia Campaign, New York, 1958.

Kilmer, George L., The Dash into the Crater, *Century Magazine*, Vol. XXXIV, No. 5, Sept. 1887.

King, Joseph E., The Fort Fisher Campaigns, 1864-1865, U. S. Naval Institute Proceedings, Aug. 1951.

Kinney, J. C., An August Morning with Farragut, Scribner's Monthly, Vol. XXII, No. 2, June 1881.

Kirke, Edmund, Down in Tennessee, New York, 1864.

Kirkland, Edward Chase, The Peacemakers of 1864, New York, 1927.

Klement, Frank L., The Copperheads in the Middle West, 1960.

Lamers, William M., The Edge of Glory, A Biography of General William S. Rosecrans, New York, 1961.

The Land We Love, various issues.

Langdon, Loomis L., The Stars and Stripes in Richmond, *Century Magazine*, Vol. XL, No. 2, June 1890.

LeConte, Emma, When the World Ended, edited by Earl Schenck Miers, New York, 1957.

Lee, Robert E., The Wartime Papers of, edited by Clifford Dowdey and Louis H. Manarin, Boston, 1961.

Letters of Loyal Soldiers, and How Douglas Democrats Will Vote, n.p., n.d.

Lincoln Day by Day, A Chronology, 1808-1865, three vols. Earl Schenck Miers, Editor-in-Chief, C. Percy Powell, Washington, 1960.

Livermore, William Roscoe, The Story of the Civil War, The Campaigns of 1863, New York, 1913.

Lunt, Dolly Sumner, Mrs. Thomas Burge, A Woman's Wartime Journal, New York, 1918.

Luvaas, Jay, Bentonville, Civil War Times Illustrated, Vol. II, No. 6, Oct., 1963; and Johnston's Last Stand—Bentonville, North Carolina Historical Review, Vol. XXXIII, No. 3, July 1956.

Lykes, Richard Wayne, Petersburg National Military Park, Virginia, National Park Service Historical Handbook, No. 13, Washington, 1951.

Lyman, Theodore, Meade's Headquarters 1863-1865, edited by George G. Agassiz, Boston, 1922.

Lytle, Andrew Nelson, Bedford Forrest and His Critter Company, New York, 1931.

McCabe, James D., Jr., Life and Campaigns of General Robert E. Lee, Atlanta, 1866.

McClellan, Carswell, Personal Memoirs and Military History of U. S. Grant versus the Record, Boston, 1887.

McClurg, Alexander C., The Last Chance of the Confederacy, Military Essays and Recollections, I, Illinois Commandery, MOLLUS, Chicago, 1891.

McKinney, Francis F., Education in Violence, The Life of George H. Thomas, Detroit, 1961.

Marshall, Charles, An Aide-de-Camp of Lee, edited by Sir Frederick Maurice, Boston, 1927.

Maury, Dabney H., Van Dorn, The Hero of Mississippi, Philadelphia, 1879.

Meade, George Gordon, With Meade At Gettysburg, Philadelphia, 1930.

Mearns, David C., and Lloyd A. Dunlap, Long Remembered, Washington, 1963.

Merritt, Wesley, Note on the Surrender of Lee, *Century Magazine,* Vol. LXIII, No. 6, April 1902.

Miers, Earl Schenck, The General Who Marched to Hell, New York, 1951.

Mills, William Howard, Chancellorsville, Magazine of American History, Vol. XV, No. 4, April 1886.

Monnett, Howard N., Action Before Westport, Kansas City, 1964; Confederate Invasion of Missouri, Missouri Historical Society Bulletin, Oct. 1951; The Battle of Westport, Kansas City *Star,* April 23, 1961; Retreat from Westport, in the Trail Guide, Kansas City Posse, The Westerners, Vol. VII, No. 3, Sept. 1962.

Mosgrove, George Dallas, Kentucky Cavaliers in Dixie, edited by Bell Irvin Wiley, Jackson, Tenn., 1957.

Mr. Lincoln's Arbitrary Arrests, New York, 1864.

Mulhane, L. W., Memorial of Major-General William Starke Rosecrans, n.p., 1898.

Muir, Andrew Forrest, Dick Dowling and the Battle of Sabine Pass, Civil War History, Vol. IV, No. Four, Dec. 1958.

Murphy, D. F., Proceedings of the National Union Convention, New York, 1864.

Nelson, A. H., The Battles of Chancellorsville and Gettysburg, Minneapolis, 1899.

Nichols, George Ward, The Story of the Great March, New York, 1865.

Nicolay, John, and John Hay, The Hampton Roads Conference, and The XIIIth Amendment, *Century Magazine,* Vol. XXXVII, No. 6, Oct. 1889.

Nisbet, James Cooper, Four Years on the Firing Line, edited by Bell Irvin Wiley, Jackson, Tenn., 1963.

Oldroyd, Osborn H., A Soldier's Story of the Siege of Vicksburg, Springfield, Ill., 1885.

Olmstead, Charles H., The Memoirs of, edited by Lilla M. Hawes, Georgia Historical Quarterly, Vol. XLIV, Number 4, Sept. 1960.

Osborn, Hartwell, Trials and Triumphs, Chicago, 1904.

Owsley, Clifford D., Genesis of the World's Greatest Speech, Lincoln Herald, Fall 1962.

Parks, Joseph H., General Leonidas Polk, Baton Rouge, 1962.

Patrick, Rembert W., The Fall of Richmond, Baton Rouge, 1960, and Jefferson Davis and His Cabinet, Baton Rouge, 1944.

Pemberton, John C., Pemberton, Defender of Vicksburg, Chapel Hill, 1942.

Pennypacker, Isaac R., General Meade, New York, 1901.

Penrose, Charles B., Lincoln's Visit to Richmond, *Century Magazine,* Vol. XL, No. 2, June 1890.

Pickett, George E., Soldier of the South, General Pickett's War Letters to His Wife, edited by Arthur Grew Inman, Boston, 1928.

Pickett, Mrs. LaSalle Corbell, The First United States Flag Raised in Richmond, from Campfire and Battlefield; and Pickett and his Men, Atlanta, 1900.

Pleasants, Henry J., Jr., and George H. Straley, Inferno at Petersburg, Philadelphia, 1961.

Pollard, E. A., Southern History of the War, New York, 1866.

Pond, George E., The Shenandoah Valley in 1864, Campaigns of the Civil War, New York, 1883.

Poore, Ben Perley, The Life and Public Services of Ambrose E. Burnside, Providence, 1882.

Pullen, John J., The Twentieth Maine, Philadelphia, 1957.

Quarles, Benjamin, Lincoln and the Negro, New York, 1962.

Record of Hon. C. L. Vallandigham on Abolition, The Union and The Civil War, Cincinnati, 1863.

Redway, G. W., Fredericksburg, London and New York, 1906.

Reed, Sam. Rockwell, The Vicksburg Campaign, Cincinnati, 1882.

Richardson, Albert D., A Personal History of Ulysses S. Grant, Hartford, Conn., 1868.

Ripley, Edward Hastings, Vermont General, edited by Otto Eisenschiml, New York, 1960.

Ritchie, J. Ewing, The Life and Times of Vicount Palmerston, two vols., London, n.d.

Rogers, Earl M., McClellan's Candidacy with the Army, Century, Vol. XL, No. 6, Oct. 1890.

Russell, John Earl, Recollections and Suggestions, Boston, 1875.

Sanger, Donald Bridgman, and Thomas Robson Hay, James Longstreet, Baton Rouge, 1952.

Schaff, Morris, The Sunset of the Confederacy, Boston, 1912.

Scheibert, Justus, Seven Months in the Rebel States, Tuscaloosa, Ala., 1958.

Schuler, Louis J., Last Battle in the War Between the States, Brownsville, Texas, 1960.

Senour, F., Major General William T. Sherman, Chicago, 1865.

Seward, Frederick W., Reminiscences of a War-Time Statesman and Diplomat, 1830-1915, New York, 1916.

Sheridan, Philip H., Last Days of the Rebellion, Military Essays and Recollections, I, Illinois Commandery, MOLLUS, Chicago, 1891.

Sherman, William T., General Sherman and the 'March to the Sea,' Century Magazine, Vol. XXXIV, May-Oct. 1887.

Simms, William Gilmore, Sack and Destruction of Columbia, Columbia, S.C., 1905.

Slocum, Charles E., The Life and Services of Major-General Henry Warner Slocum, Toledo, Ohio, 1913.

Smith, Donald V., Chase and Civil War Politics, Columbus, Ohio, 1931.

Smith, T. C., Life and Letters of James Abram Garfield, two vols., New Haven, 1926.

Smith, William Farrar, From Chattanooga to Petersburg, Boston, 1893.

Spear, Ellis, The Hoe Cake of Appomattox, War Paper 93, District of Columbia Commandery, MOLLUS, Washington, 1913.

Stackpole, Edward J., Chancellorsville, Harrisburg, Pa., 1958; Drama on the Rappahannock, Harrisburg, 1957; Sheridan in the Shenandoah, Harrisburg, 1961; They Met at Gettysburg, Harrisburg, 1956.

Stedman, Wm. P., Pursuit and Capture of Jefferson Davis, Century Magazine, Vol. XXXIX, No. 4, Feb. 1890.

Steere, Edward, The Wilderness Campaign, Harrisburg, Pa., 1960.

Stern, Philip Van Doren, An End to Valor, The Last Days of the Civil War, Boston, 1958.

Stevenson, Alexander F., The Battle of Stone's River, Boston, 1884.

Stewart, George R., Pickett's Charge, Boston, 1959.

Stine, J. H., History of the Army of the Potomac, Washington, 1893.

Stockwell, Elisha, Jr., Private Elisha Stockwell, Jr., Sees the Civil War, edited by Byron R. Abernethy, Norman, Okla., 1958.

Stripp, Fred, The *Other* Gettysburg Address, Civil War History, Vol. I, Number Two, June 1955.

Strode, Hudson, Jefferson Davis, Confederate President, New York, 1959; and Jefferson Davis, Tragic Hero, New York, 1964.

Strother, David Hunter, A Virginia Yankee in the Civil War, edited by Cecil D. Eby, Jr., Chapel Hill, 1961; and With Sigel at New Market: The Diary of Colonel D. H. Strother, edited by Cecil D. Eby, Jr., Civil War History, Vol. VI, No. one, March 1960.

Sullivan, James R., Chickamauga and Chattanooga Battlefields, National Park Service Handbook No. 25, Washington, 1956.

Talcott, T. M. R., Stuart's Cavalry in the Gettysburg Campaign, Richmond, 1909.

Taylor, Benj. F., Mission Ridge and Lookout Mountain, New York, 1872.

Taylor, Emerson Gifford, Gouverneur Kemble Warren, Boston, 1932.

Tilberg, Frederick, Gettysburg National Military Park, National Park Service Historical Handbook No. 9, Washington, 1950.

Toombs, Samuel, Reminiscences of the War, Orange, N.J., 1878.

Townsend, George Alfred, Campaigns of a Non-Combatant, New York, 1866.

Trezevant, D. H., The Burning of Columbia, Marietta, Ga., 1958.

Tucker, Glen, Hancock the Superb, Indianapolis, 1960; High Tide at Gettysburg, Indianapolis, 1958; and Chickamauga, Indianapolis, 1961.

Turchin, John B., Chickamauga, Chicago, 1888.

Turner, Edward Raymond, The New Market Campaign, Richmond, 1912.

Tuthill, Richard S., An Artilleryman's Recollections of the Battle of Atlanta, I, Illinois Commandery, MOLLUS, Chicago, 1907.

Upson, Theodore, With Sherman to the Sea, edited by Oscar Osburn Winther, Bloomington, Ind., 1958.

Vallandigham, C. C., Speeches, Arguments, Addresses & Letters, New York, 1864.

Vallandigham, Clement, Biographical Memoir of, By his Brother, New York, 1864.

Vance, Wilson J., Stone's River, The Turning-Point of the Civil War, New York, 1914.

Vandiver, Frank, Jubal's Raid, New York, 1960; and Plough-shares into Swords, Austin, Texas, 1952.

Van Horne, Thomas B., History of the Army of the Cumberland, two vols., and atlas, Cincinnati, 1875.

Van Santwood, C., The One Hundred and Twentieth Regiment New York State Volunteers, Roundout, N.Y., 1894.

Vilas, William Freeman, A View of the Vicksburg Campaign, Madison, 1908.

Villiers, Brougham, and W. H. Chesson, Anglo-American Relations 1861-1865, New York, 1920.

Von Borcke, Heros, Memoirs of the Confederate War for Independence, two vols., New York, 1838.

Wade, William W., The Man Who Stopped the Rams, American Heritage, Vol. XIV, No. 3, April 1963.

Walker, Francis A., History of the Second Army Corps in the Army of the Potomac, New York, 1886.

Walker, Peter F., Vicksburg, A People at War, 1860-1865, Chapel Hill, 1960.

Warden, Robert B., An Account of the Private Life and Public Services of Salmon Portland Chase, Cincinnati, 1874.

Warner, Ezra J., Generals in Gray, Baton Rouge, 1959; and Generals in Blue, Baton Rouge, 1964.

Warren, G. K., Proceedings, Findings and Opinions of the Court of Inquiry, three parts with maps, Washington, 1883.

Warren, Louis A., Lincoln's Gettysburg Declaration, Fort Wayne, Ind., 1964.

War Talks of Confederate Veterans, edited by George S. Bernard, Petersburg, Va., 1892.

Washburn, George H., A Complete History and Record of the 108th Regiment N.Y., Vols., Rochester, 1894.

Welch, Spencer Glasgow, A Confederate Surgeon's Letters to His Wife, Marietta, Ga., 1954.

Whan, Verin E., Jr., Fiasco at Fredericksburg, State College, Pa., 1961.

Wheeler, Joseph, An Effort to Rescue Jefferson Davis, Century Magazine, Vol. LVI, No. 1, May 1898.

Williams, T. Harry, Lincoln and the Radicals, Madison, 1941.

Wilson, James Harrison, The Life of John A. Rawlins, New York, 1916.

Wise, John S., The West Point of the Confederacy, n.p., n.d.

Wood, Thomas J., The Battle of Missionary Ridge, Sketches of War History, IV, Ohio Commandery, MOLLUS, Cincinnati, 1896.

Woods, J. T., Services of the Ninety-sixth Ohio Volunteers, 1874.

Woodward, S. L., Grierson's Raid, Journal of the United States Cavalry Association, Vol. XIV, No. 52, April 1904.

Worsham, John H., One of Jackson's Foot Cavalry, New York, 1912.

Wright, Howard G., Port Hudson, Its History from an Interior Point of View, Baton Rouge, 1961.

Yaryan, John Lee, Stone's River, War Papers, I, Indiana Commandery, MOLLUS, Indianapolis, 1898.

Young, Jesse Bowman, The Battle of Gettysburg, New York, 1913.

Young, John Russell, Around the World with General Grant, two vols., New York, 1879.

Acknowledgments

For the ten years of the writing and research for The Centennial History of the Civil War several hundred individuals and institutions have contributed in countless ways. It would be impossible to list or record all their names, but the author and research director are truly grateful.

Many gave unstintingly of their knowledge. Some were mentioned previously in the acknowledgments of Volume I and Volume II. Our debts to the various institutions and private collectors are found in the resources section of the bibliography in each volume.

Deserving of special mention in this volume, among others, are Bell Irvin Wiley and T. Harry Williams, for reading the manuscript. Allan Nevins, Ralph Newman and others continued their aid in furnishing us with valuable research material.

The following are among those whose names should be added to the roll call, although there are admittedly many others:

James L. Borroum, Corinth, Miss.; Hatchett Chandler, Foley, Ala.; J. Winston Coleman, Lexington, Ky.; Charles A. Collier, Atlanta, Ga.; Chester L. Davis, Perry, Mo.; Michael Dutton, Glen Ellyn, Ill.; Newton C. Farr, Chicago; Mrs. Francis B. Hastings, Orange, Va., for permission to use her father's account of Yellow Tavern; Robert S. Henry, Washington, D.C.; Harold Hyman, Champaign, Ill.; Wilbur G. Kurtz, Atlanta, Ga.; Alexander A. Lawrence, Savannah, Ga.; Grady McWhiney, Evanston, Ill.; Bert Maybee, Kansas City, Mo.; Howard N. Monnett, Kansas City, Mo.; Mr. and Mrs. Will Plank, Marlboro, N.Y.; H. V. Rose, Smithfield, N.C.; Wilbert Rosin and the Concordia College Library, River Forest, Ill., for the use of equipment; Don Russell, Elmhurst, Ill.; L. C. Tapp, Brice's Crossroads, Miss.; W. O. Wood, Pleasant Hill, La.; Morrison Worthington, New Canton, Ill.

Index

Index